GW00976094

BIOGRAPHICAL MEMOIRS OF FELLOWS OF THE BRITISH ACADEMY
XI

For over 100 years, the British Academy has published Biographical Memoirs—extended obituaries—of its deceased Fellows. Collectively these memoirs make up a chapter in the intellectual history of Britain, and are used as a source by biographers and historians.

These memoirs have previously been published annually within the *Proceedings of the British Academy*, most recently as separate volumes within the series. (*Biographical Memoirs of Fellows* volumes I–X were published in the *Proceedings* series between 2002 and 2011.) New Biographical Memoirs will now be made available online by the British Academy as an open-access resource, but they will still also be published in an annual hardback volume.

This latest celebrates the lives of 24 eminent scholars in the humanities and social sciences.

www.britac.ac.uk/memoirs

Biographical Memoirs of Fellows of the British Academy XI

Published for THE BRITISH ACADEMY
by OXFORD UNIVERSITY PRESS

Oxford University Press, Great Clarendon Street, Oxford OX2 6DP

Oxford New York
Auckland Bangkok Bogotá Buenos Aires Cape Town Chennai
Dar es Salaam Delhi Hong Kong Istanbul Karachi Kolkata
Kuala Lumpur Madrid Melbourne Mexico City Mumbai Nairobi
São Paulo Shanghai Singapore Taipei Tokyo Toronto

First published 2012

British Library Cataloguing in Publication Data
Data available

978–0–19–726530–7

Typeset in Times
by New Leaf Design, Scarborough, North Yorkshire
Printed on acid-free paper by
TJ International Ltd,
Padstow, Cornwall

The Academy is grateful to Professor Ron Johnston, FBA
for his editorial work on this volume

Contents

RAYMOND ALLCHIN

Frank Raymond Allchin
1923–2010

RAYMOND ALLCHIN, Fellow of the British Academy and Reader Emeritus in Indian Studies at Cambridge, died on 4 June 2010 at the age of 86. Successfully countering the threatened extinction of the long tradition of the British study of the archaeology of the Indian Subcontinent in the aftermath of Independence, he recruited and educated generations of the most able lecturers, field archaeologists and curators across Britain and South Asia. That South Asian archaeology forms a core part of the teaching and research portfolios at Cambridge, Durham, Leicester, Oxford and University College London (UCL) is a direct result of Raymond's success and dedication to his field.

Raymond Allchin, or Ray as he was also known, was born in Harrow on 9 July 1923, son of Frank Macdonald Allchin, a doctor, and Louise Maude, his wife. According to genealogical research conducted by Raymond's younger brother, Donald, the Allchin family had been village physicians in Kent and Sussex in the seventeenth and eighteenth centuries. Raymond's great grandfather, Sir William Allchin, was the first of these practitioners to obtain formal training and, after a career associated with both University College London and the Royal College of Physicians, was knighted in 1907 and appointed Physician-Extraordinary to King George V. In contrast, Raymond's mother came from a family of Lancashire tailors, the Wrights, who had moved to London and become Freemen of the City of London. Although Raymond was later to describe his memories of his first home as 'a small suburban house', his father's practice was successful enough to support the four children, a nanny, gardener, cook and housemaid and, by the time Raymond was six, the family moved to a larger home near Ealing. After kindergarten at the Haberdashers' Aske's School, Raymond was sent to Durston House Preparatory School and later recorded that he 'seemed to win a school prize every year; though whether this was because I was a star student or because the school was exceedingly liberal with its prizes I cannot now be sure'. The family moved again, this time to a villa on Ealing Common, and, after close tutoring, both Raymond and his elder brother, William, were sent to Westminster. Friendly with Michael Flanders, Tony Benn and Rudolf von Ribbentrop, Raymond and William were forced to leave the school early due to over-extended family finances accentuated by the war.

As Raymond was too young for university, he was persuaded by a friend to enrol at the Regent Street Polytechnic School of Architecture in 1940. After three years, and having passed the intermediate exam and achieving the Licentiate of the Royal Institute of British Architecture, Raymond was conscripted. Anticipating that his training in surveying and technical drawing would lead to him being attached to the Royal Engineers, he was somewhat surprised by being assigned to the Royal Corps of Signals. After initial training at Prestatyn and Catterick, Raymond was confirmed a 'Line Mechanic Class A' and found himself issued with a tropical uniform and on a troopship heading east to India. Instructed to learn Hindustani during the voyage, Raymond augmented his classes with informal coaching from Punjabi troops as well as finding their mess rather more appealing than his own. This was not without its dangers and Raymond would recall how he provided entertainment by practising some of his newly learnt Hindi phrases and only later discovered that they included the statement 'I am a donkey'. Arriving in India in early 1944, Raymond was first posted to the Indian Army Signal Corps at Mhow in Madhya Pradesh and later to Agra, Dehradun, Comilla and Chittagong. Undertaking language training as part of officer training at Mhow, Raymond quickly identified the advantages of learning Hindi, rather than Urdu, and of being able to 'communicate with local people and be increasingly involved in Indian life'. Through his tutor, or *munshi*, Raymond was also introduced to Hindi literature and first exposed to the works of sixteenth-century poet Tulsi Das.

The posting at Mhow also provided Raymond with his first taste of Indian archaeology, reawakening his interests as a schoolboy reading accounts of Ernest Mackay's excavations at Bronze Age Indus cities of Mohenjo-daro and Chanhu-daro in the *Illustrated London News*. Indeed, in later life he would also recount the impact of seeing the striking stone dome of the third century BC Buddhist *stupa* on its hilltop at Sanchi for the first time, stating that his interest in Indian archaeology started there! From the cantonment, Raymond would also cycle to and explore the medieval mosques, palaces and fortifications of Mandu in Malwa, further fuelling his interest in the architecture and cultural heritage of the Subcontinent. Transferred to Singapore and commissioned a Lieutenant in February 1945, Raymond's interests in Indian culture continued and he was fascinated by the fire-worship and sacrificial rituals that he witnessed amongst its South Indian communities.

Back in England and demobilised in 1947, he considered his options afresh and, disliking modern designs in architecture, decided not to return to the Regent Street Polytechnic to qualify as an architect but to pursue his newly acquired interest in India through a BA in Hindi with a Sanskrit subsidiary at the School of Oriental and African Studies (SOAS). After the disciplined order of his army experience, Raymond later recorded that SOAS was something of a shock 'reverting to an undergraduate experience' and 'embarking upon a newly created and virtually unstructured course'. It was also immediately after leaving the army that Raymond abandoned shaving for the rest of his life, thus initiating his signature beard. At SOAS he particularly enjoyed the lectures by Professor A. L. Basham but, more significantly, Raymond also met Professor Kenneth de Burgh Codrington and Colonel D. H. Gordon. Earlier, as Keeper of the Indian Section at the Victoria and Albert Museum, Codrington had been credited for initiating a more archaeological approach to South Asian art and in the 1940s held the only post in Indian Archaeology at a British university, although Raymond was to remain unconvinced of his field abilities. In contrast, Jock Gordon was to be of great practical help to Raymond as one of the last of the generation of Raj military antiquarians and the author of numerous papers and books, including *The Pre-historic Background of Indian Culture* (Bombay, 1958). During long vacations, Raymond also acquired archaeological field training from Sir Mortimer Wheeler's excavations at Dorchester, Colchester and Verulamium. Raymond was awarded a First Class degree in 1951 and was immediately offered a Treasury Scholarship to start a Ph.D. on the development of early culture in Raichur District of Hyderabad in the Deccan under the supervision of Codrington. This was also a year of great significance in his personal life as he married Bridget Gordon, a fellow Ph.D. student registered at the Institute of Archaeology. Raymond's grant covered the couple's travel to India as well as the purchase of an Austin pickup with which they travelled out by ship. However, before he could start his own research, Codrington invited Raymond to accompany him on an expedition to Afghanistan.

Throughout his life, Raymond was firmly attached to fieldwork and his first introduction to South Asian fieldwork was in the Bamiyan Valley of Afghanistan in 1951. Here, under the direction of Codrington, he studied the standing remains of Shahr-e-Zohak, the fortified residence and stronghold of the semi-independent Yabghu and Shansabani rulers of Bamiyan, dating to between the sixth and thirteenth centuries AD. Codrington divided up the work with Raymond undertaking the arduous survey and Codrington the photography. Raymond recalled that the slopes of the 180-metre-high site were so precipitous that it was impossible for him to map it using a plane table but that he spent up to twelve hours a day climbing, surveying and drawing during the six-week season. Looking back, he also commented that 'I still feel it to have been quite an achievement to survey this very complex site single-handed. We had succeeded in putting on record something quite unique.' This initial study was much later developed with Piers Baker as a doctoral topic and resulted in a jointly published volume entitled *Shahr-i Zohak and the History of the Bamiyan Valley, Afghanistan* (Oxford, 1991). Raymond's original sections and plans from the 1951 season feature heavily in the volume, reflecting his architecturally influenced approach to sequences and phases but also his attention to ceramic sequences. When reviewed in the *Journal of the Royal Asiatic Society* in 1992, Dr Warrick Ball stated that the volume was 'the first archaeological publication on Bamiyan since the pioneering works of Hackin and Carl' in the 1930s as well as drawing attention to the 'exhaustive detail on technical matters such as vaulting systems and squinches'—a lasting legacy of Raymond's architectural training.

Raymond remained a close observer of Afghan archaeology, particularly as he was aware how important it was to try to link the absolute sequences of Mesopotamia with the relative ones of India and Pakistan. Indeed, in reviewing the report of the excavations at the key Bronze Age site of Mundigak by Jean-Marie Casal, which he had visited in 1951, he stated that 'One is left with a feeling of the inadequacy of so much of the earlier work at some of the great sites of Iran which have for decades remained enigmas for those who attempt to trace the links between the sequences of Iraq and the Indus Valley.'[1] Raymond later subscribed to the newly formed Society of Afghan Studies in 1972 and joined its Council in 1979. He was a strong supporter of the Society's excavations at Kandahar and made a number of visits to the site. Joining forces with Professor

[1] F. R. Allchin, 'Review of *Fouilles de Mundigak* by J.-M. Casal', *Bulletin of the School of Oriental and Afrcian Studies*, 26 (1963), 662.

Norman Hammond, FBA, who had been the Society's Honorary Editor and had led an expedition in Helmand in 1966, they published *The Archaeology of Afghanistan from Earliest Times to the Timurid Period* (London, 1978). Hitherto, the archaeology of Afghanistan had been only the subject of a single chapter in Professor Louis Dupree's seminal work *Afghanistan* (New York, 1973), but now Hammond and Raymond set to work by bringing together an impressive series of specialists. Published in the same year as the Russian invasion of Afghanistan, and its subsequent descent into chaos, one can detect a certain poignancy in the words of Professor Walter Fairservis, who, in reviewing the volume, stated that 'Now when the time has finally arrived when, for example, ideas relative to diffusion or indigenous evolution might be tested, the opportunity to do so has vanished.'[2] This volume, although out of print, remains one of the core texts for the synthesis of the sequences of Afghanistan and represents what Professor Richard Frye of Harvard termed 'the most useful handbook on archaeology in Afghanistan'.[3]

With this work for his supervisor completed, Raymond and Bridget drove back from Kabul to Hyderabad and there Raymond started his doctoral research in Raichur District. The topic had been selected by Codrington due to his interest in the recent acquisition of materials from the late Captain Leonard Munn of the Hyderabad Geological Survey. This material from Raichur comprised cattle bones, ash, Neolithic-like stone tools and reports and photographs of a variety of sites. Raymond was also sent to the field with advice from Professor Frederick Zeuner of the Institute of Archaeology, who had analysed the ash and confirmed that it derived from cow dung. Significantly, Raymond had selected one of the areas of South Asian archaeology most poorly understood, the prehistory of Peninsular India, which had not had the same attention as either the Bronze Age Indus cities or those of the Early Historic period in the north of the Subcontinent. To an extent, the excavations by Sir Mortimer Wheeler at Arikamdu in 1945 and Brahmagiri in 1947 and those by Jean-Marie Casal at Virampatnam-Arikamedu in 1949 and B. K. Thapar at Maski in 1954 had begun to shed light on the Iron Age and Early Historic interface of the Peninsular but the Neolithic of the region was highly neglected although it was beginning to be explored by Dr B. Subbararo of Bombay University. Now working independently of Codrington,

[2] W. A. Fairservis, 'Review of *The Archaeology of Afghanistan from the Earliest Times to the Timurid Period*', *American Anthropologist*, 82 (1980), 421.

[3] R. N. Frye, 'Review of *The Archaeology of Afghanistan from the Earliest Times to the Timurid Period*', *Journal of Asian Studies*, 40 (1981), 809.

Raymond undertook a survey of sites within the District and selected Piklihal for further investigation, thus tackling the problem of the interpretation of the ash mounds of Peninsular India. These enigmatic circular mounds, or cinder camps as they were frequently termed, often survive up to 10 metres in height and were known to be formed of alternating layers of ash and vitrified materials. Their function was much disputed, with some previous investigators suggesting that they had been the sites of medieval iron-working and others, most notably Colonel Robert Bruce Foote in the 1870s, suggesting that the ash had been produced by burnt cow dung. Excavating in 1952, and again in 1957, with the assistance of the Andhra Pradesh Department of Archaeology and Museums, Raymond clearly demonstrated that the ash mound had a distinct Neolithic sequence with later evidence of Iron Age occupation above. When his 1960 excavation publication *Piklihal Excavations* (Hyderabad) was reviewed by Professor D. D. Kosambi, the great Marxist historian, Raymond was complimented for providing 'one of the most satisfying reports available on any Indian excavations',[4] and Dr Anthony Christie also commented that Raymond had demonstrated that 'these first settlers in the Deccan provided a number of the basic elements in the present-day culture of the region. This is a major contribution to the history of India.'[5]

Submitting his thesis 'The Development of Early Culture in Raichur District of Hyderabad in the Deccan' in 1954, Raymond was almost immediately offered a Lectureship in Indian Archaeology at SOAS and later returned to Raichur in 1957 on research leave. In order to test some of his earlier theories about Piklihal, Raymond now selected Utnur, one of the best-preserved ash mounds, to excavate, which had also been identified by Captain Munn. In a single season, he cut through metres of cinder and ash, and discovered that the mounds were contained by series of postholes, demarking superimposed circular stockades. Thus disproving the medieval hypothesis, he again dated them far earlier to the Neolithic of south India and to the fourth millennium BC on account of the associated polished stone axes. Again, Raymond swiftly published the results of his fieldwork at Utnur with a monograph entitled *Utnur Excavations* (Hyderabad, 1961) and he interpreted the stockades as annual cattle camps, whose accumulations of dung were burnt at the end of each grazing season, thus creating a regular sequence of ash and cinder. This con-

[4] D. D. Kosambi, 'Review of *Piklihal Excavations*', *Man*, 64 (1964), 164.

[5] A. Christie, 'Review of *Piklihal Excavations*', *Bulletin of the School of African and Oriental Studies*, 28 (1965), 169.

clusion allowed him to distinguish a distinct cultural sequence for Peninsular India from its Neolithic to its Iron Age megalithic cemeteries, as well as providing him with material for the humorous opening to his synthesis of this regional research, *The Neolithic Cattle-keepers of South India* (Cambridge, 1963), with the words 'This is a book about cow-dung, or rather the ash of cow-dung.'[6] This later synthesis also enabled Raymond to develop a narrative which bound together Hindu ritual tradition and contemporary pastoral practice with the archaeological narrative, and suggest that the regular burning of the stockades was not a calamity or the result of raiding but part of an annual fire rite, perhaps surviving today as *Holi*, *Divali* or *Pongal*. Professor George Dales of the University of California, Berkeley, noted that this approach was a 'courageous, often brilliant, effort conducted in the very spirit of interdisciplinary research',[7] and Raymond's pioneering work became the key reference point for subsequent studies of the Deccan Neolithic with Professor K. Paddaya, Director of Deccan College, Pune, referring to Raymond's ceramic classifications as 'Admirable and technically sound'.[8] Raymond's Deccan fieldwork, on which he was accompanied by Bridget and two small children, was also to formalise two key features in his later writing, the diffusion of culture and ethnoarchaeological analogy. The former was clearly articulated in his suggestion in *Utnur Excavations* that the cattle keepers of the Deccan 'belonged to the Neolithic of the Deccan, whose origins we have traced to north eastern Iran moving into Peninsular India in a series of waves',[9] and the latter by his suggestion that some *thali*-making techniques in the 1950s in Raichur District 'may be a survival from Neolithic times' in his 1959 paper on 'Poor men's *thalis*: a Deccan potter's technique'.[10]

In 1959 Raymond left SOAS and moved to the Lectureship in Indian Studies at Cambridge recently vacated by Dr Johanna van Lohuizen-de Leeuw; he now turned his attention to Pakistan and worked at the site of Shaikhan Dheri between 1963 and 1964 with Professor A. H. Dani of Peshawar University. Located in North West Frontier Province (now known as Khyber Pakhtunkhwa), the site had come to prominence following Sir Mortimer Wheeler's excavations at the Bala Hisar of Charsadda in

[6] p. ix.

[7] G. F. Dales, 'Review of *The Neolithic Cattle-keepers of South India*', *Journal of the American Oriental Society*, 84 (1964), 93.

[8] K. Paddaya, *Investigations into the Neolithic Culture of the Shorapur Doab, South India* (Leiden, 1973), p. 15.

[9] F. R. Allchin, *Utnur Excavations* (Hyderabad, 1961), p. 65.

[10] F. R. Allchin, 'Poor men's *thalis*: a Deccan potter's technique', *Bulletin of the School of Oriental and African Studies*, 22 (1959), 250–7.

1958. The latter was one of the largest tell sites in Pakistan, reaching a height of 23 metres above the surrounding plain, and had been dated by Wheeler to between the middle of the first millennium BC and the first century AD. Whilst excavating at the site and finding putative evidence of both an Achaemenid foundation and Alexander the Great's expedition, Wheeler commissioned some aerial photographs of the site and its immediate surroundings from the Pakistani Air Force. On examination of the images, Wheeler immediately recognised a distinctive pattern of robbed-out walls on the surface of the Shaikhan Dheri, a mound some 3 kilometres away from the Bala Hisar across the Shambor Nala. From the pattern of ghost walls, it was possible to distinguish the regular grid-iron street pattern of an Indo-Greek city, complete with major *stupa* shrine. With such clear parallels with the well-studied city of Sirkap in the Taxila Valley, the site was selected for further investigation as well as offering an ideal opportunity for the training of Pakistani students. Joining the team from Peshawar University, Raymond and Bridget supervised the processing and registration of antiquities and pottery drawing during the first season. Despite having successfully raised funds from Cambridge and the British Academy, the season still represented a major chronological and geographical challenge to Raymond in terms of his existing specialism in the prehistoric archaeology of the Deccan. What was envisaged as the first of a number of seasons of collaborative fieldwork between the universities of Peshawar and Cambridge was curtailed in 1964 with Raymond later simply commenting that the relationship had been 'ill-starred'.[11]

Raymond did, however, continue to work on his notes and later produced two papers although they did take a number of years to appear. The first was published in 1970 in the *Journal of the Royal Asiatic Society* and considered the importance of a number of small iron plates pierced with small holes around their edges, some of which had rusted together. Following his typical multidisciplinary approach with reference to Gandharan sculpture, excavation reports, textual sources and more recent Rajput examples, he suggested that they had formed part of the scale armour from the cap of a cataphract. His second paper on Shaikhan Dheri, published in *Man* in 1979, also pursued a similar methodological approach to examine a number of globular vessels. Whilst Sir John Marshall had interpreted similar examples at Sirkap for the distillation of water, Raymond again used a combination of ethnographic analogy, Vedic

[11] F. R. Allchin, 'A piece of scale armour from Shaihkan dheri, Charsada', *Journal of the Royal Asiatic Society*, 2 (1970), 113.

references and Rajput texts to reinterpret them as alcohol stills. Opening the paper by stating that 'Considering the importance of alcohol for mankind ... it is surprising that comparatively little is known of its early history,'[12] and concluding that 'it may well be that the art of distillation was India's gift to the world!',[13] one also catches an insight into Raymond's somewhat mischievous sense of humour. The experience of working at Shaikhan Dheri also provided Raymond and Bridget with future links to the University of Peshawar through a number of the younger staff as well as an insight into its place within the cultural sequences of the Subcontinent. Indeed, when reviewing Sir Mortimer Wheeler's monograph on the 1958 excavations at the Bala Hisar of Charsadda, Raymond was able to recognise its value in terms of its long cultural sequence, concluding that Wheeler's 'Charsadda excavations provide ... a foundation upon which all future work in north-western Pakistan on this period must be based.'[14]

Whilst Raymond was expanding his field experience in the early 1960s, he was also confirming his academic reputation in Hindi and Sanskrit with the publication of a volume entitled *Tulsi Das: Kavitavali* in the Indian series of UNESCO's Collection of Representative Works (London, 1964). Reviewed in the *Bulletin of the School of Oriental and African Studies* by John Burton-Page, Raymond's attention to chronology and historical context were praised as well as his 'sympathetic understanding and flair for lucid exposition'.[15] He later followed this volume with a companion translation volume, *Tulsi Das: the Petition to Ram* (London, 1966), and a shorter paper on the broader place and context of Tulsi Das in north Indian devotional tradition in the *Journal of the Royal Asiatic Society* in 1966. Whilst continuing to exploit his knowledge of the Hindi and Sanskrit textual traditions throughout his career, his final academic contribution to this field was with a paper on the reconciliation of *Jnana* and *Bhakti* in the Tulsi Das' *Ramacaritamanasa* in *Religious Studies* in 1976. This background provided him with what Professor Paddaya has recently called 'a deep appreciation of the spiritual and religious heritage of India'.

After his false start in Pakistan, Raymond shifted his focus back to India and undertook an archaeological reconnaissance of the coast of

[12] F. R. Allchin, 'India: the home of ancient distillation', *Man*, 14 (1979), 55

[13] Ibid., p. 63.

[14] F. R. Allchin, 'Review of *Charsada*', *Bulletin of the School of Oriental and African Studies*, 27 (1964), 187.

[15] J. Burton-Page, 'Review of *Tulsi Das: Kalitavali*', *Bulletin of the School of Oriental and African Studies*, 28 (1965), 403.

Gujarat in 1967, following this in 1968 with excavations at the site of Malvan with Bridget and Dr J. P. Joshi, of the Archaeological Survey of India (ASI). Raymond stressed the successful nature of this collaboration and he and Joshi jointly published a preliminary report in the *Journal of the Royal Asiatic Society* in 1970 with the full volume in the memoir series of the ASI (*Excavations at Malvan*: Cambridge, 1995). Funded by the ASI, the British Academy and the Cambridge Smuts Fund, the fieldwork was focused on investigating the presence or absence of sites associated with the Indus civilisation in western India. Such a search was timely as Sir Mortimer Wheeler had advised Indian archaeologists in 1949 after Partition that they had lost the river Indus which had provided India with her name as well as the earliest Bronze Age cities of the Subcontinent but that they now should focus on the river which had given India her faith, the Ganga. Whilst some archaeologists chose to focus on the Ganga and its early Iron Age sequences, others like Joshi were motivated by trying to find the eastern extent of those Bronze Age cities. The 1967 and 1968 expeditions were thus part of this wider campaign and focused on a small two-metre-high mound close to the mouth of the Tapti River and downstream of the old Mughal port of Surat. Whilst the wider campaign certainly succeeded, as illustrated by the discoveries of the walled city of Kalibangan in Rajasthan in 1953 and Rangpur and the port of Lothal in Gujarat in 1954, the settlement at Malvan proved to have been occupied in the post-urban Chalcolithic period. Whilst thus not formally belonging to the Indus civilisation, the site was still important as it provided evidence for the continued coastal trade of semi-precious stone as well as the presence of sufficient authority and community to excavate an 18-metre-long and 1.5-metre-wide ditch along one side of the site. The expedition also provided Raymond with valuable experience of working with Chalcolithic material as well the opportunity of collaborating with Joshi, one of India's leading archaeologists and later Director General of Archaeology between 1987 and 1990.

After a number of years, Raymond and Bridget returned to fieldwork in North West Frontier Province in the Bannu Basin, working collaboratively with their now promoted colleagues in the University of Peshawar between 1977 and 1979. Working first at Lewan and later at Tarakai Qila with Professor F. A. Durrani and Professor Farid Khan of Peshawar University, Mr Robert Knox of the British Museum, and Professor Ken Thomas of UCL, the team provided what Massimo Vidale termed 'a first step in the direction of filling a large geographical and cultural gap in the knowledge of the Early Harappan phenomenon' on the western edge of the Indus watershed.[16] Later as Joint Director of the British Archaeological Mission to Pakistan with Bridget, Raymond was to begin to focus his attention away from the Bronze Age to the Early Historic period of between *c*.900 BC and AD 350, and onto the site of Taxila in particular. Proud owners of a newly imported blue Toyota land cruiser which Piers Baker had driven up from the docks at Karachi to Taxila, Raymond and Bridget took a stroll around the Hathial ridge one February morning in 1980, not far from the Taxila Museum guesthouse. During their walk, they discovered numerous sherds of a distinctive, highly burnished red ware covering an area of 13 hectares along the foot of the spur and Raymond immediately recognised that these sherds belonged to the category of Burnished Red Ware associated with the Gandharan grave culture, and dated to the beginning of the first millennium BC at the end of the Chalcolithic period. Raymond was also aware of the parallel presence of such sherds in the basal levels of Wheeler's excavations at the Bala Hisar of Charsadda. The presence of such an early ceramic type at two of Gandharan's main Early Historic cities was most surprising as it challenged received wisdom at the time that suggested that such cities had been founded no earlier than the sixth century BC as the Persian Empire expanded eastwards and annexed the satrapy of Gandhara. Publishing a short paper in *Antiquity* in 1982 entitled 'How old is the city of Taxila?', Raymond directly challenged a model which had been particularly energetically favoured by Sir Mortimer Wheeler and suggested instead that the urban sequence of Taxila, and by extension South Asia, was under way long before Persian contact, possibly going back to the late Chalcolithic times. However, Raymond did not commence excavations at the site as it was now Bridget's turn to direct her own prehistoric research with fieldwork in the Great Thar Desert with Professor K. T. M. Hegde of the M.S. University of Baroda and Professor Andrew Goudie of the University of Oxford. Bridget subsequently developed links with the Pakistan Geological Survey and played a critical role in initiating collaborations which resulted in a survey of the Potwar Plateau directed by Professor Robin Dennell of the University of Sheffield and Professor Helen Rendell of the University of Sussex to search for Palaeolithic industries during the second phase of the British Archaeological Mission to Pakistan with the support of the Leverhulme Trust. The final activity of the Mission was for Raymond to negotiate the return of an archaeological team to Charsadda after a gap of thirty years but this time focused on the development of a chronometric

[16] M. Vidale, 'Review of *Lewan and the Bannu Basin*', *East and West*, 38 (1988), 326.

sequence for the Bala Hisar of Charsadda, jointly directed by Professor Ihsan Ali of Peshawar University and Professor Robin Coningham of Durham between 1993 and 1997, and confirming a much earlier date of *c.*1300 BC for its initial settlement.

Raymond's interest in the Early Historic period, and the emergence of its cities in particular, represented his last major academic phase of development and was largely explored through his own writing as well as through research arising from the fieldwork of a number of his later research students. For example, Dr Muhammad Usman (formerly George) Erdosy and Professor Makkhan Lal, now of the Delhi Institute of Heritage Research and Management, were to research Iron Age and Early Historic settlement patterns in Allahabad and Kanpur Districts, respectively. These data allowed Raymond to consider the presence, or otherwise, of the settlement hierarchies advocated by the great Early Historic minister to the Mauryans, Kautiliya, as contained within the *Arthashastra*. His formative views on the development of the cities themselves were developed through two papers in the journal *South Asian Studies*, one entitled 'City and state formation in Early Historic South Asia' (1989) and the second 'Patterns of city formation in Early Historic South Asia' (1990).

In 1989, and at the age of 67, Raymond initiated his last major field project in Sri Lanka at the Citadel of Anuradhapura in the island's North Central Province following a joint invitation from Dr Roland Silva, Director General of Archaeology, and Dr Siran Deraniyagala, one of his former students and then Archaeological Advisor to the Government of Sri Lanka. Recognising that he would need assistance with the execution of this project, Raymond invited his former undergraduate and new research student, Robin Coningham, to accept the role of Field Director. The project was of great significance as Sri Lanka had always been assumed to have adopted urbanism far later than any other area within the Subcontinent due to its peripheral position far away from both the Indus and Ganga alluvium. As a result, most scholars had assumed that its cities had been founded through contact with the Mauryan world in the middle of the third century BC or even later in the first century AD, as suggested by Sir Mortimer Wheeler based on his findings at the site of Arikamedu in Southern India. However, Raymond was far more open-minded and, indeed, had been one of the first scholars to recognise the impact of Jean-Marie Casal's later excavations at Virampatnam-Arikamedu and comment that the new sequence at Arikamedu was parallel to that of Brahmagiri, and that contact with Mediterranean world was with an already established settlement, one firmly linked to the earlier prehistoric cultural sequences of the Deccan.[17] Excavating trench Anuradhapura Salgaha Watta 2 between 1989 and 1993, Coningham and Allchin provided a ten-metre-deep cultural sequence for the city stretching from the ninth century BC to the tenth century AD and providing evidence of urbanism in the fourth century BC but also confirming Deraniyagala's early claim of evidence of the earliest Early Brahmi script anywhere in South Asia. Whilst some Sri Lankan newspapers offered headlines that suggested that 'Lankans wrote before Indians', analysis of the script demonstrated that it had been used to facilitate trade and commerce before it had later became adopted as an imperial tool by the Mauryans in the third century BC as argued in a joint paper in the *Cambridge Archaeological Journal*,[18] and in the discussion of the full corpus of inscriptions in the second volume on the Anuradhapura excavations.[19]

As well as undertaking almost forty years of field investigations, Raymond was also motivated by the need to record and protect heritage as the pressures of increasing population and modernisation took their toll on the cultural resource of the Subcontinent. Later, Raymond was to propose 'Allchin's Law for South Asia' which held that 'Economic progress and population expansion are certain to lead to the destruction of archaeological sites.' He was also moved by the fact that a number of the rock paintings which he and Bridget had recorded at Piklihal in 1957 had already been demolished as part of road widening when he revisited the site later in 1972. Largely forgotten now, Raymond was also one of the pioneers for the protection of heritage sites within their cultural landscape, as illustrated by his work for the UN with the Japanese Planner and Architect, K. Matsushita, in 1969. Raymond and Matsushita had been contracted by UNPD with the responsibility 'for inspiring and guiding the development of Lumbini', the birthplace of the Buddha.[20] This mission arose following the 1967 visit to the site by U-Thant, the UN Secretary General, who wished to see the site transformed from what Raymond called 'little more than a neglected field' to a site worthy of 'a collection of monuments of great importance'.[21] Interestingly for an archaeologist with

[17] F. R. Allchin, 'Review of Fouilles de Virampatnam-Arikamedu', *Bulletin of the School of Oriental and African Studies*, 19 (1957), 598–9.

[18] R. A. E. Coningham, F. R. Allchin, C. M. Batt and D. Lucy, 'Passage to India? Anuradhapura and the early use of Brahmi script', *Cambridge Archaeological Journal*, 6 (1996), 73–97.

[19] R. A. E. Coningham, F. R. Allchin and O. Bopearachchi, *Anuradhapura: the British Sri-Lankan Excavations at Anuradhapura Salagha Watta 2. Volume 2 The Artefacts* (Oxford, 2006).

[20] F. R. Allchin and K. Matsushita, *Unpublished UNDP Report for the Lumbini Development Project* (New York, 1969), p. 2.

[21] Ibid., p. 10.

a background in architecture, Raymond was also tasked with assisting the planning of a sacred garden, pilgrim village and a buffer zone around the site. This pioneering report was later to be used by the Japanese architect, Kenso Tange, as the core for his masterplan for Lumbini, which has directed the development of Lumbini over the last thirty years and will continue to do so. Raymond's contribution to the latter's masterplan made it clear that proposed major intervention at the site should be preceded by excavating and he and Matsushita suggested that a monastic area was developed, further buffering the tourist village from the core monuments. He was also clear that the excavation should be 'of a high quality so that all categories of information may be obtained and the whole range of modern scientific techniques brought to bear'.[22] As a primary document it was examined again by the current UNESCO project at Lumbini, directed by Professor Yukio Nishimura of Tokyo University, Professor Robin Coningham of Durham and Dr Constatino Merucci of Rome. Today, as in 1969, the Lumbini Development Trust and the UNESCO project continue to follow Raymond's advice that within Lumbini's context of Hindus, Muslims and Buddhists living in close proximity, it is critical that any new 'design must therefore seek to avoid any hint of narrow sectarian bias'.[23]

Active in South Asia in the immediate post-Independence period, Raymond was the first of a new generation of British archaeologists who sought to work collaboratively with South Asian colleagues as a guest. Unlike the large academic communities of Near Eastern archaeologists, however, Raymond was a single isolated scholar researching South Asia within Britain but successfully pursued a programme to make South Asian archaeology accessible and mainstream through a raft of sole, joint and edited publications. Whilst the early volumes focused on the direct results and interpretation of his pioneering fieldwork in the Deccan Neolithic (1960, 1961 and 1963), his enduring contribution was through the completion of three major synthetic works, *The Birth of Indian Civilization* (London, 1968) and *The Rise of Civilisation in India and Pakistan* (Cambridge, 1982), jointly with Bridget, and *The Archaeology of Early Historic South Asia* (Cambridge, 1995), with Bridget and three former research students. The first of these was published by Penguin and was the direct successor to Stuart Piggott's earlier Penguin *Prehistoric India* of 1950, which had been based on the latter's experience following a posting

[22] Allchin and Matsushita, *Unpublished UNDP Report for the Lumbini Development Project*, p. 8.

[23] Ibid., p. 11.

in India during the war. Reflecting on his own volume twenty-five years later when it was republished by Penguin India, Raymond suggested that *The Birth* had been 'a comprehensive summary' and 'mini reference book' although noting that 'attitudes and approaches to the study of the past have changed fundamentally, and new questions are still being asked'.[24] In parallel with Professor H. D. Sankalia's 1962 synthesis, *The Prehistory and Protohistory of India and Pakistan, The Birth of Indian Civilization* attempted to provide a review of South Asian prehistory from the earliest period until the Iron Age. As one might anticipate, Raymond and Bridget were highly reliant on the agency of diffusion for cultural change and again Aryan influences were sought, whether at the end of the urban phase of the Bronze Age Indus cities or in the advent of megalithic construction in the Deccan. The volume was replaced in 1982 by *The Rise of Civilisation in India and Pakistan*, published by Cambridge University Press, and whilst absorbing the new phenomena of discoveries over the intervening period, remained highly detailed in terms of cultural sequences but offered less in terms of explanations for changes within those sequences. It was welcomed by former student, Professor Romila Thapar of Jawaharlal Nehru University, as 'a very useful guide to the data' but she voiced some of the concerns of others in that the successor of *The Birth* continued to cite controversial archaeological and linguistic evidence for an Aryan intrusion.[25]

Raymond's earlier interest in the Early Historic period culminated in the publication of another Cambridge University Press volume, *The Archaeology of Early Historic South Asia: the Emergence of Cities and States* (1995). Edited by Raymond, it brought together a series of papers by himself, Bridget and former students, Muhammad Usman Erdosy, Robin Coningham and Dilip Chakrabarti. Raymond's contributions included a chapter entitled 'Language, culture and the concept of ethnicity' and examined their nexus and the arrival of Indo-Aryan speaking peoples into the Subcontinent. Raymond continued to make clear one-to-one identifications, for example, stating that the Gandharan Grave Culture burials of the northern valleys of northern Pakistan 'are probably the traces of a rather separate group of immigrants' but found his contribution in direct contrast with those of other contributors.[26] Representing one

[24] B. Allchin and F. R. Allchin, *The Birth of Indian Civilization* (Cambridge, 1982), pp. 7–8.

[25] R. Thapar, 'Review of *The Rise of Civilization in India and Pakistan*', *Journal of the American Oriental Society*, 104 (1984), 336.

[26] F. R. Allchin, 'Language, culture and the concept of ethnicity', in F. R. Allchin (ed.), *The Archaeology of Early Historic South Asia* (Cambridge, 1995), p. 50.

of the first synthetic volumes on this period, some like Professor Kathleen Morrison of the University of Chicago found this inconsistency problematical whilst others, like Ali, were warmer in welcoming it as 'the first comprehensive attempt to redress' the major focus on the prehistory of South Asia,[27] Professor Richard Meadows of Harvard who called it a 'welcome overview',[28] and Professor Monica Smith of the University of Michigan who referred to it as 'the classic statement of his (Raymond's) academic views on the Early Historic period'.[29] Raymond and Bridget's final synthesis, *Origins of a Civilisation: the Prehistory and Early Archaeology of South Asia*, was published in India by Viking for a more general readership in 1997 to celebrate the fiftieth anniversary of the independence of India and Pakistan.

The presence of Bridget as a major contributor to these four volumes confirms that she provided core academic support to Raymond's career, a situation which he himself acknowledged in his very earliest phase of research. Indeed, Bridget was to take on the responsibility for the two children, innumerable dogs and the house whilst successfully maintaining a core contribution to Raymond's research as well as undertaking research in her own right. Bridget was born in Oxford but raised on a farm in Galloway which she largely ran with her mother during the war with the assistance of German prisoners of war. Bridget then started a degree in History and Ancient History at UCL but, at the end of her first year, left for South Africa when her parents decided to emigrate. Interested in the culture of neighbouring Basutoland, Bridget persuaded her parents to let her leave the new farm and recommence her studies and she enrolled at the University of Cape Town to read African Studies, which included anthropology, archaeology and an African language. Taught by Professor Isaac Shapira and Dr A. J. H. Goodwin, Bridget developed a specialism in the South African Stone Age but decided to return to England to recommence her studies in London in 1950 in order to broaden her knowledge of the lithic industries of the Old World, studying under Professor Frederick Zeuner of the Institute of Archaeology. It was at lectures on the prehistory of India by Zeuner at the Institute that Raymond and Bridget first met as Raymond augmented his own lectures from Codrington. Bridget's

[27] D. Ali, 'Review of *The Archaeology of Early Historic South Asia*', *Journal of the Royal Asiatic Society*, 7 (1997), 145.

[28] R. Meadows, 'Review of *The Archaeology of Early Historic South Asia*', *Journal of Asian Studies*, 56 (1997), 515.

[29] M. L. Smith, 'Review of *The Archaeology of Early Historic South Asia*', *American Journal of Archaeology*, 101 (1997), 817.

willingness to quickly marry and travel out to India with Raymond was undoubtedly partly due to her knowledge of the Subcontinent, acquired from her father's experience as an officer of the Indian Army Medical Service attached to the Fifty-Eighth Frontier Force, comprising mainly Pathans from the North West Frontier Province. An independent author and researcher in her own right, she published *The Stone-Tipped Arrow: a Study of Late Stone Age Cultures of the Tropical Regions of the Old World* (London, 1966) and *The Prehistory and Palaeography of the Great Indian Desert* (with Andrew Goudie and K. T. M. Hegde: London, 1978) as well as holding the role of founding Editor of the journal *South Asian Studies* for over a decade. A Fellow of the Society of Antiquaries and Fellow of Wolfson College, Cambridge, Bridget also held the post of Secretary General of the European Association of South Asian Archaeologists and edited a number of its proceedings as well as *Living Traditions: Studies in the Ethnoarchaeology of South Asia* (Oxford, 1994). She also held the post of Secretary and latterly Chairman of the Ancient India and Iran Trust.

Aware of the fragmented nature of South Asian scholarship across Europe, and seeking a greater capacity than that available within Britain, together with a small band of colleagues from across Europe, Raymond and Bridget created a biannual platform for South Asian archaeologists, numismatists, epigraphers and historians of art and architecture to exchange information from ongoing excavations and research. Moreover, it provided an opportunity to enhance the bond of shared professional and regional interests which other 'oriental' conferences failed to provide and in the words of Sir Mortimer Wheeler 'one could not help reflecting that such a gathering would scarcely have been thinkable as recently as a generation ago. Then the archaeology of the East was still primarily a minor preserve of European expatriates, with relatively little interchange.'[30] Thus formed, the first meeting of the European Association of South Asian Archaeologists was organised by Raymond and Bridget and met at Churchill College in Cambridge in 1971. When the Association returned again to Cambridge in 1995, Raymond noted that the divisions into numerous simultaneous sessions was indicative of the penalties of its success whilst also stressing the need felt by those active in the field for such a common meeting ground in Europe stating that 'no one can question its usefulness, popularity, nor the international status it has achieved'.[31]

[30] R. E. M. Wheeler, 'Foreword', in N. Hammond (ed.), *South Asian Archaeology 1971* (London, 1973), pp. ix–x.

[31] F. R. Allchin, 'The South Asian Archaeologists' Conference after 25 years: some reflections', in F. R. Allchin and B. Allchin (eds.), *South Asian Archaeology 1995* (New Delhi, 1997), p. 7.

Certainly its biannual conference proceedings remain one of the core reference volumes as many of the sites reported have never been fully published. For example, the key pre-pottery Neolithic site of Mehrgarh is still awaiting a final monograph but core papers on different aspects of its excavations and post-excavation analysis allow students and academics early access. Raymond also firmly used the first volume to present considerations on 'Problems and perspectives in South Asian Archaeology', reflecting on the continued search for Indo-Aryan speakers as well as the neglect of the Early Historic cities of South Asia and, finally, the need for a shared terminology for the various phases of the Indus civilisation.[32] Continuing to argue for greater use of research-oriented excavation, he also later took the opportunity to challenge South Asian archaeologists, concluding *The Archaeology of Early Historic South Asia* with the statement that 'The volume of relevant data is certainly enormous, but the quality of so much is poor. There is an almost universal need for more problem oriented research; for a more innovative approach to theoretical problems and interpretation; and for much wider applications of scientific analysis.'[33]

Back in Cambridge, Raymond's contributions to his field were recognised and he was appointed a Fellow of Churchill College in 1963 and promoted to a Readership in Indian Studies in 1972. Externally, he was also recognised and made a Fellow of the Royal Asiatic Society in 1953, a Fellow of the Society of Antiquaries in 1957, a Fellow of the Royal Society of Arts in 1974 and a Fellow of the British Academy in 1981 as well as having an Honorary D.Litt. conferred by Deccan College, Pune in 2007. In addition to his contributions to the European Association, he also served on the Governing Council of the Society for Afghan Studies and its successor, the Society for South Asian Studies, as well as being associated with the Charles Wallace Pakistan Trust, the British Academy's Stein-Arnold Committee and the Advisory Council of the Victoria and Albert Museum. Not only did these publications, committees and conferences firmly propel South Asia into the mainstream of the English-speaking archaeological world but they also attracted research students and post-doctoral fellows to Raymond's office in Sidgwick Avenue. One of his strengths as a supervisor was never to be surprised by new or unexpected results, which would swiftly be reviewed and either assimilated or rejected.

[32] F. R. Allchin, 'Problems and perspectives in South Asian archaeology', in N. Hammond (ed.), *South Asian Archaeology 1971* (London, 1973), p. 10.

[33] F. R. Allchin, 'Concluding synthesis', in F. R. Allchin (ed.), *The Archaeology of Early Historic South Asia* (Cambridge, 1995), p. 341.

This trait, which in combination with his suspicion of theoretical trends, allowed him to update his publications and rethink his sequences as he acknowledged major discoveries such as the pre-pottery Neolithic sequence at Mehrgarh or the presence of pre-Asokan Early Brahmi at Anuradhapura. Indeed, Raymond's presence in the Faculty of Oriental Studies insulated him from the competing schools of processual and post-processual thought within the Department of Archaeology and Raymond's view of theory was made clear in one reference for a former research student which read that the individual had been 'unduly influenced by the emphasis on theoretical archaeology which was fashionable in his undergraduate days' but was now properly engaged with all aspects of cultural material! Tutored and tested by Raymond amongst an assortment of sherds, sculpture and a particularly large and animated scene of an Indic hell, these individuals form a formidably broad and diverse cohort of academics, keepers and curators of archaeology, ancient history, art and architecture, including former Directors General of Archaeology in India and Sri Lanka and at least one vice chancellor. He was also protective of his research students when necessary, and Professor Danny Miller of UCL wrote soon after Raymond's death that 'He was a genial and generous figure who fully supported my work, mainly by making sure that no one in the University tried to stop me doing what was then seen as a rather unconventional piece of research in ethno-archaeology. For those who knew him he appealed as the kind of "old-school gentleman-scholar" who maintained his affection and concern for colleagues in both South Asia and the UK.'[34] Others have remembered his and Bridget's generosity, with Professor Romila Thapar commenting that 'We were all on a shoe-string budget, given the Government of India regulations regarding foreign exchange in those years, so life was tough' but Raymond and Bridget 'had a lot of affection for South Asian students and were always ready to help with problems—from locating research journals in obscure libraries to finding unused perambulators for babies!'

Following retirement in 1989 with the status of Emeritus Reader in Indian Studies, Raymond remained concerned with the vagaries of continuing university funding for minority subjects such as South Asian archaeology and, now freed from administrative burdens, committed the next twenty years to enhancing the research profile of South Asian archaeology through the work of the Ancient India and Iran Trust. It had been

[34] Reproduced with Professor Miller's permission from <http://blogs.nyu.edu/projects/materialworld/2010/07/raymond_allchin_19232010.html>.

founded earlier in 1987 by Raymond and Bridget, Professor Sir Harold Bailey, Professor Johanna van Lohuizen de Leeuw and Dr Jan van Lohuizen, as an independent charity concerned with the study of early India, Iran and Central Asia, promoting both scholarly research and popular interest in the area. With offices and an excellent library on Brooklands Avenue, the Trust provided, and continues to provide, both Cambridge-based and visiting academics and students with open access to the founders' libraries, specialist seminars and lectures and tea parties of varying cleanliness. As critical, it also continued Raymond's earlier policy of arranging for visiting fellowships to Churchill College, which had included both Professor Romila Thapar and Professor Gregory Possehl of Pennsylvania, by coordinating funds to support a new series of both Indian and Pakistani visiting fellowships. The list of fellows is highly distinguished and its inclusion of scholars of the quality of Dilip Chakrabari, Ravi Korisettar, K. Krishnan, V. N. Misra, Lolita Nehru, K. Paddaya, Gautam Sengupta and Vasant Shinde demonstrates the phenomenal draw which the Allchin name enjoyed. Debate, enquiry and tea at the Trust would often be followed by supper at home in Barrington, where 'Uncle' and 'Auntie', as the Allchins were affectionately known in South Asia, would entertain parties as diverse as their own research interests. Raymond was particularly proud of the new house that they had built in the gardens of their old nineteenth-century farmhouse which had faced the green, because he had designed the plans himself. Reflecting their own personalities and interests, it was focused on a vast joint study and the ample dining room. Although thoroughly professional in supervisions and conferences, Raymond was also known to possess a keen sense of humour as illustrated by chanting a Sanskrit grace whilst presiding at dinner at Churchill College and by presenting a first draft chapter on epigraphy for the second volume of the Anuradhapura excavations in which he had shortened the Peninsular India Symbol System to its acronym. Hospitable but exacting on fieldwork, together Raymond and Bridget could be remarkably persuasive and Sir Nicholas Barrington, then Ambassador to Pakistan, remembered one instance when, having missed their plane from Islamabad to Delhi, Raymond and Bridget succeeded in ordering the Pakistani air traffic controller to have it return to pick them up, despite the very loud protests of crew and passengers.

Suffering from high blood pressure and failing hearing, Raymond began to grow distant from the South Asian field although he never failed to perk up to hear news of new finds and dates and continued to accompany Bridget on her visits to Brooklands House. He suffered a major stroke and went into a coma from which he never recovered and died in Addenbrookes Hospital on 4 June 2010. He is survived by Bridget and their two children, Sushila and William.

ROBIN CONINGHAM
University of Durham

Note. I am extremely grateful to James Cormick, Custodian of the Ancient India and Iran Trust, for kindly sharing the unpublished text of interviews he had recorded with the Allchins concerning Raymond's formative years and their first years in India, and also to a number of their colleagues and former students, who generously offered their recollections. This short memoir is also based on my own personal reflections as a student and colleague of FRA for the last quarter of a century.

CARMEN BLACKER

Carmen Elizabeth Blacker
1924–2009

I

Carmen Blacker was a distinctive figure in Japanese Studies in the second half of the twentieth century and a leading scholar of Japanese religion and folklore.[1] She will be remembered chiefly for her magnum opus on Japanese shamanism, *The Catalpa Bow*.[2] She also published a considerable body of work in the form of papers, lectures, contributions to edited volumes and reviews. This supporting work frequently reveals her methods and assumptions more clearly than the longer book. Nor was her research confined to religion; she also produced notable early work in intellectual history, and more broadly in a series of biographical accounts of men and women connected to Japan. She was a member of what she herself recognised proudly as 'our notable generation',[3] that included a cohort of scholars of Japan who encountered the language during the war such as, in this country, William Beasley, Geoffrey Bownas, Eric Ceadel, Ronald Dore, Charles Dunn, Douglas Mills, Ian Nish and Patrick O'Neill. The group included also scholars who later turned to the study of China, such

[1] A detailed account of her life is given by Peter Kornicki in his 'Carmen Blacker (1924–2009) and the study of Japanese religion', in Hugh Cortazzi (ed.) *Britain and Japan: Biographical Portraits*, vol. 7 (Folkstone, 2010), pp. 216–29.

[2] *The Catalpa Bow: a Study of Shamanistic Practices in Japan* (London, 1975 and subsequent editions; Japanese translation, 1979). In the references that follow, works are by Carmen Blacker unless indicated otherwise.

[3] 'Introduction' to *The Collected Writings of Carmen Blacker*, reprint of Japan Library and Edition Synapse edition of 2000 (Routledge, 2004), p. 2 (henceforward CWCB).

Biographical Memoirs of Fellows of the British Academy, XI, 27–52. © The British Academy 2012.

as Michael Loewe, whom she was to marry, and Denis Twitchett. Her own life seemed to inherit several British cultural, intellectual and scholarly traditions: the intrepid Victorian traveller in the manner of Isabella Bird; the writer of felicitous prose and cultivated lady of letters, in the general style of her own grandfather, but reinforced perhaps by her long friendship with Arthur Waley; the gifted Oxbridge woman scholar in a world still overwhelmingly dominated by men; and the participant in old-established, London-based learned societies.

Carmen was born on 13 July 1924, the eldest of three talented children. Her background was international, privileged and colourful. Her paternal great-grandfather, John Blacker, married a woman from a prominent Peruvian political family, and a cousin of Carmen, Pedro Beltran, was to become prime minister of Peru (1959–61). John Blacker was a bibliophile; his collection of Renaissance book bindings was rumoured, quite unreliably it transpired, to be worth £70,000. His son, Carmen's paternal grandfather, Carlos Blacker (1859–1928), though at one time bankrupt, seems to have recovered to live, mainly abroad, on private means. He numbered Oscar Wilde, Bernard Shaw and Anatole France among his friends. Wilde, indeed, called him 'the best dressed man in London'.[4] Carlos married Miss Caroline Frost, a descendant of a Confederate general in the American Civil War. They had two sons: the younger was killed in the First World War; the elder, Carmen's father, Carlos Paton 'Pip' Blacker (1895–1975), was a hero of both World Wars, wounded twice and awarded the Military Cross in the First World War and the George Medal in the Second World War. He was an influential psychiatrist much influenced by the Jungian tradition, and credited with the basic design of the psychiatric branch of the National Health Service. His influence on Carmen was inestimable. Not least, his bearing suggests something of Carmen's own presence; he was 'tall, spare and determined, [and] remained every inch an old Etonian and ex-Coldstream Guards officer'.[5] He was also a man of great physical vigour: 'Even in his late fifties he thought nothing of running miles and miles along a beach in sunshine in sheer exuberance.'[6] Carmen inherited these traits: she possessed great energy and was tall and slim; she dressed strikingly, often in red, in a style that projected readiness for action but at the same time elegance and authority. Carmen's mother, Helen Maude, was a daughter of Major A. J. Pilkington, from a family associated in an

[4] Richard Ellmann, *Oscar Wilde* (Harmondsworth, 1988), p. 527.

[5] Richard A. Soloway, 'Blacker, Carlos Paton (1895–1975)', *Oxford Dictionary of National Biography* (Oxford, 2004) <http://www.oxforddnb.com/view/article/47726>.

[6] G. C. L. Bertram, Obituary notice, in the *Bulletin of the Eugenics Society*, vol. 7 (3) (1975), p. 19.

earlier generation with the shipping business and the White Star Line in Liverpool. A maternal uncle, Canon Ronald Pilkington (1892–1975), turned from Anglicanism to become a Roman Catholic priest with a special interest in Eastern Christianity; he was in due course to supply Carmen with information on signs of demoniacal possession identified in the Catholic church.[7]

Carmen's early life was spent happily in the family home, 'Pasturewood', a spacious house with extensive grounds in the rural village of Shamley Green, near Guildford. Yet some influence from her father's profession was unavoidable. Carmen was to be high spirited, but also highly strung, all her life. In her early twenties, she was perceived as 'nervous', a trait exacerbated by her wartime experience. Not until 1947 did Eve Edwards, Professor of Chinese at the School of Oriental and African Studies, University of London, feel able to claim on her behalf that 'perhaps one might say that a rather "over-psychologised" childhood appears now to have been surmounted—or justified!'[8] During her Surrey childhood, there were already indications of the direction of her future life. Carmen recollected that her enthusiasm for Japan was probably aroused by her father, who 'used to read aloud to us the myths and stories of various countries, and ... when he came to the stories from the *Kojiki* [the earliest extant history of Japan] he remarked that the names of the gods were very long'.[9]

A turning point bringing the desire to learn the language was the gift from her mother to the child of twelve, at Carmen's own request, of *An Elementary Grammar of the Japanese Language, with Easy Progressive Exercises*, by Baba Tatsui (1850–88),[10] the Japanese democratic politician. This book was to 'unlock the door to a strange land which lay, radiant and shining, far over the horizon of the sea'. At boarding school at Benenden from 1938, she studied this grammar '[o]ccasionally, when bored with the school curriculum'. At boarding school, she also became friends with Juliet Piggott, daughter of Major General Piggott, a second-generation Japan hand, educated in Japan and a fluent speaker of the language, not long returned from attachment to the British embassy in Tokyo. General Piggott

[7] *The Catalpa Bow*, p. 349.

[8] Professor E. D. Edwards, 'Letter of Reference', Nov. 1947. Somerville archive. I am grateful to the Principal and Fellows of Somerville College and to Dr Michael Loewe for permission to quote this and other material from the Somerville College Archive.

[9] This and the other quotations in this paragraph are from 'Recollections of Baba Tatsui's Elementary Grammar', an essay published as a supplement to Baba's collected works in 1988; CWCB, pp. 201–3.

[10] The names of Japanese are given here in the Japanese order, with the surname first.

gave Carmen weekly lessons in Japanese during school holidays until the Second World War.

For Carmen's father, able to rejoin his old battalion, the war brought 'one of the happiest periods in my life'.[11] For his elder daughter, it meant entry into the adult world through work in intelligence and a career commitment to the study of Japan. But the war also brought lasting resentment at what she perceived as undervaluation by unimaginative and obstinate men. In 1942, she joined the School of Oriental and African Studies (SOAS), and was soon transferred to a special accelerated course in Japanese with a 'highly secret' but undisclosed job in view.[12] She was then seconded to Bletchley, the government intelligence institution. Her pay was a paltry £2 a week, explained to her as 'partly due to my age, 18, and partly due to my being a woman'. Her task was to compile a card index of vocabulary of 'any words likely to turn up in a decoded message' from Japanese captured documents and other sources. She remained convinced that she served no useful purpose in the war effort. This 'uncongenial employment', it was observed at SOAS, imposed much stress on her.[13] By the beginning of 1945, she had become 'utterly bored with the work ... and my morale began to weaken'. In February, she 'contracted an old-fashioned red-flanellist complaint known as a quinsy' [*sc.* tonsilitis] and was allowed to go home to recover. Meanwhile, confidential but successful efforts were made to transfer her back to SOAS as Special Lecturer to teach intensive Japanese courses to servicemen. She gave up her Bletchley pass with 'relief and jubilation'.

Yet this period of her life was not altogether barren. Towards the end of the war through the diplomat John Pilcher (later British ambassador in Tokyo), she met Arthur Waley, already a famous but also notoriously difficult man, of whom it has been commented that '[h]is public *persona* was of extreme shyness that became abrupt rudeness'. [14] Carmen, by her own account,[15] was a girl herself 'still paralyzed with shyness' and 'tongue tied',

[11] C. P. Blacker, *Have You Forgotten Yet?*, ed. John Blacker (Barnsley, 2000), p. 287. His battalion was now commanded 'by my old friend Colonel Lionel Bootle-Wilbraham, D.S.O., M.C. (later Lord Skelmersdale)'.

[12] This and the following autobiographical quotations regarding Bletchley are from 'Recollections of *temps perdu* at Bletchley Park', in F. H. Hinsley and Alan Stripp (eds.), *Code Breakers: the Inside Story of Bletchley Park* (Oxford, 1994), pp. 300–5.

[13] E. D. Edwards, 'Letter of Reference'; Somerville College Archive.

[14] David Holloway, 'Waley and his women' [review of Alison Waley, *A Half of Two Lives*], *The Daily Telegraph*, 8 Sept. 1982, p. 14.

[15] Quotations from 'Intent of courtesy: a recollection of Arthur Waley', first published in Ivan Morris (ed.), *Madly Singing in the Mountains: an Appreciation and Anthology* (London, 1970); CWCB, pp. 204–9;

when she first met him at his office in the Ministry of Information. Nonetheless, they formed a friendship. Waley encouraged her to learn Chinese. This she did, with texts supplied by Waley, surreptitiously while on duty at Bletchley. Carmen was to seek his advice and help on her future studies, counting for instance on his support for her application to study in America.[16] They were to remain in contact for the rest of Waley's life. She came to find in him 'a scholar of almost magical insight and ... a master of language' and she developed an intense veneration of 'a nobility of character, a tenderness, a courage in grief and adversity' that she had not at first appreciated. Waley's combination of aestheticism and cultural curiosity must be accounted an important influence on Carmen's scholarship.

Leaving Bletchley liberated Carmen; she was soon reported to have 'gained greatly in poise'.[17] Concurrently with her Special Lecturer post at SOAS, she enrolled for the BA in Japanese. She graduated with First Class Honours in 1947. Waley was an examiner. With what Carmen called his 'lofty disregard for conventions' and, it has to be said, a typical bluntness, he called her to his room and informed her of 'rather silly mistakes' in her history papers. [18] But Carmen felt that her degree in Japanese left her still under-educated. Turning down an offer of a post in Japanese at Cambridge, she wrote to Dr Janet Vaughan, Principal of Somerville College, Oxford, who had been known to her father, that 'I feel that I should read some non-linguistic subject—preferably history or sociology—before I could do anything useful.'[19] In November 1947, she successfully sat an entrance examination to Somerville, but was persuaded to change subject to Philosophy, Politics and Economics. Her wartime service entitled her to exemption from the First Public Examination, and in January 1948 she embarked on a Shortened Final Honours School, taking six, rather than the usual eight, papers in just two years. One of her tutors was R. B. McCallum (1898–1973), Professor of Modern History, later Master of Pembroke. At Somerville, entered when she was 23, a fellow student recalled that 'she subscribed to Buddhist thought and she kept a harpsichord in the Penrose Room ... She was always turned out in a distinctive fashion.' She was noted for her 'readiness to praise and encourage others (combined with active and acute criticism if occasion

[16] Carmen to Dr Janet Vaughan, 10 Sept. 1949. Somerville College Archive.

[17] E. D. Edwards, 'Letter of Reference'; Somerville College Archive.

[18] 'Carmen Blacker', in P. F. Kornicki and I. J. McMullen (eds.), *Religion in Japan: Arrows to Heaven and Earth* (Cambridge, 1996), p. xviii. This information is closely based on Carmen's own recollections.

[19] Carmen to Janet Vaughan, 10 Sept. 1947; Somerville College Archive.

demanded)'.[20] She sat finals in late 1949 and was awarded Second Class Honours, a result deemed 'most creditable' by Janet Vaughan, given that she had done 'no previous work in this field'; 'her work on Political Theory had alpha quality'.[21] By the time of her graduation, she had won respect from all quarters in Oxford. Janet Vaughan wrote of her that she was 'an extremely well balanced hard-headed, young woman'. Some traces of her earlier nervousness, however, evidently remained. Janet Vaughan cautioned on a nervous tic: her 'eye lashes which work full time are most misleading'.[22] Later, after Carmen had taken a post at Cambridge, Vaughan was to describe her as 'a young woman of real distinction of mind and person. If I saw a chance of making her a Fellow this College, I should take it at once.'[23]

After Oxford, Carmen studied at Harvard during 1950–1 under the Henry Fellowship scheme. At Oxford, she had enjoyed studying eighteenth- and nineteenth-century European political and moral thought. Curious as to how these ideas had been received in Japan, she began research on this topic at Harvard. Her mentors were the university's best-known Japan scholars, professors S. Elisseeff and E. O. Reischauer, though neither specialised in her field of research. Finally, in 1952, she succeeded in paying her first visit to Japan. A condition of the scholarship that she received from the Treasury Committee for Studentships in Oriental Languages and Cultures was that she write a thesis. She identified Fukuzawa Yukichi (1835–1901) as a pivotal figure in the adoption of Western thought in Japan, and it seemed natural to continue this study. She enrolled in Keiô University, the institution founded by Fukuzawa himself; and her supervisor was none other than one of Fukuzawa's grandsons, Kiyooka Eiichi. Like other Western foreign students in Japan in the early post-war period, she found herself privileged by the special interest and support of staff and students alike. Much of her time was spent in the 'Big Reading Room' of the gothic-style university library. But Carmen was ever a person of irrepressible energy. She 'spent as much time as I could each spring and autumn in Kyoto and most of the summer in Kamakura'.[24] In Kamakura, she stayed in the tea house of the novelist Osaragi Jirô for six weeks, which

[20] Anne Warburton 'Carmen Elizabeth Blacker, 1948, Hon. Fellow 1991', *Somerville College Report, 2008–2009*, pp. 84–5.
[21] Janet Vaughan to W. L. Atkinson, 31 Dec. 1949; Somerville College Archive.
[22] Janet Vaughan to Miss Fone, 3 Nov. 1949; Somerville College Archive.
[23] Ibid.
[24] 'Impressions of a Japanese University', first published in the *Bulletin of the Japan Society of London* (13), June, 1954; CWCB, p. 289.

she described as 'among the happiest in my life'.[25] She went everywhere by bicycle, exploring Buddhist temples and talking with people 'from all walks of life'. She recalled of this time that '[s]mall, simple actions and scenes had a wonderful intensity and reality, a kind of magic which is now more difficult to find'.

Japan was a challenge to the spirit as well as to the mind. In Kamakura, she was able to pursue her now established interest in Buddhism. She joined a *zazen* (meditation) class as an external student. Two years later she gave an account to a London audience of her experiences both of student campus activity in Tokyo and of Buddhism in Kamakura. For her, both Keiô, the modern Western style academic institution, and Engakuji, 'where the monks are seeking enlightenment by the same methods as they have followed for hundreds of years', were 'Japan as she exists now. They both exist side by side, and even interfuse.'[26] The relationship of the ancient and spiritual with the more modern was in due course to constitute a major theme in her life's work.

II

But Carmen's first commitment was to the field of intellectual history. Returning to England in 1953, she spent the next two years at SOAS, shaping her research on Fukuzawa Yukichi into a doctoral thesis. Meanwhile, in 1955 she had been appointed to an Assistant Lectureship at Cambridge, and it was Cambridge University Press that published her dissertation as *The Japanese Enlightenment: a Study of the Writings of Fukuzawa Yukichi* in 1964. This book was dedicated to her father. Its theme was ambitious: the revolution in thought that took place in Japan during the collapse of the late feudal regime and the inauguration of Japan's modern political order. Its scope is concomitantly broad; it surveys the thought not only of Fukuzawa himself, but also of other leading intellectuals of the time, most of whom wrote voluminously. Required also were knowledge of the Japanese intellectual tradition; the internal political history of Japan during a period of precipitate change; the Western intellectual tradition, including nineteenth-century positivist thinkers such as Herbert Spencer and reformers such as Samuel Smiles. The book successfully conveys the

[25] This and the following quotations in this paragraph are from 'A room with a gourd: recollections of Osaragi Jirô', first published in the *Cambridge Review*, 1985; CWCB, pp. 210–13.
[26] 'Impressions of a Japanese University'; CWCB, p. 294.

profound nature of the change in Japan: the reversal of the understanding of history as from decline from a past golden age to progress towards a future utopia; the reconstruction of the understanding of the role of the individual and of human agency in history; the position of women; the role of government and the nature and limitation of political authority. Carmen drew on new work on neo-Confucianism by A. C. Graham of SOAS, and on contemporary Japanese scholarship on Meiji-period intellectual history. She was among the first to reflect the work of Maruyama Masao, the leading Japanese intellectual historian and political scientist of the twentieth century. Carmen conveys this panorama lucidly, accessibly and elegantly, mostly through well-selected quotation and paraphrase. She is also realistic: Fukuzawa was driven partly by a spirit of rebellion against the humiliating restrictions of feudal society, and partly by a desire to use Western democracy instrumentally to arm Japan against Western expansionism. The final chapter confronts Fukuzawa's lurch to advocacy of a form of Japanese imperialism in order to resist Western expansionism.

The Japanese Enlightenment was one of the earliest British scholarly books on Japan to be published after the war. It addressed the intellectual modernisation of Japan in a generally positive spirit. Since then, much progress has been made in understanding Fukuzawa's thought. A finer-grained reading of Fukuzawa's views than Carmen could reasonably have achieved is now possible. He is recognised as a creative thinker who developed Western ideas in original ways. But Fukuzawa remains a hero, much as Carmen claimed. Her book, like the classic work of her friend and contemporary at the University of London, Ronald Dore's great *Education in Tokugawa Japan* (1965), is recognised as a pioneer work and a gesture of imaginative generosity to a defeated nation. It has been appreciated as such in Japan itself. For these reasons, *The Japanese Enlightenment* is a historically significant book. It might have inaugurated a research career in intellectual history. In fact, Carmen produced little more in that field: an article on the reactionary thinker Ôhashi Totsuan (1816–62), containing an account of Japanese neo-Confucianism that can still be recommended for its clear and accurate summary of traditional Japanese neo-Confucian thought; and a brief account of the historiography of the nationalist and pro-imperial historian Rai San'yô (1781–1832), for an edited book on East Asian historiography.[27]

[27] For a bibliography of these and other articles, see 'The principal publications of Carmen Blacker', in Kornicki and McMullen (eds.), *Religion in Japan*, pp. xxii–xxiii.

III

Even as she did the research at Keio for the book on Fukuzawa, Carmen had been drawn in a different direction. She now committed herself to the study of Japanese religion, both historical and contemporary, and the related fields of myth and folklore. Her interest in Japanese religion seems likely to have been coloured by her father's Jungian psychology and his work as a psychiatrist. Carmen may have inherited a sensitivity to the numinous from him. In his war memoirs C. P. Blacker records a powerful hierophany during an interlude in fighting near Amiens in the spring of 1917, at a place called Corbie. He was taking a walk by moonlight along a canal towpath. As he walked, the canal 'acquired a numen'. He experienced a brief vision of 'luminous bodies—meteors or stars—emitting both light and music'. He remained uncertain of its significance, but later used the metaphor of 'seeds', writing that: 'The remarkable thing, as I now see, about such seeds—stored as bare memories of past experiences which, in the past, have fallen on unreceptive ground—is their capacity to remain dormant for long periods, perhaps waiting inertly for an auspicious change in the soil which contains them.'[28]

Carmen was to share and develop her father's concern with hierophanies and their capacity to survive unconsciously in the mind. Perhaps the psychiatrist's daughter is also reflected in Carmen's focus on religion primarily as an individual, rather than social or political, experience. Throughout her life, she retained an intense sense of the power of psychic phenomena and of the mind as a volatile, but also creative, substratum of human psychology, a repository of ancient knowledge. She was to write of the 'mysterious and terrifying power'[29] associated with certain kinds of myth; of the 'magnetic force' with which the mind tends to elaborate the perception of apparitions; the 'terrifying malignity' or 'peculiar power' of 'resentful spirits'.[30] She also believed that 'altered states of consciousness', along with 'states of trance, of possession, of ecstatic flight', should, in the study of Japanese religion, be the object of 'sympathetic comprehension'.[31]

[28] Blacker, *Have You Forgotten Yet?*, pp. 159–62.

[29] 'Two Shinto myths: the Golden Age and the Chosen People', first published in Sue Henny and Jean-Pierre Lehmann (eds.), *Themes and Theories in Modern Japanese History* (London, 1988); CWCB, p. 28.

[30] 'The angry ghost in Japan', first published in H. R. E. Davidson and W. M. S. Russell (eds.), *The Folklore of Ghosts* (Cambridge, 1980); CWCB, pp. 51–9.

[31] 'Rethinking the study of religion in Japan', in Adriana Boscaro, Franco Gatti and Massimo Raveri (eds.), *Rethinking Japan: Volume II: Social Sciences, Ideology and Thought* (Folkstone, 1990), p. 238.

Her first direct encounter with Japanese religion, however, seems likely to have been with Zen. Yet the ultimate Buddhist salvation, release from the world, was for her not the main interest of the tradition. Aside from her early experience of *zazen*, Carmen appears little concerned with Buddhist soteriology itself, or in exploring the rigorous ontology, epistemology or logic that form the metaphysical basis of Zen Buddhism. The human and cultural context of the quest aroused a deeper fascination. Despite a life-long interest, she never became a Buddhist. In her Charles Strong Memorial Lecture of 1968,[32] she described two ways in which 'yoga' was used to achieve Buddhist enlightenment, a state that she described as 'a discipline, of mind or body or both, … [directed] towards the end of yoking, unifying oneself with God, the divine ground'. These two methods were found in the Zen and Shingon sects respectively. Both the *kôan* and meditation of Zen and the lesser known, esoteric, Shingon methods were 'viable'. But in Shingon esoteric practice, Carmen found a model of the religious quest based on recovery of an innate characteristic more rewarding than the fierce abstraction and renunciation of intellect of Zen. Zen's use of *kôan* had 'no aura of numinousness'; wrongly understood, it was also more vulnerable to trivialisation, witness 'most of the rubbish talked about by Beat enthusiasts of Zen'. By contrast, Shingon's luxuriant techniques of *mudra*, *mantra* and meditative visualisations employed 'symbolic imitation', and constituted a 'ritual drama'. They 'rous[ed] by means of an exterior reflection an image which already exists inside our minds'. Here was a view of the mind that resonated with Jungian psychology of archetypes and the collective unconscious. In a later address, she expanded this view of the mind explicitly to include folklore and myth as repositories of 'patterns by which [the human mind] can understand and remember historical reality'. She became interested in cultural transmission or 'how the component motifs of the legend interlock and interfuse, and how the images and symbols, with their ambivalent faces, melt into one another'.[33]

Even before the publication of *The Japanese Enlightenment* she had already begun to publish on esoteric Buddhism. Her first essay in this field, 'The divine boy in Japanese Buddhism', had drawn on early medieval Japanese texts of the *setsuwa* genre, mainly Buddhist homilies, to

[32] Charles Strong Memorial Lecture of 1968, 'Methods of Yoga in Japanese Buddhism', *Milla wa-Milla*, no. 8, 3–19.

[33] 'The Exiled Warrior and the Hidden Village' [Presidential Address to the Folklore Society, 17 March 1984], *Folklore*, 95 (2) (1984), 149. She did not find myths, folklore or religious belief incompatible with science. See her discussion in 'The seer as a healer in Japan', in H. R. E. Davidson (ed.), *The Seer in Celtic and Other Traditions* (Edinburgh, 1989); CWCB, pp. 65–6.

describe the historical phenomenon of the *gohô dôji*, boy protectors of the Law, 'a saviour, servant and wayshower of holy men'.[34] Here, the Jungian theme was particularly strong. Expressing her argument in the conceptual language of psychiatry, she concluded of this figure in words that paraphrase those of Jung himself, that the '*puer aeternus*, in his fusion of weakness and strength, seems to represent the wholeness which comes from the union of opposites, the complete man who has transcended the limitations of ordinary consciousness'.[35]

This belief in an early stratum of Japanese experience was no doubt reinforced by her reading in the works of the founding fathers of Japanese folklore, Yanagida Kunio (1875–1962) and Orikuchi Shinobu (1887–1953). For both, folklore embodied a quest for the origins of national culture but also a teleology that related these origins to the present and the prospect of revival in some form. This approach was problematic for some more left-wing scholars, but Carmen was interested in the purely religious rather than any political aspect of their work. In the same general direction another, no less strong, influence on Carmen's interest in mythology and folklore was the writing of the eminent Romanian scholar of religion Mircea Eliade whose work Carmen professed that she 'always found inspiring';[36] Eliade's belief in a primordial state and his concept of the 'paradisal syndrome' was particularly attractive to her.[37] But his influence appeared to extend further, to her basic methodological assumptions. Carmen seemed to accept his view that human nature was innately religious, reflected in Eliade's concept of '*homo religiosus*'. Experience of the sacred, she seems to assume, is itself irreducible, rather than to be explained through reductive analysis by other disciplines such as the social sciences or psychology. Though she might not have admitted to the description, Carmen is in this sense probably best viewed as a phenomenologist, largely concerned with a perceived world. She remained, at any rate, little attracted by theoretical issues or alternative theories of religious behaviour or myth. She did not explore myth from a Marxist, structuralist, let alone Freudian standpoint. She was concerned to document the religious experience of

[34] 'The divine boy in Japanese Buddhism', first published in *Asian Folklore*, 22 (1963); CWCB, p. 107.

[35] Ibid. For Jung's very similar wording, see C. G. Jung and C. Kerenyi, *Introduction to a Science of Mythology: the Myth of the Divine Child and the Mysteries of Eleusis*, trans. R. F. C. Hull, Bollingen Series XXII (Princeton, NJ, 1993), p. 83.

[36] 'The language of birds', Lecture on the occasion of the opening of the Faculty of International Studies, Ueno Gakuen University, 30 June 1996; CWCB, p. 7.

[37] Ibid., p. 12.

Japanese, both historical and contemporary, empathetically from the practitioner's standpoint. Among contemporary Japanese scholars, Hori Ichirô and Gorai Shigeru, leading students of Shamanism and of the ascetic cult known as Shugendo, are particularly frequently quoted in her writing for their empirical information.

Carmen professed a strong dislike of jargon. Her writing is clear and accessible, her style disciplined but compellingly readable, her prose often exhilarating. The approach is seldom theoretical. On the old rivalry between the 'diffusionist' and 'separate origin' theories of the origins of folklore, for instance, like one of her heroes, the Japanese antiquarian, polymath and folklorist, Minakata Kumugusu, she forbore to express an explicit opinion. In one of her last articles, 'The disguised wandering saint: an example of the stranger in folklore' (1990), she noted common features between the motif of hospitality offered to or withheld from strangers, but also crucial differences across cultures. In the case of withheld hospitality, for instance, in Europe and the West, the agent is transformed into a bird; in Japan, the food withheld becomes inedible and the whole community is affected. This led her to the conclusion that, at least in this case, here is a 'strong probability ... of a source different from the analogous European tales'.[38] Detachment from theory did not, however, mean that she avoided complexity. In another late article on divination, 'Divination and oracles in Japan', Carmen described, with illustrative diagrams, the intricate but 'cumbersome yes-no method' required in the use of turtle shells for divination, 'still employed', as she writes, 'in the course of the important and mysterious rite ... by which the Japanese emperor is consecrated and enthroned'.[39]

Later lectures and articles on historical folklore continued to view Japanese religious practice in terms of recovering or acting out an innate, pristine inheritance from primordial time. In an interview with *Japan Digest* in 1991, Carmen expressed a belief not inconsistent with Jungian teleology. She spoke of the existence of 'older levels [in the Japanese mind], which we may call mythical, ... which send up symbols which appear in dreams and folklore. These symbols will often solve a problem in a manner that rational, quantitative thinking cannot.'[40] Carmen's interest in this

[38] 'The disguised wandering saint: an example of the stranger in folklore', *Folklore*, 101 (2) (1990); CWCB, p. 183.
[39] 'Divination and oracles in Japan', in Michael Loewe and Carmen Blacker (eds.), *Divination and Oracles* (London, 1981); CWCB, p. 72.
[40] *Japan Digest*, 1 (3) (1991), p. 24.

primordial world extended to language. In 'The language of birds' (1996), she spoke with sympathy, indeed excitement, of the belief of the French philosopher Réné Guénon that folk belief in a pure ancient language was a 'safe repository for spiritual truth', a 'code', through which messages could be transmitted in times of crisis or degeneration. One aspect of this was the widespread folk belief in the 'secret language' of birds that existed before language became corrupted, accessible only to those gifted with special knowledge.[41] Here again, Carmen did not engage with the contemporary debate among scholars of Japanese history over language, domination and empowerment. She remained detached from postmodernism, structuralism or neo-Marxism in its various forms. Like Eliade himself, she saw communication and friendship with animals as a 'means of partially recovering the paradisal situation of primordial human beings'.[42]

This ancient substratum of Japanese experience had historically been overlaid or suppressed not just by modernisation, but earlier by Buddhism and by Chinese culture. It had been further damaged by the Meiji government's ruthless suppression of syncretic sects such as the Shugendô. Yet it was preserved to some extent in folklore. Thus of 'folk traditions' concerning the emperor's reputedly bizarre life style, she concludes: 'folklore . . . uniquely preserves the memory of ancient practices forgotten elsewhere but once observed by the sacral forbears of the Japanese emperors'. And this, she makes clear, referred to 'some period before history', when the 'sacred nature of the emperor was then more pronounced than in later times'.[43] This view would not now pass unchallenged; more recent scholarship would see the ritual purity of the emperor as a construct built up in the early historical period of state building in the seventh and eighth centuries under the influence of continental Daoism and of Buddhism. Uncomfortably for many historians of early modern and modern Japan, belief in a primordial ethical paradise suggests the essentialist belief in a pristine Japan propagated by the nativist school, the Kokugakusha, and their later followers, a major influence on modern Japanese nationalism.

Carmen was, of course, aware of the danger. In 'Two Shinto myths: the golden age and the chosen people', she distinguished two types of

[41] 'The language of birds', p. 10.

[42] Mircea Eliade, quoted in Douglas Allen, *Myth and Religion in Mircea Eliade* (New York, 2002), p. 15. Through recovery of this language, in Carmen's own words, 'we find ourselves looking once more at our Original Face' ('The language of birds', p. 14).

[43] 'Forgotten practices of the past: Kaempfer's description of the Japanese Emperor', in B. Bodart-Bailey and D. Massarella (eds.), *The Furthest Goal: Engelbert Kaempfer's Encounter with Tokugawa Japan* (Folkestone, 1995); CWCB, p. 161.

myth: first, explanatory, narrative myths, which 'account for the workings of the universe around us' and impose 'on the visible world an ordered scheme'. The second type consisted of implicitly irrational myths which 'possess a peculiar power over human rationality'. The latter type, perhaps more akin to ideology, 'can bind groups and whole nations together into a common purpose'. She described the chauvinistic linguistic theories of the early modern nativist scholars Kamo no Mabuchi (1697–1769), Motoori Norinaga (1730–1801) and Hirata Atsutane (1776–1843). Their beliefs, she contended, belong to the category of myth that 'possess [a] mysterious and terrifying power over the human mind'.[44] The assumption of the superiority of the Japanese language culminated in the theory that the Japanese race, too, was created superior, a belief which Carmen characterised as 'less common than might be supposed'. Such irrational views had been discredited with Japan's defeat in the Pacific War, but she added darkly that there were signs that 'their grip on the Japanese mind may not entirely have relaxed'.[45] If this hints at some of the problematic aspects the school of Japanese folklore associated with Yanagida and Origuchi alluded to above, she did not develop the theme. But her final lecture at Oxford in 2001, delivered without notes when she was already experiencing symptoms of the Parkinson's that was to disable her, fiercely exposed the fabrication of the Nationalist Shinto ideology derived from mythical traditions in the Meiji period.

IV

Carmen's early accounts of religious phenomena were based on printed published sources, many from the medieval period. Increasingly, however, her work included field study, direct observation of the present state of the phenomena whose earlier history she had researched. Already by 1963 she was visiting the Nichiren temple of Barakisan Myôgyôji in Chiba prefecture, where she observed the Abbott, 'a dignified and awe-inspiring person who had accomplished a strenuous programme of austerities',[46] implementing a detailed catechism to subjects believed possessed by vengeful spirits. This was to provide material for her later (1981) paper

[44] 'Two Shinto Myths', p. 28.
[45] Ibid., p. 37.
[46] 'The angry ghost in Japan', in Davidson and Russell (eds.), *The Folklore of Ghosts*; CWCB, p. 56.

'The angry ghost in Japan'. An early paper, 'Initiation in the Shugendô' (1965), again drew on on participant observation, here in the *akimine* [Autumn peak] ritual on Dewa Sanzan in the north of Japan. Here, library research felicitously combined with direct observation to provide a sense of how the rite had changed over its long history, leaving its typical latter-day initiate 'a faintly debased figure'.[47] Much later, her article, 'The Goddess emerges from her Cave: Fujita Himiko and her Dragon Palace family' (1994), is based entirely on Carmen's personal knowledge of Fujita, the founder of one of Japan's smaller, but most attractive, new religions, the Ryûgû Kazoku (Dragon Palace Family). Here, as elsewhere when describing apparently exotic beliefs, Carmen wrote in a nuanced style which presented her subject's sometimes bizarre views with sympathy but which delicately suspended or withheld authorial belief. Fujita claimed to be a reincarnation of the Sun Goddess, and to represent the gentle, female side of deity, to right a traditional distortion towards 'hard, war-like, masculine divinities'.[48]

Throughout her career and well into her retirement, Carmen was an annual visitor to Japan. The Cambridge summer Long Vacation could be used for the trips, first on the ten-day journey partly across Russia, latterly entirely by plane. Once there, she pursued her investigations into religious history and contemporary practice. She constantly took photos, and these and her diaries, bequeathed to the Sainsbury Institute for the Study of Japanese Arts and Cultures in Norwich, should be a valuable resource for future students of twentieth-century Japan. She took pleasure in sharing her field trips with students and friends. In Kyoto, she bicycled everywhere, as had been her wont since childhood. To accompany her was exhilarating, for she had infectious enthusiasm and a sense of fun. In 1964, visiting the Ittôen, a small religious community outside the city, she was delighted with what seemed an epiphany: suddenly, the stooped figure of the nonagenarian founder, Nishida Tenkô (1872–1968), appeared with his wife on a stone bridge over the pond in their garden, 'like Chinese immortals'. Later, touring the community farm, she delighted in the pigs poking their snouts in greeting through the bars of their cages. She took a small party to the top of Mt Hiei, the sacred mountain to the north-east of Kyoto.

[47] 'Initiation in the Shugendô: the passage through the Ten States of Existence', in C. J. Bleeker (ed.), *Initiation, Studies in the History of Religions* (Supplement to *Numen*, 10) (Leiden, 1963); CWCB, p. 193.

[48] 'The goddess emerges from her cave: Fujita Himiko and her Dragon Palace Family', in Peter Clarke and Jeffrey Somers (eds.), *Japanese New Religions in the West* (Folkestone, 1994); CWCB, p. 146.

Night came on and transport back to the city had ended for the day. The group trespassed in pitch darkness down the cable car track, fearful that at any moment a car might descend. But Carmen loudly repeated the esoteric Buddhist mantra of invulnerability, effectively, for level ground was reached without mishap. Her physical energy remained remarkable. In 1986, the historian of Victorian views of Japan, Professor Yokoyama Toshio, himself a mountaineer, accompanied her on a climb of Mt Tsurugi on Shikoku. Citing the 'nimble surefootedness of a gazelle', that William Gladstone had marvelled at in Isabella Bird, Yokoyama described Carmen's ascent. His wife left far behind, he 'had to try my very best to follow the fluttering lower ends of Carmen's trousers that were occasionally visible ever further off through gaps in the increasingly dense clouds'.[49]

V

The several qualities identified above are best exemplified in Carmen's magnum opus, *The Catalpa Bow: a Study of Shamanistic Practices in Japan* (1975). The book is named after the catalpa tree (Japanese *azusa* [*betula grossa var. ulmifolia*])[50], the hard wood of which was traditionally used to make bows. Shamans used such bows from early times to summon spirits. *The Catalpa Bow* rapidly became established as a classic, winning a readership beyond the world of Japanese Studies. The book is based on Carmen's strengths: extensive reading in the Japanese historical and ethnographic literature combined with fieldwork in sacred places, mountains, lakes, temples, and shrines, and interviews with monks, priests, shamans, pilgrims and members of the Japanese public. Carmen performed the *kaihôgyô*, a strenuous ritual circumambulation of Mt Hiei, failure at which was purported to require suicide; twice she participated in the week-long *akinomine* austerity on Mt Haguro in Yamagata Prefecture; three times she ascended Ontake, the sacred volcano that straddles the boundary between Nagano and Gifu Prefectures.

The book filled a lacuna in the Western literature on shamanism. Carmen's work forms a pendant to Mircea Eliade's seminal study of Asian Shamanism, which had largely omitted Japan. She saw Japanese shamanism as an outgrowth of its Siberian counterpart, though with a Polynesian

[49] Yokoyama Toshio, 'Memories of Dr Carmen Blacker OBE, FBA (1924–2009)', Address to memorial meeting at Clare Hall, November, 2009; published in *Sansai* (5) (April 2011), p. 132.
[50] A species of birch, less elegantly known as *yoguso minebari* or nightsoil mountain birch.

input and with the World Tree replaced by a Mountain. In this book, the 'paradisal' theme of the primordial stratum of Japanese religiosity is less obtrusive than in her articles and addresses. Lived, observed, experience interested her and she reported it with empathy and felicity. Nonetheless, she confidently identified her modern shamanism as perpetuating a pre-Buddhist 'archaic mysticism'. This tradition, overlaid in early historical times by Buddhist influences, survived 'like mycelium under the ground'.[51] The book anatomises the two realms of the shamanic world view, sacred and profane, and the figure of the shaman, who mediates between them. It describes the supernatural beings and the changing location of the other world that they inhabit as, through Japanese protohistory, it shifted from the sea to the mountains. Carmen describes the acquisition of shamanic power through ascesis, involving mastery over both water and fire. A particularly vivid chapter conjures up the prehistoric or protohistoric shaman, the 'majestic sacral woman', based on recovered ancient *haniwa* (grave clay cylinder) images and also provides a critical summary of modern reconstructions of the cult, role and initiation of ancient shamans, based partly also on modern ethnography. The book includes Carmen's own typology of shamanic practice, broadly divided into the two types of ascetic healer and exorciser on the one hand and more passive medium on the other. She identified persistent shamanic elements in certain of the 'new religions'; and, from her own compelling and vivid observation, described surviving shamanic practices, including oracles and exorcisms in village and mountain contexts. All too often, these traditional practices were found to be faltering, weakened, or abandoned. In such cases, Carmen relied on the relatively recent, extensive Japanese ethnographic literature, of which she had a thorough knowledge. Part of this book's enduring value lies in its eloquent record of practices that were fading from history.

VI

Carmen's approach to the study of Japanese religion won a degree of respect from the leading Japanese scholars of her field rarely accorded to foreign researchers. Professor Miyake Hitoshi, the *eminence grise* in the field of Japanese shamanism, wrote of how foreign scholars tended to apply their own preconceived methodologies to the study of Japanese

[51] Blacker, *The Catalpa Bow*, p. 32.

religion and to accommodate empirical evidence to these assumptions; their findings, in turn, fed back to the Japanese academic world, distorting understanding of Japanese religious experience. Carmen's approach was different:

> Even when she came to Japan, she met first not with [Japanese] researchers, but with shamanic mediums and ascetics, personally participated in their practice, and shared their experiences. Then, later, she would discuss their recollections with evident pleasure and seek their opinions. The fruits of this participatory investigation over many years are presented [in *The Catalpa Bow*].

Carmen, he claimed, had provided the basic material for an understanding of shamanism, an intercultural phenomenon.[52]

Indeed, in the eyes of Japanese, Carmen was the object of fascinated admiration, even awe. She spoke Japanese fluently, perhaps with a tinge of bookishness, in a distinctive feminine form, with honorific verb terminations and a lexicon appropriate for a woman of status. Female researchers of her generation still faced obstacles, particularly in the field of religious history, where taboos still operated. The rumour among students that in the interest of pursuing research she impersonated a man apparently has substance, at least in one instance.[53] But she largely overcame the difficulty by a combination of patent seriousness of purpose, energy, thorough preparation, personal charm and a sense of humour. At least once, at the Hayama *takusen* [oracular utterance] rite at Ôkua, near Sôma, Fukushima Prefecture, the taboo was waived for her personally.[54] Yet hindrances remained. In 1961, researching the initiatory rites of the Shugendô, she had been able as a woman only to proceed into the Yoshino hills as far as 'a spot where there stands a statue of Aizen Myôô and a stone pillar inscribed with the words, "*korekara nyonin kinsei*"—No women allowed beyond here.' By 1972, the situation was somewhat relaxed and she made the journey again. Her patience was abundantly rewarded. She was among four women 'privileged to see for the first time the deep ravines, the paths winding deeper and deeper into the hills, now through forests of pine and cryptomeria, now emerging onto open hillsides of bamboo shrub and long grass, from which could be seen layer upon layer of blue hills rising from a lake of mist as though to the edge of the world.' However, the

[52] Miyake Hitoshi, 'Kaisetsu' [Introduction], in *Azusa yumi—Nihon ni okeru shâmanteki kôi*, tr. Akiyama Satoko (Tokyo, 1995), pp. 231–8.

[53] Personal communication from Dr Loewe.

[54] *The Catalpa Bow*, p. 263.

women were inevitably soon stopped. For the rest, Carmen had to rely on the reports of male observers.[55]

Sympathy with women is abundant in her published scholarship, especially *The Catalpa Bow.* Her most conspicuous gesture in this mode was her joint editorship, with Edward Shils, of *Cambridge Women: Twelve Portraits*,[56] for which, according to Shils, she did 'most of the work'.[57] Carmen wrote the preface, which is informed by a controlled anger at the social and institutional disabilities under which women suffered in nineteenth- and early twentieth-century Cambridge, together with admiration for 'their passion for knowledge, their intellectual distinction and their powers of original and creative thinking'. She was never, however, an aggressive modern-style feminist. She had no use for what she referred to as 'gendered types, female figurations and androcentric premises'.[58]

VII

Carmen also produced article-length essays and addresses on various contemporaries or near contemporaries. This category of work was important to her, for she gave it second place after 'Religion, myth and folklore' in her collected works.[59] These lively pieces are the most literary of her writings. They have something of the panache of Lytton Strachey, but wholly lack his sardonic intent. Many were contributions to the timely and praiseworthy effort led by the former ambassador to Japan Sir Hugh Cortazzi, Professors Ian Nish, Gordon Daniels and others, to record, while personal memories still survived, the activities of men and women whose lives had involved them with Japan since the Restoration of 1868. An air of vulnerability, of failed expectation, colourful eccentricity or under-appreciation, links many of Carmen's contributions in this genre. Many of her vignettes concerned personal acquaintances and had an autobiographical aspect. But some also concerned men who lived too early for Carmen to have met. First, in chronological order, was Laurence Oliphant, the brilliant and well-connected diplomat and latterly fundamentalist Christian, with his

[55] Ibid., pp. 215–16.

[56] Edward Shils and Carmen Blacker (eds.), *Cambridge Women: Twelve Portraits* (Cambridge, 1996).

[57] Ibid., Edward Shils, 'Introduction', p. 5.

[58] Ibid., 'Preface', p. xix.

[59] CWCB, pp. 201–309.

'lilac gloves'.[60] Three English pioneers of Japanese studies, Ernest Satow, W. G. Aston and B. H. Chamberlain, are the subjects of an admiring lecture.[61] Another vivid account describes the folklorist Minakata Kumagusu, the subject of her first address when President of the Folklore Society. This must have electrified her audience: here was an individual of a kind dear to her heart, whose 'entire career was so eccentric, so flouting of every accepted convention, that for many years he was scarcely remembered, let alone honoured, in his own country'.[62] She spoke of his 'headlong erudition', and the 'demonic drive' and 'careless ferocity' of his scholarship: 'In summer he could not be bothered to wear any clothes, and would sit writing in his study stark naked. Stark naked likewise he would wander over to the other parts of the house when he needed food or company, though he was always careful to put on a loincloth or pants for meals.'[63]

Another Japanese expatriate was Yoshio Markino [Makino Yoshio],[64] the impressionist artist and writer, whose misty watercolours and prints of London and elsewhere are now eagerly collected and whose picaresque Japanese–English autobiographical writings still cause the reader to smile. Markino was repatriated to Japan early in the war and Carmen found him, living in penury, in Kamakura on her first visit to Japan. Only one of her portraits was of a woman, Marie Stopes, a friend of her father, the advocate of birth control, early enthusiast for Nô drama, and exchanger of passionate love letters with Japanese men. Carmen met her living in lonely grandeur in old age. She endorsed the view that Stopes was 'one of the most remarkable women of the twentieth century'.[65] Her tribute to Arthur Waley has already been quoted. She wrote an affectionate memoir of her friend Christmas Humphreys, the populariser of Buddhism, though she did not confront the banality of which Humphreys, a believer in Madame Blavatsky till his death, was capable.[66] Carmen's own early

[60] 'Laurance Oliphant and Japan, 1858–1888', in Ian Nish (ed.), *Britain and Japan: Biographical Portraits*, vol. 2 (London, 1997); CWCB, pp. 632–73.

[61] Carmen Blacker, 'Three great Japanologists: Chamberlain, Aston and Satow'. Lecture given at the Ueno Gakuen to mark the British Festival, 1998; CWCB, pp. 295–309.

[62] The following quotations concerning Minakata are from 'Minakata Kumagusu: a neglected Japanese genius', *Folklore*, 94 (2) (1983), 139–52.

[63] Ibid., p. 144.

[64] 'Yoshio Markino, 1869–1956', in Ian Nish (ed.), *Britain and Japan: Biographical Portraits*, vol. 1 (Folkestone, 1994); CWCB, pp. 248–61.

[65] 'Marie Stopes and Japan', in Sir Hugh Cortazzi and Gordon Daniels (eds.), *Britain and Japan: Themes and Personalities* (London, 1991); CWCB, p. 222.

[66] 'Christmas Humphreys and Japan', in Nish, *Britain and Japan*; CWCB, pp. 274–81

instructor in Japanese, Major General F. S. G. Piggott and his father, Sir Francis Taylor Piggott, were both commemorated. Both were ardent Japanophiles; both could have stepped from the pages of an Anthony Powell novel. The father had been an adviser to the Meiji government on constitutional law, and Carmen vividly evokes the social life of expatriates in the early phase of Westernisation in Tokyo. The son, fluent in Japanese and a calligrapher 'of skill and elegance', became military attaché to the British Embassy in Tokyo during the period leading up to the Second World War. It was he who, on return to England, had given the schoolgirl Carmen her first lessons in Japanese. He appears to have suffered from a military man's necessarily selective myopia, bolstered by his innocent love of the country. Amazingly, as Carmen observed '[H]e was apparently completely unaware of the ominous signs of the rise of ultranationalism, of totalitarian military rule, of the aberrant Shinto cult of the emperor'. For him, Pearl Harbor 'came as an incomprehensible shock'.[67] She venerated him, as she put it elsewhere, as 'a type of human being who was very soon to become extinct'.[68]

These vignettes will be read for their period feel and delight in human quirkiness. Carmen vividly brings to life her subjects' often remarkable talents, their colourful eccentricities and their adversities. If this category of her work tends to lionise, the same generous spirit also informs her reviews. [69] These are often descriptive as much as critical. Occasionally, there is a flash of anger, as against Edmund Blunden's ongoing exploitation of his Japanese mistress[70] and Jean Herbert's falsification of Shinto in *Shinto. At the Fountainhead of Japan* (London, 1967). This book, on grounds carefully documented in her review, Carmen declared 'deserve[s] to be ... forgotten'.[71]

VIII

Carmen's academic home for most of her life was Cambridge. She was lecturer in Japanese for nearly four decades, until her retirement in 1991.

[67] 'The two Piggotts: Sir Francis Taylor Piggott and Major General F. S. G. Piggott', in Cortazzi and Daniels, *Britain and Japan*; CWCB, pp. 231–2

[68] 'Introduction', CWCB, p. 2.

[69] A selection of her reviews is found in CWCB, pp. 313–45.

[70] 'Review of Sumie Okada, *Edmund Blunden and Japan—the History of a Relationship*', *Times Literary Supplement*, 30 Dec. 1988; CWCB, pp. 324–5.

[71] 'Introduction', CWCB, p. 4.

At first attached to Newnham, she became a founding fellow of the new graduate college, Clare Hall, in 1965. Within her own Faculty of Oriental Studies at Cambridge, Carmen would have admitted to frustrations. Yet her dedication to Japanese Studies and to learning was unquestionable. Loftily, she regarded scholarship as a vocation rather than a profession or occupation and was scornful of the unionisation of university teachers. In part, she must have seen scholarship as a humanist challenge to preserve values threatened in the modern world. As a teacher, she could be fierce, but many former students remember her with gratitude. Her erudition and the intensity of her own commitment to her field inspired, her eloquence and aura of flamboyance dazzled. Carmen gave a course of lectures on Tokugawa intellectual history for Part II of the Japanese Studies tripos, but much of her teaching consisted of reading premodern texts with undergraduates. In these translation supervisions, she insisted on good English style; arrows, for instance, were always 'loosed' or 'shot', never 'fired'. Among her students not a few pursued academic careers, several in fields related to Carmen's own: D. B. Waterhouse (matriculated 1959), distinguished scholar of woodblock prints; James McMullen (1959), researcher in Japanese Confucianism; Richard Bowring (1965), literary scholar and historian of Japanese religion; Peter Nosco (1971), intellectual historian; and John Breen (1975), specialist in Tokugawa Shinto. Others took a different path: Rupert Faulkner (1973) and Clare Pollard (1985) became art historians and museum curators primarily interested in Japanese ceramics. None of these quite followed in her particular path into folklore and mythology. In that respect, her closest heir is the French anthropologist Dr Anne-Marie Bouchy, whom Carmen never formally taught, but whom she greatly admired.

Though conscientious over her academic duties, Carmen balked at the bureaucracy of academic administration. She was detached from the technological progress in language pedagogy that made such great strides during her time. Her own experience of learning Japanese in the 1940s had been of a different sort, ascetic, almost religious in intensity. It was 'best described as a *shugyô*, a discipline of mind, body and spirit. It required dedication, concentration, willingness to sacrifice frivolities.'[72] Her early colleagues in Japanese Studies at Cambridge, Eric Ceadal, later appointed University Librarian, J. R. McEwan, intellectual historian, Douglas Mills, the historian of medieval literature, and the very reserved American historian, Charles Sheldon, had been wartime contemporaries and friends.

[72] 'Introduction', CWCB, p. 3.

After their departure by the early 1980s, she felt isolated. If a brittleness, even fractiousness, could lead to personal antipathies, there was also playfulness or mischief from her side. Visitors to her third-floor office in the Faculty of Oriental Studies were offered Japanese tea. She would open the window and, averting her face, empty the dregs onto the path below: 'I always hope that this will land on the head of Professor [x]', she once confessed. More seriously, she could be sharp tongued or impatient; old friendships could sour. Such contradictions seemed incongruous in one otherwise so conspicuously courteous, so given to imaginative generosity and gestures of sympathy. In a different direction, she could sound anti-American, yet she prided herself on being able to recite the names of all the states of the Union. She enjoyed visiting the United States and Canada, and had many North American friends.

Whatever the case, obscurely to the outside world, she was never awarded an ad hominem chair or readership within her faculty. But if her experience there was sometimes difficult, there was a momentous success. Staff retirements in the 1980s had left Carmen as the only senior full-time teacher of Japanese, and there was a real danger that the subject might be closed. There was talk of amalgamating the teaching of Japanese with Oxford. Appalled, Carmen appealed to the then British Ambassador in Tokyo, Sir Hugh Cortazzi, an old friend from her SOAS days, for help. His intervention led to a substantial benefaction from the Japanese Keidanren and Tokyo Electric Power Company. This founded a chair in Japanese Studies. Carmen herself made an eloquent speech of gratitude in the University Senate, but ruled herself out as a candidate for the chair, which was first held by her pupil Richard Bowring. Cambridge Japanese Studies had been saved. Carmen retired six years later.

In due course, Carmen's distinctive contribution to Japanese Studies was to be honoured. In addition to her Presidency of the Folklore Society 1982–4, she was elected Honorary Member in 1988; she was awarded the Order of the Precious Crown by the Government of Japan in 1988; was elected to Fellowship of the British Academy in 1989 and an Honorary Fellow of Somerville College, Oxford in 1991; received the Minakata Kumagusu Prize in 1997; a Japan Festival Award in 2001; and was appointed OBE in 2004. She received visiting academic appointments. As early as 1968, she toured Australia giving the Charles Strong Memorial Lectures. She was Visiting Professor at several North American universities: Columbia (1965–6); Princeton (1979); and Toronto (1992). In Japan, she was Visiting Fellow at the Institute of Humanistic Sciences, University of Kyoto in 1986. From 1986 annually until illness prevented her from making the journey, she was Visiting Professor also at Ueno Gakuen University, whose President, the poet and scholar of Irish literature Ishibashi Hiro, had been a friend since their student days at Keio.

In 1975, she and her partner and later husband, the notable scholar of Han Dynasty China, Michael Loewe, had settled in Willow House in Grantchester. There, they jointly brought out two edited volumes on fields of mutual interest: *Ancient Cosmologies* (London, 1975) and *Divination and Oracles* (New York, 1981). Their numerous friends and acquaintances resembled the figures whom Carmen commemorated in print and lectures. They included royalty: the present Empress of Japan and her daughter, with whom she discussed folklore; Prince Charles, whom she advised on the *Dajôsai* [Japanese coronation ceremony] and at whose invitation she spent a weekend at Sandringham; the Dalai Lama; Sir Laurens van der Post; David Wilson (Lord Wilson), formerly Governor of Hong Kong; Sir Hugh Cortazzi, sometime ambassador to Japan and biographer of Japan hands; Owen Chadwick, eminent ecclesiastical historian and vice-chancellor; Edward Shils, the Anglophile American sociologist; Laurence Picken, the eminent historian of East Asian music; Donald Keene, leading American translator of Japanese literature; and Hugh Trevor-Roper (Lord Dacre), with whom Carmen had in common wartime work in intelligence, and with whose preoccupation with the literary aspect of scholarly writing she surely sympathised. As is also reported of Trevor-Roper, Carmen was a gracious correspondent. Perhaps it was true of her as has been written of Trevor-Roper, she 'was more at ease in … letter-writing where … human contact [could] be essayed within protective limits'.[73] Carmen was also active in old-established London learned societies. In addition to the Folklore Society, she was at various times a member of the Japan Society; the Asiatic Society of Japan; the Buddhist Society; the Royal Asiatic Society; the Sherlock Holmes Society, for whom she composed a special test of knowledge; and the Victorian Association. She also acted as president of the British Association of Japanese Studies, the professional organisation for university teachers and scholars in the Japan field, in 1981–2.

[73] Blair Worden, 'Hugh Redwald Trevor-Roper 1914–2003', *Proceedings of the British Academy*, 150, *Biographical Memoirs of Fellows*, VI (2008), 259.

IX

All committed students of premodern Japan, possibly of any premodern society, are faced at some level with a sense of loss: the depletion of the distinctively traditional and particular in the face of material progress and the cultural convergence of globalisation. Carmen would surely have conceded that modern Japanese live healthier and freer lives than their predecessors, but she wrote of 'living in what René Guenon called the impoverished reality of the modern world'.[74] She reacted against the erosion of tradition with intensity.

> There is much to be said ... for being old enough to have seen Japan before tower blocks, computers, television screens and mobile phones so drastically changed the scene ... B. H. Chamberlain wrote that old Japan was like an oyster; force it open and many things beautiful and precious die. He might have said the same of the changes that have taken place since those of my generation first saw Japan.[75]

Carmen's life and work are testimony to her passionate attempt to understand and record the world whose imminent loss she deplored. She could not stop history, but, half a century after receiving Baba Tatsui's *Elementary Grammar* as her mother's gift, she expressed gratitude for 'the joys, the treasures and the enrichment of my life, which [have come] to me through the study of Japanese'.[76] Posterity, in turn, owes her no small gratitude for the eloquence and sympathy with which she has shared her exploration and documentation of a vanishing world.

In 1994, cycling into Cambridge from Grantchester, Carmen fell and broke a hip. She never fully recovered but developed disquieting symptoms, including vertigo. Eventually, she was diagnosed with the Parkinson's Disease that came to restrict her mobility, preventing her from travelling to Japan. Nonetheless, she lived to complete her English translation of the nineteenth-century Japanese novel *Mukashi-gatari inazuma byôshi* under the title *The Straw Sandal* (Folkestone, 2008). This was a farrago of magic and violence, a project begun fifty years earlier at the suggestion of Arthur Waley. But this most energetic of scholars entered a slow decline, her suffering mitigated only by the devoted care of Michael Loewe. Enigmatically, until she became too ill, she had appeared on Sunday mornings in the

[74] 'The *Shinza* or God-seat in the *Daijôsai*: throne, bed or incubation couch?', *Japanese Journal of Religious Studies*, 17 (2–3) (1990); CWCB, p. 97.
[75] 'Introduction'; CWCB, p. 2.
[76] 'Recollections of Baba Tatsui's Elementary Grammar'; CWCB, p. 203.

back of her parish church in Grantchester, to 'observe the liturgy'. She died on her eighty-fifth birthday, 13 July 2009, at the Hope Nursing Home, Cambridge. Her funeral, part Buddhist, part Christian, was held in the parish church. She would have appreciated the violent thunderstorm which broke out that morning but had cleared when the cortege left the church for her cremation.

JAMES McMULLEN
Fellow of the Academy

Note. In compiling this memoir, I have received suggestions and advice from many friends and colleagues. I should acknowledge special information from Professor Peter Kornicki, FBA, Dr Michael Loewe, Professor David McMullen, FBA, Professor Matsuzawa Hiroaki, Professor Noel Pinnington, and Professor Yokoyama Toshio.

IAN BROWNLIE

Ian Brownlie
1932–2010

I

IAN BROWNLIE, KT, CBE, QC, DCL, FBA, who died at the age of 77 on 3 January 2010, was born in Bootle, Liverpool on 19 September 1932. The son of an employee of the Liverpool and London and Globe Insurance Company, he first attended Alsop High School in Liverpool but, after the almost nightly bombing of the city by the Germans, was evacuated to the town of Heswall on the nearby Wirral peninsula. The situation there proved better, but not by much: the local school building was demolished by an air raid, and Brownlie was forced to go without schooling for a year. The time was evidently not wasted, and on his return to Alsop he quickly caught up with his contemporaries. When the headmaster asked the young man what he would like to do on leaving, he received the blunt rejoinder: 'Not teaching.'

In 1950, Brownlie won a scholarship to read law at Hertford College, Oxford. This was to prove the beginning of a lifelong relationship with the university. He took a First and was awarded the Vinerian Scholarship. He was described by Professor C. H. S. Fifoot—whose metier was contract and conflict of laws, not international law—as his ablest student.[1] Brownlie's studies were interrupted when his father died from tuberculosis. The son contracted the disease as well, but was able to return to health and Oxford in due course.

[1] R. Y. Jennings, 'Foreword', in G. S. Goodwin-Gill and S. Talmon (eds.), *The Reality of International Law: Essays in Honour of Ian Brownlie* (Oxford, 1999), p. v.

Biographical Memoirs of Fellows of the British Academy, XI, 55–77.

In 1955, Brownlie moved to Cambridge for a year's postgraduate study as the Humanitarian Trust Student in Public International Law, entering King's College. He enjoyed the company of fellow postgraduates from abroad, and discussions of the political issues of that period—apartheid, the non-aligned movement and nuclear weapons. He joined the Communist Party (which he eventually left in 1968). But it is difficult to detect any strong influence of Marxist ideas, either in his writings, in conversation or in his professional work, and he was always critical of the operation—or lack of it—of the rule of law in Eastern Europe. He always thought of himself as a lawyer, not a political activist. But in a letter of 11 January 2009 to *The Sunday Times* he headed a list of distinguished scholars and practitioners who described Israel's actions in Gaza as an act of aggression and a war crime: this was a rare exception to his practice of avoiding taking public positions on political issues.

It was also during his year in Cambridge that Brownlie began to come into his own as an international lawyer. The university attracted aspirants from all over the world.[2] Robert Jennings had just succeeded Hersch Lauterpacht as the Whewell Professor: he held monthly evening seminars in his rooms at Jesus College, with Hersch often in attendance. Other attendees included Lord McNair, Kurt Lipstein, Clive Parry, and Hersch's son Elihu, then just starting out as an Assistant Lecturer. Among Brownlie's contemporaries were Hans Blix, Theodor Meron, Georges Abi-Saab, Stephen Schwebel, Rosalyn Higgins and Hisashi Owada, who remembers fondly their time together as students.[3]

Brownlie completed his D.Phil. in 1961. His supervisor was the Chichele Professor, Sir Humphrey Waldock,[4] whom Brownlie held in high and affectionate regard. Brownlie's thesis formed the basis for *International Law and the Use of Force by States*, published in 1963. *Use of Force* was the first of several texts authored by Brownlie which could fairly claim the status of classics in their field. In the Preface, Brownlie described his decision to undertake the study as prompted 'partly by a feeling that it has not received that attention from public international lawyers which it is due

[2] H. Owada, 'Sir Ian Brownlie, Kt, CBE QC: the professor as counsel', *British Yearbook of International Law*, 81 (2010), p. 2.

[3] Ibid.

[4] Waldock was elected to the International Court in 1973, serving as President from 1979 to 1981 and dying in office. Brownlie wrote Waldock's entry for the *Oxford Dictionary of National Biography*: I. Brownlie, 'Waldock, Sir (Claud) Humphrey Meredith (1904–1981)', in *Oxford Dictionary of National Biography* (Oxford, 2004): <http://www.oxforddnb.com/view/article/31793>.

and partly by a conviction that recent changes in technology and strategy have given a new significance to the legal regulation of the use of force'.[5] The book reversed this state of affairs. Its most significant contribution was its identification of the Charter of the United Nations as the decisive moment for the rules governing the use of force by the international community.

Meanwhile Brownlie had married Jocelyn Gale in 1957, with whom he was to have three children: two daughters, Hannah and Rebecca, and a son, James. They divorced in 1975, after which Brownlie met and in 1978 married Christine Apperley, a postgraduate law student from New Zealand. Christine provided unwavering and loving support for Brownlie, invariably travelling with him to The Hague and elsewhere on cases, consultations and conferences.[6]

Brownlie was called to the Bar by Gray's Inn in 1958, although he did not undertake a pupillage until some years later. After Cambridge he took a lectureship at the University of Leeds for 1956–7, before moving to the University of Nottingham. In those days, international law was seen as possessing little more practical relevance than jurisprudence and was treated by the mainstream accordingly. In any event, it was normal to teach three or four subjects and he acquired and maintained an abiding interest in public law and tort—both of which, and especially tort, were to influence his subsequent work on state responsibility.[7]

In 1963 Brownlie was elected a tutorial fellow of Wadham College, Oxford and University Lecturer in Law. In 1966 his *Principles of Public International Law* was published by Oxford University Press.[8] This single-volume general treatment of most aspects of public international law was probably his greatest academic achievement. Its official title soon became redundant; it became known simply as *Brownlie* (though it will be referred to here as *Principles*). He took it through seven editions, seeing it translated into Russian (second edition), Japanese (third edition), Portuguese (fourth edition), Korean (fifth edition) and simplified and complex Chinese (fifth and sixth editions, respectively). Its second (and arguably best) edition

[5] I. Brownlie, *International Law and the Use of Force by States* (Oxford, 1963), p. i.

[6] Indeed they were co-authors on at least one occasion: I. Brownlie and C. J. Apperley, 'Kosovo Crisis Inquiry: memorandum on the international law aspects', *International and Comparative Law Quarterly*, 49 (2000), 878–905.

[7] See e.g. I. Brownlie, 'Causes of action in the Law of Nations', *British Yearbook of International Law*, 50 (1979), 13–41. This became Chapter V of his *System of the Law of Nations. State Responsibility Part I* (Oxford, 1983).

[8] I. Brownlie, *Principles of Public International Law* (Oxford, 1966).

was awarded the Certificate of Merit by the American Society for International Law in 1976, with the citation describing *Principles* as 'a work of great distinction'. Now in its eighth edition (2012), it retains its place as one of the lapidary texts of public international law.[9] Some of its key themes are discussed in section III below.

In 1972, Brownlie was a candidate for the Chichele Chair which became vacant on Waldock's retirement: D. P. O'Connell was however preferred. Though in some sense rivals (their views on O'Connell's subject of state succession were radically divergent; so also their attitude to international affairs in general) they maintained collegial personal relations.[10] In 1976, Brownlie was offered and accepted the chair in public international law at the London School of Economics (LSE).

A major contribution of the 1970s was his work, under the auspices of the Royal Institute for International Affairs, of a complete catalogue of African boundaries, settled and unsettled. *African Boundaries: a Legal and Diplomatic Encyclopaedia*,[11] produced with the aid of Ian Burns, was a labour of love—and was occasionally cited against him in subsequent boundary disputes.[12] Brownlie was fascinated by geography, and whatever room he occupied for an extended period of time was guaranteed to boast a collection of esoteric maps. As for *African Boundaries*, it remains the starting point for modern investigations of that continent's land borders.

During his time at LSE, Brownlie and Christine moved to London, where they continued to live following his academic return to the Chichele Chair and accompanying fellowship at All Souls College in 1980. As Chichele Professor, Brownlie assumed Senior Editorship of the *British Yearbook of International Law* (he had been an Editor since 1974) alongside the Whewell Professor at Cambridge[13]—that far from titular burden of the two titular chairs. He also served as a Delegate to Oxford University

[9] Edited by the present writer (Oxford, 2012).

[10] For O'Connell's work see J. R. Crawford, 'The contribution of Professor D. P. O'Connell to the discipline of International Law', *British Yearbook of International Law*, 51 (1980), 1–87. Brownlie's attitude to state succession was exemplified by his remark that 'it is perfectly possible to take the view that not many settled legal rules [of state succession] have emerged as yet': *Principles*, 7th edn. (Oxford, 2008), p. 650.

[11] I. Brownlie, *African Boundaries: a Legal and Diplomatic Encyclopaedia* (London, 1979). A new edition by Dr C. Beyani is in preparation.

[12] Thus he argued most of the land boundary issues in *Cameroon v Nigeria*—yet on key points *African Boundaries* supports the Cameroon position—as also did the Court: *Land and Maritime Boundary between Cameroon and Nigeria (Cameroon v Nigeria; Equatorial Guinea intervening)*, ICJ Reports 2002 p. 303.

[13] Successively Sir Robert Jennings, Sir Derek Bowett and the present writer.

Press (1984–94) and was General Editor of the successful series 'Oxford Monographs in International Law'.

Brownlie remained Chichele Professor until his (statutorily mandated) retirement in 1999—in the latter years of his tenure on a partial salary arrangement, though he maintained a normal professorial teaching load. He was awarded a DCL (1976), in 1999 elected Emeritus Chichele Professor and Emeritus Fellow of All Souls College, and in 2004 made a Distinguished Fellow of the college. The latter honours reflect his status as a stalwart of college life, tending towards conservativism on college matters. But Sir John Vickers, Warden at the time of his death, recalls that Brownlie shared a special bond with the college's younger Fellows, with whom he shared a dislike of the trendy and the pompous. He had been known to puncture name-dropping guests through comprehensive one-upmanship, usually by way of a casual reference to 'one of my clients, the United States of America'.[14]

Especially during his later years he was fond of denying that he was an academic, a term he rarely used without a note of scepticism.[15] Sir Robert Jennings referred to him as 'first and foremost a teacher';[16] I doubt Brownlie would have agreed. But he was in fact a fine teacher: he took care to get to know his students, and maintained contact with them over decades. His teaching focused not only on ensuring his students mastered the detail of international law, but also the wider perspective. Concerned about international law becoming an isolated speciality, he organised for many years a joint seminar with scholars of international relations at Oxford, notably Sir Adam Roberts. He could be tough, but he was capable of considerable sensitivity, as an anecdote by Sir Robert Jennings shows:

> I myself once had an able graduate student whose Ph.D. thesis involved some discussion of the notorious decision by the International Court of Justice in 1966 in the *South-West Africa* case; and of the point of view expressed by Sir Gerald Fitzmaurice and Sir Stephen Spender in their joint dissent in the earlier phase of the case when the Court seemed to have decided the other way ... In what I still think of as an inspired move ... I persuaded Ian to come over from Oxford to be the 'outside' examiner of the able but in places too angry thesis.

[14] J. Vickers, 'Sir Ian Brownlie', Address given at All Souls College, Oxford, 23 Oct. 2010. Brownlie first advised the United States in 1979, when counselling President Carter as to the capacity of the US to freeze Iranian assets during the Tehran hostage crisis.

[15] This was no reflection upon his attitude towards educators overall: indeed, he made a point of visiting his high school history teacher in Liverpool every year. Brownlie did, however, feel that standards had dropped within law schools over the course of his career, with far too many concessions to the latest fads and trends.

[16] Jennings, *The Reality of International Law*, p. vi.

> There was never any doubt that the candidate must get his doctorate. But in the oral examination, Ian taught him a lesson which I suspect only he could have got across to this candidate at that time. I remember Ian explaining that he felt sympathetic towards the candidate's feelings on the matter; nevertheless, he insisted, there were certain legal problems that had to be dealt with. And he took a passage from the dissenting opinion in the earlier decision and challenged the candidate to find not only a legal answer but also one as carefully and cogently argued. In this way the candidate was forced to admit to himself that the passage indeed had a point . . .[17]

It was especially as a supervisor of graduate students—doctoral and otherwise—that Brownlie shone, both as teacher and as mentor. He was no soft touch—as one distinguished former student remarked, 'he was . . . formidable . . . even when he was trying to be helpful'.[18] But he struck the right balance between attentiveness and allowing students to develop their own ideas at their own pace. A measure of this ability is the Festschrift on the occasion of his retirement from the Chichele Chair in 1999. Entitled *The Reality of International Law*—a title chosen expressly to reflect Brownlie's unapologetic pragmatism[19]—each of the twenty-five chapters was written by one of his graduate students.

II

As mentioned, Brownlie's first substantial contribution to international law was *Use of Force*. It was to establish him as an expert on the delicate relationship between the various provisions of the Charter of the United Nations and other sources of international law. In *Use of Force*, Brownlie posited that the Charter and the strictures that it placed on the use of force represented a new beginning to the oldest problem of international relations.[20] He was particularly emphatic as to the Charter's treatment of self-defence in Article 51, which provides that:

> Nothing in the present Charter shall impair the inherent right of individual or collective self-defence if an armed attack occurs against a Member of the United Nations, until the Security Council has taken measures necessary to maintain international peace and security. Measures taken by Members in the exercise of this right of self-defence shall be immediately reported to the Security Council and shall not in any way affect the authority and responsibility of the Security

[17] Jennings, *The Reality of International Law*, p. vi.
[18] Sands, *The Guardian*, 11 Jan. 2010.
[19] Goodwin-Gill and Talmon, 'Introduction', in *The Reality of International Law*, p. ix.
[20] Brownlie, *Use of Force*, pp. 107–23.

> Council under the present Charter to take at any time such action as it deems necessary in order to maintain or restore international peace and security.

Article 51 operates alongside Article 2(4) within the machinery of the Charter to limit substantially the capacity of states to employ force against other states. Article 2(4) provides that Members of the United Nations 'shall refrain in their international relations from the threat or use of force against the territorial integrity or political independence of any state, or in any other manner inconsistent with the Purposes of the United Nations'. Brownlie argued that these provisions, first, forbade the use of force generally, then created a discrete exception for cases of self-defence that subsumed completely the earlier customary law.[21]

A contrary view was taken by a young lecturer at the University of Manchester, Derek Bowett,[22] whose own contribution on the subject, *Self-Defence in International Law*, had been published in 1958. The two were to have a long working relationship: Bowett and Brownlie, having started by sharing opposed theses, would come to work opposite each other as international law professors at the Universities of Cambridge and Oxford respectively, as representing opposing parties before the International Court, and harmoniously as co-editors of the *British Yearbook of International Law*.

For his part, Bowett saw the Charter as having a strong continuity with pre-existing customary international law, which considered self-defence to be a broad and inherent right of states.[23] It also arguably conceived of a right of states to resort to self-defence pre-emptively. The pre-Charter customary law developed principally in the mid-nineteenth century. A key episode was an exchange of letters between US Secretary of State Daniel Webster and the British Special Envoy to the United States, Lord Ashburton, over the destruction of the steamship *Caroline* by British forces in 1837. At the time of its seizure, the *Caroline* was tied up at the US military outpost of Fort Schlosser,[24] but it was alleged to be involved in a rebellion against British rule in Canada. Webster, in a letter of 24 April 1841, stated that in order for the British action to be justified

[21] Ibid., p. 265.

[22] See J. R. Crawford, '*In Memoriam*: Sir Derek Bowett CBE, QC, FBA (1927–2009)', *British Yearbook of International Law*, 80 (2009), 1–9.

[23] D. Bowett, *Self-Defence in International Law* (Manchester, 1958), pp. 184–99.

[24] Further: R. Y. Jennings, 'The *Caroline* and McLeod cases', *American Journal of International Law*, 32 (1938), 82–99; A. D. (Lord) McNair, *International Law Opinions*, 2 (Cambridge, 1956), pp. 221–30; C. Greenwood, 'Caroline, The', in R. Wolfrum (general ed.), *Max Planck Encyclopedia of International Law* (Oxford, 2009).

under international law, Her Majesty's Government would need to demonstrate 'a necessity of self-defence, instant, overwhelming, leaving no choice of means and no moment for deliberation'. That strict formulation, redolent of the common law doctrine of individual self-defence, was apparently accepted by Ashburton.

The opening gambit in what would become a significant debate between the two was actually launched a good deal earlier than the publication of *Use of Force* in 1963. In 1959 Brownlie published a substantial review of *Self-Defence in International Law*.[25] He took issue with Bowett's assertion that Articles 2(4) and 51 of the Charter did not impair the customary right of states to defend themselves. In Brownlie's view, this was 'open to serious criticism':

> It is submitted that no evidence exists to support this conclusion. There is no indication ... that the right of self-defence in Article 51 [is] in contrast with any other right of self-defence permitted by the Charter ... The very terms of Article 51 preclude a view that its content is special and not general; it refers to the 'inherent right' and it is not incongruous to regard the Article as containing the only right of self-defence permitted in the Charter.... [W]here the Charter has a specific provision relating to a particular legal category, to assert that this does not restrict the wider ambit of the customary law relating to that category or problem, is to go beyond the bounds of logic. Why have such treaty provisions at all? Such an approach to the Charter ignores both the principle of effectiveness in the interpretation of treaties and the generality of Article 51 in its reference to the 'inherent right'.[26]

Brownlie repeated these criticisms almost verbatim in *Use of Force*.[27] Bowett's response, in a nice piece of symmetry, came in the form of a 1963 review of *Use of Force* in the same journal as Brownlie's earlier review.[28] He remarked:

> It will surprise no one, least of all the author, if, in this highly controversial field the present reviewer fails to share all the author's views. Perhaps the most serious issue between the author and this reviewer is whether there remains a right of 'anticipatory' self-defence or not: in other words, whether a State may react in self-defence against an attack which is imminent or only, as the author con-

[25] I. Brownlie, 'Recent appraisals of legal regulation of the use of force', *International and Comparative Law Quarterly*, 8 (1959), 707–21.

[26] Ibid., pp. 718–20.

[27] Brownlie, *Use of Force*, pp. 274–5. See also I. Brownlie, 'The use of force in self-defence', *British Yearbook of International Law*, 37 (1960), 183–68.

[28] D. Bowett, 'Review of *International Law and the Use of Force by States*', *International and Comparative Law Quarterly*, 18 (1964), 1107–8.

> tends, against one which has occurred. The author concedes that up to 1939 self-defence was conceived as being 'anticipatory' ... but he regards the Charter as having modified this position not only in the comprehensive formula of Article 2(4) but also by the phrase 'if an armed attack occurs' in Article 51. The reviewer's contention, in brief, would be that Article 2(4) was never conceived as prohibiting self-defence, and by self-defence was meant the traditional, accepted right of self-defence, including 'anticipatory' self-defence, and that nowhere in the *traveaux preparatoires* is there evidence that Article 51 was a new restriction ... The author's reaction is to say 'Why have treaty provisions at all?' ... The answer is surely that many treaty provisions are declaratory of existing rights and it is often thought useful to insert such provisions to avoid any uncertainty which might be caused by their omission.[29]

Bowett closed this particular point by noting—correctly—that a textual interpretation of the words of Article 51 would not yield a complete answer, and that state practice would be necessary to illuminate the words of the provision. He was confident that he would be vindicated, citing the early episodes of UN operations in Katanga from 1962 to 1963 and the US blockade of Cuba.[30]

Brownlie was not to be dissuaded, reasserting, most recently in the sixth and seventh editions of *Principles*,[31] the view that Article 51 displaced the customary right of self-defence. Simultaneously, he developed the fall-back position first hinted at in *Use of Force*,[32] that, even if he was incorrect as to the displacing effect of the Charter, custom—under the influence of Article 51—had moved on since the *Caroline*. Indeed, he considered it absurd that customary international law allegedly owed less to a comparatively recent treaty of near-universal acceptance than a single instance of bilateral correspondence over a century earlier.[33] Indeed state practice since 1945 has generally opposed the exercise of a pre-emptive right of self-defence, whether as a matter of customary international law or under Article 51.[34] To take but one example, the Israeli attack on an Iraqi nuclear reactor in 1981 was strongly condemned as a 'clear violation of the Charter of the United Nations' in UN Security Council Resolution

[29] Ibid., p. 1107.

[30] Ibid.

[31] Brownlie, *Principles*, 6th edn. (Oxford, 2003), pp. 701–2; Brownlie, *Principles*, 7th edn., pp. 733–4. See also I. Brownlie, 'International Law at the fiftieth anniversary of the United Nations', *Recueil des Cours*, 255 (1995), 9–228 at 202–6.

[32] Brownlie, *Use of Force*, pp. 279–80.

[33] Brownlie, *Principles*, 7th edn., p. 734.

[34] e.g. Brownlie, *Principles*, 7th edn., p. 734. This statement remains correct as a matter of international law, and was included in the eighth edition: Brownlie, *Principles*, 8th edn. (Oxford, 2012), pp. 750–2.

487, adopted unanimously.[35] In addition, although it has never specifically ruled on the subject, the International Court may have impliedly excluded anticipatory self-defence from the scope of Article 51.[36] Not even the United States—in recent years the most vociferous supporter of not only pre-emptive but also *preventive* self-defence[37]—has actually taken action on the kind of basis alluded to by Bowett. It may be noted that when the US Expeditionary Force began military operations against Iraq, the letter to the Security Council of 20 March 2003 relied upon Security Council resolutions as the primary putative legal basis of the action, not on any right to pre-emptive or preventive self-defence under general international law.[38] But to focus too much on this scholarly disagreement is, as Bowett himself conceded in the final paragraph of his review of *Use of Force*, to '[give] the wrong impression'.[39] Brownlie and Bowett valued highly each other's opinion and friendship. Indeed, they found themselves fundamentally in agreement on most issues, having emerged from the same pragmatic and workmanlike tradition of international law.[40]

Bowett was not the only colleague with whom Brownlie jousted on questions relating to the use of force. Another high profile engagement occurred with Richard Lillich,[41] for many years the Charles H. Stockton Professor of International Law at the University of Virginia. This time the participants skirmished over whether the terms of the Article 2(4) of the Charter permitted the unilateral use of force by states in order to redress a dire humanitarian situation. Brownlie's position on the position was simple: by its terms, Article 2(4) (as bolstered by Article 2(7), prevent-

[35] Security Council Resolution 487 (1981), para. 1. But no such response occurred in relation to the Israeli bombing of the Deir ez-Zor reactor in Syria in 2007: C. Gray, *International Law and the Use of Force*, 3rd edn. (Cambridge, 2008), p. 237.

[36] See *Armed Activities in the Territory of the Congo (Democratic Republic of the Congo v Uganda)*, ICJ Reports 2005 p. 168 at 223–4.

[37] *The National Security Strategy of the United States of America* (Washington, US Government, 2002), p. 15. Also: Gray, *Use of Force*, 3rd edn., pp. 209–16.

[38] United Nations Document S/2003/351, 21 March 2003 (passing reference to self-defence is made in the final substantive paragraph). The UK and Australian letters rely exclusively upon Security Council resolutions: United Nations Document S/2003/350, 21 March 2003; United Nations Document S/2003/352, 21 March 2003. On the UK position: Lord Goldsmith, Attorney-General, 'The use of force against Iraq', *International and Comparative Law Quarterly*, 52 (2003), 811–14; Lord Goldsmith, Attorney General, 'Attorney-General's advice on the Iraq War', *International and Comparative Law Quarterly*, 54 (2005), 767–78 at 768.

[39] Bowett, 'Review of *Use of Force*', 1108.

[40] H. Owada, 'The professor as counsel', 4.

[41] See B. H. Weston, 'Richard B. Lillich (1933–1996)', *American Journal of International Law*, 91 (1997), 85–8.

ing the UN from intervening in the strictly internal matters of states) permitted no such thing and thus any act of humanitarian intervention so-called—even if for the noblest of reasons—was *prima facie* illegal as a matter of international law. As with his conclusions on self-defence, Brownlie took this position early and stuck to it, writing in *Use of Force*:

> It must be admitted that humanitarian intervention has not been *expressly* condemned by either the League Covenant, the Kellogg–Briand Pact, or the United Nations Charter. Indeed, such intervention would not constitute resort to force as an instrument of national policy. It is necessary nevertheless to have regard to the general effect and underlying assumptions of the juridical developments of the period since 1920. In particular it is extremely doubtful if the form of intervention has survived the express condemnations of intervention which had occurred in recent times or the general prohibition of resort to force to be found in the United Nations Charter.[42]

Lillich's counter-argument appeared in two articles[43] on which was later based an Interim Report of the Sub-Committee of the Committee on Human Rights of the International Law Association.[44] Textually, it was predicated on the fact that the prohibition on the use of force expressed in Article 2(4) is phrased in terms of measures 'against the territorial integrity or political independence of any state': if the force used was such as to avoid compromising either of these, the argument ran, no breach of Article 2(4) would have occurred.[45] This was apparently inconsistent with the International Court's decision in *Corfu Channel*,[46] which gave a broad reading to the qualification in Article 2(4) and reduced to vanishing point the purported exception. But Lillich and other scholars—notably American—pressed on. Lillich for his part buttressed his argument with teleological assumptions as to the need for humanitarian intervention in the international community and several incidents that Lillich believed

[42] Brownlie, *Use of Force*, 342.

[43] R. B. Lillich, 'Forcible self-help by states to protect human rights', *Iowa Law Review*, 53 (1967), 325–51; R. B. Lillich, 'Intervention to protect human rights', *McGill Law Journal*, 15 (1969), 205–19.

[44] International Law Association, *Report of the Committee on Human Rights*, The Hague Conference (1970), p. 8.

[45] Lillich, 'Forcible self-help by states', 336; Lillich, 'Intervention to protect human rights', 211–12.

[46] ICJ Reports 1949 p. 4, 35. The Court's famous rejection of the UK argument has been interpreted variously as a complete rejection of narrow interpretation or as a more limited repudiation of the particular UK claim on the facts: Gray, *Use of Force*, 3rd edn., p. 32. The Court itself subsequently interpreted the position as a blanket rejection: *Military and Paramilitary Activities in and against Nicaragua (Nicaragua v United States of America)*, ICJ Reports 1986 p. 14 at 106–8.

reflected the 'essence' of state practice—i.e. what events such as the 1964 Stanleyville operation in the Congo and the landing of US troops in the Dominican Republic in 1965 were 'really' about.[47] Thus Brownlie's more cautious approach to the subject was criticised as follows:

> Balancing the need to protect human rights against the realization that non-humanitarian motives [of the intervening state] may often be at work, [Brownlie] apparently believes that world community policy requires an across-the-board prohibition of forcible self-help measures. This recommendation to forego the use of coercion, in the opinion of the writer, constitutes a classic example of throwing the baby out with the bath water. Granted the dangers inherent in accepting a decentralized determination of when it is appropriate to embark upon a humanitarian mission, the fact that a state's action in such a situation remains subject to review and revision by the world community offers some safeguard against the use of force for non-humanitarian purposes.[48]

When both he and Lillich were asked to contribute their opposing views to a volume of essays produced by the American Society of International Law,[49] Brownlie did not hold back:

> It is clear to the present writer that a jurist asserting a right of forcible humanitarian intervention has a very heavy burden of proof. Few writers familiar with the modern materials of state practice and legal opinion on the use of force would support such a view ... In the lengthy discussions over the years in United Nations bodies of the definition of aggression and principles of international law concerning international relations and cooperation among states, the variety of opinions canvassed has not revealed even a substantial minority in favour of the legality of humanitarian intervention ... When Lillich quotes my conclusion ... as a mere opinion, he does not make it clear that this view accords with that of numerous distinguished authorities. Moreover, my view is not an opinion casually thrown out, but is the outcome of a very extensive examination of state practice, especially in the period 1880–1945. Lillich's handling of the literature seems little short of arbitrary ...[50]

In his reply,[51] Lillich defended his preference for unilateral intervention over Brownlie's favoured solution of UN-backed humanitarian opera-

[47] Lillich, 'Forcible self-help by states', pp. 338–44; Lillich, 'Intervention to protect human rights', pp. 213–16.

[48] Lillich, 'Forcible self-help by states', pp. 217–18. See also Lillich, 'Intervention to protect human rights', p. 347.

[49] J. N. Moore (ed.), *Law and Civil War in the Modern World* (Baltimore, MD, and London, 1974).

[50] I. Brownlie, 'Humanitarian intervention', in *Law and Civil War in the Modern World*, p. 217 and pp. 218–20. Brownlie also contributed another essay to a book on the subject edited by Lillich: see I. Brownlie, 'Thoughts on kind-hearted gunmen', in R. B. Lillich (ed.), *Humanitarian Intervention and the United Nations* (Charlottesville, VA, 1973), pp. 139–48.

[51] R. B. Lillich, 'Humanitarian intervention: a reply to Ian Brownlie and a plea for constructive alternatives', in *Law and Civil War in the Modern World*, pp. 229–51.

tions. His ultimate conclusion, however, was that the two scholars were in reality not so far apart: at the end of the day, both agreed that suffering engendered through widespread human rights abuses and breaches of the laws of war demanded immediate and vigorous redress.[52]

As with so many of Brownlie's sparring partners, his relationship with Lillich was a cordial one. Indeed, Lillich was to spend a year at All Souls as a Visiting Fellow in 1987. As to the interaction of humanitarian intervention and the UN Charter, it appears that Brownlie again carried the day. State practice has since the 1970s steadily eroded the concept: the majority of operations in respect of which humanitarian intervention may have been invoked have instead opted for other justifications. This is reflected in, for example, the UK's shifting justification of the Air Exclusion Zones created in Iraq. The first such zone was established in northern Iraq in 1991. This involved using force with the object of excluding Iraqi air power in order to protect the Kurds of northern Iraq and was, in the view of the British government, justified by 'the customary international law principle of humanitarian intervention'.[53] The Air Exclusion Zone in southern Iraq, created in 1992, was also controversial but was, unlike its predecessor, purportedly based upon Security Council Resolution 668 of 1990.[54] The UK position over the life of the no-fly zones was, however, inconstant; on occasion, it claimed that both zones were supported by the resolution; in other instances, it claimed that even without the resolution, both zones could be justified under the supposed principle of humanitarian intervention.[55]

III

A great strength of *Principles* as a treatment of public international law is its capacity to convey international law as a *system*, based on and helping to structure a system of relations among states and other entities. Brownlie's understanding of the common themes within the system seems to have informed his choice of the term 'principles' in the title. Yet he was disdainful of 'grand theories' and similar unifying structures. Although

[52] Ibid., pp. 244–51.

[53] Brownlie and Apperley, 'Kosovo Crisis Inquiry', pp. 882–3.

[54] Ibid., pp. 906–7.

[55] e.g., G. Marston, 'United Kingdom materials on International Law 2001', *British Yearbook of International Law*, 72 (2001), 551–725 at 692–5.

certain broad trends may be observable at a distance, he thought, close inspection led only to pixilation.

Some examples are necessary to establish the point, the more so as the book's title has tended to establish in the profession's collective consciousness the idea that Brownlie's work is a sort of perennial Bin Cheng,[56] a search for and articulation of valid general principles, to be found in the materials of the subject, capable of providing an *erga omnes* justification underpinning that area of law. Nothing could be further from the truth, as the following passages show:

> Sir Gerald Fitzmaurice has attributed treaty-making capacity to 'para-Statal entities recognized as possessing a definite if limited form of international personality, for example, insurgent communities recognized as having belligerent status—*de facto* authorities in control of specific territory'. This statement is correct as a matter of principle, although its application to particular facts will require caution.[57]

> It is sometimes said that international responsibility is a necessary correlative or criterion of independence. Broadly this is true, but the principle must be qualified when a case of international representation arises and the 'protecting' state is the only available defendant.[58]

> The functional approach has been prominent in a group of cases arising from the unlawful use of force. Ethiopia was conquered and annexed by Italy in 1936. Many states gave *de jure* or *de facto* recognition to Italian control, but Ethiopia remained formally a member of the League of Nations. However, neither this principle nor that of continuity can provide an omnibus solution to the legal problems arising for solution after 1945. In all these cases, for slightly differing reasons, the occupation in fact and form went beyond belligerent occupation, since there was either absorption outright or the setting up of puppet regimes.[59]

> The position, supported by principle and state practice, would seem to be as follows. Admission to membership [of the United Nations] is *prima facie* evidence of statehood, and non-recognizing members are at risk if they ignore the basic rights of existence of another state the object of their non-recognition ... However, there is probably nothing in the Charter, or customary law apart from the Charter, which requires a non-recognizing state to give 'political' recognition and to enter into optional bilateral relations with a fellow member.[60]

[56] See B. Cheng, *General Principles of International Law as Applied by International Courts and Tribunals* (Cambridge, 1987). Cheng's work was an attempt to identify and elaborate upon the 'general principles of law recognized by civilized nations'; it remains the standard treatise on the subject.

[57] Brownlie, *Principles*, 7th edn., p. 63 (citations omitted).

[58] Ibid., p. 74 (citations omitted).

[59] Ibid., p. 81 (citations omitted).

[60] Ibid., p. 94.

> Unilateral declarations involve, in principle at least, concessions which are intentional, public, coherent, and conclusive of the issues. However, acts of acquiescence and official statements may have probative value as admissions of rights inconsistent with the claims of the declarant in a situation of competing interests, such acts individually not being conclusive of the issues.[61]

Many other examples could be given.[62]

From a certain point of view, *Principles* is a conceptualisation of international law that contains no principles; only broad brushstrokes which may be displaced by particular contexts and requirements—perhaps like any body of law in its practical application. The result is a subtle, occasionally elusive and elliptical, text which rewards (and often requires) rereading.

Underlying this key aspect of *Principles* is Brownlie's attitude towards international law as a whole. To an extent this was not based on any *a priori* theory: in his mind the system was self-evident, necessary and in no special need of justification. International law was the product of ordinary legal technique (a technique assumed to be generally valid) applied to the materials of international relations considered in detail and in all their particularity. What was presupposed was not any overarching principle or value, but an evident need for order and an assumption that the meaning of commitments, formal or customary, will yield to standard methods of textual analysis—hermeneutics without the grandeur or pomposity of the phrase.

Indeed, as Warbrick notes,[63] Brownlie's world-view was not just atheoretical: it was *anti*-theoretical. In his General Course to the Hague Academy of International Law, he went so far as to remark:

> In spite of considerable exposure to theory, and some experience in teaching jurisprudence, my ultimate position has been that, with one exception, theory produces no real benefits and frequently obscures the more interesting questions.[64]

The exception identified was the point made by Hans Kelsen that the binding nature of international law derives from a source outside international law. Kelsen identified this as the *Grundnorm*, the basal notion that states should behave as they have customarily behaved.[65]

[61] Ibid., p. 642.

[62] See, e.g., ibid., pp. 185, 300–1, 323–4, 477–8.

[63] C. Warbrick, 'Brownlie's *Principles of Public International Law*: an assessment', *European Journal of International Law*, 11 (2000), p. 634.

[64] Brownlie, 'International Law at the fiftieth anniversary of the United Nations', p. 30. When pushed, however, Brownlie admitted to a mild form of objective positivism: ibid., p. 21.

[65] H. Kelsen (tr. A. Wedberg), *General Theory of Law and State* (Cambridge, MA, 1945), pp. 115–19.

Brownlie was particularly critical of those theoreticians—notably H. L. A. Hart—who debated whether international law could be considered law 'properly so called' without displaying any real understanding of the subject itself.[66] Brownlie tackled Hart's assertion that international law's purported inability to effect adjudication, enforcement and change—due principally to its lack of courts of compulsory jurisdiction—robbed it of the status of law. In Brownlie's view:

> The lack of compulsory jurisdiction and a legislature is regarded by Hart not as the special feature of a system which operates in conditions of a certain kind, but as the marks of an outcast, of a butterfly which is not wanted for a predetermined collection. Yet ... the stability of international relations compares quite well with internal law, given the grand total of municipal systems ruptured by civil strife since 1945. And whilst it may be said that international law lacks secondary rules, this matters less if one accepts the view that secondary rules do not play such a decisive role in maintaining the more basic forms of legality in municipal systems.[67]

Thus *Principles* is a work of almost pure exposition, one which does not shy away from presenting what Brownlie considered to be the complex (and occasionally unwelcome) reality of international law: a series of discrete rules grouped under the rubric of certain general, often imperfect, principles of international law. The strength of the work is its sustained technical analysis, characterised by desire to reflect the contours of international problems and to emphasise the dispositive effect that facts may have on legal outcomes. In this vein, all seven editions of *Principles* that Brownlie oversaw lacked a general introduction that might have framed the reader's consideration of the subject as a whole: the book began, logically, with a discussion of the sources of international law and ended with a consideration of the settlement of international disputes.[68] Throughout it was characterised by a sort of normative *pointillisme*, one that made considerable demands on the reader but whose subtlety was disguised by a rather bluff style.

In his later years Brownlie was somewhat neglectful of his *magnum opus*—perhaps understandably given the demands of his practice and the sheer difficulty of updating his review single-handedly in an age where

[66] See, e.g., H. L. A. Hart, *The Concept of Law*, 2nd edn. (Oxford, 1994), chap. 10.

[67] I. Brownlie, 'The reality and efficacy of International Law', *British Yearbook of International Law*, 51 (1981), 1–8 at 8. For criticism, see Warbrick, 'Brownlie's *Principles of Public International Law*: an assessment', pp. 633–6.

[68] Though this was only the case up to the 6th edition, after which time Brownlie added his signature thoughts on the use of force: Brownlie, *Principles*, 6th edn., chap. 33; Brownlie, *Principles*, 7th edn., chap. 33.

international law is increasingly dense and specialised (and in which he disdained the computer). Lowe, in a prescient review of the fourth edition (1990), spoke of 'a faint feeling of trepidation, a slight but nagging doubt as to the comprehensiveness with which [the work] has been updated'.[69] This feeling would grow with successive editions. But the cracks—though more than merely cosmetic—were far from fatal, and the bedrock on which *Principles* was built remains a firm foundation for the eighth edition.

IV

It was undoubtedly as a barrister, a practitioner of the law, that Brownlie obtained his greatest professional satisfaction. He did not begin practice until 1967, joining chambers at 2 Crown Office Row. In 1983 he moved to Hare Court, forerunner of Blackstone Chambers, where he remained until his death. He scored some early successes in public order cases, which led to the publication of another book, *The Law Relating to Public Order*, in 1968.[70] His first contribution to the law as a practitioner was by his later standards somewhat parochial but it did, in the words of Vaughan Lowe, 'bring peace of mind [to] the parents of an entire generation'.[71] In the case of *Sweet v Parsley*, Brownlie—led by Rose Heilbron, QC—convinced the House of Lords that Miss Stephanie Sweet could not be convicted of 'being concerned in the management of premises for purpose of smoking cannabis' under the Dangerous Drugs Act as she was unaware that her lodgers were minded so to indulge.[72]

Brownlie's practice expanded rapidly into the international sphere and his eminence there was soon recognised; he took silk in 1979 and was made a Bencher of Gray's Inn in 1986. He appeared as counsel in international law matters before national courts[73] and also before a wide range of

[69] V. Lowe, 'Review of *Principles of Public International Law*, Fourth Edition', *Law Quarterly Review*, 107 (1991), 513–15 at 514. Lowe's review was still largely laudatory. A more critical and expansive review of *Principles* was undertaken by Colin Warbrick: Warbrick, 'Brownlie's *Principles of Public International Law*: an assessment', pp. 621–7. The whole of Warbrick's review should, however, be read.

[70] I. Brownlie, *The Law Relating to Public Order* (London, 1968). A second edition of the work was published in 1981, though not edited by Brownlie: M. Supperstone (ed.), *Brownlie's Law of Public Order and National Security* (London, 1981).

[71] V. Lowe, 'Sir Ian Brownlie, Kt, CBE, QC (1932–2010)', *British Yearbook of International Law*, 81 (2010), 9–12 at 11.

[72] *Sweet v Parsley* [1970] AC 132.

[73] Notably in the *Pinochet* cases, where he acted for Amnesty International: *Re Pinochet (No 1)* [2000] 1 AC 61; *Re Pinochet (No 3)* [2000] 1 AC 147.

international courts and tribunals, including the European Court of Human Rights,[74] the European Court of Justice, arbitral tribunals[75] and, of course, the International Court of Justice. He eschewed, in the words of a younger colleague, 'hand-waving or flamboyance'.[76] Instead, his advocacy was, according to President Owada, 'characterized by . . . a great eye for and an encyclopaedic knowledge of the law' coupled with 'an ability to identify the critical elements of a case, highlighting the strongest arguments on those points'.[77] To this may be added Sir Robert Jennings's observation that one of Brownlie's greatest advantages was the gift of foresight: 'his ability to see and appreciate the strengths of his opponents' probable arguments'.[78]

One of Brownlie's earliest appearances before the International Court was also arguably his most famous, and established his reputation as an advocate of skill and fortitude. In 1986, he scored a signal victory for Nicaragua against the United States of America in the case concerning *Military and Paramilitary Activities in and against Nicaragua*.[79] The case arose from the activities of the *contras*, opponents of the Nicaraguan (Sandinista) government who in 1981 commenced a guerrilla insurgency movement, operating from bases in neighbouring states and funded and assisted, covertly and overtly, by the United States. The Court found the acts of the *contras* were not generally attributable to the United States, but that, based upon actual participation of and directions given by the US, certain individual instances of paramilitary activity were attributable to it. Specifically the United States was responsible for the mine-laying and for certain other operations in which it had direct involvement. Conversely, the Court found that purported acts of self-defence undertaken by Nicaragua were not unlawful under international law.

[74] Notably in *Loizidou v Turkey* (1996) 108 ILR 443; and *Cyprus v Turkey* (2003) 120 ILR 10.

[75] Notably, Brownlie appeared as counsel for Chile in the *Beagle Channel Arbitration (Chile v Argentina)* (1977) 52 ILR 93; for Greenpeace in *Rainbow Warrior (Compensation) (Greenpeace v France)* (unreported); for Yemen in *Eritrea v Yemen (Phase One: Territorial Sovereignty and Scope of the Dispute)* (1998) 114 ILR 1; *(Phase Two: Maritime Delimitation)* (1999) 119 ILR 417; for Ethiopia in *Eritrea/Ethiopia (Boundary)* (2002) 130 ILR 1, and for Iran in various cases before the US–Iran Claims Tribunal.

[76] Sands, *The Guardian*, 11 Jan. 2010.

[77] Owada, 'The professor as counsel', 4.

[78] Jennings, *The Reality of International Law*, p. vii.

[79] ICJ Reports 1986 p. 14. Brownlie also convinced the Court in 1984 that it had jurisdiction to hear the dispute and that the claims brought by Nicaragua were admissible: ICJ Reports 1984 p. 392. Irritated by the Court's decisions on jurisdiction and admissibility, the United States refused to appear for the proceedings on the merits and subsequently withdrew from the Optional Clause entirely.

A milestone in the development of international law substantively, the *Nicaragua* case also served as an indicator of significance for the developing institution of international justice, especially for Third World states. In contrast with the endemic inequality of arms that characterises international relations at the political level, *Nicaragua* demonstrated that litigation or arbitration before international courts and tribunals could provide a relatively level playing field.

In Brownlie's own words:

> Working in a milieu in which the clients are States presents problems of a special sort, relatively unknown in a single jurisdiction practice. Within the United Kingdom the Bar would consider appearance against the government and its agencies as perfectly normal and a necessary concomitant of the Rule of Law. But should this principle apply to disputes between States, in which Counsel will appear against his own government? The principle must surely remain applicable, if the Rule of Law is to be maintained [...] In some circles the claim is made by certain lawyers that they will only work for good causes. Apparently, such good causes do not include the giving of practical reality to the Rule of Law. It is surely of the essence of the principle of legality that the law should be available to all.[80]

Brownlie was to cite this precept throughout his career, and to act on it. He appeared for Libya in the action brought against the United Kingdom and United States following the Lockerbie bombing.[81] In the *Legality of Use of Force* cases he acted for Yugoslavia against NATO,[82] after the bombing of Kosovo. In the late 1990s and until 2007, he was part of a team acting for Serbia in the series of cases concerning the *Application of the Convention on the Prevention and Punishment of the Crime of Genocide*,[83] in which the Court ultimately held that Serbia was not internationally responsible for committing genocide in Bosnia-Herzegovina. In *Armed Activities on the Territory of the Congo (Democratic Republic of the Congo v Uganda)*, he acted for Uganda.[84] He also made a substantial contribution to the development of the Court's expertise in maritime delimitation

[80] I. Brownlie, 'The perspective of International Law from the Bar', in M. Evans (ed.), *International Law*, 2nd edn. (Oxford, 2006), p. 14.

[81] *Questions of Interpretation and Application of the 1971 Montreal Convention arising from the Aerial Incident at Lockerbie (Libyan Arab Jamahiriya v United Kingdom; Libyan Arab Jamahiriya v United States), Preliminary Objections*, ICJ Reports 1998 pp. 9 and 115, respectively.

[82] e.g., *Legality of Use of Force (Serbia and Montenegro v Canada)*, ICJ Reports 2004 p. 429; *Legality of Use of Force (Serbia and Montenegro v France)*, ICJ Reports 2004 p. 575; *Legality of Use of Force (Serbia and Montenegro v United Kingdom)*, ICJ Reports 2004 p. 1307.

[83] Culminating in *Application of the Convention on the Prevention and Punishment of the Crime of Genocide (Bosnia and Herzegovina v Serbia and Montenegro)*, ICJ Reports 2007 p. 43.

[84] ICJ Reports 2005 p. 168.

matters, appearing for Canada in *Delimitation of the Maritime Boundary in the Gulf of Maine Area*,[85] for Norway in *Maritime Delimitation in the Area between Greenland and Jan Mayen*,[86] for Nigeria in *Land and Maritime Boundary between Cameroon and Nigeria*[87] and for Nicaragua in *Territorial and Maritime Dispute between Nicaragua and Honduras in the Caribbean Sea*.[88] He was involved in more cases (over 40) before the Court than any other Anglophone counsel, a record that is likely to stand for a long time.

Although some were minded to criticise his 'choice' of client (he would insist, correctly, that he never made any choice, but simply fulfilled his obligations under the 'cab rank' rule of the English Bar[89]), Brownlie's independence and integrity ensured that his sense of duty was never confused with sympathy. He was made CBE in 1993, and in 2009 (following his retirement from the International Law Commission) was knighted for his services to public international law. This was despite never having represented the United Kingdom in any international capacity.[90] Indeed on at least one occasion he proved a considerable irritant to Her Majesty's Government by joining the Mauritian delegation contesting ownership of the Chagos Islands. As another member of the Mauritian delegation relates, at one particularly heated negotiating session in early 2009 Brownlie gave the Foreign and Commonwealth Office the full weight of what he believed to be the correct position in international law, afterwards remarking that 'by the look on the face of the chaps at the FCO, the knighthood is gone forever'.[91] Happily he was incorrect.

Brownlie's career was enriched by his membership of the key professional organisations. In 1977 he was elected an Associate, and in 1985 became a Member (and eventually Rapporteur and Vice-President) of the *Institut de Droit International*, an institution devoted to lunch and therefore congenial to him.[92] In 1979 he was made a Fellow of the British

[85] ICJ Reports 1984 p. 246.

[86] ICJ Reports 1993 p. 38.

[87] ICJ Reports 2002 p. 303.

[88] ICJ Reports 2007 p. 659. This case was another significant victory for Brownlie. He convinced the Court of the merits of the bisector approach to maritime delimitation as opposed to the simple drawing of an equidistance line: see Owada, 'The professor as counsel', pp. 4–5.

[89] See Brownlie, 'International Law at the fiftieth anniversary of the United Nations', p. 22: 'In this context I act in accordance with the ethics of the English Bar, the rules of which oblige members to accept clients requiring assistance within the lawyer's area of expertise.'

[90] Brownlie had earlier received the Chilean Order of Bernardo O'Higgins (1993) and was appointed a Commander of the Norwegian Order of Merit (1993). He was made an Honorary Member of the Indian Society of International Law in 2009.

[91] Boolell, *The Mauritius Times*, 15 Jan. 2010.

[92] Brownlie was punctilious as to meals but impervious as to any soporific effect they might have—he was as sharp at the end of the day as at the beginning.

Academy. From 1982 to 1991 he was Director of Studies of the International Law Association, and for many years served as a member of its Executive Council and its institutional memory. Most significantly, he was elected to membership of the United Nations International Law Commission in 1997 (replacing Bowett),[93] and served as its President in 2007 before stepping down the following year. He was Special Rapporteur for the Commission's work on the effect of armed conflict on treaties from 2004 to 2008, in which capacity he produced several reports.[94] He was honoured by the invitation of the Hague Academy of International Law to give the General Course on public international law on the fiftieth anniversary of the United Nations.[95]

Brownlie also accepted a variety of judicial and arbitral appointments. In 1995 he was made a Judge and in 1996 President of the European Nuclear Energy Tribunal. He was nominated to the Panel of Arbitrators and the Panel of Conciliators for the International Centre for the Settlement of Investment Disputes, and sat on several arbitral tribunals in this capacity from 1988 to 1998.[96] His only inter-state role came as Trinidad and Tobago's party-appointed arbitrator in its boundary dispute with Barbados; the Tribunal unanimously determined a single maritime boundary between the exclusive economic zone and continental shelf of the two states out to 200 nautical miles.[97]

In January 2010, having just been consulted by the Indian government about a dispute with Bangladesh in the Bay of Bengal, he went to Egypt to visit his daughter and it was there that he died, tragically and suddenly, when the hotel car in which he, Christine and his daughter, Rebecca, were travelling overturned. Christine was injured but made a rapid recovery. Rebecca died in the crash. His daughter Hannah and his son James survive him.

[93] Brownlie was nominated by the UK government three times for the ILC; in his last election he topped the voting in the Sixth Committee.

[94] ILC Report 2005, chap. V; ILC Report 2006, chap. X; ILC Report 2007, chap. VII; ILC Report 2008, chap. V. On his retirement, Brownlie was succeeded as Special Rapporteur by Lucius Caflisch (Switzerland).

[95] Brownlie, 'International Law at the Fiftieth Anniversary of the United Nations', reprinted in I. Brownlie, *The Rule of Law in International Affairs: International Law at the Fiftieth Anniversary of the United Nations* (The Hague, 1998).

[96] See, e.g., *Scimitar Exploration Ltd v Bangladesh & Bangladesh Oil, Gas and Mineral Co* (1994) 5 ICSID Reports 4; *CME Czech Republic BV v The Czech Republic* (2001, 2003) 9 ICSID Reports 113. At the time of his death, Brownlie was also a party-appointed arbitrator in *Conoco-Phillips v Venezuela*, ICSID Case No ARB/07/30 (ongoing).

[97] *Barbados/Trinidad and Tobago Arbitration* (2006) 139 ILR 449.

V

As Vaughan Lowe notes:

> Ian was, above all, a lawyers' lawyer; not a pundit; not a weaver of dreams and theories; not a radical critic of outmoded intellectual fashions. He saw with clarity and perceptiveness what the law could and should do, and what it cannot and should not try to do. And he saw with the eye of a craftsman; as a cabinet-maker might eye a fine piece of oak and see in it both its potential and its limitations.[98]

His scholarly work was subtle and demanding, not an easy read but influential and long-lived. Key articles—especially those published in the *British Yearbook of International Law*—continue to be read and cited.[99] Of his books, *Use of Force* is timeless for as long as the Charter of the United Nations stands; *African Boundaries* and *Principles*, it is to be hoped, will live on in their new rescensions.

As a practitioner of the law of nations—which is how in the end he saw himself—Brownlie was determined, professional, courteous and insightful. He had a fine strategic vision, as witness his outstanding victories—*Nicaragua*,[100] *Phosphate Lands*,[101] the *Montreal Convention* cases,[102] *Loizidou v Turkey*,[103] *Cyprus v Turkey*,[104] and latterly *Serbian Genocide*,[105] *Kadi*[106] and *FG Hemisphere Associates LLC v Democratic Republic of the Congo*.[107] He was not a flamboyant advocate but he was nonetheless a formidable opponent. As a general international lawyer in his generation

[98] Lowe, 'Sir Ian Brownlie', 9.

[99] Especially I. Brownlie, 'The relations of nationality in Public International Law', *British Yearbook of International Law*, 39 (1963), 284–364; I. Brownlie, 'The justiciability of disputes and issues in international relations', *British Yearbook of International Law*, 42 (1967), 123–44; I. Brownlie, 'Recognition in theory and practice', *British Yearbook of International Law*, 53 (1982), 197–212; Unjustly neglected is I. Brownlie, 'The United Nations as a form of government', *Harvard International Law Journal*, 13 (1972), 421–80. For a fairly full bibliography of his work up to 1999 see *The Reality of International Law*, pp. xvii–xxi.

[100] ICJ Reports 1986 p. 14.

[101] *Certain Phosphate Lands in Nauru (Nauru v Australia), Preliminary Objections*, ICJ Reports 1992 p. 240.

[102] ICJ Reports 1998 pp. 9 and 15.

[103] (1996) 108 ILR 443.

[104] (2003) 120 ILR 10.

[105] ICJ Reports 2007 p. 43.

[106] Joined Cases C-402/05 P and C-415/05 P, *Kadi & Al Barakaat International Foundation v Council & Commission* [2008] ECR I-06351.

[107] [2010] HKCA 19.

he had few equals, no superiors. He left his subject richer, more complex, more diverse and more resilient for his work and service.

JAMES CRAWFORD
Fellow of the Academy

Note. I would like to thank Lady Brownlie, Sir Adam Roberts and Cameron Miles, Associate, Lauterpacht Centre for International Law, University of Cambridge, for their assistance.

JOHN BURROW

John Wyon Burrow
1935–2009

THE TERM 'INTELLECTUAL HISTORY' has had a curious history of its own in recent decades. In the middle of the twentieth century, when John Burrow was beginning his academic career, the phrase could still seem a little wilful, even *outré*, its questionable or perhaps mildly comic status reinforced by the traditional English resistance to anything that presumed to describe itself as 'intellectual'. Certainly, it was not the title of a recognised sub-discipline of History, on a par with 'political history', 'economic history', and so on. Over half a century later, usage has been quite transformed. The label has become ubiquitous, applied with little discrimination to almost any engagement with past ideas, no matter how indifferent that engagement may be to respecting the historicity of those ideas. At the same time, it has also established itself alongside its older siblings as a respectable member of History's family: there are now chairs and courses and journals that bear the title, usually with a happy ignorance of what, until recently, seemed the mark of a dubious arriviste status.

John Burrow had characteristically mixed feelings about this development: it is always vexing, having struggled against the condescension of one's elders, to be taken by one's juniors to be merely surfing the wave of fashion, and he found the promiscuous use of the label irritating. But it is no simple matter to try to disentangle the story of the development and influence of his own work from this larger transformation. By the time of his death in 2009, he was recognised as a scholar and writer of exceptional and distinctive gifts: few intellectual historians in Britain were as widely admired by colleagues from other branches of history and from other disciplines—admired for the originality and penetration of his analyses no

Biographical Memoirs of Fellows of the British Academy, XI, 81–111.

less than for the richness and grace of his prose. Yet he felt himself to be, once again, out of step with dominant academic trends. He had never cared for the paraphernalia of professionalism, and the recent industrialisation of production and work-patterns in British universities was anathema to him. In addition, the effect on the writing of history of that disparate cluster of approaches known as 'literary theory' seemed to him, on the whole, malign. The new fashion, almost mania, for appropriating the term 'intellectual history' to describe much of the work done under these two (partly complicit) impulses was prone to arouse in him feelings akin to those expressed in Dr Johnson's sardonic definition of 'patron'.[1]

Moreover, although the standing of John's own contribution to intellectual history was widely acknowledged, his career and his position in the field did not correspond to the most familiar patterns of academic success. He could certainly not be said to have founded any kind of 'school': he had admirers in plenty, but no followers—it is surely striking that such a distinguished scholar should have had only a small handful of research students, very few of whom have gone on to successful academic careers of their own. For the most part, he eschewed methodological manifestos, preferring to embody his reflective intuitions in good practice rather than attempting to legislate by means of programmatic abstraction.[2] Nor did he cultivate the conventional academic mediums of professional advancement: he abhorred conferences, he rarely wrote articles in learned journals, and it was only with great reluctance that he allowed himself to be pressed into service on academic bodies or professional associations (his well-merited reputation for not being a natural administrator anyway discouraged such invitations).

And yet, despite all this, the future historian of British academic culture in the late twentieth century will surely be forced to conclude that the sheer unignorable quality of John Burrow's books and the winning character of his personal performances made an important contribution to the process by which intellectual history came to enjoy recognition and respect from scholars in neighbouring fields. Although Cambridge was his

[1] 'Is not a Patron, my Lord, one who looks with unconcern on a man struggling for life in the water, and, when he has reached ground, encumbers him with help?' Samuel Johnson, *Letter to Lord Chesterfield* (1755).

[2] Perhaps the only significant exception to this was his John Coffin Memorial Lecture given at the University of London in 1987 and subsequently printed as a pamphlet: J. W. Burrow, *The Languages of the Past and the Languages of the Historian: the History of Ideas in Theory and Practice* (London, 1987). Some further thoughts were included in a paper he delivered on several occasions, but did not publish, entitled 'The poverty of methodology' (a copy of which is in the John Burrow papers in Sussex University library).

alma mater and always retained a strong hold on his loyalties, and although he greatly enjoyed the five years at the end of his career that he spent in Oxford, there can be no question but that his achievements were principally associated with the University of Sussex where he taught for over twenty-five years. There he helped found the first degree course in intellectual history at a British university as well as coming to occupy the first chair in the subject. Despite his own form of reticence (he could enjoy showing off but recoiled from any assertion of rank or precedence), he was increasingly recognised as an exceptionally impressive, while wholly individual, practitioner of this form of history, with a growing number of like-minded colleagues but few peers. It was not without a certain quiet pride that, on his election as a Fellow of the Academy at the age of 51 in 1986, he could, unpolemically but also undefensively, describe his professional identity as 'intellectual historian'.

I

John Wyon Burrow ('Wyon' was a family name from his father's side) was born in Southsea, Hampshire, on 4 June 1935, the only child of Charles and Alice Burrow (*née* Vosper). Shortly after his birth, the family returned to Devon, which was to be John's home for the first twenty years of his life, aside from brief periods spent at his maternal grandparents' house on the Cornish side of Plymouth Sound. His father was a commercial traveller for Shredded Wheat, supplying the small grocers of the south Devon coast; his mother had briefly been a shorthand typist before her marriage. His parents came from relatively straitened backgrounds, and never rose to financial prosperity; they each had to leave school to work before they could acquire much formal secondary education, but they shared, and imparted to their son, an enjoyment of English literature, English music, and English churches. For the final ten years of his working life, John's father found more congenial employment as a verger in Eton College chapel, and this role is nicely emblematic of the mixture of genuine cultivation, precarious or unpromising financial circumstances, and a certain genteel snobbery that characterised the son's childhood and youth, a mixture that, filtered through John's precocious intellect and responsive sensibilities, was to leave recognisable traces in his own life and character.

Much of our knowledge of his early life comes from what might be called 'the oral tradition'—knowing John involved a lot of oral tradition—but some comes from the delightful memoir of his childhood that he wrote late in life (discussed below), including the magnificently unrepentant declaration: 'I learned to talk early.'[3] During the war years John attended Bramdean preparatory school in Exeter as a day boy (his paternal grandfather paid the fees). From his childhood, he was unusually aware of the layering of historical residues in the world around him, whether culturally, architecturally, or in other terms, and he later recalled that his prep school carried 'with it into the mid-twentieth century much of the *mores* of the pre-1914 England in which it had been founded'.[4] Certainly, his own years there seem more evocative of *Stalky and Co* than of the ethos of public education at the time of the 1944 Education Act. 'The Empire was not merely taken for granted at Bramdean,' he recalled, 'but consciously celebrated. And Empire meant, above all, India; it seems to me now not inappropriate that I left Bramdean in the year the British left India.'[5] His own imaginative life was a mixture of the typical and the distinctive. He later recalled that he had, at around the age of ten, conceived the ambition to be a professional footballer, a role for which nature had conspicuously failed to endow him with any of the requisite qualities, until this was displaced by the ambition to be a stand-up comedian, a role for which he had abundant natural gifts and for which, his friends could sometimes feel, he continued to rehearse throughout his life.

In the autumn of 1947, John entered Exeter School, which at the time enjoyed, as did several others, the dual status of being a 'Direct-Grant Grammar School' and a member of the Headmasters' Conference. The grammar-school culture of the period suited John perfectly: intellectually serious yet not prematurely professional; cultured, but not precious; encouraging personal development without being egregiously experimental or simply indulgent. Apart from his deep attachment to his family and his West-country roots, one of the things the later memoir brings out most strikingly is the precocious range and sophistication, as well as the sheer quantity, of John's reading during his childhood and youth. 'I bought the Penguin classics in translation, more or less as they came out,' he records—not, he makes clear, a selection of them, but every one. In fact, his account of his teenage years largely takes the form of an annotated bibliography, and evidence of the future intellectual historian is not far to seek. 'I read Hume', he reports, adding with confident discrimination, 'especially Book Three of the Treatise, which seemed the most interesting.' No doubt there

[3] John Burrow, *Memories Migrating: an Autobiography* (privately printed, 2009), p. 2.

[4] *Memories Migrating*, p. 42.

[5] *Memories Migrating*, p. 55. Perhaps a little poetic licence was indulged here, since he elsewhere states, with some plausibility, that he left the school in 1946.

have been quite a few fifteen-year-olds who disliked the muddy military escapades associated with being in the school corps, but how many, one wonders, could have said as truthfully as John that he preferred 'to stay at home … and read Baudelaire'? And a special charm attaches to the picture of the bookish schoolboy, crouched by the family radio earnestly taking notes from a series of talks on 'Freedom and its Betrayal' by a speaker he had not previously heard of called Isaiah Berlin.[6] Decades later these two eminent historians of ideas were to recognise a certain kinship between them, perhaps not least in the humanity which they brought to their understanding of past thinkers and the volubility with which they expressed the results of those encounters.

In October 1954 John entered Christ's College, Cambridge with an open scholarship in History. Here, his Director of Studies was that talent-spotter *extraordinaire*, J. H. ('Jack') Plumb, and John became part of that galaxy of historians whose careers (and, to a much lesser extent, practice of history) were shaped by this inspiring, demanding, seductive, irascible man.[7] It was one of the marks of Plumb's gifts as a nurturer of young historical minds that he did not try to replicate himself—forming only political and social historians of the eighteenth century—but instead encouraged his protegés to follow their own bent and to cultivate some of the less well-populated fields of historical enquiry. John found the self-consciously hard-headed positivism of much political and economic history unattractive; more to his taste were the papers in the History Tripos on the history of political thought. For his work on the Part II paper on 'Theories of the Modern State' (essentially a course in the big names in political thought from Rousseau and Bentham onwards) he was supervised by Duncan Forbes, who for many years gave a celebrated course of lectures on Hegel (then little studied or little rated in the English-speaking world) and Marx (rated by many who did not study him and, as a result, studied by some who did not rate him). At this stage of his life, John was drawn to philosophical and theoretical subjects, and the history of political thought provided him (as it provided several others who have gone on to make notable contributions to intellectual history) with a way to marry his historical and conceptual interests. He obtained Firsts in both parts of the Tripos, and after graduating in 1957 he embarked on research for a Ph.D.

[6] *Memories Migrating*, pp. 105, 106, 96, 107. He had already invoked this last vignette in his Oxford Inaugural Lecture; see below, n. 37.

[7] For a perceptive account of Plumb's personality and career, see David Cannadine, 'John Harold Plumb 1911–2001', *Proceedings of the British Academy*, 124, *Biographical Memoirs of Fellows*, III (2004), 269–309.

This did not begin well, as it so often doesn't. Having expressed an interest in things Victorian, John was assigned G. R. S. Kitson Clark as his supervisor; having declared that he wanted to work on 'public opinion', he was directed by 'Kitson', as he was generally known, to study an election (that of 1886). As John later put it: 'I can think of virtually no task to which my talents are less suited.'[8] The need to keep an orderly card index recording his findings was not the least of the ways in which the talents did not match the task. But casting around to familiarise himself with Victorian ideas more generally he was led to read *On the Origin of Species*, and then, via Darwin, to Herbert Spencer, and thus, fatefully, he began to ponder the importance of 'evolutionary' thinking in nineteenth-century Britain. Kitson Clark, to his credit, accepted this change of tack and continued to provide supervision, though the topic was now far from his own chief interests. Coached by Plumb, John successfully submitted a dissertation for a Research Fellowship at Christ's, which he took up in October 1959. In 1961 he was awarded the Ph.D. for a dissertation entitled 'The concept of evolution in English social theory from Spencer to Hobhouse'; his examiners were, unusually for a doctorate in History, the anthropologist Meyer Fortes and the political philosopher Michael Oakeshott.

To revisit that dissertation is to be reminded of the unusual degree of intellectual autonomy exhibited in Burrow's early work. With hindsight, one might have expected Duncan Forbes to have played a larger role. In later life John admired Forbes as an exemplary intellectual historian, but it is hard not to feel that there was a somewhat mysteriously missed connection between the two men in the late 1950s and early 1960s.[9] Instead, John pursued his own interests in contemporary political philosophy and social theory, in part because these enquiries seemed at the time to promise to provide a progressive or broadly left-wing set of answers to questions about contemporary society and politics. Peter Laslett, an encouraging presence for many in Cambridge with these interests, had started his influential series *Politics, Philosophy, Society* while John was an undergraduate; Noel Annan published his Hobhouse Lecture on 'The curious strength of positivism in English political thought' in 1959; and W. G. Runciman gave the lectures that became his *Social Science and Political Theory* while

[8] *Memories Migrating*, p. 160.

[9] On Forbes, see Burrow's introduction to Duncan Forbes, 'Aesthetic thoughts on doing the history of ideas', *History of European Ideas*, 27 (2001), 101–13; and the reminiscences in *Memories Migrating*, pp. 149–52. See also the unpublished obituary by Donald Winch largely reproduced in the notice on Forbes in *The Clare Association Annual* (1994–5), 78–82.

John was a research student.[10] Stimulated by such sources, John began to ask what it was that social science, especially sociology and anthropology, attempted to explain that political philosophy and economic theory could not, and out of these concerns he fashioned an unusual set of questions with which to address the prevalence of social evolutionary thinking in Victorian culture.

While an undergraduate John met Diane Dunnington, who was studying philosophy at University College London; they married in October 1958. Their first child, Laurence, was born in 1961, to be followed by Francesca in 1969. John greatly enjoyed the role of father, and, many years later when Francesca produced two children, positively adored that of grandfather. Indeed, one of the historical identities in which it was easiest to imagine him was that of the Victorian paterfamilias—less remote, certainly, than some instances of the type, but relishing his central place, indulged and indulgent, in a noisy multigenerational household revolving around meals, music, and mess.

The responsibilities of fatherhood made it more imperative than ever that Burrow obtain a permanent academic appointment. At the end of his research fellowship he took up a college teaching fellowship at Downing College. Such posts, relatively ill-paid and without security of tenure, were often regarded at the time as a kind of antechamber to a permanent lectureship in the relevant faculty. During his time at Downing, John twice applied for such posts in the History Faculty and was twice unsuccessful. In later life, he could recur to these setbacks with an understandable sense of resentment, but it may not be too pollyanaish to think this local failure helped pave the way for much greater later success, and that removal to pastures new, though initially disagreeable, enabled him to pursue his own bent more freely than might have been easily possible in a junior role within the self-consciously hierarchical and sometimes intellectually intolerant community that was the Cambridge History Faculty in the early 1960s. In any event, he moved, spurred by financial need as well as local rejection, to a lectureship at the University of East Anglia in 1965, where he was promoted to Reader in 1968.

By that point he had published the book which secured his reputation and with which, in some quarters, his name is still most readily associated. *Evolution and Society: a Study in Victorian Social Theory*, an extended

[10] Peter Laslett, *Philosophy, Politics, and Society* (Oxford, 1956); Noel Annan, *The Curious Strength of Positivism in English Social Thought* (L. T. Hobhouse Memorial Lecture no. 28: Oxford, 1959); W. G. Runciman, *Social Science and Political Theory* (Cambridge, 1963).

version of his Ph.D., finally appeared, after several delays, in 1966, to numerous admiring reviews. For a first book, it was a remarkable *tour de force*: instead of cleaving closely to an intensively mined body of original sources as most first monographs do, it addressed a large question and ranged across a wide area with assurance and panache. The explicit topic on which John's doctorate had focused was the prevalence of social evolutionism in Victorian thought, but, as already indicated, he brought to this question a mind stirred by the theoretical debates in political theory and social science in the late 1950s and early 1960s. These debates had led him to meditate on the distinctive category of 'the social', and this in turn led him to read Talcott Parsons' classic work from 1937, *The Structure of Social Action*. The extent to which Parsons provided, indirectly, much of the theoretical scaffolding for the book's argument may not now be immediately obvious, though the seven direct citations of his work, once one is alerted to them, come to assume a strategic importance. In essence, Parsons had portrayed the sociology of Durkheim, Weber, and Pareto as a series of responses to the incapacity of what he, somewhat confusingly, called 'positivism' to account for 'non-rational' action. British thinkers played only a small part in Parsons' story, aside from Alfred Marshall's use of the category of 'residues' to accommodate aspects of social behaviour that did not fit the categories of neoclassical economic theory. But in emphasising the revolution in social thought which the leading Continental thinkers had effected in the early twentieth century, Parsons began his work by quoting the rhetorical question: 'Who now reads Spencer?'[11]

John Burrow read Spencer, intrigued by his fall into near-oblivion after having been such a dominating presence in Victorian thought, and he came to think that the work of Spencer and his fellow social evolutionists Henry Maine and E. B. Tylor had provided contemporaries with a way of understanding the variety of social action without abandoning their broadly positivistic commitment to rational modes of explanation. And he also came to think that the principal reason why they needed to adopt this social-evolutionary perspective from the 1850s and 1860s onwards was because Utilitarianism, the dominant rational-action model of the first half of the century, had proved incapable of fully accounting for the diversity of forms of life revealed by better knowledge both of the past and of so-called 'primitive' societies in the present. (Parsonian echoes

[11] Talcott Parsons, *The Structure of Social Action: a Study in Social Theory with Special Reference to a Group of Recent European Writers* (New York, 1937), p. 3. The question was a quotation from Crane Brinton, *English Political Thought in the Nineteenth Century*, first published in 1933.

are also audible in his treatment of Utilitarianism as a kind of 'science of social relations'.) Thus, although *Evolution and Society* ranged far beyond the standard canon in the history of political thought, the briefest formulaic characterisation of its intellectual origins might be: Theories of the Modern State meets *The Structure of Social Action*.

This bald emphasis on the conceptual underpinning of the book may seem at odds with Burrow's mature reputation as a fiercely anti-whiggish intellectual historian, intent on recovering the thoughts of past actors in their own terms. Indeed, in the second edition he was already apologising for what 'I now find tiresomely cumbersome and nagging about the constant contrasting of Spencer, Maine, and Tylor with more recent sociology and social anthropology'.[12] But at a more local level the book already displayed that ear for the intellectual quiddity of past thinkers that became such a hallmark of his later work. In addition to the book's treatment of its three principal figures, there are perceptive brief discussions of writers such as T. H. Buckle and J. S. Mill, and there is an exceptionally acute analysis of James Mill's intellectual relations to Scottish conjectural history, a topic which was not then the minor scholarly industry it has since become.[13] He also showed how the disintegration of the intellectual confidence that had underwritten Utilitarianism in the first half of the nineteenth century led to the rise of what became known as 'social anthropology' in the second half, complete with its later discarded baggage of degenerationism and of polygenism versus monogenism.

What, above all, the book was more widely thought to have established was that the prevalence of social-evolutionary thinking could not be attributed to the influence of Darwin. This was certainly part of the polemical thrust of the book, though its author trod a little more warily here than did some of its admirers. The science which, alongside philology and legal history, did help shape the redirection of English social thinking in an evolutionary direction was geology, though Burrow was, of course, well aware that this was something of a common inspiration for Darwin as well as for 'gradualist' historians and social thinkers. That his argument in the book certainly did not indicate any ignorance of Darwin or underestimation of his importance was emphatically demonstrated by his Pelican edition of *The Origin of Species* in 1968. Although he had no background in any of the relevant biological sciences, John's introduction

[12] J. W. Burrow, *Evolution and Society: a Study in Victorian Social Theory* (Cambridge, 2nd edn., 1970), p. xxi.

[13] See especially the discussion of Scottish 'conjectural history' and its fate in the early nineteenth century; *Evolution and Society*, pp. 54–64.

nonetheless gave an effortlessly lucid and authoritative exposition of Darwin's theory and its wider significance, enlivened with many characteristic touches (for example, on how 'natural history became an approved clerical hobby' with the unintended consequence that 'bug-hunting was the Trojan horse of Victorian agnosticism').[14] John always found a pleasing irony in the fact that it was as a result of writing a book that dislodged Darwin from his conventional position as the inspiration for nineteenth-century social evolution that he had been invited to edit what became for a while the most widely used version of Darwin's masterpiece.

It is important to remember, given Burrow's later reputation as an intellectual historian of Victorian England, that at this point in his career his interests were at least as much European as British.[15] At the University of East Anglia he primarily taught European history; he was to serve for several years as a co-editor of the *Journal of European Studies*; and his own statement of his current research interests when invited to Sussex towards the end of the decade emphasised projects (never completed) on Feuerbach and the young Hegelians. One expression of these interests that did reach publication was his edition of Wilhelm von Humboldt's *The Limits of State Action* (1969). John's introduction displayed an impressive familiarity with German thought of the late eighteenth and early nineteenth centuries, deftly situating Humboldt's celebration of human diversity within the aesthetic as well as social thought of German Romanticism, especially Schiller, and its later absorption into the more formalised notion of *Bildung*.[16]

II

The success of *Evolution and Society* determined the next stages of John's life in several ways. In the mid-1960s, Donald Winch was teaching at Sussex as, primarily, an historian of economic thought, and he played a

[14] Charles Darwin, *The Origin of Species*, ed. with an introduction by J. W. Burrow (Harmondsworth, 1968), pp. 18–19.

[15] For a sympathetic exploration of the European, and especially German, dimension of John's work, backed by extensive scholarship, see B. W. Young, 'J. W. Burrow: a personal history', *History of European Ideas*, 37 (2011), 7–15.

[16] Wilhelm Von Humbodt, *The Limits of State Action*, ed. with introduction and notes by J. W. Burrow (Cambridge, 1969). Characteristic touches are not far to seek here, either: for example, his observation when discussing Humboldt's ministerial career, that 'many men have looked forward to the withering away of the State but few ministers have looked forward as Humboldt did to the withering away of their own department' (p. ix, n. 3).

prominent part in establishing an ambitious course there, to be taken by all final-year students in the School of Social Studies (later Social Sciences), 'Concepts, Methods and Values in the Social Sciences', thereafter known to generations of its teachers and students as CMV. Having read John's book with admiration (and having also been working on James Mill at much the same time), Winch invited him to come to deliver a guest lecture for the historical part of this course; the two men got on, found themselves largely of one mind on the failings of the triumphalist or ahistorical accounts that often passed for the history of the social scientific disciplines, and laid the foundations for a long and close friendship. In 1969 Winch masterminded John's move to a Readership at Sussex, with a primary responsibility for teaching CMV.

In curricular terms, Sussex was perhaps the most innovative of the new 'plate-glass' universities of the 1960s. In place of the conventional departmental organisation, it instituted a structure in which both staff and students possessed dual allegiances or identities. Administratively, the chief units to which both belonged were schools of study, some of which, in the Arts area, represented geographical groupings (the School of European Studies, the School of African and Asian Studies) and other groupings by theme or method (the School of Cultural and Community Studies, the School of Social Sciences). But within and across these units were clusters, known as 'subject-groups', defined largely in traditional disciplinary terms. Thus, there were subject-groups in English, History, Philosophy, and so on, with staff members in more than one School. Students took courses in their 'major' (provided by members of the subject group), but also 'contextual courses' in their School (provided by staff in that School who could be members of various subject-groups). John's appointment was somewhat unusual, in that his was a School post, tied to the needs of CMV, not a History subject-group post that was assigned to the School of Social Sciences. But he was not unusual in having intellectual-historical interests that did not always sit comfortably with the dominant character of the subject group that one was nominally attached to: Peter Burke in History, Michael Moran in Philosophy, James Shiel in Classical Studies, similarly felt themselves to be a little uncomfortably placed (as, in a different way, did Helmut Pappé, Reader in the History of Social Thought within Sociology), and so they came together to start a new major in Intellectual History, which in time led to the formation of a separate subject-group. Though smaller than the big battalions such as English or History, Intellectual History was by no means the smallest subject-group at Sussex at a time when Religious Studies, Russian, and so on had even fewer members. Before long, the new group was able, in those expansionist days, to obtain an additional lectureship, to be held in the School of European Studies, and so it was that in 1972 Larry Siedentop was appointed to the first post in a British university to be advertised as a Lectureship in Intellectual History. (Siedentop returned to Oxford the following year, and I was appointed to the post in 1974.) Meanwhile, John, once the subject-group was established and admitting students to its major, transferred from Social Sciences to the School of English and American Studies, and that remained the disposition of forces until the mid-1980s, with sympathetic colleagues such as Donald Winch from Economics and Norman Vance from English having what, in the local patois, was known as 'secondary allegiance' to the Intellectual History Subject-Group.

Sussex, especially in the period from the late 1960s to the early 1980s, suited John intellectually and allowed him to extend the range and style of both his teaching and writing. In particular, it enabled him to move still further away from the history of political thought, not just into the history of the social sciences but also into the whole range of the intellectual life of a past period, including literary, philosophical, theological, and scientific thought. The degrees in Intellectual History at undergraduate and Master's level that he helped to establish and consolidate there were the first, and for some time the only, such courses in British universities. The interdisciplinary structures and joint teaching arrangements characteristic of Sussex at that time encouraged collaboration. John enjoyed co-teaching contextual courses with colleagues from English such as Larry Lerner and Norman Vance, and offshoots of this activity can be found in his essays on 'The sense of the past' and 'Faith, doubt, and unbelief' that he contributed to the collaborative volume on *The Victorians*, edited by Lerner, published in 1978 in the Methuen 'Literature in Context' series.[17] A more substantial expression of this collaborative ethos was *That Noble Science of Politics,* which John, Donald Winch and I wrote together (which is discussed more fully below).

John and I often taught seminars jointly, an experience from which, as anyone who knew him might imagine, I derived a good part of my education. He could, on occasion, be a brilliant teacher: he only required that the students be willing and curious, however ignorant initially—this was perhaps one reason why he later so much enjoyed his teaching in the USA

[17] Laurence Lerner (ed.), *The Victorians* (London, 1978), pp. 120–38 and 155–73. Other colleagues in English with whom he shared interests included Tony Nuttall and Stephen Prickett.

at Berkeley and at Williams College. What he hated was that strand of sullen resentment which, alas, when couched in the idiom of fashionable radicalism, was not unknown among Sussex students in the 1970s. But as long as the students were disposed to be interested, John had several natural gifts as a teacher—an extraordinary quickness of mind, the effortless finding of an apt simile or metaphor with which to illuminate otherwise opaque ideas, a quite exceptional cultural range. He also had human qualities to which, if disenchantment hadn't set in prematurely, students responded, including an utter lack of pomposity or any standing upon status, and an infectious vitality. Perhaps his command of the procedures and instruments of pedagogy was not always quite up to the highest QAA standards, but those students who were really listening—listening by the students was, in practice, the dominant mode in John's seminars—got an incomparably rich guided tour through the relevant books and ideas.

Curiously, for such a naturally eloquent speaker, he was not always so successful as a lecturer. In a class or tutorial he could respond to contributions by students in ways that deftly helped them out of their ignorance or confusion, but he rarely managed to work any such implicitly dialogic element into his lectures and the students could become restive. Although it doesn't deserve to be called a paradox, it may be mildly surprising that someone who was so unstoppably a performer in conversational settings, and visibly enjoyed being so, was not more of a success on the podium. A certain physical modesty or reticence may have played a part, as may his use of a fully written script that was not always immediately easy for the audience to follow—or, I might add, easy even for him to decipher.

The mixture of intellectual impulses that had led to the writing of *Evolution and Society* was still detectable in the work that he began at the end of the 1960s but which did not come to full fruition till the beginning of the 1980s. Always alert to the sheer variety of forms through which human beings represent and interpret their collective pasts, John became more and more interested in the ways in which certain kinds of history functioned for nineteenth-century Englishmen as a form of covert political thought. The first published fruit of this interest was an essay, entitled 'The village community and the uses of history in late nineteenth-century England', published in a Festschrift for Plumb in 1974.[18] This piece probed the ways in which accounts of the earliest forms of communal organisation

[18] J. W. Burrow, '"The village community" and the uses of history in late nineteenth-century England', in Neil McKendrick (ed.), *Historical Perspectives: Studies in English Thought and Society in Honour of J. H. Plumb* (London, 1974), pp. 255–84.

were taken to be pregnant with implications for political debate in Victorian Britain, whether in E. A. Freeman's characteristically emphatic assertion that 'our ancient history is the possession of the liberal' or F. W. Maitland's more nuanced reflections upon the ways the history of the notion of 'a trust' might underwrite a broadly Pluralist political theory. In the course of the 1970s, John began to broaden this enquiry, asking, for example (in a paper he gave several times but never published in this form), 'what kind of Whig historian was Macaulay?' Initially, one might have imagined this interest being developed into a book resembling *Evolution and Society*, a book driven by quasi-theoretical interests, in this case about the conceptualisation of 'community' and 'the state' in nineteenth-century English legal and historical thought. But, partly stirred by the interdisciplinary ethos of Sussex, especially his greater contact with literary scholars, and partly as a result of the ripening of John's own sensibility, the work took another turn. He had long been interested in and responsive to the reworkings of the past in other areas of Victorian culture, including its art and architecture, but he now extended this concern to larger questions about narrative form, questions which might involve pondering geological metaphors in Stubbs alongside evolutionary images in George Eliot, or illuminating Froude's 'plaintive threnody for lost childhood faith' by invoking Frazer's *Golden Bough* and Pater's *Marius the Epicurean*. John was also becoming more drawn to intellectual portraiture and correspondingly less charmed by theory-driven conceptual reconstruction.

The chief fruit of this expanded receptiveness was *A Liberal Descent: Victorian Historians and the English Past*, published in 1981 (and awarded the Wolfson Literary Prize for History in that year). This is, in my judgement, the most fully achieved of John's books. Its structure exhibits a deceptive simplicity: each of its four parts is devoted to one of the authors of the four most significant multivolume narratives of major periods of English history written in the Victorian period. The themes are signalled by the parts' subtitles: 'Macaulay and the Whig tradition', 'Stubbs and the Ancient Constitution', 'Freeman and the unity of history', and 'Froude's Protestant island'. But although these do provide magisterial analyses of the character of the four authors' histories of England, understood not just as commanding examples of historiography but also as literary accomplishments and cultural events, the rich texture of John's own prose serves as the carrier for a much wider range of reflections about Victorian thought and sensibility. Although there is no showy parade of generalities, the book taken as a whole offers a compelling meditation on the ways in which a complex culture understands and represents its place in history.

A Liberal Descent is, without question, a learned book—John had absorbed the work of J. G. A. Pocock as well as of Duncan Forbes on varieties of eighteenth-century whiggism, just as he was familiar with the main lines of European scholarship on the early history of the *Mark* and the *Mir*—and it is, in its uninsistent, companionable way, an analytical book. But it also has qualities that are much rarer in academic scholarship, notably the engaged imaginative sympathy with which it enters into the identifications and antipathies of his chosen subjects. This is no exercise in *Ideologiekritik*, no forensic process of unmasking assumptions judged unacceptable by later standards of cultural rectitude. Perhaps few historical subjects present easier targets for that process than Freeman, a compendium of those views which a later century regards as bigoted, all expressed with an artless vigour that leaves little for prosecuting counsel to do. Yet it is one of the singular achievements of *A Liberal Descent* not just to restore an intelligibility to Freeman's combination of manic liberalism and romantic Teutonism, but to do so without condescending to the unbuttoned zest and antiquarian zeal which give his writing its distinctive character.

As several reviewers admiringly remarked, Burrow's own prose exhibited a richness and command of register that enabled him to capture and do justice to the qualities of each of his (very different) main figures. We can, for example, hear it swelling appropriately in the long passage in which he characterises the connoisseurship about parliamentary oratory among Macaulay's circle at Holland House ('a notable orator "up" and going well was like a *diva* in fine voice'), just as he brings his analysis of Freeman's style to an appropriately rueful conclusion ('Nouns and repeated pronouns fall on the ear like successive blows of Thor's hammer; the result is predictably sometimes a headache').[19] But perhaps a better brief illustration of how the writing is the perfect medium for the temper of the book, just yet appreciative, is provided by this paragraph from his discussion of Stubbs's *Constitutional History*:

> No general account or anthology of quotations can at all convey the cautious yet precise richness of Stubbs' analyses or the fine, educated sensitivity to the tremors of social and institutional change, in names and procedural forms, in administrative, fiscal and judicial devices, in franchises, suits, fines, exactions, the growth and waning of privileges, the assumption and desuetude of functions. It is because Stubbs' own poise and control hardly falter, despite revisions; because each detail is illustrative and placed, and the steady authorial voice

[19] J. W. Burrow, *A Liberal Descent: Victorian Historians and the English Past* (Cambridge, 1981), pp. 88, 213.

> moves with unforced assurance from confident assertion to admitted conjecture, from bold suggestiveness to tentative generalisation and occasional admissions of defeat, that this mass of discriminated complexity is felt as exhilarating rather than overwhelming.[20]

If the phrase 'this mass of discriminated complexity' seems perfect for Stubbs, it is not quite right for Burrow—his writing contains relatively little technical detail and never any sense of Stubbsian accumulation—yet it surely does point to something characteristic of his work as a whole. 'Discriminating complexity', whether understood as a verbal or adjectival phrase, constituted his *forte* as an intellectual historian.

For all John's precocious intellectual development, one can detect a maturing of his intellectual style across the years in these respects. In the work of his middle and later years, theoretical scaffolding of any kind falls away and there is a richer—I am tempted to say more fully historical—engagement with the various dimensions of the mind and sensibility of past figures. Burrow was the least Procrustean of intellectual historians: he responded sympathetically and flexibly to the individuality of past thinking rather than slicing it up in any of the approved present-minded ways. And in the search for understanding, his mature work is hermeneutically generous, seeing a piece of writing as an attempt to render and make sense of a distinctive experience of life, whether in historical narratives or in philosophical theories, whether in epigrammatic fragments or in a *Gesamtkunstwerk*.

This quality connects with another emphasis in Burrow's work that became more insistent as he moved into the middle phase of his career, namely a marked hostility to those kinds of whiggish or teleological histories of past thinking which in effect selected earlier figures for attention, and praised their 'contribution', according to their success in 'anticipating' some approved state of enlightened thinking in the present. The histories of the various academic disciplines were (and in some quarters still are) particularly prone to be written in this vein, and part of what united John, Donald Winch, and me in our teaching of the history of the social sciences at Sussex was a desire to replace these complacently triumphalist narratives with less present-minded and more genuinely historical accounts. Slowly, our collective grumbling transmuted into literary ambition, and we set out to demonstrate the ways in which a preoccupation with 'things political' in nineteenth-century Britain encompassed several forms of enquiry that have subsequently been appropriated by modern disciplines

[20] *Liberal Descent*, p. 137.

such as economics, sociology, political science, and so on. Perhaps one source of the interest aroused by the book which issued from these preoccupations in 1983, *That Noble Science of Politics: a Study in Nineteenth-Century Intellectual History*, lay in the fact that it was presented as a single work collaboratively written by three authors, rather than as a collection of individually authored essays—that the authorial troika were colloquially dubbed 'Burrinchini' (initially by themselves) only heightened this effect.[21] Actually although the book was the outcome of several years of close discussion and circulation of drafts among the three authors, no secret was made of the primary authorship of its various elements: John wrote the first drafts of the chapters on the historians and on Walter Bagehot (the latter singled out by some reviewers as the jewel in the crown of the volume), and he wrote the greater part of the chapter on the Comparative Method. But much more attention was focused on the unclassifiability of the book and the distinctiveness of the methodological approach it was taken to exemplify. Though it clearly repudiated the still-prevailing forms of disciplinary history, it did not correspond to any of the methodological templates for doing intellectual history that had been propounded in recent decades, such as *Annaliste* '*mentalités*', Pocockian 'languages', Skinnerian 'intentions', Foucauldian '*epistemes*', and so on. As one reviewer sympathetically put it: 'This is going to be a perplexing book for many. Librarians will wonder how to classify it. Specialists in politics and economics will be embarrassed at its demonstration of how what they thought sewn up can be unstitched. Tutors will wonder what passages their pupils can be trusted not to misunderstand.'[22] Further reflections on the book and its reception can be found in the preface written for the Japanese translation in 1996, and the English edition was reissued in 2008, twenty-five years after its initial publication.[23]

The first half of the 1980s formed a particularly fertile and successful period in Burrow's career. *A Liberal Descent* had appeared in 1981; in 1982 he was made Professor of Intellectual History at Sussex; *That Noble Science* came out the following year. 1985 saw the appearance of his little

[21] Stefan Collini, Donald Winch, and John Burrow, *That Noble Science of Politics: a Study in Nineteenth-Century Intellectual History* (Cambridge, 1983).

[22] Wiiliam Thomas, 'Review of *That Noble Science of Politics*', *English Historical Review* (1986), 702–4.

[23] The Japanese edition was eventually published in 2002; the new preface (largely written by me, with assistance from Winch) has never been published in English, though some sentences from it are quoted in my 'General introduction', in Stefan Collini, Richard Whatmore, and Brian Young (eds.), *History, Religion, and Culture: British Intellectual History 1750–1950* (Cambridge, 2000), p. 10.

book on Gibbon, in the Oxford University Press 'Past Masters' series, a commissioning editor's dream match between author and subject. John had long enjoyed and admired Gibbon without being intimidated by him; in 1976, on the bicentenary of the publication of the first volumes of the *Decline and Fall*, he had given a scintillating public lecture at Sussex, which included a passage of adroit parody.[24] Even within the constraining format of the 'Past Masters'—the book is well under the limit of 30,000 words—John ranged far beyond the predictable topics (the Augustan periods, the footnotes), situating Gibbon's work in relation to his predecessors (mainly European) and contemporaries (mainly Scottish).[25]

These years also saw a notable rise in the number of international invitations Burrow received. A semester spent at Berkeley in 1981 was followed by a Fellowship at the History of Ideas Unit of the Australian National University in Canberra in 1983 and a British Council lecture tour in Austria in 1984. This period of notable success was rounded off by the invitation to deliver the Carlyle lectures on political thought in Oxford in 1985 (which brought with it membership of All Souls for a term, an experience John unabashedly relished), and then by election to the British Academy in 1986. (Further invitations and honours of this sort still to come included the Gauss Seminars at Princeton and the Prothero Lecture of the Royal Historical Society, as well as an honorary degree from the University of Bologna, all in 1988.) These achievements and forms of recognition were, naturally, very good for his morale, even though nationally the picture for universities was beginning to darken.

In these years John was in his prime and his prime was spent at Sussex. His personal star was rising, his children were intensely rewarding, and the institutional setting was stimulating and congenial. In addition, he enjoyed the raffish charm of Brighton (while living just over the border in genteel Hove), and he loved the Sussex countryside. But the final decade of his Sussex years marked a much less happy period in his life, during which he became discouraged about the treatment of Intellectual History at the university by both the (much larger and unsympathetic) History Subject Group and the central administration; he was also beset by financial burdens and other family worries, and generally prey to an enveloping cultural pessimism. Government cuts to public spending on higher education in the 1980s hit universities such as Sussex very hard, leading to the

[24] J. W. Burrow, 'Decline and Fall of the Roman Empire': A Bicentenary Lecture delivered at the University of Sussex, 4 Nov. 1976; this lecture remains unpublished.

[25] J. W. Burrow, *Gibbon* (Oxford, 1985).

early retirement of some of John's closest colleagues. These reductions, compounded by my departure in 1986, constrained and eventually undermined the position of Intellectual History. The appointment of Richard Whatmore and Brian Young to lectureships in the subject in 1993 promised to revive its fortunes, but John's disenchantment with the university was by then nearing its terminal phase, not helped by his encounters with the new managerialism while serving a term of office as Director of Graduate Studies in Arts and Social Sciences.

His Carlyle Lectures eventually appeared in 1988 as a slim volume entitled *Whigs and Liberals: Continuity and Change in English Political Thought*, but it was not praised as widely or enthusiastically as his earlier works had been and it was the only one of his books that John felt, with a slight sense of grievance, was always under-appreciated. His introduction to the book acknowledged that it involved revisiting figures about whom he had already written (and even in places reworking earlier material), but he hoped that this might be taken to indicate 'a long-standing interest in the impact of historicist ways of thinking on European, and above all British, culture in the post-Romantic period'.[26] The book explored continuities and transmutations in the relations between eighteenth-century Whiggism and nineteenth-century Liberalism, but it repudiated the ahistorical essentialism that often dominated discussion of 'isms', especially the all-purpose polemical construct 'liberal individualism'. Such constructions can have their uses, he readily conceded, but

> as a way of rendering something more like the vigour and activity of past intellectual life, with its complex ways of accommodating, combining, and manipulating, under various kinds of pressure, the rival theoretical languages which a rich political culture contains, [they are] severely limited and may even be misleading.[27]

Because we now tend to think in terms of the great divide between individualism and collectivism, he observed in a concluding reflection, 'we are sometimes tempted to assume that these are also the categories through which we should try to understand the political thought of the past. These lectures have been intended as a modest protest against that assumption.'[28]

[26] J. W. Burrow, *Whigs and Liberals: Continuity and Change in English Political Thought* (Oxford, 1988), p. viii.
[27] Ibid., p. 5.
[28] Ibid., p. 153.

III

Whigs and Liberals apart, Burrow published relatively little of substance in the fifteen years between 1985 and 2000, and in the late 1980s and the early 1990s his increasingly all-encompassing pessimism about the world clearly infected his energy and resolve as a writer. But then the world intervened in an unpredictable way. Having accumulated some sabbatical entitlement, he was already committed to two terms as a Visiting Fellow at All Souls in Oxford in 1994 when he was invited to apply for, and elected to, the newly established Flick Professorship in European Thought, with a Professorial Fellowship at Balliol, where he was warmly welcomed into the fellowship (it was a sign of his popularity that he was quite soon elected to the office of Steward of Common Room). He and Diane moved to a house in Witney, with their daughter and grandchildren soon coming to live nearby.

There is no doubt that the move to Oxford in 1995 revived him in more ways than one, and it was on the whole a happy final phase of his career. The duties of his Oxford chair had encouraged a return to his wider European interests, and he lectured principally on European social and political thought in the nineteenth and early twentieth centuries. As part of this revived identity, he took on the editorship of the journal *History of European Ideas* when it was relaunched in 1996. Although perhaps not in the absolute forefront of international scholarship, the journal maintained a more than respectable intellectual level, and John was particularly pleased that, under his benign editorship, it provided a home for articles by young and unknown scholars struggling to break into the world of academic publication.

But the move to Oxford also brought a wholly unforeseen complication, resulting in an episode that John found depressing and immensely distasteful. Elements in the national press began to raise questions about the propriety of Oxford's having accepted a donation from Gert-Rudolf Flick on the grounds that his fortune derived indirectly from the profits the family firm had made under his grandfather during the Third Reich, in part by using slave labour from the concentration camps. Whatever the rights and wrongs of the issue, the media coverage became sufficiently uncomfortable for Flick to agree with Oxford to withdraw his donation, since its continuance threatened to harm the university's good name. This meant that the university would be forced to provide John's salary from its own resources, but in the event a Midlands industrialist, Bob Johnson, stepped in and generously guaranteed its continuance for the remainder of his tenure. Among the aspects of this episode that John regretted was that it ensured that he would be the last as well as the first occupant of the chair, which was suppressed on his retirement in 2000.[29]

His tenure of the chair was capped by the publication in that year of *The Crisis of Reason: European Thought 1848–1914*, which partly grew out of his Oxford lectures. In the early 1990s, he had become one of the general editors of Yale University Press's new series 'The Yale Intellectual History of the West', and he agreed to write for it the volume focused on the later nineteenth century. The book was deliberately not addressed to a narrowly specialist readership, not that any of Burrow's writing had ever been inaccessible to interested readers or had failed to find them. A striking indication of the book's success in this respect was the notably warm review it elicited in the pages of the *New York Review of Books* from the Irish novelist John Banville, who pronounced: 'Burrow's superb study of a profoundly significant and formative period is a model of its kind.'[30]

It would, however, not be easy to say precisely what that 'kind' is, since the book can seem a curious hybrid in generic terms, falling somewhere between being an idiosyncratic though always interesting interpretation of certain central themes in the social and cultural thought of Britain, France and Germany (the countries to which it was in practice confined), a synthesis of familiar (and not always very recent) scholarship on European intellectual history of the period, and a series of bravura essays on an impressive range of figures—there are, for example, wonderfully illuminating meditations on figures as diverse as Wagner or Taine, and some really quite brilliant pages on Nietzsche. Students in search of a crib would be likely to find it a frustrating and resistant book, but anyone disposed to accept John's conversational rhythm and not to resent being treated as though they have long been familiar with the books and ideas he knew so well will find it a rewarding experience. The 'Prologue', in particular, is a *tour de force*, beginning with its opening conceit of seizing on the presence of both Bakunin and Wagner in the Dresden uprising of 1848–9 as a way of introducing the Promethean theme in European Romanticism that was to receive its comeuppance in the following sixty years. Yet the 'Epilogue', with its broad-brush panorama of European Modernism across the arts in the years before the First World War, matches

[29] There is an extensive collection of materials relating to this episode, including newspaper cuttings and private correspondence, in the John Burrow papers at Sussex university library.

[30] John Banville, 'Fathers and sons' [review of J. W. Burrow, *The Crisis of Reason*], *New York Review of Books*, 4 Oct. 2001, 38–40.

it for energy and command. Whatever the book may lack in usability it more than makes up for in virtuosity.

Although John had largely enjoyed his Oxford years, it is worth remembering that after his retirement he and Diane intended to move back to Sussex, and perhaps only the falling-through at the last moment of a house sale deflected them. During this period John was happy to have the honorary title of Research Professor at Sussex, happy to continue as editor-in-chief of *History of European Ideas*, where he exercised what one might call his light-touch editorial style—at least his junior editors Richard Whatmore and Brian Young might be inclined to call it that—and he always longed for the soothing balm of the Sussex Downs on a fine summer's day. But financial difficulties constrained his options, not for the first time, and the fact that his daughter and grandchildren seemed settled in Witney encouraged him to stay put (not that John usually needed much encouragement to stay put).

Stuart Proffitt, editorial director at HarperCollins and latterly at Penguin, had long recognised John's potential as a writer of books for a non-specialist market, and he now played an important part in enticing John to attempt a 'trade' book, in persuading him to undertake it on the very grandest scale, and in sustaining him through the inevitable troughs and failures of confidence. The project was to be nothing less than a history of historical writing from Herodotus to the present. This enabled John to pursue what had always been his preferred 'research strategy': to curl up in an armchair with a pile of Penguin Classics, in this case the original texts of the great (and not so great) historians. As ever, he did more reading in secondary works than was immediately visible in the eventual book, but essentially *A History of Histories: Epics, Chronicles, Romances and Inquiries from Herodotus and Thucydides to the Twentieth Century* represents the fruits of first-hand encounters between his cultivated intelligence and the works of Europe's greatest historians of the past two-and-a-half millennia. Published in 2007, the book immediately enjoyed considerable critical acclaim and commercial success (sales in the first four years, hardback and paperback combined, topped 35,000, with several translations in train). It falls to few academic historians to be the author of the most widely reviewed book of the week, as John Burrow was (according to *The Bookseller*) in early December 2007.[31] In the course of a highly positive as well as generous review in *The Guardian*, Keith Thomas struck a note which many others echoed: 'Burrow is so successful

[31] *The Bookseller*, 5312 (21 Dec. 2007), p. 39.

in this book because, in his freshness of response to many of his authors, he resembles the general, non-specialist reader for whom his work is intended.'[32]

In this respect, the book also represented a further evolution of John's style. Just as the confident question-and-answer logic of *Evolution and Society* had softened into the lusher and more richly ornamented prose of *A Liberal Descent*, so now that manner in turn was distilled and clarified into a more direct, limpid prose. Disciplined by the needs of the intended reader and stirred by what was in many cases his own first encounter with his chosen authors, John restrained his habitual riot of parenthetical qualifications, allowing the literary characters of his large cast to come through in all their vivid variousness. Reviewers responded by delightedly identifying new favourites to whom the book had introduced them, pride of place perhaps going to Gregory of Tours who, as John reported, 'begins his work with the memorable, and entirely accurate, reflection that "A great many things keep happening, some of them good, some of them bad".'[33]

But despite the catholicity of the book's embrace of past historical writing, a subdued polemic is occasionally audible in its pages. Its very architecture carries an animus against the claims of modern academic history to any monopoly of 'seriousness': John deliberately devoted half the book to ancient and medieval historians, while giving the professionalised legions of the twentieth century reprovingly short shrift. He was particularly severe on the foundation-myth of modern scholarly history, which represented 'real' history as only emerging from the primeval slime with the rise of critical archive-based scholarship in early and mid-nineteenth century Germany: 'The notion of a nineteenth-century "Copernican revolution" reinforced an enduringly distorted version of the history of historiography, slanted towards the nineteenth century and Germany, which the present book has attempted to correct.'[34] It may have been an indirect consequence of this purpose as well as an expression of John's personal tastes that the final chapter on 'The Twentieth Century' seems, despite its analytical clarity, slightly more dutiful and less engaged than its predecessors. But that may only be to register from another angle what an astonishing feat it was to write with such knowledge, insight, and sympathy about Arrian as well as Appian, Geoffrey of Monmouth as well as William of Malmesbury, Machiavelli as well as Guiccardini, Carlyle

[32] Keith Thomas, 'Review of *a History of Histories*', *The Guardian Review*, 15 Dec. 2007.
[33] John Burrow, *A History of Histories: Epics, Chronicles, Romances and Inquiries from Herodotus and Thucydides to the Twentieth Century* (London, 2007), p. 202.
[34] Ibid., p. 466.

and Michelet as well as Prescott and Henry Adams, and many others. *A History of Histories* is a fitting testament to John's enduring fascination with—to use the phrase from Burckhardt that he liked to cite—'history as the record of what one age finds of interest in another'.[35]

One final piece of John's writing, briefly mentioned earlier, deserves fuller discussion. In the early 1990s, he had composed a shortish memoir of his childhood and adolescence. He said that it was in the first instance addressed to his grandson, Julian, to explain to him a little about the corner of that far-off world in which his grandfather had grown up. The typescript had been shown to his family and a small number of close friends and then put aside. But when at the beginning of 2008 John was diagnosed with the cancer on his jaw from which he was to die within two years, he resolved to resume his narrative from the point at which he had gone up to Cambridge. Thus, the latter parts of the memoir were written in the Spring of 2008 when John was living alone while teaching as a visiting professor at Williams College (his family had stayed in England) and already displaying remarkable fortitude and uncomplaining grace in the face of increasing pain and disfigurement. Shortly before his death, a few friends, with Patricia Williams in the lead, arranged to have a small number of copies of the completed memoir privately printed and bound, so that John could give copies to a wider circle, a thought that gave him great pleasure. In what proved to be a moving occasion, those friends were able to gather at John's bedside in Witney to celebrate the 'publication' of the memoir, together with that of the selection from Macaulay's *History* for which he had written an introduction. He died 48 hours later, on 3 November 2009, aged 74.

The history of the memoir's composition goes some way to account for the different character of its two sections. The chapters dealing with his childhood and youth are among the most engaging things he ever wrote, recapturing the child's eye-view of the world with an affectionate light irony. There are vivid, fondly exaggerated portraits of older members of his family and their lives in interwar Devon; his exceptionally close bond with his mother, with whom he endured the war in his father's absence, shines through the early pages. More generally, the warm, indulgent, straitened life of his wider family is recalled with a beautifully judged mixture of gratitude for their love and amusement at their foibles. Editorial

[35] For some time John had been contracted to write, again for Stuart Proffitt, an 'Intellectual History of England', and he intended to return to this project once he had finished *A History of Histories*, but he only managed to complete a synopsis and tentative outline of chapters.

embellishment becomes a little more noticeable in the chapters on his school years, and particularly on his precocious reading, but the writing remains evocative and playful.

Although there are some literary gems scattered through the second half of the book, most readers have registered a certain falling-off in charm and attractiveness. This may be a pattern common to most autobiographies, but it may also reflect two further features of the later chapters, quite apart from the circumstances of their composition. The first is that the 'comedy of manners' genre, invoked in the book's introduction, comes to seem a little more contrived or staged in recollections of his adult life. Favourite bons mots and anecdotes are given a further polish while there is a noticeable absence of any really probing self-analysis. And the second is that the later chapters indulge a certain amount of grumpiness about the times being out of joint: a few old scores are settled, some familiar hobby-horses are taken out for a final canter, the presence of an author concerned to leave his side of the story on record is felt. Nonetheless, taken as a whole, the memoir provides a deliciously enjoyable slice of informal social history, as well as exhibiting further dimensions of John's rich literary gifts.

IV

There are, as readers of British Academy memoirs will scarcely need to be reminded, various types of successful academic—the empire-builder, the discipline-definer, the methodology-giver, the source-discoverer, and so on. John Burrow was none of these types. There is no scholarly coven of Burrovians: although his writing had been widely enjoyed and admired even before the broader public success of *A History of Histories*, that book's qualities underlined that his achievements were highly individual and practically inimitable. In recording the careers of scholars in the humanities, it is also often said that in addition to their books they produced 'a stream of articles and reviews'. This could not truthfully be said of Burrow: his standing rested, to a greater extent than has become common, on his books, and this illuminates the distinctiveness of his career from another angle. He published very little in scholarly journals: a tiny handful of articles, mostly in the earliest phase of his career, and a smattering of reviews. It is true that in the 1960s and 1970s he did a certain amount of reviewing for *The Times*, chiefly through the good offices of his undergraduate contemporary Michael Ratcliffe, then the paper's literary editor, and in the 1970s and 1980s he wrote a number of pieces for the

Times Literary Supplement and later two for the *London Review of Books*.[36] His cultural range, his readability, and his light touch might have seemed to make him a natural for the genre, especially in the longer review-essay form favoured by the literary periodicals. But from the mid-1980s onwards he pretty much gave up this kind of writing altogether. When surprise at this state of affairs came up in conversation, as it did from time to time over the years, John would explain that *starting* to write something was such an agony that he couldn't bring himself to do it very often and so he particularly hated to have deadlines hanging over him. He preferred to concentrate, and dispose of, all the agonies in one go by launching into a chapter of a book when he felt the time was ripe. This is a reminder that, for all the apparently effortless ease of his writing on the page, John suffered at least the usual agonies of composition, perhaps more, reinforcing him in his frequently repeated (but not, in truth, always consistently observed) golden rule where requests to write something were concerned: 'always say no'.

Although, as noted earlier, John found most of the manifestations of academic professionalism disagreeable, and none more so than the usual type of conference, there was one rather different kind of event that he came greatly to enjoy later in his career, and this was the series of gatherings organised by the Liberty Fund. Here, a group of largely congenial people talked in depth and in a more or less conversational manner about a particular theme or book, and this arrangement spoke to John's taste for, and flourishing in, a convivial setting that blended intellectual, social, and culinary pleasures (and strengthened his always-strong conviction of the superiority of being paid to talk rather than to write).

No one who heard him at these or other gatherings could fail to be impressed by John's intellectual and cultural range. Certainly, no one who heard his inaugural lecture as Professor of European Thought (reprinted in the journal *History of European Ideas* to mark the end of his general editorship of that journal in 2005[37]) could think of him as parochial, in terms either of geography or genre. But that range was neither limitless nor promiscuous, and in a sense it was not purely personal, either. What we might ambiguously call 'John's culture'—both his own level of self-cultivation and the cultural world he acknowledged and studied—was bounded, traditional, almost, I am tempted to say, given. Though there

[36] For full details, see the bibliography of his writings on the website of the Sussex Centre for Intellectual History. <http://www.sussex.ac.uk/cih/people/burrow>.

[37] J. W. Burrow, 'A common culture? Nationalist ideas in 19th-century European thought', *History of European Ideas*, 32 (2006), 333–44.

could be one or two additions and deletions at the edges, John implicitly took European high culture as it had taken itself in its heyday from the Enlightenment to Modernism. His own scholarly enthusiasms gather pace as the eighteenth century advances; they come to their full, voluptuous consecration in the nineteenth century; and they begin perceptibly to chill and lose interest as the twentieth century moves forward. And, as remarked above, his address to this cultural past exhibited none of the principled suspiciousness or urge to unmasking that characterises so much recently fashionable work, and nor was he concerned to rescue the once-marginalised or call attention to the systematically occluded. The great roll-call of names of European thought and literature he treated as an established possession—to be explored, certainly, even in some measure to be celebrated, but not to be dissolved or repudiated. It was another of the ways in which John exhibited some of the characteristics of the nineteenth-century gentleman-scholar rather than those of the twenty-first century professional academic. For him there was no great disjunction between the books he read so voraciously as a youth and young man and the books he later wrote about. 'I wanted', as he put it at one point, 'to learn my way around a good second-hand book shop—and I suppose that's what I've done.'

John's own aesthetic and literary tastes were of a piece with the intellectual range and focus of his work. Although he admired Augustan elegance, whether in Gibbon's periods or Georgian terraces, there was something in him that responded imaginatively to the exuberance and untidyness of Romanticism, and quite a lot of his personal as well as professional dealings with the nineteenth century involved understanding the ways in which that century extended and modified the legacy of late Romanticism. And this partly accounts, I think, for that noticeable cooling of his enthusiasms as we move through the twentieth century. He responded to Impressionism, but not, by and large, to Abstraction; to Mahleresque lushness, but scarcely at all to Schoenbergian austerity; to Nietzschean playfulness, but less so to Surrealist wilfulness; to Jamesian delicacy, but not Beckettian bleakness. Though he was immensely well read, the poetry and fiction of the past half-century scarcely touched him. I remember once enthusing to him about the merits of recent novels by Philip Roth and J. M. Coetzee. He wrinkled his nose: 'I think I'd prefer to reread Stendhal.' If he was more often to be found in galleries than in concert halls, and if perhaps he enjoyed looking at buildings even more than he did looking at paintings, it was usually with an eye to how European high culture of the eighteenth and nineteenth centuries negotiated its cultural inheritance. Incidentally, apart from writing, he practised none of the arts—they belonged, in that respect, in the company of things he had learned at school that he was unteachably bad at, such as woodwork, maths, and marching.

Pondering his cultural tastes, one is reminded that, unlike many students and young academics of his generation, John's formation did not include much exposure to or engagement with the United States. The semester he spent teaching there in 1981, when he was already 46, was his first direct experience of that country—one that he hugely enjoyed, communicating his enjoyment to friends in vivid letters that were evocative of the first European landfall in Australia or Darwin's ingenuous response to the Tierra del Fuegans. But although John developed a traveller's delight in new worlds, what really quickened the blood was Old Europe and old European culture.

The epigraph to *A Liberal Descent*, from which the book takes its title, is a passage from Burke, an author whom John held in high regard though always well this side of idolatry. The passage reads:

> Always acting as if in the presence of canonised forefathers, the spirit of freedom, leading in itself to misrule and excess, is tempered with an awful gravity. This idea of a liberal descent inspires us with a sense of habitual native dignity, which prevents that upstart insolence almost inevitably adhering to and disgracing those who are the first acquirers of any distinction.[38]

The passage is perfectly suited to the theme of the book, the elaborations and modifications of, broadly speaking, the Whig interpretation of English history. But it is a passage which also expresses an important truth about John's own sensibility and relation to the past. One of the reasons he could be irritated by intellectual fashions which trumpeted their own novelty was that he had such a strong distaste for the 'upstart insolence' of those whose claims to originality too often rested on an ignorance of, or disregard for, the achievements of the generations that had gone before them. John did not wish to 'canonise' any of those who might be regarded as our 'forefathers'—his relation to the past was neither pious nor antiquarian—but we may say that he did write with 'a sense of habitual native dignity' in part because he was so magnificently alive to that 'liberal descent' that is our common intellectual inheritance. That nice eighteenth-century phrase 'fullness of mind' sits well with John. It was more than mere learning, though he was very learned; it was more than wide culture, though

[38] Edmund Burke, *Reflections on the Revolution in France* (1790), quoted in *A Liberal Descent*, p. vi.

he was a deeply cultivated man. It had something to do with richness, something with scale and reach, and even more, perhaps, with the ready availability to him of the resources of his mind, whether in conversation or on the page.

From one point of view, it is remarkable that any of John's writings ever saw the light of day. His preferred, indeed his only, mode of composition was sitting in an armchair, with a pad of scruffy paper perched on his knee, an incontinent ball-point in his hand. The layered hieroglyphs which this produced would rival Linear B. One of the moments I would have greatest difficulty keeping a straight face was when he would explain that the sheaf of scrofulous scribbling in his hand was the 'fair copy' he had made for the typist, a role occupied by a succession of unusually talented paleographers. These technological barriers to the production of legible typescript may have strengthened John's resistance to making the changes that his friends might suggest when reading his work in draft. He tended to look favourably on comments that could be accommodated with Tippex, but to regard anything that might call for retyping as a grave failure of critical judgement.

It is notoriously hard to convey to others what it was that one so treasured and admired about a close friend. No matter how many abstract nouns one strings together, the net can never capture the butterfly. Anyone who knew John at all well will recall times when he reduced them to helpless laughter by turning some personal misfortune into high farce. It was, of course, a way of coping. He had his pride, though it was usually well hidden, and exercising his wit and inventiveness on circumstances or setbacks in life which were sometimes depressing or embarrassing for him to contemplate or admit was a way of mastering them—was, in Nietzschean vein, an assertion of the will to power, a search for the medium through which he could flourish and even dominate. Just occasionally, this rich capacity to convert embarrassing or distressing experience into hilarious narrative would assume full literary form, a rough draft having first been sketched and polished in conversation.[39]

Those who only met John on social occasions might have had little inkling of the melancholy, verging on despair, that was sometimes manifested to his close friends. On the whole, it was not John's way to take up arms against his sea of troubles; his was not what might be called an activist's temperament. He instinctively preferred the pleasures of comprehensive

[39] Some examples of these, mostly comic, flights of fancy are available on the website of the Sussex Centre for Intellectual History.

complaint to the labour of piecemeal reform. This went along with a strong streak of cultural pessimism, a characteristic that became more marked with age—a development he thought not simply justified by the facts of the world but also entirely proper to a man of advancing years. When his blood was up, the list of things which a never-exactly-identified 'they' had destroyed could be long: town centres, secondary education, red Burgundy, newspapers, literary criticism, rugby, more or less all tourist destinations, and—a note of especially passionate keening could enter the lament here—traditional hearty cooking. He reserved a particularly well-heated spot in one of the inner circles of hell for the inventors of 'nouvelle cuisine', but, then, for John anything that had 'nouvelle' in its title already had two strikes against it. It could be hard to separate genuine conviction from knowing self-satire in some of these performances. I remember sitting with him on the evening of his fortieth birthday when he declared: 'I wasn't very good at being a young man, but'—he paused to achieve the appropriately crusty effect—'I intend to be jolly good at being an old man.' He could stage the performance of being an old man brilliantly, though it should be said that it owed more to P. G. Wodehouse or Evelyn Waugh than to *King Lear*.

It would not be an exaggeration to say that throughout his years at East Anglia and Sussex John felt himself to be, in some profound if unrealistic sense, in exile from Cambridge. His years as a Research Fellow at Christ's were probably the happiest of his life in institutional terms, though becoming a Fellow of Balliol for the final five years of his employed career gave him great pleasure and allowed him once again to enjoy that conviviality of college life that he had long craved. Yet it is also only a slight exaggeration to say that throughout the last fourteen years of his life he felt himself to be, in some more superficial yet also more practical sense, in exile from Sussex (the county, not the university). Yearning for a lost Eden formed a deep part of his emotional negotiation with the unsatisfactoriness of ordinary existence.

In a famous passage, William Empson reflected that 'the waste even in a fortunate life, the isolation even of a life rich in intimacy, cannot but be felt deeply'.[40] John Burrow's was, in many respects, a fortunate life and certainly one rich in intimacy, but waste and isolation are also unignorable parts of his history. That history is, above all, a matter of deep feeling—the deep, expressive, often frustrated feelings that were central to the character of this passionate man, as well as the powerful feelings of love and

[40] William Empson, *Some Versions of Pastoral* (Harmondsworth, 1966 (1st edn., 1935)), p. 12.

admiration he evoked from those who were fortunate enough to be part of that rich intimacy. One should not rush to identify the 'waste': idleness, not a rare part of John's existence, may be the fertiliser of creativity; moodiness and depression, however stylised and camped up, may be inseparable from the trials of attempting to write less badly. But there was at times a poignancy about John that went beyond these common ailments of the writerly condition: a poignancy about a life so constantly shadowed by lack of money and lack of some of the elementary forms of orderliness; a poignancy about a short, shabby, shambolic man who had some of the gifts to be a cross between Wilde and Proust; a poignancy about an individual whose habitual self-centredness so often got in the way of that love from others that he so hungrily yearned for. Much of John is in his books, and the best of those books show an intellectual dextrousness, a delicacy of sensibility, and an exuberant but skilfully directed literary vitality that call for comparison with some of the great historians about whom he wrote so memorably. Readers of those books obtain a strong impression of their author, yet necessarily only a partial one. A wide circle of acquaintances will long recall some of his other vivid attributes, including his zest and his speed of mind. And a few close friends will always be grateful for having known an utterly exceptional individual, showered with gifts by the gods, more beset than most by the commoner plagues of human existence, yet soaring above his sometimes unpromising circumstances to reveal a richly creative, achingly vulnerable, and, above all, intensely lovable man.

STEFAN COLLINI
Fellow of the Academy

Note. Unless otherwise stated, information in this memoir comes from personal knowledge. John Burrow's autobiography, *Memories Migrating*, was privately printed in 2009; it is available in electronic form on the website of the Sussex Centre for Intellectual History, along with a range of other material by and about him, including a complete bibliography of his published writings. His papers have been deposited in Special Collections at the University of Sussex library, and a thorough handlist has been compiled by Peter Price. For advice and information in writing this memoir, I am grateful to Ruth Morse, Stuart Proffitt, Simon Skinner, Helen Small, Dorothy Thompson, John Thompson, Donald Winch, and Brian Young. A few paragraphs have been adapted from the address I gave at the memorial service in Balliol, a shortened version of which appeared in *The Balliol Record* for 2010.

PIERRE CHAPLAIS

Pierre Chaplais
1920–2006

DAUNTING EXACTITUDE, DAUNTLESS PERSISTENCE in the search for documentary evidence, and an intimidating grasp of precise detail gave Pierre Chaplais the power to identify and resolve problems in medieval historical documents that others could not approach. His successes were the result of a natural disposition to minute accuracy and observation, combined with both method and discipline in the marshalling of facts, and a sense of moral duty to commit his time and talents to unremitting labour. Such attributes might lead one to expect an austere personality behind them, but Pierre was generous, helpful, affable, and full of fun and charm. The cliché 'Nothing was too much trouble' aptly captures both his readiness to put himself at the disposal of his students and colleagues and his painstaking thoroughness in his own work. The course of his career was by any measure unusual: from small-town Brittany via Buchenwald to the Public Record Office and later to Oxford and a vineyard in Eynsham. In everything he achieved, he was untaught, schooled only by his instinctive understanding of how to examine primary documents, their forms, their words, their seals, their archival contexts. For twenty-five years he put himself under the most intense pressure. There was a price to be paid, which Pierre rarely counted, but it told on those closest to him more than on those whom he taught or advised. The cost was perhaps unsustainable, and in his fifties and sixties his concentration, his energy, and his publication declined. His skills remained unimpaired even as his eyesight faded, and his last major work, a book on Piers Gaveston, published in 1994, draws on the same command of detail in context that characterises all his best work. No one will go to his publications for the kind of new idea that

Biographical Memoirs of Fellows of the British Academy, XI, 115–150.

changes the direction of a subject. His gift was to show, by practice and example, how expertise in the handling of primary evidence bore fruit that could not be got without it. His technical virtuosity was to some historians admirable, inimitable, and unnecessary. To others it was a foundation and an inspiration.

* * *

Pierre Théophile Victorien Marie Chaplais was born on 8 July 1920 at Châteaubriant, in the département of Loire-Inférieure (now Loire-Atlantique), Brittany, almost equidistant between Rennes and Nantes.[1] Pierre's father Théophile Chaplais was the telephone engineer there, part of a family of public servants. His mother Victorine Roussel Chaplais died when he was a small boy. He had an elder sister, Renée, who would follow family tradition with a career in the telephone service at Nantes. The children were looked after by their father's unmarried sister, a Catholic with very strict views. While Pierre was still young, his father moved to the post office in Redon, in Ille-et-Vilaine, a small historic town, where the abbey of Saint-Sauveur had been founded in 832. Pierre was sent to school at the Collège Saint-Sauveur, run at that period by the Congrégation de Jésus et Marie, known as the Eudistes, and established within the former claustral buildings of the abbey. He did his baccalauréat largely in classics, philosophy, and mathematics—no history—and he hoped to go in for the navy, only to be turned down by the École navale at Brest on the grounds that he was colour-blind.

In 1938 he went up to the University of Rennes to study law.[2] The outbreak of war brought an early interruption. The invasion of Poland by Hitler's Wehrmacht in September 1939 was quickly followed by the Saar offensive, when French armed forces moved forwards from the Maginot Line into the Saarland. The advance stopped within a month, and the Drôle de Guerre set in. Pierre Chaplais volunteered for military service in October 1939 and was sent to the artillery school at Fontainebleau as an

[1]This section relies, with permission and often verbatim, on Cliff Davies's personal memoir, printed in Michael Jones and Malcolm Vale (eds.), *England and her Neighbours 1066–1453. Essays in Honour of Pierre Chaplais* (London, 1989), pp. xiii–xix. That was based largely on conversations with Pierre himself, supported by reading in the history of the Resistance. Cliff Davies also thanked Professor Jacques Brejon de Lavergnée, Pierre's old teacher, and M. Jean-Pierre Chaplet, son of his former pupil-master, for their assistance.

[2]Chaplais's *curriculum vitae* submitted when he applied for his post at Oxford in 1955 supplies facts about his university education. It shows him as enrolled in the Faculté de Droit 1938–46 and the Faculté des Arts 1940–6.

aspirant (officer designate), reaching the cavalry rank of *maréchal des logis de carrière* (equated with sergeant). The school was mobilised to fight when the German army attacked France in May 1940. During the *étrange défaite* they made their way south on horseback. Armistice came on 25 June, and Pierre's company was demobilised at Toulouse in September. He returned to Rennes to resume his studies.

At the university Pierre was now enrolled in classics as well as law. He completed his *licence* in law in July 1942 and in classics in June 1943. He fell under the spell of one of his professors, Jacques Brejon de Lavergnée (1911–93), a legal historian and historian of Brittany, with whom he completed his *diplôme d'études supérieures* in legal history in June 1943.[3] His aim was to become an academic lawyer. In France, as in England, it is useful for academic lawyers at least to qualify for practice, and to this end, at least ostensibly, Pierre had been recommended by Brejon to his near namesake, Maître Pierre Chaplet, an eminent lawyer in Rennes. Chaplet was involved in the resistance movement Défense de la France.

Défense de la France had been started in 1941 by a group of students in Paris, led by Philippe Viannay (1917–86).[4] The organisation produced in the cellars of the Sorbonne *La Défense de la France*, the most successful of the underground newspapers ('de tendance modérée et d'inspiration catholique').[5] It also produced false identity cards on a large scale. By 1943, when it was recognised by Charles de Gaulle, it was building itself up as a military force. Even so, something of the original 'boy-scout' (Pierre's words) inspiration remained in the meetings of small groups, eight or so, of would-be *francs-tireurs* in the Forêt de Paimpont, near Rennes. Pierre joined them in May 1943. In August he was with Maître Chaplet at a clandestine meeting in the forest with Pierre Dunoyer de Segonzac (1906–68), who offered a new concept of leadership among French youth, despising alike totalitarianism and the intellectualist democratic tradition and fostering a catholic and soldierly ethos.[6] Défense de la France would succeed in constituting a military force, which played a major part in the Liberation, both in Brittany and in Paris. Pierre and his group, however, were never armed. There was apparently a botched arms

[3] Brejon had only recently completed a thesis in Poitiers entitled *Un jurisconsulte de la Renaissance: André Tiraqueau (1488–1558)* (Paris, 1937), its subject a jurist who was also a humanist and friend of both Guillaume Budé and François Rabelais.

[4] Marie Granet, *Défense de la France. Histoire d'un mouvement de Résistance, 1940–1944* (Paris, 1960); Marcel Baudot, *Libération de la Bretagne* (Paris, 1973).

[5] Baudot, p. 60.

[6] Dunoyer's memoirs appeared posthumously, *Le vieux chef. Mémoires et pages choisies* (Paris, 1971). Discussion in W. D. Halls, *The Youth of Vichy France* (Oxford, 1981).

drop. Chaplet was arrested at seven o'clock in the morning of 21 December 1943; Pierre Chaplais, turning up at Chaplet's home later in the same day, walked into the arms of the Gestapo.

After interrogation at Rennes, they were taken to Compiègne, then on a three-day rail journey to Buchenwald, arriving on 29 January 1944.[7] There is no need to reproduce here the familiar horror-story of the camp, the struggle to survive the cold, hunger, and fatigue, the struggle to retain human values in a régime systematically dedicated to degradation. Maître Chaplet's published account is vivid and moving.[8] And he provides two brief glimpses of Pierre Chaplais. The first is at Compiègne: 'Mon jeune ami Ch(aplais), qui marchait à côté de moi, avec ses lèvres grasses, ses yeux en amande, et l'étrange turban dont il s'était coiffé, ressemblait à un fakir. On se le désignait du doigt. Il souriait imperturbablement comme un prince de carnaval.'[9] In the second, Chaplais discovered in a food parcel received at Buchenwald 'le portrait de sa fiancée qui fit le tour des tables. Le sourire d'Eliane eut un succès considerable. Ch(aplais) en rougissait de confusion, mais il était bien embarrassé pour dissimuler l'image qui était l'oeuvre d'un photographe d'art et prenait une grande place. Il la glissa, après avoir découpé l'entourage du carton, dans la doublure de sa veste rayée. Nous demandions à la voir de temps en temps.'[10] This wartime engagement presumably came about during Pierre's involvement with the Resistance in 1943: Eliane Daëron was herself awarded the Croix de Guerre for her work in the Resistance.[11]

During fifteen months in the concentration camp at Buchenwald, near Weimar in Thüringen, Pierre was put to forced labour in armament factories in the area. The last few weeks of imprisonment, as the Americans approached in March and April 1945, were the most dangerous. The camp authorities might well have done away with the prisoners to remove evi-

[7] Pierre Chaplais (prisoner 43478) and Pierre Chaplet (prisoner 43485) appear side by side in the list of 1584 men transported at this date, published online by the Fondation pour le mémoire de la transportation under the heading 'Transport parti de Compiègne 27 janvier 1944 (I. 173)'; out of 240 who went to Buchenwald, 149 are listed as *décédés*.

[8] P. Chaplet, *Häftling 43485* (Paris, 1947). The book begins with Chaplet's arrest and refers only briefly to his earlier resistance activities. He remained at Buchenwald only until 1 October 1944, after which he was transferred to the subsidiary camp at Dora, returning to France at the end of the war via Bergen-Belsen.

[9] Chaplet, p. 108.

[10] Ibid., pp. 280–1.

[11] She was much the same age as Pierre, having finished her schooling at the Lycée des Jeunes Filles in Saint-Malo in July 1938 (*L'Ouest-Éclair*, 14 juillet 1938, p. 6). Pierre presumably met her in Rennes. She would marry Philippe Ragueneau (1917–2003), saboteur and commander of a parachute unit, whose later career is well known.

dence of atrocities. Pierre's memory of this was hazy: in those weeks he was himself in the infirmary as a result of American bombing in Weimar, and he played no part in the 'rising' which, according to the hagiography of the official prisoners' organisations, preceded the arrival of Patton's army at the camp. Liberated by the Americans on 12 April 1945, he ran wild through the streets of Weimar. He never returned to Germany. He arrived in Paris on VE Day, 8 May 1945, when his group startled the more staid bourgeoisie as they sang the Internationale from the back of a lorry. He received the Médaille de la Résistance in 1946 and would wear it with pride for the rest of his life.

Pierre now came to the Channel resort of Deauville, where his father had become postmaster. He would go back to Brittany to resume his studies at the University of Rennes, completing his *diplômes d'études supérieures* in public law in October 1945, in private law and in classics in June 1946. For the last he wrote a thesis on Seneca.[12] In November 1945, by dint of having his war service credited, he also qualified as an *avocat* and was formally admitted to the Rennes court by Pierre Chaplet, *bâtonnier*. Academic law was still his objective, and he moved to the Faculté de Droit in Paris, where he set about preparing the substantial thesis demanded for the *agrégation* in law. He determined to work in legal history, and his supervisor was Professor Pierre Petot (1887–1966). Other significant contacts appear at this time. Michel de Boüard (1909–89), a catholic, communist, and former *déporté*, whom he had met in Deauville, introduced him to Robert Fawtier (1885–1966), professeur des sciences auxiliaires de l'histoire du moyen âge at the University of Bordeaux from 1928 to 1949, and to Édouard Perroy (1901–74), professor of medieval history at Lille from 1934 to 1950. Both had worked in England before the war, and both had been heavily involved with the Resistance. Perroy wrote *La Guerre de cent ans* while on the run from the Gestapo in his native Forez.[13] Fawtier had been arrested in 1942 and, after a period in the notorious prison at Fresnes, was deported, ending the war in the camp at Mauthausen near Linz in Austria.[14] It is not known whether Pierre's contact with Michel de Boüard

[12] Entitled 'Le Rôle de la mer dans les oeuvres en prose de Sénèque le philosophe', the essay runs to 111 pages of typescript in quarto. Inspired by the well-documented study by Eugène de Saint-Denis, *Le Rôle de la mer dans la poésie latine* (Lyons, 1935), and a thèse complémentaire, *Vocabulaire des manoeuvres nautiques en latin* (Mâcon, 1935), Pierre's work draws almost exclusively on Seneca's writings. The brief bibliography (p. 10) includes two works published in English.

[13] This is mentioned in the *avant-propos* of the book, which was published in 1945, going through nine impressions in that year. There is a brief obituary of Édouard Perroy by Étienne Fournial in *Cahiers de civilisation médiévale*, 17 (1974), 399–400.

[14] Jean Hubert, 'Notice sur la vie et les travaux de M. Robert Fawtier, membre de l'Académie', *Comptes-rendus des séances de l'Académie des Inscriptions et Belles-Lettres*, 127 (1983), 470–82.

also led to an introduction to his father, Alain de Boüard (1882–1955), who taught palaeography and diplomatic at the École nationale des chartes until his retirement in 1953.[15] The spirit of comradeship among ex-resisters no doubt did something to open doors, but only Pierre's abilities would have earned him the good offices of such austere scholars. The subject of his intended thesis was sovereignty in Anglo-French relations 1259–1453.

* * *

How the subject came to be chosen and how Pierre prepared himself for his research in English archives are now quite unknown. A grant from the French government allowed him to commence research. Taking advantage also of a three-week holiday, paid for by the newspaper *France-Soir*, successor to *Défense de la France*, he arrived in England on 2 September 1946. He carried letters of introduction from both Fawtier and Perroy to V. H. Galbraith (1889–1976), then director of the Institute of Historical Research. When term began, he remained in London to attend Galbraith's classes on palaeography and diplomatic, and by the end of October he had been induced to register for a London doctorate. He supported himself meanwhile by teaching French at the Linguists' Club in Grosvenor Place—its motto 'Se comprendre c'est la paix'—and occasionally translating into French, notably talks for the BBC. His livelihood was somewhat precarious, but he got stuck into his research. The records in the Public Record Office, Chancery Lane, had become available again in the summer of 1946 after nearly seven years' wartime closure.[16] Galbraith was greatly impressed by Pierre's single-minded devotion to medieval history. Mary Galbraith was a sixth-former at that time, who remembers Pierre 'as a quiet friendly young man, quite prepared to play charades at family Christmas parties, and as a patient, capable teacher when in 1947 he coached me in French for my Oxford entrance exams'.[17] Mrs Galbraith asked Pierre to do this, rather than a more experienced tutor, because it provided a cover for making some payments to him, when he was near

[15] PC was well acquainted with Alain de Boüard's textbooks, both on palaeography, a revision of Maurice Prou's *Manuel de paléographie*, 4th edn. (Paris, 1924), and on diplomatic, *Manuel de diplomatique française et pontificale* (Paris, 1940). He remained on friendly terms with Michel de Bouärd, who became a prominent historian and archaeologist in Normandy.

[16] The records had been evacuated during the war but returned between September 1945 and June 1946. The Long Room in Chancery Lane reopened, but reopening the Round Room was delayed until May 1947 by building work to repair war-damage (R. H. Ellis, 'Archives 1939–47', *The Year's Work in Librarianship*, 14 (1947), 258–320, at p. 263).

[17] Mary Moore, 22 Feb. 2007.

penniless. Over the next ten years, both in London and after his move in January 1948 to be Regius Professor of Modern History in Oxford, Vivian Galbraith was to be the advocate who got Chaplais's extraordinary abilities noticed and opened up for him the opportunities to develop his talents.

From 1947 a scholarship from the British Council funded his postgraduate research at the Institute in London. For three years he concentrated on his thesis, now defined as Gascon Appeals to England 1259–1453. Much of his energy was devoted to finding documents that would reveal the mechanism and context of appeals from Gascony. His concentration was not so single-minded as to let slip the opportunity to meet and woo Doreen Middlemast, who was working in the London office of *The Times of India*, around the corner from Chancery Lane. They were married in London in 1948. The thesis was examined in December 1950 by Goronwy Edwards and C. H. Williams. Pierre's own copy would subsequently swell with added material.

The subject of judicial appeals no doubt derived in the first place from Pierre's aspiration for an academic career in law and legal history. In the context of Gascony under English rule appeals depended on the contested issue of sovereignty in the French lands of the king of England. This led into the investigation of contemporary theorists' views on either side of the question. Edward III's assuming the title King of France in 1340 changed the picture, repatriating nominal sovereignty to France while it continued to be exercised by the king in England or through his officers in Gascony. The creation of a Court of Sovereignty (*Curia Superioritatis*) of Aquitaine would serve to provide the duchy with a buffer against the French king and the Parlement de Paris that would outlast English rule in Gascony. The search for evidence led Pierre into a range of little-known classes in the Public Record Office: Ancient Correspondence (SC1), Ancient Petitions (SC8), Council and Privy Seal Files (E28), Diplomatic Documents (E30 and C47/27–32), Gascon Rolls (C61), Treaty Rolls (C76), Chancery Warrants (C81), and the Accounts of the Constables of Bordeaux (among materials in E101 and E364). This exploration of the Public Record Office shaped more than one aspect of Pierre's later work. His interest widened from a focus on technical issues of appellate jurisdiction in the English Crown's French lands to the whole process of diplomatic contact between the two crowns, and then more largely the processes of diplomacy in the middle ages.

Ten articles were written and published during this period, three in English and the remainder in French.[18] In his very first paper, published in

[18] His publications to 1989, omitting reviews, are listed in *England and her Neighbours*, xxi–xxiv.

the *Bulletin* of the Institute, he thanks 'My friend Dr G. P. Cuttino for assistance in translating this article into English'.[19] George Peddy Cuttino (1914–91) was an American who had come to Oxford as a Rhodes Scholar in 1936 and written a doctoral thesis under V. H. Galbraith on a subject close to Chaplais's interests.[20] Thereafter Pierre's written English needed no such assistance—one suspects that Doreen Chaplais may have helped—but the topics were often intended for a French audience, not generally as comfortable in English as Fawtier and Perroy. One of these papers, published by the École des chartes, presents a remarkable discovery of documents missing from the Archives in Paris but found in London.[21] Another, in the *English Historical Review*, already shows how well Chaplais was attuned to the formal understanding of charters, which he would later teach. Chaplais proved that Henry III's dropping of the titles 'duke of Normandy' and 'count of Anjou' from his regnal style, a well-known concession to Louis IX of France in 1259, was actually done in two stages, and that the old and new seals were used simultaneously between May and December. For business with Louis, the new style and the new seal were used, but the change was not adopted for English or Gascon business until Henry crossed the Channel in December.[22] This detail is not observable in the documents most often used by historians, copied on the chancery rolls, which usually abbreviate the style; this perception depended on a search in the PRO for originals of the right date with seals and for documents copied with the regnal style in full. This proof demonstrates Pierre's command of his techniques in diplomatic at an early stage in his career, without specific training and at a time when his research was still primarily concerned with royal diplomacy. Attention to seals was to become a hallmark of his work.

In this period too the young Chaplais wrote what he referred to as 'sundry reviews' for the journal *Le Moyen Age*, edited in Belgium by Fernand Vercauteren (1903–79), a student of Henri Pirenne. One title he

[19] 'English arguments concerning the feudal status of Aquitaine in the fourteenth century', *Bulletin of the Institute of Historical Research*, 21 (1946–8), 203–13.

[20] Cuttino's thesis, 'The Conduct of English Diplomacy in the Fourteenth Century', University of Oxford, 1938, was published as *English Diplomatic Administration, 1259–1339* (Oxford, 1940).

[21] 'Chartes en déficit dans les cartons Angleterre du Trésor des Chartes', *Bibliothèque de l'École des chartes*, 109 (1951), 96–103. Eleven charters, still in the Archives in 1834, were bought by the British Museum in 1856 as part of the collection of Francis Moore, who had lived nearly fifty years in Paris.

[22] 'The making of the Treaty of Paris (1259) and the royal style', *English Historical Review*, 67 (1952), 235–53.

reviewed was *Relations internationales. Le moyen âge* (Paris, 1953), by François-Louis Ganshof (1895–1980), another of Pirenne's school; the book was written to order in a field where the young Chaplais was making the pace far more than the senior Ganshof. Pierre kept Ganshof's letter of acknowledgement as a souvenir.[23]

The documentary research relating to his thesis fed two volumes published by the Royal Historical Society in the Camden Series. The first, *Some Documents concerning the Fulfilment and Interpretation of the Treaty of Brétigny 1361–1369*, occupying eighty-four pages, was paired with the slightly longer collection, *The Anglo-French Negotiations at Bruges, 1374–1377*, edited by Édouard Perroy, to form the Camden Miscellany 19 (1952). Perroy had himself worked extensively in the Public Record Office twenty years earlier and would have been well connected with English medievalists such as V. H. Galbraith.[24] Pierre became a Fellow of the Royal Historical Society in the following year. The second but larger volume focused on an earlier episode, *The War of Saint-Sardos (1323–1325). Gascon Correspondence and Diplomatic Documents*, Camden 3rd Series 87 (1954). John Le Patourel found the book austere.[25]

By the Treaty of Brétigny in 1360 Jean II had ceded the sovereignty of Aquitaine to Edward III of England, subject to certain conditions, which were still unsatisfied in 1369, giving Charles V the pretext to seize Aquitaine and start a war with the Black Prince. He did so fortified with opinions provided by two Bolognese jurists, Riccardo da Saliceto and Giovanni da Legnano, which Chaplais edited along with documents concerning the treaty. He realised that 'four important passages of the two opinions' were incorporated in a French treatise, presented to Charles V in 1378, known by the title *Le Songe du vergier*, of which the presentation copy survived in the British Museum, MS Royal 19 C. iv. This work had been printed as early as 1492 and was included in Jean-Louis Brunet's edition of *Traitez*

[23] F. Vercauteren to PC, 8 Sept. 1953; F. L. Ganshof to PC, 19 Feb. 1955. The review appeared in *Le Moyen Age*, 60 (1954), 476–8. PC had had an article accepted by this journal before his thesis was examined (Vercauteren to PC, 12 Nov. 1950), 'Règlement des conflits internationaux franco-anglais au XIVe siècle (1293–1377)', *Le Moyen Age*, 57 (1951), 269–302.

[24] E. Perroy, *L'Angleterre et le grand Schisme d'Occident* (Paris, 1933). In the same year Perroy published a selection of documents considerably wider in scope than those used to support the argument of this book in *Diplomatic Correspondence of Richard II*, Camden 3rd Series 48 (1933). During the gathering of material, Perroy had taught French in Glasgow and later in London.

[25] 'Though meticulous, the edition is austere. [. . .] Probably Dr Chaplais is the only person who really knows the surviving documents in London and Paris relating to this war. It is greatly to be hoped that he will write at least a long article on the subject, and soon' (J. Le Patourel, *English Historical Review*, 71 (1956), 141).

des droits et libertez de l'Église gallicane (1731).[26] With the presentation copy accessible in London, Chaplais resolved to edit this text and to investigate the relationship between the French and the Latin original, *Somnium Viridarii* (1376), in Paris, Bibliothèque Mazarine, MS 3522, which had been printed by Melchior Goldast in 1611. He was in touch with the legal historian T. F. T. Plucknett, who wrote: 'I am delighted to hear that you contemplate a full edition of the *Songe du Vergier*: it will necessarily be an elaborate affair.'[27] And again, 'I have just heard from Fawtier who gives us the green light. A lady-chartiste wrote a thesis on the *Songe* some years ago but has married and abandoned it.'[28] The intention was to treat Latin and French together, and Chaplais laboured at this task, which demanded a considerable effort in comparing its wide-ranging legal sources. Despite Fawtier's inquiries, the chartiste reappeared with an article on the manuscript and a plan to edit the text.[29] In 1955, when Chaplais applied to Oxford, he did not refer to the *Songe* as work in progress. The eventual appearance of the French text in Paris in 1982 sent Chaplais back to his mountain of photostats and notes; returning with undimmed engagement to his ideas of thirty years earlier, he wrote up his case for attributing the work to Dom Jean le Fèvre, abbot of Saint-Vaast in Arras, who was a constant adviser to Charles V in the 1370s. Only the detailed knowledge of the text, in both French and Latin, and its sources betrays the amount of work Pierre had done so long before. His article finally appeared in 1996.[30]

[26] *Le Songe du vergier*, [Lyon]: Jacques Maillet, 20 March 1491/2 (*CIBN* S316); Paris: Le Petit Laurens, for Jean Petit at Paris and for Jean Alexandre, Jean Alisot and Charles Debougne at Angers, [about April 1499] (*CIBN* S317). The *editio princeps* was reprinted in the collection *Traitez des droits et libertez de l'Église gallicane*, ed. Jean-Louis Brunel (Paris, 1731).

[27] T. F. T. Plucknett to PC, 10 Feb. 1952.

[28] T. F. T. Plucknett to PC, 17 Oct. 1953. He alludes to Marion Lièvre's work, *Le songe du vergier*, diplôme d'archiviste paléographe, École nationale des chartes, 1947 (*Positions des thèses de l'École des chartes*, 1947, 81–4). She married Frédéric Schnerb in 1951.

[29] Marion Lièvre, 'Notes sur le manuscrit original du Songe du Vergier et sur la librairie de Charles V', *Romania*, 77 (1956), 352–60. The edition, with exiguous apparatus, followed years later: M. Schnerb-Lièvre, *Le Songe du vergier édité d'après le manuscrit Royal 19 C. iv de la British Library*, 2 vols. (Paris, 1982), pp. xcii, 501, 496. Chaplais's published findings on the legal opinions concerning the sovereignty of Guyenne were recorded, vol. i, p. lxvi, but not deployed in the commentary nor in the index of sources. The Latin text, instead of running *en face*, followed later, M. Schnerb-Lièvre, *Somnium Viridarii*, 2 vols. (Paris, 1993–5), pp. lviii, 381, –544.

[30] 'Jean le Fèvre, abbot of Saint-Vaast, Arras, and the *Songe du vergier*', in *Recognitions. Essays presented to Edmund Fryde* (Aberystwyth, 1996), pp. 203–28. In a letter to Michael Jones, dated 7 July 1998, Pierre mentioned 'Marion Schnerb-Lièvre, who has not welcomed my efforts on the *Songe* and promises to blast me and Jean Le Fèvre out of existence'. Obituaries of Mme Schnerb-Lièvre (1921–2005) concede no doubt: 'C'est celle qui a définitivement établi que l'auteur du texte était Évrart du Trémagon' (*Bibliothèque de l'École des chartes*, 163 (2005), 602–3);

Meanwhile Chaplais had found employment in the Public Record Office. He had impressed Harold Johnson (1903–73), who must have come across him when on duty in the Round Room. Johnson had oversight of editorial work, for which he sought to recruit Chaplais. There was an interview with the deputy keeper, Sir Hilary Jenkinson (1882–1961), who commiserated with Pierre over his bad luck in being taught by Galbraith.[31] It was agreed as early as March 1949 that Chaplais should work for the Office as an external editor, paid on a daily rate of three guineas. He was to prepare editions of the Treaty Rolls, the Roman Rolls, and the series of Diplomatic Documents, and as a means to that work 'to arrange and list parts of the unsorted miscellanea of the Chancery and Exchequer'.[32] The history of the Office deals with these new undertakings as the fruit of Jenkinson's overhaul of the publication policy.[33] But is it coincidence that the work planned should be so close to Chaplais's interests? By 1953 an agreement was also reached for the resumption of Charles Bémont's long-lapsed edition of the Gascon Rolls to be prepared by Yves Renouard under the supervision of Professor Robert Fawtier. The French side of the agreement was represented by Clovis Brunel, Robert Fawtier, Charles Samaran, and Georges Tessier, 'membres du Comité des Travaux historiques'. In this connection Pierre's role was 'to assist the editor of the Gascon Rolls by checking his text and rendering general editorial assistance on the documentation in England relating to Gascony'.[34]

'Confirmant une intuition d'Alfred Colville, elle a apporté la preuve que l'oeuvre était du juriste Évrart de Trémagon (†1386)' (*Annuaire-Bulletin de la Société de l'histoire de France*, Année 2006, 12). The author's access to and use of Everard's writings is not evidence of identity.

[31] Davies, p. xviii. Jenkinson had joined the office in 1920, Galbraith in 1921; from 1925 Jenkinson was a part-time reader in diplomatic at King's College, around the corner from the Record Office in the Strand, but Galbraith was the high flier who left for Oxford in 1928. He would look back on his time as an assistant keeper as 'a stick in the mud job', while doubting if he would find nicer mud to stick in (John Cantwell, *The Public Record Office 1838–1958* (London, 1991), p. 406, a book reviewed by P. Chaplais, *English Historical Review*, 110 (1995), 233–5). Chaplais made a careful study of Jenkinson's publications, but his paper, 'The study of palaeography and sigillography in England: Sir Hilary Jenkinson's contribution', in *Essays in Memory of Sir Hilary Jenkinson*, edited for the Society of Archivists by Albert E. J. Hollaender ([n.p.], 1962), pp. 41–9 (a paper omitted from the bibliography of Chaplais's works), makes no allusion to personal contacts. With the full grandeur of a deputy keeper, Jenkinson acknowledged the assistance of Chaplais and other Office juniors to his own booklet, *A Guide to Seals in the Public Record Office* (London, 1954), p. x, only through the mediation of a senior assistant keeper, Harold Johnson.

[32] Quotation from PC's CV.

[33] Cantwell, *Public Record Office 1838–1958*, pp. 446–7.

[34] Renouard's introduction gives more detail, *Gascon Rolls 1307–1317* (London, 1962), pp. ii–iii. Pierre Chaplais is particularly thanked for 'le méticuleux collationnement du texte sur l'original' and for supplying information from other material in the public records. Renouard intended one further volume to complete the rolls of Edward II's reign. The series C61 continues to 7 Edward

The first volume of the Treaty Rolls was published in 1955 with Chaplais's name on the title page—unusual recognition in those days—and a laconic preface signed by the deputy keeper, D. L. Evans. The ten rolls covered by the volume are identified according to their previous record history: 'The text of the rolls being by no means free from error, an attempt has been made to trace the sealed exemplars ("originals") of the documents enrolled, and thus useful collations of the text have been made possible; drafts and early official copies have been used for the same purpose.'[35] These few words denote a fundamental departure from normal policy in the Office and a massive search to match up the documents lying behind the rolls. The initiative was Chaplais's. He was unable, however, to thwart the parsimony of the publisher, Her Majesty's Stationery Office, which required that documents already printed in the Record Commission edition of Rymer's *Foedera* (1816) should be reduced to top and tail with a brief English summary and a note of any corrections resulting from the collation of the text. It was a grief to the editor to have prepared an improved text of the Latin or the French, only to have to delete a large part of his work in deference to the existence of an ancient edition available only in major libraries. Chaplais remained hostile to the Stationery Office until the end of its existence as a publisher in 1996. A second volume, based on the rolls without any attempt to improve their texts, was seen into print in 1972 by an American student who had completed a doctorate under his supervision.[36]

Evans's preface to the first volume had alluded to much more: 'The history of the class and the diplomatic of the documents enrolled will be

IV; an edition is now in progress under the direction of Dr Malcolm Vale (Oxford) and Dr Paul Booth (Liverpool). The Comité des Travaux historiques had been set up by the French government as long ago as 1834, its purpose 'diriger les recherches et les publications de documents inédits à l'aide de fonds votés au budget de l'État'. Clovis Brunel (1884–1971) was director of the École nationale des chartes 1930–54, where Georges Tessier (1891–1967) was professor of diplomatic; Charles Samaran (1879–1982) was at this date director of the Archives Nationales.

[35] *Treaty Rolls* i *1234–1325* (London, 1955), p. v.

[36] *Treaty Rolls* ii *1337–1339* (London, 1972), covering the next three rolls (C76/11–13), was the work of John Tyler Ferguson IV (1939–73). It was the fruit of a network centred on Chaplais. Ferguson had studied at Emory University with George Cuttino. He won a Fulbright Fellowship and came to Oxford and Wadham College in 1963 to work with Chaplais on fifteenth-century diplomacy. His thesis, 'English Diplomacy during the reign of Henry VI, 1422–1461', was defended in 1967 and published in 1972. Through Chaplais and former colleagues in the Record Office, H. C. Johnson, L. C. Hector, and R. E. Latham, Ferguson was guided into continuing the work on the rolls. He died at the age of thirty-three, leaving a third volume of the Treaty Rolls in draft and a planned two-volume work, including a selection of documents, on Edward III's claim to the Crown of France, further evidence of Chaplais's influence.

discussed in a separate introductory volume which will also cover the classes of Diplomatic Documents (Exchequer and Chancery) and Roman Rolls to be printed concurrently in parallel series.'[37] This sets out an agenda that was only ever partially fulfilled.

A further volume, *Diplomatic Documents* i *1101–1272*, was published for the Record Office in 1964, in which Chaplais presented some 444 documents, the great majority of them from the reign of Henry III. This drew in small measure on the classes officially titled Diplomatic Documents (C47/27–32, E30), printing the earliest documents in both series. By far the largest proportion of the texts was drawn from the class of Ancient Correspondence (SC1). A lot of this material was in poor condition: 'much of the transcription had to be done by using ultra-violet rays, and it required meticulous care, infinite patience, and dogged perseverance', as George Cuttino observed.[38] By this date Chaplais had come to be regarded within the Record Office as the person who could get the best results from the most difficult material.[39] With these classes, considerable effort was required before a document could be dated or its inclusion in the volume decided. The selection relied on Chaplais's increasingly refined perception of the procedures behind the conduct of diplomatic business. No second volume followed, and I find no sign of work on the Roman Rolls.

In conjunction with these volumes of texts there was to be an introduction, referred to already in 1955, which was to take the form of a book on *English Medieval Diplomacy*, of which he said: 'a large section of the work will be devoted to the history of the English diplomatic records and another to the study of the general diplomatic practice in medieval Europe, with special reference to England'.[40] The latter aspect came to predominate, and the archival history of the records is not heard of again. A characteristically understated note, published in 1958, gives a taste of what might have been: in it, Chaplais recovered the drafting and filing procedures of the Privy Seal from the endorsements on scattered

[37] PC's friend John Le Patourel said in a review, 'It is difficult to guess how many volumes will be required to complete this undertaking, but it will certainly be a very considerable number' (*English Historical Review*, 73 (1958), 667–70). This review usefully takes a page to explain the archival history of the material in the volume.

[38] G. P. Cuttino, *Speculum*, 40 (1965), 713–14.

[39] Michael Jones and Malcolm Vale have written that 'During his time as an Editor at the Public Record Office, fragmentary and decayed documents classified as "illegible" were apparently "given to Chaplais" for successful elucidation' (*England and her Neighbours*, p. vii).

[40] CV as 'in preparation'. The book was also mentioned in correspondence in 1958 between PC and D. E. Queller (1925–95), 'Thirteenth-Century diplomatic envoys: Nuncii and Procuratores', *Speculum*, 35 (1960), 196–213 (p. 198 n.).

documents.[41] Diplomacy took precedence over administration, but it is not apparent how much was written at what dates. Chaplais's prefaces tend to the same austere brevity as those printed above an official signature, with the effect that his books do not explain their own background. There appeared in 1975 a folio volume of facsimiles entitled *English Medieval Diplomatic Practice*, Part II, *Plates*; then in 1982, still from the reluctant Stationery Office, *English Medieval Diplomatic Practice*, Part I, *Documents and Interpretation*, in two volumes.[42] The 830 pages of the latter presented 420 documents, in Latin, French, and English, selected and organised thematically to illustrate the practice of diplomacy by the English Crown. Seventy-two of them were illustrated in the accompanying plates: documents of English origin preserved in the archives of foreign rulers, mainly from Paris and half a dozen other Continental archives. The coverage is concentrated in the fourteenth century, but there are also documents from the twelfth, thirteenth and fifteenth centuries. The annotation is concise, though it was sometimes allowed to include compressed essays such as that on 'The grant of Guyenne to Edward of Windsor, the great seal, and the royal style', appended to No. 49, letters patent in French from Edward II to Charles IV of France.[43] The document, from the Archives Nationales, had already been printed in *The War of Saint-Sardos*, 241 (no. 211), and the subject derives directly from Chaplais's Ph.D. thesis. Even with the publication of these large volumes, the grand plan was still far from fulfilled. The brief preface in 1982 says, 'An extensive discussion of English diplomatic practice from its origins to the end of the middle ages, originally planned as an introduction to the present volumes, will be published as a separate book, which will also contain a consolidated index.' The proposed book was halted when the Stationery Office decided no longer to handle publications for the Public Record Office, though Pierre would ever after refer to it as 'the PRO book'. It weighed on his conscience. He later revealed a still-larger plan, that two volumes of commentary should accompany these documents, 'examining the two distinct

[41] 'Privy Seal drafts, rolls, and registers (Edward I–Edward II)', *English Historical Review*, 73 (1958), 270–73. Chaplais discovered that Privy Seal drafts were arranged in monthly files with a register built up from quires corresponding to one month's drafts. He identified a surviving leaf from such a quire, subsequently used as a pastedown, in BL MS Royal 13 A. xi. Several hundreds of privy seal drafts survive, 'hopelessly scattered in various classes of the Public Record Office and elsewhere', among which he identified the best-preserved monthly files.

[42] The quality of the facsimiles was indifferent but the publication, in large format, was expensive at £19 in 1975. The two volumes of text were exorbitantly expensive at £95 in 1982 (G. P. Cuttino, *Speculum*, 59 (1984), 630–1).

[43] *Medieval English Diplomatic Practice*, Part I, vol. i, 68–70.

aspects of medieval diplomacy, the exchange of information between governments in one volume and the negotiation and conclusion of agreements between governments in another'.[44] Three substantial chapters towards the first volume were drafted, and between 1990 and 1992 efforts were made to print them. Failing eyesight and advancing age might have ended the matter there, but ten years later Pierre's friends Rees Davies, professor of medieval history, Cliff Davies, for forty years a colleague in Wadham College, and Martin Sheppard, of Hambledon Press, contrived to produce as much as was drafted under a new title, *English Diplomatic Practice in the Middle Ages* (London, 2003).

* * *

The programme of work was conceived on a massive scale. How far the plan grew in the handling, how far it was always intended to be vast, are questions that cannot now be answered. In the early 1950s, however, Chaplais's supporters in the Record Office may have recognised the desirability of harnessing his expertise and industry on a more secure basis. It is said that he would have been given a permanent position as an assistant keeper if he had been willing to take on British nationality and surrender his French passport. He chose not to do that. In 1953 he was in correspondence with Frédéric Joüon des Longrais (1892–1975) about the possibility of completing his *agrégation* in the Faculté de Droit.[45] None the less, he had little appetite to return to France, where too many senior academic positions were held by men who had not resisted Nazi occupation. His wife was English, their two young boys were English, and he was deeply engaged in his research in England. The desirability of a secure position, however, remained.

The opportunity came in 1955. Kathleen Major had been Reader in Diplomatic at Oxford since the end of the Second World War, and since

[44] *English Diplomatic Practice in the Middle Ages* (London, 2003), p. ix.

[45] F. Joüon des Longrais to PC, 31 Aug. 1953, in reply to PC's letter dated 27 June 1953: '"La souveraineté et le ressort dans les rapports entre la France et l'Angleterre de 1259 à 1453" est un sujet bien mieux délimité. Il me semble que vous avez procédé de la meilleure manière en copiant à loisir les documents anglo-français que vous étiez mieux placé que quiconque pour trouver, étudier et éditer. Vous n'avez pas à craindre que votre directeur de thèse soit effrayé par l'ampleur de vos pièces justificatives. Tout au contraire, il s'en rejouit d'avance car, comme vous le savez, aux Facultés de droit, il est bien rare d'avoir de bonnes éditions de textes dans les thèses. [...] Si votre goût vous attire vers l'agrégation de droit qui est une noble carrière, je crois, en toute sincerité, que vous aurez quand vous vous y présenterez un indéniable prestige d'éditeur de textes.'

1948 her course had dovetailed with the graduate course on the sources for English history from the eleventh to fifteenth centuries, given by the new Regius Professor, Vivian Galbraith.[46] Upon her election as principal of St Hilda's College she resigned with effect from 31 July 1955. The post was advertised in May as lecturer or Reader in Diplomatic, and the electors met on 2 June—A. H. Smith, Warden of New College (as Vice-Chancellor), Professor Galbraith, the Revd Dr [Claude] Jenkins, Mr [Goronwy] Edwards, and Mr [K. B.] McFarlane. Chaplais's application set out his *curriculum vitae* and a list of publications, actual or anticipated. His referees were T. F. T. Plucknett (1897–1965), professor of legal history in London; Harold Johnson, then principal assistant keeper and editorial director at the Public Record Office; and James Conway Davies (1891–1971), reader in palaeography and diplomatic in Durham. Conway Davies had arranged for Chaplais to give five classes in Durham, 1–5 March 1954, on 'English Medieval Diplomacy: Sources and Practice', which proved a success.[47] This was Chaplais's only teaching experience. He was elected to a lecturership at a salary of £1,200 per annum, toward the upper end of the available scale. Kathleen Major was one of those who wrote to congratulate him: 'I hope you will enjoy yourself as much as I have done. It is one of the most rewarding and interesting of posts, I think, and I am glad you are to have it.'[48] In 1957 Galbraith's recommendation got him promoted to the top point of the reader scale, then £1,650 per annum with the expectation of upward revision.[49] University appointments were made for seven years at a time then, and Chaplais was re-elected in 1962 by means of a letter circulated between the five current electors for their assent. Under a new statute he was re-elected until the retiring age in April 1963, and in February 1964 he was allowed for the first time the privilege of an office in one of the houses in Wellington Square.

* * *

[46] G. W. S. Barrow, 'Kathleen Major 1906–2000', *Proceedings of the British Academy*, 115, *Biographical Memoirs of Fellows*, I (2002), 319–29 (p. 322).

[47] J. Conway Davies to PC, 7 March 1954: 'While thanking you most sincerely for the seminars, on behalf of my department, may I congratulate you on your enticing and provocative methods of conducting them, which made all a part of the class, participating fully in discussion and deliberation.'

[48] Kathleen Major to PC, 16 June 1955. The letter also offered to show him the teaching collection of facsimiles, seal casts, and books.

[49] V. H. Galbraith to Kenneth Turpin, Secretary of Faculties, 4 Feb. 1957.

This new appointment brought new duties. Chaplais was required to lecture twice weekly every term and to cover diplomatic, primarily for students of English history, over the whole of the medieval period. He began at once to equip himself. Teaching was the driving factor in his becoming the foremost exponent of English royal diplomatic since W. H. Stevenson (1858–1924).

Anyone who has regard for chronology must be struck by the fact that, only two years after his appointment and with no previous interest in the subject, Chaplais co-authored a distinctly innovative work, *Facsimiles of English Royal Writs to A.D. 1100 presented to Vivian Hunter Galbraith*, edited by T. A. M. Bishop and P. Chaplais, produced by the Clarendon Press in 1957. This collaboration was a turning-point for Chaplais, and the circumstances merit unravelling. Galbraith's studio portrait at the front, a 'select' listing of his publications between 1911 and 1957, and a list of more than three hundred subscribers are the only outward signs that this was a Festschrift. The honorand is quoted briefly at the close of the Introduction, but there are no personal tributes. A preface of formal acknowledgements gives only one hint of the background, paying thanks 'in a special measure to Professor C. R. Cheney and Mr R. W. Southern without whom this book would not have come into existence'. Bishop himself tells us that he had attended Galbraith's classes in diplomatic at Oxford. This was presumably during the academic year 1932–3, when he was employed in the department of western manuscripts in the Bodleian between schoolmastering at Glenalmond and postgraduate work with Eileen Power in London.[50] He had had a year teaching at Balliol, replacing Richard Southern in 1946–7, before going to Cambridge as reader in palaeography and diplomatic.[51] Christopher Cheney had been Reader in Diplomatic in Oxford, teaching briefly before the war and more briefly after it before going as professor to Manchester.[52] He joined Bishop in Cambridge in 1955. Were Southern and Cheney responsible for bringing Bishop and Chaplais together to undertake this slim volume of thirty facsimiles of original documents and seals, with facing transcriptions and

[50] Bishop, *Scriptores Regis*, p. [iii]: 'For the idea of the book, which arose in his classes in Diplomatic, and for the Preface which he has now written to it, I am deeply grateful to Professor V. H. Galbraith.' If my dating is correct, the idea predates the appearance of Richard Drögereit's discussion of tenth-century royal scribes in his dissertation, 'Gab es eine angelsächsische Königskanzlei?', *Archiv für Urkundenforschung*, 13 (1935), 335–436.

[51] D. Ganz, 'Terence Alan Martyn Bishop 1907–1994', *Proceedings of the British Academy*, 111 (2001), 397–410 (at p. 400).

[52] C. N. L. Brooke, 'Christopher Robert Cheney 1906–1986', *Proceedings of the British Academy*, 73 (1987), 425–46.

commentary, and a highly compressed but brilliant introduction? In Chaplais's case this book would appear to have been undertaken from a standing start.[53] Bishop, on the other hand, had already been many years at work on royal scribes; his book, *Scriptores Regis. Facsimiles to identify and illustrate the hands of royal scribes in original charters of Henry I, Stephen, and Henry II*, was published in 1961. The idea for that book arose in Galbraith's diplomatic classes, he tells us, in an uncharacteristically loquacious paragraph of acknowledgements; it profited 'from a collaboration with Mr Pierre Chaplais, in which the advantage was very much on my side'; Cheney encouraged him to think his work was worth publishing; and Galbraith wrote a foreword, mentioning that 'at least twenty years of patient collecting and reflection have gone into this book'. Bishop was the palaeographer skilled in recognising the work of individual royal scribes, Chaplais already had experience of examining seals with equal attention to detail, but *English Royal Writs* is his first published work on documents such as these and his first to discuss script: none the less, judged against other work by the two authors, this book reads like Chaplais more than Bishop. In attention to accuracy in every detail, they were men of like mind—and different temperament—who must have come to agreement on everything that went into the book. Barbara Harvey, Pierre's friend for fifty years, recalls his saying that, when he began the collaboration, he thought those who had said Bishop was difficult were wrong but over time he changed his mind.

In the few years between *English Royal Writs* and *Scriptores Regis* Chaplais published two fundamental articles. 'The seals and original charters of Henry I', *English Historical Review*, 75 (1960), for the first time made clear the relevance of the seals both to dating and to testing the authenticity of the charters of that king, for which an unsatisfactory calendar had appeared as recently as 1956.[54] More surprisingly, in 'Une charte originale de Guillaume le Conquérant pour l'abbaye de Fécamp', published in a local volume for the thirteen-hundredth anniversary of the

[53]That start may have predated his appointment at Oxford, for Barbara Harvey recalls encountering Chaplais in Westminster Abbey Muniments, at work on the original writs of Edward the Confessor, both authentic and false, some months before their first meeting at the Galbraiths' house in Oxford in Michaelmas 1955.

[54]Charles Johnson and H. A. Cronne, *Regesta regum Anglo-Normannorum* ii *Regesta Henrici primi 1100–1135* (Oxford, 1956). This book was drafted by Johnson before the war, and the acknowledgements suggest little or no engagement with anyone working in the field thereafter. It was reviewed by PC in *Revue belge de philologie et d'histoire*, 35 (1957), 883–5. Chaplais's copy, presently in my keeping, is enriched with photographs of many of the charters that survive as originals.

abbey, Chaplais presented the Norman evidence for the earliest recognised royal scribe of the Anglo-Norman period, who worked for William I and William II.[55] Bishop's *Scriptores Regis* begins with a scribe i, who worked for William II and Henry I, but Bishop and Chaplais discuss this earlier scribe in *English Royal Writs*. Chaplais would refer to him as 'scribe nought' (he might remind those familiar with *Scriptores Regis* that this should be a lower case roman nought). I never put the question to Pierrre, 'Why did Bishop not extend *Scriptores Regis* earlier to include this one scribe?' It looks as if this discovery was a case of Chaplais's going one better than his colleague's long-term work.

A third person in the collaboration was the honorand himself. There was meant to have been another volume, *Facsimiles of Norman and Anglo-Norman Charters*, edited by V. H. Galbraith and P. Chaplais, 'à paraître à Oxford en 1962', which is cited by Mme Marie Fauroux in her *Recueil des actes des ducs de Normandie de 911 à 1066* (Caen, 1961: 15), and with plate-numbers in the source-notes of some documents. Her acknowledgements scarcely offer an explanation.[56] And Chaplais's own enthusiastic review archly says, 'One could have wished for illustrations, though it is understood that some of the original charters are to be included in a collection of facsimiles of Norman and Anglo-Norman charters by Professor V. H. Galbraith and Mr P. Chaplais to be published this year.'[57] Prints of the photographs, facing transcripts, and some commentary still exist, but the work was never completed. On one of the envelopes in which the draft is contained Pierre added dates to the title: it was to cover the years 1006 to 1135, embracing, therefore, Norman material from the reign of Henry I.[58] Permission to reproduce was refused for two of the documents, however, and there may have been difficulties arising from the cost of producing sixty plates in a large format. Galbraith's contribution is not now detectable; it may have been inspiration and conversation, but Pierre was

[55] 'Une charte originale de Guillaume le Conquérant pour l'abbaye de Fécamp: la donation de Steyning et de Bury (1085)', in *L'Abbaye bénédictine de Fécamp. Ouvrage scientifique du XIIIe centenaire 658–1958* (Fécamp, 1959), i. 93–104.

[56] 'M. Chaplais [...] a bien voulu me signaler plusieurs documents conservés en Grande-Bretagne' (p. 10). Mme Fauroux, daughter of Jacques Le Roy Ladurie (1902–88), briefly 'ministre de l'agriculture et du ravitaillement' in the Vichy government but from the beginning of 1943 active in the Resistance, and sister of Emmanuel Le Roy Ladurie, had studied with Michel de Boüard in Caen before compiling a catalogue of ducal acts for her thesis, directed by Georges Tessier at the École des chartes in 1950.

[57] *Journal of the Society of Archivists*, 2 (1960–4), 324–5.

[58] This is further alluded to in his review of the *Regesta* volume, published at the end of 1957: 'Nous espérons qu'il nous sera possible un jour de présenter ces originaux sous forme de fac-similes.'

clear that it was a joint undertaking. Another collaboration with Galbraith, to produce a guide to English documents from the earliest times to the thirteenth century, was never more than a good idea.[59] Galbraith is the one direct link between Bishop's independent work on royal scribes, the volume written in collaboration with Chaplais, and Chaplais's own work. The books also share an emphasis on reproducing original documents, which had played no part in Chaplais's earlier work but became central to his mature work in diplomatic.

Within very few years of his appointment at Oxford, Chaplais had transformed himself from an expert on the records of Gascony and more broadly on Anglo-French diplomacy to speak with a fresh authority on Anglo-Norman royal diplomatic. It was in 1960, in acknowledging an offprint of the paper on the Fécamp diploma, that Ganshof wrote: 'En vous lisant, je songeais à ce que mon maître Henri Pirenne nous disait avec insistance quand nous étions étudiants, de l'enrichissement constant et considérable que les travaux de diplomatique constituaient pour l'histoire proprement dite. Vos travaux apportent tous la preuve de la justesse de cette observation.'[60]

During the early 1960s an important paper appeared on the forgeries crafted at Westminster Abbey in the time of abbots Herbert and Gervase, in which Chaplais pointed the finger of accusation at Osbert of Clare.[61]

[59] Under the title *Nouum Formulare Anglicanum* the book first appears as Galbraith's in the Selden Society's Annual Report for 1951 and was mentioned in the first booklet listing publications and current members in 1952. Ten years later the council of the society 'received with pleasure Professor Galbraith's intimation that Dr P. Chaplais [...] would be joint editor of this volume with himself' (Annual Report 1961). In 1963 and 1965 it was advertised to members, now with a short description, which reveals that its coverage was intended to start much earlier than Thomas Madox's *Formulare Anglicanum* (1702):

> The object of this book is to plot the historical development of the Charter in England, and more especially the Royal Charter, from the earliest times until the 13th century. For this purpose it will draw on the results obtained by experts in specialised studies, though itself not a book on Palaeography or Diplomatic, but simply a book for historical students. Like Madox it will rely so far as possible on surviving originals rather than copies, chosen either as 'typical' or as indicating individual peculiarities. These charters reflect the habits of thought of the age in which they were written, and this very form, changing and growing across the centuries, is a neglected aspect of historical evolution. For they have been used, in general, merely for the dates and facts they contain. Two or three volumes are planned, one covering the time to the Norman Conquest or thereabouts, the second covering the 12th century.

It did not appear in the 1970 booklet. I never heard Pierre mention this project, but he would refer to Madox in his first lecture to his graduate class each year, 'he took great care to print in his *Formulare* original charters only'.

[60] F.-L. Ganshof to PC, 13 Feb. 1960.

[61] 'The original charters of Herbert and Gervase, abbots of Westminster (1121–1157)', in *A Medieval Miscellany for Doris Mary Stenton*, Pipe Roll Society new ser. 36 (1962), 89–110.

Other papers in both French and English came out that resulted from his continuing work on the reigns of the three Edwards, and the first and only volume of *Diplomatic Documents* finally issued from the Stationery Office in 1964. By then Chaplais had undertaken a new investigation.

* * *

His new research bore fruit in a series of articles on Anglo-Saxon royal diplomas, a form of document whose obvious formality but lack of formal authentication made it peculiarly challenging to someone with Chaplais's experience of well-organised administrative offices. By this date he was a master of diplomatic technique, and he was fascinated and frustrated by these diplomas. Frank Barlow (1911–2009), professor of medieval history in Exeter, had published an outspoken footnote, in which he said that 'no diploma is authentic in the technical sense'; rather they were to be judged as literary sources.[62] Such a notion is disconcerting to a diplomatist, but Chaplais found that, discussing Anglo-Saxon royal diplomas, W. H. Stevenson, who 'believed in diplomatic tests', none the less could be found 'arguing not a point of authenticity but one of veracity, as though he had been criticizing a chronicle'.[63] Chaplais's survey of the diplomas in favour of the monastery of Exeter, published in May 1966, belongs with four articles published between October 1965 and October 1969 in the *Journal of the Society of Archivists*, edited by Chaplais's friend, Albert Hollaender, an Austrian in exile. Their importance was recognised by the Society, which reprinted them in a volume to honour Hollaender's long editorship of the journal. These papers differ in a number of ways from his previous work. In particular, he knew that what he had to say here was controversial, and his acknowledgements show that he discussed his ideas, and perhaps his drafts, more widely than was the case with any other part of his work.

Already in 1957, Bishop and Chaplais observed that 'the names of several royal clerks have come down to us', but their role was judged to be unsupported by material evidence. Two examples of writs that may have been penned by others led them to say that 'the conclusion that the writing of at least some of our documents was left to the beneficiary cannot be avoided'. All that was secure was that sealing must have 'taken place in a royal office'.[64] While Bishop had identified dozens of later *scriptores*

[62] F. Barlow, *The English Church 1000–1066* (London, 1963), p. 127 n. 2.

[63] P. Chaplais, 'The authenticity of the royal Anglo-Saxon diplomas of Exeter', *Bulletin of the Institute of Historical Research*, 39 (1966), 1–34 (at p. 2).

[64] *Facsimiles of English Royal Writs*, pp. xii–xiii.

regis, Chaplais pursued the idea, supported by earlier Anglo-Saxon diplomas, that the writing of unsealed documents required no royal writing-office. Mary Parsons had long ago shown that the scribes from Canterbury Cathedral Priory had written diplomas.[65] And even earlier, Richard Drögereit, who elaborated on W. H. Stevenson's evidence for royal scribes from the reign of Athelstan, none the less posited a complete breakdown in the 950s.[66] Common features observed by Chaplais in the Exeter diplomas suggested local drafting. He developed this idea across a period from the seventh century to the eleventh. In the first of these papers he concluded that 'the diplomas of all the Anglo-Saxon kings were drawn up by ecclesiastics', arguing that in particular instances bishops could be shown to have composed the wording, and that they recruited scribes 'from among the personnel of near-by monastic communities'.[67] In the second he asserted that, despite the appearance of William the Conqueror's taking over a chancery from Edward the Confessor, 'there is not a shred of evidence that at any time between the seventh and the eleventh century Anglo-Saxon diplomas were drafted or written in what might be called, even loosely, a royal secretariat'.[68] The sealed writ, surviving in numerous examples from Edward's reign, was a different matter, but, rather than dealing with its emergence, he avoided the crucial point and sought instead to question the authenticity of the earliest writs, which survive only as copies. The first paper extrapolates from evidence of the tenth century, the second appears concerned to refute arguments to push the history of the writ back by a century from the reign of Aethelred II to that of Alfred. Neither paper makes a clear case that there never was an Anglo-Saxon royal chancery, and there is a reluctance to recognise change over time. The remaining papers in the series concerned very early material, ending with what was for Chaplais a remarkably speculative paper on the seventh

[65] Mary Prescott Parsons (1885–1971), 'Some scribal memoranda for Anglo-Saxon charters of the 8th and 9th centuries', *Mitteilungen des Österreichischen Instituts für Geschichtsforschung*, Erg. Bd. 14 (1939), pp. 13–32.

[66] W. H. Stevenson, 'An Old English charter of William the Conqueror in favour of St Martin's-le-Grand, London, AD 1068', *English Historical Review*, 11 (1896), 731–44; R. Drögereit (1908–77), 'Gab es eine angelsächsische Königskanzlei?' *Archiv für Urkundenforschung*, 13 (1935), 335–436. Drögereit gave an offprint to Galbraith, from whom it passed to Chaplais; it is now in Simon Keynes's possession.

[67] 'The origin and authenticity of the royal Anglo-Saxon diploma', *Journal of the Society of Archivists*, 3 (no. 2, Oct. 1965), 48–61 (quotations from pp. 61 and 59).

[68] 'The Anglo-Saxon chancery: from the diploma to the writ', *Journal of the Society of Archivists*, 3 (no. 4, Oct. 1966), 160–76.

century.[69] For a decade these papers held a defiant place in the field, confronting the prevailing suppositions of senior Anglo-Saxonists such as Stenton, Harmer, and Whitelock. Frank Stenton and Florence Harmer died in 1967, and Dorothy Whitelock's reactions were not committed to paper. Nicholas Brooks called these articles 'revolutionary', 'most revolutionary' for the tenth and eleventh centuries: 'No other scholar has ranged so widely over the entire field of pre-Conquest charters as Dr Chaplais,' he wrote, 'but his judgements may on occasion be too severe.' Brooks would later allow that Chaplais's view 'had become the prevailing interpretation', but this was for want of open challenge.[70] It was not until the late 1970s that the case for an Anglo-Saxon royal chancery was restated by Simon Keynes.[71] The study of Anglo-Saxon charters had taken a leap forward, but there was a counter-revolution.

* * *

Following the completion of this series of papers in 1969 the obvious phasing in Chaplais's published work comes to an end.

One distinctive book followed in 1971, very much the combined product of his background in the Public Record Office and his teaching. This was *English Royal Documents 1199–1461*, a slim volume of facsimiles of original documents and seals, with facing transcriptions and commentary, and a highly compressed but brilliant introduction. It illustrates the products, both internal and external, of the chancery in the later middle ages. Galbraith had come to the notice of Sir Henry Maxwell-Lyte (1848–1940) in the Record Office because of his skill in finding the references for documents deployed in the great man's *Historical Notes on the Use of the Great Seal of England* (London, 1926), and, as Reader in Diplomatic, his lectures included courses on the great seal and the smaller chancery seals. Chaplais continued that teaching tradition, accumulating photographs of documents for the purpose. This book for the first time made visible to those beyond his classroom some of the intricacies behind the increasing bureaucratisation of the seals. Hitherto the only available reproductions,

[69] 'Some early Anglo-Saxon diplomas on single sheets: originals or copies?', *Journal of the Society of Archivists*, 3 (no. 7, April 1968), 315–36; 'Who introduced charters into England? The case for Augustine', *Journal of the Society of Archivists*, 3 (no. 10, Oct. 1969), 526–42.

[70] N. P. Brooks, 'Anglo-Saxon charters: the work of the last twenty years', *Anglo-Saxon England*, 3 (1974), 211–33 (at pp. 215, 218, 220); reprinted in his *Anglo-Saxon Myths. State and Church 400–1066* (London, 2000), pp. 181–202, with a postscript, 'Anglo-Saxon charters, 1973–1998', pp. 202–15, in which he discusses the ensuing debate (quotation from p. 208).

[71] Simon Keynes, *The Diplomas of King Æthelred 'the Unready' 978–1016* (Cambridge, 1980).

designed to allow would-be readers to become familiar with the handwriting of the records, had been dominated by enrolments. Chaplais concentrated on original documents, including warrants addressed from one tier of bureaucracy to another, each with its own conventions. Even cancelled letters, retained in the mass of chancery files (C202), are retrieved (pl. 6a, 13b). Some of the plates were designed to illustrate the different methods of sealing used with the great seal, the privy seal, and the signet. Here Chaplais adopted the terminology of Jenkinson, who had described the several methods of attachment without relating them to the circumstances of their use. In his paper on Jenkinson's contribution, Chaplais justified the importance of such observation with an illustration all his own, taking three grades of diplomatic document, all sealed with the great seal, whose hierarchy was defined by the method of attachment and the colour of the wax.[72] In the book he brings to visible life the administration of late medieval England, thereby enlightening the reader needing to study great works such as Maxwell-Lyte's own or Tout's *Chapters on the Administrative History of England*. Its concision has never detracted from its value, but it is an aid to study, the fruit of much experience, rather than the working out of an argument from the records. One reviewer, recognising that the volume 'represents a major feat of exposition and compression', wished the author had expounded the link between changes of practice and the circumstances in which they occurred.[73] To do so, in line with Chaplais's standards of evidence, would have risked turning a useful aid to study into another vast enterprise that could not have been finished. The same reviewer, all unaware, picked up the one seemingly tendentious statement in the book: 'It does not seem wise to say without qualification (p. 45) that when Edward II acquired a new personal seal in 1312, the secret seal, this was done in order to replace the privy seal which he no longer controlled. The privy seal,' says Bertie Wilkinson, a student of Tout's, 'did not really escape from the king's control, though it did cease to be his personal seal.' He has read the remark in terms of the progressive distancing of the seals from the king's person, but Chaplais had in mind the precise historical circumstances in which Edward II's enemies sought to block his use of the privy seal. Tout himself had worked out the date of

[72] Jenkinson, *Guide to Seals in the Public Record Office*, 14–21; Chaplais, 'The study of palaeography and sigillography in England: Sir Hilary Jenkinson's contribution' p. 48 (see above, n. 31).
[73] Bertie Wilkinson (1898–1981), *Speculum*, 48 (1973), 122–3. There is a brief memoir of him in *Speculum*, 57 (1982), 708–10.

introduction of the secret seal but not the explanation for it.[74] Chaplais would devote a book to exploring the political importance of control of the seals in this period, but that was not written until more than twenty years later.

After 1971 Chaplais's publications became a mixture of dealing with work backlogged from years ago and, from time to time, bringing out an article to set out some discovery or interpretation first arrived at, one suspects, many years before. We have mentioned *English Medieval Diplomatic Practice* above. And in 1968 Chaplais had signed a contract with Ernest Benn Ltd for a book in their proposed series 'Contours of European History'. He treated this as an opportunity at last to publish his thesis, proposing the title *Royal Sovereignty in English Gascony 1259–1453* and composing a fresh synposis. No more was done, and the plan was firmly dropped in 1974. There were essays contributed to volumes in honour of his predecessor in office, Kathleen Major (1971), his colleague May McKisack (1971), his old friend Édouard Perroy (1973), and his counsellor on all things to do with Anglo-Saxon script, Neil Ker (1978). The only other articles he published between 1970 and 1985, 'Master John Branketre and the office of notary in chancery, 1355–1375' (1971), and 'Henry II's reissue of the canons of the council of Lillebonne of Whitsun 1080' (1973), both for the Society of Archivists, may have come to fruition on their own. While the former was in press, Chaplais appears to have failed to satisfy an earnest request from Albert Hollaender that, 'as an outstanding contributor and dear friend', he find something for the jubilee issue of the *Journal of the Society of Archivists*.[75] Nothing was forthcoming on this occasion.

* * *

Over the previous twenty years, Chaplais had gradually progressed from an exile in search of a role to a member of the English academic establishment. His professional activities were never taken lightly. Elected to the

[74] T. F. Tout, *Chapters in the Administrative History of Mediaeval England* (Manchester, 1920–33), ii. 286–90, v. 164–70.

[75] A. E. J. Hollaender to PC, 18 Dec. 1970. Offprints of John de Branketre were despatched with a letter, 20 April 1971, containing a reminder, 'Have you thought about a subject for your contribution to the *Journal* "festschrift" next April??? I *very* much hope that *some* kind of token from you will, as on so many occasions in the past, adorn our *Journal*.' On 23 April 1971 Hollaender acknowledged Pierre's instant reply, proposing a paper on the diplomatic activities of the protonotary in chancery from medieval to modern times, and stressed the need to have the typescript by 1 October 1971.

Royal Historical Society in 1953, he became, with what seems precipitate haste, literary director in succession to Denys Hay in 1958.[76] His demand for accuracy extended to this role. Barbara Harvey tells how he insisted on meeting her in the muniments at Westminster Abbey, where he took it as part of his editorial duty to check her transcriptions for the Camden series volume, *Documents illustrating the rule of Walter de Wenlok, Abbot of Westminster, 1283–1307*, Camden 4th ser. 2 (1965). One such meeting was sufficient in this case. He was reputed even to verify the footnotes of the *Transactions*, whatever period of history was concerned. And on his watch appeared the second edition of the indispensable *Handbook of British Chronology*: although not so challenging as the first edition, the revision was a complex undertaking. Hay, knowing what the task involved, wrote, 'My heart bleeds for you when I think of the *Handbook of British Chronology*.'[77] And Christopher Cheney, though sympathising with the trouble it caused, continued to send corrections to the last possible moment.[78] Pierre would surely have done the same. When he resigned as literary director in 1964, it took two to replace him. One of them was Geoffrey Barrow, who had taken Kathleen Major's course in Oxford and joined the Council in 1963. He reports how immensely thorough Pierre was in handing over the literary director's job to two tiros.[79]

Later in his career he was an influential member of the joint committee formed by the Royal Historical Society and the British Academy to direct a new edition of all Anglo-Saxon charters. In 1965 he had observed that W. H. Stevenson in 1895 and Sir Frank Stenton in 1955 had both identified the want of a really serviceable edition as an obstacle to the understanding of such documents: 'Without a critical and exhaustive edition of the Anglo-Saxon diplomas, no definitive study of their diplomatic can be contemplated.'[80] This was contested in early discussions during

[76] PC kept the invitation from the president, Dom David Knowles, 27 March 1958. His official file in the university archives shows that he was permitted to receive an annual honorarium of £200 from the Society without adjustment to his salary. Denys Hay (1915–94) had studied with Galbraith in Oxford, and in 1958 he joined Goronwy Edwards as editor of the *English Historical Review*.

[77] Denys Hay to PC, 25 Jan. 1961.

[78] C. R. Cheney to PC, 28 Feb. 1960: 'I am sorry that the Committee harrassed you about the HBC—very unfairly and unnecessarily, I thought, for you cannot do all the editorial work which the editors have failed to do: there would be no end.' On 8 Dec. 1960, Cheney asked to amend the date when Roger Northburgh was provided to the see of Lichfield.

[79] G. W. S. Barrow, 30 May 2007.

[80] Chaplais, 'The origin and authenticity of the royal Anglo-Saxon diploma', *Journal of the Society of Archivists*, 3 (1965–9), 49, citing Stevenson, *The Crawford Collection of Early Charters and Documents* (Oxford, 1895), p. viii, and F. M. Stenton, *The Latin Charters of the Anglo-Saxon Period* (Oxford, 1955), p. 9.

1964–5, but Harmer and Whitelock were outvoted, and Chaplais's view held sway.[81] The committee was formed in 1966; its membership comprised V. H. Galbraith, Francis Wormald, C. R. Cheney (the first chairman), Neil Ker, G. W. S. Barrow, Pierre Chaplais, and P. H. Sawyer (secretary until 1982). It is not hard to see that the driving force for the plan of the series was Chaplais himself. He thought diplomas had to be examined in their archival context, not only as the most appropriate means of understanding the substantive business but also as a necessary means of controlling the evidence for local drafting. By this date Peter Sawyer's *Anglo-Saxon Charters. An Annotated List and Bibliography* was in press with the Royal Historical Society—it appeared in 1968—and Sawyer undertook to edit the charters from the archive of Burton Abbey. Other editors were recruited, but progress was slow. The desire to see a new edition to the highest standards cannot of itself call such a thing into existence. By the time Pierre resigned from the committee in 1985 only Geoffrey Barrow remained active from the original membership and only two volumes had been published.

In 1975 Chaplais joined the Board of Studies in Palaeography, which had existed in the University of London since 1936.[82] This committee looked out for the concerns of the discipline nationally. He served for many years as a member of Council of the Pipe Roll Society, from 1977 until 1997; he resigned shortly before its first meeting held at Kew rather than at Chancery Lane.[83] The project to collect and edit English Episcopal Acta for the period before episcopal registers was launched by Christopher Cheney in 1973. The first volumes appeared in 1980 and 1986, and Pierre came on to the committee in 1984, serving until 1998.

On 30 April 1970 he was elected a Fellow of the Society of Antiquaries. Thirty years later he gave to the Society his collection of more than three hundred seals, signet rings, and ancient engraved gemstones.[84] The discovery of Richard I's signet ring delighted him.[85] The Commission internationale

[81] S. D. Keynes, 'Anglo-Saxon charters: lost and found', in J. Barrow and A. Wareham (eds.), *Myth, Rulership, Church, and Charters: Essays in Honour of Nicholas Brooks* (Aldershot, 2008), pp. 45–66 (at pp. 46–7), records the voting for and against the proposed new edition.

[82] T. J. Brown to PC, 5 March 1975. Brown mentions this board in his memoir, 'Francis Wormald 1904–1972', *Proceedings of the British Academy*, 61 (1975). 523–60 (at pp. 533–4).

[83] Barbara Dodwell to PC, 18 Feb. 1977; Paul Brand, 20 Dec. 2011.

[84] 'Anniversary Address 2001', *Antiquaries Journal*, 81 (2001), 1–14 (at p. 6): 'a collection of no fewer than 358 seals, generously given by our Fellow, Pierre Chaplais. They range from Mesopotamian specimens of the fifth millennium before Christ to a Japanese example later than the last War.'

[85] P. E. Lasko, 'The signet ring of King Richard I of England', *Journal of the Society of Archivists*, 2 (1960–64), 333–5. Dame Joan Evans gave the ring to the British Museum.

de diplomatique was formally established in 1970, led by Giulio Batelli (1904–2005), Robert-Henri Bautier (1922–2010), and Carlrichard Brühl (1925–97). Pierre Chaplais was a foundation member. Geoffrey Barrow accompanied him to Madrid in 1978 and Rome in 1979 for the meetings of the Commission: 'Pierre was absolutely splendid, because he refused point-blank to allow Bautier to dominate, effectively blocking our chairman's proposal that all proceedings should be in French.'[86] He became a Fellow of the British Academy in 1973 and in 1979 he was appointed a Corresponding Fellow of the Medieval Academy of America, in the same year as Bautier.

* * *

Michael Jones and Malcolm Vale opened the volume of essays presented to Chaplais in 1989 with these words:

> For over thirty years the classes held by Pierre Chaplais on diplomatic and palaeography served as the main introduction to research at Oxford for most post-graduates pursuing medieval history. [...] Whether in the formal surroundings of the History Faculty Library or in private conversation, he has shown remarkable patience and unflagging encouragement for the endeavours of countless beginners. His generosity with his time, not simply to those he was officially supervising, but for all those who brought their problems to him, has been prodigious.

The role of the Reader in Diplomatic has always been to inculcate the skills necessary for engagement with primary sources at the parchment face. The focus was very much on English documents and in particular on the public records. Pierre worked in tandem with successive readers in palaeography, N. R. Ker (who retired in 1968) and William Urry (who died in post in 1981 without replacement). They relied on a collection of books and reproductions first brought together for this purpose when Reginald Lane Poole was in post. Miss Major had further built up the collection, housed at first with the Maitland Library in Room 12 of the Examination Schools, moved in 1957 to a new History Faculty Library in Merton Street, and from 1975 in the Powicke Room of the History Faculty in Broad Street, where Pierre was able for the first time to have an office convenient for his teaching and his college. The coming of the xerox machine transformed his work, making it possible for the students to take away copies of the reproductions of original manuscripts that formed the

[86] G. W. S. Barrow, 30 May 2007.

backbone of his teaching. In the second half of his time as Reader research yielded to teaching, and for many of his students there are happy memories of a very large table covered with books, photos, and xeroxes, searching for the perfect illustration of his point. Marie Therese Flanagan writes, 'He had such a light touch that he made diplomatic seem accessible and possible and was always very positive and encouraging. It was also fun.' In the same vein, Emilie Amt wrote that 'Those classes are among my fondest memories of Oxford. He was an unfailingly generous teacher and a lovely person.' It is a token of how much these classes meant to Pierre that he kept the sheets of paper passed round at the first class of each year for his students to sign in with a brief indication of their topics, retaining them even after he gave up his filing cabinets upon retirement. Four years after that Pierre took on one last doctoral candidate, working on one of his old projects, the royal Anglo-Saxon diplomas of Exeter: Charles Insley looks back on their fortnightly sessions in the Powicke Room, 'those meetings were a real voyage of discovery, taking me into the realms of Papal, Ottonian, and Carolingian diplomatic', all of them topics on which Pierre rarely taught and never published. There was always more to his knowledge than one was likely to find in the ordinary course of business. He was often in Duke Humfrey, then the reading room for manuscripts and early printed books as well as home to the antiquarian and topographical collections. The rustle of his 'mac' presaged a greeting, a warm smile, an inquiry about whatever manuscript was on one's desk, and the risk of a long discussion. His readiness to help was unlimited. As Cliff Davies has written, 'Anybody consulting him on, for instance, some small problem in medieval Latin finds himself spending the whole morning going over the document in all its ramifications and is subject thereafter to frequent inquiries about the progress of that piece of research.'

* * *

After the important paper in Neil Ker's Festschrift in 1978, much time was taken up with finally seeing into press the two volumes of *English Medieval Diplomatic Practice*, which appeared in 1982. Three late papers followed, which highlight the difference between the younger and the older Chaplais. He was accustomed to pursuing his own investigation, having regard only for the documents and not for what other historians may have thought. He knew that his views on Anglo-Saxon charters were controversial, but he was unsettled to find his conclusion that there was never an Anglo-Saxon royal chancery called into question. Pierre could not reconsider his position in the light of new arguments. He used the opportunity of a volume in honour of his friend Ralph Davis (1918–91) to respond with 'The royal Anglo-Saxon "chancery" revisited', published in 1985. 'If we are to find an answer at all to the question of the existence or otherwise of a royal chancery in the tenth century, we must turn once again to the documents which the office is supposed to have produced, that is to say the diplomas': the argument, however, is as much external as internal.[87] He estimated the time it would take to write the diplomas resulting from a *witenagemot* three or four times a year and concluded that a royal chancery would have work for barely one month in the year; 'Anglo-Saxon kings did not find it necessary or economic to set up a royal chancery in order to deal with Latin charters.' Some diplomas provide internal indications that they were composed by bishops, and he drew the inference that such men could not write the diplomas during the course of the meeting. The two arguments are almost inconsistent, but he had a conviction that there was no royal writing office. If bishops did some drafting, so, he thought, did monastic scribes, and that produced drafting features characteristic of their own particular house. Hence the importance he attached to approaching diplomas by archive. This thinking fed into another late paper on the writing of Great Domesday Book. Well aware of Galbraith's work on this subject, and stimulated by recent palaeographical papers from Michael Gullick, Alexander Rumble, and Teresa Webber, he constructed a persuasive argument that William of Saint-Calais, bishop of Durham, was 'the man behind the Survey'. In arguing this case, two new perspectives emerge in relation to his earlier Anglo-Norman work. He now thinks that the earliest identified scribe working for William I and William II was the *only* scribe working for the king—something that can surely be disproved from witness lists.[88] And in the case of the Pyrford writ for Westminster Abbey, witnessed by Bishop William and dated 'after the survey of all England', he now sees in the hand and sealing signs that the scribe worked for the bishop rather than the king.[89] In this case he is probably correct, a judgement endorsed by Michael Gullick, but that does not go against the existence of a royal chancery. In almost every respect this

[87] 'The royal Anglo-Saxon "chancery" revisited', in *Studies in Mediaeval History presented to R. H. C. Davis* (London, 1985), pp. 41–51.

[88] 'William of Saint-Calais and the Domesday Survey', in J. C. Holt (ed.), *Domesday Studies* (Woodbridge, 1987), pp. 65–77 (at p. 71). He dated to *c.*1095 the increase in the number of royal scribes from one to two. Yet the Bath diploma, written by the one recognised scribe, names eleven members of the chapel royal alongside the chancellor.

[89] 'Consistent with what one would expect from a Durham scribe' (ibid., p. 76).

paper shows Chaplais's mind as sharp as ever and applied to material on which he had never before published. But in these two points one sees an *idée fixe* peep through. His third late paper, 'The spelling of Christ's name in medieval Anglo-Latin: *Christus* or *Cristus*?', published with the ever friendly Society of Archivists, was very much the working out of another *idée fixe*. And it was disagreement over this that saw him resign from the Anglo-Saxon Charters Committee in 1985.

He would turn back to work that had engaged him long years before. King Edward II used his privy seal to promote and reward his close friend Piers Gaveston, and warrants under the privy seal refer to him by the title Earl of Cornwall in 1308. This was a rather special earldom with powers and resources that made the Crown ordinarily keep it in royal hands. Edward II's Council, with whom he was at loggerheads, controlled the great seal, and acts drafted in Gaveston's favour consistently deny him the title of Earl of Cornwall.[90] Hardly anyone but Chaplais would have handled the actual documents, none would so consistently have sought out the warrants behind the letters patent, but Chaplais had already worked closely on the privy seal. The contrast set in train a line of thinking about Edward II, Gaveston, and what Conway-Davies called the baronial opposition.[91] Chaplais saw the working out of that opposition through competition for the control of the seals; when Council controlled the great seal, the king used his privy seal; his losing control of that, after Gaveston's death, led to the use instead of his secret seal or signet, emerging in 1312. In the precise wording of the documentary evidence Chaplais found grounds for thinking that the king and Gaveston had adopted one another as brothers. This came out as a short book in 1994, and its publication attracted more attention than Chaplais was used to, because it was seen as arguing against those who saw them as gay lovers. It was the last substantial work he was able to complete.

* * *

When Pierre took up his appointment in Michaelmas 1955, he stayed with the Galbraiths at 1 Garford Road for several days each week until a house was found for Doreen and the boys to move into Oxford.

[90] *Piers Gaveston: Edward II's Adoptive Brother* (Oxford, 1994), pp. 45–9.

[91] J. Conway-Davies, *The Baronial Opposition to Edward II, its Character and Policy. A study in administrative history* (Cambridge, 1918), pp. 158–63, intent on the bureaucratic record, missed the circumstances and reasons for the emergence of the secret seal.

Oxford cannot have been an easy place for him. The memory still rankled forty and fifty years later how during that first term he was persistently chaffed by the Clerk of the Schools, not in the friendliest way, about the fact that he could not be properly gowned for his classes until Congregation passed the decree to award him an MA; the *Gazette* reveals that this did not happen until 29 November. Although as reader Pierre held a university office, there was no obligation on any college to offer him a fellowship, and for nine years none did. There were early contacts with Balliol, where the medieval history tutor, R. W. Southern, was already well known to Pierre. At the end of 1957 Pierre was asked if he would take on a share of teaching at Balliol—on what terms is unrecorded—but he declined, saying that he had already as much work as he could handle in fulfilling his obligations in diplomatic.[92] It was through Lawrence Stone (1919–99), then history tutor at Wadham, that Pierre was invited to become a member of common room there. Galbraith's prompting has been suspected, but Pierre would deny that Stone was targeted because his wife Jeanne was the daughter of the French historian Robert Fawtier.[93] It was only in 1964 that he was made a fellow as part of a push to absorb such people into the college system.

The isolation was more acute for Doreen, an intelligent person confined to a well-ordered domestic life. The collegiate university tended to exclude wives, and the wife of someone who was not a college fellow was doubly excluded. Jeanne Stone, as one of her few contacts with the university world, was unintentionally a problem: not an academic but formidable in her own way, she had an air of rather loudly disapproving of everything around her. And there was a tendency even away from high tables for conversation to be competitive. In 1963 the family moved away from Oxford to settle at Wintles Farm House, 36 Mill Street, Eynsham, where Doreen was able to establish her own sense of community and Pierre set about cultivating his first Oxfordshire vines.[94] His rate of work

[92] Inferred from a letter from the Master of Balliol, Sir David Lindsay Keir, 12 Dec. 1957, who acknowledges Pierre's declining of the offer.

[93] Fawtier had spent seven years in Manchester, employed by the John Rylands Library and also lecturing on French history and French institutions at the university (Hubert, 476). Between January 1919 and February 1921 Galbraith was employed as a temporary lecturer at Manchester, but he appears to have spent most of the time on research in London (R. W. Southern, 'Vivian Hunter Galbraith 1889–1976', *Proceedings of the British Academy*, 64 (1978), 397–425, at pp. 404–5). I have not been able to establish whether they got to know one another in England.

[94] Pierre's oenological interests were entirely focused on French wine, and there was presumably some legacy of his early background in his lasting fondness for the unfashionable *gros plant du pays nantais*.

remained demanding, however, and Doreen would say that if Pierre did not resume work after supper she knew there was something wrong. In his fifties the self-imposed pressure slackened, and gardening became an obsession. In Wadham he was for many years keeper of the gardens, a role in which he cheerfully battled with Renée Hampshire, wife of the warden. His ambition to plant trees eventually outgrew the available space, and in 1978 Pierre and Doreen left Eynsham and its thundering gravel lorries for an exposed location between Bampton and Lew. Here he had all the land he needed, and much effort went into starting and managing his plantation. Trouble with his eyes soon began to impinge on rural life as well as on scholarship. A detached retina, treated too late, was the beginning of an increasing impairment of his vision. It soon meant an end to the yellow Triumph Spitfire that he had so enjoyed driving, and he became dependent on Doreen's driving him to catch a bus to Oxford and picking him up on the return. The isolation at Lew did not suit her. After a serious illness there in 1987—it was around the time of Pierre's retirement dinner in June—she would spend extended periods away. Her father Percy Middlemast had been a bank clerk on Tyneside, and she came to inherit a house of her own in Whitley Bay, where she could cultivate her own life in friendly surroundings.

Retirement in 1987 took away the office in the history faculty library and forced a large-scale weeding of his personal files. It put an end to the teaching that had mattered so much to him. But the cultivation of his land at Lew had been planned as a fresh interest for him, and there was still writing to do. After the completion of *Piers Gaveston*, however, he found it increasingly difficult to bring other planned work to publication, and he was increasingly troubled by his failing sight. Visits to Oxford became rare. Doreen's last illness kept him at her side, and she died on 2 July 2000, a few days before Pierre himself turned eighty. He lived on, mostly alone, at Lew for a further six years. Short-term memory loss became a concern at the end, and it was the side-effects of medication for this that put him in hospital. He died within a few days on 26 November 2006.

* * *

With no visible training Pierre had become the best reader and interpreter of difficult and damaged medieval documents. He had studied so much unpublished material, and in depth, that his perception of the writing of the king's letters and the uses of his seal was surely closer to a real understanding of the documents in context than anyone, before or since, has achieved. A reviewer of Pierre's last book spoke of 'the exploration of a field of inquiry into which the writer has unique insight that transcends everything that has previously been written on a particular subject'.[95] His work on the procedures of diplomacy was an edifice built on primary evidence and first principles. He engaged with the public records, and the administration that created them, at a level that surpassed all official expectations. His work on English royal charters and seals was entirely self-generated and put to shame almost all earlier work in the field. Method in England had not been much regarded, and Pierre appeared to many as a rigorously trained Chartiste, but he was not at all.[96] In his late twenties he had discovered in himself a natural ability to deal with difficult documents and he worked hard to cultivate it. The trained mind, he would say, reads what the eye does not see.[97] Finding the right document and appraising it with a trained eye and mind would, he thought, be sure to unlock a historical problem.

He showed little or no interest in historical argument or historiography. What historians may have thought about a problem was always subordinate to his own power to open up the documentary evidence. Historians of an earlier generation were neither venerated nor decried. In his own time, personal principles matter more than the to and fro of debate. He thought it discourteous to say that someone's opinions were mistaken, even when it was necessary for the progress of the discipline. Was this perhaps a throwback to the ways of French academic life in the 1930s? Or a reflection of his sense of obligation to those who had helped him in the early stages of his career? Galbraith revelled in debate and would not have inculcated such a principle of respect for seniority, right or wrong. Yet so adamant was Pierre about this that it comes as a real surprise to find in his own 1962 essay on the work of Hilary Jenkinson a whole series of mildly worded but cumulative negatives.[98] As he grew into

[95] N. C. Vincent, *Journal of British Studies*, 44 (2005), 922–3.

[96] Even Kathleen Major fell into error on this point, 'The teaching and study of diplomatic in England', *Archives*, 8 (1967–8), 114–18 (at p. 117).

[97] For example, A. J. Robertson, *Anglo-Saxon Charters* (Cambridge, 1956), p. 382, refers to the 'series of capital letters, cut in half', on the edge of a *placitum* in Old English (S 1454), without offering an interpretation; from the tops of the letters, Chaplais read it, realising that the letters of the expected word, CIROGRAFUM, alternated with other letters, so as to read, when taken in two sequences, 'Cirografum pletum est' (S. D. Keynes, 'Royal government and the written word in late Anglo-Saxon England', in R. D. McKitterick (ed.), *The Uses of Literacy in Early Medieval Europe* (Cambridge, 1990), pp. 226–57, at p. 250 n. 94; PC to Simon Keynes, 19 Sept. 1984).

[98] 'Some errors of detail could not be avoided in pioneer work' (p. 44), 'here I fear I must disagree with the master' (p. 45), 'it must be admitted with regret' (p. 46), 'Jenkinson's choice of technical terms was not entirely satisfactory' (p. 49).

a senior status himself, he did not like to see any criticism by the young of their elders. None the less, he had his views on distinguished historians who were satisfied without understanding, or the ambition to understand, the documentary evidence in its physical reality. Nor did he approve of putting forward ideas to catch the attention of the reader rather than to reflect the evidence. His own judgements were always arrived at only after careful consideration, and his approach was always thorough. A phrase one often heard from Pierre was that someone 'worked too fast'.[99] This might cover anything from casual error to a deeper neglect of basic research. A roll of his eyes, however, and a shake of his head were as near as he was likely to come to revealing what he actually thought.

Martin Brett relates a telling story about an occasion when Pierre did not see the joke:

> I was reading the miracles of one of the Kentish princess-saints, and laughed out loud in Bodley. Pierre was passing, and hurried over to see what provoked it, so I pointed to the first line of the story: 'It happened one day that the archbishop of Canterbury was burning some old and useless charters . . . '.[100] Pierre's face set in stone, and he left me abruptly, saying over his shoulder: 'Martin, that is not remotely funny'. I vividly recall Pierre's stumping off down to Selden End and my wondering whether I had forfeited his good opinion for ever.

The destruction of charters, even in a twelfth-century story intended to signal saintly approval for the one that survived the flames—no doubt a recent forgery—was no laughing matter. More than that, Brett's apprehension that he had irrevocably forfeited Pierre's opinion was not without some foundation. It was possible to fall from grace. There was a stubbornness, an obstinacy, about Pierre, more noticeable towards the end of his career than earlier. Those who knew him over very many years have thought it must have been there all along, helping him to survive the concentration

[99] One would not expect him to say such a thing in print, but I find the phrase used in citing Mme Schnerb-Lièvre: 'she admitted that Colville had worked too fast' (Chaplais, 'Jean Le Fèvre', 203, referring to Schnerb-Lièvre, *Le Songe du vergier*, vol. i, p. lxxxv–lxxxvi, 'mais ici, Colville veut aller trop vite', and a half-dozen errors are mentioned).

[100] The text about the miraculous survival of one particular charter from the flames can be read in the Miracles of St Eadburga in Hereford Cathedral, MS P. VII. 6 (saec. XII^{med}), fol. 190r: 'Tempore quodam contigit beate Dorobernensis ecclesie archiepiscopum quam plures habere superuacuas et inutiles terrarum cartulas, quas in unum colligens ut igne illas deleret, arripuit ignorans cum prefatis cartulis etiam cartulam circumcingentem beate Edburge territorium, eamque simul cum aliis cuidam de astantibus ad comburendum dedit. Qui cum implere quod sibi fuerat imperatum studuisset, nullo pacto beate uirginis cartula in ignis calore potuit consumi, reliquis in momento ad fauillam usque redactis. Ac ille reuersus relicta adhuc in incendio cartula, nuntiauit mirabile factum pontifici.' The occasion would have occurred around 1963, when the manuscript may have been temporarily deposited in the Bodleian.

camp, driving him to long hours of toiling through documents with a will to find the answer to his question. Once he had made up his mind on any point, never lightly or hastily done, he was unlikely to change it. The word austere has come up several times. The outward Pierre was not at all austere, but his scholarship was austere, and it is hard to believe that the inner man was not more truly reflected in his scholarship than in his entertaining presence.

RICHARD SHARPE
Fellow of the Academy

Note. Pierre Chaplais left no memoranda with the Academy, but Cliff Davies drew on conversations with him for his account of Pierre's early life. Oxford University Archives hold Pierre's *curriculum vitae* and other papers concerning his appointment in Oxford. Such letters as Pierre kept and other personal papers, including his own copy of his Ph.D. thesis, are held by Wadham College archives. I am grateful to those who have shared their memories of Pierre or otherwise provided information, and in particular Paul Chaplais, Cliff Davies, Barbara Harvey, Emilie Amt, Geoffrey Barrow, Julia Barrow, Paul Brand, Martin Brett, Marie Therese Flanagan, Jean-Philippe Genet, Michael Gullick, William Hodges, Charles Insley, Michael Jones, Mary Moore, Victor Tunkel.

KENNETH DOVER

Kenneth James Dover
1920–2010

I: 1920–55

KENNETH DOVER was a towering figure in twentieth-century Greek scholarship and on the British academic scene: head of an Oxford college, Chancellor of the University of St Andrews, President of the British Academy. He was knighted for services to scholarship in 1977, and had many honorary degrees conferred upon him. His scrupulous and untiring scholarship, like everything else he did, was governed by one commanding passion: the love of truth and rational argument. Something like this might of course be said of any good scholar, but with Dover it means something special. His commitment to truth and his confidence in reason were both exceptionally strong and exceptionally public. This was the foundation on which his enduring achievement rests. It also occasionally led him into misunderstandings and controversy, most notably in the reactions to his remarkable autobiography, *Marginal Comment*. This was a work of his seventies, and will be considered in its place. For the moment, it is enough to say that it is an essential source. What follows could not have been written without it.

Kenneth James Dover was born on 11 March 1920, the only child of Percy Henry James Dover and Dorothy Healey. His father was a minor civil servant, his mother (to whom Kenneth always had a very great devotion) the daughter of two schoolteachers. They lived at Putney, in south-west London, and Kenneth's education began at a private day-school in

Biographical Memoirs of Fellows of the British Academy, XI, 153–175.

that area. In 1932, he won a scholarship to St Paul's, where he began Greek and, as he himself says, 'was now on course'.[1]

St Paul's was—and still is—one of the great classical schools of the country.[2] Of his teachers there, Kenneth appreciated most George Bean (d.1977) and Philip Whitting (1902–88). These were not ordinary schoolmasters; they were professional scholars with recognised expertise in specialist fields, George Bean as a traveller and archaeologist in Turkey,[3] Philip Whitting as a numismatist, at one time secretary to the Academy's Sylloge of British Coins Committee. Himself to become a devoted and ingenious teacher, Dover was always ready to acknowledge such debts. In the speech he made when he was presented with the Festschrift *Owls to Athens* in 1990,[4] he spoke not only of his schooolmasters but also of some who had taught him in the Army such technical or mathematical knowledge as an artillery officer needed, and also (above all) of his Balliol tutor, Russell Meiggs, to whose stimulating and passionate example he did indeed owe very much.

He went up to Balliol as the top classical scholar in 1938, won a Gaisford Prize in his first year, and collected his First in Mods in 1940. He then joined the Army, and served as a subaltern in an anti-aircraft battery in Egypt, Libya and Italy. He was mentioned in despatches in the Italian campaign, and incidentally acquired a good knowledge of Italian and Italian life. In October 1945 he was back in Balliol, but his long service had made a deep impression on him, and he kept up something of a military bearing, as though he did not want to put it all behind him. In later years, he would stress the experience it had given him of how 'ordinary' people think and feel, and he claimed to have found this useful in his work on the 'popular' morality of the Greeks.

The Balliol to which he returned was a lively place. The group reading Greats included several (myself among them—DAR) who went on to academic careers. Dover stood out. It was humbling to share tutorials with him, and hear his lucid, elegant and cogent essays, especially on Greek history. For it was Greek history, as purveyed by Russell Meiggs, and epigraphy, as offered in classes on the Athenian Tribute Lists by the visiting

[1] *Marginal Comment: a Memoir* (London, 1994), p. 15.

[2] In 1938, Cyril Bailey congratulated Dover on his Balliol scholarship as a fellow Pauline; in 1955 Dover could do the same for M. L. West.

[3] See the memoir by J. M. Cook prefaced to later editions of Bean's *Aegean Turkey* (London, 1989).

[4] E. Craik (ed.), *Owls to Athens: Essays on Classical Culture Presented to Sir Kenneth Dover* (Oxford, 1990).

professor B. D. Meritt, that most excited his enthusiasm. He was not so keen on Latin (and it may be that this indifference persisted), though a perfectly competent Latinist and Roman historian; and he was not inspired by either of his philosophy tutors, the scholarly Donald Allan and the unsystematic and highly individual Donald MacKinnon. This too *perhaps* had a sequel in Dover's materialist and rationalist critique of Plato, most clearly to be seen in his commentary on the *Symposium* (Cambridge, 1980). Anyway, he won the Ireland Prize Scholarship and got a First in Greats in 1947. He did it all despite the distractions of early married life, for he had married Audrey Latimer in March 1947; they were to be happily married for nearly sixty-three years. He then had a brief spell as a Harmsworth Senior Scholar at Merton, before being recalled to Balliol as Fellow and Tutor in Greek and Greek History in October 1948. Roman history was left to Russell Meiggs, Latin to W. S. Watt, who shortly afterwards moved to Aberdeen and was replaced by Gordon Williams, the very congenial colleague who would later follow Dover to St Andrews.

The seven years at Balliol (1948–55) were a busy time. For most of it he was also sharing (with me—DAR) the Mods teaching at Wadham. This was quite a heavy (and somewhat unpredictable) load. All the same, he made his mark in college affairs, becoming Senior Tutor at an unusually early age, and began his own scholarly work with much enthusiasm and industry. He was a great burner of midnight oil. He had, early in 1948, enrolled as a D.Phil. student, with Arnaldo Momigliano (his own choice) as his supervisor. (We were all fascinated by Momigliano's erudition and range, even if we found his English hard to follow.) Dover's idea was to fix the chronology of forensic speeches and comedies in the early fourth century BC, after the defeat of Athens in the Peloponnesian War. The thesis was soon abandoned: in those days, a thesis was not thought necessary, perhaps not even desirable, if one had other things to do. But he did produce out of it an important study of the order and authenticity of the speeches of Antiphon.[5] The other works of these Oxford years were his revision of J. D. Denniston's *Greek Particles* (Oxford, 1954) and a (still very valuable) contribution on Greek comedy to a collective volume edited by Maurice Platnauer and called *Fifty Years of Classical Scholarship* (Oxford, 1954). Dover's piece is outstanding. At the same time, seeds were sown of enterprises to be developed later. A brave inquiry by his pupil Robin Nisbet, who asked about the rules which led Dover to suggest a

[5] 'The chronology of Antiphon's speeches', *The Classical Quarterly*, 44 (1950), 44–60 (repr. in *The Greeks and their Legacy*).

rearrangement of something in his Greek prose, stimulated the research which led to *Greek Word Order* (Cambridge, 1960); and the need to give specialist lectures on Thucydides laid the foundations of some of his most important and lasting achievements. He later said that Thucydides was the author on whom he had spent most time.

All in all, the main lines of his future achievement were settled by the time he got the call to St Andrews in 1955. They were right to say that they had 'netted the complete Grecian'. His credentials as an accomplished scholar and a sympathetic interpreter of the creative, boisterous and litigious society of classical Athens were already established. They were strengthened as time went on, but his field of interest never changed or widened.

II: 1955–76

Several considerations motivated Dover's decision to accept the chair of Greek in St Andrews. He said himself that relations within the fellowship at Balliol in the early 1950s were not entirely congenial to him; he was also despondent about the possibility of achieving the reforms in Greats which he and a few others in Oxford favoured (see further in Section III below). He was therefore attracted to a university and a post which would allow him greater academic autonomy, including the power to shape a Greek syllabus more in his own image on both the literary and historical sides. In addition, he was sure that he and Audrey would be happy in Scotland, a country whose natural landscapes, especially in the Highlands, they both loved. And he saw St Andrews as a wholesome environment in which to bring up two young children.

These factors were all to weigh increasingly with him once he was settled in St Andrews. They contributed to the fact that by the time he received the (predicted) offer of the Regius Chair in Oxford, early in 1960, he was prepared—to the incomprehension of some—to turn it down for both academic and personal reasons. By that stage, moreover, he had already been elected, in 1959, as Dean of Arts in St Andrews (an office he would end up holding twice, during 1960–3 and 1973–5): a conspicuous sign in itself of just how quickly and substantially he became embedded in, and committed to, the larger frameworks of the institution he had joined.

Despite the distinction of previous holders of the St Andrews chair, among them the outstanding Platonist John Burnet and the eccentric

Canadian polymath H. J. Rose, Dover initially had few resources to work with in the Department of Greek. His only colleague at the outset was Ian Kidd, with whom he struck up an excellent relationship that would stand the test of time.[6] Douglas Young became a third member of the Department early in 1956, and in the 1960s further Hellenists were appointed. In the St Andrews system Dover's workload included many more formal lectures (as many as nineteen a week, spread across all four years of the Scottish undergraduate degree) than he had been previously used to; he said that he had to abandon his painstaking standards of preparation and resort to a more 'journalistic' approach. While he found his students less proficient, on average, than the ones he had taught in Oxford, he also started to discover that it gave him great satisfaction to draw the best out of those even of modest talent, provided they were motivated to work assiduously. Throughout his two decades in St Andrews Dover was consistently recognised as an inspiring and meticulous teacher. He possessed superb gifts of communication and was keen to share his knowledge with students, even if many of them found it hard not to regard him as a somewhat Olympian figure. From the late 1950s onwards, his reputation led to a rapid expansion in the numbers of those—predominantly from Scottish schools and many of them women—studying Greek at St Andrews.

Dover's success in building up the size and standing of the Department owed much to his willingness to distribute his energies equally between teaching and research. This was a hallmark of the central phase of his career. He expanded the syllabus, making sure that Aristophanes, the tragedians, Thucydides, and the orators all had their place in it. Ian Kidd would later describe him as having been 'restlessly eager to experiment with better ways of teaching his subject and extending its scope'. Under Dover's leadership, St Andrews was one of the first universities in Britain to introduce (in 1967) an *ab initio* course in Greek. This was a cause he believed in deeply, a vital means of widening access to Classics at a time when the numbers learning the languages at school were falling. Dover insisted on teaching the beginners himself; he even went so far (it became the stuff of local legend) as to enroll as a beginner in Russian so that he could try to understand better the needs and problems of his own students. He also wrote the beginners' Greek textbook himself. Its rather taxing methods (requiring students to discover many grammatical rules for themselves from examples) led to its eventual replacement by more gentle

[6] They would later establish the remarkable fact that during the battle of Monte Cassino in January 1944 Dover was involved in the bombardment of a German position where Kidd had recently been taken prisoner of war.

introductions, but its very existence was a symptom of his pedagogic zeal. It was entirely appropriate, on more grounds than one, when in 1974 Dover was chosen to chair the Joint Association of Classical Teachers' advisory panel which oversaw production of the very successful *Reading Greek* primer, an event which had a radical effect on maintaining the teaching of Greek in many British universities.

One reason Dover was always able to keep his teaching, administrative, and research duties in harmony was his ferocious (and lifelong) capacity for hard work. Colleagues would observe how he could switch, almost as soon as a class or meeting finished, into a state of intense concentration on his own projects. Between his arrival in St Andrews in 1955 and his departure to the Presidency of Corpus in 1976, those projects gradually assumed proportions which made Dover an internationally renowned Hellenist, one of the finest of his era anywhere in the world. In the seven years of his Fellowship at Balliol, he had started to lay the foundations, as noted earlier, for what would turn into a long-term configuration of six main areas of interest: Old Comedy and therefore especially Aristophanes, who appealed to Dover by his paradoxical combination of earthy realism with intricate poetic virtuosity; fourth-century Attic oratory, which interested him for both rhetorical-cum-literary and broader cultural reasons; Athenian moral and religious values, as seen above all through the lenses of both oratory and comedy (a perspective he had first adopted in his D.Phil. proposal of 1948); Greek sexual mores (he had noticed the lack of any serious scholarship on Greek homosexuality when lecturing on elegiac poetry for Mods during 1952–4); the *Histories* of Thucydides, an author with whose fastidious rationality he undoubtedly felt a close affinity; and, last but by no means least, the Greek language itself, particularly from the point of view of historical stylistics and with sustained attention not only to literary texts but also to the documentary material of Athenian inscriptions.[7]

When Dover moved to St Andrews, he was in the early stages of planning an edition of Aristophanes' *Clouds*, having abandoned earlier plans to edit *Frogs* (to which, however, he would much later return after all, publishing his commentary on it in 1993). He had devoted quite a bit of his time in the early 1950s to work on Old Comedy; at one stage he contemplated producing a new Oxford Classical Text of Aristophanes. His

[7] For a fuller account of the configuration and development of Dover's interests, see the memorial lecture by S. Halliwell, 'Kenneth Dover and the Greeks', available online at <https://risweb.st-andrews.ac.uk/portal/files/6870022/Dover_and_the_Greeks_web_.pdf>.

growing authority in this field was demonstrated by his contribution (already mentioned) to *Fifty Years of Classical Scholarship* in 1954 and by his survey of Aristophanic scholarship from 1938 to 1955, published in the journal *Lustrum* in 1957: both contain numerous shafts of insight, as well as a wide-ranging command of textual, theatrical, political and other issues. In the event, much of the work on *Clouds* was not carried out till the mid-1960s, though he was lecturing on the play in St Andrews earlier than that. When the edition eventually appeared in 1968, it set the standards for a new generation of Aristophanic scholarship, and not only in the English-speaking world. The text was edited incisively on the basis of a more careful examination of the manuscript tradition than any previously undertaken; the commentary was innovative in its treatment of stagecraft (Dover said he had tried to produce the play in his imagination), unprecedentedly explicit in its discussion of Aristophanic obscenity, and illuminating on almost all the intellectual and cultural questions raised by the comedy. As in all his work, Dover was supremely assured in his observations on the poet's language. He intended, in fact, to write a monograph on the language of Attic comedy: this never materialised, though he was later to write a number of important articles on the style of Aristophanes.

Another area in which Dover worked steadily throughout the 1950s, and which was to yield his first book, was the difficult and elusive topic of Greek word order. He was fascinated by the problem of how far any clear principles could be discerned behind the considerable freedom of word order which the highly inflected nature of Greek makes available to its users. This was an area where his comparative study of inscriptions bore fruit: variations even in simple documentary formulae enabled him to establish a basic analytical model which could then be adapted, and made more complicated, for the scrutiny of literary texts. *Greek Word Order*, which was published in 1960 (after the material had been presented in the Gray Lectures at Cambridge the previous year), is the most technical of his books, partly because of its employment of symbolic notation and statistical methods; but it is also masterly in its compressed, fine-grained reasoning. The work sheds light, in a way very few scholars could even have conceived of attempting, on lexical, syntactical and logical determinants of Greek word order. And it gives glimpses of what became a salient Doverian trait: a combination of philological precision with a nuanced sensitivity to the play of style in language.

By the time *Greek Word Order* appeared Dover was already embarked on a major new venture which was to prove a prime cause of delay in the completion of *Clouds*. The death in January 1959 of A. W. Gomme, formerly Professor of Greek in Glasgow, meant that his *Historical Commentary on Thucydides (HCT)* was left unfinished; three volumes had so far been published. Dover was invited to undertake completion of Gomme's magnum opus in collaboration with Anthony Andrewes, Wykeham Professor of Ancient History at Oxford. For the fourth volume of the commentary, Dover assumed prime responsibility for Books VI–VII of the *Histories*, on which he had already lectured at Oxford; he pressed ahead with his work on these while he was Visiting Lecturer at Harvard from September 1960 to January 1961. When, because of Andrewes' other commitments, the volume was held up (it appeared eventually in 1970), Dover published his own abridged editions of Books VI and VII, aimed principally at undergraduates, in 1965. The happy and mutually stimulating collaboration with Andrewes was rounded off in 1981 by the fifth and final volume of the *HCT*, covering Book VIII of the *Histories*: Dover's primary contribution to this was a long, probing appendix on 'strata of composition', including subtle sifting of the evidence for Thucydidean changes of mind. Producing this appendix, he later said, gave him 'more lasting satisfaction' than anything else he had written.[8]

Dover's relationship to Thucydides is central to his cast of mind as a Hellenist. The historian's austere intelligence, tough realism, and artfully disciplined use of words appealed profoundly to comparable strands in Dover's own make-up. Pondering Thucydides, moreover, sometimes reminded Dover of things he had experienced himself during wartime service in North Africa and Italy; this explains in part why he could not read the narrative of the Athenians' retreat from Syracuse in Book 7 of the *Histories*, even when he had done so numerous times before, without, as he put it, 'feeling the hair on the back of my neck stand on end'.[9] But he did not idolise the historian, any more than he did other Greeks: he could identify blindspots in him, firmly resisted the tendency to regard him as an 'authority', and often stressed how few of Thucydides' claims could be independently corroborated. A useful précis of Dover's views on Thucydides is provided by the 1963 pamphlet which he wrote for the *Greece & Rome* series of New Surveys in the Classics. But he never tired of revisiting the author later in his career: he would write a series of further articles on him in the 1980s.

Dover seems always to have been prepared to work on more than one demanding project simultaneously. Even while the continuation of

[8] *Marginal Comment*, p. 76.
[9] *The Greeks* (London, 1980), p. 35.

Gomme was running alongside the edition of *Clouds* in the 1960s, and amidst all his other duties (he was, among other things, co-editor of *Classical Quarterly* from 1962 to 1968), he found time from 1962 onwards to start developing some ideas about Plato's *Symposium*, as well as writing a very substantial and original paper on Archilochus in 1963 for a colloquium at the Fondation Hardt institute in Switzerland.[10] The Archilochus piece is arguably one of his finest individual articles. It adduced comparative material from preliterate song cultures (drawing on a knowledge of Pacific languages Dover had precociously cultivated in his teens) to enrich its case for insisting that interpretation of the poet's work, and of archaic Greek song more generally, needs to be fully alert to the possibilities of fictionalised personae, rather than treating first-person utterances in such texts as straightforwardly autobiographical.

The turn to Plato's *Symposium* was to have far-reaching repercussions for Dover's work. Ever since finishing Greats in 1947, he had acquired something of an aversion to philosophy, both ancient and modern; with just a few exceptions (including Aristotle's zoology and Xenophanes' radical questioning of anthropomorphic religion) he thought its concerns and procedures mostly arid. Plato in particular, with his idealist metaphysics and his critique of bodily pleasures, Dover found antithetical to his own outlook on life (which he summed up by calling himself 'an English empiricist to the core').[11] But he was never in any doubt about Plato's greatness as a prose writer. Since the *Symposium* is the most brilliantly written of all the dialogues, it was an obvious choice when Dover was required to teach some Plato. Soon, however, it was the work's homoerotic sensibility which started to preoccupy him. Thinking about the *Symposium* reinforced his conviction of the need for a new examination of Greek homosexuality and he began to form plans for a book on the subject. Invited to give three special lectures at University College London in 1964, Dover opted to discuss aspects of the *Symposium*. The lectures produced a trio of significant articles, one of which, 'Eros and nomos' (*Bulletin of the Institute of Classical Studies*, 1964), laid out the groundwork for an account of Athenian attitudes to sexual behaviour which would eventually be elaborated into the arguments of *Greek Homosexuality* (Cambridge, MA, 1978).

[10] J. Pouilloux and nine other authors, *Archiloque (Entretiens sur l'Antiquité Classique X)* (Geneva, 1963).

[11] *Marginal Comment*, p. 146.

By the later 1960s Dover's scholarly reputation was assuming formidable proportions. He was elected an FBA in 1966, the same year in which he declined the chair of Greek at University College London. He turned down a further offer in the following year, this one from the University of California at Berkeley. That was shortly after he had given the prestigious Sather Lectures at Berkeley in early 1967. The topic of his lectures was the corpus of speeches attributed to Lysias, who worked as a speechwriter for clients in the lawcourts at Athens in the late fifth and early fourth centuries BC. Dover set himself to investigate how far disputes over the authenticity of the speeches could be clarified, particularly by stylistic analysis. In doing so he developed the heterodox thesis that individual clients may themselves have contributed to the speeches they commissioned, thus generating a kind of 'composite authorship' and complicating the whole idea of authenticity. Although the lectures had a somewhat mixed reception, and the subsequent book, *Lysias and the Corpus Lysiacum* (Berkeley, CA, 1968), did not entirely convince some specialists, the work remains an important study of the role of speechwriters in the system of forensic oratory in classical Athens; its use of stylistics exhibits Dover's ability to put his philological finesse at the service of larger historical research. Nor should it be overlooked that the project brought to fruition an idea which, on his own testimony, Dover had conceived as early as 1948:[12] the Sathers were in effect a belated fulfilment of one component of the programme of research he had proposed at that time.

In the same year that both the Lysias monograph and the edition of *Clouds* were published, Dover started to write a general introduction to Aristophanes for readers without any knowledge of Greek. This turned into *Aristophanic Comedy* (London, 1972), notable equally for its lightness of touch and breadth of coverage: it places consistent emphasis on theatrical staging, dramatic fantasy, and the ways in which Aristophanic humour manipulates elements of popular culture. While still working on that book, as well as on an edition of selected poems of Theocritus for students (published in 1971, it was to be his only substantial foray into post-classical literature), Dover began in 1969 to plan his next major venture, a study of Greek 'popular morality' as seen principally through the lens of the two genres which he thought could give access to the mentality of ordinary Greeks: oratory, especially forensic, and (with some qualifications) comedy. Significantly, this project, like his Lysias book, had its origins in the late 1940s. From the outset of his academic career, Dover had

[12] *Marginal Comment*, p. 137.

wanted to construct a picture of Greek values which would focus on the concrete, conflicted experience of 'real people', rather than the abstract theories of the philosophers (who were not, he liked to insist, *typical* Greeks).

Greek Popular Morality in the Time of Plato and Aristotle, written mostly in the course of 1972–3 (published in Berkeley, CA, 1974), rested on a principled decision not to organise its material according to Greek vocabulary and categories (though it nonetheless reckons with these in the course of the enquiry) but on the basis of topics and questions suggested by the author's 'own moral experience'. The resulting treatment of ideas of human nature, gender, responsibility, shame, death, inequality, and more besides, is therefore designed to reduce the sense of historical distance between the Greeks and 'us', though Dover's perspective on the Greeks always in fact recognised in them a composite of the 'alien' and 'familiar'. The method adopted was also intended as an antidote to the lexical emphasis (on key Greek terms), the heavily intellectualised frame of reference, and the systematising tendency of Arthur Adkins's *Merit and Responsibility* (Oxford, 1960). Adkins wrote a long, critical review of *Greek Popular Morality* (in *Classical Philology*, 1978), questioning the sharpness of the dichotomy between 'popular' and 'philosophical' thought and maintaining that Dover's method was itself more 'lexical' than he had admitted. Part of Dover's response was an article on 'The portrayal of moral evaluation in Greek poetry' (*Journal of Hellenic Studies*, 1983), in which he stressed that understanding moral discourse always requires subtle contextualisation and must take account of much more than standard evaluative vocabulary. The deep disagreements between Adkins and Dover are paradigmatic of some of the fundamental problems thrown up in the second half of the twentieth century by historical interpretation of Greek ethics.

Once again allowing the writing of different books to overlap, Dover had started working in earnest from the early 1970s on the project on Greek homosexuality for which he had perceived a need almost two decades earlier and which he had begun to plan during his study of Plato's *Symposium* in the 1960s. At one stage he had envisaged collaboration with the anthropologist and psychoanalyst George Devereux; mercifully, given the erratic nature of some of Devereux's own thinking, this idea proved impracticable. The book which Dover went on to write, *Greek Homosexuality*, was remarkable for the acumen with which it attempted to reconstruct a complex web of social and sexual mores. Pioneering in its synthesis of evidence from literature, oratory, visual art, mythology, religion, and philosophy, it addressed all aspects of the subject with a candour unprecedented in serious classical scholarship. Perhaps inevitably, it was to become the most widely known and controversial of all his books; it helped to usher in a new era of academic writing about ancient sexuality. If Dover's model of the asymmetrical attitudes to 'active' and 'passive' partners in homoerotic relationships is in places too schematic, his book is unquestionably a landmark in the modern study of Greek culture. It will retain a lasting value for the boldness and detail of its historical analyses.

By the mid-1970s, before *Greek Homosexuality* was finished, Dover had come to realise that he was ready for a fresh challenge in his career.[13] He had never ceased to devote immense energy to all his duties in St Andrews. On the departmental side, he had overseen the introduction of beginners' Greek in 1967 (see above), a new joint honours degree in Classics and Ancient History in the following year, and in 1975 the creation of a Classical Culture programme (involving study of ancient texts in translation) in subhonours, i.e. the first two years of the Scottish degree system. At the Faculty level, he served a second term (an unusual event) as Dean of Arts in 1973–5. What's more, his publications and his prowess as a speaker had turned him into a leading figure on the national Classics landscape: he was President of the Hellenic Society in 1971–4 and President of the Classical Association in 1975. But he not unnaturally found himself becoming a little stale with the routines of his undergraduate teaching, and he had been increasingly aware for some time of constraints on his opportunities for postgraduate teaching in St Andrews. He therefore allowed himself in late 1975 to be considered for the Presidency of Corpus Christi College, Oxford. When offered the position, he took only a few days to decide that, despite some misgivings (see below), this was the right time to move. But the fact that he and Audrey could not contemplate parting with their St Andrews home, to which they would eventually retire for the last thirteen years of their life together, was a sure sign of how attached they had both grown to the town and its university, whose Chancellor Dover subsequently became in 1981.[14] This would always remain the place where Dover felt that the central achievements of his career as a Hellenist had been accomplished, and St Andrews would in turn remain indebted

[13] He had in fact applied unsuccessfully for the Regius Chair of Greek in Cambridge in 1972; on this episode, see Section III below.

[14] Dover took great interest in observing the personalities of the diverse figures on whom, as Chancellor, he conferred honorary degrees, from the charming Dalai Lama to a conspicuously surly Bob Dylan. He was gratified to be able to continue as Chancellor, despite encroaching infirmity, up to 2005, the year in which Prince William graduated from St Andrews.

to him, more than to anyone else, for putting it on the map in the world of classical scholarship.

III: 1976–86

Dover stayed in St Andrews twenty-one years. There were two principal occasions when he might have left. One was in 1960, when, as noted above, he was offered and declined the Regius Chair of Greek at Oxford. The main academic reason he gave was that he could not work happily with a curriculum which confined the study of literature to the first part of the course ('Mods') and then forced everyone to do history and philosophy for the rest of the time ('Greats'). He did not think (he said) that this could be changed. It is difficult to say whether this was a solid reason or a pretext. He was of course very happy at St Andrews. He had the power there to shape the curriculum much as he wished, whereas Oxford professors (in the humanities at least) had, as he very well knew, no such power in virtue of their office, but only such personal authority as they might gradually accumulate. That may well have been the decisive consideration. He was in fact wrong about the possibility of change. It was achieved within a decade (quite quick, by Oxford standards), and it certainly helped secure the future of classical studies of all kinds, though at the cost of demolishing the Victorian concept of *literae humaniores* as a balanced and progressive education for public life, with a marked *rite de passage* in the middle.

Twelve years later, in 1972, Dover put himself forward for the Regius Chair of Greek at Cambridge, convinced that he was right for the job. The chair went instead to G. S. Kirk. Dover denied being disappointed at the time, but in later years the rejection certainly rankled, and he came to be resentful of what he supposed to be the manoeuvres that led to Kirk's appointment.

The opportunity presented by the invitation to become President of Corpus in 1976 could not have been predicted. Derek Hall had died suddenly, and the college had unexpectedly to seek a successor. Corpus is a smallish college, with a particularly strong classical tradition, which made Dover's election seem specially appropriate—though, as President, he was to be always scrupulously careful not to favour Classics at the expense of other subjects. He had some doubts about accepting. He was unsure about the future of colleges as independent institutions, and regarded the system as at any rate 'uneconomical'. However, he and Audrey soon settled in, a benevolent and hospitable presence in the newly refurbished lodgings.

They were both good at offering help where it was most needed, for example in looking after graduate students from abroad who could not get home for Christmas. Quietly and unobtrusively he steered the college through some important changes: the admission of women, the development of its graduate side, and the practice of allowing undergraduates representation at the Governing Body—this last being the most difficult to get through. He was by nature a reformer, liberal and egalitarian in his attitude in most things. (Characteristically, he was the only head of a college to vote against Mrs Thatcher's honorary degree.) His studied informality endeared him to many junior members; some seniors wondered whether he was going too far. In college business, it was his policy to seek consensus and then formulate it, rather than to give a lead or reveal his own view too soon. Meetings under his chairmanship were not likely to be short, for he did not care for fixing things up beforehand with college officers. His was the voice of reason, and he expected others to be reasonable too.

This benign and easy régime was greatly troubled by one sad event: the illness and suicide of a very talented, popular, and energetic history tutor, Trevor Aston. This was indeed a tragedy. The nature of Aston's illness made suicide always the likely outcome. Dover agonised over the situation. He took great pains to try to help his unhappy colleague; but Aston's wild behaviour became a source of serious alarm to the college and in the end there was nothing that could have been done to avert the catastrophe. A few years later, however, after he had left Corpus, Dover devoted a whole chapter of his autobiography to his exasperation with Aston. It was this chapter unfortunately on which the media fastened and which made him momentarily notorious. And of course the exposure itself did cause Aston's friends and the college very great distress. The relationship between Corpus and its former President could not now be warm; he seriously contemplated resigning his Honorary Fellowship, but was wisely dissuaded from doing so.

He did of course go on with his own research and writing while he was President. *Greek Homosexuality* (see the previous section) and his edition of Plato's *Symposium* (Cambridge, 1980) were published during these years, and his work on the development of Greek prose advanced. He became better known to a wider world through his series of television programmes on *The Greeks*, which resulted in a very popular and original book of the same name (London, 1980). The programmes themselves were not a great success, and Dover rather regretted them. But the book is a good testimony to his view of the Hellenic world, and its last chapter,

'God, man and matter', does much to explain his attitude to the philosophers: Plato's Socrates 'is wholly devoid of the genuine curiosity which makes a scientist or a historian'.[15] In 1981, too, his international reputation was confirmed by his election to the Prize Committee of the Balzan Foundation, on which he served for ten years.

He did not while at Corpus choose to play a great part in the Classics Faculty's affairs, apart from examining one or two theses, supervising an occasional graduate,[16] and giving some stimulating lectures on Greek prose. But the university did make use of his diplomatic skills, by making him chairman of a committee on undergraduate admissions in 1982. At this time, most undergraduates were admitted to Oxford on their performance in an examination set by groups of colleges, and primarily designed to choose high-flyers as college scholars. It was therefore meant not only to test achievement but to diagnose potential. It was administered with great care and a good deal of flexibility; but it seemed, not unreasonably, to be unfair to schools which could not provide a sixth-form education going beyond the precisely defined requirements of A-levels. So there was strong political pressure to change it, no easy task given the wide range of opinion in Oxford and the ingenuity with which various positions were advocated. Dover himself saw that, in this context, 'you can't make an omelette without breaking eggs'. He did in the end—exhausted, as he confessed, by the enormous amount of work entailed—succeed in finding a solution which was generally accepted. It involved abolishing entrance scholarships altogether; those were the eggs that were broken. It made the examination less important, indeed optional for many. It was thus an important stage on the way to the system which has since prevailed, selection by A-level results and interviews. The arrangement does not seem to have done much to increase the intake from state schools. What it probably did do was to add some additional pressure on all schools to concentrate more and more on A-level grades, and so make the sixth-form experience narrower and less liberal. But the pressure can only have been slight: Oxford had already lost much of its influence over secondary education.

[15] *The Greeks*, p. 115.
[16] I was myself privileged to have him as my D.Phil. supervisor (FSH).

IV: Presidency of the Academy

Dover had been elected to the British Academy in 1966 (W. L. Lorimer his principal sponsor), and was a conscientious, indeed active, Fellow in his Section. He was a key member (and later Chairman) of a Computer Committee, created to 'watch over the possibilities of exploiting computers to contribute to the solution of literary problems'; and in 1978 he served on a three-man review of the Academy's Major Projects, where he was much provoked by the 'philistinism' of the Chairman, A. J. Ayer, in relation to the classical projects which then formed the major component of the programme. In the same year he was nominated to succeed Sir Isaiah Berlin as President of the Academy.

Overcoming initial reluctance ('Oh *why* do people think I can do that sort of thing?'[17]) he brought to the office a dignified bearing and to the conduct of affairs distinguished intellectual leadership. His Presidential Addresses were a mixture of report on matters of policy and recent developments, together with reflection on a few topics of his own choosing, Olympian in tone, austere in language, in which he did not hesitate to chide, or to speak in parables drawn from Athenian history.[18] For the Academy there were challenges, above all to do with the development of public funding for the humanities, at a time when it was increasingly coming to be regarded as the main channel outside the universities for the Government's support for advanced research in these subjects. The Academy was relieved to be spared the financial cuts in public funding to which other institutions were being subjected; its research support programmes were enlarged by new funds for small grants in the humanities provided by the University Grants Committee; and its international programmes were expanding in volume and geographical range—Dover took a particular interest in the Far East, especially in the signing of an Exchange Agreement with the Chinese Academy of Social Sciences, and he visited the Japan Academy on the Academy's behalf. The most urgent organisational problem concerned accommodation. Since 1969 the Academy had occupied rent-free premises in Burlington House, shared with the Royal Society of Chemistry which was very much the senior partner. There were no facilities for Fellows, meeting rooms could only be

[17] *Marginal Comment*, p. 168. There were aspects of the job, however, to which he was never fully reconciled—formal dinners among them, and after-dinner speaking was never his *forte*.

[18] e.g. 'If I seem to be speaking didactically, even reprovingly, please attribute this to the spirit of the parabasis which I have imbibed from Attic Old Comedy …', *Proceedings of the British Academy*, LXV (1981), 66.

booked by arrangement with the chemists, and the growing staff (albeit scarcely numbering more than a dozen) worked in very cramped conditions. Dover led the search for new premises, which eventually resulted in the acquisition of a Decimus Burton house on the outer circle of Regent's Park, set back from the end of a Nash terrace. The property belonged to the Crown Estate, which agreed to a comprehensive refurbishment of the interior to meet the Academy's needs, including the erection of a lecture hall on waste ground to the rear of the building: 20–1 Cornwall Terrace, though not an ideal solution (the Academy soon outgrew it), became the Academy's home for the next fifteen years.

What came to be seen as the defining feature of Dover's Presidency, however, was 'the Blunt affair', undoubtedly the most divisive issue in the Academy's history.[19] Sir Anthony Blunt, a senior Fellow (elected in 1950), a former Vice-President and a recent member of Council, from 1975 to 1978, was publicly exposed as a Soviet spy in November 1979. He subsequently resigned from certain of his academic associations but not the Academy. A move was initiated to expel him. The Academy's constitution allowed for the expulsion of a Fellow 'on the grounds that he or she is not a fit and proper person to be a Fellow', but only on the recommendation of the Council and at a General Meeting of the Fellows—the next one was not due until July 1980. The question, on which differing views of considerable subtlety could be and were advanced, was whether Blunt's scholarly distinction as an historian of art, to which he owed his election to the Academy, was cancelled out by his treasonable (or, as some would have it, treacherous) activity. Was integrity indivisible or did moral delinquency justify expulsion? Had a *scholarly* offence been committed or was treason to be treated as *sui generis*? The membership of Council, over two charged sessions, was evenly divided, and only because of the absence at the second of an opponent of expulsion was Dover as Chairman spared from having to use a casting vote on the proposal to expel (as he understood the rules of chairmanship he would have voted against, to maintain the *status quo*). The subsequent Annual General Meeting was attended by 187 Fellows, a larger number than ever before or since. After extended discussion a motion from the floor to move on to other business was carried by a large majority, and no vote was taken on the continuance of Blunt's Fellowship. The decision provoked a small number of immediate resignations and a good deal of press coverage and comment,[20] most of it

[19] The following paragraphs draw on Dover's published account in *Marginal Comment* and on material in the Academy's archives.
[20] Some of it in the form of letters to the press by Fellows of the Academy.

adverse, over the coming weeks. There were threats of further resignations if Blunt was not induced to resign, and threats of resignation if he was. Eventually, after an exchange of letters between Dover and Blunt,[21] Blunt did resign, expressing 'the hope that my resignation will reduce the dissension within the Academy about my membership'. He also dissuaded his supporters from following his example. The total number of resignations, including Blunt's, was six.

Throughout the controversies Dover conducted himself with scrupulous even-handedness, attracting some criticism for 'failing to give a strong lead'. The contained rigour with which he addressed the issues in public was not to all tastes; but he deprecated all concession to 'feelings', and saw his role as to ensure full consideration and proper process. Indeed, he took satisfaction from the comment at the end of Council's deliberations that it had been impossible to judge which side he was on.[22] This is not to say that he did not hold strong views on the subject. As he later explained in his autobiographical memoir (p. 214), 'a decisive reason' for expelling Blunt was that 'He had transferred his allegiance to a régime which deliberately falsified history and persecuted scholars who attempted to exercise independent judgement; and nothing could have been more directly opposed than that to the purposes of the Academy.' Dover kept a meticulous record of his dealings with Fellows throughout, and though he was unfailingly courteous in correspondence, in his private annotations he could be severe in judgement, even scathing, especially when Fellows fell short of his intellectual standards.

In retrospect, Dover admitted that he had 'found the whole Affair from beginning to end, absorbingly interesting and therefore intensely enjoyable'. Nevertheless, he decided not to serve the full customary four-year term as President and did not seek re-election in 1981, confessing that his appetite for office had been somewhat jaded by the conflicts of the previous summer. He had also received invitations to lecture in Japan, North America and Australia for which his college was willing to grant him a sabbatical term, and it was clear that the Academy's new premises would not be ready for occupation until well after he would have left office. He was succeeded by Professor Owen Chadwick, whose contributions to proceedings during the Blunt affair had been notably humane and eirenic. In his own first Presidential Address Chadwick paid tribute to Dover

[21] The exchange led to the charge that improper pressure had been brought to bear on Blunt to bring about his resignation, a charge Dover vigorously refuted in a note to the Fellowship.
[22] A later President reacted with incredulity at such self-restraint.

'whose service as President happened during a period of unparalleled difficulty for the Academy and whose good humour and patience and care over detail were of high importance to our welfare'.[23]

V: 1986–2010

On leaving Corpus, in 1986, he returned, probably with some relief, to St Andrews, where he continued to be Chancellor until 2005. The next few years saw several important publications. The first was the splendid two volumes of *Collected Papers*, titled *Greek and the Greeks* (Oxford, 1987) and *The Greeks and their Legacy* (Oxford, 1988). Here are to be seen all his skills: the intimate knowledge of texts and inscriptions, the lucidity and patience, the clear insistence that classical scholarship is a form of history, and that interpreters should always seek to discover the intentions of the poets and prose-writers whom they study. Here too the very special qualities of Dover's scholarship are on view: his liberal, rationalistic temperament, his impatience with obfuscation or nonsense, whether modern or ancient, and especially with the complex of ideas which he sees as Platonic and then Christian, including the belief in the goodness of God and in life after death. Characteristic too is his choice of reference, the sorts of things with which he likes to compare the Greek phenomenon he is discussing: 'I like modern parallels', he writes, and that is a key remark.[24] He did indeed prefer to find parallels in modern culture rather than anything out of the European tradition which could be thought to be directly derived from the classical inheritance. He also liked to draw on remote cultures and languages, Vietnam for example (of which he learned something from George Devereux, who had also influenced E. R. Dodds) or the Pacific Islands. These were interests going back to his childhood, and he was genuinely learned in some of these cultures and languages. So, faced (for instance) with the need to find some parallels for the simple narrative style of early Greek prose, he turns to New Guinea or the Solomon Islands, rather than to later Greek, Latin or mediaeval story-telling. This was a settled policy. The similarities were illuminating: any suggestion of a historical link would vitiate their force. He wanted his Greeks to be seen by

[23] *Proceedings of the British Academy*, LXVIII (1983), 79.
[24] *Greek and the Greeks* (Oxford, 1987), p. 96; reprinted from *Journal of Hellenic Studies*, 103 (1983), 48.

themselves, not in the light of successor cultures, and he thought insistence on the 'canonical' a bad reason for advocating the study of the Classics.

The second major publication of this period was his long-planned edition of Aristophanes' *Frogs* (Oxford, 1993—see above). The third was quite a different sort of summing-up: the autobiography *Marginal Comment* (London, 1994). It is natural to compare this book with the autobiography of another great Hellenist, E. R. Dodds's *Missing Persons* (Oxford, 1977). But whereas Dodds's book was much admired and won the Duff Cooper Prize, *Marginal Comment* earned not so much acclaim as notoriety, with full-page spreads in several newspapers, and it led to Dover's being interviewed by Anthony Clare for the radio programme *In the Psychiatrist's Chair*.

All this was partly because of the book's explicitness in sexual matters (Dover was ahead of his time in this regard) and partly because of what seemed to many an insensitive and potentially offensive handling of the Aston affair. It is certainly a disquieting book. Someone who read it and did not know him was heard to exclaim that she didn't *want* to know 'that man'. Kenneth would have smiled indulgently and pitied her prudishness. But the trouble is not simply with the four-letter words and the possible personal offence, but with the whole tone of the narrative. It is of course absolutely honest and sincere; he brought to it all his historian's integrity. But it does not follow that it tells the whole truth. His friends knew him not only as a brilliant scholar but as a charismatic teacher, a supportive colleague, and a loyal and generous friend with whom it was always a pleasure to talk and exchange ideas and confidences. Yet in *Marginal Comment*, in all the exhaustive record of actions and reactions, successes and occasional failures, there is surprisingly little to be seen of these humane and benign qualities. Instead, many readers, not knowing him, have thought the author cold and egotistical. The very various views shown in the thirty or so reviews and articles which the book stimulated show how puzzling it was. Some were appreciative and reassuring ('Olympian objectivity', said Peter Jones in the *Scotsman*, and Bernard Knox in the *Times Literary Supplement* and Philip Howard in the *Times* were also complimentary), but others were critical: 'a sad book … will puzzle and offend many who prefer the Kenneth Dover they knew and loved', wrote Ross Leckie in *Scotland on Sunday*, and others spoke of 'exhibitionism' or suspected that he just wanted notoriety. If he did, he certainly got it: few books of the kind have stirred up such a storm. Yet it does contain a good deal of very thought-provoking observations about life and learning. Of the reviewers, Ross Leckie seems to me to have come nearest the truth: the chief character is not the Kenneth Dover we knew, and not half so agreeable.[25]

The last book of his seventies, *The Evolution of Greek Prose Style* (Oxford, 1997), was also a summation of a life-long interest. From his earliest days, Dover's enthusiasm had been for language rather than for literature. So, in this late work, he disclaimed any wish to be a literary critic. Literary criticism, he thought, had an autobiographical element and an element of preaching. Presumably, you needed to express your own reactions (which might not be anyone else's) and also to persuade others that the stuff was worth reading and would enhance life. He preferred a more objective approach. He had great gifts for the task: a marvellously retentive memory and exhaustive study. His contribution to our understanding of Greek prose is immense. It begins with *Greek Word Order* (1960; second edition, 1968), already noted in its chronological context, where he deployed his knowledge of inscriptions to supplement the literary evidence in a way that had not been done before. His analyses are subtle and generally convincing. He had pursued the same line in the important chapter of his 1968 book *Lysias and the Corpus Lysiacum*, in which he shows that the authors of these speeches did not all have the same linguistic habits. He also wrote significant articles on the colloquial element in Attic and in the language of Aristophanes. *Evolution* is his last word on these matters. It is full of fruitful ideas, not only on word order but also on vocabulary and rhythm. He perhaps did not succeed in distancing himself as completely from aesthetic and imaginative interpretations as he professed; maybe he did not really want to. At any rate, there is a striking passage in the chapter on rhythm where he connects a (quite possibly accidental) tragic trimeter in Thucydides' narrative of the Athenian disaster in Sicily with the 'tragic' nature of the whole situation.

There were many happy times in these years, not least in travels to America and elsewhere. For five years (1987–92) he went regularly as a visiting professor to Stanford—not by any means his only experience of this kind (he also greatly enjoyed his stays at Cornell during 1984–9) but a particularly rewarding one. He took a full part in the department's affairs, helping with appointments and examining. The graduate students gave him much pleasure, and he was very helpful to them. He also gave popular

[25] I made this point to him at the time. He replied that others thought the opposite, and that the reason was that different people saw different sides of him. This does not make my complaint invalid. (DAR)

lectures on Greek values. It was an excellent way of avoiding the British winters.

Dover's old age was saddened by Audrey's illness (she was wheelchair bound for some years) and by his own failing eyesight and other health problems. So he wrote rather little after *Evolution*; one notable article, very characteristic of him, was a piece entitled 'Are gods forgivable?' in a volume of essays on the subject of 'double standards' in the ancient and medieval world.[26]

Reading anything he wrote fills one with admiration not only for the acuteness of his mind but for his dedication and care. He lets nothing pass as certain if there is the slightest doubt about it. He never spared himself trouble. He says somewhere that he could spend twelve hours on a version of a Greek composition for a pupil, no doubt assuring himself that he wrote nothing he could not parallel in a classical text. Writing some Greek verses in a book he was giving to a friend, he defended a minor metrical anomaly by learned references to Theognis and Callimachus. He was a perfectionist; but unlike other perfectionists, he always finished the job.

VI

Dover was tall and spare, a figure of reassuring authority, never openly angry or perturbed. Olympian, some said; but it was as a very benevolent Zeus that he would descend on the annual Greek summer school at Bryanston. He was a superb, indeed spellbinding, lecturer, often dispensing with notes (he must have spent hours preparing his lectures) and could make an audience follow a very technical argument with understanding and pleasure. He expected a lot of his hearers (as he did of his readers) but he knew how to get it.

In youth, he had looked older than his years, and already authoritative. Later, his face was deeply lined. He was physically robust (his professed anxiety about his 'funnel chest' notwithstanding) and liked challenges, humping rocks around in his garden, to which he was devoted, and walking or camping in the Highlands. He liked, and was much moved by, grand scenery of the kind the eighteenth century would have called sublime. He also kept alive his boyhood interest in natural history. He and Audrey were knowledgeable observers of birds. So it was in lonely places, and

[26] 'Are gods forgivable?', in K. Pollmann (ed.), *Double Standards in the Ancient and Medieval World* (Göttingen, 2000), pp. 22–32.

with the wonders of nature to admire, that he probably found the most profound tranquillity he knew. His other source of deep pleasure was music; some musical experiences remained in his memory as life-changing events, and both he and Audrey were keen and appreciative concert-goers.

All the same, it was Greek scholarship that sustained and dominated his life. When he said that falling in love with Greek at St Paul's 'set him on his course', he was saying the most important thing about himself. It was not only that his expertise puts him among the greatest Hellenists of the twentieth century. The intellectual and moral attitudes of classical Athens, as he pictured them—and no one has had a clearer or better-informed vision—shaped his own attitudes and behaviour in many ways. The traffic ran also in the other direction. His deeply held rationalism and dislike of obscurity or what he saw as humbug led him inevitably to fashion his Greeks in some degree in his own image. Of course, everyone does this, and we unavoidably simplify the past by doing so. That is true even of the greatest scholars, and it is true of Dover.

Perhaps one should sum up in Greek terms. He was certainly Aristotle's *alētheutikos*, the man who never either exaggerates or understates. But he had also a touch of the *megalopsuchos*, the man of dignified bearing who believes himself worthy of great things, and in fact is so. 'The complete Grecian' is a fair verdict.

Audrey died in December 2009. Kenneth survived her barely three months: he died on 7 March 2010.

D. A. RUSSELL
Fellow of the Academy
F. S. HALLIWELL
University of St Andrews

Note. Donald Russell is the author of the first, third, fifth and sixth sections of this memoir, Stephen Halliwell of the second; but we have benefited from an exchange of comments on each other's drafts. The fourth section was kindly supplied by Mr P. W. H. Brown, former Secretary of the Academy. In addition, Donald Russell would like to acknowledge advice on various points from the following: Mrs Catherine Brown (Catherine Dover), Sir Brian Harrison, Sir Keith Thomas, Professor R. G. M. Nisbet, Mr E. L. Bowie.

PHILIPPA FOOT

Philippa Ruth Foot
1920–2010

I

Philippa Ruth Foot was born on 3 October 1920, the second daughter of William Bosanquet, who had done mathematics at Cambridge and became the manager of a steelworks in Yorkshire, and Esther Cleveland, daughter of President Grover Cleveland. She was educated mainly at home in the country by governesses, and not well. She said, many years later, that, 'unsurprisingly', she had been left 'extremely ignorant', and when the last one, 'who actually had a degree', suggested to her that she should go to Oxford, she had to work for it. She spent a year with an established Oxford entrance coach and took a correspondence course to acquire the necessary entrance Latin; the result was a place at Somerville College, where she went to read Philosophy, Politics and Economics (PPE) in 1939.

She graduated with First Class Honours in 1942, and, like many of her female contemporaries, immediately looked for 'war work'. After a year working in Oxford for the Nuffield Social Reconstruction Survey, she moved to work in London where she remained until the end of the war. There she married the historian M. R. D. Foot in June 1945 and, with him, returned to Oxford later that year where she took up a teaching position at Somerville (the marriage was dissolved in 1960). She became their first Tutorial Fellow in Philosophy in 1949, Vice-Principal in 1967, and, although she resigned her fellowship in 1969, she retained, as a Senior Research Fellow and then Honorary Fellow, very close links with the College and Somervillians, past and present, until the end of her life.

She resigned her fellowship because, with characteristic independence, she had decided that it was time for a new sort of life and that she would freelance in the US. She had already held Visiting Professorships at Cornell and MIT; in her first years of wandering she went as a visiting Professor to the Universities of California (both Los Angeles—UCLA—and Berkeley), Washington, Princeton, and Stanford, to the Graduate Center at the City University of New York and the Society for the Humanities at Cornell, and as Professor in Residence at UCLA, where she finally settled in 1976.

So, for over twenty years, from 1969 until she retired in 1991, she divided her life, flying off to the US in the autumn, and returning to Oxford, a cautious swallow, in May. In the US she was President of the Pacific Division of the American Philosophical Association in 1982–3, became a Fellow of the American Academy of Arts and Science in 1983 and the first holder of the Griffin Chair in Philosophy at UCLA in 1988, and gave well over a hundred invited lectures. To provide a secure basis for all this activity, she acquired some sort of US residency, but on one occasion forgot that this was her official status. Asked by US immigration where she lived, tired after the trans-Atlantic flight, she said 'England, of course' and was extricated from the ensuing fracas only by her lawyer's definitive statement that 'Professor Foot is not only one of the world's greatest moral philosophers but *the granddaughter of President Cleveland.*' They let her in.

Notwithstanding this official status in the US, England did remain home. As well as maintaining her association with Somerville, she became a Fellow of the British Academy in 1976, and also maintained her long association with Oxfam. She was not, as is often stated, one of the founders of Oxfam. It began in 1942 as the Oxford Committee for Famine Relief, founded by some of Oxford's leading Quakers and academics, at which point Philippa was just completing her undergraduate degree. It must have been some time after that that she became a member, and indeed, by November 1948, Oxfam's first minute book shows that the 28-year-old Philippa was the newest and, by a generation, the youngest of those running it. When she retired from UCLA in 1991, her return to Oxford happily coincided with the approach of Oxfam's fiftieth anniversary, and so she was able to give the Oxfam Gilbert Murray Memorial Lecture in October 1992, in which she managed to combine surveying Oxfam's history with philosophical reflections on the virtues of charity and justice. About ten years after this, when she was well into her eighties, Oxfam took her on a month-long visit to see their work in India. It was the sort of visit in which one stayed in peasant huts more often than in hotels and she found it exhausting but quite wonderful. Towards the end of her life she wrote: 'Oxfam has been one of the continuous threads in my life ... It's been one of the happiest things through my grown up life. I was lucky to have worked for Oxfam ... I love it.'

Her first ten years permanently back in Oxford were busy and productive, as she gave and attended classes, saw friends, became an enthusiastic gardener and worked on what was to become her book *Natural Goodness* (Oxford, 2001). For a few years after its publication she continued to work, and gave several fascinating interviews on her philosophical development, but by 2004 her health began to deteriorate badly, and by 2006 she had become bed-ridden and, sadly, unable to do philosophy any more. She hung on until 2010 when—retaining to the last her acute eye for the right moment—she died peacefully on 3 October, her ninetieth birthday.

II

By her own account, Philippa chose to do PPE, not because she was already drawn to philosophy, but only because she wanted to do 'something theoretical' and 'couldn't do mathematics'. But she came to Oxford at a propitious time for her future development as a philosopher. Mary Midgley and Iris Murdoch were in their second year at Somerville, reading Greats, and Elizabeth Anscombe, also reading Greats, was a further year ahead, at St Hugh's. Conscription had drastically reduced the number of men in Oxford, and these three girls, attending many of the same classes and (as Midgley notes in her autobiography) making themselves heard there, were friends by the time Philippa joined their group. In the 1980s, Iris Murdoch could remember that she and Philippa 'at once became close friends' in Philippa's first year, and 'the joy with which I found her, so brilliant, so beautiful. We talked about philosophy and everything.'

At this time Somerville had no tutorial fellow in philosophy, and the three Somerville girls were sent to Donald MacKinnon. He must have been a remarkable tutor, for all three recalled him with affection and gratitude decades later. Indeed, in the acknowledgements in the Preface to the first collection of her essays, *Virtues and Vices* (Oxford, 1978), Philippa singles out MacKinnon as the one to whom (perhaps) she owed most. Given the way she developed, we must suppose that this was not so much because he taught her Kant but rather that he emphasised the history of philosophy and, as a Kantian theist concerned with the reality of evil and its manifestation in tragedy, taught them a style of thinking which was very different from the Oxford moral philosophy that prevailed at the time.

This was dominated by the moral subjectivism of Ayer's *Language, Truth and Logic* (London, 1953) and Stevenson's emotivism, and was still dominant when the three young women found themselves together again in Oxford in the autumn of 1945 and Anscombe joined them a year later from Cambridge. Midgley remembers that, from then until autumn 1949, when she left, all four of them talked a lot to each other 'about Oxford moral philosophy and what should be done about it', and thinks that 'that was when we all hammered out our various thoughts on that topic'.[1]

But a diary entry of Murdoch's, from just before Midgley left, shows that it was not only moral philosophy that they were discussing. It reads, 'Argument with Pip (Philippa) and Mary (Midgley) about naming feelings. M. said, case of indefinite colour. I said at least one can *look* at the colour. Pip said she had a queer feeling which she named Hubert. Not of course a log. proper name—H. has certain characteristics otherwise couldn't be named. What is it to be Hubert again?' Clearly, they had all been picking up some Wittgenstein from Anscombe.

Anscombe had returned to a Research Fellowship at Somerville in 1946, and when Philippa was appointed as a lecturer in philosophy at Somerville a year later, she joined Anscombe in the Senior Common Room and the two of them quickly formed the habit of intensely concentrated philosophical discussions after lunch; these were a regular occurrence until Anscombe left for the chair in Cambridge in 1970. Recalling them in an interview in 2003, Philippa said 'She must have been putting to me the questions that Wittgenstein put to her. Practically every day we talked for hours. I was incredibly lucky.' This is not to say that Anscombe force-fed her Wittgenstein. Apparently, she never even suggested that Philippa should read the *Philosophical Investigations* (Oxford, 1953) after it came out, and when, some years later, Philippa did, 'voraciously', and said 'Why didn't you *tell* me?' she replied, 'Because it is very important to have one's resistances.'

[1] The quotations from Mary Midgley are taken from her autobiography—*The Owl of Minerva: a Memoir* (London, 2005). Those from Philippa Foot are taken from three interviews that she gave. Two of them are available on the web at <http://www.philosophynow.org/issues/41/Philippa_Foot> and <http://www.hcs.harvard.edu/~hrp/issues/2003/Foot.pdf>; the third has been published as 'Goodness' in Julian Baggini and Jeremy Strangroom (eds.) *What More Philosophers Think* (London, 2007), pp. 103–14.

Given her devout Catholicism, Anscombe was naturally as opposed to the prevailing Oxford moral philosophy as the other three, but Philippa, who always described herself as a 'card-carrying atheist', was convinced it must be wrong for her own reasons. She never said anything in print about what these were, but in the interviews she gave in the last decade of her life she made it clear that her philosophical conviction that morality must be objective crystallised immediately after the war when the photographs and films of Belsen and Birkenau came out. Her immediate reaction was that the separation of facts from values, the idea that, in the end, the Nazis had their values or attitudes and we had ours and there could be no grounds for saying we were right and they were wrong, '*had* to be bad philosophy'. And so she embarked on her lifelong task.

III

Foot's published work, all in moral philosophy, spans fifty years, consisting entirely of essays until its culmination in her only monograph, *Natural Goodness*. Looking at the first of her two volumes of collected papers, one is struck by how early she found her distinctive voice. Right from the beginning, we have the opposition to subjectivism in ethics and the application of the Wittgensteinian techniques. What she has always been doing is what Wittgenstein says is the work of the philosopher, namely assembling reminders for a particular purpose. The general Wittgensteinian purpose is always to '*command a clear view* of our use of words'; the particular purpose in Foot's case has always been to get clearer about our use of words when we are making moral judgements. When we evaluate someone as a good person, their action as right or wrong, their character as good or bad, what are we doing, what grounds do we typically give for our judgements, what do we expect from someone who has said it, what other uses of these words are these uses in moral judgements like, what background do these uses presuppose, what is the standard role or function of their use, and so on?

In her Introduction to the first edition of *Virtues and Vices* (Oxford, 1978), which collected most of what she had written in the previous twenty years, Foot described the last eight essays as representing 'the development of a certain line of thought on the theory of moral judgement' and also as ones in which she was making 'a painfully slow journey ... away from theories that located the special character of evaluations in each speaker's attitudes or feelings, or recognition of reason for acting'. But, given what was in the collection, that seems to be inaccurate on both counts. There was nothing *slow* about her journey away from the contemporary subjectivist theories of moral judgement that appealed to the speaker's attitudes or feelings or motivating reasons. She was utterly opposed to them when she started, as is clear in the earliest of the essays reprinted—the 'Moral arguments' paper of 1958 (published in *Mind*). But, on the other hand, we do not find her developing her own 'line of thought on the theory of moral judgement' until two papers—'Rationality and virtue' and 'Does moral subjectivism rest on a mistake?' (both reprinted in *Moral Dilemmas and other Topics in Moral Philosophy*: Oxford, 2002)—appeared over thirty-five years later, which prefigure *Natural Goodness.*

The attack on the fact–value dichotomy

'Moral arguments' already exemplifies a number of Wittgensteinian features. One is the avoidance of what he called 'a one-sided diet' of examples, another the resistance to the philosopher's 'craving for generality' which he deplored, and another, the recognition of the fact that our use of words is governed by public criteria and hence that they cannot have any meaning that a speaker chooses to give them. All these are brought to bear on the word 'rude'—not an example one would immediately think to bring up in discussions of the evaluative meaning of 'right' and 'wrong' but one which, according to Midgley, had been the topic of some of those earlier group discussions in which Foot and the others had 'hammered out' their thoughts. Foot argued that 'rude' had all the characteristics attributed to evaluative terms by philosophers, but is correctly judged to apply to a piece of behaviour when and only when that behaviour meets certain conditions, regardless of the thinker's attitudes to it. So even if it is evaluative, it is also descriptive, that is, true or false according to how things are independently of the one who makes the judgement.

Generalising the point that no individual is free to choose which facts about a piece of behaviour are relevant to its being rude, she introduced what was known at the time as 'the content restriction'. This was the claim that an action cannot be *morally* evaluated as a good action unless considerations (however insanely superstitious or wicked) of human good and harm were figuring somewhere in the background against which the evaluation was made. This was a necessary point at the time, because the philosopher R. M. Hare's widely accepted prescriptivism was thought to have the odd consequence that, as she had noted, if someone insisted sincerely that 'no-one should run round trees left-handed' and followed this rule himself, but could say nothing about why this was important, he could be correctly described as holding this as a basic *moral* principle.

Foot's metaethics is not an attack on the fact–value distinction; it is the rejection of a purported *dichotomy*. She never denied that the judgements the people she was attacking called 'evaluative' were indeed evaluative; she insisted that they were descriptive, 'logically vulnerable to facts' *too*. Moreover, she accepted that, in some as yet unexplored sense, they were related to choice and action.

At the time of writing 'Moral beliefs' (*Proceedings of the Aristotelian Society*, 1958) she was certain—perhaps because of many years of teaching Plato and reading Aquinas—that the sense in which moral evaluations were related to action was that 'moral judgements give reasons for acting to each and every man'. Further, she thought that, at least as far as judgements about the virtues were concerned, she could show that this was so. Appealing to Plato's view in the *Republic*, Foot committed herself to the ancient Greek idea that possession of the virtues benefits their possessor, arguing, albeit briefly, that even justice—so often seen as generating the paradigm cases in which morality and self-interest conflict—was 'more profitable' than injustice, and hence that everyone had reason to choose to acquire it and act in accordance with it.

Consideration of virtue terminology in the context of metaethics, at that time largely ignored, was a startling move. It was obviously true that 'just', 'courageous', 'kind', and their opposites are terms whose application is strongly governed by facts, and yet equally obvious that they are used in moral judgements. The favoured response was to preserve the fact–value dichotomy by insisting that evaluative terms could be used in two distinct ways which Hare had already introduced. There was an 'inverted comma' use, which simply described the facts, and a genuinely evaluative use in which the speaker committed herself to having some sort of favourable attitude to whatever was at issue.

This reaction may have reminded Foot, given her Wittgensteinian predilections, that concentrating on the 'thick' evaluative virtue and vice terms was feeding on a rather one-sided diet. So she turned her attention to everyone's favoured 'thin' one, namely 'good', and, in 'Goodness and choice' (*Proceedings of the Aristotelian Society*, 1961), uncovered a different sense in which evaluative judgements of the form 'a good F' are related to choice.

She begins with the obviously functional Fs—'knife', 'pen', etc.—regarding which it is generally agreed that whether or not an object is truly described as a good knife is as much a matter of fact as whether or not it is a sharp one. What 'knife' means is an object used for cutting, and the criterion for the goodness of functional objects is that they perform their function well. She then moves to 'farmer', 'rider', 'liar', noting that, although we do not say that farmers and liars have a function the way knives and pens do, nevertheless, they have a characteristic activity (what Aristotle would call an '*ergon*') which has to be done well if someone is to be a good F. So in these cases too, the criteria of goodness are determined by what the word means.

It may be objected that these are not really examples of evaluative judgements in the intended sense, and it is certainly true that none of them, so far, is what we would call a moral judgement. But the same is not clearly true of her next batch of examples. The criteria for whether someone is a good daughter, or father, or friend are determined by the meanings of the words; a good *father* is one who 'looks after his children as best he can', a good *friend* is one who is 'well-disposed' towards the man whose friend he is, and, as she notes, we may think that a 'wholly good' man could not be a bad father or friend. In support of the claim that these words have such moral connotations, she applies what might be called 'Wittgenstein's (or Quine's) translation test': if a tribe used the expression 'a good F' to apply to a man on the grounds that he offered his children up for sacrifice, we would not translate 'F' as 'father' but as, for example, 'citizen' or 'priest'.

In her discussion of these, and many other examples, Foot established the significant conclusion that a large number of evaluative judgements are not only true or false but also that their truth-conditions do not include any particular fact about the speaker's attitudes, feelings, motivations or recognition of reasons to act. They do so only when context, or the actual words used, signal this fact (as in 'This is a good knife for *my* purposes'). But she was far from denying a prevailing relation between judgements involving 'good' and there being a reason to choose what is, as a matter of fact, a good whatever. She locates it as holding, when it does, between the facts that make the judgements true and (not the individual speaker but) a general background of *people's* purposes, needs and desires. We invented pens because we wanted to write legibly and easily; unless an individual idiosyncratically wants to write illegibly or messily, she has reason to choose a good pen. We need doctors to preserve and restore our health; unless an individual wants to be unhealthy, she has reason to choose a good doctor and to be a good patient. However, the upshot of this is that anyone who does not have the relevant purposes may have no reason to choose a good so and so, and, at the very end, she says that we 'may not' be able to give a particular individual a reason for choosing to be a good, rather than a bad, parent.

The is–ought gap

This closing remark hints at her abandonment of her 'Moral beliefs' view that 'moral judgements give reasons for acting to each and every man'. She makes this explicit in the otherwise rather tentative 'Reasons for action and desires' (*Proceedings of the Aristotelian Society*, 1972) and very explicit in the far from tentative 'Morality as a system of hypothetical imperatives' (*The Philosophical Review*, 1972). Here, to the delight of the followers of Hume who maintained that one cannot get an 'ought' from an 'is', and the consternation of those who believed in the rationality of morality and had thought she was an ally, she argued vigorously against the idea that 'ought' has guaranteed reason-giving force when used to make moral judgements.

She pointed to a distinction between the 'categorical' and 'hypothetical' uses of 'ought' and 'should'. The hypothetical use, typical in the giving of helpful advice as in, for example, 'You ought to take the 5.15 train' or 'You ought to give up eating chocolate', is desire or interest-dependent. We use it as a shorthand for 'Given you want to ... or have an interest in ... or have such and such an end, you ought to ...' and this is shown by the fact that when we discover that the person addressed does not have the relevant desire or interest we withdraw the claim that they ought to. In contrast, when we are using it 'categorically', as we do, she agrees, when we intend to make a moral judgement, it is not desire or interest-dependent.

However, as she disconcertingly goes on to point out, the desire- or interest-independent use of 'ought' and 'should', far from being the distinctive mark of a moral judgement, is to be found wherever there is some system of rules; her favoured example is etiquette and the use of 'should' in the judgement 'Invitations in the third person should be answered in the third person'. Clearly, any follower of Kant will say that the etiquette judgement is not a categorical but a hypothetical imperative, and Foot takes it that their grounds must be that the fact that something is required by etiquette does not, in itself, give anyone a reason to do it, whereas the fact that something is required by morality gives everyone a reason to do it. It is assumed, that is, that moral judgements have a guaranteed reason-giving force and this Foot denies. They give reasons, she maintains, only to those who have adopted moral ends, and thereby have certain interests and desires.

Foot maintained staunchly that she did not regard this position as being 'inimical to morality', claiming in the 1978 Introduction to the collection (*Virtues and Vices*) in which this paper was reprinted that '[c]onsiderations of justice, charity and the like have a strange and powerful appeal to the human heart'. But given that she had set out to produce a theory of moral judgement which would reflect her conviction that there had to be grounds for our saying that we were right and the Nazis were wrong, she had wound up in a very strange position. We can say, with objective truth, that Hitler was a thoroughly bad person, a wicked man, that, indeed, he acted badly, but we cannot move from that to 'He had reason to be other than he was and to do other than he did', since considerations of justice and charity had no appeal to him.

Notwithstanding the staunch denials, Foot knew something had gone wrong somewhere, but, for almost fifteen years, she could see no alternative. So she abandoned her theoretical work on moral judgement and, from the mid-1970s up until 1990, she published most of her influential work in applied and normative ethics.

Applied and normative ethics

This includes her remarkable paper 'Euthanasia' (*Philosophy and Public Affairs*, 1977), which, discussing the issue in terms of charity and justice, predated any other attempt to apply virtue ethics to a contemporary moral problem by almost fifteen years and is still a frequently read classic. One of its most notable features is that she identifies most unjustified acts of killing as contrary to both justice *and* charity, pointing out that charity is the virtue that attaches us to the good of others, so when life is a good to its possessor, and death an evil to him, as is usually the case, charity forbids killing him as stringently as does justice in respecting his right to life. However, the two virtues do not always speak as one. When, as in cases of genuine euthanasia, life is truly no longer a good to its possessor, but, on the contrary, his death would be a benefit to him, charity would speak in favour of killing him. However, if he does not want to be killed, justice speaks against it. Hence the importance of the distinction between voluntary and involuntary euthanasia.

The subtle interplay of justice and charity and the different sorts of action each require is also brought to bear on the familiar distinction between active and passive euthanasia. Foot argues that, quite generally, the right to life, with which justice is concerned, is a 'liberty-right', related to the duty of non-interference, not a 'claim-right' related to a duty of service or aid; that one ought to preserve and sustain the life of others is usually a requirement of charity, but not of justice. So justice rules out killing when the person does not want to die, but does not necessarily rule out allowing to die. However it may do so, especially in the hospital context of euthanasia, where the right to life includes the claim-right to certain services from the doctors. Her complex conclusion is that non-voluntary active euthanasia is never justified, but that the other three combinations sometimes are (though noting that the question of whether they should be legalised is certainly not thereby settled and that we should be very wary of it).

The distinction between killing and allowing to die and its relation to the distinct requirements of justice and charity is prefigured in a much earlier paper, 'The problem of abortion and the doctrine of double effect' (*The Oxford Review*, 1967), though there it is largely expressed in terms of negative and positive duties. In the course of arguing that the good work done by the Doctrine's distinction between intended and foreseen outcomes of one's action could be done by the distinction between negative and positive duties, she introduced the so-called 'trolley problem', which is discussed to this day. The driver of a runaway tram can steer it onto one narrow track which will kill one man working there, or onto another which will kill five, and she discusses why it is that, in this case, we agree that the driver should steer for the one, but that, in many other cases, such as killing one man to provide needed spare parts for five others, we would be horrified by the suggestion.

In three later papers, she develops her own account of the general distinction between 'doing and allowing' (of which killing and letting die is an instance) in terms of whether or not someone is 'the agent' of harm that befalls someone else. She argues that someone brings about, or does, a harm when they initiate (by act or omission) a sequence of events that leads to the harm, or sustain a sequence leading to harm which would otherwise have petered out. In contrast, if a harmful sequence is already in train and someone could forestall it but does not, then they do not bring the harm about, but allow it.

She adds to this the distinction between intended and foreseen outcomes which she had earlier rejected, noting that allowing a harmful sequence to continue with the intention of exploiting the result, even for good purposes, is morally distinct from allowing it to continue as a foreseen outcome while one does something else. The examples are allowing a beggar to die in order to use his body to save others, and allowing a single man who will die without all of a scarce drug to die while one saves five others who need less by giving it to them.

In two of these three papers, 'Morality, action and outcome' (in *Morality and Objectivity*, edited by Ted Honderich: London, 1985) and 'Utilitarianism and the virtues' (*Mind*, 1985), Foot argued that these distinctions, so essential to our moral evaluation of action, could not be accommodated in utilitarianism, because it assumes that such evaluation is wholly dependent on an action's outcome and whether or not this is the best available state of affairs. Thereby, she concludes, utilitarianism is a deficient moral theory.

Moreover, she went on to argue, its neglect of the virtues leads us astray about 'good (or best) state of affairs'. What makes the 'best state of affairs' as the sole determinant of moral action seem irresistibly rational, she says, is the simple thought that surely it must always be right for an agent to bring about the best state of affairs that she can. How could it be *better* for her to produce a worse one! But given that this view infamously entails that one not only may but *must* do an unspeakably evil deed if that is what it takes to produce 'the best state of affairs', there must be something amiss with that simple thought, and Foot identifies it as the unexamined use of 'best state of affairs'.

She begins by arguing that 'good state of affairs', like 'good thing' and quite unlike 'good pen', 'good doctor', and the other examples she had discussed in 'Goodness and choice' (*Proceedings of the Aristotelian Society*, 1961), is far too speaker-relative to play any role in moral judgement; to do the work it is supposed to do, it has to be understood as 'good state of affairs from the moral point of view'. And utilitarians are right to say that from *within* morality, anyone with the virtue of charity—or, in modern parlance, benevolence—will indeed see states of affairs in which people are happy and free from suffering as good. Utilitarianism is often described as 'the ethics of benevolence', and, perhaps especially when we remember that benevolence encompasses compassion, this is just what attracts many good-hearted people to it.

However, Foot points out that, in a way, this is just what is wrong with it. From within morality as we have it, benevolence is but one amongst other virtues and is circumscribed by their requirements, particularly those of justice. It is only from within the utilitarian morality itself that we could always speak of someone who refuses to torture one man to save others, or who tells a hurtful truth rather than a bare-faced lie as failing in benevolence or compassion, for it is the ethics of benevolence *alone*.

IV

This was all splendid philosophy, but it was not, quite, what she had set out to do in the 1950s. She returned to her original concerns around the mid-1980s, when the work of Michael Thompson, then one of her graduate students at UCLA, suggested to her some new thoughts about moral judgements. Impressed by the ideas that Thompson would eventually publish as 'The representation of life' (in *Virtues and Reasons: Philippa Foot and Moral Theory*, edited by Hursthouse, Lawrence and Quinn: Oxford, 1995), she began the work which was to culminate in *Natural Goodness.*

Foot's original title for her book was actually 'The Grammar of Goodness'. With hindsight, it seems that this would have been a better title, making it clear that the book has little to do with the natural, biological sciences, let alone evolutionary theory. Given her commitment to Wittgenstein, this was bound to be so. Foot was anti-foundationalist and anti-reductionist to the core, and the most unlikely philosopher in the world to think that any of the natural sciences had any bearing on the philosopher's task, especially, perhaps, if that were moral philosophy; she was back in the business of talking about the logical grammar of moral judgements. For what struck her so forcibly about Thompson's work was that it represented our talk about—and hence our evaluations of—*living* things as being *sui generis*, with its own distinctive grammar.

Foot had, in fact, had the germ of this idea right back in 'Goodness and choice', but was only now able to appreciate its significance. Amongst her many examples of 'good F' judgements in that paper, she had mentioned good roots, claws, eyes, stomachs, and other parts of living things, and had pointed out that, like good knives, these were all correctly called 'good' in virtue of being such as to perform their function well. She also pointed out the absurdity of supposing that someone could set up their own criteria for 'good cactus' without any reference to the fact that a cactus is a living organism, 'which can therefore be called healthy or unhealthy'. She even noted that the goodness of the parts of a living thing, and hence its overall goodness as a specimen of its kind, had to do with the role each part played in the life of that kind of organism, and nothing whatsoever to do with us and what we want or use or need or take an interest in.

However, back then, she did not notice that, in this last respect, the evaluations of living things and their parts are grammatically distinct from the evaluations of manufactured objects, or works of literature, or riders or doctors or any of her other examples. Plants and animals have a special sort of goodness which she came to call 'autonomous' or 'natural' goodness—'autonomous' in contrast to the sort of 'secondary' goodness we ascribe to living things when, for example, we say of a specimen of a plant that it is good because it is growing the way we want it to grow, or of a horse that it is good because it wins races.

In the light of Thompson's work, she saw that when we ascribe autonomous goodness (or defect) to a living thing, we look not to ourselves but to the 'life-form' of the kind of living thing it is. The life-form of a particular kind of thing, S, is laid out in a set of 'Aristotelian categoricals'. These take the form of 'The S is (or has or does) F' or 'Ss are (or have or do) F'. These say, of a *kind* of thing, the S, that 'it' has certain characteristics or features (has a tap root, is four-legged, has eyes that can see in the dark) or that it operates or behaves in a certain way (self-pollinates, sees in the dark, hunts in packs). The Fs are the features that, in the life of the S, have the function of achieving what is needed for development, self-maintenance, and reproduction. She sometimes expresses this by saying that the Aristotelian categoricals describe a particular life-form's 'mode of operation'—how it 'manages' or 'gets along' in its life.

The Aristotelian categoricals about plants and the other animals are the sorts of factual claims that botanists and ethnologists who observe kinds of living things in what they take to be their natural habitat make. One striking thing about them is that they are not merely statistical; if things have been going badly for the Ss, it may well be that hardly any of them are F and still be true that 'The S is F'. Another striking thing is that, though factual, they supply a standard—a 'natural norm' in Foot's terminology—for evaluating individual Ss. If it is true that 'The S is F', then an individual S which is not F is defective in that respect—not 'as it should be' or 'as it is supposed to be'. But if it *is* F then it is, in that respect at least, a good F—it has 'natural goodness'. Hence they supply the norms we use to evaluate individual Ss as strong or weak, healthy or diseased, good or defective, Ss. An individual good or excellent S, defective in no respect, thereby has the Fs it needs in order to flourish, to live the life it is its good to live, notwithstanding the obvious point that whether it actually succeeds in doing so depends on chance as well as on its own qualities.

Once Foot had this idea of the distinctive 'grammar of goodness' in living things she had her new approach to moral judgements. Her thought was that they have the same 'conceptual structure' as the evaluations of other living things. She first made it public in 1989 in her Romanell Lecture on Philosophical Naturalism (a public lecture delivered annually at an American Philosophical Association meeting), which she began with the riveting remark, 'In moral philosophy it is useful, I believe, to think about plants.'

Her point is that, like plants, we are living things; when we make moral judgements about ourselves and each other, we are evaluating living things which can therefore be called healthy or unhealthy, good (or excellent) or defective specimens of their kind, just as plants can. It might be thought that moral evaluation was bound to be different, but, from her earliest days, Foot had maintained that it was a mistake to think that the uses of 'good' and 'ought' in moral judgements were grammatically distinct from their non-moral uses. Insofar as they are distinct, this is because moral judgements have a distinct subject matter, namely human character, action and will. When we evaluate an individual human being as healthy or unhealthy, or a good physical specimen of *homo sapiens*, the evaluations are not moral but medical or biological. When we drop the 'healthy' and 'unhealthy', and the use of 'specimen', but keep the terminology of excellence and defect, we find, when talking about ourselves in this way, that we are back with talk about the virtues and vices as excellences and defects, all within the same conceptual structure. The (moral) virtues are natural excellences; the vices are natural defects.

This gives her the new version of her original position on the fact/value dichotomy with respect to good, i.e. virtuous, human beings. Nothing has been said so far which determines that, for example, justice and charity are amongst the natural excellences or that an unjust human being is, in that respect at least, a bad or defective one. However, employing the conceptual structure, Foot finds many parallels between our recognition of defect in the other social animals, who, as we do, depend on each other, and the orthodox list of virtues.

One of her favourite examples is the Aristotelian categorical 'Wolves hunt in packs'. Given that this is part of the description of the wolf's way of getting on, of what wolves, in the wolf's way of life, need to do to sustain themselves, a 'free-riding' wolf which eats what the others have caught but does not join in the hunt, is thereby a defective wolf. Similarly, a chimpanzee that does not groom others is a defective chimpanzee. Part of the way we get on, Foot claims, is by making and keeping contracts, and helping each other when misfortune strikes. Such facts about human existence—different facts and details for the different virtues—figured in 'Moral beliefs' as the objective grounds for saying that everyone had a self-interested reason for aiming at virtue. Now they are fitted into the general conceptual structure, with no insistence on self-interest or the 'profitability' of justice. There are factual judgements to be made about what human beings, given what we are and what we do, need in order to flourish or live well as human beings, and in these we will find the objective grounds for maintaining that, for example, justice and kindness are virtues, or forms of natural goodness. So a just human is, in that respect, a good human being—or 'person' as, colloquially, we say when making moral judgements.

But what of the is–ought gap—the idea that 'moral judgements give reasons for acting to each and every man'? At the beginning of *Natural Goodness* she describes this problem as 'the fence at which I myself have repeatedly fallen, trying now this way, now that, of getting over it', reminding her readers that her first attempt dated as far back as 1958, with 'Moral beliefs', and that it was the problem that had brought her to a halt after she had written 'Morality as a system of hypothetical imperatives' in 1972 and concluded, but not happily, that moral judgements did no such thing. She now locates the source of her persisting difficulty in her unquestioning acceptance of an instrumentalist account of practical rationality, namely that its function is to achieve the maximum fulfilment of the agent's desires or the agent's self-interest. It was a mistake in strategy to start with a pre-established concept of practical rationality and then try to bring moral action under it. What is needed is a fresh start in which one sees goodness in reason-recognition and reason-following as another form of natural goodness.

That 'The human being acts for reasons' is certainly an Aristotelian categorical about the human life-form; indeed philosophers have long had a term for this aspect of our behaviour; it is the operation of our 'practical reason'. Viewed one way, our practical reason is, as far as moral philosophy is concerned, our most significant feature, the thing that, in philosophical tradition, makes us distinct from the other animals in being moral agents. But viewed another way, it is just one of our features, albeit unique, *as* an animal, a living thing, namely a faculty like our sight and hearing, which can be, or fail to be, in good working order in a good, or defective, human being. And it is as the latter that Foot could now view it.

She argues that the two forms of instrumentalism each capture *an* aspect of practical rationality in human beings, given the nature of the human life-form. The human being desires pleasure and enjoyment; an individual who does not is sadly defective. Moreover, many human pleasures are harmless and innocent, and it is rational to satisfy desires for them when there is no reason not to. A human being who does not ever recognise 'That would be enjoyable' as an 'all things considered' reason for doing it, or, recognising it, self-denyingingly fails to act on it, is defective. That is one aspect of practical rationality. The human being can look out for itself much better than anyone else can. (She notes that, in theory, there could be a kind of rational being which found it impossible to think calmly about its own future and had invented a 'buddy system' in which each person had someone else to look out for him. But we are not like that.) An adult human being who does not often recognise 'That might well be my undoing' as an all things considered reason for avoiding it, or recognising it, does it anyhow, is defective. That is a second aspect of practical rationality.

So we have it, in both cases, that practical rationality—good practical reason, or the faculty in good working order—is goodness in reason-recognition and reason-following. Her argument for the third aspect connects this with the concept of a virtue. What distinguishes someone with a virtue from someone who lacks it, she points out, is not simply how they act, but their reasons for acting in that way. Virtuous people, defective in no respect, recognise certain considerations as powerful, and in many circumstances compelling reasons for action, and follow them. So any virtue is a form of goodness in reason-recognition and reason-following and hence a further aspect of practical rationality.

In rejecting the instrumentalists' restriction of reasons for action to considerations related to the agent's desires or interests, Foot agrees with Kant in accepting what is called 'externalism' about moral reasons—the view that someone who says of them 'That's not a reason for me' is defective in practical reason. But, for Foot, there are no such things as the principles of *pure* practical reason; practical reason, as we know it, is not a feature of rational beings or rational agents as such, but simply a feature of us—terrestrial hominids. Kant's purely formal account of practical rationality is displaced in Foot by a substantive conception of non-defective, particularly human, agency.

To establish, within the conceptual structure, that a certain character trait is a virtue, is also to establish that a human being who does not recognise certain considerations as reasons for acting is thereby defective in practical rationality. As she recognises, common usage does not really allow describing the actions of the Great Train Robbers as 'irrational' which was what had led to her earlier rejection of externalism in 'Morality as a system of hypothetical imperatives', but she can now express the point she wanted in terms of defect, and she is happy to say that what they did was 'contrary to reason', or that in saying truly that what they did was dishonest and callous we *would* be giving them reason to do other than they did, regardless of whether they recognise it or not.

Throughout the book she emphasises the fact that she is outlining a conceptual structure which our moral evaluations share with the botanists' and ethnologists' evaluations of the individual members of whatever kind of living thing they are studying. In both cases, the evaluation is based on natural facts about the nature of the kind of living thing being evaluated and how it lives. However, she also argues that, within this structure, a great 'sea-change', as she wonderfully puts it, occurs when we move from the talk about the other living things to talk about ourselves, for what we are and how we live is, indeed, rich and strange. The life that is the human good is far from being merely a matter of development, self-maintenance and reproduction as it is for all other living things, but essentially related to the concept of happiness, and facts about the nature of human beings and how human life goes, in the relevant sense, though natural facts, are far from being a matter on which the human sciences have authority. All of this is taken into account, but the differences between us and the other living things still fit into the same conceptual structure.

V

Philippa inspired love in many of her colleagues and pupils, and those of us who loved her find *Natural Goodness* expressing many of the qualities we loved in her: her delightful sense of humour, her rich capacity for enjoyment, the clarity of her thought, her originality, her tender consciousness of lives less fortunate than her own, her generosity, her willingness to admit to past mistakes, her moral wisdom, and, perhaps, above all, the evidence of her steely determination to work things out about moral judgement, no matter how difficult it seemed or how long it took her. Few academic philosophers wrestle with a single problem throughout their careers, and of those that do, few bring it to a successful culmination. But Philippa did. At the remarkable age of eighty, she achieved what she had always been aiming at—a satisfactory theory of moral judgement. Had she managed to publish *Natural Goodness* just two years earlier, many would have hailed it as the greatest work in moral philosophy of the twentieth century. It is very short and hence, philosophically, very dense. But it is written with such lucid simplicity, and filled with such a wealth of real life examples, that non-philosophical readers frequently describe it as 'beautiful', which, indeed it is.

ROSALIND HURSTHOUSE
University of Auckland

NORMAN GASH

Norman Gash
1912–2009

BORN ON 16 JANUARY 1912 at Meerut, in the Indian state of Uttar Pradesh, Norman Gash was one of seven children, two of whom died in infancy; his mother Kate Hunt, a bootmaker's daughter, had married his father Frederick Gash in 1902. From a family long established as agricultural labourers in Berkshire and Oxfordshire, Frederick was stationed in Meerut. Rising from private to regimental sergeant major in the Royal Berkshire Regiment, he retired from the army in 1921, and then worked for the Inland Revenue. So authoritarian was he that his son, even when a professor in his forties, would be summoned when needed with the cry 'Boy! Boy!' Yet Norman was deeply upset when his father died, and in 1982 asked a colleague, then about to visit India, to find the elderly Sikh ex-soldier who maintained the baptismal font in Meerut's old Garrison Church, and 'give him some annas from me'. The favourite children were (for Frederick) the eldest, Billy; and (for Kate) the youngest, Tim. So Norman's childhood saw relative emotional deprivation. All the Gash children received a good education, however, and Norman attended two elementary schools in Reading, Wilson Road School and Palmer School, before winning a scholarship to Reading School, an ancient grammar school. There he excelled at Latin, French and English, canvassed for the Liberal Party, and published at seventeen in the school magazine a rather mannered but eloquent and learned essay on 'Meredith's and Hardy's conception of Napoleon'. Yet in this somewhat cold, unpolished, and unintellectual family, scholarly achievement did not improve relations with his brothers; their uncomprehending reaction was more to jeer than tease. Norman escaped into books, taking them with him on solitary cycle

Biographical Memoirs of Fellows of the British Academy, XI, 199–236.

rides in the country, and later on solitary cycling holidays. A lifelong pattern was already established: emotional and intellectual self-sufficiency combined with an almost obsessive valuation of his privacy.

A Sir Thomas White scholarship from Reading School took Norman to St John's College, Oxford (founded by White) in 1930 with fifty-two others, and in 1933 he won a First in modern history. He and his fellow-historians owed much to the well-known history tutor W. C. Costin, and included Frank Barlow (launched with a First as a distinguished medieval historian), the prominent civil servant Sir Martin Flett (also with a First), Norman's friend Arnold Taylor (later Chief Inspector of Ancient Monuments and Historic Buildings, nursed by Norman through examination nerves into a Second), and C. L. Mowat (also with a Second, and later a pioneer of contemporary British history); one other among his history contemporaries won a Second and two got Thirds. Gash was for two seasons in the College's football team and was elected to its Essay Society, yet his undergraduate life was not happy, perhaps because his rough-edged personality and manners ill-suited what was then a highly class-conscious community. None the less, he embarked on a B.Litt. thesis, supervised by the Oxford agricultural historian Reginald Lennard, on 'The rural unrest in England in 1830 with special reference to Berkshire'. A fast worker, he had completed it by 1934. His topic reflected his local roots and loyalties, and decades later Douglas Hurd, who knew the area well, could detect in Gash's accent a Berkshire flavour.[1]

Situating the unrest geographically in its agricultural and poor-law context, Gash found that 'everywhere poverty was the driving force behind the riots'. Owing little to outside influences or radical agitators, the labourers were uniformly practical in their grievances: 'there should be work for all, and ... all work should be justly rewarded'. In a fractured society, the gentry were losing influence to farmers who increasingly substituted commercial for traditionalist values. Symbolic of this was the farmers' treatment of their men in winter, when poverty was at its worst: as one labourer said, 'they keep us here like potatoes in a pit and only take us out for use when they can no longer do without us'. Gash thought the less literate labourers naive to expect the authorities' sympathy and even endorsement for their protests, yet noted that the justices were more lenient to the rioters

[1] Brian Harrison's interview with Lord Hurd, 10 Sept. 2010. This memoir relies heavily upon Brian Harrison's interviews and correspondence with Norman Gash's relatives, colleagues and students. Though they are too numerous to mention here, we are deeply grateful to them all. The footnotes indicate where any individual has been quoted.

than central government recommended, even bringing pressure to bear upon the farmers. From its epigraph onwards, Gash's thesis showed marked sympathy with the rioters: they were neither vindictive nor thirsting for violence.[2] The one publication growing out of the thesis was Gash's short article on 'Rural unemployment, 1815–34' in the *Economic History Review* for October 1935. There he saw the labourers as 'not entirely unreasonable' in regarding threshing machines as a primary cause of unemployment and poverty in winter. For the most serious riots in the county, at Kintbury, the death sentence was pronounced upon three rioters, but it was implemented in 1831 only on William Winterbourne: 'life had not dealt so tenderly with him', wrote Gash, 'for death at last to hold much bitterness' (p. 79). As for agricultural labourers who chose to emigrate, 'those who know the conservatism and intense local feeling of country people, can appreciate the courage and the sacrifice involved in such a decision. It was a venture undertaken only by a valiant few' (p. 85).

With hindsight, the thesis is remarkable in at least three respects. First, its empathy with organised labour in its more primitive forms was more akin to a paternalist Tory Radical or leftish orientation than to the Peelite Conservatism whose historian Gash became, and still less to the free-market Thatcherism that he later espoused. No doubt such empathy owed much to the Hammonds, whose *Village Labourer* (London, 1911) is the one secondary source Gash's bibliography cites. Second, the thesis anticipates in its agenda, its technique, and its findings the historiography of the Sixties.[3] Its attempt to interpret popular protest from the inside, its geographical and even topographical approach, and its embracing of a highly analytic and close-textured social history became fashionable only decades later. Its resourceful research involved consulting original records for Berkshire in the County Record Office and in what was then the Public Record Office in London, together with Berkshire newspapers and parliamentary papers. Its eighty-five single-spaced pages with four learned appendixes and a set of maps were a labour of love, and Gash typed it himself. It has been frequently sought out: consultations before November 1972 are not recorded, but fifty-one people read it between then and February 2011, a large number for a B.Litt. thesis examined in 1934. Why, then, was it never published? The Oxford University Press did after all publish Beloff's *Public Order and Popular Disturbances 1660–1714* in 1938.

[2] Quotations from, respectively, pp. 33, 37, 22; see also pp. 6, 8, 11, 13, 59–60, 68, 74–7.

[3] See, for example, E. Hobsbawm and G. Rudé, *Captain Swing* (London, 1969), pp. 180, 203, 288 on the limited nature and incidence of violence and arson.

Gash's reception from the examiners, J. L. Hammond and G. N. Clark, may provide the answer. Their report was bland enough: his research was assiduous, his interpretation original, and his style and arrangement 'well up to the required standard'.[4] Years later, however, Gash complained that Lennard had known too little about his subject, and that in the oral examination Clark (whose views before 1914 on Oxfordshire's class relations had been far more radical than anything in Gash's thesis) had been aggressive and inaccurate in his criticisms.[5]

Gash taught for two terms at Clayesmore School, Iwerne Minster, and first met his first wife, (Ivy) Dorothy Whitehorn, at a gathering of Oxford undergraduates from Reading. After holding a scholarship at the girls' section of Christ's Hospital, she was reading French at St Hugh's College, Oxford, and a contemporary told Gash afterwards that on this occasion he had behaved badly to her. To apologise, he invited her out to tea, and soon fell deeply in love. He persuaded her to abandon her studies before her Finals term; to fund this term she would have been required to teach in a school for two years, which precluded marriage. They married on 1 August 1935. It was a union of opposites: she spontaneous, good-looking, vivacious, gossipy, opinionated and fun: he quiet, measured and scholarly. She fascinated him, and the marriage went ahead despite hostility from both Gashes and Whitehorns. Education had enabled both families to rise in the world, but the Whitehorns had risen further, and to them Gash seemed bad mannered: as her mother told Dorothy, 'he may be a diamond, darling, but he's a very *rough* diamond'. Dorothy's young husband felt socially insecure, and she gave him polish: 'you've done wonders with him', his history master at Reading School, J. W. Saunders, confided to her when visiting several years into the marriage. Gash gradually developed a courteous manner towards women which in later life seemed old-fashioned and even unintentionally patronising. He preferred the separation of spheres then usual in academic circles: children and housekeeping were the wife's responsibility, men did the breadwinning. Dorothy received an allowance which was not always updated for inflation. She was an excellent housekeeper, cook and hostess, and did much to smooth his way. Though never overtly feminist, she eventually came to regret his curtailing her degree course, and often felt lonely and unfulfilled.

[4] Oxford University Archives: Modern History agenda papers 1934 (OUA, FA 4/11/2/9), f. 186 Examiners' report in Clark's hand. We are grateful to the University Archivist Simon Bailey for generous help here.
[5] Brian Harrison's interview with Professor Bruce Lenman, 5 Oct. 2010.

A secure income was now essential, and Gash explored several options before getting on to what later seemed the right track. He hankered to write fiction: the half-written novel begun in the 1930s was discarded after the war, but in the 1970s he published four short stories with a Buchan flavour in *Blackwood's Magazine* under the pseudonym 'William Hunt'. He considered joining the Indian Civil Service, but thought it doomed, and disliked the idea of the home civil service.[6] He wanted to write, and was enabled to do so as temporary lecturer in history (1935–6) at the University of Edinburgh and as Assistant Lecturer (1936–40) at University College London under Sir John Neale. Gash soon settled upon his lifetime preoccupation: the early nineteenth-century aristocratic political system whose values his thesis had defended against the Webbs and Hammonds. The Peel papers in the British Museum nearby were a goldmine. He exploited them in two short articles for the *English Historical Review*;[7] and his two articles of 1938–9 in lesser-known Oxford periodicals first brought Peel to the fore.[8] Already evident was his skilful and meticulous integration (more widely publicised from 1953 in his *Politics in the Age of Peel*) of research in leading politicians' papers and in constituency sources.

For some months the Gashes lived in Exeter, where University College was evacuated. Norman Gash disliked Neale's authoritarian style, which lacked any paternalist justification. The distaste was mutual: in a much retailed episode, Neale told Barlow in a urinal that his assistant lectureship could not be renewed, 'nor Gash's, for that matter, although I can say to you what I could not say to Gash, that you are a good scholar'.[9] War closes many options but opens others, and to Gash and Barlow it offered liberation: on the day after war was declared, they went to the local recruitment office to join up. Many years later Gash explained how they had been turned away with 'we won't be calling up gentlemen for a while yet, sir',[10] so as poor eyesight ruled out his first choice (the navy), he volunteered in 1940 to enlist as a private in the army. He could now make his

[6] Here we draw upon ff. 3–4 of Professor W. Arnstein's typescript interview with Gash on 10 June 1985 which he generously made available to us, and which lay behind his essay 'Norman Gash. Peelite' in his *Recent Historians of Great Britain. Essays on the Post-1945 Generation* (Ames, IO, 1990), pp. 147–72.

[7] 'Ashley and the Conservative Party', *English Historical Review*, 53 (1938), 679–81; 'The influence of the Crown at Windsor and Brighton in the elections of 1832, 1835, and 1837', *English Historical Review*, 54 (1939), 653–63.

[8] 'Oxford politics in the Chancellor's election of 1834', *Oxford Magazine*, 28 Apr., 543–4 and 5 May 1938, 574–5; 'Peel and the Oxford University election of 1829', *Oxoniensia*, 4 (1939), 162–73.

[9] P. Collinson, *The History of a History Man* (Woodbridge, 2011), p. 79.

[10] Geoffrey Parker, email to Brian Harrison, 10 Dec. 2010.

own way within the army on merit, like his father; given that his father was recalled as RSM during the war, enlisting as a private had the additional advantage of avoiding potential family embarrassment. As a good linguist, however, Gash could not remain a private for long, and in 1941–3 he served as an intelligence officer at HQ Southern Command, then on the General Staff (War Office) in 1943–6. He was well qualified, as his German was good: in 1930 he had used a leaving scholarship to take a six-month German language and literature course in the University of Berlin, and when at Oxford he had joined a reading party in the Black Forest. He joined MI14 (the department concerned with intelligence about Germany) and focused on the Waffen SS.

This was a difficult time for Dorothy: her husband spent long hours away on secret work which he could not discuss; they lived in London during the bombing; in 1945 their flat was wrecked in a rocket attack; and in 1944 and 1946, respectively, their two daughters Harriet and Sarah were born. At least as alarming for Dorothy must have been Gash's intelligence work in Germany immediately after the war. Stories of Gash's speeding into Berlin across Russian-occupied Germany on his motor-bike seemed incongruous to subsequent acquaintances, yet hearsay evidence suggests that through interviews he was (among other duties) gathering information on events in the bunker shortly before Hitler's suicide. When compiling his *The Last Days of Hitler* (London, 1947), Hugh Trevor-Roper used the report compiled by himself and fellow intelligence officers without acknowledging colleagues' roles. Many years later, several of Gash's academic colleagues independently recall his indignant claims about his substantial and unacknowledged contribution to the report. Gash was not the sort of man to make such claims lightly, but he never provided or preserved a written record of his role, and no independent evidence corroborating his claims has been found. Trevor-Roper's *Last Days* is so brilliantly and distinctively Trevor-Roper's that Gash's claims can refer only to the book's raw material. Though he shared Trevor-Roper's Conservative alignment, three factors may have fuelled Gash's long-standing distaste for the man: Gash's upright and patriotic reticence, which chimed in with a secretive temperament; an inevitable ignorance about how the secret service had itself encouraged Trevor-Roper to publish the book under his own name; and a failure to recognise how limited was Trevor-Roper's freedom in 1946–7 to publicise the names of colleagues. Compiling for a world readership a document with a vital practical purpose, he was far indeed from wishing to prepare an academic article respectably peppered with footnotes freely acknowledging help from others. Yet such restraints need not have shaped the book's many later editions because Trevor-Roper's former tutors included J. C. Masterman, whose *Double Cross System* (London, 1972) opened up wartime intelligence to public view.

The war's many other consequences for Gash included an enhanced taste for the military virtues; the latter led him to provide much-valued insider help to the Officer Training Corps from the 1950s as Convenor of St Andrews University's Military Education Committee. When asked in 1946 by the head of the university's history department Professor Williams why he wanted its advertised lectureship, Gash is said to have disarmingly and puzzlingly replied that he was not sure that he did, yet he got the job. This remark may reflect the marked salary cut involved, and perhaps also his equivocal experience of pre-war academic life in Oxford, Edinburgh, Exeter, and London. However, once appointed, he threw himself into the task; indeed, as with many in his generation this was essential if he was to recoup six lost years of academic study. The early years at St Andrews were happier for Dorothy, who enjoyed entertaining young people and visitors, saw more of her husband, and helped him in his first book with proofreading and constructive suggestions; she was one of two singled out in the book for generous acknowledgement. Gash took a genuine interest in his students and postgraduates as individuals, holding coffee evenings in his home for those in his pastoral care, and later taking them sailing in the Dysart yawl which he owned in the late 1950s.

With his articles on the Conservative Party manager 'F. R. Bonham' in the *English Historical Review* for 1948 and on 'Peel and the party system 1830–50' in the Royal Historical Society's *Transactions* for 1951, Gash sketched out much of the ground his publications covered later, and in the second he brought out the themes that he soon rendered familiar: the consistency of Peel's objectives, his determination to ensure stable government in difficult times, and hence his subordination of party to what he saw as the national interest. It now seems extraordinary that Gash submitted the book which made his name, *Politics in the Age of Peel* (London, 1953), to twelve publishers before Longmans Green took it.[11] In its three parts, 496 pages, and ten appendixes, it developed its major theme: the fact that 'landmarks are usually more conspicuous at a distance than close at hand', and that 'turning-points rarely show any abrupt change'.[12] For Gash the first Reform Act exemplified the continuity in British politics that he so valued, though he was not the first to pursue this line: J. R. M. Butler, for

[11] Arnstein interview, f. 5.

[12] *Politics in the Age of Peel*, p. x (Introduction).

one, in his classic study published in 1914, saw the Bill as a measure designed to perpetuate aristocratic rule.[13] But until 1953 there was no full-length, thoroughly documented study of politics at national and local level which forced the point home. Governments might move more warily after 1832, but both before and after that year small pocket boroughs, corrupt constituencies open to the highest bidder, extensive political patronage, electoral violence and bribery all persisted, together with the monarch's electoral involvement.

Part 1 ('The representative system') drew heavily and fruitfully on parliamentary debates, but the book was especially pathbreaking in its second section ('The working of the system'). There Gash carried his investigation down to the humblest levels of day-to-day party-political practice, with studies of electoral expenditure, violence, 'influence' and corruption. As recently as 1950 J. A. Thomas had found it 'curious that so little attention has been paid, by historians and political theorists, to the rise of party organization in Britain':[14] three years later he could not have written thus. Spurning facile generalisation, alert to local diversity, the book provided brisk well-informed vignettes of individuals where needed, but focused primarily upon evoking lost values and forgotten patterns of conduct as seen through an empathetic, non-censorious, almost social-anthropological eye. Its third section ('Direction from above'), looser in structure than its precursors, returned to the national level, and described how the parties tried to control the new situation through exercising political patronage, court 'influence', and the formation of party clubs. Oddly truncated, the book lacked an integrating conclusion. And yet the conclusion was in a sense subsequently provided by others, for this was one of those books which, with few secondary sources to draw upon, prompt their rapid creation. *Politics in the Age of Peel* prised open a whole new research area. It was Gash's personal influence which in the 1950s urged E. J. Feuchtwanger to write about urban Conservatism;[15] and it was from Gash's work that J. R. Vincent, K. T. Hoppen, Royden Harrison, D. A. Hamer and many others took their cues for transcending 'constitutional' history through studying political practice.

It was often alleged that Lewis Namier provided Gash's inspiration, yet Gash's work is more akin to Moisei Ostrogorski's, though the latter

[13] *The Passing of the Great Reform Bill* (London, 1914), p. 266.

[14] 'The system of registration and development of party organisation, 1832–1870', *History*, 35 (1950), 81.

[15] Letter to Brian Harrison, 28 Sept. 2010. We are grateful for Dr Feuchtwanger's letter and for his permission to cite it.

nowhere features in Gash's indexes. Namier does not feature in the index to *Politics in the Age of Peel*, which Gash had largely drafted before reading Namier's *Structure of Politics at the Accession of George III* (London, 1929). While respecting Namier, Gash did not view himself as a disciple, and criticised Namier's approach to politicians' motives, his valuation of collective biography, and his faith in collaborative research. Only after his first book was published did Gash make personal contact with Namier, whose respect for Gash stemmed from their experience in jointly examining Manchester students.[16] Gash contributed to *Essays Presented to Sir Lewis Namier* (London, 1956) on 'English reform and French revolution in the general election of 1830'. This was an incisive appendage to both Gash's B.Litt. thesis and his *Politics in the Age of Peel*. It exemplifies how Gash in his prime could combine economical argumentation with deep knowledge of the British electoral system, at local and national levels, to crack a clearly delimited problem. Little more than a quarter of the seats in England and Wales had been contested in 1830, nor was there any chronological fit between the revolution and its British domestic impact. Long before 1830, Roman Catholic emancipation had opened the way to parliamentary reform, and the new government was formed on the day after the riots in Paris, yet by then most of the electoral contests were over. Only after the election did Radicals liken English reform to French revolution; it was widely assumed in Britain that France was merely catching up with England's revolution in 1688; and during the election campaign domestic issues predominated. Dr Quinault's critique of Gash's article rightly stresses the scale of the revolution's overall impact on Britain, but Gash would have agreed.[17] His concern was, rightly or wrongly, to focus more sharply on the election itself, as one would expect from the historian of the electoral system, and his aim was characteristically and convincingly to illustrate how complex was the early nineteenth-century relationship between public opinion and public policy.

In the *Times Literary Supplement* on 3 July 1953 Roger Fulford's two-page review of *Politics in the Age of Peel* offered 'the warmest acclamation' to the book's 'unflagging skill and zest' in unravelling a complex area of British history. But instead of advancing further along his pioneering path, Gash in his next major work *Mr. Secretary Peel. The Life of Sir Robert Peel to 1830* (London, 1961) and *Sir Robert Peel. The Life of Sir Robert Peel after 1830* (London, 1972) for a second time in his career as historian

[16] This discussion owes much to Brian Harrison's interview with the late Professor F. A. Dreyer on 16 Dec. 2010 and to Hamish Scott's e-mail of 5 Apr. 2011.

[17] 'The French Revolution of 1830 and parliamentary reform', *History*, 79 (1994), 377–93.

stepped back to take a more traditional course: this time into high-political biography. In doing so, he did not anticipate the insights of Cowling and Vincent into the complexities and mixed motives of politicians manoeuvring within a closed system: Gash's focus rested upon a single individual, his relationship to policy and to a single political party. Nor is there any echo here of Namier's rather cynical outlook on the political process, for Gash's politicians, most notably Peel, are committed to public service, as highlighted by the biography's epigraph: they are doing their best in very difficult social and constitutional circumstances. A new biography was much needed. Among the big Victorian political biographies, C. S. Parker's three-decker on Peel (*Sir Robert Peel from his Private Papers*: London, 1891–9) was a Trabant, not a Rolls Royce, and the biographies by Anna Ramsay (*Sir Robert Peel*: London, 1928) and Kitson Clark (*Peel and the Conservative Party*: London, 1929) did not rise fully to the occasion. Much as he admired Kitson Clark, a dedicatee of his *Aristocracy and People* (London, 1979), Gash found this 'very Christian gentleman' too moralistic in his perspective, with 'no feel for the real problems of politics'.[18]

Where Gash's biography did innovate, by mid-twentieth-century standards, was in its scale. Of the fifteen prime ministers from Liverpool to Salisbury, only four received authorised biographies in fewer than two volumes, but eleven of the seventeen from Salisbury to Callaghan. Asquith's biography (Spender and Asquith, *Life of Henry Herbert Asquith*: London, 1932) was the last in the two-decker mould: twentieth-century prime ministers have received on average half as many volumes in their authorised biographies as his predecessors. With his two volumes on Peel, however, Gash was doing for political biography what Michael Holroyd was simultaneously doing for literary biography: restoring the genre to its Victorian scale. The complaint that Gash did not sufficiently control his material in the last part of *Politics in the Age of Peel* reappeared in criticism of his 1965 Ford lectures,[19] but biography relieves this problem by prescribing its own shape, and in its 1,436 pages Gash's two-volume *Peel* adopts a broadly chronological arrangement. Especially in the first volume it opened up neglected areas of Peel's career: his private life, marriage, friendships, aesthetic interests and intellectual connections. None the less, Gash's perspective as biographer is, like Peel's, 'executive and governmental'.[20]

[18] Arnstein interview, f. 5

[19] D. Beales in *Historical Journal*, 10 (1967), 314.

[20] Gash, *Peel*, II. 707.

The biography highlights the neglected importance of Peel's period as Chief Secretary for Ireland (1812–18), and always stresses the complexity of a governmental structure which reformers were complicating still further. In a society changing at an unprecedented rate, Gash's small group of beleaguered politicians struggles to operate a political system with its earlier props removed. Peterloo is barely mentioned, and Irish unrest during the Napoleonic wars and after is, like Chartism, seen as a 'problem' for government to tackle. Beset by irresponsible backbenchers and by fractious and uncomprehending monarchs with waning electoral influence, Gash's men of government deploy party structures with only precarious control over an increasingly restive public opinion. Yet in 1890 W. E. Gladstone had famously and somewhat mischievously remarked that 'in point of ability and efficiency ... the country had never been better governed than in the period preceding the first Reform Bill'.[21] Gash was intrigued to see how it was done, and in his *Peel* he seemed at times to be combining two books in one: an account of Peel's career, but also a manual of statesmanship with Peel as exemplar, Peel's 'maxims and reflections' being deployed in six pages at the end of the second volume.

Gash tried not only to see the problems of government through Peel's eyes, but felt an instinctive sympathy with the sheer difficulty of governing in any period, an outlook that fell increasingly out of fashion during his career. 'In terms of mental capacity alone', Gash wrote, Peel 'was one of the ablest prime ministers in British history';[22] his 'master passion in politics', however, was not theory, but 'the desire to get things done', and he aimed always for 'the practical measure rather than ... the political gesture'.[23] He 'throve on power, responsibility and action', his 'fundamental courage and ... spirit' were evoked by 'action and responsibility, especially when spiced with danger'.[24] By 1817 Peel had perfected his administrative technique: first question the knowledgeable to collect the relevant facts, then use them to test generalities and opinions, then pursue consensus pragmatically through a judicious compromise which gets people to work together, then reach a decision only cautiously and slowly, aim to present it as a middle course, choose effective agents through recognising that 'the great art of government' is 'to work by such instruments as the world supplies', and then act energetically once decision has been reached: 'Facts

[21] C. R. L. F[letcher], *Mr. Gladstone at Oxford. 1890* (1908), p. 43.
[22] Gash, *Peel*, I. 712.
[23] Ibid., II. 711, 297.
[24] Ibid., II. xvii; I. 548.

are ten times more valuable than declamations' said Peel.[25] Gash illustrates Peel's methods by dwelling upon his successful introduction of the Metropolitan Police, on his penal reforms and on his Forgery Bill when Home Secretary (1822–7, 1828–30), and likewise on his constructive approach to Irish policy and banking reform when prime minister (1841–6). Although public opinion was for Peel 'something to scrutinise rather than to follow', his 'sense of timing ... was one of his superlative qualities as a politician'.[26]

Gash credits Peel with setting up the mid-Victorian 'age of equipoise', a workable settlement that had never been inevitable. He presents Peel's government of 1841–6 as more effective than its Whig precursors in enforcing public order while tackling the underlying causes of unrest. Peel's doubts in 1842, that perilous year, about the continued viability of the Corn Laws indicated that 'not Ireland but the Condition of England Question was the underlying motive' for their repeal. Paisley was 'a town that haunted Peel all through 1842', and his courageous reintroduction of the income tax enabled him to pursue the cheap government, free trade and lower taxes that the Chartists wanted, for they 'were, in fiscal matters at least, good Peelites'. Gash later claimed that Peel's budgets of 1842, 1845 and 1846 probably 'did more for the working classes of Britain than all Shaftesbury's reforms put together'.[27] The invitation to deliver Oxford's Ford Lectures in 1964, which Gash proudly accepted, enabled him to consolidate this position at the denominational and party-political levels. Published as *Reaction and Reconstruction in English Politics 1832–1852* (Oxford, 1965), the lectures explained how Peel and the Whigs marginalised militant dissent and energised the established church by pressing it to make concessions at its weak points, creating 'in the complex, divided, and emotional society of early Victorian England a kind of self-acting principle of equilibrium which prevented any party or interest from gaining too much power'.[28] In party politics, too, consolidation and a move from the extremes towards the centre had occurred in the Reform Act's aftermath, with the Whigs digesting their radicals and the Conservatives digesting their Ultras. A rather carping anonymous reviewer in the *Times Literary Supplement* (14 April 1966, p. 331) regretted the lectures' somewhat myopic focus, but could not deny Gash's mastery of his subject

[25] Gash, *Peel*, II. 717; I. 226.
[26] Ibid., I. 4; II. 615.
[27] Ibid., II. 554, 358, 362; Gash, *Aristocracy and People. Britain 1815–1865* (first pub. 1979, pbk edn. 1987), p. 4.
[28] Gash, *Reaction and Reconstruction in English Politics 1832–1852*, p. 91.

matter; J. R. Vincent saw them as providing 'a classical example of the genre of consolidation, of scholarship recollected in tranquillity, which Ford lectures ideally should provide'.[29]

Peel's consensual omelette required him to break party eggs: for him 'the essence of Conservatism was a governmental ethic and not a party interest', and in his parlance the word 'mere' often preceded the word 'party'. The need in dangerous times to strengthen the executive accentuated in Peel the tendency among so many prime ministers to gravitate towards seeing themselves as national rather than partisan leaders. For Gash the paradox of Peel's position lay in his role as 'defender of a system of which he was the intellectual critic and active reformer; which he upheld in principle and amended in detail'.[30] Gash fully acknowledged how serious was the friction between Peel and his party well before 1846. In forcing the House of Commons in 1844 to reverse its vote on the sugar duties, for instance, Peel's manner 'was sharp and offensive, and he spoke as though completely detached from the benches behind him', handling the episode 'as badly as any in his long parliamentary career'.[31] He 'tended to overestimate the influence of reason in human affairs', seeming sometimes 'more anxious to win support among his opponents than to make friends among his supporters'.[32] Overworked, plagued by hearing problems, and alert to the scale of national dangers, Peel in his stiff pride grew increasingly impatient with the backbenchers on whom he depended.

Where does this leave him in Conservative Party history? Not seriously damaged for, on the widest definition of Conservatism, Gash's Peel even in 1846 was promoting its long-term interests: his Conservatism 'was not a party label, still less a class interest, but an instinct for continuity and the preservation of order and government in a society ... confronted with the choice between adaptation or upheaval'.[33] Gash later claimed that 'Peel's diagnosis of the true interests of Conservatism cannot easily be faulted':[34] his strategy from 1830 safeguarded church, state, social stability, and aristocracy. Yet there were casualties from such an interpretation: not just Whigs and radicals, but broad swathes of his own party—Ultra Tories, Tory Radicals, Lord George Bentinck, Lord Shaftesbury, and above all

[29] *Victorian Studies*, 10 (1966), 89.

[30] N. Gash, 'Peel and the party system 1830–50', *Transactions of the Royal Historical Society*, 5th series, 1 (1951), 56; Gash, *Peel*, II. xx.

[31] Gash, *Peel*, II. 450, 453.

[32] Ibid., II. 706.

[33] Ibid., I. 14.

[34] In R. A. Butler (ed.), *The Conservatives* (London, 1977), p. 104.

Disraeli. Gash later saw Bentinck as possessing 'few qualities necessary for a political leader and many which positively disqualified him for such a position'. It was 'at least arguable' that the savagery of protectionist attacks on Peel in 1846 had ultimately been counterproductive, failing to advance protectionism, further discrediting Disraeli, and inflaming ill-feeling within a party that long remained divided thereafter.[35] Gash had no time for Disraeli, 'the most cynical and unscrupulous of all the men who have held the leadership of the Conservative party'. Opportunistic in his quest for inter-party parliamentary alliances, short-term in his perspectives, bereft of constructive ideas on policy, unprincipled in pursuing his own career, Gash's Disraeli pursued power with 'very little notion of what to do when he had it'; if he led the Conservatives out of the wilderness, 'he had originally led them into it'.[36] He was 'essentially a comedian', 'a political impresario and actor-manager' and phrase-maker who bewitched posterity with the romance of his career, the glitter of his speeches, and the sparkle of his novels, for 'with posterity literature is more potent than history'. Hence Disraeli's prominence in Conservative historiography.[37] This view clashed with that of another glittering Victorian whom Gash undervalued—Walter Bagehot, whose diffuse but famous essay on 'The character of Sir Robert Peel' (1856) claimed that Peel lacked imagination and originality; Gash saw such complaints as betraying 'a curious misconception. A politician is not a mother but a midwife.'[38]

Gash conducted his defence of Peel as founder of the Conservative Party at a second level, by respectfully chronicling the long-distance voyage he devised for his party, trimming to catch the Liberal wind through a middle-class alignment. A class-hybrid himself, Peel was well equipped to stabilise aristocratic government by aligning aristocrats with the middle classes. It was 'a curious feature of the Conservative Party' that 'though its practice has almost invariably been Peelite, its myth has been largely Disraelian'. Because Disraeli's re-education of his party after 1846 'was inevitably a return to Peel's principles', Peel as founder of modern Conservatism was 'unchallengeable'.[39] Gash's was also the view taken by

[35] N. Gash, 'Lord George Bentinck and his sporting world', in N. Gash, *Pillars of Government and Other Essays on State and Society c.1770–1880* (London, 1986), p. 175; Butler (ed.), *The Conservatives*, p. 102.

[36] 'The founder of modern Conservatism [Peel]', *Solon* (Jan. 1970), 11.

[37] Quotations from Gash's 'Review of Blake's *Disraeli*', *English Historical Review*, 83 (1968), 363; *Solon* (Jan. 1970), 11.

[38] Gash, *Peel*, II. 711.

[39] *Solon* (Jan. 1970), 11; Gash, *Peel*, II. 709.

the prominent mid-twentieth century historians of Disraelian Conservatism, Robert Blake and Paul Smith.[40] Gash dismissed Young England as electorally impracticable, and Disraeli's franchise reform option of 1867 as 'an astounding piece of opportunism'. As for the 'Tory democratic' alternative taken by Disraeli's disciple Lord Randolph Churchill in the 1880s, it was merely 'pseudo-radical': the genuinely radical strategy was for 'a new line of policy which will outflank your opponents and force them back on the defensive'.[41] Lord Salisbury despised Peel, yet Gash thought that Salisbury 'in many respects ... carried on the Peelite Conservative tradition': like Peel he invoked the state to improve the condition of the people, and like Peel he demonstrated 'that political pessimism and a sense of history could be combined with a shrewd grasp of electoral realities, utilitarian common sense, and active reform'.[42] Ultimately, then, the Conservatives 'returned to the road along which he [Peel] had guided them; but belatedly and without gratitude'.[43]

Gash's critique of Peel as party leader has already been noted, but Gash highlighted other faults too. Drawn from outside the aristocracy, Peel resented aspersions on his honour and integrity, and 'on several occasions his sharp and sometimes unreasonable resentment at insult led him to the time-honoured demand for satisfaction or apology'.[44] Peel's 'curious self-consciousness and lack of assurance ... formed the one great flaw in his emotional equipment'.[45] Insecure in relation to his social superiors, he could be arrogantly dismissive of inferiors denied his financial security and educational background: Peel 'never had to struggle; and he had too much scorn for politicians who could less afford to be nice in the methods they used in making their careers'.[46] As an idealist in politics, with an 'ambition ... not just for power but for the right use of power', Peel made enemies through his high-mindedness, and in lacking flexibility 'he lacked an instinct for political self-preservation' and skill 'at the manipulation of private interest for the public good which is an indispensable feature of representative politics'. Yet in outlining Peel's defects Gash often comes near to portraying them as virtues. In Peel's two notable reversals of

[40] Blake, *Disraeli* (first published, London, 1966, pbk edn. 1969), p. 211; Smith, *Disraelian Conservatism and Social Reform* (London, 1967), pp. 3–4.

[41] N. Gash, *The Radical Element in the History of the Conservative Party* (Swinton Lecture, Conservative Political Centre, 1989), pp. 7, 5.

[42] N. Gash, 'Review of Robert Taylor's *Lord Salisbury*', *Victorian Studies*, 20 (1977), 341.

[43] *Solon* (Jan. 1970), 18.

[44] Gash, *Peel*, II. 187, cf. 103.

[45] Ibid., I. 5.

[46] Ibid., I. 667.

view—on Catholic emancipation and the Corn Laws, for instance—'his sense of public duty drove him to take up large issues; his intelligence provided him with radical solutions; his integrity denied him ordinary safeguards'.[47] In truth, Peel became Gash's hero: 'to read some of his parliamentary speeches, still more some of his cabinet papers, is to be conscious ... of an outstanding intellect at work. Few things are more impressive in an examination of Peel's career than the actual quality of mind which he brought to bear on every aspect of administration.'[48] Is it fanciful to detect an affinity between these two upwardly mobile but socially insecure men launched on the world from Oxford? Suffice it to say that, like many biographers who home down on one person, Gash eventually came to resemble his subject, evoking the sympathetic jokes which circulated widely among students at St Andrews.

Gash's indictment of Peel's contemporary critics was formidable, but given the British historiographical mood of the 1960s and after, so provocative a case could hardly go unchallenged. The challenge had been mounted by Disraeli: when confronted by Peel's high-mindedness, he had seen the roots of political integrity as being institutional rather than personal: it was 'only by maintaining the independence of party that you can maintain the integrity of public men'.[49] Peel, by contrast—in pursuing consensus, national rather than party interest, and ultimately coalition—undermined the directness of Parliament's responsibility to the electors. As for Peel's twentieth-century critics, even Blake thought there was 'a better case for dating the modern Conservative party from 1846 than from 1832',[50] if only because Peel as leader had failed to prevent a major split; from 1846 there emerged what was in effect a different party with the same name. The Whigs, too, had their defenders. Reviewing *Reaction and Reconstruction*, Derek Beales praised Gash's deep learning in the parliamentary politics of the period, but thought the contribution made by the Whigs (especially Lord John Russell) to the mid-Victorian compromise more positive than Peel's: 'the book's greatest weakness ... lies in its author's strong Conservative bias'.[51] Beales and Boyd Hilton later adduced statistics to show that as the criminal law worked out in practice, the Whigs

[47] Quotations from Gash, *Peel*, II. xvii, 706.

[48] Ibid., p. 712.

[49] W. F. Monypenny and G. E. Buckle, *The Life of Benjamin Disraeli* (first published London, 1910–20, rev. 2-vol. edn. 1929), I. 754–5 (speech on 22 Jan. 1846, countering Peel).

[50] R. Blake, *The Conservative Party from Peel to Thatcher* (London, 1985), pp. 58–9.

[51] *Historical Journal*, 10 (1967), 314.

(and especially Russell as Home Secretary, 1835–9) contributed far more to mitigating its severity than Peel's much-lauded legislation.[52]

Gash's view of Peel as founder of modern Conservatism was also readily challenged. What precisely was involved in 'founding' the party? How could Peel be credited with the growth in the 1830s of a party grass-roots organisation which sprang up largely spontaneously from below? Could Peel really be exonerated from seriously damaging his party when in the mid-1840s he almost wilfully accentuated its internal divisions? Was he not partly to blame for its languishing in opposition for nearly three decades after 1846? Gash did not conceal the fact that Peel spent four years 'propping up a Whig administration' (1846–50); that 'the natural outcome' of twenty-five years of weak government would have been Peel's consent (if he had survived beyond 1850) to head a coalition of Whig and Peelite Liberals; and that Peel's leading disciples gravitated not to the Conservative but to the Liberal party.[53] Hence Peel's subsequent neglect by his party: his name 'Salisbury and Balfour could hardly bear to hear mentioned, regarding him as little better than a traitor'.[54] Gash himself later scaled down Peel's role from the opposite end by including Liverpool with Peel as 'the great though unacknowledged architects of the liberal, free-trade Victorian state',[55] unacknowledged, because unintended.

Bruce Coleman's *Conservatism and the Conservative Party in Nineteenth-Century Britain* (London, 1988) unobtrusively challenged Gash by stressing the need for a closer and more sympathetic focus on the party's periods out of power and on its rank-and-file, though Coleman scarcely mentions Gash by name.[56] More direct was the challenge from Hilton. Like many young history postgraduates in his day, he found Gash's work stimulating, and in 1979 referred to Gash's 'marvellous biography'.[57] Gash had been one of the two examiners for Hilton's Oxford doctoral thesis (1973), which in 1977 became his first book: *Corn, Cash, Commerce. The Economic Policies of the Tory Governments 1815–1830* (Oxford, 1977). Hilton and Gash both knew that Peel as early as 1830 favoured restoring the income tax as facilitating a tariff-cutting programme.[58] They disagreed only on how far Peel's

[52] Beales, *Historical Journal*, 17 (1974), 880: cf. B. Hilton, 'The gallows and Mr. Peel', in T. C. W. Blanning and D. Cannadine (eds.), *History and Biography. Essays in Honour of Derek Beales* (Cambridge, 1996), p. 91.

[53] Gash, 'Peel and the party system 1830–50', 69; *Solon* (Jan. 1970), 12.

[54] B. Hilton, *A Mad, Bad, and Dangerous People? England 1783–1840* (Oxford, 2006), p. 513.

[55] Gash, *Lord Liverpool* (London, 1984), p. 253.

[56] See especially pp. 4–5.

[57] B. Hilton, 'Peel: a reappraisal', *Historical Journal*, 22 (1979), 588.

[58] Gash, *Peel*, I. 618; II. 299. Hilton, 'Peel: a reappraisal', 606.

economic outlook had been fully formed by the early 1820s. Hilton emphasised that Peel's doubts about preserving the corn laws also dated from the 1820s, and constituted a potential source of division within his Party that was masked in the 1830s by the salience of franchise and Church issues. When later in the decade such issues faded from prominence, and when Whig/Liberal commitment to free trade advanced, the protection issue increasingly threatened Conservative unity.

At the general election of 1841 Peel publicly upheld protection, and at this point the disagreement between Hilton and Gash opens out. Whereas Gash's Peel gradually thereafter became more flexible on the Corn Laws, Hilton's Peel had been flexible all along, though only in his own mind: on the Corn Laws in 1841, as on Catholic emancipation in 1829, Peel's resolute public stance diverged from his private views.[59] As with most politicians, Peel's public statements could not be taken at face value: he was 'uncandid and self-deceiving', says Hilton, and 'ideologically so reticent that his beliefs and assumptions have often to be inferred (with caution) from those of his closest associates'.[60] Hilton's Peel remained in 1841 what he had been in the 1820s: not pragmatic, but doctrinaire: not Cobdenite but 'liberal tory'; that is to say Malthusian, moralistic, providentialist, and ultimately pessimistic on prospects for sustained economic growth. Not until later in his 1841–6 ministry does Hilton's Peel find in the 'condition of England question' and the Irish famine, with help from the Anti-Corn Law League, a heaven-sent opportunity to emerge in his true colours, and repeal the Corn Laws in 1846. If Gash saw Peel as gradually and incrementally moving towards repeal in an empirical response to what he saw as changing circumstances, with a liberal-Conservative destination in the longer term, Hilton saw repeal as the logical end-point of a political economy that Peel had espoused since 1819. The secularised and more optimistic ideology of free trade that Cobden was advancing in the early 1840s, later espoused by Gladstone, never captured Peel the liberal Tory. For him, free trade duly rewarded intelligence and hard work, and rendered the economy natural by removing the artificial stimulus of protection; but he never claimed that it would bring economic growth or even stability.[61]

Gash had impatiently dismissed Bagehot's interpretation of Peel: 'rarely can such a clever character sketch by such an intelligent man have been

[59] B. Hilton, 'The ripening of Robert Peel', in M. Bentley (ed.), *Public and Private Doctrine. Essays in British History Presented to Maurice Cowling* (Cambridge, 1993), pp. 70–1.
[60] 'Peel: a reappraisal', 605, 606.
[61] Ibid., 612–14.

based on such false premises'.[62] Not only had Bagehot exaggerated the importance in politics of constructive imagination (as distinct from administrative and executive skills): he too readily implied that Peel should have moved faster towards the obvious Liberal destination, an assumption that left no ongoing role for 'liberal Conservatism' as a distinct grouping or political location. For Hilton, however, it is the moral imperatives of free trade that shape Peel's stance in 1845–6, not 'the claptrap about a new conservatism, based on national consensus, sound government, and universal caring'.[63] Hilton therefore shares with Blake the view that the Conservative Party of Derby and Disraeli was not Peel's, but a reinvented party. Not till the 1920s did historians begin to think otherwise, and rediscover Peel as ancestor of a party whose anti-socialism was by then causing it to cultivate Liberal individualist recruits.[64] For Hilton, therefore, Peel could be seen as founder of the Conservative Party only through bypassing a large Liberal detour between 1846 and the 1920s.

Rare is the scholar who relishes being controverted, and within his family Gash found it difficult to deal with criticism, seldom confessing to a mistake. Professionally, he was intellectually self-contained, and little affected by fashion or criticism. Self-sufficiently he held aloof from controversy, seldom engaging closely with other historians. He was an exemplary reviewer, bearing in mind the author's intentions, and well aware of how difficult it is to write a good book. His reviews were careful, fair-minded, shrewd, well-versed in relevant earlier publications, alert to errors large and small. He almost always qualified criticism by finding something to praise. There was, however, one exception: his long review of Hilton's *The Age of Atonement* (Oxford, 1988).[65] Acknowledging the 'impressive display of erudition' in this 'fresh and original book', he chose to offer a battery of objections to the small part of it that concerned political aspects, thereby failing adequately to acknowledge its extraordinary range. Gash might have reflected that to have prompted controversion of this calibre testified to the importance of his own achievement. For whatever detailed objections Gash's work might encounter, they did not preclude his bestriding for four decades the political history, broadly interpreted,

[62] Gash, *Peel*, I. 14.
[63] Hilton, 'Peel: a reappraisal', 615.
[64] See Hilton *Mad, Bad and Dangerous People?*, p. 513. Our discussion in these two paragraphs owes much to Brian Harrison's interview with Boyd Hilton on 21 Feb. 2011 and subsequent correspondence.
[65] *English Historical Review*, 104 (1989), 136–40.

of Britain from the 1810s to the 1850s with his meticulous scholarship and firm grasp of the period.

How was Gash able single-handedly to conduct such powerful research on such a scale? He used his time efficiently, answering letters promptly and working quickly, though his departmental and domestic work-space looked chaotic, and was beset by heaps. Yet he could always find what he wanted, and his typing skills, developed in the early 1930s when quite rare in academic life, remained with him for life. On technology he was deeply conservative. He and his pre-QWERTY Remington machine aged together into the twenty-first century, with no thought of computers and word-processors. The absence of 'Gash papers' is misleading: he threw little away, and used extensive card-indexes, but his daughters obeyed his instructions and destroyed everything at his death. During his last eleven years at St Andrews he worked harmoniously with his self-effacing and very efficient departmental and personal secretary, Miss Elizabeth Anderson; she was among the few who could decipher his handwriting. While holding tightly to professorial power, he was good at devolving; he trusted subordinates to do what was asked, encouraged them to consult him about their difficulties, and then staunchly backed them. 'Whatever you do, don't upset my secretary', he told the department's new recruits; colleagues were reminded that 'she could get another job at any time, which is more than any of us could do.' She devised a filing system for his departmental papers, and soon learned to draft letters which he could confidently sign. He was fluent in dictating, but typed the first drafts of his books himself, then sent chapters one by one for Miss Anderson to produce a fair copy, never bridling at her suggestions and corrections tentatively offered; his *Peel* (London, 1976) and *Aristocracy and People* (1979) were both produced in this way.[66] In retirement he relied upon a secretarial agency for his fair copy.

Gash conserved time and effort at a second level, through being highly focused. He had few interests outside work, the media did not seduce him, and he did not fuss about historical method or diffuse his energies by publishing long review-articles. Nor did he spread himself into publishing on non-British history, or outside the first half of the nineteenth century, or beyond political history (broadly defined). He was focused by temperament. When in later life he did take up leisure interests, they sometimes came to resemble research projects, and he would read around enjoyed

[66] This paragraph owes much to Brian Harrison's interview with Miss Anderson on 8 Oct. 2010 and subsequent correspondence.

experiences before moving on. His single-mindedness may help to explain why Gash's career culminated in a CBE (1989) rather than a peerage (like Lords Briggs and Blake) or a knighthood (like R. C. K. Ensor and E. L. Woodward). He was neither prominent for public duties undertaken, nor popular for cultivating a gentlemanly amateur image, nor did he pronounce publicly upon things in general. His public visibility may also have suffered through being remote from the centres of power. Travel to London libraries and archives in England was expensive, and there was little time or taste for metropolitan social, professional and political distractions. Yet this in itself conserved Gash's time, and he warned ambitious young colleagues contemplating a southward move that Oxbridge colleges' clever pupils would never compensate them for the burdens of collegiate teaching and administration, and their research would suffer.

Furthermore, like many scholars in his day, Gash was cushioned at home. He was good at winning research grants, and for much of the time when not on research trips he was alone in his study while Dorothy shielded him from distractions. From the early 1950s onwards Gash's family paid a price for his success as an historian, for the family picnics and swimming expeditions became less frequent, family holidays were rare, and as a parent he became remote. Helpful when advice was needed, encouraging and proud of his daughters' careers, but distant from their daily lives, he was too preoccupied with his own thoughts to be companionable. Well able to rebuke an undergraduate for eating in the street, Dorothy was no doormat, but her self-assertion took the form of identifying closely with her husband's career, of which she could be fiercely defensive. She was devoted to her daughters, but given the academic potential which marriage had terminated so early, she felt intellectually unfulfilled and often lonely; she loved company, whereas Gash fended people off, and did not accumulate friends, often not perceiving how his manner affected others. Much historical research is necessarily solitary, but its solitude also reflected Gash's preference acquired in teenage years for his own company: for him, to be alone was never to be lonely. As a young professor when sailing in races in the bay he would begin with the others at the start line, but whereas they would sail to a marker buoy, turn to another and then return home, he kept sailing out to sea alone and returned hours after the rest had gone home. In later life, when sea-bathing, he would alarm companions by swimming far out on his own.

Gash put much of the emotional energy denied to his family, much of the public work absent at national level, into local causes where his scholarly reputation could enhance his influence. At St Andrews, heads of department were powerful. 'Participation' even of lecturers, let alone of students, had yet to become the vogue word, and Gash's sense of hierarchy within university and department was firm. Going with the post initially was a big house in The Scores, the street where three professorial houses were located, as well as a seat in the Senate. The informality of decision-making left much discretion to the professors, and Gash's was an unusual combination: skill and productivity in research, efficiency in administration, successful lecturing, sympathetic tuition, and influence in university politics. Yet his departmental success was hard won. In 1953 he had applied successfully for the chair of modern history at Leeds with the aim of qualifying as an external candidate for the chair of history at St Andrews, which he knew would become vacant in 1955. The plan succeeded: he returned to St Andrews, much to Dorothy's relief. She had found Leeds an unfriendly place, its schools were less good, and Sarah had a serious road accident there. Yet Gash's second move in two years brought trouble, for he returned to St Andrews with two Leeds colleagues, Anthony Upton and Cedric Collyer, in a threesome nicknamed 'Leeds United'. They soon became decidedly disunited, with Gash and Collyer notoriously at loggerheads within the department for many years until Collyer departed. Gash's appointment of John Erickson and Margaret Lambert also caused trouble: both felt under-appreciated, friction turned into hatred, and both departed. None of this was good for Gash's self-confidence, a situation worsened by the St Andrews structure of historical study. Gash was Professor of History, and head of the modern history department, and his letter-heading throughout his time described him as '*The* Professor of History'. There were two other history departments outside his parish, however: for mediaeval and Scottish history. This prompted argument about the professors' relative status, with yet more bad feeling and departures. The department's internal relations were sometimes so bad that outside conciliators were invoked.

During the 1960s, however, things improved: younger appointments were made, enemies departed, and Gash's self-confidence grew. 'Formidable' was a word that came to be used about him. His old-fashioned steel-rimmed spectacles with thick lenses sharpened his gaze on interlocutors, and he reminded Bruce Lenman of Velasquez's cardinal inquisitor.[67] Always formal in dress, speech, manner, and modes of address, he had little taste for gossip. With a large head and grey hair brushed back rather severely, he inspired awe among colleagues even when posthumously

[67] Brian Harrison's interview with Bruce Lenman on 5 Oct. 2010.

recollected in tranquillity. Yet beneath all this there was an elusive humour: he could tell a good story, and then there would be a thin smile and a slight laugh. 'He had an engaging way of putting his fingertips together and considering a point carefully before answering in measured tones', Madsen Pirie recalled. '… Sometimes his eyes would twinkle as he made a humorous point, his face only just betraying the humour. He spoke slowly and with gravitas. His immaculate greying hair added to his authority.'[68] In the 1970s Gash's growing power within the department accorded more closely with his authoritarian style; there was never any doubt that it was *his* department, and to younger colleagues he was never 'Norman', always 'Professor Gash'. His sense of mutual responsibility, however, made the outcome very different from what he had observed in Neale during the 1930s. With his strong sense of duty and justice, Gash gained the trust of his staff, and they came to realise how deep was his concern for their welfare, and how resolutely he would defend them against outsiders.

Students knew that as a teacher he set high standards and commented carefully and honestly on their written work; the more closely they knew him, the more they realised how much he cared about them as individuals. His lectures to the second year were delivered in a good carrying voice, and were clearly arranged. By the 1970s their audience was shrinking because their nineteenth-century British subject matter was moving out of fashion, but he showed no sign of resenting the success of younger and more charismatic lecturers with more fashionable subjects. Not for him the fireworks, the slides, the mischievous asides, and the latest news from the research front; students felt instead the weight of his years of learning. Yet he never talked down to them, and commanded respect from his powerful reputation and patent seriousness. Gowned behind a podium, he came to seem rather old-fashioned in style, perhaps too unremittingly erudite, and his personality was (if only for reasons of age) somewhat austere and remote by comparison with colleagues. 'He seemed foreign both in terms of place and century', writes Andrew Gailey (1973–7). 'I remember thinking that if Robert Peel was to walk in, the Professor would have felt far more at ease with his hero than with his own time or his contemporaries [and certainly his students]. Indeed he could have been, perhaps was, Peel.'[69] In the 1970s students who attended his seminars later in the course were struck with how misleading was his student image as 'Gash the Fash'. He could unravel complexity and require high standards while simultaneously

[68] Interview with Brian Harrison, 19 Oct 2010.
[69] E-mail to Brian Harrison, 21 Feb. 2011 which Dr Gailey kindly allowed us to quote.

showing himself intellectually receptive and rather kindly; indeed, his way of leading them on by planting subversive but stimulating questions in their midst was almost mischievous.

High standards were also applied to colleagues, and there was some resentment at Gash's reluctance to promote, and even complaints that he had failed to honour promotion promises. But to students and colleagues alike, he was receptive to sensible suggestions for curricular change, ensuring that history at St Andrews harmonised old with new. Upton found that his own strongly socialist views never complicated relations: what mattered to Gash was the quality of Upton's teaching and scholarship. With Dorothy's help, Gash did his best to overcome subordinates' small-scale personal difficulties, storing colleagues' property in his house in emergencies, entertaining them at home, and reducing teaching commitments in situations of overload. He was keen to leave his younger colleagues space to research and publish, and was at his best when colleagues sought careers advice. Geoffrey Parker thought him 'a wonderful mentor', and discovered that he had been thinking more about his subordinates than he had revealed.[70] In recruiting staff Gash preferred a broad specification which would attract a wide field of candidates who could adapt later to departmental need. Thus did St Andrews become a first-rate history department for studying the so-called 'middle period'. Claims that Gash disliked appointing women were unfounded. He was susceptible to flattery from women, who appreciated his old-style courtesy, but his women colleagues were appointed on merit. One of them had twice quietly to remind him (with ultimate success) that, with one woman present at his Friday coffee mornings for staff, 'gentlemen' was not an appropriate way in which to begin; after initially being wary of him, she came to admire his way of running the department, and appreciated a wry sense of humour so quietly subtle that it sometimes went unperceived.[71]

The coffee mornings in his office were his way of holding the department together, and became larger and rather more formal as staff numbers grew. Collyer, who had earlier made embarrassing scenes at them, eventually ceased to attend. Their purpose was more to inform than decide, since Gash kept decisions almost entirely in his own hands. He served the coffee

[70] E-mail to Brian Harrison, 15 Nov. 2010. We acknowledge here the enormous trouble Professor Parker has taken to illuminate for our benefit every aspect of Norman Gash's personality and career, and to encourage former colleagues to do likewise.

[71] M. J. Rodriguez-Salgado, 'Recollections of Norman Gash' (e-mailed to Brian Harrison, 28 Nov. 2010). We are most grateful to Professor Rodriguez-Salgado for permission to cite her valuable memoir.

himself, then sat behind his large desk and colleagues sat on chairs and sofas around it. Some of the meetings were quite long, with questions answered and incoming letters sometimes read out. In discussion Gash led from the front, but where there was disagreement he usually got his way by not weighing in until everyone had talked themselves out, and sometimes prevailed with the aid of a joke. Keith Wrightson recalls that 'his manner when chairing these meetings was that of an affable laird. He could be very witty, and encouraged the same manner in others, and the room was often filled with laughter.'[72] One of his woman appointees recalls that at the end of his career many colleagues were in awe of Gash, 'some revered him, many were afraid of him. It was rare to hear of someone who disliked him ... I never saw anyone treat him or refer to him with anything less than respect.'[73] For Parker, Gash's courtesy to colleagues is exemplified in the care he took in 1980 to tell them individually about his impending resignation before making the news public.[74] When Gash announced this at his Friday coffee morning, Wrightson recalls that 'we were stunned. A long silence followed; then rather stuttering efforts to respond to this bombshell ... many of us shared an inability to envisage the department without Gash. Where would the university find someone of his stature? ... It was clear that an era was over.' Serving under Gash for five years before he retired, Wrightson thought him 'head and shoulders the best head of department that I have ever encountered. He had enormous authority.'[75]

There was a two-way traffic between departmental authority and influence within the university. Gash's secure departmental power-base made him a major figure in the university senate, especially given his wit and forcefulness as debater, and from 1978 to 1980 he held a key post as Dean of the Faculty of Arts. He felt little respect for J. Steven Watson, Principal of St Andrews from 1966 to 1986, either as historian or as Principal. This became clear in several much-relished senatorial exchanges between two wily operators: the easy-going and somewhat disorganised Labour sympathiser and the efficient and astringent Conservative scholar. In the circumstances, Gash's memoir of Watson for the *Oxford Dictionary of National Biography* is generous indeed. In 1980 Gash's relations with another

[72] 'Some memories of Norman Gash' (e-mail to Brian Harrison, 21 Nov. 2010). Professor Wrightson allowed us to quote from this valuable memoir.
[73] Rodriguez-Salgado, 'Recollections of Norman Gash'.
[74] 'Remembering Norman Gash' (e-mail to Brian Harrison, Dec. 2010).
[75] 'Some memories of Norman Gash'.

prominent St Andrews personality, Sir Kenneth Dover, President of the British Academy,[76] became of major importance in the Academy's discussions about whether the art historian Sir Anthony Blunt's espionage for Soviet Russia should invalidate his fellowship. Historians were at the heart of the controversy, not least Gash, who had been a Fellow since 1963. The annual general meeting (which Gash was unable to attend) decided on 3 July 1980 not to expel Blunt. This prompted four resignations, and Gash publicly and inaccurately claimed that the meeting had been 'packed' by Blunt's supporters from the south-east. With three other Fellows, he threatened to resign his fellowship at the end of the year if Blunt then remained a Fellow.

Dover despised pressure of this kind, but feared a mass exodus, so on 13 August in St Andrews he visited Gash, 'a resolute man'[77] with whom he had not always agreed. This meeting turned out to be crucial. Dover, perhaps unduly scrupulous as President of the Academy in forcing himself to conceal his personal views on Blunt, had been surprised that nobody at Council or at the annual general meeting had used what he saw as the crucial argument. For Dover 'there was only one justification for expelling Blunt: that he had worked treacherously for the supremacy of a totalitarian nation which has consistently frustrated and persecuted scholarship, and by so doing he tried to defeat the purposes for which the Academy exists'. Dover held this view strongly: as he later recalled, 'I have always felt, and still feel, that a nation which fails to tear a traitor to pieces is doomed.'[78] He recalled that at their meeting Gash 'said something which touched my sorest nerve' when pointing out that what Dover saw as 'the real charge' against Blunt had not been raised at the annual general meeting, and that when people were alerted to this, as they would be, many would resign. Dover then told Gash that he would encourage Blunt in the course which Gash recommended in the *Daily Telegraph* two days later: to rescue the Academy from 'the worst crisis in its 80-year history' by resigning.[79] In 'one agonised afternoon' some ten days after meeting Gash, a meeting to which Dover did not subsequently refer in public, he confessed that 'I had gone to see Gash to tell him to stop [*sc.* encouraging resignations] and had come away one hour and two sherries later prepared to do his bidding.'[80]

[76] See the memoir of Sir Kenneth in this volume, pp. 153–75.
[77] British Academy archive, BA2249: President, Correspondence etc. 1979–81, f. 91.
[78] Ibid., f. 219. For Dover's published recollections see his *Marginal Comment. A Memoir* (London, 1994), pp. 212–21.
[79] Ibid., f. 91 (Dover's notes).
[80] Ibid., f. 92.

Dover's letter to Blunt produced the desired result and terminated public debate on the main issue, though not without controversy about Dover's conduct. His and Gash's recollections of the episode illuminate their personalities as vividly as their conduct. Gash's reflections appeared in the Winter 1981 number of *Policy Review*, organ of the American right-wing Heritage Foundation. In criticising 'the liberal progressive mind' in western societies, Gash identified with 'the less intellectual people' who 'have simpler ideas and more direct instincts', and distanced himself from the professionalised scholarship that breeds 'a certain exclusiveness and distortion of values … Scholarship is not a religion but scholars sometimes behave as if it is, with themselves as a kind of priesthood immune from conventional obligations.' Deploring what he saw as declining standards, Gash claimed that in the 1930s Blunt would have been forced out of public life or even out of the country, and regretted 'the fashionable tendency to regard moral standards as purely subjective.… The only test seems to be the sincerity of the doer, not the consequences of his actions.' Noting 'the sudden tenderness which comes over left-wing intellectuals when the Soviet Union is implicated', he was surprised that the Fellows were so coy about publicly taking a resolute line during the affair.[81]

Gash's conservatism was multilayered. In his personal life he relished his daily routine, dressed conservatively, discouraged his wife and daughters from using make-up, loved being in his study with his books and ancient typewriter, and deplored change at home and elsewhere. J. B. Conacher, reviewing his *Reaction and Reconstruction* in 1966, saw him as 'a conservative historian in the best sense … sceptical, discriminating, detached, ever on his guard against easy generalizations or sentimental enthusiasms, cautious and clearheaded'.[82] In the Blunt affair Gash regretted that the governmental perspective so prominent in his publications was now less central to scholarly values. He deplored 'the tendency to be critical of all traditional and prescriptive authority both in society and in the state. For many self-conscious liberals,' he continued, 'loyalty and patriotism have become intellectually indecent words which, uttered in public, cause mild embarrassment.'[83] In his historical writing Gash was not above taking the occasional unobtrusive pot-shot at anti-governmental attitudes: 'few things are so dangerous in politics as the enunciation of principles', for instance; or his reference to Peel's twenty-year experience by 1830—'in

[81] 'Over there. A scholar and a traitor', *Policy Review* (Winter 1981), 159–60.
[82] *American Historical Review*, 72 (1966), 191.
[83] 'Over there', p. 159.

the art of getting things done; an asset which idealists do not usually acquire'.[84] Common sense, that supreme governmental quality, Gash often praised in conversation, together with (in his writings) political continuity. The more extreme radicals in the 1830s were, he thought, 'distinguished, as political crusaders are apt to be, more by obsessive zeal than by practical sense'.[85]

The villagey mood and somewhat secluded location of St Andrews in the 1950s suited Gash, as did its students' rather traditionalist outlook in the 1960s and 1970s. It witnessed no major 'Sixties' protests, and even his support for Ian Smith in Rhodesia could not make Gash a hate-figure. St Andrews students liked wearing their red gowns, their procession to the pier on Sundays, and their 'Raisin Monday'. They were distinctive for supporting a Student Conservative Association much larger and more influential with students than in other universities.[86] This lent the Association national influence, especially in the 1970s and 1980s when the university became a cauldron of free-market Conservative ideas. Free-market student meritocrats were particularly influential, privately but not maliciously labelling the more traditionalist and privileged Conservative students as UCTs ('upper-class twits') or 'Yahs' (mimicking their English public-school way of speaking). Here was a breeding-ground for key figures in the 'Thatcherite' revolution such as Douglas Mason, Michael Forsyth and Madsen Pirie, with close links to Enoch Powell, Michael Fallon, Christopher Chope, Ralph Harris, Rhodes Boyson, and the Institute for Economic Affairs. From St Andrews came the three graduates who founded the influential free-market Adam Smith Institute in 1977, and several Conservative founder-members of the No Turning Back Group. Whatever their earlier views, the Gashes by the 1970s were in student circles 'sort of "royalty", in a way', Lord Forsyth recalls: they were interested in young people, and enjoyed holding an annual garden party in their garden. For Pirie, Norman Gash was 'an avuncular figure, a kind of godfather', and 'a benign presence' if there were disputes with authority. The Gashes took a proud, close and generous interest in Pirie's unusual self-help career, and it was to them that he dedicated his first book.

Gash was sceptical about the history of ideas and the political role of abstract thinking. He knew well enough that intellectuals can be influen-

[84] *Reaction and Reconstruction*, p. 68; *Peel*, II, xvii.

[85] *Aristocracy and People*, p. 162.

[86] This paragraph owes much to Brian Harrison's discussions with Lord Forsyth of Drumlean on 14 Dec. 2010, Dr Madsen Pirie on 19 Oct. 2010, and Professor Michael Prestwich on 9 Oct. 2010.

tial: dissolving conventional thinking, harnessing discontent, stimulating action, forming 'the cutting-edge of social and political movements, enabling them to move faster and with more assurance', and sometimes prevailing even when in a minority.[87] Unlike Blake or Beloff, however, Gash focused his contribution to Conservative national politics where he felt best qualified: through publishing in the right-wing press on relevant historical topics. In his long-ranging analysis of political-party evolution published in 1978, he argued that 'the ratchet effect of collectivist legislation' had ended the mutual accommodation which had hitherto made the two-party system practicable. A corporate state entailed the end of the Conservative Party because the 'logical end' of collectivism is a one-party state. He put little faith in such devices as written constitutions and electoral reform as shields against socialism, and like the rest of his party soon found an alternative way out through Thatcher's vigorously anti-socialist leadership.[88]

Gash's expertise seemed still more relevant in the mid-1980s when Peel, Disraeli, and Salisbury became short-hand terms for factions within Thatcher's Conservative party. In 1984 Edward Heath urged 'the pragmatism of Peel, not the dogmatism of "There is no other way"' in his speech to the Peel Society on the one hundred and fiftieth anniversary of Peel's Tamworth Manifesto: Conservatives should steer between 'doctrinaire radicalism from the left, and the reaction of ... Tory ultras'.[89] By contrast, Gash and St Andrews students likened Peel's free-trade campaign to Thatcher's move towards the free market: both had forced their way from minority status to become the intellectual mood of the moment, and it was Thatcher's 'wet' critics who were the aberration, straying from the true Conservative path.[90] For Gash, Baldwin's decision to join the National Government coalition in 1931 had entailed 'a certain intellectual flabbiness'; Macmillan's *Middle Way* 'represented a slip-way to Socialism rather than a new path for Conservatism';[91] and in the mid-1980s centrist Conservative attempts to discover a radical Disraeli in their pedigree were doubly mistaken, for the radicals were Peel and Thatcher, not Disraeli and

[87] N. Gash 'The power of ideas over policy', in A. Seldon (ed.), *The Emerging Consensus ...?* (London, 1981), p. 236.
[88] N. Gash, 'The British party system and the closed society', in W. H. Chaloner *et al.*, *The Coming Confrontation. Will the Open Society Survive to 1989?* (London, 1978), pp. 53–4; see also pp. 56–8.
[89] *The Times*, 1 Dec. 1984, 4.
[90] Gash, 'Power of ideas', pp. 236–7; *Radical Element*, p. 6.
[91] Gash, *Radical Element*, p. 11.

the 'wets'.[92] Thatcher's was the third Conservative 'radical initiative' to force the Party's enemies on to the defensive, Peel's being the first, and Chamberlain's tariff reform the second.[93] Historical parallels are never exact, however, and from this particular political parlour game no convincing winners seem in retrospect to have emerged.

There were push and pull impulses behind Gash's early retirement from St Andrews in 1981 to Langport in Somerset. Pushing him was a university scene decreasingly attractive in a world of funding cuts and even less attractive for the protests against them; he soon came to feel that there were too many universities, and that they tried to fund too much arts research.[94] Pull factors included concern for Dorothy's health; desire to publish more; and a yearning to get closer to his roots in southern England, Langport being the nearest he could get to them in a house that he could afford. He was, after all, still fit: Miss Anderson recalls a man who always ran up and down stairs, never walked, and was 'always in a hurry'. He told his former graduate student, Fred Dreyer, that he would 'rather get out while I am reasonably sound in wind and limb—a good deal more so than some of my younger colleagues, I like to think. And the next ten years in university life in this country is [*sic*] going to be a difficult one.'[95] In the relative isolation of Langport he inevitably drew largely upon materials already collected, but if his many publications in retirement did not enhance his reputation, they left it intact.

In the mid-1970s, despite all his administrative distractions, Gash was still writing high-quality history; by then his earlier publications were so important that in new publications he could often paraphrase his own conclusions, though with a tendency to move back in time and showing more interest in Liverpool and Wellington than in Peel. As one of four authors, he contributed eighty-seven authoritative and lucid pages on 'From the origins to Sir Robert Peel' to the synoptic collaborative history of the Conservative Party edited by R. A. Butler, *The Conservatives* (London, 1977). Then, in 1979, he published *Aristocracy and People. Britain 1815–1865* in Edward Arnold's 'The New History of England', a series which he edited jointly with A. G. Dickens. Alert in this volume to the formidable difficulties experienced by governments after 1815, he saw the Napoleonic wars as compounding the problems presented by rapid

[92] N. Gash, 'The enigma [Macmillan] who strayed', *The Times*, 31 Dec. 1986, 12; see also Gash's 'Myth of the two Tory parties', *Daily Telegraph*, 8 Oct. 1984, 18.
[93] Gash, *Radical Element*, pp. 7, 12.
[94] See Arnstein interview, f. 8.
[95] Photostat of t/s letter, 27 Jan. 1980.

industrialisation, urbanisation, and population growth. Yet for Gash, industrialisation in the long term brought its own cure, for in the historians' 'standard of living controversy' of the 1950s and 1960s he was an optimist. After two descriptive chapters he adopts a narrative approach while admiring the resilience, pragmatism and flexibility with which aristocratic politicians prolonged their influence. Far from idle, they were thoroughly integrated into national life, and helped to secure the mid-Victorian 'age of equipoise' with which the volume's final chapter (in revived descriptive mode) 'takes stock'. Never inevitable, this peaceable outcome had seemed improbable in 1815.[96]

Early in retirement Gash published a substantial two-part article in *Parliamentary History* for 1982: it filled out his earlier work by fully explaining how the Conservative Party had evolved at parliamentary and constituency levels between 1832 and 1846. He moved on to Lord Liverpool, on whom he had contributed an informative, concise and respectful essay to Van Thal's *The Prime Ministers* (London, 1974), stressing Liverpool's continuous influence and the unimportance for policy of the ministerial changes in 1822.[97] In *History Today* for May 1980 and March 1982 he published two incisive articles illuminating aspects of Liverpool's career, but his *Lord Liverpool* (London, 1984) was smaller in scale than his two volumes on Peel. It complemented them, though, through portraying Liverpool as Peel's exemplar and precursor in (admired) personal characteristics, in surmounting constitutional and social problems, and in economic remedies devised. This unassuming, likeable, unself-advertising prime minister infused public life with 'qualities which in aggregate few prime ministers have equalled. In grasp of principles, mastery of detail, discernment of means, and judgement of individuals he was almost faultless,'[98] so he 'clearly ranks as one of the great though unacknowledged architects of the liberal, free-trade Victorian state, second only to Peel in importance' (p. 253). Gash had found another hero, and his biography's main aim was to rescue Liverpool from undue neglect. Its wartime narrative chapters were unexciting, but the book perks up when Liverpool becomes prime minister, and there is a fine chapter on Liverpool's personality, prime-ministerial methods, and cultural interests. Gash found in Liverpool's career, as in Peel's, an object lesson in the art of politics, for Liverpool 'had learned the most valuable lesson that politics has to teach:

[96] For a shrewd and nuanced review see B. Hilton in *Welsh History Review*, 10 (1980–1), 435–7.
[97] N. Gash, 'The Earl of Liverpool', in H. Van Thal (ed.) *The Prime Ministers*, I (London, 1974), p. 289.
[98] Ibid., p. 287.

to see men for what they really are and to know how, with all their faults and weaknesses, they can be used for a common purpose' (p. 102).

Gash's *Pillars of Government* (London, 1986) was a stocktaking or mopping-up operation: most of its articles had already been published, but one was new and important: an essay on 'Cheap government'. Peel's achievement was again highlighted, this time with contributions hostile to his antagonist, Lord George Bentinck. Gash never sought to limit his readership to other scholars, and his three articles for the *Modern History Review* in 1990, 1992 and 1994 show him concisely and clearly unravelling for a wider public complex issues that he had earlier discussed at length: on Peel and the Conservative Party, on Peel and Ireland, and on the Peelites, respectively. His lightly footnoted book *Robert Surtees and Early Victorian Society* (Oxford, 1993) is his first publication to show a certain loss of grip. Concerned more with context than with Surtees himself, it was a social history of Britain in disguise; indeed, Gash discussed Surtees almost as an afterthought, giving his novels no close analysis, and never really integrating them into the book. Furthermore, he came near to subverting his book's purpose when he confessed that Surtees was a decidedly untypical Victorian.[99] To an expert reviewer the book seemed slightly anticlimactic, containing little new material, and citing no recent sources on social history.[100] Yet Gash was still publishing substantial articles in the *Oxford Dictionary of National Biography* in his eighties, most notably on Wellington and Liverpool, together with an article on Peel in the *Dictionary of Irish Biography*. Gash's contribution to Anthony Seldon's *How Tory Governments Fall* (London, 1996), published in his eighty-fourth year, showed no loss of grip on his chosen period, and in his nineties he performed the signal service to J. T. Ward's widow of compressing Ward's biography of the Conservative MP and factory reformer W. B. Ferrand into publishable shape; it came out in Gash's ninetieth year (*W. B. Ferrand: 'the working man's friend', 1809–1889*: East Linton, 2002). This had indeed been a fruitful 'retirement'.

The Old Gatehouse, close to the busy main road from Langport to Taunton, was originally an eighteenth-century toll house, somewhat awkwardly set at different levels on the ground floor, with three rooms below, one of them a much-valued wine cellar. The house was comfortably but not lavishly furnished, with maps, paintings and engravings on its walls.

[99] Gash, *Robert Surtees*, p. 389; see also Gash's article on Surtees in the *Oxford Dictionary of National Biography*, <http://www.oxforddnb.com/view/article/26791>.
[100] D. C. Itzkowitz, *American Historical Review*, 100 (1995), 161.

Gash had a library built on at the back, with book-filled shelves and a big working table, and in the garden he enthusiastically cultivated roses and apple trees. In retirement he led a quiet life, and when not in his study or garden he enjoyed watching televised sporting occasions, and followed the fortunes of Reading's football team up to his death. In the 1960s the World Cup had been the occasion for his first hiring a television, and a year or two later he had bought one. With his savings he was careful, but he had no taste for shrewd investment, let alone tax avoidance. He lacked practical skills, and at fifty-three had obtained a driving licence only after several attempts. He was adventurous behind the wheel: the old road from St Andrews across Fife to the motorway was slow and winding, Wrightson recalls, and 'more than once while trundling along in my Mini I was overtaken by a Peugeot dancing through the traffic at high speed. It was Gash.'[101] To some passengers he could as a driver seem frighteningly unobservant, yet no accidents occurred.

Gash in retirement was still mobile enough to promote several good causes from Langport. His interest in the Prince Albert Society grew naturally out of his expertise on the history of early nineteenth-century monarchy. The Society promoted contact between British and German historians of Britain through regular conferences in Coburg, and Gash not only backed it from the outset but addressed its meetings in 1983 and 1984. He put even more into Southampton University's care for the Wellington papers, joining the advisory committee on its formation, and attending its meetings until he retired from it in 2002. He also spoke at its conferences, and edited the proceedings of one. His third cause was the R. S. Surtees Society, formed in 1980 to keep Surtees' novels in print. Again he backed the Society from the start, staunchly supported Lady Pickthorn in running it, and gave the Society the paperback copyright to his *Surtees*. His favourite cause, though, was the Peel Society, founded in 1979 to keep Peel's memory alive in the Tamworth area. Yet again, Gash was a firm backer from the outset; he also made donations to its museum, published pamphlets for the society, and gave expert help when asked. He and Dorothy attended and always seemed to enjoy its social events, and in his will he left the Society his Peel-related books and some of his papers.

Gash was lucky with his health, gave up smoking in the 1970s, did exercises every morning, and was still swimming in the sea in his early nineties. Usually tight-lipped, he seemed every inch 'the professor', the epithet he often attracted, but he smiled easily, and in 1982 he described

[101] 'Some memories of Norman Gash'.

himself as leading 'a kind of mellowed undergraduate life', in his study in the morning, exercising in the afternoon and writing letters and reading in the evenings, with no tutorials to give or essays to mark. He was living in 'a private All Souls of one's own, with one's colleagues conveniently dead or immured between the covers of books to be taken up or laid down at one's convenience'.[102] It was a misleading self-portrait because strokes and other problems were by then causing Dorothy's mental and physical health to disintegrate; he had to run the house and teach himself to cook, and eventually she needed constant nursing care and moved into a nursing home nearby. There he visited her devotedly until she died from pneumonia on 30 December 1995.

He now lived alone, but he loved cats, and adopted one from next door. He had never cultivated close relationships with friends or relatives, and was often curt on the phone. Yet he was assiduous in keeping up contacts with former students and colleagues through message-bearing Christmas cards, ideal vehicles for protecting privacy while enjoying a firmly controlled sociability. The occasional scholarly visitor would be welcomed to tea or something more: Douglas Hurd seeking advice and receiving encouragement for his biography of Peel; Paul Smith pursuing local colour at Bagehot's nearby family home, Herd's Hill, for his edition of Bagehot; an annual affectionate visit from the President and Director of the Adam Smith Institute. His daughters, living far away, worried about him and maintained a tactful oversight, but he resolutely maintained his independence. In 1997 he married a widow, Ruth Jackson, whom he met locally through friends, but neither this nor their divorce in 2004 greatly affected their life-styles: each retained a separate home, but together they continued to entertain friends, attend concerts, go on outings and conduct long phone conversations in the evenings. Only towards the end of his life did he substitute a siesta for gardening in the afternoon, and experience the stiff joints and the macular degeneration which made reading and writing difficult, and in his last two months (much to his distress) impossible. His morning walk into Langport to collect the newspapers persisted into the last year of his life, and his growing deafness made him seem more confused than he really was. He was well able to issue instructions to his carer about the shopping he required on the day of his death, 1 May 2009, and on her return she found him dead, sitting upright in his favourite chair, alone. At his own wish, his gravestone was inscribed 'In loving

[102] G. Parker, 'Remembering Norman Gash', quoting Gash to Parker, 3 Nov. 1982.

memory of Ivy Dorothy Gash 1914–1995 and Norman Gash 1912–2009 Historian.'

Norman Gash lived well into the tape-recording age, yet Walter Arnstein's is the sole surviving interview, and many puzzles about Gash cannot now be solved. Wanting his papers destroyed at death reflects Kipling's injunction: 'seek not to question other than the books I leave behind'. Yet Gash's attitude to history is readily inferred from his abundant writings. In Archilochus's famous dichotomy between the fox who knows many things and the hedgehog who knows one big thing, Gash is a fox. Specialisation such as Gash's on Peel does not make him a hedgehog because no single driving idea shaped his view of Peel; Gash's cast of mind was empirical rather than theoretical, and about British society in Peel's time he knew many things. A consistent mood in all his writing was empathy: like the social anthropologist, he soaked himself in the context of his subjects, reached out for the implicit and often unconscious attitudes moulding their conduct, and was never seduced by familiar vocabulary into neglecting important shifts in meaning. In the 1830s, for example, patronage was morally distinct from bribery, and attitudes to electoral bribery varied with social location. Again, absurd as the opponents of Roman Catholic emancipation in the 1820s might now seem, they should be comprehended rather than merely condemned: their view of British history, their patriotism and their concern for social stability should be acknowledged. Gash sometimes tried to widen sensitivity to contemporary context with deftly provocative remarks: in their high hopes of reform, the emancipationists in 1829, like the electoral reformers in 1832, were wrong and Peel was right.[103] During Gash's career such provocation from the right was thought decreasingly acceptable, though it was less often condemned when emanating from the left. Gash fought against the 'ethical association' conveyed by the word 'reform': it might have purified British politics after 1832, but change by then had already begun, and was not rapid thereafter.[104] Gash opposed condemning the Victorians out of their own mouths; in their reforming zeal, they publicised what was bad about their society, but were 'virtuous propagandists', not to be taken at their own valuation. Nor should the 'social novelists' receive undue attention, given their tendency to exaggerate: 'they have done more to confuse than enlighten posterity on the real nature of Victorian society'.[105]

[103] Gash, *Peel*, I. 596. *Politics in the Age of Peel*, pp. 3–4.

[104] *Politics in the Age of Peel*, p. x.

[105] *Aristocracy and People*, p. 1.

Historiography was not Gash's strong point, and his essays on biography and history are thin.[106] None the less the importance of human agency is a second theme running through his published work, as through that of many Conservative historians. When he thought it underplayed by other authors—as, allegedly, in Asa Briggs's *Age of Improvement* (London, 1959)—he said so: the book's 'chief lack', he wrote, 'is perhaps humanity'.[107] He thought biography a broadening art form, in that the biographer must follow wherever his biographical subject goes, and must 'make himself master of a number of different activities ... which left to his own devices he might never have felt any inclination to explore'.[108] Yet biography is a difficult art, if only because the biographer must not lose sight of the man when describing his times, and must 'give the physical appearance, the voice, the gestures, the little human touches familiar to contemporaries'.[109] In praising Blake's *Disraeli* (London, 1966) Gash outlines biography's essentials: 'to portray a human being in the round, to make a dead figure live in the printed page, to dissect a complex temperament with subtlety and judgment, to give the reader a sense of seeing as vividly as contemporaries but with more knowledge'.[110] Some would say that Gash's *Peel*, especially its second volume, does not meet these stringent demands: that it is unduly narrowing in its high-political preoccupation, and in its failure to portray Peel as others saw him.

Like G. R. Elton, Gash saw politics as 'the Queen of History', given its power, together with war, to shape social change.[111] This lent higher status to political than to social history, but such a pecking order both exaggerated politicians' influence and neglected the many impulses to change that stem autonomously from social structures and attitudes, whether demographic, recreational or cultural. It also played down his own achievement, for in his own publications he had blurred the arbitrary distinction between political and social history; as he himself pointed out, politics is 'after all only one aspect of society itself'.[112] He more than anyone opened out the study of early nineteenth-century British politics beyond 'constitutional' history towards politics at the electoral and grassroots level, arguing that 'only on an established basis of local history can national

[106] Chaps 14–15 of Gash's *Pillars of Government*.
[107] *English Historical Review*, 75 (1960), 174.
[108] *Pillars of Government*, p. 181.
[109] Ibid., p. 183.
[110] *English Historical Review*, 83 (1968), 360.
[111] Arnstein interview, f. 7.
[112] *Politics in the Age of Peel*, p. 152.

history of this kind be written'.[113] His historian exemplars, Kitson Clark and W. L. Burn (both dedicatees of his *Aristocracy and People*), took a broad view of history, seeing it as a rich brew which did not segregate the political from the social, the social from the economic, or the history of men in action from the history of the mind. Towards the end of his long scholarly life Gash with his *Surtees* returned more overtly to the social history with which he had begun, though without the originality and penetration that his B.Litt. thesis had displayed.

Gash repeatedly distanced himself from the history of ideas, distinguishing it from 'ideas in history'; even when he did focus upon politicians' ideas he showed less interest in their substance than in the political intention that lay behind them. He thought it 'an occupational weakness of intellectuals to attach excessive importance to ideas in the abstract', and took a Tocquevillean view of the link between British pragmatism and British social and political stability. The only ideas that interested him as historian were 'ideas in action' as distinct from 'ideas in the head', and he often teasingly feigned puzzlement at Fred Dreyer's interest in great thinkers. Indeed, Gash's playing down of 'ideas' sometimes elided into a playing down of 'ideals': dismissing the notion that benevolent ideas produce a benevolent outcome, he claimed that 'most people, once they emerge from adolescence, tend to shed ideals and, as recompense, acquire motives.'[114]

None of this led Gash to shelter coyly from public affairs in scholarly reticence, as witnesses his conduct during the Blunt affair. He devoted his professional life to pioneering the scholarly historical treatment of Britain in the nineteenth century at a time when most respectable history stopped at 1815 or even earlier, and he long outlived his fellow pioneers W. L. Burn and Kitson Clark.[115] Gash believed that professional scholars should not hold themselves aloof from controversial company: historians should fertilise public debate.[116] Here there was shared ground with left-wing historians such as E. P. Thompson, whose *Making of the English Working Class* Gash praised in the bibliography (p. 355) to his *Aristocracy and People* as 'eminently readable' and as providing 'a quarry of information even for those who do not accept his interpretation'. Gash was not starry-eyed about history's influence, telling Arnstein in 1985 that though undoubtedly

[113] Ibid., p. xvii.
[114] Quotations from Gash, 'Power of ideas', pp. 230, 232; see also pp. 231, 233–4 and *Peel*, II. 711.
[115] We owe this point to Professor Arnstein.
[116] N. Gash, 'The state of the debate', in R. M. Hartwell *et al.*, *The Long Debate on Poverty* (London, 1972), p. xxiii.

interesting, its study has little impact upon 'how a society behaves'. Still, a society with no knowledge of history would, he thought, be 'intellectually lamed or crippled'. For him, history is related to other arts subjects as is mathematics to the natural sciences: 'it is the common language, the essential framework', and given that, 'it must be studied for its own sake by those who have no other motive'.[117]

BRIAN HARRISON
Fellow of the Academy
K. THEODORE HOPPEN
Fellow of the Academy

[117] Arnstein interview, f. 6.

JOHN GOULD

John Philip Algernon[1] Gould
1927–2001

John Gould was a leading scholar of Greek literature (especially tragedy) and religion, a pioneer in the serious use of anthropological theory and practice, and an inspiring teacher of all aspects of ancient Greek language, literature and culture; he was a lover of modern Greece and its people, and delighted to explore continuities between the two worlds, despite the differences to which he was equally alive. Many wished he had published more; but his work on the festivals and performance of Athenian drama, his book on Herodotus, and the eighteen or so papers, many of them achieving the status of classics, collected and published just before his death,[2] constitute a powerful and lasting memorial. It was above all the exceptional quality of these classic articles, which were of greater significance than many books and set agendas for subsequent research, which made him a scholar of the highest international importance. His impact on the thinking of scholars in many countries and many disciplines was greatly enhanced by the excitement of his teaching and his informal conversation, with its constant flow of fresh ideas and profound observations.

John Gould was born on 20 December 1927. His father was Harold Ernest Gould, a Classics teacher first at Wellingborough School and then at Kilburn Grammar School. From the 1930s to the 1950s Harold Gould published, mostly in collaboration with J. L. Whitely, two Latin textbooks and nearly twenty school editions of Cicero, Caesar, Livy, Horace, Virgil,

[1] John hated the Algernon and if asked would refuse to say what the A. stood for.

[2] John Gould, *Myth, Ritual, Memory and Exchange*: *Essays in Greek Literature and Culture* (Oxford, 2001): henceforth *MRME*.

Biographical Memoirs of Fellows of the British Academy, XI, 239–263.

and Ovid, many of which are still in print. John's mother Marjorie Gould was also a language teacher, employed as a lecturer in French at Birkbeck College, London between 1922 and 1955, and the author of school text-books on French language and prose composition. For his pupils at school Harold was apparently 'too august a figure to have had a nick-name'. He had a characteristic bark of a laugh, with head thrown back (e.g. when a pupil made an inept translation); this was equally characteristic of his son John when amused or outraged. It was evidently a cultivated family, and John became a literary scholar whose intellectual interests included a deep knowledge and love of French and English literature and language as well as those of Greece and Rome. His approach however was to be very different from those exemplified by his parents.

After moving to London the Goulds lived in the upmarket part of Kensal Rise, and John moved from Wellingborough School to University College School, Hampstead, where he formed a lifelong friendship with George Forrest—a friendship he movingly recalled in his last public talk in July 2000 at a conference in honour of Forrest in Wadham College, Oxford. At this stage too he began a relationship with Pauline Bending, the daughter of an East End secondary school headmaster. Both families were Catholic. Though John lost his faith, the attempt to comprehend and explain the essential characteristics of Greek pagan religion was to be a constant feature of his scholarship, and he would later profess that an upbringing in Catholic traditions in a northern European context did no harm to this endeavour.[3]

In 1945 he won a scholarship to Jesus College, Cambridge, where he took a double first in the Classical Tripos, with 'special merit' in Part Two in Ancient Philosophy (1948). Before starting postgraduate research, he left to perform the necessary eighteen months of National Service (1948–9) where, under a procedure known as 'Emergency Commission', he served as an army captain in the Educational Corps. Of his commission Gould would say that it showed how desperate they were. Not surprisingly, he did not greatly enjoy army life, and was happy to return to Cambridge. His intellectual interests at Cambridge were remarkably wide-ranging, and already displayed the commitment to modern cultural movements which lasted throughout his life.[4] He attended lectures by Wittgenstein, Pevsner and others, as well as those by distinguished classicists; he was friends

[3] See the end of his paper on 'Herodotus and religion', *MRME*, pp. 376–7.

[4] For details here and elsewhere I am indebted especially to a memoir written by his lifelong friend, Roy Waters, who was at St John's.

with poets like Thom Gunn, attended early music concerts or performances of new works, and listened to recordings of French singers such as Trenet and Brassens. Above all he and his friends were devoted to films, especially the new European cinema. His first publication seems to have been an undergraduate review of *La règle du jeu*. He was a founding member of a small dining club with the indicative name of the Gin & Baudelaire Society. Additional members of the society, the patrician New Englander Charles van Doren and his then girlfriend, brought glamour and an emotional disturbance, as John became hopelessly enamoured of the girlfriend, both in Cambridge and during a summer vacation on the Left Bank in Paris.[5]

On his return in autumn 1949 to Jesus he began research on Plato's Ethics, funded by a scholarship, a travel exhibition and a College Research Studentship, and under the supervision of John Raven, while Francis Cornford was a major influence. This resulted in a research fellowship thesis and an appointment as a Research Fellow; a few years later the work became his first book, published at the age of 28, *The Development of Plato's Ethics* (Cambridge, 1955). This was an original attempt to understand profound developments in Plato's ethical thought from the *Apology* to the *Laws*. A number of characteristic features distinguish this book from the main trends of Platonic scholarship at the time. One is the focus on Plato's changing approaches to the major moral questions as a key to his thought, whereas contemporary philosophers were perhaps more interested in the Theory of Forms and related metaphysical issues. This led Gould to devote much closer attention than was usual at the time to the *Laws* and its educational views; the structure of the book brings this out clearly, as the *Laws* is considered in Part Two, immediately after the discussion of initial 'Socratic' positions, as an indication of how far Plato's conceptions of human capabilities for right action moved in a pessimistic direction over his long life. We can also see the signs of the subtle literary critic operating with the widest frames of cultural reference, for example in the attention paid to the developments of Plato's style, with frequent comparisons to other exponents of highly elaborate and baroque styles such as Henry James and Proust. Some found these 'far-fetched'.[6] The book starts with an argument which shows already the commitment to the

[5] Van Doren was later to be embroiled in a famous Quiz Show scandal, admitting at a Congressional Subcommittee hearing that the contest in the TV show *Twenty One*, at which he had won more than $129,000, had been rigged. The story became the subject of a 1994 Robert Redford film starring Ralph Fiennes.

[6] T. G. Rosenmeyer in *Classical World*, 50 (1956), 72–3.

historical study of Greek words and concepts from Homer onwards: he made a case (which was not in fact widely accepted at the time or later) that *episteme* in Plato's Socratic works has more of the sense 'knowledge of how to be good' than 'knowledge of the good', a question of technique rather than intellectual knowledge. The book, however, stands rather apart from his subsequent interests, and he does not seem to have commented much on it in later life. He only rarely returned to Plato, most significantly in a brief but powerful paper, first published in 1992, on Plato's deeply felt and contradictory relations with the most profound forms of literature, Homer and tragedy.[7] The central and characteristic argument of this paper is that Plato responded with such puzzling hostility to the complex imaginative literature of his culture precisely because its acceptance of plurality and contradictions were irreconcilable with his philosophic commitment to univocal answers to the questions of reality.

In 1953 Gould, now married to Pauline, who had trained as a nurse, was enticed from Cambridge and appointed for a first probationary year as Lecturer at Christ Church, Oxford (as was then usual). A year later he became a permanent Student and Tutor in Greek and Latin Literature. Following Denys Page's departure for the Regius Chair at Cambridge in 1950, Greek and Latin language and literature ('Mods') at Christ Church had been taught for a year by Anthony Chevenix-Trench who then, to the surprise of his colleagues, returned to Shrewsbury School as a housemaster, and from there to various headships.[8] It took a couple of years after that for the college to find the 'right man'. R. H. Dundas's comment in the Christ Church Annual Report was: 'We have for some time been lacking a Classics tutor. Now we hope and believe we have found what we are looking for.... All the omens are favourable.' Dundas had praised Chevenix-Trench, at his departure, for the 'vast' work he had done to revive the college's rowing tradition. He would not find Gould shared such sporting concerns.[9] It is noticeable that after a record of his appointment as Student and the birth of his first child, 'Mr Gould' appears only rarely in the Dundas reports. It is said that the appointment owed very much to Eric Dodds, the holder of the Regius Chair of Greek (1936–60) and *ex*

[7] 'Plato and performance', in A. Barker and M. Warner (eds.), *The Language of the Cave: Apeiron*, 25 (1992), 13–25: *MRME*, chap. 13.

[8] Chevenix-Trench went on to hold headships at Bradfield, Eton and Fettes. Revelations in 1979 and in the 1990s of an extreme predeliction for flogging might suggest one reason for his return to public school life.

[9] Gould's response—NO—survives to the invitation issued to freshmen at Jesus to declare what college games they intend to play.

officio a member of Christ Church Governing Body, who had been impressed by the Plato book. Invited to lunch in Christ Church, Gould was surprised at the end by Dodds's asking 'Well, are you going to take this job?' Dodds then persuaded him it would be a good idea. Christ Church had more than its fair share (even for Oxford) of rich undergraduates educated at Eton, Westminster and other public schools, and a good few traditional members of Governing Body were happy to fit such men for the world; but Dodds and the tutors concerned with *Literae Humaniores* ('Greats') shared more intellectual and egalitarian values and expected serious study and hard work from their students.[10]

Dodds was to matter greatly to Gould as he settled in Oxford. The breadth of his intellectual interests, his leftist politics, and his commitment to renovate the teaching of Classics in Oxford and throughout the UK, were all very congenial;[11] Gould became and remained a close friend, and a collaborator in Dodds's attempt to bring about curriculum reform in Oxford. In particular, Dodds's pioneering use of comparative anthropology and psychology, seen best in his work on Euripides' *Bacchae* and in *The Greeks and the Irrational* (Berkeley, CA, and London, 1951), was to exercise a profound influence on Gould's development throughout his life (cf. the preface to *MRME*).

Like many colleges, Christ Church expected its Latin and Greek tutor to cover the whole range of the syllabus in tutorials, though, less usually, it gave Studentships to both a Greek and a Roman historian; for most of Gould's time there these were David Lewis (appointed in 1955, in succession to Dundas)[12] and Eric Gray. Teaching support was given by younger Lecturers, Research Fellows and Senior Scholars, who included Michael Winterbottom, Peter Parsons (one of his earliest undergraduate pupils), Colin Austin and John Rae. Gould undertook to acquire what he saw as the required mastery of the texts, scholarship and criticism across the whole syllabus from Homer to Late Latin. The time-consuming work of preparation and teaching, carried out with scrupulous devotion and commitment, to say nothing of extra pastoral care, was initially exhausting, and was undoubtedly one reason why during the fifteen years at Christ Church he published no more than a few reviews of books on Greek Tragedy. Other reasons included the absence of pressures to publish in

[10] Cf. Christopher Robinson's memoir, *Christ Church Annual Report for 2003*.

[11] Cf. Dodds's autobiography, *Missing Persons* (Oxford, 1977) and Donald Russell's memoir, 'Eric Robertson Dodds 1893–1979', *Proceedings of the British Academy*, 67 (1981), 357–70

[12] See Simon Hornblower's memoir, 'David Lewis 1928–1994', *Proceedings of the British Academy*, 94 (1996), 557–96.

days long before the introduction of such things as Research Assessment Exercises (it was then still possible to complete an Oxford career without publishing anything, but with a secure reputation as a great teacher and college man); but most of all it was a perfectionism which would remain through his career and inhibit the completion of many of his ideas. During the Oxford years Gould was working on a number of projects concerned with Greek Tragedy, only one of which was to be completed as planned.

This project reached publication in 1968, just as Gould moved to Swansea. David Lewis and he formed the ideal team to collaborate on the major revision of Pickard-Cambridge's already classic study of *The Dramatic Festivals of Athens* (Oxford, 1953); their work, in effect done by 1964, was a very significant improvement (and was further updated in the final edition of 1988). All later scholars of Greek Drama have relied on it, and many have spoken of its pervasive influence;[13] Peter Wilson has observed that in some ways it has become too much of a 'classic', and may be taken as too authoritative.[14] Wilson is engaged with his Sydney colleague Eric Csapo and others on a major collaborative project ('The Theatrical Revolution: the expansion of theatre outside Athens') to renew, and broaden, the work and provide a much fuller understanding of the 'documentary base of the Greek theatre, across the Greek world'.[15] Fundamental to Pickard-Cambridge's book was the determination to offer a detailed presentation of the evidence for all aspects of the Athenian dramatic festivals—texts (many of them antiquarian reports from periods much later than the time of the plays), inscriptions, images on vases, terracottas, and so on, as well as the material remains of the theatres. The book operates in 'hard-core' mode, with page after page of testimonia in untranslated Greek. Gould and Lewis maintained this tradition unashamedly, a noble tribute, though one already perhaps becoming anachronistic, to the assumption

[13] e.g. for Simon Goldhill the revision is 'a marvellous example of careful, scholarly criticism that is never less than constructive: 'Representing democracy: women at the Great Dionysia', in R. Osborne and S. Hornblower (eds.), *Ritual, Finance, Politics: Athenian Democratic Accounts presented to David Lewis* (Oxford, 1994), pp. 347–70.

[14] See P. Wilson (ed.), *The Greek Theatre and Festivals: Documentary Studies* (Oxford, 2007), p. 3. 'Hundreds of these interpretative studies blithely refer to the relevant pages of Pickard-Cambridge's *Dramatic Festivals of Athens* and *Dithyramb, Tragedy and Comedy*, and take all that is said in them on trust.'

[15] This project reflects a major shift in current thinking away from Athenocentrism and the domination of the City Dionysia, achieved by works such as O. Taplin, *Comic Angels: and Other Approaches to Greek Drama Through Vase-Paintings* (Oxford, 1993), and *Pots and Plays. Interactions between Tragedy and Greek Vase-painting of the Fourth Century BC* (Los Angeles, CA, 2007); E. Csapo, *Actors and Icons in the Ancient Theatre* (Oxford, 2010) and P. Wilson, *The Greek Theatre*.

that serious English-speaking students of ancient drama had sufficient Greek to cope. This decision was made in contrast to that taken by T. B. L. Webster when he had revised Pickard-Cambridge's *Dithyramb, Tragedy and Comedy* (first edition London, 1927, revised edition Oxford, 1962); the need, which of course became ever more pressing, for students and the general public to have reliable English translations of many of these texts and inscriptions would later be met by Eric Csapo's and William Slater's excellent *The Context of Ancient Drama* (Ann Arbor, MI, 1995).

It was a work of complete collaboration, and reveals well the breadth of conception of their subject that the two shared. Lewis was an epigraphically based historian whose conception of the subject none the less embraced literature, religion, archaeology and art,[16] though he was totally committed to making ancient historians understand the centrality of inscriptions to all these topics. Gould was a literary specialist, though one with the deepest interest in historical and cultural contexts (for his final refusal to be labelled a historian see the *MRME* preface). Lewis had initial responsibility for chapters I and II (the Festivals), and VI and VII (the Audience and the Artists of Dionysus), and greatly improved the accuracy and breadth of the presentation of the epigraphic material; Gould was more responsible for the chapters on the visual appearance and production of the plays and the roles of the performers (III–V, Actors, Costumes and Chorus). The revision was thoroughgoing, but discreetly carried out (Pickard-Cambridge's name remains on the cover), and the text only rarely offers explicit dissent from Pickard-Cambridge's views, or signals where the material is essentially new, though the authors indicate in summary form in the preface areas where major changes were made (for example a new paragraph on the politics of the plays and their productions).[17] Chapter III on actors and their styles alters the emphasis in a number of places, often to insert more caution against assuming naturalistic gesture, or underestimating the degree of stylisation; and chapter IV on costumes and masks was given a more drastic recast and revision, in order to place greater emphasis on precise presentation of the visual evidence in chronological order and to privilege the Athenian material over the South Italian.[18]

[16] Cf. Hornblower's 'David Lewis'.

[17] p. 90. Cf. Hornblower's 'David Lewis', pp. 578–80.

[18] In 1988 they published a second edition of their revision, with seven pages of updating addenda, setting out and discussing new evidence, particularly iconographical, and offering a typically concise and sceptical note on the disputed issue of official censorship of political satire.

Gould's preparedness to accept highly unnaturalistic modes of representation, hinted at in the revision, became more explicit when he returned to the theme of 'Tragedy in performance', in a chapter written for a more general readership in the *Cambridge History of Classical Literature*.[19] Here he asserts positively that Euripides' supposed taste for showing unfortunate characters in rags may be the result of Aristophanes exploiting the intensification of descriptive language, rather than a significant change in actual costumes,[20] and suggests that the experience of Japanese theatre should teach us not to underestimate the extent to which an audience's acceptance of a tradition of stylisation in performance can persuade it to experience it as naturalistic and emotionally powerful. In the mid-1960s Gould was already thinking hard about the relevance of Noh and Kabuki theatre, and engaged in discussions with Masaaki Kubo, a Japanese classical scholar whom he knew both in Oxford and during the year he spent at the Hellenic Centre in Washington (1962–3), under the Directorship of Bernard Knox. This continued to have an effect on his thinking.

In the Oxford years, Gould was engaged in detailed thinking about how the formal elements of Greek tragic drama, so different from the practices of contemporary bourgeois theatre, worked in performance: elements such as the choral songs, the actor's lyrics, the convention of masking and duplication of parts, the combination of elaborate rhetorical speeches and dramatic, if 'unrealistic', stichomythia, the distancing effects of the verse and choral idiolects. He was influenced by German work such as Kranz's book on the choral songs (*Stasimon*: Berlin, 1933); but his concern was to go beyond this formal approach towards more satisfactory analysis of what these elements all contributed to the plays' effects and polyvalent meanings. In his mind at this time were a book on Euripidean techniques, and a general book on tragedy; neither ever approached completion, but the central ideas found their way, revised in the light of later developments in scholarship, into the later influential articles on tragedy (see below).

His tutorials were a combination of rigour, inspiration and fun. Christ Church pupils were taught both in seminar classes (e.g. on Homer and Virgil) and in individual essay tutorials. I remember how the class on Homer (1963–4) threw first term undergraduates into the main topics of

[19] P. Easterling and B. M. W. Knox (eds.), *Cambridge History of Classical Literature: I: Greek Literature* (Cambridge, 1985), pp. 263–91: *MRME*, chap. 6.

[20] Merely a tentative footnote in the second edition of *Dramatic Festivals of Athens* (Oxford, 1969: see above, n. 14). See now the work of Eric Csapo on Euripidean developments in music and representation in *Actors and Icons in the Ancient Theatre* (Oxford, 2010).

current scholarship in that rather positivist age, such as the theory of oral poetics, the historical contexts of the poems and the historicity of the Trojan war, and also, more interestingly for some of us, the political structures of Homer's own time, and the conceptions of society, personality and morality conveyed by an often puzzling language (Finley's *The World of Odysseus* (London, 1956), Snell's *The Discovery of the Mind* (Oxford, 1953), and Adkins's *Merit and Responsibility* (Oxford, 1960) were much discussed). He persuaded us we could participate in these detailed and technical debates with scholars like Milman and Adam Parry, Page, Finley, Snell, Dodds and Adkins; at the same time he did not let us lose sight of the underlying point of the project, to appreciate that these were great texts, with fundamental connections to all subsequent Western literature. It was not clear to me that he then had reached the conviction, which would be powerfully developed, for example by his successors at Christ Church, Colin Macleod and Richard Rutherford, and his friend Oliver Taplin, that the greatness of the *Iliad* and *Odyssey* lies above all in their presentation of coherent—or coherently contradictory—fictional societies, and a complex and balanced picture of war as both heroic and tragic; and that this demands the assumption of an essentially unified structure and single author for each poem. Such conceptions certainly pervade his later forays into Homeric issues, the articles on 'Supplication', 'Homer and the tragic moment', and 'The idea of society in the *Iliad*' (*MRME*, chapters 2, 5 and 15).

Gould's tutorial method approximated more to the traditional Oxford ideal of exploring students' ideas and encouraging their intellectual development; there was little sustained exposition (as, for example, Christ Church undergraduates got from Eric Gray or those at New College or Magdalen from Geoffrey de Ste. Croix).[21] One felt drawn into a deeply serious engagement with issues of interpretation and the shared pursuit of understanding poetry and ideas through precise attention to the words and their linguistic and cultural contexts. The style was in the best sense democratic and open, conducted in a room of friendly disorder shrouded in Woodbine smoke. Some of the less confident of us might have wished for a more explicit indication of how good or bad our essay had been (one somehow knew not to seek anything as definite as a mark); but a different and more valuable form of confidence—and determination to study further—came from the experience of being opened up to a vast range of

[21] Cf. Robert Parker's memoir of 'Geoffrey de Ste. Croix 1910–2000', *Proceedings of the British Academy*, 111 (2000), 461.

cultural references and connections across languages, centuries and cultural patterns (for example comparable discontinuities in form in Euripides and Bartok). One was guided to realise that understanding a literature from a very different culture was a vitally important, if demanding and difficult, activity.

In addition to the ceaseless flow of ideas and connections between classical texts and the modern world at tutorials, his students benefited tremendously from the regular and generous hospitality and friendship offered by the whole Gould family: his wife Pauline, now planning to retrain as a teacher, and their four children Rachel, Jessica, Christopher (Kit) and John Mark (Yanni) in their large Christ Church house ('Compas') at 62 Iffley Road. They shared the house with John Burrow and his family. Burrow was an English tutor at Christ Church and a close friend, who would later take up a Chair at Bristol, like Gould; he, and later his son Colin, currently a Senior Research Fellow at All Souls, Oxford, like many scholars in other disciplines, found much stimulation over the years in Gould's conversation and writings on literature. We found Sunday afternoons there a delightful relief from the pressures of undergraduate life, and enjoyed inspiring absorption into cultural forms ranging from Webern and Kurt Weill to the Stones and Dylan. It was there too that we became aware of what was to become increasingly vital to his development and his life, the engagement with the language, culture, poetry, music, landscape and people of modern Greece; we would read Seferis and listen to the Theodorakis versions. The family summers were occupied with travels across Greece in VW camper vans, all too liable to break down. It seemed an idyllically happy family.

Another feature of his time in Oxford was the work he and other colleagues such as Donald Russell undertook, under the initial leadership of Dodds, towards the major reform of the traditional Classics syllabus ('Literae Humaniores'): the aim was to end the division between the initial (five terms) study of language and literature ('Mods') and the subsequent (seven terms) exclusive concentration on Ancient History and Philosophy ('Greats'). Agreement took a long time to arrive (opposition being especially strong among the philosophers), and Gould was a strong and influential voice on the committee, though, as at other times, he was not always to be relied on with regard to punctuality or deadlines. The eventual reform introduced some history and ancient philosophy into Mods, and conversely established literature as one of three options in Greats from which undergraduates would select two; thus those who wished could intensify their studies of ancient literature throughout their four-year degrees. The reform was only enacted after Gould had left Oxford (and long after Dodds had retired).[22]

Gould's politics were consistently on the left. In 1956 he had joined with other Christ Church dons in writing a letter condemning the Suez invasion, and the use of college notepaper incurred official disapproval. During the 1960s he was active in local Oxford politics, for example canvassing along with colleagues such as Forrest for Labour candidates in local elections (one of whom was Gerry Fowler, then a Roman historian at Hertford College, and later MP for The Wrekin and a Minister of Education and Science). From 1967, again with many colleagues, he was vocal in his opposition to the rule of the Colonels in Greece, and did not visit the country during the time of the junta. Much later, he left the Labour Party in despair at its anti-socialist policies.

In the summer of 1968 he took over from Kenneth Dover as an editor of the *Classical Quarterly*. He served until 1974, sharing the duties first with Donald Russell and then with Michael Winterbottom. The editors at that time took most decisions themselves, only seeking external referees on rare occasions where neither felt able to make a judgement or where they disagreed. Gould performed these duties very conscientiously, and it is doubtful whether he heeded sufficiently the advice Dover had given him not to spend too long improving β+ articles; his lack of an adequate filing system could also cause problems, as when he had to confess to an anxious author that he had yet not been able to give a decision on publication, as he could not remember from which scholar he had asked for an opinion.

Between 1968 and 1974 he held the Chair of Classics in the University College of Swansea. Those were years of profound change both for the politics of British universities and for Classics departments in the UK, and Gould played a part in bringing about significant reforms in both areas. As an ex-officio member of the Senate, Gould was drawn, in those years of student protest and agitation, into the debates about university government, and his voice was heard, naturally enough, in favour of some student participation in most areas of decision-making, from the Council and Senate down to the departmental student/staff committees. His effectiveness in college politics, however, was not aided by an administrative vagueness and disdain for procedures, and perhaps also a reputation as something of a middle-aged radical.

Reforming the Classics Department was more successful. Gould saw the pressing need for immediate and fundamental change and welcomed

[22] Dodds, *Missing Persons*, pp. 177–8.

the chance to effect reforms much more rapidly than was possible in Oxford. When he succeeded George Kerford, nothing had been done about the crisis which faced Swansea in common with many Classics departments: a traditional and rigid syllabus focused on the ancient languages and philology, and far too few students qualified or interested enough to follow or enjoy it. Gould worked closely with sympathetic colleagues, especially Alan Lloyd and Roger Ling, against the instincts of traditionalists, to 'save the Department'. The essence of the plan was first to open up the serious study of ancient literature, history and philosophy to those who had not hitherto had the opportunity to learn Latin and Greek, by introducing courses in literature in translation and a Joint Honours degree scheme in Ancient History, also taught in translation; and second to enliven the teaching of traditional Classics by a greater concentration on the serious study of the meaning of literary texts as wholes, with close attention to their language, their structures and their historical and social contexts. New appointments (e.g. Joan Booth and David Hunt) brought fresh commitment to the programme. Gould set out the basic principles in his powerful inaugural lecture.[23] This combined a rather Cantabrigian moral passion, redolent of Leavis and Eliot, for the purity of the language, the seriousness of the study of literature and the sense of a single Western literary tradition, with the growing belief in the importance of social anthropology in general, and the ethnography and experience of contemporary Greek cultures in particular, for the understanding of what is distinctive in ancient Greek experience. This approach, informed by Dodds's example, and the work of scholars like J. K. Campbell, Clifford Geertz and Godfrey Lienhardt, was enhanced by personal contact with Margaret Kenna, a social anthropologist in Swansea doing field work on the Greek islands, and by his own increasing familiarity with modern Greek language and literature and its rural world. In the Swansea years, he came to believe all the more strongly that the anthropology of those in the Evans-Pritchard school working in the Mediterranean, and particularly in rural Greece, had a particular value and relevance for students of ancient Greek history and literature, especially if reinforced by direct personal contact with rural Greek life.[24]

[23] 'Ancient poetry and modern readers': *MRME*, chap. 1. See also his contribution to a debate on the teaching of literature in Classics departments, *Didaskalos*, 3 (1970), 218–26.

[24] He told me *c.*1969, when we discovered that we had independently been inspired by Campbell's *Honour, Family and Patronage* on the transhumant Sarakatsani in north-west Greece, that he felt such modern ethnography could fill out many of the missing pieces of the complex jigsaw of ancient Greek social values.

Teaching at Swansea was very different from Oxford, conducted more by formal lectures than seminars or tutorials, and the students arrived with less familiarity with the texts and the ancient world in general. Gould's lecturing style, stronger on intellectual inspiration and the spontaneous development of ideas than on systematic exposition, had been successful in Oxford, for example in lectures on tragedy or on Thucydides VI and VII; but at Swansea this somewhat freewheeling style was not universally popular among students seeking more basic help and organised coverage of the syllabus.

Gould's passionate commitment to promote more effective learning of Ancient Greek for students of all ages, in the changing educational climate, led to a long-standing involvement in the Reading Greek project run by the Joint Association of Classical Teachers (JACT). Initially, John was a regular teacher at the JACT Greek Summer Schools, for sixth-formers, undergraduates and adults, then held at Dean Close School, Cheltenham. He is remembered as an inspirational figure: very tall and thin, a mass of sandy curls, in white shirt and jeans, sitting on a table and talking about any aspect of language or culture. From 1974 to 1979 he chaired the JACT Steering Committee which produced the influential and successful series of *Reading Greek* textbooks (published by Cambridge University Press) aimed at university students and adults. The committee was composed mostly of experienced teachers and supported by a team of academic advisors chosen by Gould, and he was the overall intellectual driving force and guiding spirit. The founding principles he laid down were that the language must be presented as clearly and helpfully as possible, without compromise, that the Greek to be read should, from the outset, be based on real texts (hence stories based on Aristophanes and Demosthenic forensic speeches featured early, followed by extracts from Homer, Herodotus and tragedy), and that the Greeks' different cultural values and assumptions should be presented and explained from the start, with sensitivity to cultural meaning extending from individual words to whole situations. The resulting textbooks, readers, grammars and companion volumes have been a triumphant success.

The results of Gould's concern for the contribution anthropology could make to the understanding of Greek social institutions and literary texts, originally fired in Oxford by the work and personal inspiration of Dodds, are clearly seen in his first major article (1973), on the ritual of supplication (*hiketeia*) as a social institution and its significance in Greek literature.[25] This masterly paper, written from 1969 to 1972, and finished

[25] 'Hiketeia', *Journal of Hellenic Studies*, 93 (1973), 74–103 (a volume produced in honour of Dodds): *MRME*, chap. 2.

at the Fondation Hardt, immediately established itself as an exemplary and classic study of a curiously neglected topic, and has become the starting point for all subsequent treatments, some of book length.[26] Gould established firmly the procedural requirements of this specific ritual, whereby those facing death at the hands of an enemy, or arrivals in a strange and dangerous land, made contact submissively, touching knees or chin, with those with power (or with an altar), and uttered appropriate words and arguments; the effect was to apply moral pressure (strong, but not irresistible) on the recipient to enter into a reciprocal relationship akin to friendship and reciprocal hospitality (*philia* and *xenia*). Gould went on to explore subtly its ramifications and changes over time, and established the motif as a dramatic and morally significant action in major scenes in Homer, Herodotus, Thucydides and tragedy.

Gould's commitment to the JACT Summer School at Cheltenham was to have transforming consequences for his personal life and family. Shortly before he left Swansea in 1974, he started a love affair with Gillian Tuckett, a modern languages teacher, who was following the Greek course. The affair led to the break-up of both the Gould and the Tuckett marriages and in time to John and Gillian's remarriage, and John's becoming stepfather to her three young children, Thomas, Tabitha and William. In 1974 Gould was appointed to the H. O. Wills Chair of Greek at the University of Bristol, in succession to Nicholas Hammond;[27] this move coincided with the marriage break-up, and a new house in Bristol. Gould attempted to make these two major changes into a complete new start in his life. But for Pauline and their children, and the Tuckett children, the ruptures were extraordinarily bitter and unhappy, and the wounds were never healed. Pauline recovered to retrain again and work as a social worker, before dying of cancer some twenty years later. After an uneasy period where some of the Gould children lived with John and Gillian and her children

[26] e.g. K. Crotty, *The Poetics of Supplication* (Ithaca, NY, 1994); S. Goldhill, 'Supplication and authorial comment in the *Iliad*', *Hermes*, 166 (1990), 373–7; M. Lynn-George, *Epos: Word, Narrative and the Iliad* (London, 1988); A. Chaniotis, *Kernos*, 9 (1996), 65–86; S. Gödde, *Das Drama der Hikesie: Ritual und Rhetorik in Aischylos' 'Hiketiden'* (Munster, 2000). Most recently, F. S. Naiden, *Ancient Supplication* (Oxford and New York, 2006) offers the fullest account, including a valuable survey of innumerable cases of supplication in both Greek and Roman texts. His criticism of Gould's treatment (pp. 8–14), however, rests in part on reductive misunderstanding; for example he claims misleadingly that on Gould's view Greek supplication was 'invariably successful, provided the requirements of the ritual are met', and that he had as a result paid insufficient attention to other crucial aspects of the process, the justification of the request and the decision whether to accept it.

[27] See Anthony Snodgrass's Memoir, 'Nicholas Geoffrey Lemprière Hammond 1907–2001', *Proceedings of the British Academy*, 120, *Biographical Memoirs of Fellows*, II (2003), 242–59.

in Bristol, there was a complete and devastating break, and John's children were to have almost no contact with their father for the rest of his life; John ceased to make attempts to stay in touch and would not discuss with others how they were. Contacts between the Tuckett children and their father became equally minimal. These difficulties also damaged relations between Gould and some of his academic friends who had known his first family well.

Gould's years in the large and flourishing Classics Department in Bristol (1974–91), where he shared leadership with Niall Rudd, the Professor of Latin, were successful and harmonious. Substantial changes to degree schemes were not required. He shared research interests in tragedy and anthropology with Richard Buxton, and they had a common admiration for, and friendship with, the Parisian *équipes* of Jean-Paul Vernant and Pierre Vidal-Naquet, both of whom visited the department and were given honorary degrees by the university. His teaching—whether on the most basic Greek texts or the complexities of religion or tragedy—continued to be a source of inspiration and admiration for the better students, while he seems also to have improved his ability to adjust his methods for the less able; he retained the capacity to develop his ideas in mid-lecture. His distaste for the details of administration and increasing levels of bureaucracy was in no way diminished (though 'managerial' styles and governmental interference were of course to intensify greatly after his retirement); nor, apparently, was there any increase in his own powers of organisation, as demonstrated by the anarchy of his desk, where student essays might lurk undiscovered for months.

The Bristol years were much more productive in terms of publication, resulting in a series of classic articles, some reviews in the *Times Literary Supplement*, and a major book. Having given lectures on Thucydides in Oxford, at Bristol he lectured for many years on the highly congenial Herodotus, and this resulted in his *Herodotus*,[28] described as a 'wonderful book, still the best introduction in English to that author'.[29] It was later supplemented by two papers: 'Give and take in Herodotus' and 'Herodotus and religion'.[30] The book is concerned not so much with Herodotus'

[28] *Herodotus*, London, 1989. It won the Runciman Prize for 1990, awarded by the Anglo-Hellenic League.

[29] T. Rood, 'Review of John Gould, *Myth, Ritual, Memory, and Exchange: Essays in Greek Literature and Culture*', *Bryn Mawr Classical Review*, 2002.05.29.

[30] 'Give and take in Herodotus', J. L. Myles Lecture, Oxford 1991: *MRME*, chap. 12; 'Herodotus and religion', in S. Hornblower (ed.), *Greek Historiography* (Oxford, 1991), pp. 91–106: *MRME*, chap. 16.

reliability for constructing historical accounts as with his 'mind' as a historian: his handling of different types of sources, his understanding of other peoples, his method of structuring a narrative with explanations, and his conceptions of humanity, morality and divinity; and it breathes throughout a warm and sympathetic love of its subtle, entertaining, exhilarating and humane author. It presents him as pursuing radically different, but not necessarily more 'primitive' or simplistic, methods and purposes from his great successor Thucydides. Major features of the book continue the subtle and detailed application of the continued immersion in social anthropology and in the world of rural Greece.[31]

Gould brings to the debate on Herodotus' trustworthiness in reporting sources (both Greek and non-Greek) a sophisticated awareness of the complexities of oral traditions (both among distinguished families and in communities) and the mythologising or politically motivated transformations that 'social memory' can create; this enables him to resist persuasively the arguments of Fehling and others that the historian's wide travels and many of his stories were free inventions. Second, Gould finds the key to the work's complex structure and its favoured forms of historical explanations in the fundamental ideas of honour, shame and reciprocity, both positive and negative. Hence the work is packed full with long-term obligations of friendship reinforced by hospitality and gift-exchange (themes also explored in the 'Give and Take' paper); and long chains of events, where initial acts of hostility and aggression provoke retaliations (hence 'revenge', *timoria,* is a vitally important motivating force, for individuals and states).[32] The fundamental modes of expressing causation are characteristically personal, yet this does not prevent Herodotus from expressing in such moralising terms as 'greed', *hybris*, revenge and so on ideas of more generalised or collective causes which later historians might express in more abstract terms such as aggression or imperialism. Finally, Gould opposes any attempt to identify the historian's main purpose as delivering a clear 'message', whether moral lessons of divine punishment of the proud or the aggressors, or a contemporary political warning against the new imperialism of the Athenians; for Gould, the *Histories*, like the *Iliad*, offer morally significant, complex and often over-determined, accounts of

[31] Much of the book was written in a monastery in Western Crete, where Gould was staying with his wife Gillian and her daughter Tabitha; in the preface he acknowledges their substantial collaboration.

[32] The centrality of reciprocity to Herodotean narratives and explanations is accepted and extended by David Braund, in C. Gill, N. Posthlethwaite and R. Seaford (eds.), *Reciprocity in Ancient Greece* (Oxford, 1998), pp. 159–80.

motives and actions, and their chains of consequences, though awareness of current examples of Greek aggression, comparable to the Persian, may be present as well.[33] On religious explanations, in the book and in the later article ('Herodotus and religion', *MRME*, chapter 16), Gould charts a delicate balance: he insists, against those who see Herodotus as a thoroughgoing sceptic, that the historian was persuaded that some events did display divine as well as human causation, but also that his frequent expressions of uncertainty reflect his firm adherence to a typically Greek awareness of the limitations of human knowledge; this helps to explain also his readiness to explore, open-mindedly and tolerantly, other religious systems.[34] Here Gould suggests that what can seem a rather limited concentration on matters of ritual, especially sacrifice, and on the different names of gods, has its roots in the centrality of ritual to the Greeks' conception of their own religion, and in the lack of evidence available to Herodotus of the theogonies or theology of (for example) the Persians or the Egyptians.

Probably the most read and cited of Gould's classic articles is the 1980 piece on 'Law, custom and myth: the social position of women in classical Athens'.[35] This paper, written in the early days of the application of feminist and structuralist ideas to Greek society, marked a considerable advance in its sophistication and use of anthropological and psychological theory. It dealt a death blow to the opposing, oversimplified, positions, that Greek men kept their womenfolk in 'oriental seclusion' and regarded them with contempt, or that they treated them with respect and allowed them much freedom (a position whose best exponent had been Gomme). Each side tended to over-emphasise alternative categories of evidence (imaginative literature or law court speeches), and both ignored the laws. Gould's methodological principle, which has now become standard, was to consider separately evidence falling under his three categories (laws, norms and customs, and the representation of myths in literature), and to argue that each category displays complementary, if significantly different, complexities and contradictions. Intelligent and eclectic use is made of anthropological and psychological studies of gender and religion and of the contrasting approaches to Greek religion and myth of both the Paris

[33] On the second issue, see for example, the comparison of Fornara and Gould by P. Derow, *Classics Ireland*, 2 (1995), 29–51, and K. A. Raaflaub, in *Brill's Companion to Herodotus* (Leiden, 2002), pp. 177–81.

[34] T. Harrison, *Divinity and History: the Religion of Herodotus* (Oxford, 2000), argues in detail for a Herodotus who firmly offered religious explanations, arguably dissipating too much the operation of Gould's 'uncertainty principle' (see pp. 11–18, 191).

[35] *Journal of Hellenic Studies*, 100 (1980), 38–59: *MRME*, chap. 4.

school of Vernant and Vidal-Naquet and the Swiss of Meuli and Burkert. This paper ends with a reflection on the difference between modern romantic 'Love', which Gomme had invoked as a familiar element in Greek literature, and the '*Eros*' of the chorus from the *Antigone*, which Gomme had cited in support of his view, but which the chorus describes as a power undefeated in war, destroying properties, driving its victims to madness, the just to injustice, and provoking quarrels between kin.[36]

A comparably powerful article which has also become a standard and unrivalled introduction to a broad topic is 'On making sense of Greek religion', published in a collection of essays offered to John Sharwood Smith, the prime mover behind JACT, with whom Gould had worked for many years.[37] This also makes detailed use of anthropological theorists (Evans-Pritchard and Lienhardt on African systems and above all Geertz's general idea of religion as a system for making some sense of unbearable chaos), and combines a high level of generality with telling exegesis of Greek rituals and texts. Beyond its succinct identification of the salient differences between Greek polytheism and modern monotheisms, the paper pursues a crafty balancing act between apparently contrasting ideas. Greek polytheism was a mass of rituals, festivals and myths, located in the political units (polis, deme etc.) at various levels, all infinitely various, open to change, unstructured, and free of any dogmatising church or priests; yet it contained a broadly systematic, coherent and complex attempt to make sense of the infinite plurality of the world. Rituals and myths alike present divinities—contradictorily—both as human in appearance, thought and emotions, yet also uncanny and terrifying, encouraging morality yet capable of imposing inexplicable destruction and suffering (neatly summed up in Solon's phrase to Croesus in Herodotus 1.32: 'divinity is envious and disorderly').[38]

In 1989, Gould delivered the Jackson Knight Memorial Lecture at Exeter (republished as *MRME*, chapter 11) with the then topical title 'Dionysus and the hippy convoy: ritual, myth and metaphor in the cult of Dionysus'. This offered a valuable qualification to the approach to the cults of Dionysus being then developed by Albert Henrichs, who argued that the wild maenadism and social subversion of literary representations, above all in Euripides' *Bacchae*, were no guide to the ritual practices of

[36] It is difficult not to sense a certain irony in this point, in view of the effects of 'Love' and *Eros* on the Gould and Tuckett families at the time of writing.

[37] P. E. Easterling and J. V. Muir (eds.), *Greek Religion and Society* (Cambridge, 1985), pp. 1–33: *MRME*, chap. 7.

[38] For a sympathetic recent assessment of Gould's approach to Greek religion, in the context of a critique of the widely accepted category of 'polis religion', see J. Kindt, *Kernos*, 22 (2009), 9–34.

organised women's *thiasoi* in Greek *poleis* revealed by inscriptions, and that there was a firm division between the exclusively male cults involving ritual wine-drinking and female cults involving maenadic dancing. Gould argued plausibly that this was in danger of reductionism, of creating over-rigid boundaries, and simplifying the god who was—in ritual and myth—irreducibly contradictory, always 'on the move', both an unsettling outsider from (various parts of) the East and 'coming home' as a native Greek, and associated with luxuriant and uncontrollable vegetation (vines and ivy). Here again, it is the insistence on the acceptance of plurality, ambiguities and contradictions as central to the Greek understanding which marks out the approach.

Greek Tragedy remained the main focus for his research, and a long series of influential articles from 1978 to 2000 develops themes first worked out in Oxford, in discussion with other scholars in the UK, France and Germany. The prevailing concerns are characterisation, modes of narrative and the functions of the chorus. First, and most generally, he tackled the delicate issue of 'Dramatic character in Greek tragedy',[39] in a response to two papers by Pat Easterling.[40] In effect Gould sought to locate Greek drama along a spectrum of psychological realisation of individual personality, whose two extremes are formed by the ultra-naturalistic, highly detailed, physical and psychological presentation found in Eugene O'Neill and the most highly stylised forms of Noh theatre; Gould placed Greek plays closer to the Noh end than would many others. Formal aspects of stage-presentation (costumes, masks, staging) and of language and metrical forms (stylised or rhetorical styles, stichomythia, Dorianisms, musical accompaniments), illustrated with some telling examples, are held to militate against any great interest in the psychological details of individual characters or their back stories. Gould prefers to replace Easterling's (relatively minimal) talk of the 'human intelligibility' of the differentiated characters in a play, whose actions and words make sense to us, with an awareness that the play as a whole presents an intelligible, morally significant, metaphor for human experience. Many subsequent discussions have engaged with Gould's paper as the most influential and important example of this type of approach; especially helpful are further papers by Easterling and Goldhill, and the more general work by Christopher Gill on Greek conceptions of character and personality.[41]

[39] *Proceedings of the Cambridge Philological Society*, 204 (1978), 43–67: *MRME*, chap. 3.

[40] *Greece and Rome*, 20 (1973), 3–19 and 24 (1977), 121–9.

[41] e.g. P. Easterling and S. Goldhill in C. Pelling (ed.), *Characterization and Individuality in Greek Literature* (Oxford, 1990), pp. 89–99, 100–27; C. Gill, *Personality in Greek Epic, Tragedy and*

A paper published in 1983 titled 'Homeric epic and the tragic moment' concerned the relation between Homer and tragedy.[42] It started from the position developed by Gould's French friends Vernant and Vidal-Naquet on the 'tragic moment': the argument that fifth-century Greece saw radical new forms of thinking about many aspects of human experience, and that tragedy dealt with clashes of vision and values between the world of myths and heroes and of rationality and the citizen. While accepting this in general, Gould proceeded to argue that one should in no way underestimate the extent to which already in Homer complexity and ambiguities of values and social structures produced powerful tragic realisations.[43]

His Corbett lecture delivered in Cambridge in 1991, '"And tell sad stories of the deaths of kings": Greek tragic drama as narrative' (later published as *MRME*, chapter 14), engages with Gérard Genette's apparently clear distinction between dramatic representation and narrative (and ultimately with Plato's much earlier attempt at a similar distinction in *Republic*, 3). Greek tragedies, as Gould shows, may have no single narrative voice, but they have a controlling mind in charge of the manipulation of the story, which regularly includes narrations (often choral) of past, concurrent or future events which then guide or condition the stage actions. They also have intra-dramatic narratives, *in primis* the so-called 'messenger speech'; these may stand as models of an authoritative account from an outsider, but other narratives, even those delivered by divine figures, may also be partial or misleading. In this, the competing narrative discourses and strategies of drama prevent acceptance of a single privileged narration, and contribute to a sense of pervasive ambiguities and multiplicity (the conclusion thus coheres with Gould's other papers). As in all his papers, the analysis includes penetrating and convincing treatment of details, for example on the complexities of time-management and narratives of the past in *King Oedipus* and *Agamemnon*.

Philosophy (Oxford, 1996), especially pp. 107–24; see also recently B. Seidensticker in M. Revermann and P. Wilson (eds.), *Performance, Iconography, Reception: Studies in Honour of Oliver Taplin* (Oxford, 2008), pp. 333–48

[42] T. Winnifrith, P. Murray and K. W. Gransden (eds.), *Aspects of the Epic* (London, 1983), pp. 32–45: *MRME*, chap. 5.

[43] Cf. also J. Redfield, *History of Religion*, 31 (1991), 73–4. The nature of the reciprocal social relationships and obligations in the *Iliad*, and the conflicts and contradictions inherent in this relatively unstructured (fictional) society are penetratingly explored in Gould's unpublished paper on 'The idea of society in the *Iliad*' (*MRME*, chap. 15). There are clear similarities with ideas on Homer which Oliver Taplin was developing at the same time in *Homeric Soundings* (Oxford, 1992).

Between 1987–9 Gould was also writing papers focused on specific plays, elucidating their characteristic language and imagery: they treat the *Bacchae*, *King Oedipus* and *Antigone*. 'Mothers' Day', a contribution to a day in honour of Reginald Winnington-Ingram and published in 1987,[44] focuses on the mothers in the *Bacchae*, victims and perpetrators of horrific violence (Semele, Agaue, the Theban wives on the mountain), and plots the connections between the beauty, fertility, wildness and terror of their actions and emotions, and those of the landscape and its vegetation revealed in narrative and imagery. 'The language of Oedipus', published in 1988,[45] explores, with typical sensitivity, linked ironic contrasts in the presentation of Oedipus. It shows how Oedipus' characteristic language, which contrasts in different ways from that of Teiresias and Creon, and which changes as his journey to self-discovery progresses, combines the increasingly haunting play with the key sites in the landscape (Delphi, the three-road crossing, Thebes, Corinth, Cithairon) to convey a profound sense of Oedipus' isolation from the other characters. The others appear more firmly rooted in geographical and political space and in control of their own identities and language, while the set of ambiguities surrounding Oedipus brings him into close, if opaque, connection with the world of the gods whose responsibility for the events is undeniable, if impossible to state with precision. A previously unpublished lecture ('Oedipus and Antigone at Thebes'; *MRME*, chapter 10) briefly compares and contrasts the narratives and overall meanings of *King Oedipus* and *Antigone*. Gould finds a number of parallels between the two plays, and suggests that the *Oedipus* can be profitably seen as a radical reworking of themes important in the earlier play: imagery, characterisation and the final portrayals of divine operations, human suffering, and indestructible heroism.[46]

While projected books on Euripides and Greek tragedy never emerged, there is no doubt that the greater productivity of the Bristol years owed a great deal to Gillian. She acquired sufficient knowledge of the texts and scholarship to discuss his work with him, and offered constant encouragement and organisational support. They spent much time renovating a large rather run-down house in Clifton, which became a warm centre of hospitality. Gould was a loving and caring stepfather (as he had previously

[44] *Papers given at a Colloquium on Greek Drama in Honour of R. P. Winnington-Ingram*, Hellenic Society Supplementary Papers, 15 (London, 1987): *MRME*, chap. 8.

[45] H. Bloom (ed.), *Sophocles' Oedipus Rex* (New Haven, CT, 1988): *MRME*, chap. 9.

[46] There are connections here with the discussion of the opacity of knowledge in the *Oedipus* by Claude Calame and Gould's colleague Richard Buxton in M. S. Silk (ed.), *Tragedy and the Tragic* (Oxford, 1996), pp. 17–37, 38–48.

been a father), and took much delight in Tabitha's music, in her and Thomas's studies in Classics and English, and William's training in the Royal Ballet School and subsequent success as a dancer and choreographer; John and Gillian attended many first nights, in London and Athens.

They spent many extended periods travelling across Greece, though money was short, and journeys hampered (still) by unreliable vehicles. In 1983 Gould's Philhellenism found a new cause. Following Melina Mercouri's clarion call in August 1982, Gould was present at the initial discussions on Euboea on a plan for action, convened by the architect James Cubitt and his wife Eleni. This led to the foundation of the Committee for the Restitution of the Parthenon Marbles in 1983. Eleni Cubitt was the first secretary, and Robert Browning the first Chairman; the initial members of the Committee were Christopher Price, Brian Clark, Michael Dummett, George Forrest and Gould. This has operated ever since as a powerful lobbying and informative pressure group.[47] While the main aim is yet to be achieved, the Committee has done a great deal to change the climate of opinion and Gould contributed much to its initial progress.

In this period the Goulds' lives were blighted by disease and tragedy. Thomas, Gillian's older son, after years of drug-taking and schizophrenia, killed himself while an undergraduate studying Latin at London. Gould himself began to suffer from serious ill health, from Sjögren's syndrome, an autoimmune disease which attacks the exocrine glands, and from detached retinas in both eyes, only one of which could be saved. Subsequently, lymphatic cancer was diagnosed, which was eventually to kill him, after periods of false hope. He bore his pain with great courage, and Gillian cared for him devotedly. They remained close and mutually dependent, but their remaining years were full of tensions and grief.

By 1991, as his tenure at Bristol was coming to an end, his reputation as a scholar of the first rank was assured, and he was elected a Fellow of the British Academy, on the basis of the Herodotus book and the string of major and fundamental articles. In the next few years in retirement, though his health remained poor, he undertook some teaching in New College, Oxford,[48] and in 1993 he spent some months as a visiting Fellow at Stanford University.

The last two papers Gould published during the 1990s were the final development of his long contemplation of the Greek tragic chorus. The

[47] It is now known as the Committee for the Reunification of the Parthenon Marbles: see <http://www.parthenonuk.com>.

[48] Coincidentally, Tabitha was also in Oxford at the time, preparing for her finals in Greats and later for a doctorate in Classics and English.

more general one, originally delivered at a 1993 conference in London on 'Tragedy and the tragic', with a response from Simon Goldhill, was among his most important and influential.[49] It focuses on the status and gender of the choral personae, and what the positions and emotions expressed by their songs and speech contribute to the meaning of the plays. Assuming the unsatisfactory nature of traditional reductive formulae such as 'the ideal spectator' or 'poet's voice', Gould directs gentle corrective fire at more recent and subtler formulations offered by Vernant, Vidal-Naquet and others, that choruses tend to represent the collective 'truth' of contemporary citizens, or the collective, moderate, values of the city, as opposed to the individual heroism or excess of the leading characters. While accepting that the chorus are indeed a distinct collective entity, separate from the characters, Gould emphasises that the choruses in the surviving plays are clearly distinguished from moderate Athenian citizens, both by their language, even more distanced than that of the actors from 'ordinary' language in metre, dialect (literary Dorianisms) and diction, and, more importantly, because they are only rarely active, adult male citizens of the mythical community, and are typically marginal figures, often (and especially in Aeschylus and Euripides) women, foreign or slave (sometimes all three). The collective memory of a community is central to their presentation, but that 'community' needs to be more precisely and carefully defined for each play. Where a chorus might seem to fit the Vernant model, i.e. a group of elderly citizens, advisors to a kingdom (e.g. *Agamemnon, Antigone, Oedipus Tyrannus*), it is often cowardly, morally inadequate, or prone to dissolve into disunity and confusion; conversely, when the chorus is composed of foreign or slave women, it is present inside the play's action, as a collective, not (usually) actively causing events, but responding emotionally to them and commenting on them from the perspective of its members' relation to the place, social memory and the oral traditions of the play's city and the practices and values of its rituals and institutions.[50]

[49] 'Tragedy and collective experience', in M. S. Silk (ed.), *Tragedy and the Tragic* (Oxford, 1996), pp. 217–43: *MRME,* chap. 17. Gould's paper is declared 'seminal' by M. Revermann in M. Revermann and P. Wilson (eds.), *Performance, Iconography, Reception: Studies in Honour of Oliver Taplin* (Oxford, 2008), p. 42.

[50] Goldhill's critique (*Tragedy and the Tragic*, pp. 243–56), while applauding much, adduces strong arguments challenging Gould's emphasis on the marginality of choruses' statuses and positions, the distancing of their language and their lack of any authority; in many cases the tension between a chorus's marginality and the apparent authority of their moral, political or religious comments contributes much to the questioning of authority characteristic of the genre. See also the critique of C. Sourvinou-Inwood, *Tragedy and Athenian Religion* (Lanham, MA, 2003), pp. 265–84.

The second paper was a brief contribution to a Bristol conference entitled 'Myth, memory and the chorus: "tragic rationality"'.[51] This built on the previous paper to explore ways in which choral songs contribute to the rational arguments and debates of the plays, by their awareness of relevant mythical stories and associated moral conclusions (*gnomai*). During the last two years of his life came the preparation with Oxford University Press for his collected papers (*Myth, Ritual, Memory and Exchange: Essays in Greek Literature and Culture*). Despite much pain, he fought to have all his papers included (at one stage the Press wished to exclude some previously published in its own volumes), and added the two unpublished pieces and a few mildly polemical addenda, one attacking Burkert's sociobiological view of supplication, one dissenting from Finkleburg's view of Homeric values, and one commenting on Connerton's view of collective memory. The publication in February 2001 gave him much pleasure.[52]

The Goulds spent the years of retirement divided between Somerset, where they had a cottage at Nunney near Frome, France, where they had bought a delapidated chateau near Angers, and Greece, where they had bought a small house in the hills above Stoupa in the northern Mani. The houses abroad needed much work, and money remained very tight. There were happy times, especially in the Mani, where they had more friends, and continued to feel that rural Greek customs and social relationships strengthened understanding of ancient culture and values. Eventually, the renovation problems became too much, as John's health further deteriorated, and they sold the foreign properties and returned to Nunney.

His last academic paper was delivered in July 2000, when he was gravely ill and in much pain, at the conference in Wadham in memory of his old friend George Forrest.[53] This was the last occasion on which many of us saw him. His elegant, elegiac, piece brought together stories of divine interventions told in Herodotus with stories of the miraculous preservation of Piero della Francesca's *Resurrection* in the Borgo San Sepolcro during the Second World War; a British officer, remembering that it

[51] R. Buxton (ed.), *From Myth to Reason? Studies in the Development of Greek Thought* (Oxford, 1999), pp. 107–16: *MRME*, chap. 18.

[52] Like the Herodotus book, this appropriately won a major prize offered by an Anglo-Hellenic association, the John D. Criticos Prize awarded by the London Hellenic Society: the prize for 2001 was presented posthumously on 4 October 2002.

[53] 'Herodotus and the resurrection', in P. Derow and R. Parker (eds.), *Herodotus and his World* (Oxford, 2003), pp. 297–304. It was of course too late to be included in the collected papers volume, *MRME*.

housed the painting Aldous Huxley had called 'the best picture in the world', allegedly delayed shelling the town, in the hope that the German troops would abandon it; and they did. Gould imagines the explanation which Herodotus would have given—an imprecise but firm supposition of the work of a supernatural power—and asks how this might contrast with various modern explanations or a modern reluctance to offer any explanation. His death came a little over a year after this conference, on 19 October 2001.

John Gould was a great scholar and inspiring teacher who had a profound influence on our thinking about Greek literature, religion and culture, and who in person had a rare power to convince one of the seriousness and the fun of the intellectual life. I was not the only person after his death to apply to him the concluding words he used of Herodotus: 'the lasting impression is exhilaration ... he made you laugh, not by presenting experience as comic, but by showing it as constantly surprising and stimulating; he made you glad to have known him, as one who responded to suffering and disaster with energy and ingenuity, resilient and undefeated'.[54] Throughout his work he brought out the power of the Greeks' awareness of complexities and contradictions and of the potential for conflict and tragedy in human nature and the 'natural' world. Contradictions, tensions and tragedy were also not foreign to his own life.

NICK FISHER
Cardiff University

Note. I have had much help, in conversations, letters and emails, from Rachel Gould, Gillian Gould, Tabitha Tuckett, Roy Waters, Christopher Robinson, Martha Livingston, Peter Parsons, Antony Duff, Oliver Taplin, Donald Russell, Robert Parker, John Burrow, Colin Burrow, Michael Winterbottom, Richard Rutherford, Christopher Collard, Alan Lloyd, Richard Buxton, Peter Jones, Anthony Snodgrass and Robin Howells.

[54] Obituary in *The Independent*, 30 Oct. 2001; Parker and Derow, *Herodotus and his World*, p. vi (applying the terms also to Forrest, as had Hornblower, ibid. p. 37). Other obituaries: Richard Buxton, *The Times*, 1 Nov. 2001, and Peter Jones, *The Daily Telegraph*, 2 Nov. 2001.

MARGARET GOWING

Margaret Mary Gowing[1]
1921–1998

IF SOME HISTORIANS are born great, few acquire greatness. But some have greatness thrust upon them. This was certainly true of Margaret Mary Gowing, civil servant, archivist, and Britain's first official historian of the nuclear age. From modest origins, but armed with a good education, and favoured by the circumstances of Britain at war, Gowing met and seized opportunities that led her eventually to occupy a position of national prominence that few historians—and, at the time, few women historians—could have anticipated, and which even fewer achieved. Her greatest, lasting scholarly contribution takes the form of two books, which in their mastery of official records laid the foundations of archival research upon which later generations of scholars have built. But her progress was never easy, nor were her successes complete. Ever entwined, her personal and her professional life were deeply touched by moments of acute stress, tinged with tragedy, that came to affect not only her academic performance but also the lives of family, friends, colleagues, and students.

The following memoir traces the outlines of her career and measures the significance of her work, against a background of personal and professional struggle. Inevitably, this says much about the writing of official history, the special circumstances of Britain's nuclear history, and Britain's role in the nuclear age. It also says something of the difficulties that have, over the years, attended the proper institutional recognition of her field, and its contribution to the discipline of modern history in Britain.

[1] A similar memoir appears in *Biographical Memoirs of Fellows of the Royal Society*, 58 (2012), 67–111.

Biographical Memoirs of Fellows of the British Academy, XI, 267–327.

Beginnings

Margaret Mary Elliott was born on 26 April 1921, the youngest of three children of a working class family. She was brought up in North Kensington, where her father suffered from poor health and (like many workers of his generation) long periods of unemployment; her mother, a primary school teacher by training, was forbidden to work by the marriage bar. Despite these difficult circumstances, all three children—Audrey, Donald and Margaret—were clever, and made their way in the world. Audrey and Margaret showed academic promise; and after finishing Portobello Elementary School, in 1932, at the age of eleven, Margaret (or 'Babs' as she was known in the family) won a scholarship to Christ's Hospital. She didn't enjoy the school, but thanks to the encouragement of her headmistress, as she later recalled, she enjoyed learning, otherwise she might have ended as a clerk with the London Council, which is what her parents had in mind.[2] Taking her School Leaving Certificate in 1936, she won a Leverhulme Entry Scholarship to the London School of Economics (LSE), where she made friends with many who shared her social background and who, like her, were ambitious for academic success. At the same time, she never forgot her family, or the fragilities of family life. In later interviews, she recalled sending half her scholarship money to help her parents.[3] Her father died of tuberculosis, after being out of work for months. She became and remained a staunch advocate of the welfare state, the National Health Service, the Labour Party, and state education.[4]

Entering LSE in 1938, Margaret won the Gladstone Memorial Prize and the Lillian Knowles Scholarship for economic history. With the coming of war, she was evacuated with LSE to Cambridge, where in 1941 she graduated with a B.Sc. (Econ.) degree with First Class Honours. Her courses focused on economics, banking, economic history, and international history. That she specialised in economic history she attributed to the stimulating lectures of Eileen Power, in many ways a powerful role model, who encouraged Margaret to continue in academic life. In 1941, however, academic prospects were few, so from September she found work as a temporary statistical assistant in the Prices and Statistics Section of the Iron and Steel Control directorate in the Ministry of Supply. The civil service suited her, and by 1945 she had moved to the Board of Trade, and

[2] Margaret Gowing, in an interview with Sarah White, 'Nuclear historian', *New Scientist*, 28 Nov. 1974, 656–9 at 656.

[3] Nik Gowing to author, 7 May 2004.

[4] Museum of the History of Science, Oxford (MHS), Gowing Papers, Perrier Box, Gowing to Neville Mott, 26 June 1986.

the Directorate of Housing Fitments, where she rose to the rank of Assistant Principal.[5]

In 1944 Margaret married Donald Gowing, an accomplished young singer, who had also been a scholarship student at Christ's Hospital. In 1939, Donald won a choral scholarship to King's College, Cambridge, and went up to read History. He is remembered by contemporaries at King's as having 'a happy disposition and an infectious enthusiasm', qualities that would have recommended him to Margaret.[6] In 1941, after Margaret and he graduated, Donald joined the RNVR. He was posted first to Combined Operations, then to naval intelligence. With the marriage bar suspended for the duration, he and Margaret were married in Wimbledon Registry Office just before he was posted overseas; he learned Japanese at a US military college in Colorado. Due to the imperatives of secrecy, for well over two years Margaret had no idea where her new husband was. Their only contact was through the occasional military 'bluey' letter, but with no originating location permitted. Unknown to her, Donald went on to serve as a translator for the US Naval Command in the Pacific; he was a member of General MacArthur's staff on board the *USS Missouri* when the Japanese surrender was accepted. After the war, he stayed on in Japan for a year as a political adviser at the British Embassy in Tokyo, and returned to England in 1946. Such a long period of separation from her new husband was a key factor in sharpening her personal determination to succeed in a male-dominated civil service and Whitehall environment: such single-mindedness—some described it as stubbornness—marked the whole of her career, largely in positive ways.

Whitehall after the war

In June 1945, with her husband overseas, and with Whitehall's war work winding down, Margaret looked to her future. Fate took a hand when she was spotted by Keith (later Sir Keith) Hancock, the brilliant, 'quizzical, kindly, energetic, pipe-smoking' Australian historian,[7] author of an

[5]CAB 160/5. Gowing Employment File. Her salary at the Board of Trade was £335 plus war bonus of £48 and special allowance of £50, or a total of £433.

[6]Donald Gowing (1921–69), later Director-General of the Musicians Benevolent Fund. See *King's College Magazine*, Nov. 1970, p. 37. For this information I am indebted to Ms Sue Turnbull of the Development Office, King's College, Cambridge.

[7]This description I owe to Ann Oakley, *Man and Wife: Richard and Kay Titmuss: My Parents' Early Years* (London, 1996), pp. 146–7.

acclaimed survey of the British Commonwealth,[8] who in 1941 had taken leave from the University of Birmingham to join the Historical Section of the Cabinet Office.[9] In June 1941 Sir Edward Bridges, Secretary to the War Cabinet, had suggested the idea of preparing a civil counterpart to the military history series that the Cabinet Office had produced since the end of the Great War.[10] 'Nowadays,' Bridges said, the 'armed forces … were no more than the cutting edge of the nation at war.'[11] To supervise this 'civil series', Bridges approached Hancock (who was, like him, a former Fellow of All Souls, Oxford).

Thanks not least to his reputation as an imperial historian, Hancock had Whitehall connections that opened doors. He took on the job at a lower salary than he might have had at Birmingham, by way, as he put it, of doing his 'national service', which, he took 'all the more seriously because it seemed so peculiar'.[12] In fact, he enjoyed remarkable freedom. To academic authors of his own choosing, he wrote his own instructions, subject only to the nominal approval of an advisory committee—under Dr E. A. Benians, Master of St John's College, Cambridge—that seldom met—and overseen by a Cabinet committee, chaired by R. A. Butler (newly appointed President of the Board of Education), that never interfered. For sceptics, it was legitimate to ask, Hancock said, whether there was any point in writing the history of the war before it was won. But few such doubts troubled him. For Hancock, the argument turned on the principle of 'funding experience for government use'.[13] With some reluctance,

[8] See W. K. Hancock, *Survey of British Commonwealth Affairs*: vol. 1: *Problems of Nationality, 1918–1936*; vol. 2: *Problems of Economic Policy, 1918–1939* (Oxford, 1937–42).

[9] See Jim Davidson, 'Sir William Hancock (1898–1988)', *Australian Dictionary of Biography*, vol. 17, 482–5; and his definitive *A Three-Cornered Life: the Historian W. K. Hancock* (Sydney, 2010). See also A. Low, 'William Keith Hancock, 1898–1988', *Proceedings of the British Academy*, 82 (1992), 399–414.

[10] The seed may have been sown earlier by Brigadier Sir James Edmonds, who since 1919 had led the Historical Section (established by the Committee for Imperial Defence (CID) in 1906), and who urged the need for a civil companion series. See Lorna Arnold, 'A letter from Oxford', *Minerva*, 38 (2) (2000), 201–19 at 203.

[11] Quoted in W. K. Hancock, *Country and Calling* (London, 1954), p. 196. Hancock credits Bridges with the idea for the series, whose activities are described in CAB 98, CAB 102 and CAB 103. For background, see Denys Hay, 'British historians and the beginnings of the Civil History of the Second World War', in M. R. D. Foot (ed.), *War and Society: Historical Essays in Honour and Memory of J. R. Western, 1927–1971* (London, 1973), pp. 39–55. See also Davidson, 'Sir William Hancock'.

[12] Oakley, *Man and* Wife, p. 300; Hancock, *Country and Calling*, p. 197.

[13] W. K. Hancock and M. M. Gowing, *British War Economy: History of the Second World War: United Kingdom Civil Series* (London, 1949), Preface, p. xi.

the Treasury approved payment for ten historians; eventually, the Series employed over twenty-five.[14]

As Hancock accepted, his authors faced the prospect of reading, digesting, and delivering summary conclusions based on some two million files. Bridges advised Hancock to begin at the top; and so he did, starting with the decisions of the War Cabinet, and working through their implications and consequences. With this 'top-down' protocol, an Olympian perspective inevitably pervaded the Series—whose individual volumes were to be written not in terms of 'one department, one history', but in reference to 'salient subjects', administrative functions of relevance to civil government.[15]

Hancock met Gowing for the first time in June 1945. He was in his forties, she was 24. She was impressed by his 'charm, his grin and kindliness', but 'scared stiff by his great erudition'.[16] Their relationship was, in a professional sense, love at first sight. In July, he requested her transfer, and Sir Edward Bridges persuaded the Treasury to agree. Reluctant to lose her, the Board of Trade delayed for months, until Hancock threatened to resign, on the grounds that without her, the central volume to 'which, for political reasons, great importance is attached', may have to be abandoned. The transfer was approved in September, and she was finally released in October. She moved from a salary of £433 to £548.[17]

Immediately, it seemed the pair were ideally matched. She was educated, attractive, agreeable, ambitious, amenable, and hard working. They shared interests in world travel and left-wing politics. They were both keen archive scholars. Hancock thought true talent was wasted in administration, and so (as she amply demonstrated in later years) did she. Both belonged to a meritocracy *avant la lettre*—'outsiders' by birth, keen to know how the Establishment worked, and to make it work for them. In this, they resembled Hancock's friend (and Gowing's idol) Richard Titmuss, whom Hancock pulled from an insurance office to produce the Series volume on *Problems of Social Policy*, and who pioneered social policy at the LSE. Like Titmuss, whose British Academy memoir she later

[14] These included W. H. B. Court, a friend and colleague from Birmingham, and Michael Postan, professor of economic history at Cambridge and a former official in the Ministry of Economic Warfare. Hancock, *Country and Calling*, p. 200.

[15] Hancock and Gowing, *British War Economy*, Preface, p. xi.

[16] M. Gowing on 'Hancock in Whitehall', in 'Hancock: some reminiscences', *Historical Studies*, 13 (1968), 302.

[17] CAB 160/5. Gowing's personal file relates Hancock's persistence in prising her away from the Board of Trade. Minute, 9 Aug. 1945.

wrote,[18] in joining Hancock Gowing left behind a life that was culturally thin and exchanged a job as a clerk for a career with a future.

On 17 September 1945 Gowing signed the Official Secrets Act and began work at the Cabinet Office. She was styled, in the Trollopian lexicon of the Civil Service, a 'Narrator'. Formally, she was Hancock's assistant, but she quickly became his apprentice, penetrating the mists of administrative history in the company of a magus of the art.[19] Hancock's Series had to embrace the war work of twenty agencies, including war production, food, agriculture, fuel and power, building, the social services, civil defence, land transport, shipping, manpower, and economic warfare. Predictably, authors (and departments) at first insisted that each was a special case, requiring special treatment. Diplomatically, Hancock found a way through the minefield by commissioning a few 'synoptic' volumes, which he intended to follow with specialised volumes dealing with departmental issues in greater detail. His authors had to exercise, as Hancock put it, 'a good deal of ingenuity', circumspection, and discrimination in working from documentary to oral evidence and back again.[20] Much time was spent in revision. Perhaps there were some, like Titmuss, who produced drafts that were 'too intimate, too revealing ... for the ministry, full of gossip, rife with unflattering facts'.[21] In such cases, Hancock had to coerce and cajole, even to threaten.[22]

In 1947 Gowing was given the title of Historian, and the rank of Principal.[23] If, at first, Hancock treated her like a research assistant, she soon became his right hand, revealing what many later saw as 'a drive and ability for decisive action that other historians usually lacked'.[24] In dealing with difficult authors, diffuse sources, and dissonant departments 'she was my saviour', Hancock said.[25] During the next two years, she consolidated her reputation with the formidable *British War Economy* (1949), of which Gowing drafted a third, managing the statistics, so as to leave Hancock free to concentrate on broader themes of political economy, finance and

[18] Margaret Gowing, 'Richard Titmuss (1907–1973)', *Proceedings of the British Academy*, LXI (1975), 401–28. See also D. A. Riesman, *Richard Titmuss: Welfare and Society* (London, 1977), and J. Kincaid, 'Richard Titmuss', in P. Barker (ed.), *Founders of the Welfare State* (London, 1984).

[19] Margaret Gowing, 'Hancock: some reminiscences', *Historical Studies*, 13 (1968), 291–306.

[20] Hancock and Gowing, *British War Economy*, Preface.

[21] Oakley, *Man and Wife*, pp. 146–7.

[22] Ibid.

[23] CAB 160/5 Gowing File, Summary Sheet, 1959.

[24] Gowing Family Papers, Box 3, Webster to Nik Gowing, 23 Nov. 1998.

[25] Davidson, 'Sir William Hancock', p. 211.

manpower.[26] Later, according to Hancock, Gowing rescued the Series volumes on agriculture, land transport and the Board of Trade. No wonder he dubbed her his 'mobile reserve'. The next book in the Series she wrote with E. L. Hargreaves (Fellow of Oriel College, Oxford), *Civil Industry and Trade* (1952), which was followed by a chapter in *Studies in the Social Services*, edited by S. M. Ferguson and H. Fitzgerald.[27] By 1958, Hancock ranked Margaret as effectively co-editor of the entire Series, which eventually ran to twenty-eight volumes. Of the women who worked with Hancock at the Cabinet Office, two were especially dear to him—one, his secretary (Marjorie Eyre), whom he later married; the other, Margaret, who remained a friend for life.[28]

For Gowing (as she was now in print), the Hancock legacy was equally enduring. Being midwife to the series meant having to reconcile the wishes of historians and officials, without sacrificing the integrity of either. Thanks to Hancock 'the whole concept of official history ceased to represent the prostitution of the profession and became rather an important contribution to understanding in an age when Government policy bulks so large'.[29] From Hancock, Gowing took away lessons about how Britain managed economic mobilisation and planning, squaring civil liberty with efficiency, against an extemporised and flawed but remarkable history of interdepartmental and interservice cooperation. With Hancock, she shared a sense of outrage at America's early termination of Lend Lease, and the severe economic difficulties into which Britain had thus been put. Her reservations about the extent of American cooperation were to last the rest of her career, and to influence critical parts of her writing.

By the end of 1959, 32,000 copies of *British War Economy* had been sold, and a post-war generation of historians saw in it a narrative of victory through national unity and central management, heralding the advent of the 'social service state'. Thanks to Hancock and Gowing, the war for

[26] The book remains one of the best read and cited volumes in the series. See Jose Harris, 'Thucydides amongst the Mandarins: Hancock and the World War II Civil Histories', in D. A. Low (ed.), *Keith Hancock: the Legacies of an Historian* (Melbourne, 2001), pp. 122–48 at 133. See also Harris, 'If Britain had been defeated by the Nazis, how would history have been written?' in William Roger Louis (ed.), *Still More Adventures with Britannia: Personalities, Politics and Culture in Britain* (Austin, TX, 2001), pp. 211–28.

[27] Margaret Gowing, 'Introductory: the growth of government action and the ups and downs of the family', in Sheila Ferguson and Hilde Fitzgerald (eds.), *Studies in the Social Services* (London, 1954).

[28] Hancock, *Country and Calling*, p. 200. Gowing's account of 'The Civil Histories of the Second World War', delivered as a lecture in 1988, is preserved in her papers in Oxford. See also Fred Alexander, A. Boyce Gibson, Margaret Gowing and Robin Gollan, 'Hancock: some reminiscences', *Historical Studies*, 13 (1968), 291–306.

[29] Gowing on 'Hancock in Whitehall', p. 303.

the peace would be read as similarly requiring cooperation and planning.[30] In the words of Alan Bullock, the distinguished economic historian, the book was a 'perfect vehicle' for describing the career of Ernest Bevin.[31] Much later, British historians—winning for themselves belated access to the same official files—would beg to differ, and see in the Series' narratives more evidence of division and disunity, of conflict rather than consensus.[32] In their own time, some volumes met deep official opposition—Postan's history of British war production, for example, was blocked by the War Office and Supply and Service departments, on the grounds that it revealed too much. The Series volume on *Design and Development of Weapons*, almost shelved in 1955, appeared only in 1964. A later generation of historians saw them as narrative without dissent (or as Hancock himself liked to say of official histories generally, 'dead mutton'). This experience, too, Gowing took away with her—along with a cautious appreciation of the power of Whitehall to defend, deny, and delay.

Against this, Gowing enjoyed the prestige of working with the Cabinet Office. As such, she had entré to top secret papers, and everyday access to leading politicians and civil servants. Gowing remained in the Cabinet Office, working on the Civil Series until 1959. During the early 1950s, Margaret and Donald celebrated the birth of their two sons: Nicholas (Nik)—christened Nicholas Keith, after Hancock—in 1951, and James in 1954. In 1952, her experience of official archives was tapped by the Chancellor of the Exchequer, who appointed her—then aged only 30—to Sir James Grigg's Committee on government records. The Grigg Report in 1954 laid the foundations of the modern state records system in Britain, and was to have a dramatic effect on her own life.[33] Gowing later remembered a race between finishing her report and giving birth to James.[34] Fortunately, it proved to be a race, as in Alice, where all were winners.

[30] In Gowing's words, public enterprise, rationality and altruism had succeeded where markets and muddle had failed. See her 'The organisation of manpower in Britain during the Second World War', *Journal of Contemporary History*, 7 (1972), 147–67.

[31] Alan Bullock, *The Life and Times of Ernest Bevin*, vol. II (London, 1968), cited in Harris, 'Thucydides amongst the Mandarins', p. 141.

[32] See, e.g. Correlli Barnett, *The Audit of War* (London, 1986) and *The Lost Victory* (London, 1995).

[33] The Committee on Departmental Records (1954. Cmd 9163) was chaired by Sir James Grigg, Permanent Undersecretary at the War Office, 1939–42 and Secretary of State for War, 1942–5. The Grigg report recommended that the Lord Chancellor be responsible for the Public Record Office; that Records Officers should be appointed in each department; and that official papers should be reviewed after twenty-five years, and in principle transferred to the PRO after a fifty-year interval.

[34] [Lorna Arnold], 'Professor Margaret Gowing', *The Times*, 11 Nov. 1998, p. 23.

During the 1950s, Donald's singing ambitions met with mixed success. He hoped that being appointed as a member of the Royal Opera House, London, choir would launch a professional career but it did not, despite acclaim in many productions. The need for a reliable income to supplement Margaret's earnings led him to take an administrative post with the Musicians Benevolent Fund, and he rose to the position of Director-General during the 1960s. But the combined pressures of an unfulfilled musical career in parallel to Margaret's growing professional success and recognition led to alcoholism, which steadily darkened his and the family's lives. To look after the boys, the Gowings employed a college-trained nurse, Vera ('Va'), who stayed for seventeen years and became the family's best friend. But Margaret had to pay her, and to support her widowed mother as well. As it was, in the post-war years, a married woman with children, holding an *ex-tempore* post, could count on little sympathy (let alone superannuation) from the Civil Service Commission. Another future, preferably well paid, was needed.

As Hancock feared, the wartime History Office was never intended to be a permanent fixture. Hancock himself began to return to academic life as early as 1944, working on the Civil Histories only part time until 1957. As early as 1950, Sir Norman Brook (later Lord Normanbrook), then Head of the Civil Service, put the case for having a permanent Historian in the Cabinet Office, to which it was said he would have appointed Gowing; but the proposal met stiff formal opposition from the Treasury and the Civil Service Commission. In 1951, Gowing was told she had no prospect of being retained at the rank of Principal (with full pension benefits) without her post first being made subject to open competition. Apparently, she did not seek a permanent appointment in the Administrative Class, for which she was certainly eligible.[35]

In 1955, with the Civil Series coming to an end, with Hancock moving to the chair of economic history at Oxford, and with young children to support, Gowing faced a daunting choice—to continue on an unestablished basis in the Cabinet Office or, in her words, to 'move to different territory'.[36] With Hancock's encouragement, she applied in 1955 for the LSE's Readership in Social Administration—'work with a more human content', as she put it[37]—and in the following year she applied for the

[35] CAB 160/5 Gowing Employment File, RMJ Harris, Treasury to A. B. Acheson, Cabinet Office, 17 July 1951.

[36] MHS, Gowing Papers, Gowing to Appointments Board, NIESR, 21 Sept. 1956.

[37] MHS, Gowing Papers, Gowing to Secretary, LSE, 13 Sept. 1955.

Secretaryship of the National Institute of Economic and Social Research (NIESR). Her referees for the first were Hancock, Sir Keith Murray (chairman of the University Grants Committee), and Professor G. C. Allen (of University College London). Her applications reflect her well-tested confidence in speaking knowledgeably about public policy. But neither application was successful. She remained in the Cabinet Office until 1959, during which time she worked for the Radcliffe Committee on the monetary system, and for Sir Norman Brook himself, on what she called 'experimental work on historical work for administrative use'[38]—the results of which were never published.

In 1958, following the successful reception of the Grigg Report, the Macmillan government passed the first Public Record Act, which required all executive departments to set up archives and records management systems, and to appoint Departmental Records Officers (DROs) to oversee the review, collection, listing, and conveyance of papers to the Public Record Office (PRO). This was the origin of the 'Fifty-Year Rule'.[39] Not all agencies, however, were included in the Act's catchment. This omission notably included the United Kingdom Atomic Energy Authority (UKAEA),[40] which had been set up in 1954, following the first British bomb tests in 1952, to manage Britain's civil nuclear policy and power production. The Authority had inherited the functions and assets of the 'Tube Alloys' department of the Ministry of Supply (1940–54), along with the records of several defunct wartime agencies. But to the surprise of Whitehall, the Authority—a government corporation, rather than a department—asked to be voluntarily included under the Act. This created an unprecedented opening for an 'Historian and Archivist'.

The UKAEA's decision had important consequences. Without it, the flow of nuclear history materials to the PRO would have been slowed to a trickle, and the earliest would not have reached the public until the 1990s. The decision also made Britain's early nuclear history better known to a general public whose understanding of wartime developments had been dominated by American narratives since 1945, and which had only recently been given much information about Britain's wartime achievements, following Macmillan's Bermuda accord with Eisenhower in 1957.[41]

[38] MHS, Gowing Papers, Curriculum Vitae for the University of Kent, 1967.

[39] By the Public Records Act of 1967, the 'Fifty Year Rule' was replaced by a 'Thirty Year Rule'.

[40] The constitutional concept of such an Authority was new to the civil service. For its history, see AB 48/252 and AB 16/3851, 3852; 4185, 4286, and 4589.

[41] The American nuclear story was highly influenced by the Smyth Report in 1945. Later, more detailed accounts, but which also paid relatively little attention to Britain's contribution,

For Gowing, the Authority's decision created a golden opportunity—at a single stroke—to continue as an historian, to become 'established' as a permanent civil servant, and to retain her rank as Principal (later rising to Assistant Secretary).[42] In the summer of 1959, backed by Hancock, she applied for and was offered the job. Having failed to find an administrative loophole by which he might have kept her as an historian in the Cabinet Office, Sir Norman Brook reluctantly let her go.

The atomic age, 1959–1966

Gowing departed from the Cabinet Office on 14 June 1959.[43] Looking back, she later recalled her fourteen years there as among 'the happiest in my life'.[44] Her new job was not easy. Just one person was meant to organise, from scratch, and bring under a unified system of reference, a vast quantity of relevant archives, originating in the Cabinet Office, the War Office, the Supply Departments, and the Services, from at least 1939 to 1959; and to devise a records system appropriate to a rapidly growing organisation that was already employing over 40,000 people, working in more than ten offices, laboratories and factories across Britain. It also meant reading up a subject about which she knew nothing. Her archival *nous*, polished by long practice in the Cabinet Office, was certainly relevant. But her role, as she saw it, was not merely custodial nor, for that matter, managerial. To an historian, archives are a means to an end, not an end in itself. As to this part of her work, she later recalled, 'very little thought at all had been given to the historical side of the task or its implications'.[45] It was a testament to her own vision and energy that, within

appeared in three volumes: R. G. Hewlett and O. E. Anderson, *The New World, 1939–1946, Volume I: a History of the United States Atomic Energy Commission* (University Park, PA, 1962); R. G. Hewlett and F. Duncan, *Atomic Shield: a History of the United States Atomic Energy Commission, 1947–52* (Washington, DC, 1972); and R. G. Hewlett and J. M. Holt, *Atoms for Peace and War, 1953–1961* (Berkeley, CA, 1989).

42 MHS, Gowing Papers, Brown Archive Box, Jobs and Applications, MG to C. P. Myers, 21 July 1964.

43 Gowing later remarked that she had declined the offer of an Assistant Secretaryship in the Cabinet Office because she 'looked forward to writing another book for publication'. MHS, Gowing Papers, Brown Archive Box, Jobs and Applications, MG to Peirson, 2 May 1962. Norman Brook was prepared to make her Cabinet Office Archivist, but could not offer her a pension. See CAB 160/5 MG to S. Anderson, Establishment Officer, Cabinet Office, 4 May 1959.

44 CAB 160/5, MG to Theobald, 26 Dec. 1969.

45 MHS, Gowing Papers, Brown Archive Box, Jobs and Applications, MG to C. P. Myers, 21 July 1964.

two years, she had immersed herself sufficiently in the subject to embark upon what would become her life's work—the history of Britain's atomic energy programme.

In Gowing's day, writing nuclear history meant navigating uncharted seas. As her colleague Lorna Arnold recalled, 'there was no secondary material, and the subject, which had been wrapped in wartime secrecy, was still largely secret'.[46] Gowing also had no scientific training ('I didn't know an atom from a molecule', she liked to say).[47] And she knew nothing of the history of science. But she did have several advantages, whose value she understood from her years at the Cabinet Office. The UKAEA would let her work with the minimum of interference. There were few strings attached—no deadlines, no designated methods of work, or periods or themes to be covered. She was given secretarial support, a salary, and she reported directly to the Chairman of the Authority. She was free to get on in her own way, at her own speed. Thanks to an early Authority agreement with the Cabinet Office, she had access to all departmental, Cabinet Office, Downing Street, and Foreign Office records, however secret, except for an undisclosed quantity of intelligence material.[48] An advisory committee was mooted, but apparently not appointed.[49]

All Gowing wrote, of course, would be subject to vetting, but within the Authority there was the presumption that some form of publication would ensue. Above all, she had the inestimable advantage of writing on a subject of intense national and contemporary interest, about which little was publicly known, but for which there was a growing audience, eager to learn, and likely to respond well to a lively narrative. Her only competition came from American historians, and their account of the nuclear story, in her eyes, needed a British companion.[50]

From the early 1960s, Gowing set out to apply to Britain's nuclear history the methods she had learned from Hancock and the Cabinet Office—that is, begin at the top, and work your way through the people who

[46] MS Memo, Lorna Arnold to author, Nov. 2004, section 5, p. 3. Lorna Arnold joined the UKAEA's Health and Safety Branch around the time that Gowing was appointed; their offices were nearby, and they often lunched together. Ead., section 4, p. 1, 6.

[47] MS Memo, Arnold to author, Nov. 2004, section 5, p. 3. This mantra appears repeatedly. See Sarah White, 'Nuclear Historian', p. 656; [Lorna Arnold], 'Professor Margaret Gowing', p. 23.

[48] Official Historians were appointed by the Cabinet Office, but Gowing was appointed and employed by the UKAEA.

[49] See PRO AB 16/3851, Sir Roger Makins to Hitchman, 7 Nov. 1960.

[50] The first American official nuclear history was published in 1962, two years before Gowing's *Britain and Atomic Energy* appeared in 1964. See Hewlett and Anderson, *The New World, 1939–1946, vol. I.*

actually made the history. In this, she was fortunate in writing at a time not long after the events she was describing, and could command the help of many who knew these events at first hand. She played by the rules—she produced drafts, and sent them for comment to senior officials. As during the war, she excelled at asking awkward questions of senior scientists and officials. The first time they met, Sir Christopher Hinton gave her two hours, and 'bared his soul'. Sir James Chadwick, the Nobel-Prize-winning physicist who had refused to cooperate with a Cambridge historian sent earlier by the Cabinet Office, pursued their conversation with 'a glow of warm letters'. She became good friends with the physicists Nicholas Kurti and Sir Rudolf Peierls, both now at Oxford. In France, she met Bertrand Goldschmidt, and in the United States, J. Robert Oppenheimer and General Leslie Groves. She got on so well with Nils Bohr, the distinguished Danish physicist, that he invited her to Copenhagen.[51]

Within the Authority, the competing roles of archivist and historian were not always well understood, and for the latter Gowing had to fight for support. Among her closest allies was Sir Roger Makins (later Lord Sherfield),[52] chairman of the UKAEA, and an historian by education. Makins had served in Washington, DC, during the passage of the McMahon Act, 1946, the implementation of which denied Britain access to American nuclear know-how—especially the production of nuclear materials—and he knew first-hand the limitations of the 'Special Relationship'. In 1964, the news of his forthcoming retirement brought Gowing a moment of despair: 'the future of myself and my history seem very gloomy and I wonder if I can face it', she wrote.[53] Revealing sentiments that she made more vocal over time, Gowing reflected:

> I suspect that people think I collect files together and then sit down in an academic calm so enviable compared with the administrative hurly burly and, with a bit of [luck] and inspiration, write a chapter. In fact it is a gruelling intellectual job which requires intense concentration and involves very difficult problems of analysis, judgement and selection, as well as literary skill. Quite apart from this, I have had to cope with very eminent, sometimes very difficult people.

[51] MG to C. P. Myers, 4 March 1964. Their friendship contributed to Margaret Gowing, 'Niels Bohr and nuclear weapons', in A. P. French and P. J. Kennedy (eds.), *Niels Bohr: a Centenary Volume* (Cambridge, MA, 1985), pp. 266–77.

[52] Roger Makins, Baron Sherfield (1904–96), Fellow of All Souls, diplomat and civil servant at the British Embassy in Washington, DC (1945–7) and British Ambassador to the US (1953–6), served as chairman of the UKAEA between 1960 and 1964. He was elected a Fellow of the Royal Society in 1986, under Statute 12.

[53] MHS, Gowing Papers, MG to J. Charles, 21 July 1964.

> If I had put a foot wrong the opprobrium on the Authority might well have been considerable.[54]

Fortunately, Gowing's relations with the Authority improved when—after just two years and two months, without research assistance, and amidst difficulties at home—she researched, wrote and published her first work in nuclear history, *Britain and Atomic Energy, 1939–1945*.[55] This was the first civil official history to appear outside the Cabinet Office series. As such, publication could not be guaranteed—certainly not if it contained footnotes, even if they were to documents that other historians could not see for the next thirty years. However, once Gowing had submitted her manuscript for vetting, few changes were suggested, and opposition melted away. The UKAEA retained copyright and, with a nod to security, removed her footnotes.[56] But they let the book be published by Macmillan, with an eye to a wide potential readership. It was a canny decision, profitable to publisher, agency, and author.

Conceived by Gowing as the first of three chronological volumes, '*BAE*' was a triumph. Hancock, who had read the text in draft, pronounced it 'first rate'. Its success inspired Mark Oliphant, FRS—the distinguished Australian veteran of the Manhattan Project, and Hancock's former colleague at Birmingham, now returned to Australia—to seek the appointment of an historian to work with the new Australian Academy of Science in Canberra.[57] Stephen Toulmin, the philosopher of science, then exploring new frontiers at the Nuffield Foundation and Sussex University, thought that 'No better example of contemporary narrative history of science has yet appeared . . .'. The media played a similar tune. Even the Cabinet Office was impressed, and in 1966 decided to sponsor a new series of peacetime official histories, which took Gowing's readable book as a model.[58] To a degree unusual among academics, and remotely rare among civil servants, Gowing was suddenly launched into the limelight, and proclaimed a national treasure.

[54] MHS, Gowing Papers, MG to J. Charles, 21 July 1964.

[55] Margaret Gowing, *Britain and Atomic Energy, 1939–1945* (London, 1964).

[56] Not until 1980 were Gowing's footnote references made available to readers at the Public Record Office, where they are available today in the form of typescript booklets.

[57] MHS, Gowing Papers, Correspondence Files, Hancock to Gowing, 12 Nov. 1961.

[58] MHS, Gowing Papers, Official Histories, Cabinet Office, C. J. Child to David Allen, 24 Aug. 1972. At the end of 1960, the Prime Minister announced three new volumes—on colonial development, by D. J. Morgan; environmental planning, by J. B. Cullingworth; nationalisation, 1945–60, by D. N. Chester; followed possibly by a fourth on external economic policy by L. S. Pressnell (Memo by Gowing, 4/1972). Subsequently, the series has included three volumes on the National Health Service by Charles Webster.

The reason was simple. *Britain and Atomic Energy* told a story that was unfamiliar to the British public, and little known even to many in senior government circles. Working from documents and interviews, Gowing charted Britain's heroic contributions in Cambridge, Manchester and Birmingham, through the Military Application of Uranium Detonation (MAUD) Committee of 1941, preparing the way for the Manhattan Project. At a time when the United States was keen to monopolise the story, Gowing reminded the world what Britain had contributed to its success. Her point was clinched by an appendix that, for the first time, reprinted the original February 1940 memo sent by Otto Frisch and Rudolf (later Sir Rudolf) Peierls to Mark Oliphant, showing that, contrary to Heisenberg's calculations, a uranium bomb was technically feasible. The story that Gowing came across this priceless paper in an old cornflakes packet may be apocryphal, but its retelling had an instant appeal that heavyweight official history could not match. Suddenly, there was an interest in the contemporary history of science, and in preserving archives on both sides of the Atlantic. In Gowing's phrase, the bomb had 'drawn a line across history'.[59] A new age of science had begun. If scientists had 'the future in their bones', as C. P. Snow put it, the nuclear scientists were in charge of reading the auguries.

In retrospect, Gowing was both lucky and inspired in her timing. '*BAE*' appeared just as Harold Wilson's newly elected Labour Government pronounced its determination to lead a 'white hot technological revolution'. Here was a textbook showing what Britain could do. But this was not the only attraction. Amidst the gray precincts of official history, traditionally dominated by worthy accounts of transport policy and export controls, hers was possibly the most *interesting* book to trace its origins to Hancock's benevolent influence. Although she escaped becoming a 'teledon', in an age that coined the art form, her mail now included invitations to join government committees,[60] and to write for the literary press. That her contributions relied upon a thin background in science did not diminish her influence, or her reputation, which in any case was augmented by displays of secret documentary knowledge that few, if any, could match. Overall, the response of the UKAEA was gratifyingly positive. Public

[59] Gowing, *Britain and Atomic Energy, 1939–1945*, p. 386.

[60] Including the SSRC's Committee on Social Science and Government, the Publications Advisory Committee of the Public Record Office, the Executive Committee of the Association of Contemporary Historians, and the International Committee on the History of the Second World War.

acclaim had won the Authority a rare form of *kudos* that politicians admired and administrators understood.

This Niagara of near-universal praise had a tremendous effect on Gowing's self-esteem, at a time when professional encouragement and support was dearly needed. Her husband, Donald, had by now long suffered from depression and alcoholism, and his continuing tragedy weighed upon her to such a degree that she sought a separation.[61] She thought time spent apart from Donald would benefit the boys.[62] Of course, she had also to earn a living. She had produced her first volume in less than five years, but the next—covering at least the next decade of Britain's nuclear story—would take longer, and involve the mastery of more complex organisations, structures, and technical issues, not to mention the contributions of many more scientists and engineers. She began to look for a university post where she could take the boys, one that would let her relinquish her role of Authority archivist, while keeping a hand in writing its history.

When, in 1966, such an opportunity arose to take on 'work with a more human content', as she put it, she seized it with enthusiasm. In September 1966, backed by her usual sponsors, and basking in the success of her book, she was appointed to a newly created Readership in Contemporary History at the University of Kent. This post she hoped would help her promote the study of science and society—perhaps along the lines of the University of Sussex, which had begun similar activities in January the same year.[63] A senior academic appointment was surely her due—and Kent could have been her solution. But, as time revealed, it was not to be her destiny.

Canterbury tales

The University of Kent was founded in 1964 and, like other post-Robbins 'new universities', was determined to play its part in 'redrawing the map of knowledge'. Gowing was actively encouraged to come, in the hope that she would help 'close the gap' between Snow's 'Two Cultures' and develop

[61] Nik Gowing to author, 7 May 2004.

[62] MHS, Metal Bookcase, Bullock file, Gowing to Bullock, n.d. but *c.* Dec. 1971.

[63] See Roy MacLeod (ed.), *Technology and the Human Prospect: Essays in Honour of Christopher Freeman* (London, 1986), Introduction. Later correspondence suggests that Gowing may have been offered a position at Sussex, before she accepted Kent, but this has not been confirmed. See MHS, Gowing Papers, I&D File, Gowing to Asa Briggs, 3 Oct. 1974.

the academic study of science and society. Leaving Donald in London, she moved to Canterbury in October, 1966, with high hopes all round.

When she took up the Readership, the UKAEA made her a consultant, with an annual retainer of £1,000, a three-year contract (to September 1969), and a deadline of 1970.[64] 'It is a condition of the present agreement', the Authority said, 'that you will, subject to the normal exigencies of life, continue the project with undiminished vigour; and in particular use your best endeavours to achieve or improve upon our estimate of the time required for [its] preparation.'[65]

It was soon clear that Gowing's late entry as a 'mature academic' was to be a challenge for all concerned. As she discovered, taking time to research and write a major book, based on close contact with primary sources in distant archives, was bound to sit uncomfortably with the timetables of routine university business. Nonetheless, she began well, and contributed to lectures, tutoring, committees, and sixth form conferences. As a single parent, home life with the boys proved difficult, but manageable. She christened their new home in Nackington Road, 'Elliotts', after her own family name. In the coming months, preoccupied with university work, and with snatches of research, she published nothing new on atomic energy. However, she also took important steps in a wider direction. Reflecting on her own experience, she began to talk about the main problems besetting the writing of contemporary history—the disappearance of leading personalities, and the loss or destruction of their records.[66] While many in Britain were interested in conserving political, military and literary records, there was no national effort to preserve the papers of Britain's leading scientists and engineers. Gowing recalled how, in the course of interviewing James Chadwick at his retirement home in North Wales, the two sat in his attic, surrounded by wooden filing cabinets full of priceless documents. She was greatly worried when, asking what Chadwick was going to do with them, he 'shut his eyes, groaned, and said, "burn them"'.[67] Such episodes helped set in motion what was to become perhaps one of her most significant contributions to British scholarship, the Centre for the Archives of Contemporary Science (CACS).[68]

[64] Institution of Mechanical Engineers, Hinton Papers, MG to Hinton, 27 Jan. 1978.

[65] MHS, Gowing Papers, Jobs and Applications, Contract with UKAEA, Oct. 1966.

[66] M. Gowing, 'The Records of Science and Technology—with Thoughts about their Disposal', British Records Association, Annual Meeting, 5 Dec. 1966.

[67] Bodleian Library, Special Collections, Gowing Papers, Retirement speech at the Royal Society, 1 Sept. 1986.

[68] This episode is recounted in Gowing, 'The Contemporary Scientific Archives Centre', *Notes and Records of the Royal Society*, 34 (1979), 123–31.

In 1961, in the course of interviewing her nuclear physicists, Gowing had the good fortune to meet Nicholas Kurti, FRS, the distinguished Hungarian émigré physicist, who was deeply interested in the history of Britain's wartime Tube Alloys project.[69] Kurti read and commented on *BAE* in draft, correcting several factual errors but broadly welcoming her work, and giving it a fine review.[70] During the mid-1960s, interviewee and interviewer became steadfast allies, and bonded to mobilise support for something like a national archive for contemporary science. By 1966 their 'open conspiracy' included Alan (later Sir Alan, later Lord) Bullock, the acclaimed contemporary historian and founding Master of St Catherine's College, Oxford; Roger Ellis, of the Historical Manuscripts Commission; and William (later Sir William) Paton, FRS, the noted Oxford medical scientist, who represented the Royal Society's interest in the papers of its Fellows. A meeting in July 1966 led to the establishment in 1967 of a Joint Standing Committee of the Royal Society and the Historical Manuscripts Commission which, after many meetings, commissioned in 1969 a pilot survey of the surviving papers of three British scientists to demonstrate whether Gowing's ideas were feasible.[71]

Under Gowing's supervision, this survey was conducted by Miss Joan Pye, formerly Sir John Cockroft's secretary, and currently the UKAEA archivist at Harwell.[72] Miss Pye processed the three collections in only three months. In 1969, acting on the advice of Dr Michael Hoskin, the principal historian of science at Cambridge (and founder of the Churchill College Archives Centre), Gowing proposed the establishment of a processing centre, rather than a national archive, in the interests of economy and cooperation with existing institutions. A meeting at the Royal Society confirmed the idea of a Centre for Contemporary Scientific Archives—not a single site, but an active service, set up with private funding to catalogue papers and find permanent homes for them.[73] Money was obtained

[69] John Sanders, 'Nicholas Kurti', *Memoirs of Fellows of the Royal Society*, 46 (2000), 299–315.

[70] Bodleian Library, Special Collections, Kurti Papers, J. 807A, Kurti review, *c.*16 Nov. 1965.

[71] The three were Sir Francis Simon, Sir John Gaddum and Professor L. R. Wager.

[72] Gowing, 'The Records of Science and Technology . . .'; M. Gowing, N. Kurti, J. M. Pye, and R. H. Ellis, 'The archives of twentieth century scientists and technologists', *ASLIB Proceedings* (March 1971), 118–32.

[73] During the next decade, disagreements would emerge as to the degree of detail into which catalogues would enter, thus how long they would take, and how much they would cost. Gowing preferred a rudimentary system, such as she had known in Whitehall. Professional archivists preferred more detailed catalogues. Eventually, Gowing lost the point of principle, although in practice the degree of cataloguing detail would vary. See Bodleian Library, Special Collections, Gowing Papers, Retirement Speech, Royal Society, 1 Sept. 1986.

in 1972 from the Wolfson and other foundations for a three-year project, to begin in 1973. In 1972, Gowing also launched an SSRC-sponsored project to prepare guides to newly opened papers at the Public Records Office; and organised a conference with the SSRC on the use of historical data in the social sciences.[74]

Inevitably, all this missionary activity competed for attention with Gowing's central task—for which, in fact, she was being paid—viz., preparing the second volume of her nuclear history. In 1967, to keep the history on the rails, the UKAEA persuaded Mrs Lorna Arnold, an experienced civil servant, to transfer from the Authority's Health and Safety Division to become the Departmental Records Officer (DRO) and Gowing's Assistant Historian. Arnold had taken an honours degree in English and Latin from the University of London (1937), and then taught secondary school for two years before entering the civil service at the outbreak of the war.[75] Like Gowing, she had two sons. She had not studied history. On paper, she was a talented generalist. But she was adaptable, resourceful, and eventually became something of a 'boffin'—a description she would, with characteristic modesty, deny. By the beginning of 1968, she and Gowing had researched and begun to draft parts of the second volume of the nuclear history, which took the story from 1945 to 1952. Much remained to be done, and both were hard pressed. When the Public Records Act of 1967 reduced the mandatory 'closed period' from fifty to thirty years, the Authority's deadlines for reviewing and transferring records to the PRO quickly drew closer. As Gowing had little time to visit the several sites at which nuclear archives were kept, Arnold took on more and more of the work. Showing great ingenuity and initiative, she became to Gowing what Gowing had been to Hancock—and, in certain respects, overtook her senior.

[74] MHS, Gowing Papers, Jobs and Applications, CV (1972). The Guide was compiled by Dr Brenda Swann and Miss Turnbull, and published in Oct. 1971.

[75] Lorna Arnold (1915–), born in Surrey, studied at Bedford College, 1937–9 (BA Hons. in English and Latin) and Cambridge (Diploma in Education, 1938). During the war, she served in the Army Council Secretariat. Between 1945 and 1947 she was on the staff of the Allied Control Commission in Germany and in its Washington, DC, office. For a time, she was the only woman in the British diplomatic service. In May 1949, she left the service to be married, and had two children. In 1955 she returned to official work, and in 1959 was recruited by the newly formed UKAEA to work on a report following the Windscale accident of 1957. In 1967, she joined Gowing, and became the UKAEA's Departmental Records Officer (DRO). Later, she was made UKAEA historian. In 1976 she moved to Harwell to be closer to her work. The same year, she was appointed OBE. Today, she lives in retirement in Oxford. I am grateful to Mrs Arnold for this information.

Given the circumstances, the completion of volume two—*Independence and Deterrence, 1945–1952* (or *'I&D'*, or *Indy*, as it was familiarly known to Gowing and Arnold)—was considerably delayed. The amount of material was huge, and as new sources were discovered a projected one-volume product became, on paper, two. More than *BAE*, these second volume(s) involved close vetting by the UKAEA, the Foreign Office, and the Ministry of Defence. In a reflective moment, Arnold describes how the two women researched the chapters on the 'Hurricane' tests, which involved trekking to the Atomic Weapons Establishment at Aldermaston. There it was ruled that, despite their being official historians, and so under the rule of the Official Secrets Act, they could not take their notes out of the office, and so must do all their writing *in situ*, under the watchful eye of the Departmental Records Officer. The ordeal was complicated by the tyrannies of transport. To get to Aldermaston, Gowing had to leave her boys, catch a very early train from Canterbury to Waterloo, thence by Underground to Paddington for a train to Reading. Meanwhile, Arnold drove from Amersham to collect Gowing at Reading, for the drive to Aldermaston. They finally arrived at 10.00. 'We worked like mad in the archives,' Arnold recalls, 'with a sandwich and a cup of tea at our desks ... until the office closed at 5 pm and we started the journey home.' 'Once', she adds, 'we stayed two nights at a nearby riverside hotel,'[76] but their domestic duties could seldom permit such indulgences.

Practical difficulties were compounded by changes in the directorate of the UKAEA. By the early 1960s, many of Gowing's wartime contacts had died or retired. In their absence, she began to rely on a few advisors, notably including Alan Bullock as well as her 'nuclear friends' Nicholas Kurti and Rudolf Peierls. Her mentors at the UKAEA included Robert Spence, the chief chemist and later director of Harwell, and Sir Christopher (later Lord) Hinton, the towering and formidable director of the Industrial Group of the British nuclear power project based at Risley, which formed a triad with Harwell and the Atomic Weapons Research Establishment at Aldermaston. Hinton was active in the House of Lords, and later became chairman of the Central Electricity Generating Board (CEGB) and the first Chancellor of the University of Bath. Gowing found in him a loyal ally.[77]

[76] Memorandum, Arnold to author, Nov. 2004, section 7, p. 11.

[77] Christopher Hinton, Baron Hinton of Bankside (1901–83). Gowing wrote Hinton's entry in the *Dictionary of Business History*, vol. III, 1985, followed by his entry in the *Dictionary of National Biography* (1981–5), 1990, pp. 195–6. At his request, Gowing delivered the eulogy at Hinton's memorial service in Westminster Abbey. According to Lorna Arnold, Hinton was 'a

Miraculously, the end of 1968 saw the authors of '*I&D*' nearing a first draft. Gowing focused on Volume 1, and Arnold on Volume 2. They had no clerical help beyond the secretarial pool at Harwell. Margaret worked against the odds—in her words, writing until 3 a.m. every night after getting the boys to bed, and every weekend, while looking after an ill housekeeper (whose salary she had to pay).[78] Sending greetings to Gowing from Canberra on Christmas Day, 1968, Hancock guessed that she 'must have been working like a b[...] at Atomic Energy II'.

> In times of great distress, as I well know, work is medicine, but try not to give yourself an overdose of it. I have no apprehension at all of your second volume not equaling, or even surpassing, the first one; but I suspect that it is at present in what I call the 'slinging together stage'? Whatever happens, you must give yourself time to fuse every sentence and paragraph and chapter in the crucible of your final drafting, an agonising, exhausting, exhilarating task. My prayers will be with you when the time comes for you to face it.[79]

However, a completed final draft was still far distant. If commuting to London and Harwell two days a week was stressful, so were the pressures to conform to her department's expectations of undergraduate teaching, an occupation for which she was neither trained nor especially gifted. She made herself unpopular by writing an article comparing grants to Kent's student union with the funding available to patients at the local mental hospital. She recounted how, as a member of her local education committee in London, 'she had to struggle to get £2000 to replace the lavatories in a slum school'.[80] Like the other 'new universities', Kent required staff to socialise to a degree that she found difficult to match with family commitments. Amongst the staff, she made few friends. These included Robert Spence, FRS, who was Master of Keynes College. But her head of department in Canterbury, Professor Theo Barker, became an implacable enemy. To Barker, she was a troublesome priest. She was not martyred but, according to a colleague, was instead hived off into a 'department' by herself.[81]

With Donald in London, her sons at school, and few friends at work, sadness and loneliness soured her correspondence. The ever-supportive Hancock counselled patience:

---

brilliant man, a kind and delightful man, who could be very difficult at times. He and MMG had a love-hate relationship for many years'. Memorandum, Lorna Arnold, section 7, p. 20.

[78] Institution of Mechanical Engineers, Hinton Papers, Gowing to Hinton, 27 Jan. 1978.

[79] MHS, Gowing Papers, Hancock Files, Hancock to MG, 25 Dec. 1968.

[80] White, 'Nuclear historian', p. 657.

[81] Pers. comm., Maurice Crosland, University of Kent, to author, 29 April 2004.

> For James' sake, you have to stay a few more years in Canterbury, which you have no cause to love. But since you have to live in it a while, you may as well look for a *modus vivendi*. Take Barker … if you can find a *modus vivendi* with him, life will be more tolerable for you both …[82]

This proved impossible. Worse news befell her on 16 December 1969, a day she was away doing research, when Donald suffered a massive stroke and died in hospital in London. Nik was in the midst of his 'A' levels, and James was still in school. Remarkably, the family survived its heavy loss. Nik won a place at Bristol, where he read geography. James took up a place at Wye College, and later began to farm in the Orkneys. The boys made their own way. But Donald's death left Gowing coping with a great sadness that grew ever more intense with time.

From mid-Summer 1969, Gowing had begun looking for another job. Her morale was boosted by the warm reception given her paper to the Anglo-American Historical Conference, meeting in London, on the contemporary history of British science. Kurti recommended she send it to Hugh Trevor-Roper, Regius Professor of Modern History at Oxford, adding that the recent TV series by Kenneth (later Lord) Clark on 'Civilisation' had failed to mention Galileo, Newton, or Einstein.[83] In July, 1969, Gowing answered an advertisement for the Keepership of the Public Records, effectively the head of the Public Records Office, a position for which her expertise and experience amply qualified her. To her grief, but perhaps not to her surprise, she was the 'only outsider' amongst the three interviewed, and was passed over in favour of the Deputy Keeper, whom she dismissed as a 'medievalist', 'competent but very pedestrian', and suggested the office was 'anti-feminine'. 'I desperately wanted it and was very disappointed', she confided to Kurti, and excused herself from meetings with him, pleading domestic duties: 'I long to finish vol. II', she said: 'the thought I might is all that keeps me going sometimes. Then perhaps I'll escape Canterbury, which is *not* my spiritual home.'[84] In 1970, she tried another tack, and

[82] MHS, Gowing Papers, Hancock to MG, 9 July 1969.

[83] Bodleian Library, Special Collections, Kurti Papers, Gowing to Kurti, 25 July 1969, Kurti to Gowing, 25 Aug. 1969.

[84] Bodleian Library, Special Collections, Kurti Papers, H 127, Gowing to Kurti, 9 Nov. 1969. The successful candidate at the PRO was Jeffery Raymond Ede (1918–2006), CB, 1978, Assistant Keeper, 1947–59, Principal Assistant Keeper 1959–66, Deputy Keeper 1966–9, who served as Keeper of Public Records 1970–8. He was also a Lecturer in Archive Administration, School of Librarianship and Archives, University College London, 1956–61, and President, Society of Archivists, 1974–7. *The Independent*, 23 Dec. 2006. For histories of the PRO, see Philippa Levine, 'History in the archives: the Public Record Office, 1838–1886', *English Historical Review*, 101 (1986), 20–41; Philippa Levine, *The Amateur and the Professional: Antiquarians, Historians and Archaeologists in Victorian England, 1838–1886* (Cambridge, 1986); and John D. Cantwell, *The Public Record Office, 1838–1958* (London, 1991).

applied for the newly vacated chair in the History and Philosophy of Science at University College London, the oldest chair in the subject in England.[85] This was perhaps the first indication that Gowing saw herself as contributing to the history of science as a discipline, rather than to the contemporary history of science and politics. However, the UCL Department had no discernible interest in the history of contemporary science, and few were surprised when a scholar of early modern science was appointed.[86] Nonetheless, for Gowing these applications were useful trial runs. Her referees inevitably included Hancock, as well as Alan Bullock, Nicholas Kurti, and Sir Rudolf Peierls, all in Oxford. Peierls respected her work, and probably sent her the UCL advertisement. All three knew she was unhappy at Kent.

A break point came in January 1972, when Gowing applied for a personal chair at Kent in order, as she put it, to finish her book. To her surprise, her application was declined, and appeals to the Vice-Chancellor, Geoffrey Templeman, proved unavailing.[87] The conversation ended badly. Accusing Templeman of putting administration above scholarship, Gowing told him that Kent was 'no place for my type of activity'.[88] She was probably right.

Given all the difficulties Gowing either made or met, it was largely thanks to Lorna Arnold that the UKAEA history made any serious progress at all over the next two years. A year earlier, in the spring of 1971, Gowing promised Christopher Hinton that final drafts would be circulated in the autumn that year.[89] But it was not until early 1972 that draft chapters finally went to departments for comment—almost three years late. In the meantime, the entire first draft was read by Alan Bullock—perhaps the first person outside government to have done so—who

[85] See William A. Smeaton, 'History of Science at University College London, 1919–47', *British Journal for the History of Science*, 30 (1997), 25–8.

[86] Dr P. M. Rattansi, a student of Walter Pagel, was appointed to the chair.

[87] Geoffrey Templeman, first Vice-Chancellor of the University of Kent, was an historian, well known for his history of Warwickshire. He retired in 1980 and died on 22 Feb. 1988. For context, see Graham Martin, *From Vision to Reality: the Making of the University of Kent at Canterbury* (Canterbury, 1990). Regrettably, this account says nothing about Gowing's presence at the university. I am grateful to Ms Anna Miller of the Templeman Library, University of Kent, for this information.

[88] 'In the academic world at large, such chairs have been regarded as the recognition of outstanding scholarship. You, however, feel that they should serve the more pressing needs of the university administration, believing that anyone who makes scholarship a major part of his interests should be content with a Readership ... I believe that this concept will be damaging to the university.' (Draft of message to Dean of the Faculty of Social Sciences, following a meeting with the Vice-Chancellor, initialed by MMG, Feb. 1992). MHS, Gowing Papers, Kent File.

[89] Institution of Mechanical Engineers, Hinton Papers J 21, Gowing to Hinton, 28 March 1971.

pronounced it 'a book of first class importance'.[90] Bullock offered to help Gowing, despairing of Kent, find a new job—an offer he repeated in January 1972:

> I think you have written some of the best contributions of 20th century history I have read and I am convinced the further volumes will establish ... your reputation as one of the leading contemporary historians in the English-speaking world. How to cash in on this and turn it into the sort of job you want? If there is any job you see for which you would like my support, you can rely on me to write enthusiastically about your work ... I beg you not to lose heart. I cannot believe that work as good as yours can go unrecognized for long when the next two volumes are published.[91]

Bullock began to enquire about possibilities at Oxford, including research fellowships at Nuffield and St Antony's. Kent had become a problem, and Gowing looked for a solution.

Oxford revisited

In February 1972, Oxford University advertised a chair in the history of science, the first in the university's long history. Despite having rich scientific traditions, and the oldest science museum in Britain (and one of the oldest in the world), Oxford had few students and fewer dons who took a professional interest in the subject. But the need to do something for the subject was recognised, and in 1953 the Faculty of Modern History established a university lectureship, in accordance with its practice of creating posts in small subjects not already covered by the college system. The appointment went to A. C. Crombie, an Australian-born biologist with an omnivorous interest in the history of science, then a lecturer at University College London.[92]

At a time when England boasted few professional historians of science, Crombie brought Oxford an impressive reputation. Following early academic work in physiology in Australia and at Cambridge, Crombie had been identified with the new discipline since the 1940s. He helped establish the British Society for the History of Science in 1947, and was the first editor of the *British Journal for the Philosophy of Science* in 1950. In 1952, he published *Augustine to Galileo,* which became one of the best-

[90] MHS, Gowing Papers, Jobs and Applications, CV 1972.
[91] MHS, Brown Archive Box, Oxford Professorship File, Bullock to Gowing, 22 Jan. 1972.
[92] For the early history of science at Oxford, see Robert Fox, 'The History of Science, Medicine and Technology at Oxford', *Notes and Records of the Royal Society*, 60 (2006), 9–83.

selling textbooks in the history of medieval and early modern science.[93] This he followed in 1953 with *Robert Grosseteste and the Origins of Experimental Science, 1100–1700*, which elaborated his view of science as a quintessentially rational activity, with a logic and dynamic of its own.[94]

During the mid-1950s, under Crombie's direction, the subject had developed steadily, with five to seven graduates each year reading for a one-year Diploma; and by 1957, five-to-ten science undergraduates were taking a Supplementary Subject offered in the history of scientific thought. From 1958, undergraduates reading chemistry could also write on the history of chemistry for Part III, whilst a few read for the B.Phil. in Philosophy either in Greek mathematics or medicine, seventeenth-century physics, or nineteenth-century biology.[95]

In seeking ways to develop the history of science, Crombie was ambitious for himself, and for Oxford. In 1962, with Michael Hoskin, his contemporary and counterpart at Cambridge, he launched a new professional journal, *History of Science,* which attracted wide attention across the fledgling field. In 1963, with Rom Harré (recently appointed University Lecturer in the Philosophy of Science), Crombie convened at Oxford a massive international conference on 'The Structure of Scientific Change', fresh on the heels of the publication of Thomas Kuhn's *Structure of Scientific Revolutions*, and remembered still as one of the most significant congresses in the discipline since the Second World War.[96] From overseas, these efforts were seen as almost unprecedented acts of cooperation between the ancient universities, and between Oxford and the rest of the world; and brought Crombie a degree of international celebrity he warmly desired and fully deserved.

[93] J. D. North, 'Alistair Cameron Crombie (1915–1996)', *Proceedings of the British Academy*, 97 (1998), 257–70 at 259; A. C. Crombie, *Augustine to Galileo: the History of Science, AD 400–1650* (London, 1952 and 1959).

[94] A. C. Crombie, *Robert Grosseteste and the Origins of Experimental Science, 1100–1700* (Oxford, 1953). These views he elaborated in a lengthy (3 vols.) account, which took nearly thirty years to write, and which was published after his retirement, two years before his death in 1996: A. C. Crombie, *Commitments and Styles of Scientific Thinking in the European Tradition: the History of Argument and Explanation, especially in the Mathematical and Biomedical Sciences and Arts* (London, 1994).

[95] A University Committee for the History and Philosophy of Science was established in 1958. See Archives, Faculty of Modern History, Oxford University, MH (83) 101—letter from Dr Crombie (n.d., *c.*1983). Ref FQ 7/1/HM. For a recent appreciation, see Robert Fox, 'The History of Science, Medicine and Technology at Oxford', published online, and repr. in *Notes and Records of the Royal Society*, 60 (2006), 69–83.

[96] Conference papers and commentaries appeared in A. C. Crombie (ed.), *Scientific Change: Historical Studies in the Intellectual, Social and Technical Conditions for Scientific Discovery and Technical Invention* (London, 1963).

From the early 1960s, Crombie argued that a chair in the history of science was needed to stimulate the subject, as well as to complement Oxford's traditional strengths in the philosophy of science.[97] By 1964, History undergraduates could take a Special Subject on the Scientific Revolution of the seventeenth century. This attracted between eight and ten students each year. But in a period of rapid growth in the discipline, and increasing interest in the history of science to help bridge the 'gap' between C. P. Snow's 'Two Cultures', Oxford's modest course offerings did not go far enough. To achieve his objective, Crombie needed allies. His careful cultivation of American scholars at his conference of 1963 gave him international stature. But this seemed to count for less in Oxford, where he enjoyed some support in the Natural Sciences, but little in Modern History, where any such chair was bound to be placed. Worse, he had an enemy in Hugh Trevor-Roper (later Lord Dacre), then of Christ Church and later (as Regius Professor) of Oriel. Trevor-Roper fumed against historians of science, whom he collectively dismissed as 'antiquarians'—that is, 'historians of science who knew science, but not history'.[98]

Nonetheless, the subject grew steadily in popularity and, from the early 1960s, students reading for diplomas and higher degrees rose from seven to thirty-two.[99] Recognising that 'a higher post seems essential to the teaching of a subject of such growing importance to the History School', the Faculty of Modern History twice accorded the chair 'Priority 1' in its submissions to the University Grants Committee for funding in the quinquennia 1962–7 and 1967–72. In 1971 the Faculty's application was successful, and in January 1972 a chair was finally advertised. After a decade-long campaign, Crombie rejoiced. Looking back, an external observer, unfamiliar with the ways of Oxford, and knowing nothing of the Faculty, could be excused for thinking the chair to be his for the asking.

Such, however, was not to be. On paper, Crombie was the outside favourite. His twenty years at Oxford had seen some fifty students take the Diploma in the history and philosophy of science, and some thirty arts and science undergraduates read for special subjects. But Crombie had few friends. His missionary fervour for his subject, conflated with per-

[97] Dacre Papers, Trevor-Roper to Sir Peter Medawar, 16 April 1970; Blair Worden to author, 7 Jan. 2005. I warmly thank Professor Worden for making these letters available to me.
[98] Dacre Papers, Trevor-Roper to Sir Peter Medawar, 16 April 1970.
[99] Archives, Faculty of Modern History, LE/7, Professorship of the History of Science, Quinquennial Submission, 1967/72, p. 15. I am grateful to Mr A. P Weale, Secretary of the Faculty of Modern History, for permission to consult these files.

sonal ambition, had not made him popular.[100] His critics were quick to find fault. He was not a natural lecturer; he was said to show little patience with undergraduates, and was thought opinionated and pedantic.[101] His faux-English mannerisms masked a certain bunyip arrogance. The chair was by no means his for the asking.

Within days of the advertisement appearing in the press, and knowing well her unhappiness at Kent, Sir Rudolf Peierls alerted Gowing, and Nicholas Kurti rang, suggesting she apply.[102] The deadline was 20 February. Gowing was intrigued, but thought her chances poor. In the event, she applied only at the last minute, with Lorna Arnold rushing to get the application in the post.[103] The Board of Electors met to review applications on 3 March. Gowing's *curriculum vitae* was impressive but, by modern standards, incomplete. By way of publications, she could offer her books with Hancock, but these were in economic history, and were by now decades old; more recently, she could offer *Britain and Atomic Energy*, but even that had appeared eight years earlier. *Independence and Deterrence*, which in any case was co-authored with Arnold, was still in proof.

There were eight applicants. To her surprise, Gowing was one of the four interviewed. Hinton was among her powerful referees, and Hancock coached from the benches.[104] On 26 May, she met the electoral board of nine, chaired by Alan Bullock, then Vice-Chancellor.[105] On the science side, there was Rudolf Peierls, her champion, and Frederick Dainton, who knew her work; among the historians, Peter Mathias, who shared her

[100] North, 'Alistair Cameron Crombie (1915–1996)', pp. 264–5.

[101] 'Had Crombie taken a narrower view of his subject', his biographer writes, 'he might have avoided the common complaint that he was empire-building'. North, 'Alistair Cameron Crombie (1915–1996)', p. 264.

[102] Lorna Arnold, Interview with Tony Simcock, 25 Aug. 1999. I am grateful to Dr Simcock for permission to use his notes of this interview.

[103] Institution of Mechanical Engineers, Hinton Papers, J 21, MG to Hinton, 4 June 1972; 'I should not have dreamt of applying for the history of science chair if Rudi Peierls had not written urging me to do so. I dreaded the interview as my ignorance seemed fathoms deep. But I was able to relax because of you and Alan Bullock's kindness'. Dacre Papers, Gowing to Trevor-Roper, 2 Sept. 1988.

[104] MHS, Gowing Papers, Brown Archive Box, Oxford Professorship File, Hancock to Gowing, 4 March, 16 April 1972.

[105] The Board of Electors comprised Alan Bullock, J. B. Bambrough (Lincare), Dr T. G. Halsall (Linacre), Professor Hugh Trevor-Roper, Sir Rudolf Peierls, Professor Peter Mathias, and Sir Frederick Dainton, FRS (Professor of Chemistry, soon to be chairman of the University Grants Committee). The external assessors included Professor A. R. Hall (Imperial College) and Professor William (later Sir William) Paton, FRS, Editor of *Notes and Records of the Royal Society*, and member of the Wellcome Trust. I am grateful to Mr A. P. Weale for this information.

interests, and Trevor-Roper. To her surprise, Trevor-Roper took her part. Possibly he warmed to the idea of a chair going to a working class scholarship girl.[106] In any case, he was vehemently anti-Catholic.[107] And Crombie, the internal candidate, was a Catholic.

'I was in a blue funk by the time I got to the electoral board,' Gowing later told Christopher Hinton, 'however, once having got my sea legs, I quite enjoyed it.'[108] The affair was, Peierls told her later, 'touch and go', but she 'got it on the oral'. Kurti was a 'little surprised', and thought the 'pundits would have elected someone devoted to looking out obscure facts about Newton, Harvey, Boyle *et al.*'.[109] A. Rupert Hall[110]—the distinguished historian of science, then at Imperial College, acting as an external elector—supported Crombie. In reaching the final decision, Alan Bullock, the chairman—who alone on the Board had read Gowing's (and Arnold's) book in draft—played an influential role.[111] When votes were cast, Crombie lost. The Board appointed to Oxford's first chair in the history of science a person who had degrees neither in science nor in the history of science; the first woman to be a professor in the history of science in Britain; and one of the few women then to hold a chair in any subject at the university.[112] Modestly, Gowing said she had not expected to get the job:[113] 'If anybody had said I would one day be a professor of the history of science, I would have said they were crazy ... I dropped both subjects at school.'[114] But the die was cast.

Election to the Oxford chair marked a turning point in Gowing's life, and potentially a turning point in the history of the discipline in England. Academically, it amounted to a vindication of her contribution to a national discourse. Institutionally, it revealed the high regard in which she

[106] Blair Worden, 'Hugh Redwald Trevor-Roper, 1914–2003', *Proceedings of the British Academy*, 150, *Biographical Memoirs of Fellows*, VI (2007), 247–84 at 257.

[107] Ibid., p. 256.

[108] Institution of Mechanical Engineers, Hinton Papers, J.21, MG to Hinton, 4 June 1972.

[109] Gowing Family Papers, Giana Kurti to Nik Gowing, 30 Nov. 1998.

[110] For an appreciation, see David Knight, 'Rupert Hall (1920–2009), pioneering historian of science and editor of Isaac Newton's letters', *The Guardian*, 27 May 2009, and the memoir in this volume by Frank James.

[111] Institution of Mechanical Engineers, Hinton Papers, J 21, MG to Hinton, 4 June 1972: 'Alan Bullock told me ... I'd done a marvelous interview.' MHS, Gowing Papers, Metal Box. 'One of the episodes of my period of office ... which I look back on with most satisfaction was your appointment.' Bullock to Gowing, 4 May 1978.

[112] Institution of Mechanical Engineers, Hinton Papers, A 123, MG to Hinton, 4 June 1972.

[113] 'No one except the British Society for the History of Science was more surprised than I when I was appointed.' Dacre Papers, Gowing to Trevor-Roper, 2 Sept. 1988.

[114] This quotation dates from an interview in 1986 (if not earlier). See her obituary in the *Oxford Times*, 27 Nov. 1998.

was held by contemporary historians, as well as by the community of nuclear physicists, who were among Britain's most influential scientists. In university terms, her election sent a message to the world—that Oxford, struggling to modernise, could do just that, when opportunity arose.

Gowing's election struck a conspicuous blow for modern, as against medieval and early modern, science, and for a reading of history that favoured social, economic and political perspectives, as against the examination of scientific practice. Some American historians, including a few who had thought to apply but who were put off by the salary, were reportedly nonplussed. A Cambridge friend warned her that 'Oxford may give you a bitter welcome'.[115] Still, Gowing was at last free of Kent and, moreover, going to a place that set the highest value on academic achievement.

The UKAEA was pleased with the appointment, as it seemed to augur well for her writing:[116] 'I hope to write another installment of the saga,' she assured Lord Plowden, former chairman of the AEA (1954–9) in October 1972. However, she added cautiously, 'It will not be immediately because (to my surprise) I have been appointed to a new chair in the history of science at Oxford from January 1973, and I must concentrate on that for a time. But it is important to begin collecting evidence and once Oxford is under control, I should have more time for writing.'[117] To Roger Makins (later Lord Sherfield), Chairman of the UKAEA, she was even more cautious: 'I am looking forward to Oxford with enthusiasm and some panic. I am anxious to bring the history of science firmly into the mainstream of history and get "ordinary" historians interested in it. To do this, it is necessary to give some good lectures even if only a handful of students turn up at first.' 'At present', however, she added thoughtfully, 'I can't see when I shall write them.'[118]

Gowing's caution was well founded. She left Kent in November 1972, and arrived in Oxford in January 1973. With memories of Kent's limitations fresh in mind, she had expectations of Oxford that belied the reality. Oxford gave its new professor a generous salary. But there was no actual department, no secretary, no research funds, and no office. Her first desk

[115] MHS, Gowing Papers, Brown Archive Box, Oxford Professorship File, to Margaret, 7 June 1972.

[116] MHS, Gowing Papers, Brown Archive Box, Oxford Professorship File. 'All of us here will be delighted that in this one instance your judgement was at fault,' wrote A.M. Allen of the UKAEA (7 June 1971). Congratulations from over twenty well-wishers are preserved in the files.

[117] MHS, Gowing Papers, Oxford Professorship File, Gowing to Plowden, 18 Oct. 1972.

[118] MHS, Gowing Papers, Oxford Professorship File, Gowing to Sherfield, 31 Aug. 1972.

was in a room at the top of the Registry Annex; but ultimately she acquired a small space at the top of the Indian Institute, above the Faculty library, five floors without a lift. The chair was attached to Linacre, a recently established graduate college, which offered an air of informality she welcomed, and an absence of undergraduates that seemed to suit her well.[119] Almost immediately, she took to Linacre, and Linacre took to her, and many happy memories survive.[120]

During the next two decades, Linacre became the principal college for Oxford postgraduate students in the history of science. Gowing inherited few students, and had to build her own flock from scratch. Overall, Oxford enrolled about twenty research students in various fields of the history of science, but their supervision was distributed between the History Faculty, the Museum, and the newly established Wellcome Unit for the History of Medicine.[121] There was no university-wide core course for postgraduates in the history of science, and few research students in History were interested in the history of contemporary science. For History undergraduates, there was a Special Subject, and in Science, a two-term course, with one term in philosophy of science and one in history of science. College dons could let their undergraduates take these courses, but few did. To advance the subject across the university, Gowing would have to enlarge the existing Special Subject, and to persuade at least one faculty to accept a new graduate degree. But the Faculty Board of Modern History had little reason to create courses for which there were no tutorial funds. The School of Natural Sciences was reluctant to create a graduate course that was principally concerned with History and Philosophy. Administratively, the history of science lacked institutional autonomy. Much to her annoyance, Gowing's first attempt to chair her own faculty committee was overruled by a policy that gave the Faculty the right to appoint the *ex-officio* chairman. Crombie continued as a lecturer in the subject, doing much of the

[119] In 1962, Linacre had elected to its fellowship Dr Rom Harré, University Lecturer in the Philosophy of Science, who advocated a close association with the history of science. In 1965, Francis Maddison, Curator of the Museum, was also elected a Fellow. In 1971, following unsuccessful attempts to raise external funding to establish a college-based enterprise in the social studies of science (as at Sussex University) the college secured the chair of the history of science, on the grounds of its 'special interest in interdisciplinary studies'.

[120] The Master of Linacre, John Bamborough, became a good friend. See Robert Fox, 'Linacre and the History of Science', *Linacre News*, Issue 27 (Spring 2004), 4–5.

[121] The Wellcome Unit for the History of Medicine was established in 1972. The Wellcome Trust paid (but did not appoint) its director. Administratively, the Unit came under the Faculty of Modern History, in cooperation with the Faculty of Medicine.

same teaching as before, leaving Gowing a narrow window through which to develop student support.

All this added up to a less than optimistic prospect.[122] Gowing's task was to develop the history of science. As Oxford professors lecture, but do not tutor, and she had few natural allies amongst the History dons who furnished her undergraduate numbers, her best strategy was to develop a graduate degree. But for this, through no fault of her own, she was singularly ill-equipped. Her innocence of the subject that she was appointed to teach she once shared with the Oxford University Scientific Society, where she disarmingly observed that 'I think it would be very unfortunate if the history of science becomes the preserve of people who say we can't study the subject because we have no scientific or mathematical training.'[123] Not only had she—*pace* her distant dealings with the Vice-Chancellor of Kent—no administrative experience, she also had an arms-length relationship with students. Most important, perhaps, she lacked basic training in the language, methods, and ideas that dominated professional practice in the rapidly changing discipline of the history of science, and knew little of the many professional projects that were making headway throughout the world.

All this she fully acknowledged. To Hinton (and possibly others) she appealed for 'tuition, literally from scratch—in electricity, history of, all the way . . .'[124] Once the initial surprise of her appointment had passed, colleagues rallied round—packages of books, journals, and course reading lists were sent her from Edinburgh and Sussex—in the sure knowledge that the Oxford chair was, and would rightly be seen as, the jewel in the crown of the profession in Britain.[125] Hancock also sent her references to articles on 'science and society'. Gowing read quickly, if unsystematically, into the subject matter of her newly acquired and rapidly moving discipline—which in Cambridge was eventually to have several chairs to Oxford's one.

On the personal side, domestic matters at first claimed much of Gowing's time in Oxford. House hunting proved a challenge until she found a home, first at 25 Hayward Road, and later at 5 Northmoor Road.

[122] MHS, Gowing Papers, CBE file, Dorothy (?) to Gowing, 5 June 1981.

[123] MHS, Gowing Papers, Brown Archive Box, 'Early Days in Oxford', Interview with the Oxford University Scientific Society, 1972.

[124] Institution of Mechanical Engineers, Hinton Papers J21. MG to Hinton, 4 June 1972.

[125] The Cambridge chair in the philosophy of science was then held by Mary Hesse, FBA. There were at the time several Readerships but, outside University College London, no other established chairs in the subject in England.

Living alone and out of college, she seldom entertained.[126] Once a routine had been established, academic life was enjoyable. Hancock advised, '*à bas* all Crombies! ... don't use up adrenalin on their account',[127] and diplomatic relations with Crombie were simplified when he went on sabbatical leave the term she arrived. Rupert Hall advised her to treat him kindly, and so she did,[128] although for the next decade, until his retirement in 1983, they had little to do with one another, either socially or professionally. Crombie remained the sole lecturer in the 'department' that Gowing never had.[129]

In her first full teaching year (1973), progress was slow. As ever, Hancock was full of advice: 'By now', he wrote in May 1973, 'you will be nearly through your summer term's lectures. Numbers don't matter if the teaching is good. Anyway, numbers may rise in later years. And soon your house will be in order and Oxford—always a slow welcomer—will be growing more human.'[130]

She made no secret of her reform agenda. To Alan Bullock's joy, her Inaugural Lecture—'What's Science to History or History to Science?', delivered in 1975—gave promise of a brave new world, with Oxford at its pinnacle. 'Science and history', she said, 'are divided not by deep chasms but by man-made frontiers.'[131] Despite the decades since C. P. Snow's memorable assault on the 'Two Cultures', her message still resonated across the land. Regrettably, at Oxford, the cultures were more deep than she imagined, and the trenches dangerous to cross.

Not unexpectedly, Gowing used her lecture to criticise the 'academic isolation' that was the 'painful experience of some newcomers to Oxford', and noted that the decentralisation of undergraduate teaching among the colleges made curricular reform 'peculiarly difficult'. If the history of science were to thrive, it would need a larger place in the examinations. But there was the rub; this would require her listeners in the History Faculty to 'Be not afraid of science.' The second half of her lecture argued that 'history and science intermingle and cannot be separated by tenses', and that the politics of science must be part of History. She approved of the

[126] Although when she did, it was much appreciated, especially by her research students. Pers. comm., Dr Peter Morris to author, 31 May 2006; pers. comm., Dr Catherine Crawford to author, 2006.

[127] MHS, Gowing Papers, Hancock File, Hancock to MG, 31 Jan. 1974.

[128] MHS, Gowing Papers, Oxford Professorship File, Rupert Hall to Gowing, 22 June 1972.

[129] North, 'Alistair Cameron Crombie (1915–1996)', pp. 264–5.

[130] MHS, Gowing Papers, Hancock to MG, 22 May 1973.

[131] Margaret Gowing, 'What's science to history or history to science?' *Inaugural Lecture delivered before the University of Oxford*, 27 May 1975 (Oxford, 1975), 25 pp.

recent administrative separation of the history from the philosophy of science, and welcomed the history of technology, economic history, and politics, in shifting the terminal date of the Modern History syllabus beyond 1939. Doffing her hat to Peter Medawar, she insisted that 'Whether we like it or not, science—the art of the soluble—is inextricably linked with politics—the art of the possible.' With perhaps a glance at her colleagues in the History of Science Museum, the discipline, she said, had 'tended to be an esoteric profession in the past, too often uncongenial to mainstream historians and scientists alike'. Divisions between 'internalists' and 'externalists' were unfortunate, and unnecessary. Collaboration between science and history was urgently required. Offering perhaps too generous a hostage to fortune, she concluded with a promise: 'If we do not achieve this collaboration by the time I leave this chair, I shall have failed to fulfil the purposes for which it was established.'[132]

By the late-1970s, Gowing had developed a lecture course in the history of science in the nineteenth and twentieth centuries that, with minor modification, continued to serve through the 1980s. To these, she recruited Allan Chapman (an erudite expert in the history of astronomy), Paul Weindling (then a promising research student in the history of medicine and biology, later a professor at Oxford Brookes), and Nicolaas Rupke (later a distinguished professor of the history of science in Göttingen). With Lorna Arnold, she contributed to a Nuffield project on Science and Society,[133] and convened seminars with colleagues—including Alastair Buchan in 1975 on 'Science Technology and the International System'.[134] Less happily, she did not keep up with rapid movements in the history of science, such as at Leeds, Durham, Sussex, Kent, Lancaster, and Edinburgh, and was almost entirely ignorant of developments in Europe, the United States and Australasia that were reshaping the discipline. Indeed, what she did not follow she tended to reject, sometimes to the professional cost of colleagues whose work she disliked, or whom she thought fell short of her high standards. As correspondence in her papers reveals, in not supporting colleagues for grants or promotion her word as an Oxford professor was often taken as definitive, whether or not the assessment expressed was well informed.[135]

[132] Ibid., pp. 4, 11, 14, 17, 23, 25.

[133] Margaret Gowing and Lorna Arnold, *The Atomic Bomb*; *Science in a Social Context (SISCON) Unit No. 3* (London, 1979), 56 pp.

[134] Institution of Mechanical Engineers, Hinton Papers, F 85, Oxford Seminar, 17 Nov. 1975.

[135] MHS, Gowing Papers, Perrier Box, Alphabetical Files; Promotion Files.

Research students did come her way, and some became friends, although, living alone, Gowing found it difficult to combine professional life with domestic entertaining.[136] Much less friendly were the unwritten rules of the university, with its predominantly masculine and traditional biases. As she learned, academic life at Oxford, as elsewhere, revolves around strategic alliances. Some, knowing nothing of the actual circumstances of her appointment, found it convenient to see her as the 'scientists' candidate', and her success in a competition run by an Arts Faculty as a victory for Science. Others regarded her as a mere archivist,[137] or, as one put it privately, Hancock's 'best research assistant'. Her powerful allies in Physics had few counterparts in History, even among the economic historians, who might have been expected to offer her sanctuary. Peter Mathias (All Souls) and Hugh Trevor-Roper (Oriel) remained good friends, but were not always there to support her discipline. Perhaps her closest academic colleague was Charles Webster (Corpus), the distinguished historian of science and medicine, who had arrived from Leeds the same year as she, as Oxford's first Reader in the History of Medicine and Director of the Wellcome Unit for the History of Medicine.

Gowing and Webster cooperated closely in university affairs.[138] For her part, Gowing supported Webster and his unit against what she called the 'forces of darkness', among which she counted, at one time or another, William Paton, Rupert Hall, and various Wellcome Trustees.[139] Webster reciprocated with generous advice on a wide range of issues, including student supervision, promotions, and appointments. Gowing thought Webster the best living British historian of early modern science and medicine. At the time, he was also hard at work on the official history of the National Health Service, a task for which she had both personal sympathy and professional respect.[140] She hoped Webster would succeed her on her retirement.[141]

[136] Lorna Arnold recalls Gowing saying (more than once) that what she needed most was a wife. Memo Arnold to author, 2004, Section 9, p. 7.

[137] Pers. comm., Dr Peter Morris to author, 31 May 2006.

[138] Gowing Family Papers, Box 3, Webster to Nik Gowing, 12 Nov. 1998 and 12 July 1999.

[139] Gowing Family Papers, Box 2, Gowing to Hugh Trevor-Roper, 28 July 1986.

[140] Webster's memorable study of the Baconian tradition, *The Great Instauration: Science, Medicine and Reform, 1626–1660* (London, 1975; New York, 1976; 2nd edn., Bern, 2002) grew from his earlier lectures at Leeds. At Oxford, he continued his work in early modern science, while completing *Problems of Health Care: the National Health Service before 1957* (London, 1988) and *Government and Health Care: the National Health Service, 1958–1979* (London, 1996). A further study, *The National Health Service: a Political History* (Oxford, 1998, 2nd edn., 2002), was followed by a celebrated return to early Modern Europe: *Paracelsus: Medicine, Magic, and Mission at the End of Time* (New Haven, CT, 2008).

[141] Gowing Family Papers, Box 2, Gowing to Hugh Trevor-Roper, 28 July 1986.

Contemporaries were sometimes surprised to find that in Trevor-Roper Gowing found an improbable, but loyal, ally.[142] Their friendship—polar opposites on the political and social spectrum—was a mystery to those who cared to think twice about it. Possibly it was nourished by a shared, anti-elitist (or at least contrarian) view of academic *mores;* possibly they shared a dislike of the 'new Right'.[143] But there was also a shared respect for the integrity of scholarship. Years later, Gowing expressed her thanks to Trevor-Roper for his help in making 'the history of science real history, rather than a public relations exercise of failed scientists'.[144] Such praise has failed to find its way into recent scholarship on Trevor-Roper, but its deeper dimensions are worth exploring.

By way of contrast, from the curators of Oxford's glorious but introspective Museum of the History of Science Gowing preserved a professional distance. Their reaction to her appointment was courteous, but not over-friendly. Her response was to keep calm and carry on. She had much work to do. Hancock advised, '... don't, for heaven's sake, remain perpetually submissive to deadlines. They are incompatible with civilised living.'[145] Such sensible advice, which she ignored. Between 1972 and 1973, she and Lorna Arnold struggled to complete a text for vetting. There seems to have been no pressure to publish with HMSO. So, encouraged by Alan Bullock, Burke Trend (formerly Head of the Cabinet Office), and Richard Hewlett, the historian of the American Atomic Energy Commission,[146] she asked Tim Farmeloe at Macmillan, which had done well with her first book, to send it out widely for review. Significantly, perhaps, Gowing signed her Preface as from Linacre College, where she had been made welcome, rather than from the Faculty of Modern History, where she had few friends.

The two volumes of *Independence and Deterrence* appeared in November 1974,[147] and were received with great fanfare—perhaps not quite as much

[142] 'I was very scared when I came to Oxford,' she wrote to him years later; 'I hardly knew it at all and I also felt a phoney in the history of science. Your unfailing kindness, helpfulness and support made an enormous difference and I am deeply grateful.' Dacre Papers, Gowing to Trevor-Roper, 19 May 1980.

[143] Dacre Papers, Gowing to Trevor-Roper, 20 Dec. 1983. They joined forces in a much publicised contretemps with Lord (John) Vaizey, concerning his criticism of Gowing's wartime heroes. See Vaizey's *In Breach of Promise: Gaitskell, Macleod, Titmuss, Crosland, Boyle: Five Men who Shaped a Generation* (London, 1983). Vaizey died the following year.

[144] Dacre Papers, Gowing to Trevor-Roper, 2 Sept. 1988.

[145] MHS, Gowing Papers, Hancock File, Hancock to MG, 31 Jan. 1974.

[146] MHS, Gowing Papers, I&D File, Burke Trend to Gowing, 31 Oct. 1974; Hewlett, 6 Dec. 1974.

[147] Margaret Gowing, assisted by Lorna Arnold, *Independence and Deterrence: Britain and Atomic Energy, 1945–52, Vol. 1: Policy Making; Vol. 2: Policy Execution* (London, 1974);

as greeted her first book, but enough to satisfy Hancock and Makins,[148] the UKAEA, and probably Gowing and Arnold as well.[149] Complimentary reviews appeared in *The Guardian*, *New Society*, and the academic press. Even *l'Express* and *Le Figaro* published notices. Thanks to the Insight team, which did a double-page spread on Gowing and her work, for two glorious weeks, Michael Howard wrote, 'you had the *Sunday Times* virtually to yourself'.[150]

Dividing her story into two parts, the first volume was concerned with 'why' and the second with 'how' Britain had developed its atomic project from the end of the war in 1945 to its first weapons tests in 1952. The story was, in her words, 'woven into almost every part of the post war history of Britain, and involved almost every layer of government, military and civil'. Although not part of the new series of peacetime official histories underway in the Cabinet Office, it was the first official history for the post-war years authorised for publication by Her Majesty's Government. Even so, in her account, there were significant omissions. No attention was given to the wider context of the Cold War, nor to the highly sensitive area of nuclear intelligence, where discussion of the 'Fuchs incident' and the 'Cambridge spies' was still highly topical, and secret. Still, within her chosen compass, Gowing had enough to say. She took few hostages, and none by name. Her overriding theme in volume one—on which Makins (by then Lord Sherfield) seems to have agreed—was that critical decisions had been taken without adequate consultation; that British considerations of British self-interest had been sacrificed to the goal of closer collaboration with the US; and that this goal was not attained, because it was unattainable. In the post-war period, British nuclear diplomacy had mirrored British foreign policy—to the dismay, and eventual disarray, of both.

Kenneth Younger, reviewing *Indy* in *Nature*, took Gowing's readings as read, and marvelled how she and Arnold had so clearly shown that the key nuclear decisions in the years 1945–52 had been taken—in secret by a small circle around Attlee, Bevin and Morrison—and executed in ways that now seemed profoundly muddled, even chaotic. Makins and Hinton agreed that much had been a muddle, but how much more it would have

separately (and subsequently) published: *Independence and Deterrence: Britain and Atomic Energy, 1945–52: References to Official Papers* (London, April 1983).

148 MHS Gowing Papers, I&D file, Hancock to Gowing, 4 Dec. 1974—a 'handsome job of book production'. Makins to Gowing, 26 Nov. 1974, 'I am sure they will be a big success.'

149 MHS, Gowing Papers, I&D File, Arnold listed forty reviews.

150 MHS, Gowing Papers, I&D File, Michael Howard to Gowing, *c.*26 Nov. 1974.

been so, they said, had Britain's atomic policy actually been considered by the full Cabinet. Apologetics were the order of the day.

Gowing revealed how, and why, Whitehall had persistently refused to confirm the link between Britain's civil and military programmes. She made public the fact that Calder Hall, Britain's first reactor, opened by Her Majesty the Queen in September 1956, was specifically designed to produce not only civilian electricity but also military plutonium. She revealed that the fire in 1957 at Windscale (now Sellafield, in Cumbria)—the world's first, and largest, nuclear accident before Chernobyl—neglected warnings received from Washington, DC, that underlined a continuing lack of consultation and communication.

Overall, Gowing revealed the failures of Anglo-American governments to share information, and demonstrated how Britain, having sacrificed Commonwealth and European ties for the sake of the 'Special Relationship', had been left to find its own, very expensive way forward in nuclear research and development. This was especially the message of volume two—how Britain, deprived of the cooperation it deserved, had nonetheless brought its 'enterprise' to a remarkably successful outcome.

Gowing's message was not warmly received by all in Government. Her revelation that the Americans 'led us up the garden path time after time' was not what the Foreign Office wanted to hear, or see read.[151] Some thought Gowing had indulged in hindsight. But she spoke from the written record and, in effect, told some of the nuclear barons (Sir William, later Lord, Penney among them) things they say they had never known.[152] For the first time, those involved in small parts of the story could now see the whole. Even those personally involved found material they had known of only second-hand.[153] The first archive-based account of post-war British nuclear policy instantly became required reading. When the second volume of the history of the American nuclear programme appeared the same year, Richard Hewlett warmly acknowledged her contribution to the Anglo-American story.[154]

However, the two volumes of *Indy* took that story only to 1952. The pity, as Hinton mournfully noted, was that it 'had to stop at a point where all that could be said for us was that we had produced an obsolete bomb

[151] AB 376, Circulation of Drafts, 1969. Penney, Imperial College, to Gowing, 27 Jan. 1969.

[152] Ibid.

[153] MHS Gowing Papers, I&D file, G. R. Strauss, MP, to Gowing, 4 Dec. 1974.

[154] See Richard Hewlett, 'Margaret Gowing (26 April 1921–4 November 1998)', *Isis*, 90 (1999), 326–8.

more slowly than the Russians'.[155] Britain had laid foundations for world leadership in a field 'that were so quickly lost'.[156] For Hinton, Gowing confirmed (a view from which Makins, the diplomat, dissented) that Britain had given America 'all our nuclear power technology in return for a ballistic missile that would not work'.[157] Such issues would not go away. Gowing more than hinted at the way in which the initial requirement of British Cabinet 'consent' for a British-based American nuclear deterrent was gradually diluted to mere 'consultation'—an issue that proved controversial in the 1980s, and may be so again.

To this pioneering work, a sequel was meant to come—not instantly, perhaps, but sometime soon—possibly again in two volumes. In the meantime, Gowing was optimistic. The science media made her a feminist pin-up. The *New Scientist* praised not only her book, but also the 'shining example of the liberated woman, who has managed to combine career and home successfully'.[158]

Given her overnight celebrity, Hancock advised Gowing to take time out—'for fallowing and for the pleasures of teaching, talking, dining, wining, reading, sleeping and lying in the sun before you throw yourself in to another battle against time'.[159] Hancock was displeased at the prospect of her engaging in 'more obsessive work', as he put it: 'Why not leave atomic energy to the young—teach, enjoy Oxford, make new friends and give yourself a fallowing period?'[160]

Wise advice, which Gowing ignored. The obligation (thanks to pressure from the UKAEA) weighed heavily. But how to organise the next volume, and what ground should it cover? All of '*Indy*' dealt with a period of only seven years. How to handle the next decade? One plan was to cover a similar period—the next seven years, 1952–9—between the 'Hurricane' tests that gave Britain the Bomb, and Britain's first H-Bomb test in 1958. This volume could be called either *Independence to Interdependence*, or *Interdependence Regained*, and would bring the narrative to a positive, if

[155] MHS, Gowing Papers, I&D File, Hinton to Makins, 8 May 1975.
[156] Ibid.
[157] Ibid.
[158] Sarah White, 'Nuclear historian'. Interestingly, Lorna Arnold—whose feminist credentials shone as brightly—was not mentioned in this essay, although she appeared as Margaret's co-author of an article following the interview, on 'Health and safety in Britain's nuclear programme', which was supremely Lorna's subject. Ead., 659–61.
[159] MHS, Gowing Papers, I&D File, Hancock to Gowing, 4 Dec. 1974.
[160] MHS, Gowing Papers, Hancock File, Hancock to Gowing, 26 April 1975.

fleeting closure, with the US/UK agreement between Macmillan and Kennedy that ended twelve years of nuclear estrangement.[161]

Another possible outline was given the title *Equipoise and Energy*, to cover the period 1952–63, in two volumes—the first, dealing with administrative and international events, including the all-important Anglo-American relationship, arrangements within NATO and the Commonwealth, the development of the H-bomb, the advent of nuclear submarines, the Partial Test Ban Treaty, and Britain's civil nuclear power programme—as well as the emergence of CND and the question of nuclear security. The second volume would complement this, with the consideration of several special topics, such as the Windscale accident in 1957, the development of nuclear health and safety standards, the fall-out debate, continuing weapon trials, the supply of uranium and other raw materials, the history of nuclear production programmes, and developments in fast reactor and fusion research.[162]

A third plan, equally ambitious—and possibly inspired by Lorna Arnold—was called simply 'Britain and Atomic Energy, 1952–1958', and is dated as late as November 1991. This outline covered similar ground, beginning with the origins of the UKAEA, the development of Harwell, the expansion of plutonium production (especially in the form of dual purpose reactors), the resumption of an 'unequal interdependence' with the United States, and the development of civil nuclear power and thermonuclear weapons. This version would also have traced the euphoria that first greeted nuclear power, but then fell victim to public scepticism, especially after Windscale; the role of atomic energy in international affairs; and the development of a civil energy programme, with special reference to health and safety. Finally, it would have looked forward to the changed world once the McMahon Act was amended, and would have considered the future of British policy after the American moratorium on atmospheric weapons testing in 1961.[163] Even so, there was no mention of nuclear strategy, or nuclear intelligence; and the 1991 outline left what would be the next 'natural' period, 1958 to 1978, in total darkness.

In fact, none of these three outlines—nor the third volume—was destined to appear. Indeed, 'volume three' failed to progress beyond the

[161] MHS, Gowing Papers, Perrier Box, Gowing to Sir Solly (later Lord) Zuckerman, 3 Dec. 1985.
[162] See Authority Historians Office (AHO) 2.1.1 Synopsis for AE History, 1953–59/60; MHS, Gowing Papers, Jobs and Applications, Annexe II 'Outline of next volume of the history of the British Atomic Energy Project' (n.d., but probably 1972–4).
[163] Draft Outline, Lorna Arnold to author, dated Nov. 1991.

outlines of 1972–3. Research continued on massive archives in many locations, driven by the indomitable Arnold,[164] but the book's strategic structure remained unresolved, and most of its text remained unwritten. Gowing continued to be retained as a consultant to the UKAEA, which, as before, expected her to come up to London and work steadily on the book. Increasingly, however, her energies turned in different directions. Following '*I&D*', Hancock prophesied that new opportunities would come her way ('How are the Templemans confounded', he trumpeted),[165] and he was right. In 1974, she was invited to give the Wilkins Lecture to the Royal Society,[166] and was appointed a member of the Lord Chancellor's Advisory Council on Public Records (1974–82). In July 1975, she was elected to the Fellowship of the British Academy—one of the few historians of science to be so honoured, her success again facilitated by Alan Bullock.[167]

In 1976, she was made a member of the BBC Archives Committee. This was followed by the award of honorary degrees from Leeds (1976), Leicester (1982), Manchester (1985), and Bath (1987). She delivered the Bernal Lecture at Birkbeck College in May 1977,[168] and in 1978 the Rede Lecture at Cambridge, in which she defended the utility of history against the undermining effects of secrecy, which in her view had distorted Anglo-American relations and undermined constitutional government in Britain.[169] In 1978 she began two years' strenuous work as one of the three members of Sir Duncan Wilson's Committee on Public Records (1978–81)—her appointment welcomed by Trevor-Roper, who thought it 'a great blow struck for the forces of Reason, Sense and Enlightenment'.[170] She was eminently qualified, as the only historian who had also been a Departmental

[164] See, e.g. Margaret Gowing and Lorna Arnold, 'Health and safety in Britain's nuclear programme', *New Scientist*, 28 Nov. 1974, 659–61.

[165] MHS, Gowing Papers, Hancock to MG, 26 April 1975.

[166] Margaret Gowing, 'Science, technology and education: England in 1870', Wilkins Lecture for 1977, *Notes and Records of the Royal Society of London*, 32 (1) (July 1977), 71–90; repr. in *Oxford Review of Education*, 4 (10) (1978), 3–17.

[167] MHS, Gowing Papers, Brown Box, Gowing to Bullock, 1 July 1975.

[168] Margaret Gowing, 'Science and politics', *The Eighth J. D. Bernal Lecture* (London: Birkbeck College, 17 May 1977), 16 pp. 'As all the previous lecturers were Bernal's (mostly Marxist) friends', she wrote to Roger Makins, 'I thought it time to break the party up.' MHS, Gowing Papers, Perrier Box, Gowing to Makins, 13 June 1977.

[169] Margaret Gowing, 'Reflections on Atomic Energy History', *The Rede Lecture, 1978* (Cambridge, 1978), 26 pp. at 14; repr. as 'Reflections on Atomic Energy History', *The Bulletin of the Atomic Scientists*, 35 (3) (1979), 51–4.

[170] MHS, Gowing Papers, Perrier Box, Trevor-Roper to Gowing, 21 Aug. 1978. Dacre Papers, Gowing to Trevor-Roper, 30 Aug. 1978. Duncan Wilson was Master of Corpus Christi College, Cambridge, a former Ambassador to the USSR.

Record Officer, and as a veteran of the Grigg Committee a quarter of a century earlier.[171] The Wilson enquiry took her to the United States, welcome travel, made onerous by a painful back. In 1979, she was invited to Jerusalem for the Einstein Centenary, where she was feted as one of Britain's leading science historians. Her back pain she bore stoically—as she did her lack of progress on 'volume three'.

As the decade ended, back pains were complicated by signs of a mysterious chronic illness that remained undiagnosed, but whose effects markedly slowed her down. Friends remarked that she returned time and again to call upon the same material, with variations for different audiences.[172] Reading her Rede Lecture back at her, Hinton teased, 'It is interesting, but you must be getting a bit tired of boiling the same cabbage over and over again.'[173] Lost time was a constant theme. To Nicholas Kurti, in December 1978, she lamented the effort she had devoted to the Contemporary Scientific Archives Centre [CSAC]—'it has involved for me a great deal of financial and staffing detail of the kind I especially dislike, (and which I said I would not do!), and after all I do not even have a secretary'.[174] It was hardly the first time. Perhaps illness was taking its toll.

In February 1979, in witness of a brave denial, Gowing assured Christopher Hinton that any fears that she was 'fed up' with atomic energy were totally unfounded, and promised him that she would retire from her chair in 1981, at the early age of 60, to concentrate on finishing 'volume three'.[175] She had been saying this since at least 1976, when she confided in Kurti that she might go even earlier 'if a good college research fellowship arose'. She repeated the point to everyone: 'I want to stay in Oxford but I must spend more time on writing atomic energy history—also important for posterity—and I want more time to see my friends and family.'[176] 'The

[171] MHS, Gowing Papers, Perrier Box, Gowing to Arnold Thackray, 11 Sept. 1978.

[172] See, for example, Margaret Gowing, 'Britain, America and the Bomb', Lecture given at the University of Leeds, 10 Oct. 1977, *University of Leeds Review*, 21 (1978), 50–65; developed in David Dilks (ed.), *Retreat from Power: Studies in Britain's Foreign Policy of the Twentieth Century, Vol. Two: After 1939* (London, 1981), pp. 120–37; rewritten for Michael Dockreill and John W. Young (eds.), *British Foreign Policy, 1945–1956* (London, 1989), and Margaret Gowing, 'How Britain produced the bomb: Anglo-American relations and the nuclear deterrent', *The Guardian*, 8 April 1985, p. 9.

[173] AHO 5, Articles, Reviews and Lectures, Hinton to Gowing, 25 June 1979.

[174] Bodleian Library, Special Collections, Kurti Papers, Gowing to Kurti, 18 Dec. 1978.

[175] Institution of Mechanical Engineers, Hinton Papers, H 32. Gowing to Hinton, 7 Nov. 1977.

[176] Bodleian Library, Special Collections, Kurti Papers, Gowing to Kurti, 19 April 1976. As to the future of her archival interests, she added, 'As long as I am in Oxford I would take an interest in the 'academic side' of the Centre (i.e. CSAC), but not a legal-financial responsibility. The RS is bigger, stronger and richer than me!'

trouble', she wrote to Hinton, 'is that I feel tired in my '50s and increasingly find it difficult to cope with no secretary—even for phone calls ... I can't do more in a week than I do and even so I feel guilty over undone chores (and of friendships unpursued). I hope I shall get a clear run for 1981; I can't think how I did *I&D*.'[177]

In mid-1979, having completed six years at Oxford, Gowing took her first sabbatical—a visit to Canberra, where friends and admirers—including the Hancocks, F. B. Smith, Oliver MacDonagh, and Noel Butlin—made her feel welcome, even cherished. On her return, however, there was always 'the Book'. In September 1979, she delivered on a promise to herself, and applied for a Research Fellowship at All Souls. Hancock agreed that 'Election ... would mean release from the strain which you have suffered without intermission for the last 30 years and more. You would do the things which you are bound to do professionally, and the things which you want to do as a person ...'. [178] The Fellowship would also have given her a clear run at 'vol. three'.[179]

Election to the Oxford college where Hancock had thrice been a Fellow—however stuffy its reputation, and rear-guard its influence—would have pleased her greatly. However, her application failed—despite supporting letters from Bullock and Trevor-Roper, as well as Hancock.[180] The blow deeply dented her self-esteem. Failure in such a competition could be construed as personal rejection, anti-feminist prejudice, or even as a dismissal of the history of science. But in all likelihood, these considerations were irrelevant. Peter Mathias and Michael Howard, both Fellows of All Souls, would have supported her candidacy. But the contest was of epic proportions—with 175 candidates competing for a single place—and that the vote went to an internationally distinguished mathematical logician could easily be mistaken for something it was not.[181] Nonetheless, for Gowing, failure was a form of rejection, leaving a bitter taste that refused to go away.

During her years at Oxford perhaps Gowing's greatest satisfaction, if also her greatest frustration, came with her efforts for the Contemporary Scientific Archives Centre (CSAC). The preparatory work that began in 1967 under the aegis of a Joint Committee of the Royal Society and the Historical Manuscripts Commission was continued under a subcommit-

[177] Institution of Mechanical Engineers, Hinton Papers, F 198, Gowing to Hinton, 6 Feb. 1979.
[178] MHS, Gowing Papers, Hancock File, Hancock to Gowing, 9 Sept. 1979.
[179] Dacre Papers, Gowing to Trevor-Roper, 7 July 1979.
[180] MHS, Gowing Papers, Hancock to Gowing, 9 Sept. 1979.
[181] MHS, Gowing Papers, All Souls Fellowship.

tee of the Royal Society's British National Committee for the History of Science, Medicine, and Technology, which included representatives from the British Library, the Wellcome Trust, and the Council of Engineering Institutions. When, in 1972, the Wolfson Foundation gave a grant to establish a Centre—which, according to Gowing, neither the Royal Society nor the Historical Manuscripts Commission wanted to run—Gowing agreed to take it with her to Oxford, for three years in the first instance. Since the overall majority of 'eminent scientists' whose papers were to be surveyed and catalogued were Fellows of the Royal Society, Gowing continued to insist that the Royal Society should take responsibility for the project. This, however, Sir David Martin, the Executive Secretary, resisted, as did his successors. In the event, the Centre was launched with funds from the Royal Society, but also with grants from other sponsors, including the Wolfson and Pergamon Foundations and, later, the Ernest Cook and McRobert Trusts.

Work began in April 1973 with two salaried staff (Mrs J. B. Alton and Mrs Harriot Weiskittel), based first at Gowing's office in the Indian Institute, and then at 10 Keble Road. Within six years, following the principles established by Joan Pye of Harwell—a simple survey, not an elaborate cataloguing—sixty-two collections had been prepared, and the Centre had proved its worth.[182] Gowing recalled spending 'more time on the Centre than on anything else for my first two years at Oxford',[183] but gradually (and reluctantly, some said) she left her staff to get on with it. At her request, the Bodleian agreed to assign the two staff professional salary grades. This gave them due recognition, even if it committed the Centre to meeting their annual increments.

In 1976, when the Centre completed its first three years, Gowing discovered she had few prospects of further funding, as foundations typically limited their grants to single awards. Time and again, she appealed to prospective sponsors, and to Ronald Keay, who succeeded David Martin. Keay eventually agreed that the Royal Society should take over about half the cost, in the form of a line budget in its annual government grant.[184] With this in hand, Gowing generated matching grants from the Rhodes Trust, the Wolfson and Nuffield Foundations, and the Institution of Mechanical Engineers.[185] The Centre lived to fight another day. But in

182 Gowing, 'The Contemporary Scientific Archives Centre'.

183 Bodleian Library, Special Collections, Gowing Papers, Gowing to Sir William Paton, 15 July 1985.

184 Ibid.

185 Ibid.

1980 the Wellcome Trust, which had set up a medical archives project of its own, announced the end of its sponsorship, and the 1980s began with the Centre's future unresolved. Gowing's twice-yearly reports reveal her continuing anxiety: 'Is this really', she wailed to Kurti, 'what life in one's declining years should be comprised of?'[186]

In fact, the 1980s proved to be a busy mixture. In 1980, James was married, followed by Nik (at St Cross, Oxford) in July 1982. Both sons were successfully launched in life. In 1981, Gowing's work for the Wilson Committee on Public Records finished, and in 1983, her four-year term with the Lord Chancellor's Public Records Advisory Council came to an end. She was unhappy with the Wilson Committee's recommendations for the preservation of records, which effectively postponed further reforms for many years.[187] But Sir Richard Wilson, later Secretary of the Cabinet, spoke in glowing terms of her reputation throughout Whitehall.[188] In June 1981, she was appointed CBE—'a fitting reward for all your hard work', Alistair Crombie generously sang, and many chorused.[189]

In 1982, Gowing was invited to deliver the Herbert Spencer Lecture, on 'Science and Politics: an Old and Intimate Relationship', in which she reversed the 'popular image of a British Empire created and governed by Oxford Greats'. This, she said, 'obscured the pervasive role of those scientists, such as the botanists and the geologists who, with their professional institutions, were deeply involved with imperial and economic power . . .'. In time, politics embraced scientists—who proved 'both wise and foolish, both myopic and far-sighted, both judicious and ridiculous, both clear-headed and muddled. They turned out to be, indeed, remarkably like politicians.'[190] This was pontifical Gowing at her best—but her reflections on science and politics won her few new friends in either Faculty.

Her academic ribbons and honours—what Kurti called her 'alphabetical adornments'[191]—Gowing wore with sober grace. But these seemed to bring little satisfaction. Family and friends were especially dear, as were

[186] Bodleian Library, Special Collections, Kurti Papers, Gowing to Kurti, 2 Dec. 1982.
[187] MHS, Gowing Papers, Perrier Box, Gowing to Sir Solly Zuckerman, 3 Dec. 1985.
[188] Gowing Family Papers, Box 3, Sir Richard Wilson to N. Gowing, 18 Nov. 1998.
[189] Gowing Papers, CBE file. Her well-wishers included Asa Briggs, Kenneth Lucas, Sir Michael Perrin, William Marshall, and Michael Howard.
[190] Margaret Gowing, 'Science and politics: an old and intimate relationship', in Vernon Bogdanor (ed.), *Science and Politics: Herbert Spencer Lectures, 1982* (Oxford, 1984), pp. 52–69; repr. in A. Boserup, L. Christensen and O. Nathan (eds.), *The Challenge of Nuclear Armaments: Essays Dedicated to Niels Bohr and his Appeal for an Open World* (Copenhagen, 1986), pp. 21–37.
[191] MHS, Gowing Papers, Kurti to Gowing, 4 July 1978.

memories of her past. The phrase 'She never forgot her roots' recurs in letters to and from those who knew her. In the academic world, however, she failed to present a smiling face. Apparently to create more time for writing, as she put it, she once considered letting her name go forward for the headship of an Oxford women's college. When this did not eventuate, she withdrew into a self-protecting silence. Her response to a similar suggestion made years later, a friend recalled, was a swift and firm 'no'. Bitterly, she wrote, that even 'if all the Fellows walked on their knees from the station to Northmoor Place to supplicate her, she would not change her mind'.[192] The record suggests they did not, nor did she.

Winding up, slowing down

'Death and disaster' were the leading words of Gowing's letter to Hancock in August 1982, reporting the death of George Allen, the economist, who had long been amongst her closest friends. Christopher Hinton's death followed in 1983. Gowing wrote moving memoirs of both.[193] In Oxford, she felt she could still call upon Peter Mathias, who shared her interest in science and society; and Michael Howard, whose long experience of journalism and military affairs gave them common cause. She continued a close friend of Charles Webster, who became a Research Fellow of All Souls in 1988. She greatly enjoyed a gossipy correspondence with Trevor-Roper, elevated to the peerage in 1979, who in 1980 swapped a fitful absence of harmony at Oxford for 'seven contentious years' in Cambridge.[194] The frustrations that he met as Master of Peterhouse recalled to Gowing her own struggles in Oxford.[195]

Gowing often repeated her plan to retire early, and clearly wanted to do so. The target year of 1981 conveniently coincided with the publication of the Wilson Report and the end of the Royal Society's grant to CSAC. But against early retirement loomed the prospect of a lower pension and, with it, came the logic of staying on until 1986, and age 65. Her younger son, James, needed financial help with his farm in the Orkneys; and she worried about the risks that her elder son, Nik, took when covering trouble

[192] Gowing Family Papers, Box 3, Brian (Eyre?) to Nik Gowing, 13 Nov. 1998.

[193] M. Gowing, 'George Cyril Allen (1900–1982)', *Proceedings of the British Academy*, LXXI (1985), 473–91.

[194] Worden, 'Hugh Redwald Trevor-Roper', p. 271.

[195] Dacre Papers, Trevor-Roper to Gowing, 10 Dec. 1983, and Gowing to Trevor-Roper, 20 Dec. 1983.

spots in the world for ITN and Channel 4 News, as senior correspondent and then Diplomatic Editor. As these tyrannies took their toll, Gowing's ability to focus seemed to ebb away. She fell prey to a kind of nervous exhaustion that her doctors failed to identify, let alone remedy. By 1982, she was complaining to all who would listen that 'there is far too much to do to keep my head above water. I find it increasingly difficult to keep track of everything, especially with the flood of paper, with no secretary.' 'The privilege of Oxford', she added.[196] In fairness, Oxford was not especially unkind to her.[197] Her life at Linacre was a source of pleasure. But the university seemed indifferent to many of its professors, and such indifference she read as opposition. Those few research students whom she supervised speak warmly of her help, 'conscientious (to a fault) and very hard-working in terms of reading drafts, writing copious comments and offering advice'.[198] But she seldom commented on Oxford intellectual debates, and played little role in university administration. Oxford was not her game.

During the mid-1980s, Gowing published several papers, which drew on her earlier research,[199] but expressed concern that her 'life work' would never be finished. A decade had passed since *I&D*, and a sequel was nowhere in sight. Her prospects were not improved between 1980–6 by a flutter with a history of solid state physics that did not materialise, and by several time-consuming visits to Geneva in preparation for a history of CERN, in which she soon lost interest.[200] Her chapter on 'Nuclear weapons and the special

[196] Institute of Mechanical Engineers, Hinton Papers, A 123, Gowing to Hinton, 13 July 1982; 'I have no secretary (and) my filing is unreliable,' she reminded him. Hinton Papers B 96, Gowing to Hinton, 17 Jan. 1983.

[197] Gowing's experience was not unique. Robert O'Neill, Chichele Professor of the History of War, and Fellow of All Souls, met similar frustrations. As Professor O'Neill recalls, 'I did supervise some graduate students and a couple of visiting fellows in the nuclear weapons field, but that was as far as Oxford allowed the subject into the doorway ... I ran graduate classes and lectured every week, but I could get no teaching assistance and no secretary. So it was a "DIY" university as far as I was concerned.' Pers. comm., Robert O'Neill to author, 22 Nov. 2009.

[198] Pers. comm., Dr Peter Morris to author, 31 May 2006.

[199] Margaret Gowing, 'How Britain produced the bomb: Margaret Gowing on Anglo-American relations and the nuclear deterrent', *The Guardian*, 8 April 1985, 9; 'Niels Bohr and nuclear weapons', in A. P. French and P. J. Kennedy (eds.), *Niels Bohr: A Centenary Volume* (Cambridge, MA, 1985), pp. 266–77; 'Les Savants Nucléaires dans la Tourmente', *Echos du Groupe CEA*, No. 1 (1984), 12–15, trans. Bertrand Goldschmidt, 'En Gammel og intim Forbindelse', in *Naturens Verden*, 11 (1984), IX–XVI, in *Om Videnskab og politik, tre essays med udgangspunkt I Niels Bohrs overvejelser* (Rhodos), pp. ix–xvi; 'Sir Nevill Mott: an appreciation', *Philosophical Magazine* B, 52 (1985), 215–16.

[200] The project teetered on the edge of tears until it was rescued by Dr (now Professor) John Krige, an outstanding historian of science and technology, previously a member of the pioneering History and Social Studies of Science Subject Group at Sussex University. He and his team produced

relationship' in a collection edited by Roger Louis and Hedley Bull marks the end point of a journey that, in happier circumstances, might have had a different outcome.[201]

As the years went by, Gowing increasingly left Arnold to 'her own salvation'.[202] In Gowing's absence, the Authority Historians Office produced what Arnold called 'a modest flow of papers, articles and lectures', and furnished information to industry and academics in Britain and overseas.[203] But no real progress was made on a 'third volume'. Research assistants were hired to write up sections that might one day be folded into a master narrative.[204] John Hendry, one of these assistants, remembers Gowing as being 'quite impossible to work with'; 'the only way to get anything done was to work around her. During the period I worked there (1980–4), she produced nothing but just stormed in occasionally, had a tantrum, and stormed out again.'[205] Given what we now know of her health, her behaviour is perhaps understandable.

Gowing asked Hendry and Arnold to write up a few 'special topics'. For Hendry, this included important work on fusion; for Arnold, on health and safety.[206] Arnold proceeded to write the first published account of the British atomic tests in Australia, the research for which made available for the first time archival information then used by a Royal Commission in Australia.[207] The book made Arnold's name, both in Australia and Britain, whilst buying time against the completion of 'volume three'.

At Gowing's request, Arnold also wrote a chapter on the Windscale accident of 1957, for which she conducted interviews that would have

John Krige *et al.*, *History of CERN*, 3 vols. (Amsterdam, 1987–96). For the work of the Subject Group, see Roy MacLeod, 'Fifty Voices, Fifty Faces: the University of Sussex Oral History Online Exhibition' (Falmer, 2011)—see also <http://www.sussex.ac.uk/fiftyyears/50voices50faces>.

201 'Nuclear weapons and the "Special Relationship"', in Roger Louis and Hedley Bull (eds.), *The Special Relationship: Anglo-American Relations since 1945* (Oxford, 1986), pp. 117–28.

202 Memo, Arnold to author, Nov. 2004, section 7, p. 7.

203 Lorna Arnold, 'A letter from Oxford', *Minerva*, 38 (2000), 210.

204 These included John Hendry, 'Technological Decision Making in its Organizational Context: Nuclear Power Reactor Development in Britain' (University of Cambridge Engineering Department, 1991), and (with J. D. Lawson, FRS), 'Fusion Research in the UK, 1945–1960' (AEA Technology Report, AHO 1, Jan. 1993). A paper by Stephen Keith, 'The Fundamental Nucleus: a Study of the Impact of the British Atomic Energy Project on Basic Research' (AHO 2, May 1993), was prepared for internal use. Other papers that appeared in this series are held at Harwell.

205 Pers. comm., John Hendry to author, 21 May 2004.

206 MHS, Gowing Papers, Gowing to Makins, 2 Aug. 1984.

207 Lorna Arnold, *A Very Special Relationship: British Atomic Weapon Trials in Australia* (London, 1987).

been impossible a decade earlier, or later. The incident came to the fore following the Chernobyl disaster of 1986, which occurred near the date (January 1988) when official files concerning Windscale were to be released by the Public Record Office. Given the prospect of wide media interest, Arnold suggested producing a book. Gowing agreed, and the result was Arnold's *Windscale, 1957: Anatomy of a Nuclear Accident.*[208]

'Not long from now, you will be free from the distractions of your chair,' Hancock wrote to Gowing, in December 1984, 'no need for you to worry. You will bring to a triumphant conclusion your magisterial history of the Atomic Energy Authority.'[209] The long promised moment of retirement came finally in 1986, when Gowing turned 65, two years before the official (and customary) retirement age at Oxford. The event was marked by collegial courtesy and civility. Lincacre College made Gowing an Emeritus Fellow, and Nicolaas Rupke edited a fine Festschrift—which, appropriately, included a Preface by Alan Bullock.[210] More surprising—to her colleagues, and to Gowing herself—came the news of her election to the Fellowship of the Royal Society, under the provisions of Clause 12 of its Charter, which permits the election of non-scientists who have made distinguished contributions to science.[211] This honour elevated Gowing into the ranks of a select few—at the time, only two others (Joseph Needham and Karl Popper)—who were Fellows both of the British Academy and of the Royal Society. Jon Turney in the *Times Higher Education Supplement* (*THES*) acclaimed Gowing as one who 'has done more than anyone to establish the importance of science in social, political and economic inquiry'.[212] She was fond of saying to friends that, at one time, she had been undervalued; now, she was overvalued. Genuine modesty masked deep delight.

Gowing was not sad to leave her chair. Oxford University held no high place in her affections: 'Inevitably,' she wrote to Trevor-Roper, 'I am conscious of my failures here rather than my successes.' Among the latter, she counted her continuing support of the Wellcome Unit, which had thrived

[208] Lorna Arnold, *Windscale, 1957: Anatomy of a Nuclear Accident* (London, 1992; 2nd edn., 1995).

[209] MHS, Gowing Papers, Hancock File, Hancock to Gowing, 8 Dec. 1984.

[210] Nicolaas Rupke, *Science, Politics and the Public Good: Essays in Honour of Margaret Gowing* (London, 1986).

[211] Hancock, prescient as ever, foresaw this possibility in Jan. 1985. MHS, Hancock File, Hancock to Gowing, 23 Jan. 1985. Hancock said (8 Oct. 1985) that he was asking Oliphant to mobilise others to propose her.

[212] Jon Turney, 'Chronicler of Big Science at the Heart of the State', *Times Higher Education Supplement*, 22 July 1988, 6.

under the direction of Charles Webster.[213] Her most conspicuous legacy to the university was CSAC which, on her retirement in 1986, and Mrs Alton's in 1987, Oxford proposed to close. The Centre had processed some 110 collections, and had won international acclaim. But this had come at a cost. To Michael Hoskin of Cambridge, Gowing confessed that 'over the 11 years of the Centre's life, money has been a constant nightmare'. The Royal Society was meeting 50 per cent of its budget (£32,000 in current pounds), but the other half required hard canvassing. Gowing did 'not envy any other body which might take over the job of raising money on this hand-to-mouth basis', and expressed 'great exasperation' with the Royal Society for declining to take it over completely.[214]

Under the circumstances, Gowing was obliged to let other universities 'bid' for CSAC. In the end, the only offer forthcoming came from the University of Bath, where Rodney Quayle, FRS, then on the Royal Society's Council, was Vice-Chancellor. With Royal Society support, CSAC continued at Bath from the Spring of 1987, rebranded as the National Cataloguing Unit for the Archives of Contemporary Scientists. Many collections were processed, and several more were underway, under the direction of Dr Peter Harper, and with the continuing assistance of Mrs Alton, when in December 2009 the Royal Society withdrew its funding. The University of Bath declared itself unable to continue its support.[215]

Fortunately, Gowing did not live to see the demise of her beloved Centre. For a time, the history of science at Oxford also remained in a parlous state. The university lectureship that Crombie held disappeared with his retirement in 1983, and Gowing had been unable or unwilling to seek funds to replace him. The Museum of the History of Science slumbered under erudite but unenterprising management, and undergraduate numbers in the history of science remained small. In 1986–7, only about twelve History undergraduates, in each of the first two years, took one of the two History options on the Scientific Revolution and on Intellect and Culture in Victorian Britain. In science, some ten to twenty undergraduates took a Supplementary Subject or did a Part III thesis in the history of

[213] This is perhaps not an appropriate place to discuss the vexed history of the Wellcome Trust and the Wellcome Unit in their complex and sometimes bitter relations with the Faculty of Modern History. This history is abundantly surveyed in the Minutes of the Faculty Board.

[214] Bodleian Library, Special Collections, Gowing Papers, Gowing to Sir William Paton, 15 July 1985; Gowing to Dr Michael Hoskin, 2 Aug. 1984; Hoskin to Gowing, 4 Aug. 1984.

[215] Pers. comm., Professor Angus Buchanan to author, 17 March 2011. There are proposals to continue its work, possibly at Imperial College or the Science Museum. I am grateful for information and assistance from Dr Peter Harper and Dr Timothy Powell.

chemistry, and a few undergraduates from other Schools, reading for other degrees, attended lectures. In the undergraduate courses, Gowing's participation had receded, and none of the seventeen research students working in different areas of the history of science were hers. Her passionate plea for the integration of science and history—the key theme of her Inaugural Lecture in 1975—had been forgotten. The vacant chair went onto Oxford's Register of Suspended Posts. With the freezing of academic appointments in 1986, some feared the chair might disappear. [216]

At the time, it was common knowledge that Gowing had retired to write the celebrated 'third volume',[217] a Homeric task that had achieved almost mythic status. But what had been a near certainty at the project's dawn, and even feasible at midday, appeared at twilight quite out of reach. Even a 'synoptic' volume, of the kind that Gowing had written with Hancock during the war, was too awesome to contemplate.

Following Gowing's retirement, the UKAEA closed the historian's London office, and the AHO at Harwell was run down. Had there been an Advisory Committee, its decline might have been arrested, and its work continued. But there was none. As it was, work was delegated principally to Lorna Arnold. Not surprisingly, Gowing grew envious of her extremely able, loyal, and dedicated colleague, whom age had (and has) never wearied.[218] Over the next two years, Arnold produced a fine history of Britain's H-bomb, recounting events between July 1954 and the Christmas Island tests in September 1958. This for the first time made public the work of William (later Lord) Penney and the 'weaponeers' of the Atomic Weapons Research Establishment (AWRE), Aldermaston, in designing, fabricating and testing Britain's first thermonuclear weapon.[219] Along with other political factors, this demonstration of technological capability had won for Britain the 'great prize' of restored cooperation with the United

[216] In 1986, given the freeze on appointments, only two of the thirteen posts on the Register were filled (the chair in the History of War, vacant for four years by 1986, and a CUF lectureship). Bodleian Library, Special Collections, Gowing Papers, Gowing to Paton, 15 July 1985. Dacre Papers, Gowing to Trevor-Roper, 28 July 1986. Observers suggest that the timely intervention of Professor Mary Hesse of Cambridge, who led a UGC review of the history of science in Britain, helped rescue the Oxford chair for the discipline, and for the nation. In 1988, Charles Webster considered applying for the chair, but instead accepted a Senior Research Fellowship at All Souls. The same year, Robert Fox was appointed to the chair. Fox retired in 2006, and his successor was appointed in 2007. At this writing, there is no lectureship, but undergraduate numbers are up, research student numbers are stable, and the Museum of the History of Science, under the direction of Dr Jim Bennett (formerly of Cambridge) is an outstanding success.

[217] See, for example, Dacre Papers, Gowing to Trevor-Roper, 28 July 1986.

[218] I owe this observation to Nik Gowing.

[219] Lorna Arnold, *Britain and the H-Bomb* (London, 2001).

States—the goal of nuclear diplomacy on which Gowing had put such great store, and on the absence of which she had so passionately written.

In all she then wrote, and in all she has since written, Lorna Arnold proved Gowing's worthy successor. Arnold's 'H-Bomb' marked the last formal production of the UKAEA History Office.[220] Since the UKAEA was closed in the 1990s,[221] nuclear history in Britain has become 'fragmented and there is no government body with an overall responsibility for nuclear matters'.[222] The Authority's recent past has involved extensive privatisation—of which Gowing would have certainly disapproved[223]—and there appears to be no interest at the Cabinet Office in sponsoring a history of the last half-century of Britain's affair with the atom.[224]

With hindsight, the publication of *Indy* in 1974 marked the UKAEA history's high water mark. But those volumes were limited to the period 1945–52. The next period, 1952–8, was dealt with in a few *ad hoc* publications, of which Arnold's were memorable; but for the decades since 1958 'there was (and is) nothing'.[225] As of this writing, the absence of a 'third volume' leaves a major gap. There remains today no official study of the deliberations surrounding US/UK nuclear collaboration after the UK/USA agreement of 1958; no official study of Britain's civil nuclear power policy, nor of the many organisational changes that have transformed Britain's nuclear enterprise since 1953.[226] Nor, indeed, has there been a definitive history of Britain's role in respect to reactor safeguards and radiological protection.

[220] See Arnold, 'A Letter from Oxford', p. 203.

[221] In the Thatcherite 1980s, the AEA was required to become a commercial enterprise, and during the 1990s many of its activities were transferred to a public company, AEA Technology. By the early 2000s, the Authority was reduced to a residual body, charged with managing and restoring former nuclear sites, decommissioning, and policing nuclear materials.

[222] Arnold, 'A Letter from Oxford', p. 213.

[223] In April 2008, a new subsidiary, UKAEA Ltd, was created to oversee decommissioning and environmental restoration. In February 2009, a wholly owned subsidiary of the Authority was formed to operate the sites at Harwell and Winfrith. Research Sites Restoration Limited (RSRL) continues work for Harwell and Winfrith on behalf of the Nuclear Decommissioning Authority (NDA). In Oct. 2009, UKAEA Ltd. and its subsidiaries were acquired by Babcock International Group PLC.

[224] The only 'official' historian now in post is Ms Kathryn Pyne, the technical historian of Aldermaston, who assisted Lorna Arnold in the preparation of her book on the H-bomb. I am grateful to Ms Pyne for an introduction to Aldermaston and its work.

[225] Arnold, 'A letter from Oxford', p. 213.

[226] In 1971 the Authority was partitioned. Research activities remained with the Authority, a Radiochemical Centre was assigned the production of radioisotopes, and British Nuclear Fuels, Ltd took over weapons production facilities at Springfields, Capenhurst, Windscale, Calder Hall and Chapelcross. In 1973, the weapons sites were transferred to the Ministry of Defence.

We may take it as given that, in Lorna Arnold's words, Britain's official nuclear history project is now 'dead beyond hope of resurrection'. But if nothing of the original plan survives, it is surely appropriate to foster in other ways the work that Gowing and Arnold memorably began. Given the continuing role of nuclear technology in Britain's civil and military policy, it remains essential that we know the routes by which science, technology, industry and government have brought us to the present we know, and to a future we will all have to deal with.

The final curtain

From the early 1980s, family and colleagues noticed signs of Gowing's illness. Symptoms of failing memory and chronic tiredness were at times compounded by a troublesome back, which required her to wear a metal corselet. After retirement in 1986, she began to suffer what she called a 'virus', variously described as a myalgic encephalomyeltitis, or as 'post-viral fatigue disease'.[227] These diagnoses may have masked her real condition. Some recall that, when she was elected a Fellow of the Royal Society in 1988, she had difficulty in taking in the news.[228] Others recall having to help her find her way in the street. Her mental condition was all the more distressing for not being properly understood, and was never correctly diagnosed. She is now thought to have suffered from multi-infarct dementia, and from what are by now the all-too familiar features of Alzheimer's disease.

During the late 1980s, Gowing remained a visible presence at academic gatherings. Although she could not do new research, publications from her pen continued to appear.[229] Some of these repeated earlier work, but

[227] MHS, Gowing Papers, Perrier Box, Gowing to Martin Rudwick, 29 Feb. 1988; Dacre Papers Gowing to Trevor-Roper, 2 Sept. 1988.

[228] Pers. comm., Dr Peter Morris to author, 31 May 2006.

[229] 'How Nuclear Power Began', *Second CEGB Lecture* (Southampton: University of Southampton, 1987); 'Britain's postwar industrial decline: commentary on Corelli Barnett, *The Audit of War*', *Contemporary Record*, 1 (2) (1987), 18; 'Britain and the bomb: the origin of Britain's determination to be a nuclear power', *Contemporary Record*, 2 (2) (1988), 36–40; 'The Civil Histories of the Second World War', Lecture, 1988; 'The origins of Britain's status as a nuclear power', *Oxford Project for Peace Studies*, OPPS Paper 11, 1988; 'Prologue: early Western nuclear relationships', Center for International Security Studies, Nuclear History Program, Occasional Paper 4 (Bethesda, MD, 1989); 'The origins of Britain's status as a nuclear power', in John Baylis and Alan Macmillan (eds.), *The Foundations of British Nuclear Strategy, 1945–1960*, International Politics Research Papers No. 12, Department of International Politics, University College of Wales (Aberystwyth, 1992), pp. 7–19.

her memoirs of Bohr, Hinton, and Chadwick were and remain fundamentally important contributions to the literature.[230] In 1992, she retired from the Trusteeship of the National Portrait Gallery, and in the next few years her social life wound down. Recalling her post-war struggles with the Treasury, her last years were troubled by struggles with the pension service. Although she had worked in the civil service and academic life for forty-five years, she was reckoned to have only twenty-seven pensionable years, so was not eligible for a full pension. Her son Nik and his family were called upon to support her.[231]

In the early 1990s, Gowing moved from Northmoor Road to Ritchie Court, a block of purpose-built flats on Banbury Road, and then to a nursing home. With both cunning and foresight she had identified these flats some years earlier, fearing a deterioration in her health, which she seemed to comprehend but also hoped to hide for as long as possible. In February 1994, after a lumbar puncture, her general health began to fail. With her mental condition worsening, Nik and James moved her to even more sheltered care in a home in London, much closer to them. As the inexorable but little understood process of dementia consumed her, she was admitted to Putney Hospital, then to Kingston Hospital.[232] The end came, after the onset of pneumonia, on 7 November 1998.

Gowing willed her brain to the Oxford Project into Memory and Ageing (OPTIMA) at the John Radcliffe Hospital. With her passing, tributes flowed in abundance.[233] A memorial service was held at the University Church of St Mary the Virgin, Oxford, at which Alan Bullock spoke. Margaret had led a distinguished life, of memorable service to her country and her calling. During her lifetime, she entered the history she had herself

[230] Margaret Gowing, 'Niels Bohr and nuclear weapons', in J. de Boer, E. Dal and O. Ulfbeck (eds.), *The Lesson of Quantum Theory* (Amsterdam, 1986), pp. 343–54; 'Niels Bohr and nuclear weapons', Discourse, *Proceedings of the Royal Institution*, 59 (1987), 47–56; 'Lord Hinton of Bankside (12 May 1901–22 June 1983)', *Biographical Memoirs of Fellows of the Royal Society*, 36 (1990), 219–39; repr. as 'The life and times of Lord Hinton of Bankside', *Atom* (June 1991), 20–4 and (July/Aug. 1991), 21–6; 'James Chadwick and the atomic bomb', *Notes and Records of the Royal Society*, 47 (1) (1993), 79–92.

[231] MHS, Hancock File, covering memo; pers. comm., Nik Gowing to author.

[232] Nik Gowing to author, 20 May 2012.

[233] Obituaries include (in chronological order): Richard Norton-Taylor, 'Exploding the myth of the bomb: Professor Margaret Gowing', *The Guardian*, 9 Nov. 1998, 15; [Lorna Arnold], 'Professor Margaret Gowing', *The Times*, 11 Nov. 1998, 23; Charles Webster, 'Margaret Gowing', *Daily Telegraph*, 12 Nov. 1998; Robert Fox, 'Professor Margaret Gowing', *The Independent*, 20 Nov. 1998, 6; Anon, 'Professor Margaret Gowing: Oxford's first Professor of History of Science who turned official files into lively reading', *Daily Telegraph*, 23 Nov. 1998; Richard Hewlett, 'Margaret Gowing (26 April 1921–4 November 1998)', *Isis*, 90 (1999), 326–8; Charles Webster, 'Margaret Gowing, 1921–98', *History Workshop Journal*, No. 47 (1999), 327–30.

written; at her death, she became part of the national record that she had helped to preserve.[234]

Remains of the day

A memoir seeks to be objective and even-handed, and this memoir is unlikely to be the last word said about Margaret Gowing. Rather, this should be viewed as an invitation to study in greater detail the life and times of a woman of intelligence, ability and drive who left a memorable body of work. This essay offers no more than tentative suggestions, upon which a later biographer may wish to build.

Given existing evidence, it is hard to resist the conclusion that Gowing's life embodied a fortuitous combination of intelligence, good luck, timely chance, careful tutelage, opportunity, integrity and hard work that, in the circumstances of post-war Britain, enabled her to rise from unpromising social, economic and educational origins to reach the summits of English academic life. Of all the opportunities presented to her, she made the most. Her contributions to official history are regarded as monumental. Amongst her staff, she was said to be 'difficult', and Sir Crispin Tickell spoke of her 'spikey side'; yet, she was cherished by many historians who knew her. As Lawrence (now Sir Lawrence) Freedman wrote to her son, 'knowing that Margaret Gowing took you seriously was a boost to anyone's confidence'.[235]

Domestically, Gowing found herself in an unhappy marriage, but took great pleasure in her children, friends, and extended family. For her generation of women academics in Britain, she became a portrait in how to square the eternal circle of family, life, and work. She lived for her subject, and for her children. Her early social and economic background left its mark. As Lorna Arnold, perhaps her closest colleague recalls:

> Of non-professional and non-academic interests, she had few. She was not much interested in music, or opera, or the theatre, and so far as I ever discovered, did not reach much outside her own subjects of economic and nuclear history. She wasn't interested in sport. In fact I think all her interest was really focused on her two sons, Nicholas and James, to whom she was devoted, and on her career and professional work.[236]

[234] Robert Fox, 'Margaret Gowing, 1921–1998', *Oxford Dictionary of National Biography* (Oxford, 2004), vol. 23, 147–9. <http://www.oxforddnb.com/view/article/71257>.
[235] Gowing Family Papers, Freedman to Nik Gowing, 27 Nov. 1998.
[236] Memorandum, Arnold to the author, Nov. 2004, section 9, p. 7.

She was not without contradictions. She enjoyed the hallmarks of the Labour left, of men with northern accents and working class sympathies, but she could be autocratic towards her staff. Social climbing runs as a subtext throughout her career. She never seemed to overcome an early, deep-seated lack of self-confidence, which the receipt of academic awards and national honours failed to remedy. With her staff, or with those she felt not quite in her league, she could appear ungenerous. With some students, Gowing could also appear cold; yet, in her assessment of those she valued, she was full of praise. Most of her few students went on to professional success, and attest to her kindness and readiness to help.

Extremely sensitive to criticism—intended or otherwise—she was quirky, ingenuous, abrupt, and awkward with others. Reading her correspondence, one finds she could be oblivious to the implications of gossip, or what effect her words might have on others. 'Outsiders' to Oxford relished her readiness to say what she thought, without regard for the consequences. But this had a downside. Whilst she greatly admired people she approved of, she was sharp in dismissing those whom she did not. Difficult to please, both personally and in print, she could find credit difficult to share. She was selective in her praise, and could be accused of playing favourites. The obligation to recommend all too easily becomes an opportunity to reward or punish. Her worst invective she reserved for those whom she considered morally or academically weak. Her letters are peppered with the vocabulary of the censor, with an implicit arrogance—works she disliked were deemed 'worthless' or, scarcely less terrifying, 'disreputable'. As often with those espousing high principles, her broadsides could backfire. She could rebuke what she called 'dealers in sneers', yet in private correspondence sail perilously close to using their own language.[237]

In a familiar, self-deprecating phrase, one that wearied with repetition, Gowing seems to have rejoiced in the admission, once appointed, that she had never studied science. In an interview with the *THES*, seventeen years after she took the chair at Oxford, she admitted it was 'completely improbable that she should move into the history of science'.[238] But to rise to the challenge is what the work demanded, and once her drafts had been read—and corrected, if necessary, by the brightest scientists in the land—her ignorance of science did her no lasting damage. Indeed, faced with large, usually masculine egos, in what were, in her day, the most masculine

[237] Dacre Papers, Gowing to Hugh Trevor-Roper, 20 Dec. 1983.
[238] Turney, 'Chronicler of Big Science', p. 6.

fields of science and engineering, the *de facto* necessity of cultivating a stereotype of female innocence, if not ignorance, could work powerfully to her advantage. Knowing little of the technicalities, she showed herself willing to learn from those who gave her time. Her account of events in turn helped reflect their considered views. As caricatures of Margaret Thatcher beckon, it could be that women more powerful than Gowing have played the same game with similar success.

For Gowing, academic life at Kent and Oxford was a disappointing experience. However much she may have been viewed as the 'scientists' candidate' (and advocate), Gowing never strayed far from her wartime interests in archives, government, politics and contemporary history. University life had its compensations, but also its limitations; one had to teach, which she disliked; and to help students who might not share her passion. At Oxford, she was handicapped in having little formal knowledge of the subject she was meant to profess; and was unfairly (if somehow, properly) called upon to pontificate upon subjects, people, and periods she hardly knew. For all her networking, she knew little of academia, and those features she did, she generally deplored. She had several research students assigned to her, but having no research degree herself, she could be insecure and overbearing in their supervision. On the other hand, she did not weigh her position lightly, nor had she any sense of entitlement. A more modest, meritocratic Oxford professor would be hard to find, and her students remember her with affection.

It was a tragedy that Gowing did not have an opportunity—whether in her academic appointments, or in her writing—to build upon her training in economic history, and to contribute to economic policy, rather than to be repeatedly, relentlessly pilloried for her admitted ignorance of the sciences and their history. Nonetheless, the opportunities to engage with economic historians and historians of technology were many—both at Oxford, and elsewhere in Britain. It remains surprising that she chose to stand so far apart from their traditions and debates.

As an official historian, Gowing's style and methods reflected her years of apprenticeship with Keith Hancock, a master of the craft. Edward Bridges once told Hancock that he must begin his research at the highest level—and not to write of one department only, nor of one project or personality, but instead to develop key subjects, and pursue them.[239] From her twenties, Gowing took these lessons to heart—formal but fair, reject-

[239] Hancock, *Country and Calling*, p. 198.

ing secrecy and conspiracy, and cultivating close contact with men (*sic*) who made the key decisions. She enjoyed the company, and earned the confidence, of the influential and powerful, to which her wartime experience of the Cabinet Office and its grandees greatly contributed. Learning from Hancock to work 'from the top' was not only how to practise a trade, but how to tell a story. Her work embodied a central perspective more characteristic perhaps of Whitehall than Westminster, a focus on tactics, details, avoiding contention, and letting commentary speak for itself. Policy and politics as viewed from the centre, informed by disinterested elites, form the perspective for which she is remembered.

In an age before the dominance of computers, Gowing's methods of research and writing reveal a masterful approach to the collecting, cataloguing, and use of public records. Lorna Arnold recalls once remarking to Gowing on the disorderly appearance of her desk, only to be told that she did not need a system, or to be neat, because she had such a good memory. Certainly, Gowing had a powerful mind, capable of cutting through masses of documentation to see the big picture. To this, she added a direct, forceful, straightforward if inelegant style. This brought enormous advantages. If she were never difficult to read, it was difficult for her readers (and departmental vetting officers) to disagree with what she wrote.

Gowing's appointment to the UKAEA—surely, one of the most patient and tolerant government departments in Britain ever to commission a history—was both timely and promising. The perspective of official historian required knowledge both of the machinery of government, and of the people who made policy. Gowing was fortunate in that Britain's nuclear history—the story of building a Bomb, and a Super Bomb, and developing civilian nuclear power—had engaged some of the best minds in the country, and their records had been carefully kept. If the Authority had decided not to accept the rule of the Public Records Act, its archives would have remained under the Official Secrets Act; and even those released to the public, and eventually reaching the PRO, would have been thin, and greatly delayed—indeed, either until the 1970s (under the Thirty Year Rule) or the 1990s (under the Fifty Year Rule). This would have delayed historical analysis for at least a generation, long after the death of many of the key actors, whose memoirs could not be relied upon in the same way.

To her task, Gowing brought ability and energy, and opened the subject of nuclear history for others. In the words of Lorna Arnold, her legacy forms 'an incalculably important piece of British history'.[240] She was fortunate, as her account of British nuclear policy between 1945–52 has never been superseded, nor seriously questioned. It was once said of her friend Hugh Trevor-Roper that his writing showed more brilliance than depth. In Gowing, these features are reversed. Her writing is deep, rather than brilliant; her measured prose unfolds a narrative that brooks no distraction. Thanks to the rules of official history, it is also unhindered by the presence of qualifying footnotes, or intellectual crossfire. Tangential discussion or debate are not the stuff of policy.

But if this must be the way with official history, it is not the way with fast moving, nuanced fields of scholarship, such as the history of science and technology. Gowing's grasp of the moving research front in the history of science and technology was, at best, unsure. To her credit, she never promised otherwise. She never hid her respect for high scholarship, and encouraged those who looked to her for guidance and supervision. And given a life of state papers and prose, she had little time for changing scholarly fashions. Her letters and papers reveal remarkably little interest in historical events or ideas before the twentieth century, or outside her own compass, or even in the mainstream of current economic and social history, as then taught at Kent, Oxford, or elsewhere. She reveals even less interest in American history, or European let alone Asian history, and whilst enjoying the company of émigrés in England and holidays in France, sensed no professional need to follow nuclear developments over the Channel or across the Atlantic.

In assessing Gowing's legacy, our conclusions must remain tentative. Gowing's reputation rests principally on her two books and a large number of articles and book chapters, many of which are repetitive. This corpus contributed significantly to the emerging fields of nuclear history, nuclear politics, and strategic studies, which in the 1980s were carried forward by scholars such as Andrew Pierre, Peter Malone, and John Simpson.[241] In ways that all historians admire, Gowing was cited by them, and is still cited today. However, it is indeed disappointing that her account ended in 1952, with the publication of her second volume(s) in 1974. The next thirty years of the Cold War were to prove transformative for Britain's defence policy, its nuclear deterrent and force posture, and its relationship with the United States, and, in many ways, that story remains to be writ-

[240] Memo, Lorna Arnold to author, Nov. 2004.

[241] Andrew Pierre, *Nuclear Politics* (Oxford, 1982); Peter Malone, *The British Nuclear Deterrent* (London, 1984) and John Simpson, *The Independent Nuclear State* (London, 1983).

ten. However, Gowing is hardly alone among historians in leaving books unfinished;[242] and in any case, a comprehensive 'third volume' along the lines that she and Arnold contemplated between 1972 and 1985 may have proved in the end impossible to produce. Even by the 1970s, the quantity of official documentation had grown too large, too varied, too complex; and future official histories—if there were to be such—would be obliged to divide the subject into periods, problems, places, and personalities. The result could be more thorough, but possibly less comprehensive. Such was the approach that Lorna Arnold decided to take with her studies of Windscale, the British Tests in Australia, and the British H-Bomb. It remains unclear why Gowing did not attempt to do the same, writing on specific topics of her own choosing—unless, of course, her illness provides the simplest explanation.

Given the conventions of official history, Gowing's writing is a model of probity and integrity. At times, her sense of civic duty seems to restrict the public expression of views she must have deeply held. By upbringing and choice, Gowing was left-wing. Yet, her writing takes a vow of neutrality, or at least follows a style that relies upon narrative to speak for itself. It is well known that she, like Hancock, distrusted the unequal terms of engagement that defined the 'Special Relationship' with the United States, and her respect for liberal democracy was at times compromised by the conduct of British nuclear decision-making. Her message in *Independence and Deterrence*—and after—was that, by the decisions of a few, taken without consultation with the people, Britain had made itself hostage to a fortune that, for a time, seemed to favour membership in a nuclear club, that cost a great deal and guaranteed little. Regrettably for Britain, the price of admission was such that the country gained neither 'independence' nor a real deterrent. This was a conclusion Gowing did not wish, nor wished to see, but it was an outcome that few could deny. The missing 'third volume', with its apparent emphasis on 'interdependence', could perhaps have set the story straight, or at least have given it greater balance.

In the decades immediately before and after her early retirement, Gowing's health made serious new work difficult, if not impossible. As her illness became more widely known, her physical limitations, and her loss of memory, were accepted as a condition for which she bore no blame. The famous 'third volume' would no doubt have ensured her a more prestigious place in the pantheon. But a younger generation of scholars, having access to public records she fought hard to make available, has overtaken

[242] Trevor-Roper left at least five, possibly more. Worden, 'Hugh Redwald Trevor-Roper', p. 267.

her, and new questions are being put. The Cabinet Office Historical Series continues, if at a glacial pace that may prove too slow for the internet. Perhaps the high tide of official history, as Hancock knew it, has passed. But if so, the issues that Gowing took up have not lost their salience. Sixty years ago, in *British War Economy*, she and Hancock recalled Britain's struggle to overcome the consequences of policies that heavily burdened the nation, and poorly distributed its resources.[243] Gowing did not live to see the end of that struggle. Possibly, neither have we.

ROY MacLEOD
University of Sydney

Note. For information about Gowing and her family, I am greatly indebted to Mr Nicholas (Nik) Gowing; I am also grateful to Dr Tony Simcock, Archivist of the Museum of the History of Science, Oxford, for assistance with the Gowing Papers that are deposited there; and to Mr Michael Hughes for assistance with the Kurti Papers. The Gowing Papers, given specifically by Professor Gowing's instructions to the Museum, remain uncatalogued and difficult of access. They are an important source for the social history of science, for the history of Oxford, and for the history of British science and technology in Gowing's lifetime.

Correspondence from the Dacre Papers at Christ Church, Oxford, is cited by courtesy of the Literary Estate of Lord Dacre of Glanton. I would also like to thank Professor Blair Worden for giving me access to the letters of Trevor-Roper, and Dr Jim Davidson for sharing his insights into the relationship between Gowing and Sir Keith Hancock. For information about Gowing's life in Oxford, and her professional life in general, I wish to express my appreciation to Mr Robin Briggs, Professor W. H. Brock, Mr Charles Crombie, Professor Robert Fox, Professor A. Rupert Hall, Professor Peter Hennessy, Professor Mary Hesse, Dr Michael Hoskin, Professor Peter Mathias, Professor John North, Dr Gerard Turner, Dr Jerome Ravetz, Professor John Simpson, and Sir Keith Thomas.

Among Gowing's colleagues at Oxford, I would like to thank Ms Jeannine Alton, Mr Alan Chapman, Mr Rom Harré, Professor Robert O'Neill, Dr John Roche, Professor John Rowlandson, and Professor Charles Webster. Among Gowing's former students, may I include in my thanks: Dr Catherine Crawford, Dr Peter Morris, Professor Nicolaas Rupke, and Professor Paul Weindling. For assistance with records of the History Faculty, I am grateful to Ms Judith Muskett and Mr A. P. Weale. For their careful editorial assistance, I am indebted to Dr Kimberly Webber, of Sydney, to Peter Brown and Ron Johnston, and to all the British Academy Publications staff.

At Kent, my thanks go to Anne Miller of the Templeman Library. At Aldermaston, my thanks go to Ms Kate Pyne; at the University of East Anglia, Ms Bridget Gillies; at the Authority History Office (ARO), Harwell, Professor John Hendry, Mrs Margaret Gardiner, and Ms Sue Connell. For assistance in consulting Gowing's extensive records

[243] Gowing and Hancock, *British War Economy*, p. 555.

at the PRO (Kew) and at the Cabinet Office, I am indebted to a host of Records Officers, among whom Mr Stephen Twigg is deserving of special thanks. For Gowing's work with the Contemporary Scientific Archives Centre (CSAC), Bath, I am indebted to Professor Angus Buchanan and Dr Peter Harper. For their views on Gowing's contribution to nuclear history, I am grateful to Professor John Bayliss and Dr Richard Hewlett. Above all, I wish to express my deepest appreciation to Mrs Lorna Arnold, OBE, Gowing's closest colleague and co-author, together with my thanks for her kindness, encouragement, and patience during the preparation of this memoir.

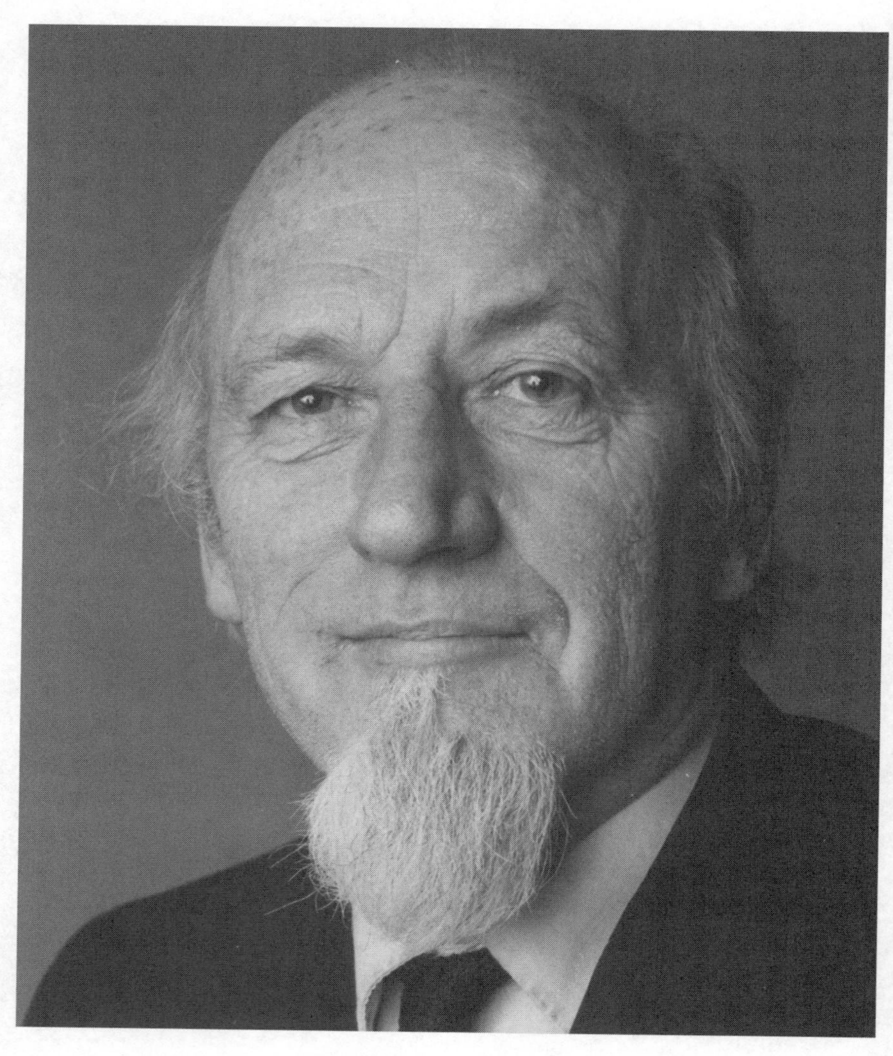

JOHN GRIFFITH

John Aneurin Grey Griffith
1918–2010

Life

John Aneurin Grey Griffith was born in Cardiff on 14 October 1918, shortly before the end of the First World War, to a Baptist minister, the Revd Benjamin Grey Griffith, and his wife Bertha. His first years were spent in Wales but the family later moved to London and he became a boarder at Taunton School in Somerset, where he played rugby for the school. From 1937 to 1940 he was a student at the London School of Economics (LSE), spending his final year in Cambridge, where the School spent its wartime, refugee days. Here he met his wife Barbara Williams, a student of economic history, whom he married in 1941. The marriage was both rich and long-lasting; it lasted seventy years. John died on 8 May 2010 and Barbara died a year later in May 2011. The three children of the marriage, Adam, Ben and his daughter Sarah, five grandchildren and three great-grandchildren, of whom he was inordinately fond and proud, all survive.

After the Second World War, John took a teaching job at the University College of Wales, Aberystwyth, where he spent two years, returning to the LSE in 1948 as lecturer. Despite some differences with Sir David Hughes-Parry, a long-standing Head of the Law Department, who frequently advised John to look elsewhere for a chair, John became Professor of English Law in 1959 and acceded to the Chair of Public Law in 1970. Aside from visiting professorships at the University of California at Berkeley in 1966 and York University, Toronto in 1985, John never left the LSE; on retirement in 1984, he had spent around forty years there. As he

Biographical Memoirs of Fellows of the British Academy, XI, 331–350.

himself said, 'When one has been in an institution this length of time, really one ought not to continue to be there unless one has a very considerable feeling of respect for the institution and also affection for the institution. I certainly have had that very strongly.'[1]

After his retirement, John was elected—much to his own surprise—as Chancellor of Manchester University. The post was contested and John had stood at the request of students and lecturers against the 'official' candidate, the Marchioness of Anglesey, believing his chances to be minimal. He took up his post with enthusiasm in 1986 and held it for seven years. John took his duties seriously, breaking with convention by attending council meetings, where he demonstrated his usual independence of mind in frequent challenges to the university establishment, becoming a 'thorn in the flesh of university managers'.[2]

There are some clues to all this in his background. John was Welsh and had a 'chapel background' and, although he lived for most of his life in England, these Welsh roots were very obvious. He was not and never wished to be a member of the English establishment. John's radical socialism was associated with the long tradition of dissent in this country; he was a natural dissenter and, despite his many successes, including election as a Fellow of the British Academy in 1977, he proudly remained and saw himself as an outsider. He enjoyed controversy, knew his own mind and was never afraid to stand alone and out from the crowd. He was proud of being Welsh, even though he left Cardiff with his parents in 1927. He was a strong supporter of the Welsh rugby team, always kept an eye on how Cardiff City FC was doing and enjoyed watching cricket. Norman Dorsen, a long-time friend and president of the American Civil Liberties Union, recalls of his time at LSE that John and he spent 'many an afternoon at Lord's drinking beer and deciding the fate of the world', an experience shared by law department colleagues and students and, no doubt, many others. Up until retirement, John spent a day annually at Lords with younger colleagues, preferably watching Test cricket.

In his obituary, Martin Loughlin called John 'a singular, often eloquent voice' and 'the last link with the radical socialist tradition that shaped the LSE in its founding years and exerted such influence over post-war politics'.[3] Less formally, John called himself 'A Labour Party person and all that.' There can be no doubt about John's devotion to the socialist

[1] In an interview with Richard Rawlings, recorded for an oral history of the School compiled in the context of the centenary in 1995.

[2] *Times Online Obituary*, 19 May 2010.

[3] M. Loughlin, 'John Griffith obituary', *The Guardian*, 25 May 2010.

cause, evidenced not only in his academic writings but also in a steady stream of contributions to the *New Statesman*, *Marxism Today* and the quality press. Michael Zander, an LSE colleague for many years, described him 'not just as a towering figure in the law department but as the quintessential LSE person: feisty, eloquent, controversial, scholarly, engaged. His was an independent and free spirit. And, with it, though deeply serious, he always seemed to have a twinkle about him.'[4] How well this captures John's highly individual and disputatious personality!

The Celts, as Nora Chadwick reminds us,[5] were the professional orators and demagogues of classical Rome, and John possessed the 'hwyl' to an extraordinary degree. The wit and eloquence of his lectures carried generations of students with him and permeates his writing. His literary and eclectic style was epitomised in 'The political constitution',[6] the Chorley Lecture delivered towards the end of his long LSE career in June 1978 and in some ways an *apologia* for his career and beliefs. The lecture is notable for the wide range of the reading on which it is based and contains in particular copious quotations from Paul Fussell's literary study of the 1914–18 war,[7] which he was then reading with enthusiasm and lending to colleagues.

The pity of war

The shadow of the First World War never left John, a fact recorded in 'The political constitution':

> For my generation, born during or immediately after [the First World War], the significance of that war cannot be overstated. We were brought up in the period of delayed shock which followed. And no doubt also in the penumbra of the images which began to merge as reflections of terrible events. These are not the same as myths, except in the Jungian sense. They are kind of impressions, of recollections, caught by those who wrote the later memoirs of the time ... [The] war of 1914–18 seriously damaged the concept of legitimate authority. Orders were being given which resulted in the death of tens of thousands to no purpose ... Faith in authority which, I suggest, is essential to the working of that form of government known as liberal democracy, was never recovered. And authority, not for the first time in history, was replaced by authoritarianism.[8]

4 Speech at the LSE *In memoriam* for John Griffith, hereafter *In memoriam*.

5 Nora Chadwick, *The Celts* (Harmondsworth, 1970).

6 J. A. G. Griffith, 'The political constitution' (1979) 42 *Modern Law Review* 1.

7 P. Fussell, *The Great War and Modern Memory* (Oxford, 1975)

8 'The political constitution', p. 4.

Significantly, at the start of the Second World War, John registered as a conscientious objector and served as a field ambulance-man in the Middle East; later, however, he applied for deregistration and went on to serve in the Indian army, an experience that left him with a deep affection for India and things Indian and a correspondingly deep disaffection for British colonialism. The Foreign Office files that came to light in 2011 implicating Britain in torture and inhumane treatment in colonial Kenya would not have surprised John, though he would certainly have been shocked by the combination of arrogance, secrecy and authoritarianism, all qualities he attributed to government.

Fussell's book had a double appeal for John, first because of Fussell's awareness of literature. What distinguished Fussell's book from other critical accounts of the world wars was, as a journalist later put it, its literary emphasis and clear nostalgia for a more literate age.[9] These were preoccupations John shared. He remarked somewhat ruefully that the First World War was the last time that everyone, officers and private soldiers, had in common the language of the King James Bible and Shakespeare. He certainly loved the rhythms of both, quoting by heart into old age reams of Shakespeare, Macaulay's *Lays of Ancient Rome* and other epic poems that he had learned in his youth, together with more modern poets, such as Peter Porter and his great love, W. H. Auden. Undergraduates were often badly thrown when tutorials took an unexpected turn from the intricacies of public law into these 'realms of gold'. In *Who's Who* John listed amongst his hobbies the writing of 'bad verse', a hobby he carried with typical irreverence into a review of a book in an academic journal written in vivid doggerel.[10] Whatever John wrote reads well and he took great care that it should. He was a wordsmith who used words with precision. For years he agonised whether to call the judges in the *Politics of the Judiciary* 'Conservative' as he thought them, or simply the more restrained 'conservative'. On other occasions, like many fine orators, he was carried away by the passion of his own rhetoric, a trait that unfortunately allowed his opponents to downplay his ideas.

The second appeal of Fussell's book lay in the fact that he set out to record the 'everyday texture of life at the front' and the appalling circumstances of the ordinary soldiers in their own language. Concern for the ordinary people who make up the building blocks of society infused all John's work and underpinned his view of the constitution. Squarely inside

[9] S. Rustin, 'Hello to all that', *The Guardian*, 31 July, 2004.

[10] J. Griffith, 'Review of *Poetic Justice*' (1948) 11 *Modern Law Review* 374.

the LSE tradition in which he worked, John believed with William Robson that

> [T]he great departments of state . . . are not only essential to the well being of the great mass of the people, but also the most significant expressions of democracy in our time. Considerations of this kind, however, could scarcely be expected to weigh with the predominantly upper middle class conservative legal mind.[11]

From this belief in the need for government strong enough to undertake much-needed political reform and redistribution of wealth sprang John's faith in the 'political constitution', which vested power in democratically elected governments rather than non-elected judges. To translate this into the language of political science—which John usually avoided—in a 'model of government' the checks on power come from within the political process, rather than, as in the 'model of law', from an autonomous and unelected judiciary, which both checks and balances the elected government.[12]

Realist empiricism

From his early days at the LSE, John had been trained in a realist or functionalist style of public law, working with Ivor Jennings and William Robson, later Professor of Public Administration at LSE. Jennings taught John as a first-year student and his elegant rebuttal of Dicey, *The Law and the Constitution*,[13] was later selected by John as the work that had most greatly influenced his student days. A further significant influence was a series of ten lectures on theories of law delivered at LSE in 1932 in which Jennings propounded the 'institutionalist' theory of law,[14] according to which the focus of administrative law should be the work of government departments, statutory authorities, public utilities, etc., rather than judicial decisions or individual rights. This was a formula to which much of John's work conformed. *Central Departments and Local Authorities*,[15] a book that attained classic status, was one of a handful of empirical studies by public lawyers. Basing himself on his study of housing policy and provision, John concluded that localism would come into conflict with the

[11] W. Robson, *Justice and Administrative Law*, 3rd edn. (London, 1951), p. 421.
[12] See M. J. C. Vile, *Constitutionalism and Separation of Powers* (Oxford, 1967).
[13] W. I. Jennings, *The Law and the Constitution* (London, 1933, rev. 1938, now 5th edn. 1959). And see J. Griffith, 'A pilgrim's progress' (1995) 22 *Journal of Law and Society* 410.
[14] W. I. Jennings (ed.), *Modern Theories of Law* (Oxford, 1933).
[15] J. A. G. Griffith, *Central Departments and Local Authorities* (London, 1966).

need for effective provision of housing, thus presaging modern debates over community, localism and central government as regulator.

Robson, for many years a colleague, was referred to by John as 'the master' and one of his two 'guiding spirits', the other being Jeremy Bentham. As John explained, the group's functionalist aim was to strip away the 'stage paraphernalia' used by the holders of political and economic power to screen their true motivation and expose the *reality* of political and economic power:

> We were not surprised to discover that the trappings of democracy concealed rather than adorned the body politic. But who was pulling the levers, where the levers were being pulled, who were the puppets and who the puppet-masters, these were questions to which we sought answers. We are still seeking them.[16]

The LSE motto, 'to find out the causes of things', exactly epitomises John's scholarly creed.

John's twin commitments to sceptical realism and to law as a social science permeated his teaching. He taught and worked closely with Professor George Jones in the LSE department of government, like John an authority on local government. In his own public law course, John simply invited his many friends, politicians, practising lawyers and academics to tell students 'what actually happens' by describing the jobs that they did. The result was random but fascinating, though it would in these days of evaluation and bite-sized learning—which John would certainly deplore—be thought very idiosyncratic. But John was content to trust students: 'the fact is that the students who come to LSE are on the whole very, very, good students; they are very competent people. They wouldn't have got to LSE unless they were pretty intelligent characters.' He was in fact a fine teacher, who devoted a great deal of his time to helping, talking to and drawing the best out of students to whom he was devoted and saw as an 'inspiration'. But he was modest about his contribution: 'you have them for three years as undergraduates and the great joy, I think, of being a university teacher, is that you can see how they can develop over those three years. You mustn't claim much credit for it because they are going to develop between the ages of 18 and 21 anyway. But at least you can see the way in which they do develop.'[17]

[16] 'The political constitution', p. 5.
[17] Interview with Richard Rawlings, see above, n. 1.

Functionalist administrative law

The realist method also marks the student textbook designed as 'a compact introduction to administrative law', co-authored with Harry Street. The Preface introduced a further element of John's academic credo. Law and politics are holistic and should never be treated as discrete subjects of study; law is, in other words, a component part of the social sciences:

> We have tried to emphasise throughout how limited a view of law or politics or public administration is obtained if any one of these social sciences is surveyed to the exclusion of the others. It is not so much that the study of one is incomplete without reference to the others, but rather that the landscape is single and entire. There are not different views to be seen, but only different viewers with variously adjusted blinkers.[18]

John's views on judicial review, which became a central theme in his later work, were shaped by his view of himself as a 'new positivist'. John did not advocate the abolition of judicial review, insisting that:

> ... those who rule must be subject to the rule of law. It is this last principle that is crucial to the preservation of any measure of liberty and to the control of Governments. This is not to denigrate political checks on power, but such checks are greatly strengthened by the insistence that all governmental activity which encroaches on the rights of the individual must have a firm basis in rules of law.[19]

John believed that judicial discretion was too wide and wanted to see it confined to cases where public authorities acted outside their statutory powers (*ultra vires* in the classical sense of the term) or had violated rules of procedure laid down by or under statute in accordance with natural justice. His sympathies lay with the formalist tradition of judges like Lord Greene MR, in his celebrated '*Wednesbury* unreasonableness' test of the ambit of ministerial discretion;[20] or Lord Morris of Borth-y-Gest, dissenting in *Padfield's* case on the ground that the statutory language was clear and unambiguous and did not lend itself to judicial interpretation.[21] To put this differently, John hoped to see judicial review limited to Lord Wilberforce's category of 'narrow ultra vires' as distinct from 'principles of administrative law',[22] which he saw essentially as 'invented' by the judiciary.

[18] J. A. G. Griffith and H. Street, *Principles of Administrative Law* (London, 1963).

[19] T. C. Hartley and J. A. G. Griffith, *Government and Law*, 2nd edn. (London, 1981), p. 8.

[20] *Associated Provincial Picture Houses v Wednesbury Corporation* [1948] 1 KB 223. For Griffith's assessment of Lord Greene, see J. Griffith, *Judicial Politics since 1920: a Chronicle* (Oxford, 1993), pp. 51–7.

[21] *Padfield v Minister of Agriculture, Fisheries and Food* [1968] AC 997.

[22] *Bromley London Borough Council v Greater London Council* [1983] 1 AC 126.

Parliament should intervene to structure judicial discretion by providing 'more positive, black-letter provision by statute which will define where the balance of public interest lies'. Express provision as to justiciability should be made in new legislation and clearer directions as to where power was in the last resort to lie. But John was not particularly sanguine about the outcome, being generally 'pessimistic about the possibilities of progressive legal change':[23]

> In our system for two principal reasons, the judiciary have a wide scope for the making of political decisions. First, statute law does not seek with any precision to indicate where, between Ministers and judges, final decision making should lie. Secondly, judges themselves, in the common law tradition of judicial creativity, frequently invent or re-discover rules of law which enable them to intervene and to exercise political judgment in areas that hitherto had been understood to be outside their province. In the event, for these two reasons, legislators and Ministers and public authorities are continuously being surprised to discover that, in the view of the judges, they do not have the powers they thought they had.[24]

Judges and politics

The double disagreement over the function of the state in modern society and the balance of power in modern governance occupied John greatly and in his later years brought him into dispute with influential and articulate members of the judiciary. It is for *The Politics of the Judiciary*, mischievously called by John his 'little book', that he is best known outside academic circles. He both hoped and foresaw that it would prove controversial. Written in a series part-edited by political scientist Professor Bernard Crick, a long-standing colleague and friend, the book's preface acknowledges the help of (amongst others) Crick, Ralph Miliband and Lord Wedderburn—a clear indication of the stable from which his ideas came and of those with whom he shared them. *The Politics of the Judiciary* exposes in entirely accessible style and language the relationship between the judiciary and politics, examining in some detail the way that judges had dealt with political cases that came before them. John defined 'political' loosely to cover 'cases which arise out of controversial legislation or controversial action initiated by public authorities, or which touch impor-

[23] M. Loughlin, *Public Law and Political Theory* (Oxford, 1992), p. 197.
[24] J. A. G. Griffith, 'Constitutional and administrative law', in P. Archer and A. Martin (eds.), *More Law Reform Now* (Chichester, 1983), p. 55.

tant moral or social issues'. The core argument was that members of the judiciary formed a class 'broadly homogeneous in character' which, faced with 'political' cases, would act in broadly similar ways. This added up to 'a unifying attitude of mind, a political position, which is primarily concerned to protect and conserve certain values and institutions'. His case was *not*—though it was widely supposed to be—that judges belonged to a particular political party or invariably supported the government; it was that judges were 'protectors and conservators of what has been, of the relationships and interests on which, in their view, our society is founded. They do not regard their role as radical or even reformist, only (on occasion) corrective.'[25]

Had the argument stopped there, it might have been seen as largely non-contentious, but of course it did not. The book tackled several controversial issues, including the background and social position of the judiciary, the antiquated appointments system, the judges' extrajudicial activities in chairing commissions and inquiries, and their legislative role. The chosen case-studies of industrial relations, social security, student affairs and race relations were contentious. They were suggestive of an anti-left-wing bias on the part of the judges and the implication was that a left-wing attempt to curtail individual freedoms would meet with more immediate judicial opposition than a right-wing attempt.[26] A further three chapters strongly critical of the way judges dealt with civil liberties undercut their claim to be the rock on which freedoms were founded; judges did not by and large stand out as protectors of liberty, of the rights of man or of the underprivileged. Judicial views of the public interest were not the views of the extreme right but they could be seen as 'reactionary conservatism'. This conservatism did not necessarily follow the day-to-day political policies of the party currently associated with that name but it did nonetheless add up to a political philosophy.[27]

Twenty years later, after a decade in which the judges had regularly annulled decisions of right-wing Conservative politicians, these conclusions were rewritten in the fifth edition to blunt charges of political prejudice. Judges were still said to be the product of a particular limited class with the characteristics of that class, which would naturally incline them always to uphold the status quo but the judiciary was expressly absolved of 'a conscious and deliberate intention to pursue their own interests and

[25] J. A. G. Griffith, *The Politics of the Judiciary* (London, 1977), pp. 7–8.

[26] Ibid., p. 208.

[27] Ibid., pp. 212–13.

the interests of their class'. It remained the case that only occasionally had 'the power of the supreme judiciary been exercised in the positive assertion of fundamental values' and part of their 'present robustness' was clearly attributable to an effort 'to maintain their position as part of established authority' and 'to regain what status they have lost'.[28] It was, however:

> idle to criticize institutions for performing the task they were created to perform and have performed for centuries. The principal function of the judiciary is to support the institutions of government as established by law. To expect a judge to advocate radical change is absurd.[29]

This conclusion, which presumably represents John's final position, moves the argument to a more constitutional level, where the judges would be further engaged.

Rights talk

John had previously sparred with Lord Hailsham on the subject of rights, increasingly invoked by members of the judiciary—and notably Lord Scarman in his Hamlyn lecture series[30]—as a platform for an extended role. Shortly before his appointment as Margaret Thatcher's Lord Chancellor, Lord Hailsham—later described by John as a 'highly political holder of the office'[31]—had published *The Dilemma of Democracy*,[32] a book that advocated a comprehensive package of constitutional reforms. Lord Hailsham saw modern Britain as an 'elective dictatorship' in which the executive dominated Parliament and deprived it of all effective power of scrutiny. His projected reforms were designed to introduce 'limited government'; he would end parliamentary sovereignty, introduce a second chamber elected by proportional representation, and a written Bill of Rights. In 'The political constitution', John riposted with an attack on the whole rights movement. In courts of law, arguments over rights were couched in legalistic jargon designed to disguise their political nature, the effect being to exclude the general public from the debate and 'fob off' attempts at necessary reform. Law was not and should never be a substitute for politics and political decisions should be taken by politicians, which 'in our society

[28] J. A. G. Griffith, *The Politics of the Judiciary*, 5th edn. (London, 1997), pp. 338–42.
[29] Ibid., p. 343.
[30] Sir Leslie Scarman, *English Law—the New Dimension* (London, 1974).
[31] *The Politics of the Judiciary*, p. xiv.
[32] Lord Hailsham, *The Dilemma of Democracy: Diagnosis and Prescription* (London, 1978).

means by people who are removable'.[33] Famously—but to many infamously—John redefined rights as 'political claims', ending his lecture with his usual flair for controversy:

> As an individual I may say that I have certain rights—the right to life being the most fundamental. But those who manage the society in which I live will reply 'Put up your claim and we will look at it. Don't ring us, we'll ring you.'
>
> In this political, social sense there are no over-riding human rights. No right to freedom, to trial before conviction, to representation before taxation. No right not to be tortured, not to be summarily executed. Instead there are political claims by individuals and groups.[34]

This passage was designed to shock and shock it did. It was one thing to assert that arguments from rights allowed questions of politics or economics to be 'presented as questions of law'. The question of overlap between socio-economic rights and public policy is and remains a highly debatable question and one which has survived the passage of the Human Rights Act in 1998. But to call the right to life a 'claim' that could be defeated by 'those who manage society' went too far and seemed to position John with 'those in authority' whom he had most stubbornly opposed. This was not his intention. He wished only to stress that adopting the language of rights not only meant changing the nature of the debate but was also a way of disguising a change that would have the practical effect of shifting controversial decisions over policy from the political to a judicial forum. John who, as an active socialist, had participated in a post-war political revolution, which had engineered a substantial transfer of resources to the poor and underprivileged, regarded the judiciary as a protector of property and the status quo. He was never open to the counter-argument put forward by human rights lawyers that the establishment of a 'right' in a court of law could act as a springboard for, rather than a barrier against, reform. Not unnaturally, he did not foresee the halfway-house solution of the Human Rights Act which, with the innovative 'declaration of incompatibility', leaves parliamentary sovereignty intact.

John's encounter with Sir John Laws, who had argued in a series of articles that the judges were custodians of moral values, defenders of rights and of the constitution,[35] dragged him onto metaphysical terrain where he least liked to be. John espoused Bentham's view of rights as

[33] 'The political constitution', p. 16.

[34] Ibid., p. 17.

[35] Sir John Laws, 'Law and democracy' [1995] *Public Law* 72; 'The constitution: morals and rights' [1996] *Public Law* 622; 'Is the High Court the guardian of fundamental constitutional rights?' [1993] *Public Law* 59.

'nonsense on stilts',[36] and thought the very idea of a 'community morality', on which judges often relied to legitimate their discretionary decision-making,[37] 'nonsense at the top of a very high ladder'.[38] Society, he insisted, was inherently disputatious and there could be no fixed consensus over morality. The term 'community morality' simply covered the collective, or sometimes individual, ethos of judges, which he had tried to expose in *The Politics of the Judiciary*.

Was it perhaps paradoxical that John, who believed so strongly in the fusion of law and politics, believed with equal fervour that law and morality must be severed? Like Bentham, he derided the idea of natural law, presenting himself as a pragmatic 'new positivist', whose views derived from the sociological school of Comte, Durkheim and the French constitutional lawyer, Léon Duguit. Duguit, whose works John had read 'avidly' in his youth, presented 'the nearest thing to a solid, positivist, unmetaphysical, non-natural foundation for analytical jurisprudence' that he knew of.[39] It followed that he would find Sir John's thesis of a 'higher-order law', which could not be abrogated by government legislation and of which the judges were trustees, extremely unpalatable; it set the judiciary above Parliament and did so on the basis of 'mythology'. Sweeping aside Sir William Wade as a 'pantomime horse', John declared that the judges, when claiming a power of judicial review, which was 'of their own making and owe[d] nothing to statute', would be wise to accord a similar autonomy to Parliament.[40] The judges could not single-handed set aside the constitutional settlement that rested on history and 'political realities'; their claims amounted to a 'take-over bid' which might, if it failed, devalue the reputation and trustworthiness of the judiciary.[41] The forthright argument and robust language, typical of John, did little to endear him to his opponents.

[36] 'Anarchical fallacies', in J. Bowring (ed.), *The Works of Jeremy Bentham* (Edinburgh, 1838–43, vol. 2, 1843).

[37] See the celebrated Hart/Devlin debate: H. L. A. Hart, *Law, Liberty and Morality* (Oxford, 1963); Sir Patrick Devlin, *The Enforcement of Morals* (Oxford, 1965).

[38] 'The political constitution', p. 11.

[39] Ibid., p. 6.

[40] J. A. G. Griffith, 'Judges and the constitution', in R. Rawlings (ed.), *Law, Society and Economy* (Oxford, 1997); 'The brave new world of Sir John Laws' (2000) 63 *Modern Law Review* 159; 'The common law and the constitution' (2001) 117 *Law Quarterly Review* 42.

[41] 'Judges and the constitution', p. 306.

Constitutionalism, responsibility and accountability

John engaged Sir Stephen Sedley on the high ground of the constitution over the issue of sovereignty. Sedley's argument, that 'the rule of law recognises two sovereignties, not one and not three',[42] distressed John by its implication that 'the institution of Government is declared to be not sovereign, but subordinate to the courts and to Parliament'.[43] This thesis, in John's view both ahistorical and at variance with the actual constitution, was, he thought, yet another argument to justify and promote further expansion of judicial power. Ministerial government in the sense that government could largely control proceedings in Parliament was the 'heart of the style of our present system of parliamentary democracy'. Government was neither theoretically nor otherwise 'subordinate' to Parliament; the two institutions were interlocked in 'a complexity of powers and relationships which together make the machinery of the state':

> [T]o deny the sovereignty of one or other of the three major institutions is to deny that complexity of the constitution which is its peculiar strength. If the definition of sovereignty is that it lies with that institution which has 'the last word' then Government is sovereign not only in its own role (the part it plays in the working Constitution) but also in relation to other institutions.

It was not that John put great trust in governments. In 'The political constitution' he firmly asserted that 'my distrust of governments and of the claims made by those in authority is as profound as any man's and more profound than most.'[44] It cannot be too often reiterated that John saw government—and indeed, society generally—as inherently authoritarian. But there was a dichotomy in his beliefs. On the one hand he was convinced of the need for imaginative and effective government, the 'great departments of state' theme; on the other, he was deeply sceptical of authority and its capacity for lapsing into authoritarianism. Moreover, as he attempted to show in *The Politics of the Judiciary*, he saw the judiciary as part of the establishment, inclined by temperament to side with those in authority and not particularly amenable to 'claims' from underprivileged sections of society. Positively, he believed firmly in the responsibility and accountability not only of ministers but of all public figures—including judges. Thus, along with the colleagues with whom he worked and

[42] Sir Stephen Sedley, 'The sound of silence: constitutional law without a constitution' (1994) 110 *Law Quarterly Review* 270.
[43] 'The common law and the constitution', pp. 45 and 50.
[44] 'The political constitution', p. 16.

fraternised at the LSE, he looked for controls inside, and not separate from, the democratic process.

Throughout his writing, John emphasised the need for a free and powerful press, for access to information and open government. The dangers lay not in an 'elective dictatorship',

> not in the powers of minority governments, not in the sovereignty of Parliament as the legislative institution, but in the prosecution of investigative journalism ... Excessive legislation does not seem to me to be where the dangers lie. The dangers are in excessive administration designed to limit criticism and to protect governments.[45]

We cannot know whether he would have agreed with political scientist Geoffrey Marshall (a longstanding friend and member of the editorial board of *Public Law*, which John edited for twenty-five years) that 'the most obvious and undisputed convention of the British constitutional system is that Parliament does not use its unlimited sovereign power in an oppressive or tyrannical way'.[46] His position on constitutional convention was equivocal and hard to understand. Speaking of the convention that a government defeated in an election must resign and cede power to the victors, he starts out confidently but begins to sound uncertain, even a little puzzled:

> That new government is recognized by everyone as having legal authority to govern. This is because such a transfer of power is, as we say, constitutional and, in that sense, legal. In our constitution there is no document which lays down the principle that power may be properly so transferred from one group to another. But an unwritten constitution is still a constitution. Such transference of power is part of 'the set-up'. It is one of the basic rules which all political parties accept. It is how the game is played. And we speak of the law of the constitution as including these basic rules. So we say that the transference is 'lawful' because it follows the recognized practice. Yet this is a misleading identification of 'law' and 'practice', for we shall see that there are many constitutional practices which are denied this legal status; that the distinction between law and practice is regarded by many writers as fundamental; and that the courts themselves recognize this distinction. 'Law' in this context is therefore a word used in two different ways. First, there are some, very few, practices which are so fundamental to the working of the constitution that they are recognized as providing the absolutely basic framework ... But the fundamental practices derive their authority from nowhere; or, if you prefer, from the constitution itself, from the set-up.[47]

[45] 'The political constitution', p. 18. See also 'Official secrets and open government', in J. A. G. Griffith, *Public Rights and Private Interests* (Trivandrum, 1981); 'The Official Secrets Act 1989' (1989) *Journal of Law and Society* 273.

[46] G. Marshall, *Constitutional Conventions* (Oxford, 1984), p. 8.

[47] Hartley and Griffith, see above, n. 19, pp. 5–6.

This somewhat tentative passage seems at one and the same time to confirm John's celebrated aphorism that the 'constitution is what happens'—a polemical metaphor that earned him the undeserved reputation amongst his opponents of an anti-constitutionalist who thought in terms only of political expediency—but also to undercut it by suggesting that some parts of what happens are more lawful and constitutional than others.

In actual fact, John always argued for a reformed and strengthened Parliament and put in solid work together with members of the Study of Parliament Group, a group made up of parliamentary officials and academics with a special interest in Parliament. He published two important studies of Parliament, which gained great respect. The first, a meticulous study of parliamentary scrutiny of legislation, has been described by Meg Russell, a younger reformist, as a 'classic text'.[48] John once more set out to clear the ground by establishing *facts* but he was not one to blind himself to unwelcome truths. Hostile in principle, as might be expected, to the hereditary and unelected House of Lords, he did not draw back from the conclusion that the House of Lords was the best scrutinising body for legislation.

John's second book on Parliament was co-authored with Michael Ryle, Clerk of Committees to the House of Commons.[49] It again epitomises the realist academic method. On the one hand, the authors aimed to provide an accessible alternative to Erskine May's great work on parliamentary practice and a successor to Jennings's now outdated study of Parliament;[50] on the other to show how parliamentary procedures are used by the three main participants—Government, Opposition and backbenchers—'as tools for political purposes'. Robert Blackburn records disagreements between the two authors, attributable to their different temperaments: 'Michael Ryle was a great optimist, things are going to get better with Parliament. John was fairly gloomy, nothing ever changes etc.'[51]

[48] J. A. G. Griffith, *Parliamentary Scrutiny of Public Bills* (London, 1974). The citation is from M. Russell, 'Bicameral parliamentary scrutiny of Government Bills: a case study of the Identity Cards Bill', *Political Studies*, 58 (2010), 866–85.

[49] J. A. G. Griffith and M. Ryle, *Parliament: Functions, Practices and Procedures* (London, 1989). The quotation is from the preface to the 1st edition.

[50] Erskine May's *Parliamentary Practice* (London, 2011); I. W. Jennings, *Parliament* (Cambridge, 1939).

[51] Rob Blackburn, *In memoriam*.

The scholarly record

Shortly before his death, John's contribution began to be evaluated by a younger generation of academic writers, schooled in a more conceptual and normative approach to public law than John's mainly positivist generation. From such an angle, failure to ground the model of the political constitution in theory or to explain the norms and values on which it was founded is a defect. Unsurprisingly, Adam Tomkins criticises John's work for its descriptive character and the very atheoretical emphasis on fact and reality that John saw as the major contribution of sociological positivism to public law.[52] His omission to explore diverse meanings of the term 'political' has also attracted some criticism. For Graham Gee and Grégoire Webber, however, this is not a problem:

> [I]n neither ['The Political Constitution'] nor his writings more generally did Griffith purport to grapple with the question 'what is a political constitution?', perhaps because he never conceived of it as anything distinct or separate from the British constitution itself. Rather, Griffith's contribution was to offer what was, in 1978, a novel account of Britain's constitutional arrangements and, for some, a faintly disturbing account of what he took to be the distinctively political character of the constitution. Through this, Griffith laid the foundations for the emergence of the idea of a political constitution as a fresh and provocative way of thinking and talking about the British constitution. To be clear, the novelty of his lecture lay less in making claims not found in his previous scholarship or in describing the British constitution as distinctively political; rather, the novelty was in bringing claims (and aphorisms) present in his earlier scholarship together into a reading of the British constitution that was political inasmuch as it was characterized by conflict, disagreement, messiness and chaos—a reading that was fresh, provocative, even unsettling for some.[53]

Thomas Poole calls 'The political constitution' 'one of the key texts of late twentieth-century British public law scholarship' and the 'founding text of an influential style of public law thinking'. For Poole, Griffith's contribution lies in his consistent 'positivist debunking' of constitutional mythology. And Poole puts his finger unerringly on the reason why 'The political constitution' continues to resonate: it is 'brilliantly constructed: concise, punchy, provocative and, above all, candid almost to a fault'.[54] Its capacity to aggravate has not declined but, however much one dislikes John's ideological

[52] A. Tomkins, *Our Republican Constitution* (Oxford, 2005), pp. 36–40.

[53] G. Gee and G. Webber, 'What is a political constitution?' (2010) 30 *Oxford Journal of Legal Studies* 273.

[54] T. Poole, 'Tilting at windmills? Truth and illusion in "The political constitution"' (2007) 70 *Modern Law Review* 250.

standpoint, it is hard to forget 'The political constitution' and its brilliant aphorisms.

The activist

If, as close friends testify, John had 'a streak of melancholy due perhaps to his high expectations of achieving real change, and feelings of impotence when nothing much happened',[55] this did not mean that he did not try to make things happen. He was something of a 'mover and shaker'. Throughout his career, he supported a robust and autonomous free-thinking university system. He was a founder member of the Council for Academic Freedom and Democracy (CAFD, later CAFAS) and gave generously of his time in helping academics who found themselves at odds with the university establishment. In 2005, for example, a group of Swansea academics publicised the fact that the university had awarded some fifty MA degrees without the Examination Board reading the dissertations or even troubling to meet. Colwyn Williamson, a well-respected philosophy lecturer and founder member of CAFAS, was one of the main authors of a complaint to the University Visitor. When he was dismissed on charges of 'vilification and denigration' and of hacking into the university computer system, John stepped in to defend him. Williamson recalls John's unstinting support: he 'represented us throughout and devoted a substantial chunk of three years of his life fighting to prevent Swansea sacking us'.[56]

John felt very strongly that lawyers owed a particular duty towards those who were victimised by public or private power especially when the law was obscure or arcane. This helps to explain the sometimes puzzling role that he played in the LSE 'Troubles' of 1966/7, one of the School's most controversial episodes.[57] On the appointment of Walter Adams as Director, students protested through letters and at meetings. The authorities reacted high-handedly with disciplinary proceedings, resulting in the suspension of the President of the Students' Union, who was subsequently cleared by a Board of Discipline. Further disciplinary proceedings followed, however, after the death of a porter from heart failure while controlling a

[55] Judith Chernaik, *In memoriam*.

[56] Colwyn Williamson, *In memoriam*.

[57] A concise account of 'The Troubles' is given by Lord Dahrendorf in R. Dahrendorf, *A History of the London School of Economics and Political Science 1895–1995* (Oxford, 1995), pp. 443–75.

crowd of students protesting at the intransigent banning of a meeting by the School authorities. Concerned at the 'incompetence and paternalism' of the authorities and their 'lack of comprehension' of the students' viewpoint, John tried to act as mediator and also acted as counsel for the students in the disciplinary proceedings. Where his sympathies really lay is not entirely clear; probably, like many who were involved, he had mixed feelings. At the heart of the dispute lay questions of authority and issues of governance, involving openness on the part of the School authorities and participation by the student body in the affairs of the School. These were issues of importance and principle on which John had always held strong views. But John undoubtedly loved a fight, relishing rebellion and challenges to authority. As Richard Kuper, a student who participated in the Troubles, put it:

> He loved the fact that we did things, that we challenged, that we took on the School, even if, as I said, he didn't always agree with what we were doing. Sometimes I'm sure he thought we were quite mad, but that didn't stop him from kind of valuing the fact that we were trying to make sense of the world, and trying to change the world, and trying to change it in ways that he valued and respected.[58]

In a different sort of fight, John's expertise in local government proved pivotal. In 1957, he became aware of plans to demolish Marlow's famous Grade I listed suspension bridge over the Thames completed by William Tierney Clark in 1832 and to replace it with a concrete bridge of two or four carriageways. John sprang into action. The Marlow Bridge Preservation Society was formed and in 1961, after a hard fight in which John was a fully engaged participant, the bridge was saved and remains in place today. Again in 1993, John and a small group of Marlow Society members pushed the executive committee into opposing a proposal to build a Tesco superstore in the heart of Marlow. Armed with the result of a privately organised poll of Marlow Society members, which showed that over 90 per cent opposed the plan, the group persuaded the committee to reverse its position and fight the District Council, which finally refused planning permission for the Tesco proposal. History was repeated in 2006 when Waitrose applied to build an inappropriately sized new supermarket in the heart of Marlow's conservation area. This time a 'parish poll' was organised, which showed beyond any doubt the degree of opposition to the application. Again the council was persuaded to turn down the planning

[58] Richard Kuper, *In memoriam.*

application. So John left a very permanent mark on the landscape of Marlow. His long experience of local government and deep knowledge of local government law undoubtedly stood the protestors in good stead. He had represented Marlow, where he lived for over fifty years, on Buckinghamshire County Council from 1955 to 1961. On his retirement, Councillor Venner, Chairman of the Council, said:

> We have from time to time disagreed with him, but if honesty, strength of purpose, and courage to hold a predetermined course, regardless of the opinion of others, constitute grounds for respecting the character of a public man, then I regard John Griffith as one of the most conscientious men I have met in public life.[59]

The tribute is endorsed in a different context by Lord Dahrendorf, Director of the LSE. He described John as 'the conscience of the School and guardian of its tradition in critical times' and wrote in his official *History* of the School that John's 'devotion to the LSE was great, which made his criticism of School policy all the more weighty. Those who were exasperated by him may not have realized his indispensable contribution to the sanity of LSE.'[60] It has to be said that 'the School' was not always grateful, sometimes viewing John as a maverick, accusing him of bringing the School into disrepute, or christening him the 'Professor of Law and Disorder'. John, who saw dispute as an essential element in society, would not have been unduly worried!

John hated fuss. He refused a retirement party; as Michael Zander, then Convenor of the Law Department, recalls, 'we had a boat party going down the Thames because John refused absolutely to countenance anything with speeches'. He refused the formal Festschrift that he so much merited; instead, a group of friends got together surreptitiously to publish a set of essays 'as a small gift from a few of the people who share John Griffith's interests and have enjoyed talking and working with him'.[61] He refused the request from his old friend Cyril Glasser to be allowed to organise a party at LSE to celebrate John's eightieth birthday. His family was all-important to him and his son Ben recalls total love, keen interest in his children's intellectual development, support, comfort and reassuring advice that was calming and sensible. But he was also unusual in giving his complete and absolute support to people in trouble who needed legal

[59] Quoted by Adam Griffith, *In memoriam.*

[60] Dahrendorf, *History*, see above, n. 57, p. 455.

[61] C. Harlow (ed.), *Public Law and Policy* (London, 1986), p. v.

and other support—political, personal or social. He was a warm and generous friend who could always be relied upon to give good, sympathetic advice and a devoted teacher, who dedicated much time to his students for whom it was a coveted privilege and an honour to be invited to his home at Marlow for the afternoon. This is how he would like to be remembered.

CAROL R. HARLOW
London School of Economics

RUPERT HALL AND MARIE BOAS HALL AT THEIR RETIREMENT IN 1980

Alfred Rupert Hall
1920–2009

Marie Boas Hall
1919–2009

THIS MEMOIR, perhaps unusually for the British Academy, is essentially a love story. It is set against the war of 1939–45, the Cold War and the threat of nuclear annihilation, the decline of British imperial power, the cultural arguments that consequently arose, and the post-1945 growth of academia including the establishment of the new discipline of the history of science which would contribute significantly to our understanding of the nature of scientific knowledge and its various relations with society and culture.

Unlike many love affairs that are conducted across continents and between individuals from radically different backgrounds, this one had a happy conclusion for the two principal figures involved, albeit with a period of considerable pain and unhappiness. In September 1957 Marie Boas, who came from a New England academic family, and Rupert Hall, who belonged to a family of shoemakers in the English Midlands but, by then a Fellow of Christ's College, Cambridge, fell in love with an intensity that came as a shock to them both.

This memoir will first trace their separate and rather different lives for the nearly forty years before that event and then move on to their lives and work thereafter which became so inextricably linked that it would be pointless, indeed repetitious, even to attempt to disentangle them. Indeed without their intimate relationship the landscape of the history of science during the past half century would have been very different in a number of respects, including publications and the training of the next generations of historians of science.[1]

Rupert Hall

Background, early life and education

On Hall's mother's side, her grandfather, Thomas Ritchie (*c.*1833–1917), a draper born in Ayrshire, had moved to Stoke-on-Trent by 1856 when he married Margaret McLellan (*c.*1830–98), born in Dumfriesshire. One of their sons, Andrew (*c.*1859–1931), continued in the drapery trade and at the time of his marriage in 1883 to Janet Ferguson (1856–1943) was a travelling draper. Their eldest daughter, Margaret (1885–1961), married into the Hall family of shoemakers who had lived in Staffordshire since the early nineteenth century. William Cade Hall (*c.*1852–1919) worked and lived in Stafford and in 1874 married Eliza Dawson. They had six children most of whom also worked in the shoe trade. Their third child, Alfred Dawson Hall (1879–1961), married Margaret Ritchie in June 1911 in the Wesleyan Chapel in Basford located between Stoke-on-Trent and Newcastle-under-Lyme, close to the Wedgwood pottery works at Etruria. By then he had risen to the position of foreman in a Norwich shoe factory and later moved into shoe sales. The peripatetic nature of this role presumably explains why his children were born in different towns—Doreen Janet (1913–72), later a musician, in Norwich, and Enid Catherine (1915–64), later a nurse, in Leicester. He served in the army during the Great War and it seems possible that his wife returned to her family for the duration, which

[1] The papers of Hall and Boas Hall are in the archives of Imperial College. As they have yet to be sorted or catalogued, they are simply cited here as IC MS Hall. Both wrote a number of autobiographical reminiscences, some of which were published. Their unpublished accounts, mostly it appears written in the 1990s, exist in typescript in the archives of Imperial College and the British Academy. For Hall they are (1) 'Biographical Notes', (2) 'How I became an Historian of Science and the Author of Books A Sidelight on the Twentieth Century' and (3) 'An account of Alfred Rupert Hall Litt.D. F.B.A.'. For Boas Hall they are (1) 'Marie Boas Hall A Brief Autobiography' and (2) 'How the partnership of Hall & Hall came into existence The Junior partner's tale'. These are cited as Hall or Boas Hall, followed by the number. Also in 1993 Scott Mandelbrote interviewed the Halls on two occasions which formed the basis for his 'A. Rupert Hall', *Metascience*, 1994, issue 5, pp. 64–84 which on pp. 77–84 contains a significantly shortened and edited version of the interviews. However, a transcript of the entire interviews is in All Souls College MS LX.2.6 [Box 1] 0 and is cited as Mandelbrote interview.

would explain why Alfred Rupert (though he never used Alfred) was born at 8 Victoria Street, Basford, on 26 July 1920.[2]

Hall first attended May Bank Infants' School in Newcastle until 1928 when the family moved to Leicester, which also had a large shoemaking industry. It is not known which primary school he attended in Leicester, but he passed the scholarship examination and in 1931 entered Alderman Newton's School, 'not the most fashionable grammar school in Leicester',[3] but it did have strong connections with Christ's College, Cambridge. Hall's mathematics teacher, Tom Pickering (1907–2000), and his physics teacher, H. S. Hoff (1910–2002, better known as the novelist William Cooper), had both been taught at Christ's by the ex-Newtonian Charles Snow (1905–80) who was originally a chemist before becoming a novelist, civil servant and pundit. Indeed Snow's brother was in the sixth form when Hall entered the school.[4] Such connections had improved the quality of the school compared to when Snow had been a pupil and laboratory assistant there (between 1916 and 1925) and were to prove decisive for Hall. Hoff became a significant figure in Hall's schooling since he interested him in the theory and practice of wireless, a very popular hobby in the 1930s. In his early teens Hall made his own wireless sets, bought books such as *The Admiralty Handbook of Wireless Telegraphy* (first published in 1925) and subscribed to *Amateur Wireless*.[5] Nevertheless, Hall later thought that had the teaching of science been better, he might well have become a scientist.[6]

But perhaps the most influential teacher on Hall was the head of history, Herbert 'Bert' Howard (1900–63). Clearly a quite remarkable and inspirational teacher, Snow modelled the character George Passant on him in his *Strangers and Brothers* novel sequence.[7] Howard would ask his pupils to answer absurd questions such as 'Which was the bigger fish: the Habsburg or the herring?'[8] Each year Howard selected the six brightest pupils when they entered the school at the age of eleven and then guided them through their time there. By this mentoring during his forty years at the school his pupils obtained thirty-nine awards from Cambridge alone.[9]

[2] Sources for this paragraph are Hall (1), p. 1, the General Register Office records of births, marriages and deaths and the ten yearly census from 1841 to 1911 in The National Archives.

[3] Hall (1), p. 1.

[4] Hall (3), p. 2.

[5] Hall (3), p. 12 and (2), pp. 6–7.

[6] Mandelbrote interview, p. 3.

[7] C. P. S[now], 'Mr. H. E. Howard', *The Times*, 15 Nov. 1963, p. 21, col. b.

[8] Hall (3), p. 8.

[9] Neil McKendrick, conversation with FJ, 21 Oct. 2011.

These included at least three other distinguished historians besides Hall ('conscious all my life of a real indebtedness to Bert'[10]): Jack Plumb (1911–2001, FBA 1968), Neil McKendrick, and Peter Bowler (FBA 2004). Although Hall and Plumb, whose social backgrounds were remarkably similar,[11] had lived only 200 yards apart, and indeed their mothers knew each other as Tory activists, they first met only in 1935 in Howard's house;[12] thereafter they socialised quite frequently when they were in Leicester.[13]

Howard played a crucial role in ensuring that Hall won an Open Minor Scholarship to read history at Christ's College. The competition, held in December 1937, Hall described as 'gladiatorial'.[14] Neither Sidney Grose (1886–1980, who would be his tutor[15]) nor Anthony B. Steel (1900–73, who would be his supervisor) liked the seventeen-year-old Hall much, but Howard's 'prestige saved him', and so he came second from the bottom in the £60 class.[16] He entered Christ's College a few days after the Munich crisis at the end of September 1938. In such circumstances it should not be found surprising that Hall joined the Cambridge University Socialist Club, though he resisted suggestions to join the Communist Party. However, by the end of his first term he had given up on the Socialist Club, writing later that 'the undergraduate futility and its public-school cum working-class solidarity was too apparent'.[17] His social life centred on Snow's Sunday evenings at Christ's, where he formed lifelong friendships, for example with the chemist Philip George (1920–2008).[18]

The lecturer whom Hall found most inspiring was the economic historian Michael Postan (1899–1981, FBA 1959) and much later Hall considered doing his Ph.D. in that area.[19] Following the departure of many faculty for various parts of the war effort, Plumb took over supervising Hall for his second year, 1939–40,[20] but failed to prevent him taking an Upper Second in the Part I examination, which bitterly disappointed Hall, just as the British Expeditionary Force retreated to Dunkirk in May 1940.

[10] Hall (2), p. 2.

[11] David Cannadine, 'John Harold Plumb 1911–2001', *Proceedings of the British Academy*, 124, *Biographical Memoirs of Fellows*, V (2004), 271.

[12] Hall (3), p. 4.

[13] Hall (2), pp. 3–4.

[14] Hall (3), p. 3.

[15] Hall (3), p. 2.

[16] Snow to Howard, 17 Dec. 1937 and 18 Dec. 1937, Snow file, ULC MS Plumb papers.

[17] Hall (3), p. 7.

[18] Hall (3), pp. 10 and 9.

[19] Mandelbrote interview, p. 1.

[20] Hall (3), p. 10–11.

The army

As a result of both these events, Hall left Cambridge and, after spending a couple of months in the Home Guard,[21] in September 1940 volunteered as a Signalman in the Royal Corps of Signals, his first choice of regiment,[22] doubtless accounted for by his long-standing interest in wireless. Recommended very quickly for officer training, he was sent to Catterick training camp in Yorkshire. After a year there, his colonel commented that Hall 'Possesses certain qualities of leadership and should develop. Has unusual technical ability and had done very well indeed;'[23] he was immediately commissioned as second lieutenant.

With the prospect of service overseas he married in December 1941 Anne Hughes (1913–80) seven years his senior. The daughter of a pottery manager and a friend of one his sisters, Hall had known her since they were children. She spent the war in the Land Army[24] and in April 1942 he was posted to Egypt, arriving towards the end of June (the ship went via Cape Town[25]). From there he joined the 10th Army in Persia and Iraq. Promoted to lieutenant whilst there, he established a direct wireless link between Baghdad and London which he later regarded as one of his better pieces of work.[26] His section then returned to North Africa where they participated in the operations of the 8th Army following the battle of El Alamein. After the end of the war in Africa, Hall participated in the invasions of Sicily (July 1943) and the Italian mainland and in the subsequent slow 'zigzag advance northwards to the Alps'[27] until March 1945 when he flew (in a Lancaster bomber) back to England to attend a special wireless course at Catterick. A brief sojourn in occupied Vienna followed before demobilisation in time to resume his studies in Cambridge, though not formally discharged until the start of November 1945.

Hall, as a signals officer, spent virtually the entire war in rear areas. Indeed the only action that involved him directly was when an enemy bomb destroyed the telephone exchange and signals office whilst he was stationed at Cesena (10 December 1944).[28] Hall's later recollections of the

[21] Hall (3), p. 12.
[22] Cadet Record Sheet.
[23] Cadet Record Sheet.
[24] Hall (2), p. 15.
[25] Hall (3), p. 17.
[26] Hall (2), p. 8.
[27] Hall (3), p. 21. On a single sheet of paper in IC MS Hall, Hall listed the places, with precise dates, where his unit was located in Italy.
[28] Hall (1), p. 2.

war were of 'intense tedium & drunkenness, with playing poker somewhere in between'.[29] Nevertheless, his less than five years in the army clearly made a strong impression and it dominates disproportionately his various unpublished autobiographical writings. He attended El Alamein reunions[30] and with Paul Randall (1912–2007), who later became a colonel and was one of the few fellow officers with whom Hall formed a lifelong friendship, he edited a selection of songs from the 8th Army signal corps.[31]

Cambridge

Hall's tutor, Grose, had applied for his early release from the army,[32] and so in the middle of October 1945 Hall found himself back in Cambridge to read for Part II of the history tripos, for which he successfully obtained the first class degree that had eluded him six years earlier. As a consequence of this degree Christ's awarded him a Bachelor Research Fellowship and he put aside his original intention to work as a teacher (he had been offered a position at Queen Elizabeth's Grammar School, Blackburn).[33] Together with some supervision and marking,[34] the Fellowship gave Hall the financial security to start a family; indeed he and Anne only really began their married life on his return to Cambridge where their first daughter, Alison, was born in November 1947.

As to the subject of his research, the Regius Professor of Modern History, George Clark (1890–1979, FBA 1936), suggested that Hall should research some aspect of the history of science, specifically ballistics. This choice of history of science intersected with the interests of both Charles Raven (1885–1964, FBA 1948), the Master of Christ's between 1939 and 1950 who had worked on the history of early English naturalists, and also Hall's friend Philip George.[35] To some extent Hall embracing the specific topic of ballistics in seventeenth-century England was not as surprising as it might seem. Interested in science at school in his teens, he had been fascinated by books such as Albert Neuburger's *The Technical Arts and*

[29] Hall to Boas, 18, 19 Oct. 1957, IC MS Hall.
[30] Programmes etc. in IC MS Hall.
[31] A. R. Hall and P. Randall, *1941–1945 Songs of the Eighth Army Signal 1647 Fifty Years On* (no place, *c*.1992).
[32] Hall (1), p. 2.
[33] Hall (2), p. 15.
[34] Hall (2), p. 15.
[35] Hall (1), p. 2 and (3), p. 16.

Sciences of the Ancients (1930) and had read related works such as Johann Beckmann's *A History of Inventions and Discoveries* (many nineteenth-century editions) and one of the chemistry books by Eric Holmyard (1891–1959), which contained much historical material, that his sister Enid had acquired.[36] Furthermore, Philip George, who had remained in Cambridge during the war, had begun collecting historic chemistry books which Hall read through.[37]

During his research Hall became connected with those few at Cambridge who took an interest in the history of science. These included Raven as well as Herbert Butterfield (1900–79, FBA 1965), whom he first met at the end of 1947.[38] Hall had a distant relationship with Raven,[39] but he did arrange an informal seminar in the Master's Lodge at Christ's. There Hall met, among others, Alistair Crombie (1915–96, FBA 1990) and Samuel Lilley (1914–87).[40] Although Crombie taught at University College London from 1946 until 1953 (when he went to Oxford), he retained strong connections with Cambridge. A close friend of Hall, Crombie, a zoologist by background and a Roman Catholic, argued strongly for a continuity of natural knowledge from the medieval period to the seventeenth century.[41] Lilley, a mathematician by background taking a Marxist view of science, with which Hall fundamentally disagreed, held a fellowship in the history of science at St John's College between 1946 and 1949, before going to Birmingham in 1950.[42]

Hall became close to Butterfield who acted as a lifelong patron and supporter, both within and outwith Cambridge. Plumb, who had been elected a Fellow of Christ's College in 1946, was Hall's other major patron, but he seems to have concentrated most of his efforts in the college. The details are opaque, but Hall was elected a Research Fellow in 1949 (renewed in 1952), and an official Fellow in 1955, the same year in which he was appointed College Steward. As a number of commentators have pointed out,[43] Hall belonged to a quintet of historians teaching at the

[36] Hall (2), p. 1.

[37] A. R. Hall, 'Beginnings in Cambridge', *ISIS*, 75 (1984), 22.

[38] Hall (2), p. 18.

[39] Hall (2), p. 17.

[40] Hall, 'Beginnings', p. 23.

[41] John North, 'Alistair Cameron Crombie, 1915–1996', *Proceedings of the British Academy*, 97 (1998), 257–70.

[42] Vidar Enebakk, 'Lilley revisited: or science and society in the twentieth century', *The British Journal for the History of Science*, 42 (2009), 563–93.

[43] Neil McKendrick, Obituary of Kenyon, *Independent*, 10 Jan. 1996. David Cannadine, 'The era of Todd, Plumb and Snow', in David Reynolds (ed.), *Christ's: a Cambridge College over Five Centuries* (London, 2005), p. 188. See also Cannadine, 'Plumb', p. 278.

college in the 1950s, the other three being Frank Spooner (1924–2007), John Kenyon (1927–96, FBA 1981) and Barry Supple (FBA 1987), all of whom Plumb appears to have selected.

Butterfield, who had published his famously iconoclastic *The Whig Interpretation of History* in 1931 (possibly a source for Hall's distrust of the notion of progress), had been appointed Professor of Modern History in 1944. He was thus in a position to play a key role in reviving the study of the history of science in Cambridge which had begun in 1936 with the establishment of the History of Science Committee by the Marxist biochemist Joseph Needham (1900–95, FRS 1941, FBA 1971) and the pathologist Walter Pagel (1898–1983, FBA 1976). That committee was chaired by Needham and dominated by scientists. However, in 1942 Needham went to China on a British Council mission and the chair was taken over by Butterfield. Needham did not return to Cambridge until 1948 by which time the committee was dominated by historians.[44] This was one of the reasons why there was continual friction between Butterfield, Needham and Raven.[45]

Butterfield was determined that the history of science should be taught and practiced by trained historians. To illustrate this view he delivered for the committee in the Lent and Easter terms of 1948 a course of lectures in the Arts Building[46] to an audience of about fifty to sixty (including Hall[47]) on 'The Origins of Modern Science', published the following year.[48] In this he concentrated on the 'scientific revolution' which he asserted, in an oft-quoted passage, 'outshines everything since the rise of Christianity and reduces the Renaissance and Reformation to the rank of mere episodes, mere internal replacements, within the system of medieval Christendom'.[49] The scientific revolution was thus an extraordinary significant event in human history which needed to be studied primarily by historians, with all their available tools, and not by scientists. This view was shared by Raven who told Needham that there was a real danger that history of science would become a refuge for second rate scientists which, he hinted, was the case with Herbert Dingle (1890–1978) who had recently been

[44] Anna-K. Mayer, 'Setting up a discipline: conflicting agendas of the Cambridge History of Science Committee, 1936–1950', *Studies in the History and Philosophy of Science*, 31 (2000), 665–89.

[45] Mandelbrote interview, p. 7.

[46] David Dewhirst, conversation with FJ, 4 Aug. 2011.

[47] Mandelbrote interview, p. 7.

[48] Herbert Butterfield, *The Origins of Modern Science 1300–1800* (London, 1949).

[49] Ibid., p. viii.

appointed Professor of the History and Philosophy of Science at University College London.[50]

Butterfield wanted to expand the subject in Cambridge and to this end, despite being unanimously urged by the committee to repeat his lectures during the 1948–9 year,[51] he declined and instead suggested the creation of a lectureship and specifically mentioned Hall in this regard, and also the possibility that he might in addition be appointed curator of the Whipple collection of scientific instruments.[52] In 1944 Robert Whipple (1871–1953), chairman of the Cambridge Scientific Instrument Company, had donated his collection of old scientific instruments and books to the university, together with some money. Because of the war it took some time to decide what to do with the collection and by 1948 Butterfield clearly saw an opportunity to use the collection to promote both the history of science and Hall's career.

At a meeting of the committee on 3 June 1948 it was decided that an application should be made to establish a lectureship in the history of science (which was not accepted).[53] In the meantime, while this was going through the Cambridge administrative process, the committee decided to appoint a temporary part-time curator (for an honorarium of £100) and invite someone to deliver a course of lectures similar to Butterfield's. Three candidates were discussed: Crombie, Hall and Lilley. Needham's notes of the meeting refer to Crombie as 'R' (right wing) and Lilley as 'L' (left wing) with the clear implication that the committee viewed their political positions as *ipso facto* ruling them out of consideration.[54] So Hall was appointed to the Whipple and invited to deliver eight lectures on sixteenth- and seventeenth-century science (for £25).[55]

The issues at stake are clearly seen in correspondence. A few years later Butterfield praised Hall for being neither Roman Catholic nor Marxist.[56] Needham, from his Marxist perspective, agreed with this analysis, but not with the practical consequences: 'The general criticism of Lilley is that he is too Marxist, and of Crombie that he is too Thomist.

[50] Raven to Needham, 6 May 1948, ULC MS NEEDHAM B309.
[51] History of Science Committee minutes, 12 March 1948, ULC MS NEEDHAM B309.
[52] Butterfield to Needham, 27 May 1948, ULC MS NEEDHAM B309.
[53] History of Science Committee minutes, 10 March 1949, ULC MS NEEDHAM B310.
[54] Needham's notes of History of Science Committee meeting, 3 June 1948, ULC MS NEEDHAM B309. For further details and also the background to the decision see Anna-K. Mayer, 'Setting up a discipline, II: British history of science and "the end of ideology", 1931–1948', *Studies in the History and Philosophy of Science*, 35 (2004), 55–6.
[55] History of Science Committee minutes, 3 June 1948, ULC MS NEEDHAM B309.
[56] Butterfield to Downs, 8 Jan. 1955, ULC MS BUTT/531/H6.

Hall here in Cambridge has never much impressed me; he is wafted on by the Butterfield circle, to which I do not adhere.'[57] But beyond the issue of individual ideological beliefs existed the question of who was qualified to do the history of science. A few days after the appointment meeting Needham wrote a long letter to Charles Singer (1876–1960), perhaps the leading historian of science in the country at that time, in which he complained about the assumption that only trained historians could do history of science, and about the committee's decisions, saying that they clearly wanted Hall appointed and asking if Singer knew anything about Hall.[58] To the latter point Singer responded 'I don't know H. [*sic*] R. Hall at all, but to suppose that you can make an historian of science from a man untrained in science seems to me silly.'[59]

Hall took up his new positions, whilst still completing his Ph.D. thesis. For the Whipple collection, he had the assistance of David Dewhirst (to whom he had been introduced by Snow[60]), then a research student in metallurgy, who helped Hall gain some basic knowledge of scientific instruments.[61] Hall began unpacking the objects and he added to the collections items from various colleges and also persuaded the Director of the Cavendish Laboratory, Lawrence Bragg (1890–1971, FRS 1921), to donate some early apparatus from the laboratory.[62] Whipple was delighted that something, at last, was happening with his collection[63] and on 5 May 1951 the first Whipple Museum opened on a site in Corn Exchange Street.[64]

Since plans were well advanced to include a paper in the history and philosophy of science in the Natural Sciences Tripos, the disappointing decision not to create an assistant lectureship in 1949 was reversed the following year with the establishment of the position from October 1950.[65] John Ratcliffe (1902–87, FRS 1951), head of the radio group at the

[57] Needham to Taylor, 2 Oct. 1950, quoted in Enebakk, 'Lilley Revisited', p. 575.

[58] Needham to Singer, 7 June 1948, ULC MS NEEDHAM B309.

[59] Singer to Needham, 20 June 1948, ULC MS NEEDHAM B309.

[60] David W. Dewhirst, 'The opening of a new gallery at the Whipple Musuem', in Liba Taub and Frances Willmoth (eds.), *The Whipple Museum of the History of Science: Instruments and Interpretations to Celebrate the Sixtieth Anniversary of R. S. Whipple's Gift to the University of Cambridge* (Cambridge, 2006), pp. 75–6.

[61] A. R. Hall, 'The first decade of the Whipple Museum', in Taub and Willmoth, pp. 58–9.

[62] A. R. Hall, 'Whipple Museum of the History of Science, Cambridge', *Nature*, 167 (1951), 878–9.

[63] Whipple to Hall, 2 March 1949, quoted in Frances Willmoth, 'Documents from the founding and early history of the Whipple Museum', in Taub and Willmoth, *The Whipple Museum*, pp. 7–8.

[64] Hall, 'The first decade', p. 61.

[65] History of Science Committee minutes, 16 Feb. 1950, ULC MS NEEDHAM B310.

Cavendish, was very keen to include a non-scientific component in the Tripos and saw the history of science as an effective way of achieving this.[66] Hall, as the incumbent, became the assistant lecturer which in 1953 was converted into a full lectureship with Hall appointed for three years.[67] Hall's lectureship entailed an increase in his workload and, following the opening of the Whipple Museum, he wrote a memorandum asking for the appointment of a part-time curator under his general direction. He suggested his research student, Derek Price (1922–83), for the position, which was agreed.[68] The inclusion of philosophy of science in the Tripos meant that a lecturer had to be appointed to cover this and in 1952 Norwood Russell Hanson (1924–67) took up the position. American-born, Hanson had studied philosophy at both Oxford and Cambridge, and took history very seriously indeed, which is probably why he and Hall got on very well indeed, spending much time in discussion and reading each other's work.[69]

While during 1948 and 1949 Hall's positions in Cambridge were being established, he continued work on his Ph.D. thesis, which he submitted in April 1949. His examination, held in the Athenaeum Club, was conducted by Clark (by now Provost of Oriel College, Oxford) and Singer.[70] On Singer's recommendation to Cambridge University Press, the thesis was published three years later and contained many of the themes that would recur throughout Hall's scholarly career.[71] His fundamental conclusion, that the 'practice of artillery contributed nothing to seventeenth-century science',[72] reflected his firm view that science had its own logic which had little to do with technology, at least before the nineteenth century, if then: 'At the time of their composition Newton's propositions were as irrelevant to the technical practice of the age as Maxwell's electromagnetic waves; and the practical applications of the one and the other were equally unforeseen.'[73]

[66] Mandelbrote interview, p. 9.

[67] Sartain (Cambridge University) to Hall, 12 Aug. 1953, IC MS Hall.

[68] A. R. Hall, 'Memorandum on the Staffing of the Whipple Museum', 26 Aug. 1951 and Minutes of the History of Science Committee, 14 Nov. 1951, both in ULC MS NEEDHAM B314.

[69] Mandelbrote interview, p. 22. N. R. Hanson, *Patterns of Discovery: an Inquiry into the Conceptual Foundations of Science* (Cambridge, 1958), p. 196.

[70] A. R. Hall, 'Review and reminiscences', in Richard L. Dalitz and Michael Nauenburg (eds.), *The Foundations of Newtonian Scholarship* (Singapore, 2000), pp. 197–207, on 204.

[71] A. R. Hall, 'Ballistics in the Seventeenth Century' (University of Cambridge Ph.D. thesis, 1949) and *Ballistics in the Seventeenth Century: a Study in the Relations of Science and War with Reference Principally to England* (Cambridge, 1952).

[72] Hall, *Ballistics* (1952), p. 161.

[73] Ibid., p. 164.

One is tempted to speculate whether Hall's wartime experiences of using a science-based technology influenced him in developing these views. He would have known, first hand, of the serious problems that almost inevitably arise when using scientific knowledge for practical purposes. Furthermore, Hall appears to have been deeply concerned with the way science had been used during the war, especially in the development of atomic weapons. He was always equivocal in his attitude towards the idea of progress and this may have influenced him into arguing for a history in which science, contrary to the Marxist interpretation and indeed modern practice, was unrelated to technology.

He read widely in the subject and was heavily influenced by the work of Alexandre Koyré (1892–1964), especially his three volume *Etudes galiléennes*, published in 1939, which Hall read at some point in the late 1940s.[74] Koyré stressed the importance of the change in theoretical outlook brought about by science rather than the establishment of facts—a non-positivist view of science. He was particularly critical of the experiments made by Galileo Galilei (1564–1642), some of which he doubted had happened, and emphasised the philosophical method of the *exposition des textes* in historical writing. Inspirational for Hall, Koyré's approach showed him that the subject need not be a dull one of simply establishing facts and order of events as Hall found in journals such as *ISIS* or *Annals of Science*.[75]

Thus in his thesis Hall traced the development of the theoretical understanding of projectile motion through the work of figures to whom he would continue to devote much time to studying: Galileo, Christiaan Huygens (1629–95, FRS 1663) and above all Isaac Newton (1642–1727, FRS 1672). Hall's first paper, published in the *Cambridge Historical Journal*, discussed the significance of one of Newton's notebooks that he kept while an undergraduate at Cambridge in the first half of the 1660s. Hall read this in the University Library whilst undertaking his thesis research.[76] What is striking about this paper was the way Hall helped understand a historical problem (in this case the origin of Newton's *annus mirabilis*) by the use of manuscript material. At the time it was almost unheard of to use manuscripts in the history of science in this way, but, as

[74] Hall (2), p. 19–20.
[75] Hall (2), p. 20.
[76] A. R. Hall, 'Sir Isaac Newton's note-book, 1661–1665', *Cambridge Historical Journal*, 9 (1948), 239–50.

Hall pointed out, knowing anything about what Newton was doing before 1665 was 'precious'.[77]

Although not published in a history of science journal, Hall's article was noticed by Henry Guerlac (1910–85), Professor of the History of Science at Cornell University, who wrote asking Hall for two offprints.[78] Hall at this time was expanding his horizons—for example, he attended the sixth International Congress of the History of Science held in Amsterdam in 1950, where he met Koyré.[79] He also came to the attention of Thomas Kuhn (1922–96) who taught history of science at Harvard University from 1948 to 1956 and met Hall in 1950 when he was sent by the President of Harvard, James Conant (1893–1978), to find out about history of science in England.[80] When, the following year, Kuhn heard that Guerlac's former student Marie Boas, then teaching at the University of Massachusetts, was going to England to study the papers of Robert Boyle (1627–91, FRS 1663) at the Royal Society, he suggested that as they were interested 'in the same kind of subjects',[81] she should 'look up' Hall.[82]

Marie Boas

Background, early life and education

Boas's ancestors mostly originated in the Jewish communities of the German speaking countries. Both her grandfather, Herman Boas (1854–98), a tailor, and his wife Sarah Eisenberg (b.1857) had emigrated as children from Germany to the United States. They eventually settled in Providence, Rhode Island, where they had six children including Boas's father, Ralph Boas (1887–1945), and George Boas (1891–1980) the historian of ideas. Both brothers attended Brown University in Providence, where Ralph Boas read English, graduating AB in 1908 and AM in 1910. Boas's other grandfather Rudolph Schutz (b.1858), a jeweller, emigrated from Austria as a child and married the Vermont-born (but half-Austrian) Esther Beckman (b.1860). They too settled in Providence where their daughter,

[77] Hall, 'Newton's note-book', p. 241.
[78] M. B. Hall, 'Recollections of a history of science guinea pig', *ISIS*, 90 (1999), S76.
[79] Mandelbrote interview, p. 21.
[80] Steve Fuller, *Thomas Kuhn: a Philosophical History of Our Times* (Chicago, 2000), p. 173.
[81] Boas Hall (1), p. 10.
[82] Boas Hall (2), p. 22.

and Boas's mother, Louise Schutz (1885–1973) was born. She too studied English at Brown, graduating AB in 1907 and AM in 1910.[83]

Not only did Ralph Boas and Louise Schutz (who married in September 1911) both teach English, they also collaborated on a study of New England puritan minister and scholar Cotton Mather (1663–1728, FRS 1713) and on a self-help book for new Americans.[84] Ralph Boas was a prolific writer of textbooks,[85] which was financially rewarding,[86] whilst Louise Boas published studies of Walter Scott (1771–1832) and Elizabeth Barrett Browning (1806–61), as well as an account of the development of women's colleges in the United States.[87]

Ralph Boas had a fairly peripatetic teaching career, beginning in Whitman College, Walla Walla in Washington State. There their son, also called Ralph (1912–92), later a distinguished mathematician who wrote the classic paper on the 'mathematical theory of big game hunting',[88] was born. However, they returned to New England in 1917 where Ralph senior taught in Massachusetts at the Central High School in Springfield, Mount Holyoke College, and finally, from 1928, Wheaton College in Norton, a rundown agricultural town about thirty miles south of Boston.[89] The latter two institutions were women's liberal arts colleges and in 1929 Louise Boas was also appointed Associate Professor of English at Wheaton; in 1950 she became full professor, a position that she held until 1952.

It was at Springfield, 'a manufacturing town noted only for its arsenal',[90] that Marie Boas was born on 18 October 1919. When she was aged about four the family moved to South Hadley which she recollected, with fondness, as 'an attractive village in lovely rolling countryside where I learned to enjoy walking, recognising wild flowers, and when I recovered

[83] Information for this paragraph is taken from the births, marriages, deaths and census records of both Rhode Island and the United States, and the graduate files of both R. P. Boas and L. S. Boas held in Brown University archives. These latter also inform the following two paragraphs.

[84] Ralph and Louise Boas, *Leading Facts for New Americans* (New York, 1923); *Cotton Mather, Keeper of the Puritan Conscience* (New York, 1928).

[85] These include Ralph Boas, *The Study and Appreciation of Literature* (New York, 1931); (with Barbara Hahn) *Social Backgrounds of English Literature* (Boston, 1923); (with Katherine Burton), *Social Backgrounds of American Literature* (Boston, 1933).

[86] Boas Hall (2), p. 1.

[87] Louise Boas, *Woman's Education Begins; the Rise of the Women's Colleges* (Nonton, IL, 1935); *Elizabeth Barrett Browning* (New York, 1930); *A Great Rich Man; the Romance of Sir Walter Scott* (New York, 1929).

[88] H. Pétard (pseud.), 'A contribution to the mathematical theory of big game hunting', *American Mathematical Monthly*, 45 (1938), 446–7.

[89] Boas Hall (2), p. 2.

[90] Boas Hall (1), p. 1.

from a series of illnesses, starting school'.[91] Being the daughter of English teachers meant that she was surrounded with books and 'imbued from an early age with the idea that one's parents wrote books'.[92] At the age of twelve she was helping them proof read and a few years later her mother acknowledged her contributions to the compilation of a bibliography.[93]

Boas attended a private boarding school in Norton and then spent the year 1935–6 studying English and chemistry at Wheaton College. Her work there included an essay on the printing innovations introduced by William Morris (1834–96) which she regarded as her real introduction to scholarship and recollected that 'factual writing and the use of secondary sources came to me easily'.[94] But it was chemistry that captured her imagination and when she entered the women-only Radcliffe College, 'then a curious subsidiary'[95] of Harvard University, in 1936, despite her family background she chose that subject to study. She progressed steadily until February 1939 when her parents were granted sabbatical leave and decided to visit Europe, where her brother, who had studied mathematics at Harvard, was spending a year in Cambridge. After short periods in France, Switzerland and Italy, Boas and her parents settled in London. In the reading room of the British Museum, Boas helped her mother with her researches on Harriet Westbrook (1795–1816), the first wife of Percy Shelley (1792–1822), not completed until the early 1960s.[96] They took a brief holiday in Devon and visited Poland, before returning to Massachusetts in August 1939, landing the day Britain declared war on Germany.[97]

Wartime

Although the United States was not yet fighting, the outbreak of war had a direct effect on the remainder of Boas's education. Due to a change in Harvard's admission policies, she became one of the first two women to attend lectures alongside male students there and following the completion of her degree in 1940 was then among the first women to be allowed to work as a postgraduate in the Harvard chemistry laboratories, obtaining her Masters degree in 1942.

[91] Boas Hall (1), p. 1.
[92] Boas Hall (2), p. 1.
[93] Louise Boas, *Woman's Education*, p. xi.
[94] Boas Hall (2), p. 1.
[95] Boas Hall (2), p. 4.
[96] L. S. Boas, *Harriet Shelley. Five Long Years* (London, 1962).
[97] For a vivid account of the tour see R. P. Boas, 'Mr. Boas says . . .', *Wheaton Alumnae Quarterly* (1939), 12–15. There is a copy of this in the graduate file of Boas in Brown University archives.

After the United States declared war against the Axis powers in December 1941, Boas, not wishing to work on either poison gas or explosives to which Harvard chemistry had switched, volunteered in the summer of 1942 to work as a civilian for the Army Signals Corps at Fort Monmouth, New Jersey. She learned how to wire radios and write instructions for their use. Having done this in a variety of mid-west towns, she began to doubt the usefulness of her work and, despite her job classification as 'essential', was able to leave the Corps in the middle of 1944. She then moved to the secret (she had not previously heard of it) Radiation Laboratory at the Massachusetts Institute of Technology, which developed new types of radar including those stemming from the cavity magnetron invented at the University of Birmingham in 1940.[98] She was placed in the technical manual section and, as with her previous work for the Signals Corps, this involved understanding how to work various new forms of radar and write the instructions for their use, but in this case she found the work far more congenial.[99] In total, however, she 'hated the war years ... & felt I was missing out on life'.[100] Despite this, one might plausibly suggest that the clarity that she later displayed in both her writing and her lectures stemmed from this period when she had to explain the use of unfamiliar and complex pieces of equipment to those lacking the necessary technical skills and knowledge.

Cornell

After the end of the war Boas, with two others from the technical manual section, joined the Historian's Office in the laboratory. This had been founded in 1943 and was headed by Henry Guerlac. Though for her the project lasted only eight months, it proved to be decisive in Boas's move to the history of science, all the more so because Guerlac was one of the very few practitioners of the subject in America. In the early 1930s he had studied chemistry and biochemistry at Cornell University, before moving to Harvard where his interest turned to the history of science. His Ph.D. thesis was entitled 'Science and war in the old regime. The development of science in an armed society' (1941) and following its completion he moved to the new history of science department at the University of Wisconsin, Madison. However, two years later he was granted leave of absence to

[98] M. B. Hall, 'Guinea pig', pp. S68–9.
[99] Boas Hall (1), p. 6.
[100] Boas to Hall, 16 April 1958, IC MS Hall.

lead the team of about half-a-dozen to work on the official history of the United States radar programme.[101]

Guerlac and Boas shared an office,[102] and she later recounted that 'The whole operation was conducted in a joyous spirit of historical adventure, with each member of the highly diverse staff being given jobs suitable to his or her talents.'[103] The results of the project were not properly published until 1987, after Guerlac's death,[104] though he and Boas in 1950 wrote a joint paper on naval radar.[105] At the end of the project he agreed to take her on as a Ph.D. student when he returned to academia in 1946 as professor in the history department at Cornell. There she was the first research student in the history of science and course assistant on Guerlac's historical course for chemical engineers, although he quickly expanded both the number of students and course assistants. It was, however, this work that gave her the funds to pursue her research.

As someone who, aside from her work at the Radiation Laboratory, had done no historical research, Boas followed courses on medieval history and astronomy as a science.[106] She originally proposed the history of atomism for her thesis, not then realising how large a subject it was. Guerlac suggested the history of pneumatics and eventually, after further prompting, she wrote her thesis on Boyle and the corpuscular philosophy as a study of theories of matter in the seventeenth century; evidently her research was conducted in the same spirit as at the Radiation Laboratory. During her final year (1948–9) she was awarded Cornell's George Boldt Fellowship in history, which was a 'reluctant admission'[107] of her status as an historian and allowed her to complete writing her thesis free of teaching duties.

It was at Cornell that Boas began to develop her own style as an historian. Even though she had respect for the Belgian-born positivist George Sarton (1884–1956), one of the earliest practitioners of the subject in the United States, founder of the journals *ISIS* and *Osiris* as well as the History of Science Society, she rejected what she saw as his biographical

[101] Material on Guerlac is taken from M. B. Hall, 'Henry Guerlac, 10 June 1910–29 May 1985', *ISIS*, 77 (1986), 504–6. For his brief time at Wisconsin see Victor L. Hilts, 'History of Science at the University of Wisconsin', *ISIS*, 75 (1984), 71–2.
[102] M. B. Hall, 'Guinea pig', p. S69.
[103] M. B. Hall, 'Guerlac', p. 505.
[104] Henry E. Guerlac, *Radar in World War II*, 2 vols. (Los Angeles and New York, 1987).
[105] Henry E. Guerlac and Marie Boas, 'The radar war against the U-boat', *Military Affairs*, 44 (1950), 99–111.
[106] M. B. Hall, 'Guinea pig', p. S70.
[107] Ibid., p. S72.

and bibliographical approach, although he was helpful to her in publishing her early work. Nor was she enamoured of the work of sociologists such as Robert Merton (1910–2003) which linked the development of science in the seventeenth century to the Puritan ethic. Her (then) radical historiographical edge came, like Hall's, from her study of Koyré's *Etudes galiléennes*. As she recollected: 'Koyré's call for the study of texts and concentration on ideas rather than on social and economic influences greatly appealed to me and justified my approach to my thesis topic.'[108]

Her thesis covered not only Boyle but also the influence in the Renaissance and seventeenth century of the views expressed by Hero of Alexandra (*c.* AD 10–70) in his *Pneumatica*,[109] and concluded with a chapter on the theory of attraction in the work of Newton. Here she attributed the source of his ideas to his chemical experimentation (a view she quickly retracted) and expressed some puzzlement as to why Newton's biographers had found his alchemy discreditable. Altogether it was an impressive achievement; especially as it was based entirely on the printed sources she had available at Cornell and at Harvard during the summers. The bulk of her thesis was published as a 138-page paper in *Osiris*, entitled 'The establishment of the mechanical philosophy'.[110] The change of title was significant in that it embraced her view that the key to seventeenth-century natural philosophy was understanding particles in motion, rather than the nature of matter; presumably the title of her thesis had to be approved at Cornell before it was written. Her thesis introduced many of the themes that were to occupy her professional career; for example, a concentration on the Renaissance and seventeenth century (though not exclusively so) and the primacy for historical study of the relations of ideas and texts. In many ways Boas was fortunate to choose a period and a topic that would be central to the interests of historians of science in the ensuing decades, as she seems to have recognised in her foreword to the 1981 reprint of the paper.[111]

In her time at Cornell she had also shown hard work and great strength of character in her achievements, learning much in areas where she had not previously been trained. It was these qualities that put her in a good position when the need to find a job arose. She was quickly appointed an

[108] M. B. Hall, 'Guinea pig', p. S72.
[109] M. Boas, 'Hero's *Pneumatica*: a study of its transmission and influence', *ISIS*, 40 (1949), 38–48.
[110] M. Boas, 'The establishment of the mechanical philosophy', *Osiris*, 10 (1952), 412–541.
[111] M. B. Hall, *The Mechanical Philosophy* (New York, 1981).

assistant professor in the history department at the University of Massachusetts, Amherst, very near her childhood home at South Hadley. The appointment was made on condition that she taught nineteenth-century history and so she spent the summer of 1949 reading up on the topic. Though she had little opportunity to teach her own subject, she found that routine teaching needed little preparation[112] and so was able to write and publish a few articles, but overall found her time there 'rather dismal'.[113]

Guerlac had given her one of the offprints that Hall had sent him of his paper on Newton's early notebook, which, as she later wrote, she found 'an eye-opener for manuscript scholarship was in its infancy as regards 17th century history of science'.[114] At that time virtually all historians of science wrote from published sources and indeed some, such as I. Bernard Cohen (1914–2003) at Harvard, thought, even as late as 1956, that this was a virtue.[115] Hall's paper prompted her to wish to look at one of Newton's notebooks on chemistry. The microfilm that she ordered took two years to arrive from Cambridge University Library; as Hall later told her, they had mislaid it.[116] As with Hall and Newton's unpublished work, she turned, also influenced by Koyré, to thinking about Boyle's unpublished papers which, so far as she could see, had not been studied seriously since the eighteenth century.[117] In the summer of 1951, using her own savings and accompanied by her mother, she visited London to work on them in the library of the Royal Society, then located in Burlington House. Following Kuhn's introduction Boas and Hall met for the first time during her visit.[118] But aside from her later recollection that they 'did indeed find that our interests were similar and friendly',[119] no other trace of this encounter has been found and they appear to have had no further contact for a couple of years.

[112] Boas Hall (1), p. 8.
[113] Boas to Hall, 16 April 1958, IC MS Hall.
[114] Boas Hall (2), pp. 19–20.
[115] Boas Hall (2), p. 20.
[116] Boas Hall (2), p. 20.
[117] M. B. Hall, 'Guinea pig', p. S76.
[118] Ibid.
[119] Boas Hall (2), p. 22.

Hall and Boas

1951 to 1957, friendship

Boas returned to Massachusetts for the 1951–2 year, towards the end of which she was told that her contract, along with that of two of her colleagues, appointed at the same time, would not be renewed since otherwise they would automatically receive tenure. She recollected that 'rather bitterly I noticed that only the man without a PhD was not fired'.[120] Through an 'old friend'[121] she secured an interview for a position in the history department at Brandeis University which had been recently founded, amidst some controversy. She was appointed there but, as at Massachusetts, the position was not related to the history of science and she had to teach introductory history, which at Brandeis was dominated by Frank Manuel (1910–2003). The great advantage for Boas of Brandeis was that she easily became part of the network of historians of science centred on Harvard. Because of the disruption occasioned by the move to Brandeis, Boas was not able to visit England during 1952.

But she did so the following year and renewed contact with Hall, meeting him for lunch at Millbank which she enjoyed so much she invited herself to see him in Cambridge in mid-July 1953 and he met her off the train.[122] The reason why they lunched in Millbank was that Hall had become one of the editors to publish *A History of Technology* in five substantial volumes. This project was funded by ICI and despite holding three jobs in Cambridge Hall seems to have felt short of money.[123] The initial editors were Singer and Holmyard; Hall joined them at the end of 1951,[124] with the fourth and final editor, Trevor Williams (1921–96), joining in time for the publication of volume one in 1954, the year in which Hall's second daughter, Clarissa, was born. *A History of Technology* involved Hall in making weekly journeys to London to the project office housed in ICI's Millbank headquarters. He was largely responsible for volume three,[125] published in 1957, which covered the period roughly from 1500 to 1750. He contributed the chapter on 'Military Technology' (as he had done for volume two) and concluded the volume with a chapter on the rise

[120] Boas Hall (2), p. 21.
[121] M. B. Hall, 'Guinea pig', p. S77.
[122] Boas to Hall, 13 July 1953 and 16 July 1953, IC MS Hall.
[123] Hall (2), p. 20.
[124] Worboys (ICI) to Hall, 27 Nov. 1951, IC MS Hall.
[125] Hall (2), p. 23.

of the West which he ascribed to increasing technological sophistication. In this Hall softened his earlier stance on the relations of science and technology and commented that by about 1700 there was already some justification for a linkage between them. But he ended on a pessimistic note: '[Men] saw science as the inspiration of technology, and technology as the key to a life of richness and prosperity: what they could not see, however, was the infinite and tortuous complexity of man himself'.[126]

The project was valuable to Hall not only in providing him with additional income but also in giving him a fair acquaintance with the development of Western technology. Despite the tensions that inevitably arise in this kind of collaborative project,[127] it did lead Hall to a close association with Singer who invited him on occasion to stay at his home on the Cornish coast, Kilmarth, just outside Par.[128] Nevertheless, Singer never changed his mind that only those trained in science could do history of science; perhaps history of technology was different in his mind.

At the same time as running the Whipple Museum, undertaking his college and teaching duties and working on *A History of Technology*, Hall published his book on seventeenth-century ballistics in 1952. At the start of that year, following Plumb's suggestion and recommendation, Hall signed a contract with Longmans to write a book entitled *The Scientific Revolution 1500–1800*, the manuscript to be delivered in the autumn of 1953;[129] possibly the timing was related to his need for money. This learned and highly readable book, based on Hall's lectures to undergraduate students, popularised the term scientific revolution which thereafter for a few years became the metaphor of choice for historians and writers on science—for example Kuhn's *The Copernican Revolution* (1957), whilst the full title of Snow's 1959 Rede lecture at Cambridge University was *The Two Cultures and the Scientific Revolution* and finally in 1962 Kuhn's *The Structure of Scientific Revolutions*.

Furthermore, the subtitle of Hall's book, *The Formation of the Modern Scientific Attitude*, confirmed his belief that modern science originated in this period: 'Much more has been learnt about Nature, from the structure of matter to the physiology of man, in the last century and a half than in

[126] A. R. Hall, 'The rise of the west', in C. Singer, E. J. Holmyard, T. I. Williams and A. R. Hall (eds.), *A History of Technology. Volume 3 From the Renaissance to the Industrial Revolution c.1500–c.1750* (Oxford, 1957), p. 721.

[127] See, for example, Hall to Singer, 8 Nov. 1955; Singer to Hall, 14 Nov. 1955; Williams to Hall, 14 Nov. 1955; Hall to Singer, 15 Nov. 1955; Williams to Hall, 18 Nov. 1955. IC MS Hall.

[128] Hall (2), p. 23.

[129] Mandelbrote interview, p. 9. Blagden to Hall, 24 Jan. 1952, IC MS Hall.

all preceding time. Of this there can be no doubt. But the scientific revolution ends when this vastly detailed exploration began, for it was that which made such investigation possible.'[130] Furthermore, Hall related none of this to practical issues; the words 'engineering' and 'technology' are notably absent from the index. This is peculiar both because Hall was working on *A History of Technology* at the same time and also his view, echoing Butterfield, that science 'is the one product of the West that has had decisive, probably permanent, impact upon other contemporary civilizations. Compared with modern science, capitalism, the nation-state, art and literature, Christianity and democracy, seem regional idiosyncrasies, whose past is full of vicissitudes and whose future is full of dark uncertainty.'[131] Why, it might be asked, should science be regarded as so generally important other than as a driver for technological change? Furthermore, once again Hall's pessimism comes through as does his view that the original creation of modern science was largely unrelated to practical concerns.

Following the completion of *The Scientific Revolution*, Hall began to contemplate a series on the history of science to be published by Cambridge University Press. It is not clear precisely what he had in mind, as Boas pointed out in replying to his invitation to contribute to the series—the same letter in which she suggested, as a 'brash American', that they should be on first name terms henceforth.[132] Boas had been kept busy with her duties at Brandeis as well as Secretary of the History of Science Society, a position she held from 1953 until 1957 apart from 1956 when Kuhn took on that role. She found her early meetings of the Council dull, but became involved in a 'junior revolution' which, together with a financial crisis, improved things.[133] Nevertheless, she had time to do some writing on Boyle and help establish a discussion group of younger historians of science in the Boston and Cambridge area, including Kuhn.[134]

Boas had not expected to visit England during 1954, but at the end of June she and her mother were touring the Forest of Dean from where she wrote to Hall saying that she would be in Cambridge in a couple of weeks and hoped 'to have a good history-of-science talk' with him and to hear the latest news about his book.[135] On 19 July she arrived in Cambridge and

[130] A. R. Hall, *The Scientific Revolution 1500–1800: the Formation of the Modern Scientific Attitude* (London, 1954), p. 364.
[131] Ibid.
[132] Boas to Hall, 6 March 1954, IC MS Hall.
[133] Boas to Hall, 18 Nov. 1955, IC MS Hall.
[134] Boas to Hall, 6 March 1954, IC MS Hall.
[135] Boas to Hall, 4 July 1954, IC MS Hall.

invited Hall and Anne (whom she had met during her 1953 visit)[136] to dinner the following day.[137] Boas returned to Massachusetts in time for the October hurricane season which she described experiencing, both in Cambridge and at her mother's home in Orleans on Cape Cod. In the same letter she asked Hall for support in her application for a Guggenheim Fellowship to allow her a year off from teaching and to study in England, hoping that she was not presuming on their friendship.[138] That month *The Scientific Revolution* was published and Hall sent her a copy;[139] she also reviewed it enthusiastically for *ISIS*.[140]

By this time, Hall's reputation was rising. With Butterfield's (and presumably Plumb's) support, he was elected to an official fellowship at Christ's in early 1955[141] and at the beginning of the following year his lectureship was made permanent.[142] At the same time Gerald Holton wrote inviting him to move to Harvard, an offer which though Hall found tempting he declined, citing, among other things, family reasons.[143] Nevertheless, doubtless to remind Cambridge of his existence, he showed the correspondence to Butterfield, who found it sufficiently alarming for him to tell Hall that he would have his support should Cambridge decide to establish a chair in the history of science.[144]

Boas was successful in obtaining a Guggenheim Fellowship and in July 1955 she moved to London for a year and lived at 12 Buckland Crescent, in Belsize Park. She mostly worked on Boyle and completed the text of what would become her first book: *Robert Boyle and Seventeenth-Century Chemistry* (Cambridge, 1958) won the first Pfizer Prize to be awarded by the History of Science Society.[145] She also became acquainted with the historians of science at University College London, including Douglas McKie (1896–1967), none of whom she found stimulating.[146] She stayed with Hall and his wife during the first week of November[147] and he

[136] Boas to Hall, 6 March 1954, IC MS Hall.
[137] Boas to Hall, 19 July 1954, IC MS Hall.
[138] Boas to Hall, 12 Oct.1954, IC MS Hall.
[139] Boas to Hall, 13 Nov. 1954, IC MS Hall.
[140] *ISIS*, 46 (1955), 304–5.
[141] Downs to Hall, 3 March 1955, IC MS Hall. Butterfield to Downs (draft), 8 Jan. 1955, ULC MS BUTT/531/H6.
[142] Taylor to Hall, 3 Feb. 1956, IC MS Hall.
[143] Hall to Holton, 2 Feb. 1956, IC MS Hall.
[144] Butterfield to Hall, 6 Feb. 1956, ULC MS BUTT/531/H7.
[145] *ISIS*, 51 (1960), 85.
[146] Boas to Hall, 16 Nov. 1955, IC MS Hall.
[147] Boas to Hall, 21 Oct. 1955, IC MS Hall.

invited her to the Ladies night at Christ's.[148] In line with inviting other scholars, such as the civil engineer at Imperial College, Alec Skempton (1914–2001, FRS 1961),[149] to deliver lectures on their specialist topics to his students, Hall asked Boas to lecture twice during the Easter term of 1956.[150] In September they both attended the eighth International Congress of History of Science held in Florence and Milan, between the 3rd and the 9th. Boas later wondered whether it was that trip that began to move their relationship beyond friendship as she remembered their being cross with each other and was surprised;[151] thereafter she began keeping Hall's letters to her.

After her year in England Boas returned to Brandeis for the start of the new teaching year and began corresponding with Hall almost monthly, though mostly on professional matters. Thus she asked if he would be 'angelic enough' to find out what had become of the manuscript of the Boyle book that she had given to a typing agency in London. But she also discussed her car, an MG, and the political situation, being staunchly opposed to the idea of the Republican Dwight Eisenhower (1890–1969) serving a second term as President.[152] In reply Hall asked if she would care to change her E for Britain's E (the Prime Minister, Anthony Eden, 1897–1977) and said that he had rung Cambridge University Press and found that the typescript of her book had arrived.[153] This was at the time of the Suez debacle and he felt moved to write Boas a letter entirely devoted to the crisis: 'There has been nothing like this since Munich. It is worse than Munich.'[154]

At this time, Hall was contemplating a sabbatical for the entirety of 1958. Most of this he told Boas would be spent in England because of school commitments, but he thought he could manage three months in America and asked her advice as to how practicable this was.[155] She made some helpful suggestions about lecture fees, travel etc. to confirm her view of its feasibility, adding, in pen, against that passage '& very nice too'.[156] What threw these plans off track was that Marshall Clagett (1916–2005)

[148] Boas to Hall, 20 Dec. 1955, IC MS Hall.
[149] Hall to Boas, 9 Nov. 1957, IC MS Hall.
[150] History of Science Committee minutes, 12 June 1956, ULC MS NEEDHAM B324.
[151] Boas to Hall, 14, 15, 16 April 1958, IC MS Hall.
[152] Boas to Hall, 25 Oct. 1956, IC MS Hall.
[153] Hall to Boas, 30 Oct. 1956, IC MS Hall.
[154] Hall to Boas, 3 Nov. 1956, IC MS Hall.
[155] Hall to Boas, 30 Oct. 1956, IC MS Hall.
[156] Boas to Hall, 3 Nov. 1956, IC MS Hall.

at the University of Wisconsin invited Hall to contribute a paper on the scholar and craftsman idea (something which Hall later said he did not know much about,[157] but in which he continued to separate science and technology)[158] to a major conference to be held in Madison during September 1957 on 'Critical Problems in the History of Science'.[159]

1957–1959, a transatlantic love affair

Early in 1957 Boas decided to leave Brandeis following their decision not to promote her. She was aware of three available positions; two at the University of California (Los Angeles and Berkeley) and one at the University of Leeds. She wrote asking for Hall's advice, especially about Leeds.[160] Hall commented that there were not any strong candidates in England, so if she did apply for Leeds he would withdraw his support from a name he had put forward.[161] She corresponded with Stephen Toulmin (1922–2009) at Leeds and appears, with Hall's help, to have been offered the position there.[162] However, she quickly decided to accept the appointment to the Department of History at UCLA to teach history of science entirely, for the first time.[163] She was anxious about Hall's reaction,[164] but he said he would have done the same thing in her position.[165] Between June and August, Boas was back in Buckland Crescent and met Hall a number of times and they both attended a conference at Royaumont near Paris.[166]

According to Hall, his marriage, at least on his side, was already in trouble by 1947[167] as the tone of his letters to Boas at this time reflects, Hall writing on one occasion a letter which began 'My dear Marie' and ended 'Please don't think it doesn't give me great pleasure to hear from you';[168] their frequent meetings suggests that if they had not, unknowingly

[157] Mandelbrote interview, p. 12.
[158] This was later published as A. R. Hall, 'The scholar and the craftsman in the scientific revolution', in M. Clagett (ed.), *Critical Problems in the History of Science* (Madison, WI, 1959), pp. 3–23.
[159] Hall to Boas, 22 Dec. 1956, IC MS Hall.
[160] Boas to Hall, 5 Feb. 1957, IC MS Hall.
[161] Hall to Boas, 11 Feb. 1957, IC MS Hall.
[162] Boas to Hall, 23 March 1957, IC MS Hall.
[163] Boas to Hall, 11 March 1957, IC MS Hall.
[164] Boas to Hall, 23 March 1957, IC MS Hall.
[165] Hall to Boas, 26 March 1957, IC MS Hall.
[166] Boas to Hall, 22 May 1957, IC MS Hall.
[167] Hall to Boas, 11 to 14 Sept. 1957 and 8, 9 Oct. 1957, IC MS Hall.
[168] Hall to Boas, 10 May 1957, IC MS Hall.

as yet, already fallen in love, then the conditions were right for it to happen. As indeed it did at the Madison meeting held from 1 to 11 September 1957 which was Hall's first visit to America. The day before the conference ended Hall spoke to Boas about his feelings for her, exchanging two kisses;[169] after that there was, could be, no going back: 'I could almost be angry with you' she wrote two days later 'because I would not have known how much you meant to me if you had not spoken—but after that I knew what would happen.'[170]

The immediate problem was that both flew out of Madison on the 11th—Boas to UCLA to start her new job and Hall, first to the University of Indiana at Bloomington, then to Pennsylvania to meet his old friend Philip George and to Massachusetts to meet the historians of science there, before returning to Cambridge. Although both suggested that they would soon return to normality, or rationality set in, as Boas put it,[171] these declarations were half-hearted, as they must have known, especially as they began writing daily to each other. These were very long letters usually on five sheets (the maximum permitted by postage) of air letter paper written over a period of two or three days in moments snatched from their very busy schedules. At the best it took four days, but usually five, for letters to go between Cambridge and Los Angeles, so replies tended to be to letters sent ten days to a fortnight earlier.

The development of their relationship and their deep, passionate and enduring love went through four very well defined periods. The first, from September 1957 until February 1958, was conducted entirely by letter. In these they explored, sometimes with painful honesty, their feelings and quickly consolidated their love. Very early on they decided that Hall should return to America, originally in the summer of 1958, but their impatience to meet again eventually brought this forward to February. Both had attacks of guilt, especially in regard to Anne's position, and the unwritten long-term future implications of their relationship. They were clearly living in their own world and Boas commented that they were 'both behaving in a particularly young & foolish way';[172] Hall referred to living a double life[173] and they told no one.

The second phase of their relationship lasted from February 1958 until the first week of April. Hall returned to America and by delivering lec-

[169] Hall to Boas, 1, 2 Oct. 1957, IC MS Hall.
[170] Boas to Hall, 12, 13 Sept. 1957, IC MS Hall.
[171] Boas to Hall, 12, 13 Sept. 1957, IC MS Hall.
[172] Boas to Hall, 28, 29 Sept. 1957, IC MS Hall.
[173] Hall to Boas, 3, 4, 5 Oct. 1957, IC MS Hall.

tures in Bloomington, Seattle, Berkeley and Los Angeles he was able to pay for his visit. They spent time together there and later during his visit an idyllic period at Cape Cod: 'We did manage an amazing range of life, in our time together—work & play & social life, & holiday idling & domestic contretemps—& it was all equally & deeply satisfactory.'[174] If there had been any doubts about the rightness of their relationship when he arrived, there were none when he left, but again they did not talk about their long-term future. Writing on the plane taking her back to Los Angeles, Boas told Hall that 'perfect bliss' had come to an end but not permanently.[175] Hall, likewise writing on his plane back to England, wrote to her 'Dearest heart, we do belong, we are wonderful together and for each other.'[176]

His return to England signalled the start of the third and infinitely most painful phase of their relationship, conducted mostly by letter but with fairly frequent transatlantic telephone conversations. Instead of going directly to Cambridge, Hall went to Buckland Crescent where Boas's mother, Louise, was living. She 'made me [Hall] face what I mean to do. She wouldn't have if I'd refused to face it, but I knew myself I have to. We can't go on like this.'[177] Hall went to Cambridge where he told Anne about the affair and asked for a divorce, but, of course, she had suspected that he was having an affair and with whom.[178] Thus began a very emotional and hellish time for everyone involved, and especially for Hall who had serious scruples about what he was proposing to do (especially in regard to his daughters, who were still very small), scruples for which Boas said she loved him all the more for holding.[179]

At first Anne refused to divorce him and Hall agreed to try for a year to see if their marriage could be saved,[180] but would be with Boas in August and during 1959 as they had agreed—indeed almost the first thing that Boas did when she got back to Los Angeles was to make a reservation on a flight to London for early August.[181] Such desperate solutions were simply untenable even in the short term, and Boas, clearly very unhappy, uncertain and depressed in Los Angeles, explained to Hall that he must consider himself as well as others and that he needed to make a decision

[174] Boas to Hall, 7 April 1958, IC MS Hall.
[175] Boas to Hall, 6 April 1958, IC MS Hall.
[176] Hall to Boas, 6 April 1958, IC MS Hall.
[177] Hall to Boas, 8 April 1958, IC MS Hall.
[178] Hall to Boas, 9 April 1958, IC MS Hall.
[179] Boas to Hall, 10, 11 April 1958, IC MS Hall.
[180] Boas to Hall, 21, 22 April 1958, IC MS Hall.
[181] Boas to Hall, 8, 9 April 1958, IC MS Hall.

one way or the other within eighteen months, or else all their lives would be shattered.[182] After much further anguish, many letters (including an exchange between Boas and Anne), phone calls, and a meeting between Anne and Louise Boas,[183] it became clear that there was no point in even trying to keep the marriage going and Anne agreed to divorce him. Louise Boas dealt with the last remaining practical problem so far as the relationship was concerned by, at the end of May, paying Hall's air fare to fly on 3 June to Los Angeles and Boas.[184] Thus began the final phase of their relationship which lasted for more than fifty years, for thereafter Hall and Boas would never be separated again for any significant period of time.

They spent the summer in Los Angeles and in the autumn returned to London to live at 24 Montague Square, though it is not clear on what basis Boas was able to leave UCLA to come to London. Derek Price saw them at the beginning of October, shortly after their return, and reported to Singer that 'They seemed to be quite happy together.'[185] Hall worked in Cambridge teaching twenty-one hours weekly ('a great strain'[186]) and lived in Christ's whilst Boas stayed in London. They usually spent the weekends in London and when he was in Cambridge continued to write to each other daily, although somewhat shorter letters than when the Atlantic was between them. Occasionally she would visit Cambridge and Leicester, where Hall introduced her to Bert Howard who found her 'company very stimulating!'[187] It was during this period that Hall spent much of his research time exploring the Newton manuscripts in the University Library. Towards the end of November he commented to Boas that 'we may have to bring out a book of unpublished remains',[188] a suggestion to which she responded enthusiastically: 'a joint book would be wonderful'.[189] It was in this context of these Newton studies that Hall got to know D. T. 'Tom' Whiteside (1932–2008, FBA 1975),[190] then completing his doctorate on late seventeenth-century mathematics and shortly to embark on his eight volume *Mathematical Papers of Isaac Newton*, published between 1967 and 1981, a project so massive that aside from papers and lectures he published nothing else.

[182] Boas to Hall, 14, 15, 16 April 1958, IC MS Hall.
[183] Hall to Louise Boas, 11 May 1958, IC MS Hall.
[184] Hall to Singer, 2 June 1958, Wellcome Collections PP/CJS/A.42.
[185] Price to Singer, 8 Oct. 1958, Wellcome Collections PP/CJS/A.47.
[186] Hall to Butterfield, 23 Feb. 1959, ULC MS BUTT/531/H9.
[187] Hall to Boas, 12 Jan. 1959, IC MS Hall.
[188] Hall to Boas, 25 Nov. 1958, IC MS Hall.
[189] Boas to Hall, 26 Nov. 1958, IC MS Hall.
[190] Hall to Boas, 18 March 1959 and 19 March 1959, IC MS Hall.

Hall and Boas's major concern during the period was, however, finalising the divorce which proved protracted, with Hall seeking speed and Anne showing no sign of haste. This prompted Boas to accuse her of making everyone unhappy, 'a futile thing since it can't be constructive, & only hurts herself & the children as well as you'.[191] Although Anne slowly dealt with the paperwork, it would seem that she was still harbouring hopes of Hall returning to her, though her methods of persuasion were such as to ensure that he 'couldn't go back to <u>that</u> kind of life'[192] as he put it following a particularly harrowing exchange of letters. The petition was not served until the end of January 1959.[193] Following its completion, Hall and Boas married in Marylebone Register Office on 10 June 1959, the witnesses being her mother and Hall's sister Doreen.

1959–1963, America

Just before he asked Anne for a divorce, Hall had written to Boas 'I shall get a job in America as soon as possible'[194] and a few days later: 'We can only live together in America, now.'[195] There was no pressing institutional necessity for him to leave his Cambridge jobs as his return to work there in October 1958 illustrates. Butterfield (who had had his own passionate affair in the 1930s though it did not lead to divorce and remarriage[196]) and the Master of Christ's, Brian Downs (1893–1984, who was himself divorced), both wanted Hall to stay,[197] whilst Plumb despaired at being left behind in a 'dreary college'.[198] Indeed the only criticism from his colleagues that Hall seems to have encountered came from a mathematics fellow at Christ's, Stourton Steen (1897–1979).[199] But Hall also sensed that he was stuck in Cambridge, which was unlikely to create a senior post in the near future. It is clear from his correspondence that he did not enjoy undergraduate teaching, had no opportunity for teaching advanced students and indeed had been 'fed up with Cambridge' since at least the middle of

[191] Boas to Hall, 22 Oct. 1958, IC MS Hall.
[192] Hall to Boas, 11 Nov. 1958, IC MS Hall.
[193] Hall to Boas, 29 Jan. 1959, IC MS Hall.
[194] Hall to Boas, 8 April 1958, IC MS Hall.
[195] Hall to Boas, 12, 13 April 1958.
[196] Michael Bentley, *The Life and Thought of Herbert Butterfield: History, Science and God* (Cambridge, 2011), pp. 78–94.
[197] Hall to Singer, 2 June 1958, Wellcome Collections PP/CJS/A.42.
[198] Hall to Boas, 13, 14 May 1958, IC MS Hall.
[199] Hall to Boas, 2 Oct. 1958, IC MS Hall.

1956.[200] Furthermore, Anne wanted him to leave Cambridge: 'I think I owe her that much.'[201] The divorce settlement meant that Hall had to pay half his salary to her in alimony[202] and so Boas Hall had to remain employed so they could support themselves. Since there were no positions available in England, unless they lived apart for significant periods of time on opposite sides of the Atlantic, it really meant finding a job for Hall in America.

Hall had strong possibilities of positions at Michigan, Wisconsin and Indiana; Boas had done a good job of spreading the word that he was looking for a job in America, although not the reason. In the end the key figure was Horace W. Magoun (1907–91), a distinguished neuroscientist, who in 1950 had moved to UCLA where he founded the Brain Research Institute. He had also established in 1953 UCLA's programme in the history of medicine with funding from the National Institute of Health and was 'quite well acquainted' with Boas Hall.[203] He created 'an unexpected niche'[204] for Hall as Associate Research Medical Historian, based in the Medical Center. Hall had met Magoun when he had lectured at UCLA in early 1958 and from Hall and Boas's correspondence it is clear that she had done some gentle lobbying to secure this position for him. Thus on 23 February 1959 Hall resigned his posts at Cambridge with effect from 30 September. He told Butterfield that he was sorry to leave Cambridge, and asked to be considered if there was a chance for him in the future.[205] Downs, as Master of Christ's, wrote a fulsome letter of thanks and praise for all of Hall's time at Cambridge and wished him well for the future.[206]

At UCLA Boas Hall returned to her teaching and research whilst Hall concentrated on his research. He worked with the historian of Renaissance medicine Charles O'Malley (1907–70) who in 1959, much to Hall's annoyance since it meant that there would be no possibility of a permanent job for him at UCLA, had been appointed Professor of Medical History there.[207] Nevertheless, O'Malley and Hall organised a seminar series on scientific literature in England during the sixteenth and seventeenth cen-

[200] Boas to Hall, 13 July 1956, IC MS Hall.

[201] Hall to Singer, 2 June 1958, Wellcome Collections PP/CJS/A.42.

[202] Hall to Linstead, 28 Jan. 1962, IC MS KH/2/2.

[203] Mandelbrote interview, p. 36.

[204] A. R. Hall, 'Introduction' to *Science and Society: Historical Essays on the Relations of Science, Technology and Medicine* (Aldershot, 1994), p. viii.

[205] Hall to Butterfield, 23 Feb. 1959, ULC MS BUTT/531/H9.

[206] Downs to Hall, 26 Feb. 1959, IC MS Hall.

[207] Hall to Boas, 28 April 1959, IC MS Hall.

turies;[208] Hall put the museum experience he had gained at the Whipple to use when he acted as consultant for an exhibition of microscopes held in 1961;[209] and he wrote a paper on the understanding of the cardiovascular system by the second-century AD physician Galen.[210] Hall later recollected that they had enjoyed their time at UCLA, but apart from Boas Hall there was no one else there to talk to about the history of science.[211]

Hall probably did enough to justify his place at UCLA as an historian of medicine. But it is clear that most of his and Boas Hall's research efforts were concentrated on Newton and related topics. They published a number of articles and in 1962 Cambridge University Press issued their edited selection of previously *Unpublished Scientific Papers of Isaac Newton*, which mainly dealt with the development of Newton's ideas on the nature of matter. This was the end of the project that they had started in late 1958 during Hall's last year at Cambridge. Most significantly, perhaps, they began their joint work on the correspondence of Henry Oldenburg (*c*.1619–77, FRS 1663), who had been the first Secretary of the Royal Society between 1663 and his death in 1677.[212] Hall had first come across Oldenburg's correspondence when he had been researching his Ph.D. thesis in the late 1940s. In the Royal Society he had found letters from Oldenburg to the poet John Milton (1608–74), a Christ's man, and this had sparked Hall's initial interest. He began transcribing and came to realise that Oldenburg's correspondence represented a vast clearing house of scientific exchange in the early history of the Royal Society at a time when science in England was beginning to flourish as never before.[213] As early as 1953 it was known that he was working on an edition of Oldenburg's letters,[214] but with all his other commitments during this time progress would undoubtedly have been slow.

Aside from combining their formidable knowledge and skills in editing Oldenburg's correspondence, quite how they saw their future at that point is not certain, but judging from his output Hall clearly did not see himself as an historian of medicine and presumably as a consequence his

[208] A. R. Hall and C. O'Malley, *Scientific Literature in Sixteenth & Seventeenth Century England* (Los Angeles, 1961).
[209] Papers and text of captions in IC MS Hall.
[210] A. R. Hall, 'Studies on the history of the cardiovascular system', *Bulletin for the History of Medicine*, 34 (1960), 391–413.
[211] Mandelbrote interview, p. 36.
[212] Boas Hall (1), p. 12.
[213] Mandelbrote interview, p. 27.
[214] Sister M. Marion to Hall, 30 July 1953, IC MS Hall.

time in this role at UCLA could only be limited. The late 1950s was a time when new departments devoted solely to the history of science and medicine were established in the United States due, in part, to the establishment by the National Science Foundation in the late 1950s of its programme in the history and philosophy of science.[215] During 1960 alone three new departments were founded at Princeton, Yale and Indiana. Both Hall and Boas Hall were on the advisory committee of the new Department of History and Logic of Science at Indiana, then chaired by Russell Hanson, who had left Cambridge for Bloomington in 1957 and was very keen to have the Halls move there.[216] His idea was to create a department that would cover the scientific revolution in its entirety with Edward Grant on late medieval science, Boas Hall on the Renaissance and Hall on the seventeenth and eighteenth centuries, together with three philosophers of science. The Halls did not make the move from Los Angeles to Bloomington until the autumn of 1961 because of the need to address the rules of Indiana University about the employment of a husband and wife in the same department.[217] They enjoyed Bloomington and later recollected 'we never found such an exciting and creative intellectual environment again as we had there'.[218]

There they completed writing Boas Hall's *The Scientific Renaissance, 1450–1630* (London, 1962) and Hall's *From Galileo to Newton, 1630–1720* (London, 1963), which he regarded as a better book than *The Scientific Revolution*.[219] These two books, both published by Collins, became very influential and at least one was awarded as a prize at Alderman Newton's school.[220] These books were intended to be the second and third volumes in a series conceived by Hall in the late 1950s entitled 'The Rise of Modern Science' covering, in eight volumes, the history of science from the ancient world to the twentieth century.[221] Although no further volumes were published, the Halls did however cover this large topic in their joint *A Brief History of Science* (New York, 1964, with the preface dated Indiana,

[215] Margaret W. Rossiter, 'The History and Philosophy of Science Program at the National Science Foundation', *ISIS*, 75 (1984), 95–104. Boas served on the grants committee for a number of years, Boas Hall (1), p. 9.

[216] Boas Hall (1), p. 11.

[217] Kevin T. Grau, 'Force and nature: the Department of History and Philosophy of Science at Indiana University, 1960–1998', *ISIS*, 90 (1999), S304.

[218] Mandelbrote interview, p. 39.

[219] Norman Cantor, 'The Scientific Revolution: A. R. Hall', in *Perspectives on the European Past: Conversations with Historians*, 2 vols. (New York, 1971), Vol. 1, p. 346.

[220] Recollection by Peter Bowler.

[221] Hall to Bragg, 18 Sept. 1958, RI MS WLB 51B/200.

15 December 1962) which, despite selling 40,000 copies, was not deemed a success by the publishers (New American Library) who pulped the remainder.[222]

Furthermore, the Halls took on research students including David Lindberg (1935–) and Victor Thoren (1935–1991), who had originally worked with them at UCLA on Tycho Brahe (1546–1601) but who followed them when they moved to Indiana. They continued work on Oldenburg's correspondence, for which they received a $12,000 grant from the National Science Foundation,[223] and completed the first two volumes,[224] though not immediately published. They spent the summers in England working on the project and attending meetings such as the 1961 conference on scientific change organised by Crombie and held in Rhodes House in the University of Oxford.

At this meeting Kuhn presented what was essentially the first third of his *The Structure of Scientific Revolutions*, which would be published the following year. Hall, who later said he could not see any connection between Kuhn's *The Copernican Revolution* and *The Structure*,[225] concluded his commentary on Kuhn's paper at the Oxford meeting by saying that he seemed 'to be concerned rather with the minor tactics than with the grand strategy of scientific change'[226] and suggested that Kuhn's paradigms were monolithic. Hall continued his attack on Kuhn's views a couple of years later in November 1963 at one of the famous fortnightly seminars organised by Karl Popper (1902–94, FBA 1958, FRS 1976) at the London School of Economics, much to Popper's approval.[227] Despite the criticism of Hall and others, Kuhn's work became and remains massively influential in the academic world and beyond, mostly in the area of science studies and philosophy of science. Historians of science, right from the beginning as indicated by Hall's comments, found, and still find, the framework of scientific change proposed in Kuhn's *Structure* to be unhelpful and very few historians have analysed science in those terms.

[222] Boas Hall (1), p. 12.
[223] Grau, 'Force and nature', p. S306.
[224] Mandelbrote interview, p. 39.
[225] Mandelbrote interview, p. 23.
[226] A. R. Hall, 'Commentary on T. S. Kuhn, "The function of dogma in scientific research"', in A. C. Crombie (ed.), *Scientific Change: Historical Studies in the Intellectual, Social and Technical Conditions for Scientific Discovery and Technical Invention from Antiquity to the Present* (London, 1963), p. 375.
[227] Private communication, 2 Sept. 2011, from Jagdish Hattiangadi to FJ. See also Jagdish Hattiangadi, 'Kuhn debunked', *Social Epistemology*, 17 (2003), 175–82, especially p. 177.

Hall continued his critique of what was beginning to be labelled the externalist view—as opposed to his internalist view—of the factors that were claimed by historical sociologists, such as Merton, to have caused the scientific revolution. He outlined his views in a paper entitled 'Merton revisited' published in 1963,[228] which was strongly criticised by Robert Young (1935–) in a Festschrift for Needham that, amongst other issues, discussed the development of the history of science in Britain.[229] Young described Hall's views, as seen ten years later, as apparently 'bizarre', as coming to the reverse conclusion to Marxists in regard to the relationship between science and society, and stressing the 'severe limitations' to his approach and that of others.[230]

Looking back at the debate between externalism and internalism, as exemplified by the writings of Hall and of Young, it is striking how it was conducted in the realm of ideas, rather than in terms of historical and biographical contexts. While this was entirely in line with Hall's views and practice, it is a bit surprising that Young followed suit. Familiar with history of science in post-Hall Cambridge—he arrived there in 1960 to do his Ph.D.—Young was clearly unacquainted with the battles that had been fought out in the 1940s and 1950s. It would seem, also, that he was unfamiliar with the impact that wartime service had on the previous generation. Both these factors contributed significantly to the formation of Hall's historiographic views. Leaving aside the various ideological commitments, the internal–external debate emerged from the argument as to who was qualified to do history of science—scientists or historians—and this did not necessarily conform easily with other ideological considerations. Marxists and scientists such as Needham and Lilley at Cambridge and those who belonged to the 'Visible College'[231] elsewhere, were mostly very high-level scientific practitioners, who analysed science in terms of social and economic structures and modes of production. Non-Marxist scientists tended to view modern science as contributing crucially to material prosperity and a general improvement in living standards. Either

[228] A. R. Hall, 'Merton revisited or science and society in the seventeenth century', *History of Science*, 1 (1963), 1–16.

[229] Robert Young, 'The historiographic and ideological contexts of the nineteenth-century debate on man's place in nature', in Mikuláš Teich and Robert Young (eds.), *Changing Perspectives in the History of Science: Essays in Honour of Joseph Needham* (London, 1973), pp. 344–438.

[230] Ibid., pp. 346 and 356.

[231] Gary Werskey, *The Visible College: a Collective Biography of British Scientists and Socialists of the 1930s* (London, 1978).

way, science was a critically important activity and thus its creation needed to be understood. Historians, such as Butterfield and Hall, who accepted the rhetoric, sought to do this.

At one level the criticisms made by Needham or Singer of Butterfield and Hall, that only a training in science qualified someone to work in the history of science, referred to the specialised knowledge of the various sciences. But there was another feature of this argument which affected Hall's historiography. Although he had considerable experience of the difficulties of applying science in practice, he had never undertaken any scientific research and this seems to have contributed to a mild positivism and idealism stemming from his concentration on the history of theory through reading Koyré and a consequent tendency to downplay the significance of experiment. Thus, for example, Hall accepted Koyré's view of the impossibility of the experiment where Galileo described the motion of water and wine without mixing, until the present author demonstrated it to him. Boas Hall, on the other hand, had undertaken some scientific research and consequently knew the problems inherent in experimental work. Partly as a consequence of this experience, and partly as a reaction to Sarton, she tended to be rather less positivist in outlook, despite the influence of Koyré, but, like Hall, she followed Koyré in concentrating on the history of ideas approach to the history of science.

All this fitted in very well with their colleagues at Bloomington where the experience of working with philosophers strengthened Hall's analytical interests.[232] And this goes a long way to explaining the explicit historiographical turn that Hall's work took in the early 1960s. Yet despite the intellectual excitement at Indiana, the Halls' freedom to do research, to visit Europe in the summers, and the financial benefits of being there, all was not happy and there were tensions within the new small department. The Halls turned down an invitation from Pennsylvania, but Hanson formally accepted an offer from Yale in early 1963.[233] Before that, indeed within months of taking up their positions at Indiana, Hall wrote a letter of enquiry when a new chair in the history of science and technology was announced at Imperial College late in 1961.

[232] Mandelbrote interview, p. 37.
[233] Grau, 'Force and nature', pp. S306–7.

Imperial College, 1963–1980

Appointment

The origins of what became the Department of the History of Science and Technology at Imperial College can be traced to some correspondence in the autumn of 1958 between the Rector, Patrick Linstead (1902–66, FRS 1940), the head of physics, Patrick Blackett (1897–1974, FRS 1933), and Charles Singer. The immediate cause of the correspondence was the emigration of Derek Price to the United States after failing to find a job in England, despite having an enormously powerful patron in Lawrence Bragg, first as Director of the Cavendish Laboratory until 1953 and then as Director of the Davy–Faraday Research Laboratory at the Royal Institution.[234] Singer bemoaned the loss of Price to Britain and suggested to Blackett approaching ICI to found a chair for him at Imperial dealing with the humanistic relationships of science.[235] Blackett copied this correspondence to Linstead who turned this proposal into developing history of science which he was very keen to do, but for which there was no funding provision.[236] Nevertheless, a college committee was formed and on 22 May 1959 it convened a dinner for outside experts to discuss the matter. Those who attended included Hall, Singer and McKie, whilst those from the college, in addition to Linstead and Blackett, included a number with strong historical interests such as Skempton and the theoretician, philosopher and historian of mathematics, Gerald Whitrow (1912–2000). Singer continued to insist that for the historian of science 'scientific training was more important than historical'[237] and later suggested that Price should be appointed[238]—this was shortly after Price had failed, much to his disgust, to be appointed as Hall's successor at Cambridge.

What was not in contention at the dinner was the idea that the humanistic relations of science should be interpreted as meaning the history of science. Coming less than two weeks after Snow had delivered his diatribe against the supposed separation of scientific and literary cultures in his 'Two Cultures' lecture, the timing of the dinner could hardly have been more apposite. How many of those at the dinner knew of the lecture is not

[234] See the Price file in Bragg's papers, RI MS WLB 55F.
[235] Singer to Blackett, 10 Sept. 1958 and 12 Sept. 1958, IC MS KH/2/1.
[236] Blackett to Linstead, 23 Sept. 1958, IC MS KH/2/1.
[237] Notes of a dinner meeting held on 22 May 1959 at 178 Queensgate, IC MS KH/2/1.
[238] Singer to Linstead, 24 July 1959, IC MS KH/2/1.

known—it would be a little while before Frank Leavis (1895–1978) supplied his incendiary rejoinder that would make Snow's lecture far more significant than it deserved.[239] At this time Hall and Boas were working on radio talks for the BBC Third Programme to be part of a series on the history of science. These were published in *The Listener*[240] and collected together in a book to which Hall provided the foreword dated 1 January 1960. He began: 'If it is true, as Sir Charles Snow has argued, that our present educational system produces two cultures, the history and philosophy of science occupies a central position between them,'[241] and then proceeded to make a strong case for the expansion of the subject to provide a solution to the cultural problems of science that Snow had focused on. The idea that history of science (combining, as Hall pointed out, elements from both science and history) would help solve the two cultures problems seems to have been one attractive to the higher reaches of university administrations on both sides of the Atlantic. In the ensuing years many new departments devoted to the subject would open as well as individual appointments made across a wide range of academic departments.

So far as Imperial College was concerned, throughout the remainder of 1959 discussions continued about possible figures to fill a chair in the history of science, should it be established, as well as how it should be funded. In early 1960 ICI agreed to contribute £1,500 annually for seven years towards the chair[242] and by the middle of 1961 it had been included in the University Grants Committee quinquennial funding settlement for the college to start in October 1962.[243] The position was announced in December 1961 and was framed explicitly in the rhetoric of the two cultures: 'the first holder of the chair will have the opportunity to bridge one of the gaps between the humanities and the sciences'.[244] In early January 1962 Hall wrote to Linstead asking for details, mentioning Boas Hall and adding that he was not sure that he wanted to leave the United States.[245] Linstead replied that he had not regretted his own moves to and fro across

[239] Guy Ortolano, *The Two Cultures Controversy: Science, Literature and Cultural Politics in Postwar Britain* (Cambridge, 2009).

[240] M. Boas, 'The machinery of nature', *The Listener*, 61 (1959), 1106–8; A. R. Hall, 'The experimental way', *The Listener*, 62 (1959), 131–3.

[241] A. R. Hall, 'Foreword', in A, R. Hall (ed.), *The Making of Modern Science Six Essays* (Leicester, 1960), p. 3.

[242] ICI to Linstead, 2 Feb. 1960, IC MS KH/2/2.

[243] Linstead to Blackett, 17 May 1961, IC MS KH/2/2.

[244] 'History of Science and Technology at the Imperial College', *Nature*, 192 (1961), 1131.

[245] Hall to Linstead, 4 Jan.1962, IC MS KH/2/2.

the Atlantic and referred to Boas Hall as a 'special opportunity',[246] a phrase that would recur in correspondence as 1962 progressed. Hall, after a slight hesitation, responded by saying that he would not apply for the position, that Boas Hall was 'In many ways … far more able than [he]', adding that they could not afford to live on a single salary because of the alimony. He concluded by expressing the hope that the college would employ a professional historian—surely a riposte to the views of the now dead Singer.[247]

Sixteen people applied for the chair including the historians Samuel Lilley (1914–87), Frank Greenaway (1917–) and Donald Cardwell (1919–98), but also the science communicators Magnus Pyke (1908–92) and Anthony Michaelis (1916–2007).[248] The appointment board of the University of London, whose membership included Butterfield, Blackett and Linstead, met on 15 February 1962 and decided that none of the applicants was appropriate for the position. Instead they decided that Linstead would approach, in order of preference, Joseph Needham and then Hall and if both declined the Board would reconvene. Needham declined, and since his rejection does not seem to have been followed up this suggests that it had been couched in a non-negotiable way.

At the beginning of March 1962 Linstead was considering how best to approach Hall. At this point Butterfield intervened to say that Hall must be brought back and suggested, as an inducement, that Boas Hall should be offered a position, although he had never met her.[249] Linstead told Butterfield that he did not rule out this option, again referred to it as a 'special opportunity' and added that he had invited Hall to London in May to discuss the matter.[250] Hall took some time to respond[251] and eventually suggested that as they were coming to England at the end of June they should meet then, to which Linstead agreed.[252]

They met at the start of July and with Blackett's approval Linstead offered them both jobs, with Boas Hall to be appointed at Senior Lecturer level (which Imperial could offer) with it being understood that she would be promoted to Reader the following year, this being an appointment

[246] Linstead to Hall, 12 Jan. 1962, IC MS KH/2/2.
[247] Hall to Linstead, 28 Jan. 1962, IC MS KH/2/2.
[248] File relating to board of advisors meeting on 15 Feb. 1962, IC MS KH/2/3.
[249] Butterfield to Henderson, *c*.7 March 1962, IC MS KH/2/2.
[250] Linstead to Butterfield, 16 March 1962, IC MS KH/2/2. Linstead to Hall, 9 March 1962, IC MS KH/2/2.
[251] Hall to Linstead, 22 March 1962, IC MS KH/2/2.
[252] Linstead to Hall, 4 April 1962, IC MS KH/2/2.

which only the University of London could make and thus could not be done immediately.[253] Hall then hesitated for two months about whether to accept or reject the offer, a delay that clearly irritated Linstead. But during this period some of the details were worked out, such as where they would have their offices and departmental library—180 Queensgate. Furthermore they were offered a flat (on very reasonable terms) next door at 179 while they found somewhere to live permanently. Against the move was their enjoyment of working in Indiana, although Hanson's imminent departure lessened that attraction, and they would take a significant cut in salary. On the other hand there was the near impossibility of continuing work on Oldenburg while based in Indiana, and, but probably significantly, the personal reason to be nearer Hall's daughters.[254] Eventually on 3 September Hall accepted on both their behalves agreeing to start at the beginning of October 1963.[255]

On 19 November 1963 Hall delivered his inaugural lecture entitled 'Historical relations of science and technology'.[256] In this he surveyed both disciplines, noting the institutional weakness of the history of technology compared to that of science, criticised the undue optimism of nineteenth-century historians and spent a significant proportion of his time talking about Newton. On such an occasion Hall could not ignore the cultural context which had brought the department and his chair into existence. He commented that he preferred to leave bridge building to civil engineers (one imagines Skempton's chuckle in the audience), but repeated the position he had taken four years earlier that he believed the subjects had 'a large role waiting for them in the more liberal scheme of British education that I hope will come'.[257] *Nature* published Hall's lecture in its entirety over nearly five pages which is an indication of the importance attached to his appointment and the subjects, both by the college and also more broadly by the scientific and engineering communities.

Teaching

The new Department of the History of Science and Technology, of which Hall and Boas Hall were the only members for the first few years, was

[253] Note by Linstead, 3 July 1962, IC MS KH/2/2.
[254] Mandelbrote interview, p. 39. Boas Hall (1), pp. 12–13.
[255] Hall to Linstead, 3 Sept. 1962, IC MS KH/2/2.
[256] A. R. Hall, 'Historical relations of science and technology', *Nature*, 200 (1963), 1141–5.
[257] Ibid., p. 1145.

always intended to be a research department; Blackett had used the comparison of the Department of Meteorology.[258] Hence undergraduate courses were only very slowly built up. In part this was due to the reluctance of individual departments to permit their students to take courses outside their control, although Chemical Engineering allowed Boas Hall to deliver a popular course on the history of technology to their students.[259]

To make an immediate impact on the consciousness of the college following their arrival, the Halls put on a course of lectures (some of which were delivered by others), entitled '400 Years of Mechanism: Theory and Practice 1500–1900', which was open to the entire college. The following year Hall delivered a series of six lectures on the early history of the microscope and in 1965 they provided a series on the history of chemical theory.[260] Thereafter, following the establishment of a postgraduate programme, these series were discontinued, but the Halls retained their college-wide presence by contributing to the lunch time lectures organised by Associated Studies.

The development of the postgraduate programme was delayed by Imperial College's then status as a school of the University of London, the degree-awarding authority. This meant that to establish masters courses in the history of science and technology necessarily required going through the committee structures of both college and university and this took time. However, the college on its own could establish one-year postgraduate diploma courses, awarded on the basis of a short research project, which is what the Halls did initially. Their first student, Richard Hills, wrote his 60,000 word dissertation on the drainage of the fens for which he gained his Diploma of Imperial College in 1964.[261]

By the middle of 1966 the Halls had received the necessary authorisations to establish masters courses in the history of science and in the history of technology which first ran in 1967–8. Each year thereafter around half-a-dozen students took the history of technology course and slightly more did the history of science. Both courses could be done full time in a year or part time over two or more years. Because neither history of science nor technology were studied at undergraduate level, the Halls insisted that before anyone pursued doctoral research they should first do one or

[258] Notes of a dinner meeting held on 22 May 1959 at 178 Queensgate, IC MS KH/2/1.
[259] Boas Hall (1), p. 13.
[260] Lecture course announcements in IC MS KH/1/2 and Hall to Linstead, 27 Aug. 1963, IC MS KH/2/4.
[261] Richard Hills, conversation with FJ, 6 July 2009.

other of the masters courses, or at the very least attend the lectures. Most students for both masters and research possessed first degrees in a science or engineering subject or, occasionally, history or design. Thus the Halls viewed the master degrees as conversion courses before going on to undertake research.

However, both masters and research students were, they found, slow in coming because of the funding arrangements, or rather lack thereof, an issue that particularly frustrated the Halls. The history of science groups at Oxford and Cambridge Universities were given quotas from the Department of Scientific and Industrial Research (from 1965 the Science Research Council) or from the Department of Education and Science from which they could directly allocate grants to students. History of science at Imperial College was not part of this quota system which the Halls found discouraged a number of students from studying with them.[262] Students could apply directly to these sources for support, but in practice very few were successful.

But in the end they produced many students who subsequently went on to pursue distinguished careers in the history of science. Among research students, of whom more than twenty completed their theses, can be counted Andy Wear (who worked on Renaissance anatomy), Albert van Helden (Saturn's rings in the seventeenth century), Janet Browne (mid-nineteenth-century biogeography), J. V. Field (Kepler's geometrical cosmology), Nick Russell (early modern animal breeding), Frank James (the beginnings of spectroscopy) and Steve Pumfrey (William Gilbert, but he completed at the Warburg Institute).

It is apparent, both from the work of these individuals and from the others, that the Halls were more than happy to supervise students on almost any topic or scientific speciality, although it is noticeable that there was only one thesis on the twentieth century and none on any pre-sixteenth-century subjects. Nearly half of the theses dealt with the nineteenth century which reflected a growing trend in the subject and the beginnings of doubting the view of the Halls and others that the origins of modern science lay in the sixteenth and seventeenth centuries alone. There was little in the way of research training and methodological teaching (possibly because the Halls believed that what was necessary had been covered in the masters courses), although research students were strongly encouraged to read and discuss the various works of Robin Collingwood

[262] Hall to the Secretary of the Science Research Council, 27 July 1967, IC MS KH/2/4. This was a very strongly worded letter and it is not clear whether it was sent.

(1889–1943, FBA 1934), especially the *Autobiography*.[263] The Halls ran a closed seminar for their students in order to keep them 'free of the sometimes vicious personal attacks that formed part of the intellectual argument in the history of science community in the 1970s'.[264] Whilst the overwhelming preponderance of the theses submitted at Imperial were internalist in outlook, the lack of explicit methodological training meant that students were not indoctrinated with this view. Indeed most of those who pursued careers in the history of science moved into more socially oriented historical studies of science, but with a clear respect for the value of the content of scientific knowledge. All in all 'As teachers the Halls were inspiring, painstaking, approachable and kind.'[265]

Amongst their diploma and masters students who went elsewhere for their doctorates can be counted Richard Hills, Nick Fisher, Andy Cunningham and Anne Sant (later Secord). Furthermore the Halls hosted research students from overseas (mostly American) universities, such as Bob Westman, Patri Pugliese, David Roos and Jim Secord, for a year. Amongst senior scholars who visited the department for extended periods were Emory Kemp, L. J. Jones, Jim Taub, Rod Home and Martin Rudwick (FBA 2008). All in all, the Halls built up, from scratch, a scholarly department which became, for a while, one of the major centres for the history of science both nationally and internationally.

To mark Hall's seventieth birthday in 1990 a group of their former students organised, on behalf of the British Society for the History of Science, a conference, 'Renaissance and Revolution', held at Keble College, Oxford. It is a testimony to the esteem in which they were held that the meeting was very well attended by historians of science at all stages of their careers including those who held somewhat different views from them.[266] A smaller meeting was held at the Royal Institution in 2000 to mark their eightieth birthdays.

[263] For Hall on Collingwood see A. R. Hall, 'Presidential Address: can the history of science be history?', *British Journal for the History of Science*, 4 (1969), 217–18.

[264] Andrew Wear, 'Obituary Rupert Hall (1920–2009) Marie Boas Hall (1919–2009), *Medical History*, 53 (2009), 588.

[265] J. V. Field, 'Obituary. Alfred Rupert Hall (26 July 1920–5 February 2009) and Marie Boas Hall (18 October 1919–23 February 2009)', *British Journal for the History of Science*, 43 (2010), 103.

[266] A selection of some of the papers presented at the meeting was published as J. V. Field and Frank A. J. L. James (eds.), *Renaissance and Revolution: Humanists, Scholars, Craftsmen and Natural Philosophers in Early Modern Europe* (Cambridge, 1993).

Research and projects

The Halls were also expected to pursue their own research. At Imperial the first volume of Oldenburg's correspondence was published in 1965 by the University of Wisconsin Press. This contained a foreword by Linstead as Foreign Secretary of the Royal Society, but the Halls dated their preface Indiana September 1962. In the following twelve years they published a further ten volumes, the last two published by Mansell in London—that is one every year until 1971 and then a volume every other year. They then encountered problems with finding a publisher who was willing to complete the project by publishing the final two volumes, but eventually in 1986 (after they left Imperial) volumes twelve and thirteen were produced by Taylor and Francis. Their preface, dated February 1980, commented that 'We have at last, after twenty years work, come to the end of a task we undertook light-heartedly.'[267] But they were satisfied that all the effort had been worthwhile and that Hall's original vision of the scope of the project had been borne out. If much of the Halls' work has suffered the usual fate of historical writing to be superseded by later work and interpretations, their edition of Oldenburg's correspondence will surely remain invaluable to historians for many years to come—a permanent monument to their relationship, quite possibly something that might never have come into existence but for that. Furthermore, Hall firmly believed that it was the duty of historians to make documentary contributions to the subject.[268]

The reputation of the Halls, and the department as they built it up, ensured that they and it would attract funding for key projects. Although Hall had extensive expertise in the history of technology and Boas Hall some, clearly the subject was not as well covered by them as the history of science. To rectify this, in 1966 Linstead successfully applied to the Leverhulme Trust for a five-year research fellowship in the history of technology.[269] This application was probably stimulated by the presence in the department during 1965–6 of Norman Smith (1938–2009), who had returned from a three-year stint teaching civil engineering in New Zealand. He had a very strong interest in the history of water engineering and had obtained a Science Research Council research fellowship which he used to spend the year in the department. Smith was mentioned specifically in the application to the Leverhulme and his help in the second half of the 1960s

[267] A. R. Hall and M. B. Hall, *The Correspondence of Henry Oldenburg*, 13 vols. (Madison, WI, and London, 1965–86), Vol. 13: p. xv.

[268] Mandelbrote interview, p. 15.

[269] Linstead to Murray, 4 March 1966; Murray to Linstead, 30 June 1966, IC MS KH/2/4.

was invaluable to the Halls in ensuring the success of the diploma and masters course in the history of technology.

Following the demolition of most of the Imperial Institute in the late 1950s, the Doric Portico at Euston Station in 1962, the closure of the Transport Museum in Clapham and the proposed closure of St Pancras Station, the 1960s saw the emergence of an influential and effective group opposed to further destruction of Britain's Victorian industrial heritage led by figures such as the poet John Betjeman (1906–84), his friend the film-maker Arthur Elton (1906–73) and the writer L. T. C. 'Tom' Rolt (1910–74). In 1968 the Duke of Edinburgh (FRS 1951) chaired a committee to consider a proposal by Betjeman to move the Transport Museum to St Pancras which would become a museum of industrial technology.[270]

Before anything could be done the magnitude of what would be involved had to be established. To this end the Director of the Leverhulme Trust, Lord Murray of Newhaven (1903–93), asked the department to undertake a pilot survey to identify what survived and the Trust provided the necessary funding for the project. Smith was appointed Principal Investigator for the project, the report of which was published a couple of years later.[271] Following Smith's work, another meeting was held at Buckingham Palace, the outcome being the establishment by the Standing Commission on Museums and Galleries of a working party to consider the issues. Chaired by the Earl of Halsbury (1908–2000, FRS 1969), its membership included Elton, Rolt, and Hall, who was a key figure in making the recommendations.[272] In a plethora of activities directed towards the preservation of industrial heritage, the working party and Smith's report were two strands that were both praised by the arts minister, Viscount Eccles (1904–99), in the ensuing debate in the House of Lords. But he enfolded most of them into a more general review of museum provision in Britain.[273] However, one recommendation of the working party that was implemented was the establishment of a fund to support the purchase and conservation of items of scientific, industrial and technological significance. Called the PRISM fund and chaired initially by Paul (later

[270] Standing Commission on Museums and Galleries, *The Preservation of Technological Material: Report and Recommendations* (London, 1971), p. 2.

[271] Norman A. F. Smith, *Victorian Technology and its Preservation in Modern Britain* (Leicester, 1970).

[272] Standing Commission on Museums and Galleries, *Eighth Report 1965–1969* (London, 1970), p. 24.

[273] House of Lords debate, 15 May 1972, *Hansard*, v.330, cc.1255–71.

Lord) Wilson (1908–80), Hall was one of its 'livelier' members for the ten years he served on it.[274]

Another key project that came to the department shortly afterwards was the completion of a printed edition of Isaac Newton's correspondence. The Royal Society had been considering such a project since the start of the twentieth century, but it was not until 1939 that they appointed the astronomer Henry Plummer (1875–1946, FRS 1920) to the position of editor.[275] Because of the war not much progress was made and in 1947, following Plummer's death, the metal physicist Edward Andrade (1887–1971, FRS 1935) was appointed chair of the Royal Society's Newton Letters Committee. The mathematician Herbert Turnbull (1885–1961, FRS 1932) became editor, but the project ran into difficulties,[276] as might be expected from anything that involved Andrade,[277] together with an unwieldy and editorially active committee. Nevertheless, Turnbull produced the first volume in 1959, with volumes two and three appearing in succeeding years, though the latter volume was published posthumously. His assistant Joseph Scott (1892–1971) took over and published the fourth volume in 1967.[278]

Andrade died in 1971 and the Royal Society invited the mathematician James Lighthill (1924–1998, FRS 1953) to take over as chair of the Newton Letters Committee. After reading through the papers Lighthill wrote at the end of July 1971 'Quite honestly the invitation seems comparable to that given to Hercules to clean the Augean stables!', and went on to outline the conditions on which he would accept the chairmanship. These included retiring Scott, reforming the structure and functions of the committee and above all appointing a leading Newton scholar as editor, mentioning Hall by name.[279] Matters were made easier when Scott died less than three weeks later[280] and it would appear that Lighthill's other demands were agreed to. He acted quickly and invited Hall to undertake the task, which he accepted on a number of conditions including the appointment of a research assistant on the project.[281] For this position Hall had Laura

[274] John Robinson, conversation with FJ, 9 Jan. 2012.

[275] Minutes of Newton Letters Committee, 23 May 1939, RS MS CMB120A.

[276] Boas to Hall, 18 July 1955, IC MS Hall.

[277] Frank A. J. L. James and Viviane Quirke, 'L'affaire Andrade or how not to modernise a traditional institution', in Frank A. J. L. James (ed.), *'The Common Purposes of Life': Science and Society at the Royal Institution of Great Britain* (Aldershot, 2002), pp. 273–304.

[278] For further details see the editors' preface to R. H. Dalitz and M. Nauenburg (eds.) *The Foundations of Newtonian Scholarship* (Singapore and London, 2000), pp. xi–xii.

[279] Lighthill to Maunsell, 29 July 1971, RS MS RMA 663 NL/3 (third file).

[280] Martin to Lighthill, 27 Aug. 1971, RS MS RMA 663 NL/3 (third file).

[281] Hall to Lighthill, 20 Sept. 1971, IC MS KH/2/5.

Tilling in mind; she was then a research student of his working on a thesis on eighteenth-century observational error that she completed in 1973. By the first week of October negotiations had been completed[282] and at the start of February 1972, at what proved to be the final meeting of the Newton Letters Committee, Hall's appointment was formally agreed and he was awarded a grant of £3,000 (later increased to £4,000) annually to cover his honorarium, expenses and research assistant.[283]

The final three volumes of Newton's correspondence went from 1709 until his death in 1727, covering much of his time at the Royal Mint. Furthermore, undated letters, those that should have been published in earlier volumes as well as corrections, were included. Because of the chaotic state in which the papers were given to Hall and Tilling, they effectively started locating, editing and researching from scratch.[284] However, by the middle of 1976 their work had been completed.[285] Volume five appeared at the start of the previous year and the remaining volumes in 1976 and 1977.

Another major project was editing and publishing the *ISIS Cumulative Bibliography*, which appeared in six volumes between 1971 and 1984. The proposal to do this arose at the time of the fiftieth anniversary of *ISIS* in 1963. The original idea was simply to index the volumes, but this was complicated by the inclusion of a critical bibliography in *ISIS* (one of Sarton's ideas) which comprehensively listed all the publications in the history of science. Eventually it was decided that the *Cumulative Bibliography* would include all the entries in the critical bibliography—in effect it would be a large comprehensive bibliography of publications in the history of science and allied subjects between 1913 and 1965. A professional librarian (and wife of Gerald Whitrow), Magda Whitrow (1914–2010), was appointed editor and Hall gave her office space at Imperial to house the project and the tens of thousands of index cards on which the bibliography was based. In 1968 the office was moved to the Science Museum but returned to Imperial in 1976. It was perhaps the last major bibliography to be produced before the advent of computers (the entries were typed onto new camera-ready index cards using IBM golfball typewriters), but it provided

[282] Lighthill to Martin, 7 Oct. 1971, RS MS RMA 663 NL/3 (third file).

[283] Minutes of Newton Letters Committee, 2 Feb. 1972, RS MS CMB120B. This decision was ratified by the Royal Society Council the following week.

[284] A. R. Hall and Laura Tilling, *The Correspondence of Isaac Newton Volume V 1709–1713* (Cambridge, 1975), p. xiv.

[285] Hall to Robinson, 18 Dec. 1975 and Hall to Le Grand, 6 June 1976, RS RMA 1194 File A.63.

gainful employment for some of the Halls' research students lacking financial support.

Expansion and Closure

While the Halls and their colleagues had done exactly what they had been invited to do when they moved to Imperial in the early 1960s, by the end of the decade and into the 1970s this was not what the college wanted; history of science was no longer seen as the, or even a, solution to the cultural problems of science. The Halls lost their major backer in the college when Linstead died suddenly on 22 September 1966, to be eventually replaced as Rector by the atomic scientist Lord Penney (1909–91, FRS 1946) in 1967. Blackett, one of the Halls' other supporters, had left the college in 1965 to become President of the Royal Society, but they continued to enjoy the support of Whitrow and Skempton who, as head of Civil Engineering, was particularly helpful with the issues surrounding Norman Smith.

Penney was concerned with the poor state of the college's finances, and on one occasion raided the department's reserves which, though small in absolute terms, he regarded as disproportionately large for its size.[286] He was basically as unsympathetic to the humanities and social sciences as Linstead had been supportive.[287] The problems this created for the Halls were played out in their struggle to obtain a permanent appointment for Smith, once his Leverhulme Fellowship ended in the middle of 1970. Smith had been appointed a temporary lecturer in August 1969, but as the next quinquennium did not begin until 1972–3 (the earliest point at which any funding resulting from a successful college bid would become available) there was a two-year gap. The departmental reserves would cover the first year and if they did not Hall wrote that he would be willing to make up the difference from his own salary and made a strong case for Smith's appointment beyond July 1971.[288] Key to making Smith's appointment permanent, as Penney pointed out, was how many students there would be in the department during the coming quinquennium, an issue that Hall had already addressed.[289] Hall was successful as in April 1971 the college

[286] Penney to Hall, 11 Feb. 1970, IC MS KH/2/5.

[287] Hannah Gay, *The History of Imperial College London 1907–2007: Higher Education and Research in Science, Technology and Medicine* (London, 2007), p. 571.

[288] Hall to Penney, 9 July 1970, IC MS KH/2/5.

[289] Penney to Hall, 8 Sept. 1970 and Hall to Jackson, 26 Nov. 1969, IC MS KH/2/5.

increased the department's budget by £2,500 for 1971–2[290] which allowed Smith to be made a permanent member of the department, thus increasing its size by 50 per cent. He continued to take most of the responsibility for the history of technology masters course and supervising most of the research students in that area. In 1976 he and Hall edited the first of an annual volume of essays entitled *History of Technology*, a series which continues to be published.

However, securing Smith's appointment would be the Halls' last success so far as the college was concerned. In 1973 another atomic scientist, Lord Flowers (1924–2010, FRS 1961), became Rector. As the 1970s unfolded with the oil crisis, industrial unrest and high levels of inflation, amongst much else, university budgets started to come under pressure. The appointment of Shirley Williams in September 1976 as Secretary of State for Education and Science marked the beginning of retrenchment, a process that continued with vigour following the election in May 1979 of the Conservative government, led by Margaret Thatcher (FRS 1983).[291] Flowers was not necessarily opposed to government higher education policy, indicated by his being the first peer to join the short-lived Social Democratic Party which Williams and others founded in 1981.

At the start of 1976, the Halls sought to expand the department again by the addition of a junior lecturer, specifically to undertake the undergraduate teaching that was slowly increasing. They also pointed out that since they would both reach the age of sixty (the earliest possible retirement age, although they could have both continued for a further seven years) during the 1979–80 academic year, they intended to retire then and therefore there was a need to plan for their succession.[292] The reference to their retirement was a serious tactical error and Flowers pounced, saying that he could not promise a new lectureship, but that the prospect of their retirement changed things;[293] all he had to do was to wait for three years and the future of the subject at Imperial would no longer be in the Halls' hands.

The Halls confirmed in the spring of 1979 that they would be leaving in the summer of 1980, thus permitting, as they thought, ample time to find successors. When there was no movement, Hall wrote to Flowers, shortly after the general election that brought Thatcher to power, asking

[290] Penney to Hall, 2 April 1971, IC MS KH/2/5.
[291] Gay, *Imperial College*, pp. 466–7.
[292] Hall to Flowers, 11 Feb. 1976, IC MS KH/2/5.
[293] Flowers to Hall, 12 Feb. 1976, IC MS KH/2/5.

for assurances that his chair would be continued. Flowers declined to provide this and added that he hoped that Hall would not write round the country about the matter.[294] Matters came to a head in June when Boas Hall sought permission to accept part-time students on the M.Sc. course and experienced 'considerable distress' when this was refused on the grounds that students who would go beyond 1980 could not be accepted.[295] The implication was clear: it had been decided to close the department, although Flowers did ask the Professor of History of Science at Oxford University, Margaret Gowing (1921–1998, FBA 1975, FRS 1988), who seems to have been a personal friend, for her views, but she only told him who was not suitable.[296] The Halls were distressed when it was decided that after they retired what was left of the department (i.e. Norman Smith) would be merged with Associated Studies to form a new Department of Humanities with only a single lecturer as their replacement.[297] Hall's last contribution to the college was to write a short history for its seventy-fifth anniversary in 1982. It was published in October that year, but contained no Rectorial foreword or preface.[298] One does wonder whether Hall had adopted the view implied in the letter that he had written to Flowers asking for reassurance about the future of the department: 'When I came to Imperial College sixteen years ago I believed it to be an institution seriously devoted to education, learning and research and I have not yet abandoned that position.'[299]

Rewards

With such a distinguished record, especially in research, it should not be found surprising that the Halls were widely recognised for their work. However, it was mostly Hall who received the rewards and this was probably what they wanted, as suggested by the subtitle of one of Boas Hall's autobiographical pieces: 'The junior partner's tale'. With this she did herself somewhat less than justice, since, according to Butterfield, she was

[294] Hall to Flowers, 17 May 1979, IC MS KH/2/6 and Flowers to Hall, 18 May 1979, IC Hall.
[295] Hayman to Flowers, 20 June 1979, IC MS KH/2/6.
[296] Gowing to Flowers, 6 July 1979 and 6 Nov. 1979, IC MS KH/2/6.
[297] Flowers to Hall, 5 Dec. 1979, IC MS KH/2/6.
[298] A. R. Hall, *Science for Industry: a Short History of The Imperial College of Science and Technology and its Antecedents* (London, 1982).
[299] Hall to Flowers, 17 May 1979, IC MS KH/2/6.

sometimes considered the better of the two,[300] which was also Hall's opinion[301]—doubtless such mutual admiration and respect of one another goes a long way to accounting for the success of their relationship.

They of course took part in running the British Society for the History of Science. Boas Hall served on its Council between 1970 and 1973 whilst Hall served from 1964 to 1969 (during which he was President, as a 'benevolent dictator',[302] between 1966 and 1968) and again 1973 to 1979. Hall served on the British National Committee for the History of Science (which was based at the Royal Society) and was also President of the International Academy of the History of Science from 1977 until 1981. Both these roles meant that he was a key figure when in 1978 Britain hosted the fifteenth International Congress for the History of Science held in Edinburgh. Hall's connections with the Royal Society meant that he was invited to deliver two of their named lectures, Wilkins (1973) and Leeuwenhoek (1988)—the only occasion on which a non-scientist has thus far delivered that lecture. In 1994 he was President of the History of Science section at the annual meeting of the British Association in Loughborough and it thus fell to him to chair the famous discussion between Harry Collins (1941–) and Lewis Wolpert (1929– , FRS 1980) on the sociology of science, a spat that provided the *Times Higher Education Supplement* with copy for some weeks afterwards.

Hall's status as an historian, even of science, meant that he was not eligible for election to the Royal Society, although Snow thought he was one of the few people who should be both FRS and FBA.[303] Hall's connections were mostly with the scientific community, especially at Imperial College and the Royal Society, and this meant that he was somewhat isolated from the humanities community and its reward systems. In 1975 Hall applied for the Litt.D. degree from the University of Cambridge. Butterfield wrote a supportive, if somewhat equivocal ('Hall is not a genius') report[304] and the degree was conferred on him. The same year Hall was considered for Fellowship of the British Academy, but the proposal found little favour at that time. However, Whiteside was elected then and

[300] Butterfield to Williams, *c.* 13 Jan. 1977, ULC MS BUTT/531/H12.
[301] Hall to Linstead, 28 Jan. 1962, IC MS KH/2/2.
[302] David Knight, Obituary of Hall, *Guardian*, 27 May 2009.
[303] Neil McKendrick, conversation with FJ, 21 Oct. 2011.
[304] H. Butterfield, 'Report on the work submitted by Dr. A. R. Hall for the Litt.D. degree', 1975, ULC MS BUTT/531/H12. Presumably due to the close similarity in content with Butterfield to Williams, *c.*13 Jan. 1977, the cataloguer assumed they were versions of the same document and thus allocated them the same manuscript number.

two years later he proposed Hall.[305] Butterfield was asked for his opinion, and, as with the D.Litt., was supportive, writing that Hall had the authenticity and originality to qualify as a Fellow. Yet there was the same caveat: 'at no point does he [Hall] emerge as having the sort of "genius" which makes Whiteside unique'.[306] Presumably independently, later in the year Flowers, realising Hall's position and possibly out of a slight sense of guilt, wrote to Gowing (another of the 1975 intake) asking for her to support Hall for the fellowship[307] to which he was elected the following year. As Plumb wrote in his letter of congratulation: 'It has been a long haul since Leicester.'[308]

Hall in his reply to Flowers's congratulatory letter commented that 'I certainly hope I shall not long remain a unique FBA at IC.'[309] But for reasons that are not clear Boas Hall had to wait sixteen years before she was elected to the British Academy, this despite being jointly awarded with Hall the highest award of the History of Science Society, the Sarton Medal, in 1981.[310] Nevertheless, she was elected to the Academy in 1994, her principal sponsor being Whiteside.[311]

After Imperial

With their departure from Imperial and the completion of Oldenburg's correspondence coinciding, the Halls now had the freedom to pursue other interests. Furthermore, having first lived in Chiswick and then in a flat in Bayswater on the other side of Hyde Park from the college, they were tired of living in London. In 1968 they had purchased a country cottage in Tackley, a village to the north of Oxford with the immense convenience of a railway station. They enlarged the cottage to take their books,[312] owned a cat (Isaac Newton Felis), they had a garden and an allotment, they walked in the countryside, entertained their friends and former students, ran the bookstall at the church fete, attended evensong[313] (though

[305] Williams to Butterfield, 11 Jan. 1977, ULC MS BUTT/531/H11.
[306] Butterfield to Williams, *c.*13 Jan. 1977, ULC MS BUTT/531/H12.
[307] Flowers to Gowing, 27 June 1977, IC MS KH/2/5.
[308] Plumb to Hall, 18 May 1978, IC MS Hall.
[309] Hall to Flowers, 3 July 1978, IC MS KH/2/5.
[310] F. L. Holmes, 'Award of the Sarton Medal for 1981', *ISIS*, 73 (1982), 266–8.
[311] Information from Peter Brown.
[312] Boas Hall (1), p. 14.
[313] Stephen M'Caw, Funeral sermon, 4 March 2009.

by no means believers) and were prominent in the Tackley Local History Group. Their involvement here included a paper by Hall on Tackley's water supply and collaboration in publishing wills relating to the village.[314]

However, they did not entirely abandon London in the early 1980s. In 1974 Hall had been appointed chairman of the Wellcome Trust's Advisory Panel on the History of Medicine and had become a close friend of the Director of the Trust, Peter Williams; indeed his wife Billie (1925–2007) had taken the history of science masters course and had then undertaken her doctoral research at University College, submitting her thesis in 1976 on the work of Luigi Galvani (1737–98).[315] During Hall's chairmanship, the academic role in the history of medicine undertaken by the Wellcome Trust expanded. This included the establishment of the close links with University College London and medical history units elsewhere in the country. However, when the Director of the Wellcome Institute for the History of Medicine retired in 1979, Hall as chairman tried to provide direction through the committee, but this was not a success. Despite their friendship, Williams was not blind to Hall's difficulty with administration and thought he was not 'stern' enough with the committee.[316] The result was that in 1981 Williams added the duties of Director of the Institute to his tasks (which he did for two years) and Hall took on the role, for four years, of coordinator of the history of medicine programme at the Trust, for which he was paid £10,000 annually and had the use of a flat in Euston Road.[317] In the course of working for the Wellcome Trust, Hall wrote, with B. A. Bembridge (a Deputy Director of the Trust), its history from its founding in 1936 until 1986 and included a foreword by the then chair of Trustees, David Steel (1916–2004).[318]

Despite their commitments, of which the Wellcome Trust was by far the most significant, during the 1980s and 1990s the Halls mostly researched and wrote, which is what they had intended to do following Imperial. It is noticeable that during their time at Imperial, aside from the volumes of the Oldenburg and Newton correspondences, and a steady

[314] A. R. Hall, 'Tackley streams and water', in *Watery Tackley: Publication Number 4 of the Tackley Local History Group* (Tackley, 2000), pp. 1–12. *Tackley Wills 1463–1707: Publication Number 6 of the Tackley Local History Group* (Tackley, 2004).

[315] Published, with a foreword by Hall, as B. I. Williams, *The Matter of Motion and Galvani's Frogs* (Bletchingdon, 2000).

[316] Peter Williams, *The Story of the Wellcome Trust: Unlocking Sir Henry's Legacy to Medical Research* (Hindrigham, 2010), p. 68.

[317] Barren to Hall, 23 Dec. 1981, IC MS Hall.

[318] A. R. Hall and B. A. Bembridge, *Physic and Philanthropy: a History of the Wellcome Trust 1936–1986* (Cambridge, 1986).

stream of papers and reviews, they had not produced a book during those seventeen years. In 1980, however, Hall published *Philosophers at War; the Quarrel between Newton and Leibniz* (Cambridge, 1980) on which he had been working during the 1970s. In this he analysed the quarrel between Newton and Gottfried Leibniz (1646–1716, FRS 1673) over the invention of calculus.

Hall's first post-Imperial book, published in 1983, was listed as the third edition of *The Scientific Revolution*, but was substantially an almost entirely new book. Entitled *The Revolution in Science 1500–1750* (Harlow, 1983) and with no subtitle, it drew upon much of the research that had been undertaken by the Halls and others in the preceding thirty years. Nevertheless, and despite giving a significant role to technology and an entire chapter to experimentation, Hall stated that he would 'unashamedly follow a positivist or even a whiggish line'.[319] This was a carefully thought out position which he defended in detail in a paper published the same year.[320] In terms of *The Revolution in Science*, he meant that he was writing a history of science which culminated in the work of Newton, not one that necessarily led to today's science beginning in 1800 as he had suggested in 1954; hence the lack of a subtitle and taking the end-point back by fifty years. This striking change in approach showed how the history of science was now part of a contextual history, rather than something studied just by scientists usually with some modern aim in view, and was thus worth studying in its own right.

As one of the leading experts on Newton, Hall was the obvious choice to write his biography when Blackwell's began their series of science biographies under the editorship of David Knight, a former student of Crombie's. Hall agreed to this commission on the condition that he could also write a biography of the Platonist Henry More (1614–87, FRS 1664), a Christ's man, who would not have been an obvious choice for the series. Hall delivered this book first and was not sympathetic to More;[321] as Knight wrote, it was 'inimical, detailing the metaphysics and psychical research with fascinated distaste'.[322] There were, however, no such feelings in his Newton biography, published two years later. Hall began by saying: 'I have endeavoured here to write an account of the greatest mind in British history'[323] and concentrated on the scientific work for which Newton

[319] A. R. Hall, *The Revolution in Science 1500–1750* (London, 1983), p. 2.
[320] A. R. Hall, 'On whiggism', *History of Science*, 21 (1983), 45–59.
[321] A. R. Hall, *Henry More and the Scientific Revolution* (Oxford, 1990).
[322] David Knight, Obituary of Hall, *Guardian*, 27 May 2009.
[323] A. R. Hall, *Isaac Newton: Adventurer in Thought* (Oxford, 1992), p. xiii.

remains famous. In addition to a couple of volumes in which he collected some of his papers,[324] Hall was to publish two more books, both on Newton. The first was devoted to Newton's *Opticks* (1704),[325] which doubtless contained material that could not be included in his biography, whilst in the second he published a collection of eighteenth-century biographies written in English, French and Italian.[326] Hall's last publication, appropriately, took him back to the start of his career with an account of his work at the Whipple Museum in the 1950s published in a collection of essays to mark the sixtieth anniversary of Whipple's gift.[327]

While Hall in the 1980s and 1990s concentrated on Newton, Boas Hall worked on the history of the Royal Society. Immediately after leaving Imperial she began working on a history of the Society during the nineteenth century. The then President Andrew Huxley (1917–2012, FRS 1955) took a strong personal interest in the project due to the impending celebrations to mark the centenary of the Presidency, between 1883 and 1885, of his grandfather, Thomas Henry Huxley (1825–95, FRS 1851); indeed the Society paid her travelling expenses.[328] The book, with a foreword by Huxley, was published as *All Scientists Now: the Royal Society in the Nineteenth Century* (Cambridge, 1984), and is a useful case study showing how the scientific community in the nineteenth century deliberately sought to give itself an exclusive professional identity, thereby moving science away from other areas of culture, thus sowing the seeds of the cultural problems of science during the mid twentieth century. This work, together with her service on the Royal Society's Library Committee, led to her being invited to write the history of the library, which was published in 1992.[329]

But in the latter part of the 1980s and into the 1990s she returned to studying the early Royal Society, which provided the subject for her last two books. In the first, *Promoting Experimental Learning* (Cambridge, 1991, and dedicated to her former students), she explored what actually happened at meetings of the Society between its founding in 1660 and Newton's death in 1727. The second, a biography of *Henry Oldenburg*,

[324] A. R. Hall, *Newton, his Friends and his Foes* (Aldershot, 1993), and *Science and Society*.
[325] A. R. Hall, *All Was Light: an Introduction to Newton's Opticks* (Oxford, 1993).
[326] A. R. Hall, *Isaac Newton: Eighteenth-Century Perspectives* (Oxford, 1999).
[327] Hall, 'The first decade'.
[328] Boas Hall (1), p. 15.
[329] M. B. Hall, *The Library and Archives of the Royal Society, 1660–1990* (London, 1992).

had for its subtitle *Shaping the Royal Society* (Oxford, 2002). This was really an extended introduction to his correspondence and was her last published work.

By now into their eighties, the Halls began to suffer the usual infirmities associated with being in one's ninth decade. They were visited weekly by Peter Williams who lived in a nearby village and, despite advice from friends and colleagues, they refused to move from their cottage which was not really suitable as they began to markedly deteriorate first physically and then mentally. This was painful both for themselves and for those who had known them in their prime. The end came quickly in the early part of 2009 when Hall died in the John Radcliffe Hopital on 5 February. Boas Hall lasted less than three weeks longer, dying in the Horton General Hospital in Banbury on the 23rd. There was a joint funeral service in St Nicholas's Church, Tackley, on 4 March, a sunny but fresh spring day with the daffodils already out. Well attended by former students, colleagues and their friends, Peter Williams delivered the address on their lives, and they were laid to rest side by side in the churchyard.

As so often happens with successful pioneers, the very success obscures the magnitude of the achievement. Some of the things that we now take for granted simply did not exist when they started their careers. For the Halls, perhaps the two most significant changes they contributed to bringing about were making history of science a proper branch of history and emphasising, both by their historical writings and by their practice, the value of studying and publishing manuscripts. Both these are now so taken for granted that it requires considerable historical imagination to understand that in the 1940s and indeed into the 1950s such views would have been generally regarded as perverse and that the Halls were both historiographically radical in their day.

Both Hall and Boas would have undoubtedly enjoyed successful careers individually. But by bravely defying the prevailing social conventions, by having confidence in their joint future during the very difficult and emotional closing years of the 1950s, Hall and Boas created the formidable partnership in the history of science that has been outlined in this memoir. Their passionate love, respect and admiration for each other surely produced historical work of a quality and influence much greater than anything they might have done separately.

FRANK A. J. L. JAMES
The Royal Institution

Note. I wish to thank the following for a wide variety of help, especially in permitting access to documents and spending time providing (in both written and verbal form) information about the Halls and their times: Anne Barrett, Michael Bentley, Harold Boas, Peter Bowler, Peter Brown, Angus Buchanan, David Cannadine, Catherine Harpham, Maurice Crosland, A. E. L. Davis, David de Haan, David W. Dewhirst, Julia Elton, Nick Fisher, Jagdish Hattiangadi, Richard Hills, Rod Home, Desmond King-Hele, David Knight, David Lindberg, Stephen M'Caw, Neil McKendrick, Anna-K. Mayer, W. A. Noblett, John Perkins, John Robinson, Norman Robinson, Clarissa Thomas (née Hall, especially for obtaining a copy of her father's army service record), Albert van Helden, Bob Westman and Peter Williams. I also thank the following archives for access to their holdings: Imperial College (IC); University Library, Cambridge (ULC); the Royal Society (RS); Royal Institution (RI); Wellcome Collections; Brown University; Christ's College, Cambridge; All Souls College, Oxford—as well as the collections of the British Library and the London Library. Finally, I am grateful for the comments I received when sections of this memoir were read to the University of London Institute of Historical Research seminar on the philosophy of history. Nevertheless, responsibility for the content of the memoir is mine alone.

IAN JACK

Ian Robert James Jack
1923–2008

IAN ROBERT JAMES JACK was born on 5 December 1923 in Edinburgh, the only child of John McGregor Bruce Jack, Writer to the Signet, and Helena Colburn Buchanan. His mother died early, when he was only eight, and he was then looked after by his paternal aunt. One anecdote only comes down from his earlier childhood. An uncle had bought a great house on the Black Isle, with stags' heads on the walls. When first going on holiday there he was sure (he said) that the rest of the stags' bodies must be on the other side of the walls.

He is likely to have had a relatively lonely childhood. He was afflicted, like his father, by asthma, which he suffered from all his life and which may have been the immediate cause of his death. 'Ventolin', the great palliative for asthmatics, was not much known before the early 1960s. He seems, however, to have been happy at his father's old school, George Watson's, which he attended from 1931 to 1942. Despite asthma he played cricket for the Second XI for three years, but scored a duck on his one appearance in the First XI.

The great importance of George Watson's for him was the study of Latin and Greek under the guidance of 'Ikey' Penman, his classics master, the son of a Fife miner, one of whose hobbies was watching all-in wrestling. Knowing that Ian's class would have learned nothing in their first year, under another master, Penman started them off with elementary Latin grammar and ended by teaching them Homeric Greek. We know this from a memoir of Mr Penman by Ian Jack himself, published in *The Watsonian* (1991–2, pp. 23–6; see also the following article, 'Laudari a viro laudato … laudatur temporis acti' by Christopher Rush, the editor of *The Watsonian* that year). At one point Ian fell out of the important 'U' class, to which Penman taught Classics, but managed (in his own words) 'to clamber back, rather ingeniously, by saying I wanted to take Greek'.[1] He hated science (as it was then taught) but had done well in Latin. Penman recommended to his class the words of Glaukos to Diomedes in Book VI of the *Iliad* (l. 208):

> always be best [bravest], and pre-eminent above all.

In the competition for university entrance scholarships Ian's friend Ronnie and he came first and second, in that order, in the John Welsh Classics List, each becoming a John Welsh Scholar: 'I shall never forget,' Ian wrote, 'the incredulous delight with which my father heard that I had been well placed, when I managed to ring him on a public telephone on the way home. He put it down to good teaching.' However Ian had already impressed his father by the 'relative fluency' with which he translated an unseen passage of Cicero.

Ian concludes his tribute to Mr Penman by noting that he hardly could have commented on the verse of Gray's *Elegy* or Tennyson's 'Crossing the Bar' without having known the different but often recalled rhythms of Latin verse. When he came to edit Robert Browning, his last major undertaking, he knew that this 'delightful task' could not be performed with success by an editor unacquainted with Greek, 'since Greek poetry was never far from Browning's mind'.

While it is clear that Ian Jack had particular satisfaction at his success in Latin and Greek, he must also have had good teaching in English literature from, among others no doubt, Edward Albert, author of a two-volume novel, *Kirk o'Fields*, on Mary Queen of Scots, the Earl of Bothwell, and the question of the Darnley murder. It seems likely that Ian Jack always intended to devote himself to the study of English literature, and he now was admitted to the University of Edinburgh to read English. He left George Watson's for university in 1942, became James Boswell Fellow in 1946, and took his MA in 1947. He was, to his disappointment, turned down for National Service on account of his asthma.

One would like to know more about Jack's undergraduate period reading English, but information is relatively sparse. I am the more grateful to Mr John McCann, a fellow student of Ian's, perhaps in the latter's fourth year at the university. From him we learn that Ian much admired the

[1] Other biographical quotes from Ian Jack in this memoir are taken from his piece in *The Watsonian*.

poetry of John Clare, a recondite subject then and not as now a popular subject of research. Ian was in those days interested in the theatre, amateur and professional, and persuaded John to join him in two walk-on parts in an amateur performance. Ian was passionately interested in the election of a new Rector of the University, persuading Sir William Beveridge, author of the Beveridge Report and one of the founders of the National Health Service, to stand and canvassing for him with energy, though without success in the end. Perhaps, however, John McCann's most interesting memory of Ian is of their rambles together: 'We used to go for long walks together, mostly on the Pentland Hills, and as fellow-asthmatics we understood each other's difficulties in climbing steep gradients. During these walks we talked nineteen to the dozen, about anything and everything, and a very stimulating companion he was … He knew I was hard up, so when he knew I was going to terminate my studies at Edinburgh without graduating he misinterpreted the reason and offered me the money from a bursary he had been awarded which he said he did not need. It was an extraordinarily generous offer (which I did not accept), but I have often thought about it, and have remembered it with gratitude' (Letter to Elizabeth Jack, 30 October 2008).

Ian Jack now won a place at Merton College, Oxford, to pursue research on English literature of the seventeenth and eighteenth centuries. This was in 1947. On 8 July 1948 he and Jane Henderson MacDonald were married in the Parish Church of St Peter in the East, Oxford. Jane Jack became a scholar in her own right and the two continued to collaborate after their marriage was dissolved some twenty years later. Meanwhile Ian's research was supervised by Nichol Smith and, in his final year, Helen Gardner. This was the work which became his first book, *Augustan Satire* (London, 1952), a well-known and successful study. Meanwhile he had become Lecturer in English Literature at Brasenose (1950–5), and was later elected Senior Research Fellow there (1955–61). Jack could surely have made his career in Oxford, but Cambridge attracted him, partly perhaps as the home of the New Criticism. He successfully applied for a Lectureship in the Cambridge English Faculty in 1961. Professor Basil Willey encouraged him to come to Pembroke and (as Ian later told me) he gratefully agreed though he might have hankered after a larger and grander college than Pembroke then was.

Jack may have been impressed by the New Criticism, but he lacked the dogmatic intensity of F. R. Leavis, I. A. Richards's steely commitment to the words on the page, and the brilliant eccentricity of William Empson. (There was of course more to all these critics.) The Cambridge English

Faculty, for the most part, did not think Ian Jack was one of them. The Faculty set him down as a learned traditional scholar whose critical judgements were little better than common sense. While Ian, who had a high opinion of common sense, might have settled for this judgement, his coming work, both critical and editorial, would show that Cambridge was wrong. Meanwhile the difficulties of his adjustment were made more sad by the break-up of his marriage with Jane.

It was not long, however, before he met the lady who would become his second wife, Elizabeth Crone, a school-teacher who shared his literary interests. They were married on 12 August 1972, and soon after bought Highfield House, Fen Ditton, near Cambridge, a spacious and comfortable home which could accommodate all Ian's growing collection of antiquarian and modern books, and which had beautiful views over meadows and on to the river Cam. The many friends of Ian and Elizabeth, colleagues, students and former students, recall with delight the unfailing hospitality of Highfield House, and feel we can attest to a long period of happiness there, during which their son Rowland grew up, and Ian addressed himself to what one may think was the most important and successful part of his academic work.

In fact the new development may already have begun to happen. Those who recall Ian Jack's *English Literature, 1815–32* (Oxford, 1963), *Oxford History of English Literature*, Vol. X, and then turn to *Keats and the Mirror of Art* (Oxford, 1967) will immediately see a breakthrough and a fresh critical mode. This, it may be thought, is Ian Jack's finest work of criticism, and a brilliant example of the close reading of poetic texts in relation with painting—especially Nicholas Poussin and Claude—who meant so much to Keats.

Not long after this, however, Ian Jack seems to have turned away from the eighteenth century and Romantic period to the Victorians. He had for some time been General Editor of the Clarendon Edition of the Novels of the Brontës, *Jane Eyre* (edited by Jane Jack and Margaret Smith) having been published in 1969. In 1976 he published with Hilda Marsden the edition of Emily Brontë's *Wuthering Heights.* His part of the Introduction, which he states as beginning on p. xxv, shows what a detailed and decisive grip he had on the notorious textual problems of that novel. He shines a new light on the obviously faulty text of T. C. Newby, the first edition, yet does not take the easy way out by choosing as copy-text the later, conventionalised, edition by Charlotte Brontë (1850). Jack wrote:

> Newby's text possesses some features which probably derive from the manuscript and which Emily Brontë may well have wished to see retained. The text is

> not so bad as to render it likely that an editor will get closer to the author's intention by adopting the punctuation and other accidentals of Charlotte (and Smith Elder) than by a careful recension of Newby's edition. (p. xxxi)

It would seem that Jack and Marsden have given us the first reliable text of this famous novel.

Jack may, at some moments, have been uncertain which way to proceed: back to the seventeenth century, perhaps to Jacobean drama, or forward into the high Victorians. The higher common sense prevailed. He had already edited a one-volume edition of Browning's *Poetical Works, 1833–64* (London, 1970) followed by his critical study, Browning's *Major Poetry* (1973). He decided to build on foundations already laid and become the general editor of a major Clarendon Press edition of the whole *Poetical Works of Robert Browning*.

This was a remarkable decision. Jack, always a practical and realistic man, was now nearing his sixties. Even with early retirement and a trusted team of collaborators, surely he could not have hoped to see this great edition completed? Perhaps as well as having laid down the guidelines of the edition, he expected to see at least Browning's well-known middle poetry done. In this he was not disappointed. Together with Rowena Fowler, Robert Inglesfield and Margaret Smith, he brought out the first five volumes—Volume V *Men and Women* (Oxford, 1995) being the one with which he was most engaged—within perhaps fourteen years of his original decision. *Men and Women* contains some of Browning's most well-known and moving poems: 'Childe Roland', 'Andrea del Sarto', 'Cleon', 'Two on the Campagna' and many others. Volume V was not an unfitting place for him to halt.

As an undergraduate in the mid-1950s, I absorbed the view that there was only one Victorian poet worthy of attention: Gerard Manley Hopkins. Christopher Ricks's edition of Tennyson taught me, later, that I had been wrong about this particular Poet Laureate. Ian Jack's *Poetical Works*, Vol. V, taught me that I was at least partly wrong about Browning. He did this by his annotations. Consider the last two lines of 'Childe Roland':

> Dauntless the slug-horn to my lips I set,
> And blew: 'Child Roland to the Dark Tower came.'

On the word 'slug-horn' Jack says, in a short note (n. 203), that Browning was misled by Thomas Chatterton. The word should mean something like 'slogan' or 'battlecry'. Chatterton was, on his part, misled by Thomas Ruddiman's 1710 edition of the fifteenth-century Scot, Gavin Douglas's translation of Virgil's *Aeneid*. The modern reader is here taken away from the intentionality of the fortunate Browning to contemplate the coalescence, in the poem, of the sound of the horn and the words of Roland's (no doubt) doomed challenge.

'Bishop Blougram's Apology'—to take a more difficult poem—is very long and fully annotated here. It deals with a revival of Catholicism in Victorian England, led partly by Cardinal Wiseman and also of course by Cardinal Newman. Browning, certainly not a Catholic, perhaps scarcely a Christian, disliked Wiseman, the subject and speaker of this protracted monologue. The other person present is allowed to say nothing. It must be admitted that Browning's depiction of the pleasantly drunk and interminably talkative Blougram, though the poet is not agreeing with him, does portray him as a shrewd, friendly and subtle man. The length of the poem enacts the confidence of the speaker and Browning's almost Shakespearian capacity to dramatise a character he distrusted, and most nineteenth-century Protestants loved to hate, leave the reader with a less than doctrinaire vision. Ian Jack's own view was probably close to Browning's, but the subtle learning of his commentary seems to leave Blougram still holding forth, untouched.

When this volume of Browning's *Poetical Works* was published, I followed Pembroke College tradition and asked permission for an entry to be made in Wine Book. It runs: 'Mr. Erskine-Hill gave a bottle to congratulate Mr. Jack on his conquering of the Tower and bringing out *Men and Women*.' Foolishly pleased with myself, I showed it, soon after, to Ian. 'Nobody will understand it' was all he said. Much chastened I obtained permission to add a footnote, and thus even the Wine Book entry was annotated.

Ian Jack had a very good reputation with the undergraduates he taught. It was certainly well deserved and yet in some respects surprising. Other supervisors at Cambridge at least would want to get an interesting conversation going, Ian tended to be curt and dismissive. Others urged their pupils to still greater efforts; Ian made up his mind early as to how well they would do. But all worked out well for several reasons. First, his pupils respected him for his learning and achievement. Secondly, they soon realised that he respected *them*, though not necessarily as high intellectuals. Thirdly, they understood, in due course, that he was a kind man. Professor Christopher Salveson, one of his earliest pupils, has a telling anecdote:

> As my tutor at Oxford, Ian had to deal with an ex-National Serviceman who, over two years had lost a good deal of scholarly momentum; he was supportive and sympathetic in helping me recover some proper sense of direction—I

> remember, in my first term, his abandoning a not particularly productive tutorial for a bracing walk round Christ Church Meadows and some constructive discussion of life in general. When I eventually became a University lecturer I gradually realised how much I owed to Ian's example in the business of reading, teaching and criticism. (Letter to Elizabeth Jack, 30 October 2008)

In his later years Ian frequently sought to pass his students over to other supervisors. In my first year as a lecturer in Cambridge I was surprised to be asked by him to take over all his first years for the Easter Term. I was glad to and they were an excellent group. I got to know one better than the others because he was interested, as I was, in the poetry of Hugh MacDiarmid (Christopher Murray Grieve). This undergraduate, Christopher Smith, became Minister for Culture, Arts and Sport in Tony Blair's first administration and was then responsible for restoring free access to art galleries and museums. As Lord Smith of Finsbury he is (at the time of writing) Chairman of the Wordsworth Dove Cottage Trust. Another example stands out. One day at High Table Ian spoke to me of an absolutely first-rate research student he had had for one year, but now wished to pass on to me. I tried to dissuade him but his mind was made up. This accomplished graduate student thus came to me, the subject of his thesis was then settled, and in due course he was elected into a Research Fellowship at Pembroke. The name of this graduate was Richard A. McCabe, now Fellow of Merton, Professor of English, and FBA.

Some have enquired where Professor Jack stood in the deconstructionist debates which so troubled the Arts Faculties in Cambridge in the 1980s. He did not play a part in the public controversy and was out of the country for some of this antagonistic period. When something of it was explained he set down deconstructionism as such an obvious folly that it could never prevail. A slightly younger generation was more troubled, since it appeared to them not just that established truths were being challenged, which happens continually and rightly, but rather that the philosophic *concept of truth* was being relegated from academic discourse. Of those who supported this trend, some were incredulous that any new idea could be unwelcome in Cambridge, while others thought that the concept of truth was the social tool of a middle-class hegemony. This last claim defeated itself, obviously, by deploying the concept of truth, as all political, historical and literary discourse is bound to do.

Since the question of religion has been touched on above in relation to Browning, a word of two more may be said. Ian once said to me that if God existed it was in the mind of man. He may have meant that God was a delusion or, possibly, a presupposition of the enquiring mind—as Kant considered causality to be. On a related point Ian may, despite much talk about folly, have been a relatively hopeful humanist. Among his papers found after his death were two cuttings placed together. Each concerned accounts of children or youths marooned on a desert island. One, from the *Times Literary Supplement*, 19 September 1986, recounted the story of the first publication of William Golding's *Lord of the Flies* in September 1954, a novel which Ian already knew well. The second, from *The Times*, 17 September 1966, recounted the story of six boy castaways from Tonga who lived for fifteen months on the uninhabited south Pacific island of Ata, living on raw seabirds to keep alive. They built a hut, drew up rules, managed to burn an area of scrub as a signal, said prayers morning and evening and, though completely naked, were reasonably healthy and cheerful when they were rescued. Ian set this cheerful narrative against the dark vision of Golding.

* * *

Ian Jack was Reader in English Poetry at Cambridge, 1973–6, and Professor 1976–89. He was elected FBA in 1986. He died on 3 September 2008.

HOWARD ERSKINE-HILL
Fellow of the Academy

Note. I am grateful to Elizabeth Jack for her assistance in the preparation of this memoir.

GEORGE KANE

George Kane
1916–2008

For half a century and more George Kane was a leading scholar in medieval English literature and the acknowledged authority on Langland. As general editor of the London edition of *Piers Plowman*, published 1960–97, he was solely responsible for the first of its three weighty volumes, and he co-edited the second and third volumes. With the publication of the first of these editions, a contemporary reviewer wrote that 'for Mr. Kane there is a secure place in the history of medieval scholarship'.[1] These volumes continue to engage academic debate, and they remain an indispensable tool for all who undertake serious work in later Middle English literature. They are complemented by Wittig's *Lemmatized Analysis* (London, 2001) and Kane's own *Glossary* (2005). Their influence is everywhere plain to see, not just in Carl Schmidt's widely used editions and in the framing of Hoyt Duggan's *Piers Plowman* Electronic Archive,[2] but in a host of monographs and articles that continue to build on and examine their contents. The editorial responsibilities handed on by W. W. Skeat to R. W. Chambers at University College London found, in George Kane, the last of Chambers's research students, a worthy successor.

The greater part of Kane's academic teaching life was spent in the University of London, where he was an influential and greatly respected figure, first in University College, then as Professor of English Language and Literature and Head of the English Department at Royal Holloway College from 1955–65 and finally as Professor of English Language and

[1] J. A. W. Bennett, *Medium Ævum*, 14 (1963), 68–71 at 71.
[2] <http://www3.iath.virginia.edu/seenet/piers/>.

Medieval Literature, 1965–76, and Head of the English Department from 1968–76 at King's College, becoming Professor Emeritus of London University from 1976. Then he went on to the William Rand Kenan Jr Professorship of English in the University of North Carolina at Chapel Hill, where he was to serve as Chairman of the Division of Humanities, 1980–3. In 1987 he became, for a second time, Professor Emeritus, and this retirement was marked by a Festschrift, *Medieval English Studies presented to George Kane*, edited by Edward Donald Kennedy, Ronald Waldron and Joseph S. Wittig (Cambridge, 1988). Throughout his life many honours came his way, notably: Fellow, British Academy, 1968, serving on its Council from 1974–6; Fellow, University College London, 1971; Fellow, King's College London, 1976. He was twice awarded the Sir Israel Gollancz Memorial Prize by the British Academy, in 1963 and again in 1999. Elected a Corresponding Fellow of the Medieval Academy of America in 1975, he became a Fellow in 1978, the year in which the Academy awarded him the Haskins Medal, and served on its publications committee and on the editorial board of *Speculum*. He held Leverhulme Trust Research Fellowships in 1962 and 1975 and visiting professorships of the Medieval Academy of America in 1970 and 1982. He was a Fellow of the American Academy of Arts and Sciences 1977–91, a Fellow of the National Humanities Center, 1987–8, and a Senior Fellow of the Southwestern Institute of Medieval and Renaissance Studies, 1978; and he served on the committees of the New Chaucer Society and the American Council of Learned Societies. Other service on boards and governing bodies included: Council, Early English Text Society, 1969–88; Governing Body, School of Oriental and African Studies, 1970–6; and Governing Body, University of North Carolina Press, 1979–84. An excellent lecturer, he acted as Public Orator of the University of London across the years 1962–6, and he received many invitations to speak all over the world. Among his most important public lectures were: the Chambers Memorial, University College London, 1965; Accademia Nazionale dei Lincei, Rome, 1976; the John Coffin Memorial, University of London, 1979 ; the Annual Chaucer Lecture, New Chaucer Society, 1980; the M. W. Bloomfield Memorial, Harvard, 1989; and the Tucker-Cruse Memorial, Bristol University, 1991. Kane's was a distinguished career, rewarded with honours on both sides of the Atlantic.

George Kane was born in Humboldt, Saskatchewan, on 14 July 1916, an eighth-generation Canadian on his father's side—his father's mother was descended from one of the original settlers of Acadie (Nova Scotia). The Kanes were more recent arrivals in North America, early nineteenth-century immigrants from the North of Ireland. He was a posthumous child—his parents married in September in Muenster and went to live in Hudson Bay Junction where, in late December 1915, his father died suddenly of a heart attack—and spent his early childhood on his mother's parents' farm in St Peter's Colony, Saskatchewan, a few miles from Humboldt, moving with them, when his grandfather retired, into the nearby village of Muenster. His mother, who was, as he was proud to relate, a 'career woman', was a librarian before her brief first marriage and after it a teacher. Her father had come originally from Switzerland, and her mother from Hanover, so George Kane grew up bilingual in English and German, in a household headed by first-generation immigrants. From 1922 he spent his summers with his mother and stepfather, in farming countryside sixty miles north-west of Muenster, as big brother to a growing family of three brothers and a sister. Those summers on the shores of Lake Wakaw were idyllic: swimming, messing about in rowing boats, mostly in a bathing suit. Kane looked back on them and the cottage at Lake Wakaw as his 'Walden, but better than Thoreau's'. In Muenster during the rest of the year he first attended the local parish school and then went on to St Peter's College (1930–4), the school run by the nearby Benedictine abbey where, one of three day boys, he had an excellent education which included a good grounding in the classics. It was a highly academic school, but also played games seriously: baseball, handball, tennis, ice hockey. For his last two years at school Kane was the college's sports correspondent, writing reports for the weekly diocesan newsletter, the *Prairie Messenger*, which the abbey published. There was tobogganing, and skiing too, in a nearby ravine. In winters the journey cross country to and from school was quickly made, on skis. His years at the abbey school left Kane with a sense of admiration for the religious life and a deep understanding of a life of dedication with its daily Gregorian chants, even though he ceased to be a practising Catholic soon after leaving school.

In his final year at St Peter's College, Kane took and completed the First Year Arts course of the University of Saskatchewan, so that in 1934, when he moved west to Vancouver with his mother, stepfather and their four children, he was able to enrol into the second year at the University of British Columbia. His first choice of subjects—English, French and German—was not an available course, and he therefore opted for honours in English and Latin. There were eighteen hours of classes spread over the five week-days, a schedule few universities would impose on Arts students in Britain today. Because of the large content of Latin and Greek language work, it was heavier than Kane, in his King's College London days, himself thought appropriate for first year undergraduates in English. Then he deemed eleven hours ideal, and ruled that all should, as a matter of discipline, be expected to be in college four days a week (Wednesdays were for the library, intercollegiate lectures and, for the athletic, sports in the afternoon). In his second semester in Vancouver, he joined the University Officers' Training Corps, which met three times a week, an extra-curricular activity that was, unexpectedly, to come in useful a few years later. The decision to weight his undergraduate work towards English came with his selection of the topic 'Critical Opinions in the Plays of Shakespeare' for the substantial essay required of all finalists. He graduated in 1936 with first class honours in English and Latin, and an application to the University of Toronto netted him a generous graduate fellowship that included fees and accommodation for his MA year.

The boy from the plains had first moved west, to British Columbia, but now he travelled east across the continent to Toronto, by ship to Seattle and onwards by the Great Northern Line railway. It was too long a journey to consider going home for the Christmas vacation. He concentrated his MA work at the University of Toronto in medieval and early modern literature, working in some depth on Ben Jonson and elaborating a future research topic on Milton and the theory of the epic in the renaissance. His year as an assistant warden at Toronto's Massey College passed quickly, and was followed by a research fellowship at Northwestern University (1937–8). He had, however, already decided that he wanted to undertake research in Britain and set about seeking funding. The year at Evanston he found academically challenging, 'a good year', even though he knew he was marking time. Taking courses without any examination pressures, he concentrated again on medieval and renaissance literature, adding Old French to his skills and enjoying reading *Beowulf* alongside the *Chanson de Roland*. The former, he discovered, more than repaid the chore of having to learn to read Old English and, in its 'greater sophistication', outshone the 'crude execution and vitality' of the latter. But his two-year graduate studentship, awarded by the Imperial Order of Daughters of the Empire, beckoned and it must have seemed an academic career of promise would follow seamlessly. He knew of course that the Munich crisis was mounting, that there was war in Spain and that Mussolini had invaded Abyssinia, but he was not deterred.

Kane arrived at University College London in September 1938, eager to work on the Milton project he had already mapped out, but was soon to find out that no supervision in that area was being offered. Assigned to R. W. Chambers for research direction, he was sucked into preparatory editorial work for what would today be called the *Piers Plowman* project. From 1909 onwards Chambers had both separately and with J. H. G. Grattan published a series of preliminary articles in which they spelled out the difficulties of arriving at a final edition of any of Skeat's A, B and C texts before full consideration of the others. Some of Chambers's students, including Elsie Blackman, B. F. Allen (Mrs Tapping), F. A. R. Carnegy and Alex (A. G.) Mitchell, had already accomplished a considerable amount of work towards a new edition, but overall the labour of collation moved slowly. For his Ph.D. topic Kane set about collating the final three passus of the B-text, working for the most part in the Students' Room at the British Museum, where he discovered the helpfulness of a young librarian, later a firm friend, called Francis Wormald, who was to become an eminent palaeographer. There were visits too to the Duke Humfrey reading room of the Bodleian Library in Oxford and to the University of Cambridge Library. For the Huntington Library manuscript he had the photographs made for Chambers's use. In the early summer of 1939 he got down to pulling together his critical edition and by mid-August had begun checking the whole. War intervened, however, and, unable in London to join a Canadian regiment, he enlisted in the Honourable Artillery Company. Chambers insisted that Kane's completed collations and working papers should go to Aberystwyth to be stored with the college's rare books and muniments for the duration: a lucky decision. All the other possessions he left in London were lost in a house bombed in 1942.

From 1939 to 1946 Kane served in the British Army. Although he had enlisted in the Honourable Artillery Company, he was posted to the Artists' Rifles, by then an officer training unit, and he chose to move on from there to the Rifle Brigade. Towards the end of training he volunteered for a battalion to be made up of experienced skiers and mountaineers, the fifth battalion of the Scots Guards, newly formed to help Finland, which had been attacked by the Red Army, an aborted enterprise because Sweden refused the permission necessary to cross into Finland. Briefly, therefore, he was a guardsman (like other officers, he resigned his commission to join this special battalion). Eventually the unit was disbanded, but not before it had as its highlight a week's skiing in ideal conditions at Chamonix (March to April 1940). Meanwhile Kane had missed posting to Egypt with the Second Battalion of the Rifle Brigade, so now he proceeded to his first post as a regimental officer of the Rifle Brigade, Second Lieutenant, with the Motor Training Battalion at Tidworth. By May 1940 he was in Essex, in charge of C Company, digging entrenchments for the defence of England, and then in Suffolk. A call came suddenly on 21 May to move to

Southampton, and next day he embarked for France. There he took part in the chaotic stand at Calais. Leading a fighting patrol towards the end of the defence, he was hit by a bullet that went right through his body. He had to be left behind with other serious casualties, and got taken into Calais by the Germans as a prisoner of war, where he received treatment in a field hospital until fit enough for travel. The first of his escape attempts made while in hospital was foiled by an officious chaplain. In 1984, with his wife and daughter, he visited the place in Calais where he had been captured, only to find it was now the site of a large supermarket.

The journey to his first prison camp was not an easy one. There was transport on 19 June as far as Lille, but after that it was a slow circuitous trudge through much of north-western France and Belgium. He spoke later of spending a night in a condemned cell, the only place with a roof, and of being given an omelette hot from the frying pan straight into his hands, as he walked through Belgium. The column of well over a thousand prisoners reached Antwerp on 1 July, to be herded into goods wagons and taken to a transit camp at Dortmund. Kane was a prisoner first in Oflag VIIC, once a country palace of the Archbishops of Salzburg, near Laufen in Bavaria (July 1940 to September 1941). In January 1941 he was adopted into a tunnelling team, which gave some sense of purpose to his life until its discovery late in June. Otherwise the days were spent mainly in reading Tauchnitz fiction reprints (their purchase was arranged by the senior British officer, Major Charles Shears, who had before the war worked in a publishing firm). Autumn brought a move to Oflag VIB at Dössel bei Warburg in Westphalia, a huge camp into which the Germans had poured most of the prisoners taken after the retreat from Dunkirk, some from the North African campaign and all from Greece, as well as RAF people shot down over Europe, some two and a half thousand officers together with 450 orderlies. An enormous amount of effort went into tunnelling, but managed to get only three officers outside Oflag VIB. One tunnel in which Kane was involved was holed by a collapse in freakish spring weather. From September 1942 to January 1943 he was in Oflag VIIB at Eichstätt, in southern Bavaria. As a fluent German speaker he was much in demand and he was one of the group that escaped through a gate on 24 November, getting as far as Talmühle, about eight miles from Switzerland. His last prison camp was Oflag IXA, not the lower camp in the middle of Elbersdorf but the upper camp, Schloss Spangenberg, where he remained until its evacuation. Spangenberg, a small camp, even had a library, well run by Charles Shears. Somehow Shears managed to arrange for good supplies of new books to be sent over, and others were given to the library from book parcels received by individual prisoners. Shears invited Kane to become assistant librarian, a role that gave him ready access to the books it became his duty to catalogue. At Spangenberg, he read avidly, and not just English books. He schooled himself through many French novels and he set about learning Italian well enough to read Dante. On 30 March the Germans evacuated Spangenberg, marching their prisoners out to the noise of gunfire. A few days later Kane was one of the small group who slipped away from the column and came across an advance troop of Patton's army. Their adventures were made famous by Terence Prittie who, in *South to Freedom* (London, 1946), describes Kane as having 'exceptional nervous energy' and 'a remarkable determination which serves to keep him awake and alert long after physical exhaustion has claimed the average man'. For his part, Kane remembers rather different detail of the escapes in which both he and Prittie were involved and his account adds significantly to the published records. There are many stories told about Kane's war years, often false. He was not at Dunkirk, despite tales of being seen lying in a ditch there. Nor did he work on *Piers Plowman* collations in Spangenberg, a myth built on a parcel of books Chambers sent to him in 1942.

Kane got back to England in early April 1945, among the first of the 160,000 British and Commonwealth prisoners of war to be liberated. His return to London was to a city horribly changed. At University College the central buildings were 'reduced to first floor level, the fine dome gone, grass growing on the floor where the English Library had been'. The English Department was still in Aberystwyth and not to return until September. C. J. Sisson was with the department, but A. H. Smith was a Wing Commander in the RAF and Chambers had died in April 1942. As far as the War Office was concerned, his time was his own until leave in Canada would come up. He was still in London for VE Day, but later in the summer sailed on the Queen Mary to North America, to travel across the continent and, for the first time in seven years, catch up with his family. An unexpected interruption during his leave was an invitation to the University of Saskatchewan by John Lothian, who wanted him to take over and build up the English Department—it must have been a disorienting experience for someone as yet to be demobilised and with a half-finished Ph.D. VJ Day he spent in New York, just before crossing back to England in the *Queen Elizabeth*. At Southampton Docks he was handed an order to report to the Rifle Brigade Regimental Training Battalion in Nottinghamshire, where there was so little for him to do that out of boredom he demanded a posting—and was told to take some leave. He went back to London, where he found waiting for him a job offer, an Assistant Professorship in University College Toronto to start in September: an ideal job, except that by now he was planning to marry and settle in London. In the months in London after liberation, before going on leave to Vancouver, Kane had met the girl he was to marry, Bridget Montgomery, sister of a fellow prisoner at Spangenburg, and they wanted to stay in England. Another enticing job offer did come up: Charles Shears of Hutchison's, a fellow prisoner at Laufen, offered him a well-paid post once his Ph.D. was finished, but it was an offer never taken up.

By September 1945 Kane had applied to resume his Ph.D. and he was appointed a Departmental Assistant (unpaid) at University College for the second year of his interrupted scholarship, with an Assistant Lectureship to follow on in 1946. His demobilisation came up in late February 1946, the month in which his collations and notes returned to London from Aberystwyth. So he set about writing up his Ph.D., an edition of Passus XVIII–XX of *Piers Plowman*, submitted in June that same year. He took up his University of London appointment to an Assistant Lectureship in the autumn, and was appointed to a tenured lectureship in 1948. The thesis presented 'a critical text of the archetype of the B-manuscripts of *Piers Plowman*, Passus XVIII–XX' together with 'full notes of the lines in B-XVIII–XX which are likely to be emended from the C- manuscripts', a list which he described as 'the first statement of a project which, with Dr Mitchell's help, I hope before too long to produce in a final form. When it is completed I believe that, where it was possible to work with B- and C-manuscripts, we shall have produced a text very near to what the author of *Piers Plowman* wrote' (50–1). In his first teaching years, however, there was little time to give to editing, for he turned his attention to writing his first book, *Middle English Literature* (London, 1951), daringly a work of literary criticism at a time when historical and language-based approaches were general. A Readership followed soon afterwards, in 1953. This work engaged directly with romances, lyrics and *Piers Plowman,* and was described by an early reviewer as 'one of the best books so far written on any aspect of Middle English literature'.[3] It quickly came to command a wide undergraduate audience, both in Britain and North America, and for its 1970 reprinting Kane was to reflect ruefully 'I could not now revise, let alone rewrite it; what has persuaded me to consent to its reproduction is the consideration that it has become a period piece, such as librarians might wish to include in their documentation of the history of medieval

[3] A. I. Doyle, *The Review of English Studies*, NS 4 (1953), 69–70.

studies.' Further editions were to follow, the most recent in 2000, and it remains a book in student use.

Kane's 1948 paper '*Piers Plowman*: problems and methods of editing the B-Text' (*The Modern Language Review*) formulated in print the task to which he had decided to square up: editing the B-text, with Skeat's chosen basic manuscript, Oxford, Bodleian Library, Laud Miscellany 581, as his base text. Already he recognised that major problems lay ahead, not least that although the B manuscripts preserved a relatively homogeneous text, the many errors they had in common derived from corruption in the B archetype; and that for these the C-text tradition held valuable evidence. He stated the desirability of bringing to his editorial task the methods and insights on the principles of editing practised in New Testament and *Commedia* scholarship, and he foresaw that the B-text would be edited not from the B manuscripts alone but from the forty or so B and C manuscripts together. Pointing out that 'the question of authorship has been allowed to take precedence for a long time over the problem of the text, when in actual fact no point regarding this poem, and certainly not that of its authorship, can be settled upon internal evidence until the text itself has been fixed', he demonstrated the need for a full examination of the B and C texts and for the reconstruction of the 'best possible texts ... from the evidence to be found there'. Commenting on the lack of an 'established text' for any of the three versions of *Piers Plowman*, he observed: 'The task has, from the outset, been enormous. Dr Skeat and his approved successors Professors Chambers and Grattan, and their students and early co-workers, Mrs Blackman, Mrs Tapping [B. F. Allen] and Mr F. A. R. Carnegy, have contributed in varying degree to bringing it nearer completion.' Kane presents an optimistic picture: 'Professor Grattan now hopes to take up the A-text again where he left off before the war; Professor A. G. Mitchell of Sydney University has almost completed the collation of the C-text manuscripts; and we may hope that critical texts of at least these two versions of *Piers Plowman* will be in print within the next three years.' When he wrote this paper he did not know that Grattan's edition of the A-text, interrupted by the war years, would not be completed and that Mitchell's work on the C-text would drag on endlessly, but he was soon to realise that if ever the A-text were to be completed, and he needed access to it for editing the B-text, Grattan would require his help.

During the war the Chairman of the Advisory Committee of the Medieval Academy of America had, after Chambers's death, asked Grattan for a statement on the progress of the critical edition of *Piers Plowman*. Grattan's note, published in *Speculum* in 1945, makes depressing reading, apart from its mention of 'a newly discovered A-MS, which has proved to be of high textual importance'; Kane figures, though not by name, in the statement as an 'important worker who was last heard of as a prisoner of war in Germany'.[4] A revised report, outlining 'plans for a comprehensive critical edition' drawn up after a meeting held in September 1949, was published by Grattan in *Speculum* in 1951, the year of his death.[5] In all, six volumes were proposed, to be published by the Athlone Press under the editorship of Grattan, Kane, Mitchell and A. H. Smith: I A-text (Grattan and Kane, with general introduction by Smith); II B-text (Kane); III C-text (Mitchell); IV linguistic apparatus and glossary (Grattan, Smith and C. R. Quirk); V notes 'under the general direction of Kane, with the collaboration of Professors Morton W. Bloomfield of Ohio State University, and E. T. Donaldson of Yale University'; and VI discussion of background, authorship, etc., 'by the authors of Volume V'. At that point it was thought that the first volume would be ready to go to print in late 1951, that Mitchell's volume was 'almost ready', that II would 'be ready by 1953, and the other volumes would 'follow at short intervals thereafter'. In effect, Kane was now the successor of Skeat and Chambers. The A-text collations, assembled haphazardly in non-compatible layers over many years, were being replaced, and from 1950 Donaldson was working with Kane towards the B-text. In time, editing of the C-text was to descend to George Russell, and Kane would join him in getting it to press. The glossarial work by Kane and Wittig was eventually to bring the critical editions of the A, B and C versions to completion.

Piers Plowman: the A version, Will's Visions of Piers Plowman and Do-Well, first of the three volumes of the Athlone Press edition, was ready for press early in 1956 and appeared in 1960. It was a huge achievement. Kane had himself undertaken a completely new classification of the seventeen manuscripts surveyed in the edition and prepared full collations. He established his text not through what he regarded as the straitjacket of recension but by the exercise of editorial judgement, reading by reading. Not only did he furnish word-for-word collations of the manuscripts, in itself a task not previously undertaken on such a scale in the editing of Middle English, but he attempted to excavate the originary reading at every point of variance. He did not, as had Skeat, use the earliest manuscript, Oxford,

[4] George R. Coffman, 'The present state of a critical edition of *Piers Plowman*', *Speculum*, 20 (1945), 482–3.

[5] J. H. G. Grattan, 'The critical edition of *Piers Plowman*: its present status', *Speculum*, 26 (1951), 582–4.

Bodleian Library, MS Eng. poet. a.1 (the Vernon manuscript), as his base manuscript, but Cambridge, Trinity College, MS R.3.14, a manuscript already identified both by Chambers and Grattan, and by Knott, as preferable and now confirmed as needing less correction than the recently discovered Chaderton manuscript (Liverpool University Library, F.4.8). In a tightly argued Introduction Kane set out an impressive discussion of how variants arise, drawing in great detail on the collations to show the grounds on which his editorial decisions were made. His aim was to determine the authorial word or words behind the variants that confronted him. With the A-text, Kane's emendations, although many, gained wide approbation as judicious. The edition was acclaimed as superseding Skeat's, and was to prove influential in editorial work more generally. The disputed twelfth passus was set apart in an Appendix, an eminently sensible decision, and twenty-eight pages of Critical Notes admirably complemented the lengthy and detailed Introduction. The edition was widely and justly praised. C. L. Wrenn, for example, described it as 'probably the nearest to a definitive text of the A version of *Piers Plowman* that human wit and diligence can hope to attain',[6] and it was awarded the Gollancz prize by the British Academy in 1963. But the edition did not address the issue of authorship, which rumbled on. Knott and Fowler's edition of the A text (Baltimore, MD, 1952) had assumed multiple authorship, as had Fowler's monograph *Piers Plowman: Literary Relations of the A and B Texts* (Seattle, WA, 1961). The latter provoked from Kane a swingeing review,[7] in which he commented that to deal with Fowler's arguments in any detail 'would take two books, one for the evidence for authorship of *Piers Plowman*, another comparing the A and B versions'. Kane followed the review up promptly with *Piers Plowman: the Evidence for Authorship* (London, 1965), a clear and cogently argued analysis that was to quash the issue of authorship for the next couple of decades. A major omission of Kane's A version was any mention of the 'Z' text, Oxford, Bodleian Library, MS Bodley 851, an AC splice, although he did draw attention to 'the extreme possibility, that even the worst of the surviving A manuscripts was set down from memory, or is descended from a manuscript so set down', only to dismiss the possibility as 'altogether remote' (p. 144); in his 1975 book (pp. 14–15 n. 95) he was to describe Bodley 851 'as worthless for editorial use', commenting that he should have noted its rejection in the A-text volume. It was an omission that was, later, to reopen the authorship question.

[6] *Modern Language Notes*, 76 (1961), 856–63 at 863.
[7] *Medium Ævum*, 33 (1964), 230–1.

Even while the A-text was being edited, work had continued on the collations for the B-text. In his prisoner-of-war years, Kane had been involved in a great deal of tunnelling, of which he said, in the memoir he wrote late in life for his grandchildren, 'Except for the absence of physical hazard collation was like tunnelling in that a man's sense of progress, if he paused to think, was slow. But unlike tunnelling in good soil it was never monotonous: its diversity lay in the response by scribes to the text as it passed through their heads and hand.'[8] From 1950 Kane had the help of E. Talbot Donaldson (Yale University) as collaborator on the B-text, a task that together took them a quarter of a century to complete.

In 1955 he became Professor of English Language and Literature and Head of Department at Royal Holloway College, still at that time a women's college. He was, for a while, one of the very few men in the college. There he inherited the courses of his predecessor, Gladys Willcock, including two years of English poetry from Skelton to Herrick, the period in which he had originally planned to do research. It was a small department, and he was able to tutor each of the ten or twelve finalists every year. It was a good period too for research, for steady attention to the readings in the *Piers Plowman* manuscripts. These were the years in which the children were small: Michael, born January 1948, and Mary, born in the autumn of 1950, shortly after the family moved to Englefield Green. In 1961 they were to move to Shandon Cottage in Beaconsfield, their home for fifteen years. They managed a long summer visit to Canada in 1960, when Kane returned to the University of British Columbia to teach at the July summer school, an opportunity to see his mother and many other members of his family properly as well as to catch up with old friends.

In 1965 Kane returned to central London on his appointment as Professor of English Language and Medieval Literature at King's College in the Strand, where, although his lectures and tutorials were mainly on Middle English literature, he greatly enjoyed his share of tutoring undergraduates on a wide range of topics in their first term. Keenly aware of the changing profiles of university entrants, he whole-heartedly supported first-year work in the classical background for English literature and himself was tutor to the first batch of students admitted without a classical language at O-level among their entrance requirements. Somehow he managed to juggle undergraduate teaching and graduate supervision, a distinguished scholarly output and a heavy administrative burden with a kindly patience and quiet humour that made it all seem effortless. He

[8] To be published by the Arizona Center for Medieval and Renaissance Studies, Tempe, AZ.

cared also for getting to know and work with his medieval colleagues. When I joined the English Department at King's in 1969, for a few years George Kane organised a small reading group which he, Ron Waldron, Janet Cowen and I all went to, one evening a week during term time. One year we read Old High German with Martin Jones, other years Old French and then Provençale with Mary Hackett; and Julian Brown was bludgeoned into doing a huge course on medieval Latin for far larger numbers from the Faculty of Arts more generally. It was all rather hard work but invigorating and, for me, marvellous top-ups to a degree in English and French. In those days the English Department at King's still taught Old Norse as a matter of course, and overall there was a fine array of medieval languages within Arts, giving a strong sense of cohesion to medievalists. Looking back, I realise this was the springboard for CLAMS (the Centre for Late Antique and Medieval Studies), which began as a fairly low-key group set up by four of us from Spanish, German, Byzantine Studies and English, a few years before formal procedures took over. And Ron Waldron has reminded me of Kane's stimulating postgraduate seminars, attended by many medievalists of his acquaintance, for example Tauno Mustanoya and E. T. Donaldson, who happened to be in London at the time, and of the many hours we spent reading aloud (and recording with the help of Nick Budd of the Audio-Visual department) the poems of Chaucer and other Old and Middle English poetry. Within the college Kane served on many senior committees, shouldering disparate commitments that included much of the planning of the new Strand building, and he was noted for his efficiency and impartiality. His remarkable ability to concentrate people's attention was evident also in his chairmanship of the University Board of Studies in English, 1970–2.

Kane retired from King's in 1976, acquiring the first of two titles of Professor Emeritus. Throughout his three decades as a teacher in London University George Kane was a force to be reckoned with in the dealings of the intercollegiate Board of Studies and on its examination boards. Warwick Gould remembers him at an examinations meeting of the University of London Board of Studies in English: asked to comment on a question he had set, he replied sternly, leaning on his silver-tipped walking stick, 'I do not intend to lecture the Board upon *Piers Plowman*', bringing the room to silence (an unusual feat). In addition to his departmental roles and a myriad committee responsibilities, he was the University's Public Orator from 1962 to 1966 and Dean of the Faculty of Arts at King's from 1972 to 1974. Internationally too he had become a force to be reckoned with, invited to lecture in many European universities and in North

America, serving on appointment panels for senior posts, on the editorial boards and councils of learned societies, delivering keynote lectures. In 1970 he directed a summer seminar at Harvard for the Medieval Academy of America in palaeography and textual criticism, and in 1975 he became a Corresponding Fellow of the Medieval Academy of America.

Across these years Kane published papers and lectures of note, as well as shorter pieces and reviews. His Chambers Memorial Lecture of 1965 confronted 'The autobiographical fallacy in Chaucer and Langland studies' in a paper complementing his analysis of the evidence for the authorship of *Piers Plowman*. Arguing that our sense that we know both these men is 'logically dubious', he pointed to the absence in the late fourteenth century of 'any convention of detached, impersonal narrative'. The author may seem to project himself, yet may be presenting a literary fiction. In a footnote he qualified the argument, noting that 'any considerable poet of the time would be writing for a coterie, that set of people, comprising his patrons and their associates, to whom he read, and thus in effect presented and published his work'. For Chaucer, 'there is a reasonable presumption that his patrons and public were to be found in the court', but nothing is known of Langland's patrons. Yet, because of the nature and quality of his work, he envisaged for him 'an educated and intelligent audience' that, 'unless he had independent means', 'in some way maintained the poet'. Attempts to weave up life stories for Langland and Chaucer from their writings have burgeoned wildly in recent years, yet Kane's notion of the poet's supportive 'coterie' continues influential. In 1966 he revisited 'Conjectural emendation', by now an editorial procedure closely associated with his name. This paper was first published in the Festschrift (1969) for G. N. Garmonsway, his predecessor in the Chair of English Language and Medieval Literature at King's, and was soon to be reprinted in the collection *Medieval Manuscripts and Textual Criticism* (Chapel Hill, NC, 1976). In 'Some reflections on critical method', an address to the English Association in 1967 (published as 'Criticism, solecism: does it matter?' in *Essays and Studies* 1976), he reflected on the 'affective element' in our understanding of literature that makes it impossible for literary study ever 'to develop an exact science'. Discussing some of the more nonsensical readings of *Venus and Adonis* and *Sir Gawain and the Green Knight*, he identified as the central problem in both poems the misunderstanding of tone: critics, at sea in what is 'an essentially ludicrous situation', too often prate about ambivalence.

Throughout these years Kane continued to work steadily on the editing of *Piers Plowman*, and 1975 saw the publication of *Piers Plowman: the*

B Version, Will's Visions of Piers Plowman, Do-Well, Do-Better and Do-Best (London), edited with Donaldson. The sub-title, 'An edition in the form of Trinity College Cambridge MS. B.15.17, corrected and restored from the known evidence, with variant readings', reveals that they had abandoned Skeat's base text, Oxford, Bodleian Library, MS Laud Miscellany 581, choosing instead an earlier manuscript, exceptional for the consistency of its spelling and in grammar resembling late fourteenth-century usage as found 'in the best known manuscripts of Chaucer and Gower' (coincidentally the 'best' text chosen earlier by Wright). Some objected to the change from Laud Misc. 581. There is after all a substratal layer of south-west Worcester dialect features both in Laud 581 and Oxford, Bodleian Library, MS Rawlinson Poet. 38, probably reflecting Langland's own usage, although such features have on the whole been eliminated from B-text manuscripts by London copyists. Yet, as Michael Samuels pointed out in defence of Kane and Donaldson's choice, 'it is perfectly reasonable to read the B-text in the form in which it would have been understood by the London audiences for which it was intended'.[9] The choice of copy-text was less controversial than the whole-hearted way in which Kane and Donaldson emended its readings in their search for the readings of 'the archetypal B text' and, beyond that, the 'historical truth' of the poem.

Whereas with the A-text Kane's choices had for the most part gained approval as appropriate or at least judicious, the B-text edition met with mixed reviews. The criteria laid down for emendation on metrical grounds drew particular criticism. From their own analysis of the metre Kane and Donaldson argued that Langland 'would not have written lines without discernible alliteration' (p. 137), thus going against Skeat's view that as a variation a line could be wholly without alliteration. There was little to fault in the identification of the alliterative pattern aa/ax as the metrical norm, or in the exceptions they allowed to this norm, but the principles laid down were adjudged overstrict. For example, they claimed that lines with the pattern aa/xa were absent from Langland's verse system and, arguing that such lines were the result of scribal corruption, firmly rearranged them. There was resistance also to the idea that the line's binding alliteration could sometimes fall on unstressed syllables. On this score,

[9] M. L. Samuels, 'Langland's dialect', *Medium Ævum*, 54 (1985), 232–47 at 244. Repr. in M. L. Samuels and J. J. Smith (eds.), *The English of Chaucer and his Contemporaries* (Aberdeen, 1988), pp. 70–85.

Kane's response, 'Music "Neither unpleasant nor monotonous"'[10] should be read alongside the more recent paper, 'Measured discourse', by Ronald Waldron.[11] Because the B-version had so long and widely been read in Skeat's edition, there was a general sense of dismay at the disappearance of accustomed readings with the dislodgement of Laud 581 as basic text. But the excellence overall of the new edition as an authoritative overview of the B tradition and of the detailed information it contains has made it an indispensable tool for future generations of scholars. (Ironically, indeed, the excellence of the editorial materials provided by the Athlone volumes has enabled Laurence Warner to argue against the very identity of a B version of the poem.) Kane himself commented wryly on the usefulness of their collations to later editors. Even as the Athlone edition progressed, new student editions of *Piers Plowman* were already benefitting from the discoveries and procedures of the first two volumes. Inevitably there was little time to make more than running repairs in the new editions of the A and B volumes published in 1988, a decision that drew criticism but must be balanced against the imperative of completing the third volume.

Some critics still objected to Kane's turning aside from recension, but the insights to be gained from variational groupings of the Langland manuscripts were clear and the thickets of the Chaucer manuscripts must have seemed to him an enticing prospect. Together with Janet Cowen, a King's College London colleague, Kane embarked on the first 'open' edition of a Chaucerian work. In their 1995 critical edition of Chaucer's *Legend of Good Women* they presented full variants, plus the detailed evidence that underlies their classification of the manuscripts and underpins the text established. As an exercise testing the methodology and procedures of the *Piers Plowman* texts, the edition was a triumph. Its lack of literary introduction, full language analysis of the copy-text, explanatory notes and glossary means, however, that its audience is scholarly rather than general, which is unfortunate, for it deserves to be more widely used. In particular, the clearly thought-through punctuation of the text makes it a joy to read by comparison with earlier editions of the *Legend*. The detailed work required to produce such editions is inordinately time-consuming, whether for a printed text or for machine-held files as is now becoming customary. The temptation to present accompanying ancillary materials is

[10] P. L. Heyworth (ed.), *Medieval Studies for J. A. W. Bennett, Aetatis Suae LXX* (Oxford, 1981), pp. 43–63.

[11] Ronald Waldron, 'Measured discourse; the fourteenth-century alliterative long line as a two-tier system', *Approaches to the Metres of Alliterative Verse*, Leeds Texts and Monographs, NS 17 (2009), 235–54.

best avoided in the interests of achieving the central task, the establishment of an edition. Papers on Chaucer published by Kane and Cowen during the years their edition was in preparation are paradoxically better known than the edition itself, for example Cowen's discussion of the grounds on which final *-e* should be restored in Chaucer and her literary analysis of the *Legend*,[12] and Kane's analysis of their copy-text.[13] In addition, Kane was to publish a formidable series of more general articles, some on the 'obligatory conjunction' of Langland and Chaucer, others on a variety of Chaucerian topics—integrity, romantic love, philosophy, the idea of poetry. Most are to be found conveniently gathered together in his 1989 collection *Chaucer and Langland: Historical and Textual Approaches*.

Kane's final teaching position was at the University of North Carolina at Chapel Hill (1976–87), where he held the William Rand Kenan Jr Professorship of English. He had been approached by that university to ask if he would consider moving there whilst still at King's. By that time Michael was 28 and training to become a doctor of medicine. Mary was 26 and working as a solicitor in the West End of London. Bridget's mother and father were dead. George and Bridget agreed that a move to America would be a new adventure. The only full professor on the medieval side when he arrived, he carried on the strong tradition of teaching and mentoring graduate students vigorously, taught courses in the Comparative Literature department as well as in English, and acted energetically to support and encourage medieval studies across the liberal arts departments. Graduate students who worked with him remember vividly how they scurried to the *Oxford English Dictionary* and the *Middle English Dictionary*, poring over the meanings of words before they felt ready to appear for each session in one of his Langland or Chaucer seminars. He was a congenial and invigorating colleague to his juniors in the Middle English field, and he saw to the department's hiring of two new assistant professors in Anglo-Saxon, whose careers he took pains to foster. And at the end of each semester, George and Bridget gave memorable parties to which they invited all the medieval students and faculty with whom George's teaching and other activities brought him into contact. Colleagues at Chapel Hill remember those parties fondly. He served on many

[12] 'Chaucer's *Legend of Good Women: Structure and Tone*', *Studies in Philology*, 84 (1985), 416–36; 'Metrical problems in editing The Legend of Good Women', in Derek Pearsall (ed.), *Manuscripts and Texts: Editorial Problems in Later Middle English Literature* (Cambridge, 1987), pp. 26–33.

[13] 'The text of The Legend of Good Women in CUL MS Gg.4.27', in Douglas Gray and E. G. Stanley (eds.), *Middle English Studies Presented to Norman Davis in Honour of His Seventieth Birthday* (Oxford, 1983), pp. 39–58.

university-wide committees, and was for three years the chairman of the Division of Humanities (1980–3). He slipped back easily into the wider scholarly community of North America. He was elected to the American Academy of Arts and Sciences in 1977, and in 1978 he became a Fellow of the Medieval Academy. During the summer of 1978 he directed a seminar at Duke University for the Southwestern Institute of Medieval and Renaissance Studies, and in 1982, for a second time, he directed a summer seminar in palaeography and textual criticism for the Medieval Academy of America at Harvard. After his retirement from North Carolina, Kane spent the following two years at the National Humanities Center, on a National Endowment for the Humanities Fellowship, as he describes in the 'Acknowledgements' to the *Glossary*. The Center is an easy drive from Chapel Hill, so he and Bridget were able to enjoy two more years in the house they built within walking distance from campus.

In 1989, Professor Emeritus for a second time, George and Bridget returned to live in England, where their son Michael and daughter Mary and their families lived. They had travelled back and forwards across the Atlantic over the Chapel Hill years, and Kane remained an important figure in the lives of his London colleagues. Ron Waldron (King's College) joined Don Kennedy and Joe Wittig (Chapel Hill) in editing the Festschrift presented to him in 1988, drawing together a collection of papers that reflected Kane's international stature. Now it was good to have him back during the university year as well. He lived first in a tiny Georgian house near the British Museum, moving to a house in Hampstead, round the corner from Mary and her family, after Bridget had fallen on ice and broken her ankle, which later necessitated hip operations as well. They moved to West Sussex in 2002, again to be close to Mary. Kane was a welcome figure at seminars and lectures in the University of London for many years, and from time to time he came to the weekly medieval postgraduate seminars held in the English Department at King's. He belonged to two London clubs: the Athenæum; and the Flyfishers'—both still traditional gentlemen's clubs.

His work on Langland continued steadily, and the third volume, edited with George Russell (of the University of Melbourne), the C-text collaborator recruited long before by Mitchell, was published in 1997. For the C-text, again the editors diverged from Skeat's choice (Phillipps 6231, now Huntington Library MS Hm 137), as they had done both for the A- and B-texts. Earlier work by Allen had shown that Skeat's base manuscript came from a sophisticating group and that British Library MS Additional 35157 was to be preferred, the manuscript adopted as base-text by Carnegy in his 1923 thesis, but in 1924 a previously unknown manuscript came up for sale at Sotheby's: Huntington Library MS HM143. Chambers was able to make a preliminary examination of this new manuscript before it went to San Marino. In 1935 he went to the Huntington Library for more extended work upon it, to discover it was far superior to Additional 35157. HM 143 was to provide the base text for Mitchell's edition of the C Prologue and Passus I–IV, the completion of his thesis overlapping with Kane's first year of postgraduate work in London. The acknowledged superiority of HM 143 as copy-text for editing C was therefore uncontroversial. However, as had been the case with the B-text edition, there were reservations. Indubitably, the edition was an important addition to scholarship, not least for the wealth of excellent detail contained in the lengthy footnotes that accompany the text. As before, there was much praise for new, clever and satisfying conjectural emendations, but there was disquiet again about the degree of editorial interference. The editors were considered over-prescriptive in their treatment of the copy-text, making many changes, particularly relating to grammar and alliteration, which seemed unwarranted. Moreover, during the long years during which Russell and Kane had been forming their idea of the C archetype, Derek Pearsall's best-text edition (1979) had become justly popular, its deft introductory matter, annotations and glossary establishing it as a widely admired textbook undergraduates enjoyed working with. (Pearsall has recently pointed out that its 2008 revision, benefitting particularly from the publication of the Athlone C version, is 'a "critical" edition of a critical edition').[14]

As a mark of his achievement in completing the editing of *Piers Plowman* Kane was in 1999 awarded the Gollancz prize for a second time. For Kane, however, the task he had undertaken was not complete until he got to press in 2005 his glossary for the English vocabulary of the three Athlone volumes. Sustained work on the glossary was under way in the 1980s, with funding from the National Endowment for the Humanities providing the springboard for the great deal of preparatory work still to be undertaken. Under Acknowledgements Kane describes the mechanics of making the glossary. Wittig's electronic files contained some 150,000 words reduced to 5,000 headwords for his 2001 concordance. From 2002 Wittig fed copy to Kane in a variety of appropriate typefaces, for Kane to enter his 'revisions and corrections accumulated over the years', to arrive at a contextual meaning for each word in the three Athlone editions. An

[14] Derek Pearsall, 'The text of *Piers Plowman*: past, present and future', *Poetica*, 71 (2009), 75–91 at 90 n. 30.

intensive week of cross-checking the corrections together in the summer of 2004 was sufficient to enable Wittig to 'set up the resulting glossary in page format as camera-ready copy'. In the Introduction Kane wrote of the particular difficulties presented by terms such as *charite*, *conscience*, *leaute*, *pardon*, *reson*, or *treuthe*, identifying as the most challenging feature of undertaking the glossary 'the undebatable remoteness of the substance of the poem, an intellectually honest man's response to the major religious, thus cultural and in our language social crisis of his time, of a nature quite alien to the libertarian world of today'. It is an assessment that somehow encapsulates George Kane's own intellectual honesty and his deep understanding of late fourteenth-century English literature. He once noted that Chaucer and Langland 'in their combination of similarities and differences [were] the best company a man could wish for',[15] a love of and enthusiasm for his research field that he communicated to undergraduates, graduate students and colleagues in many universities.

The impact of George Kane's editorial and critical work was wide-reaching, and his influence continues to be important in Middle English scholarship. When the Athlone C version appeared, a century had gone by since Chambers and Grattan published the first results of their work on *Piers Plowman*. At last Skeat's parallel texts of 1886 had their true successor, although already new editorial procedures were gathering momentum. It is sobering to reflect that The Piers Plowman Electronic Archive published its prospectus as long ago as 1994, emphasising 'the provisional nature of scholarly editing'.[16] Seven manuscripts have now been edited in the SEENET series: stunning digital facsimiles accompanied by meticulous textual detail and analysis. But CD-ROM publication looks like giving way to on-line publication, as newer PCs struggle to open files held in older technological formats. Two of the five volumes of the *Penn Commentary* have appeared, a project that got under way in 1986. The three volumes that comprise the Athlone *Piers Plowman* will continue to provide an unparalleled amount of invaluable textual detail for some time to come, even to readers who decry the authoritarianism of its critical editions. That they exist at all is down to the unflagging energy of their chief editor who, at the outset of his career, inherited opinions that we now find it hard to credit. Back when Kane completed his Ph.D. thesis, no sustained work had been done on the language of the *Piers Plowman* manuscripts and it was thought that little was to be garnered from them about the poet's dia-

[15] Preface: *Chaucer and Langland: Historical and Textual Approaches* (London and Berkeley, CA, 1989).

[16] <http://www3.iath.virginia.edu/seenet/piers/archivegoals.htm>.

lect—the huge changes brought to our understanding of late Middle English by Angus McIntosh and Michael Samuels lay far in the future.[17] That Kane in 1946 described as the purpose of an editor's work the rejection of errors from the text and opposed emendation for the sake of metre, alliteration and spelling is, with hindsight, a surprise. Perhaps the very orderliness of the copy-text chosen for their B version nudged Kane and Donaldson towards emulation of its norms.

Kane's superbly argued assessment of 'the evidence for authorship' freed a generation of scholars from worrying about Langland's identity and the attribution of the A, B and C texts to him. In Derek Pearsall's words: 'Everyone decided to agree with him and get on with things. Enough was enough, Langland studies began to blossom.'[18] In time, inevitably, discussion of the integrity and sequence of versions came back into play. Two significant publications were to draw Kane's fire. Charlotte Brewer and George Rigg argued for a version that preceded the A version in their 1983 publication of the first part of the Z text (Oxford, Bodleian Library, MS Bodley 851). Kane's 1985 *Speculum* review article was, if you enjoy the cut and thrust of argument, splendidly rebarbative, but to at least one reader the tone felt 'bitterly dismissive'.[19] Nevertheless, an early *Piers Plowman* text comprising the first two visions gained its adherents as an authentic fourth version, and it is included as such by Carl Schmidt in his 'parallel-text edition of the A, B, C and Z versions' (1995–2008). A decade later Jill Mann, in her paper 'The power of the alphabet',[20] stood the generally accepted sequence of texts on its head, suggesting that the A text originated in an authorial abridgement of the B text. Langland himself, she argued, could have made a simpler version for a non-clerical audience, shortening his text, tidying the story line and cutting back on Latin and sexual references. Kane was not the first to mount a refutation of Mann's ingenious reworking of Meroney's 1950 proposition, but once both the *Legend of Good Women* and the Langland C-text editions appeared he had 'time and space' to pen 'an open letter to Jill Mann', firmly arguing that Langland's poem 'unquestionably developed as he wrote it' and that it remained unfinished.[21]

[17] Angus McIntosh, M. L. Samuels and M. Benskin, with the assistance of Margaret Laing and Keith Williamson, *A Linguistic Atlas of Late Mediaeval English*, 4 vols. (Aberdeen, 1986).

[18] Pearsall, 'The text ...', p. 78.

[19] Derek Pearsall, *An Annotated Critical Bibliography of Langland* (New York, 1990), p. 25.

[20] Jill Mann, 'The power of the alphabet: a reassessment of the relation between the A and B versions of *Piers Plowman*', *Yearbook of Langland Studies*, 8 (1994), 21–50.

[21] George Kane, 'An open letter to Jill Mann about the sequence of the versions of *Piers Plowman*', *Yearbook of Langland Studies*, 13 (1999), 7–33.

When Kane came to write his *Oxford Dictionary of National Biography* entry on Langland (2004) he revisited fully the details known or surmised of Langland's life, now dated by him *c.*1325–*c.*1390. Earlier he had placed the making of the C text early in the 1380s, maintaining that Langland was 'dead by 1387'. In a review article he found Anne Middleton's argument that C V 1–104 shows the influence of three provisions of the 1388 Statute of Labourers so persuasive that he put forward 'an alternative possibility, that just as *Piers Plowman* was a catalyst in the uprising of 1381, so this C passage might be reflected in, have influenced the detail of, the Statute'. Speculatively he suggests that 'Langland of whom it must be recalled we know nothing beyond his parentage and place of birth', had to do with its drafting.[22] Kane does allude to Langland's 'fluency in legal terminology' in the *Oxford DNB* piece, but draws back from involving him in the framing of the Statute. Placing the poet's putative birth in *c.*1325 lengthens his life, a change made in the light of recent discoveries about a cleric named William Rokele, tonsured in the Worcester area by 1341 and (possibly the same man) beneficed within the jurisdiction of the Bishop of Norwich in 1353. Clearly Kane viewed the identification as attractive, if unprovable. A Norfolk connection, he points out, could help explain the distribution of some of the earliest manuscripts of the A version, but does not ultimately affect how *Piers Plowman* is to be read and understood. For Kane, 'Langland stands, for the quality of his art, with Dante and Chaucer among the supreme poets of the European middle ages.' This succinct overview of Langland's life demonstrates clearly the admiration and affection *Piers Plowman* inspired in him and which he communicated so effectively to others.

Kane admitted to one hobby only, which he took up seriously in 1958. A keen flyfisher, the holidays spent wading into rivers or tumbling about in small boats on cold loughs were, apart from reading, his main relaxation, although this could be combined with seeking out little known and often isolated ruins of castles in Scotland and Ireland. There were many visits to Ireland, which began soon after the war: arriving on a ferry into Waterford, George's first encounter with an Irish 'fry' sealed what was to become a love affair with Ireland. But his family was the centre of his life. When Michael was ill, he and his father developed an interest in genealogy, spending time, before the arrival of the internet, in the Mormon library in London, chasing up links from Ireland, France and Germany leading to his family's various arrivals in North America. Michael died in

[22] George Kane, 'Langland: labour and "authorship"', *Notes and Queries*, 243 (1998), 420–5.

1998. In 2008, George and Bridget moved into sheltered accommodation in Eastbourne, as she had developed Alzheimer's disease and he and Mary were unable to care for her on their own. There he continued to work slowly at his typewriter, on requested articles and his autobiography, up to six weeks before his death. He remained interested in politics and academic gossip and delighted in being asked to look through and comment on his grandson's dissertation for his history degree, needless to say on a mediaeval period. He died in Eastbourne, on 27 December 2008, and is survived by Bridget, his wife of sixty-two years, their daughter and four grandchildren.

JANE ROBERTS
University of London

Note. In preparing this memoir I am particularly grateful to Mary Kane for all her help and for letting me read a copy of the memoir her father wrote for his grandchildren, from which quotations are taken. I should also like to thank friends and colleagues of George Kane for their help and advice: Don Kennedy, Patrick O'Neill, Joe Wittig (Chapel Hill); Ros Allen, Janet Bately, Janet Cowen, Warwick Gould, Ron Waldron (London). Obituaries for Kane were published in the *Guardian* (19 March 2009), *The Times* (2 April 2009), and *Speculum*, 85 (2010), 782–8.

Bibliography of works by George Kane

Although the 1988 Festschrift for Kane contained a list of some of his publications, this was far from complete and so a fuller listing is provided here.

'The B-text of Piers Plowman, Passus XXIII–XX' (Ph.D. thesis, University of London).

'Review: *The Pardon of Piers Plowman* by Nevill Coghill', *The Modern Language Review*, 41 (1946), 424–6.

'*Piers Plowman*: Problems and Methods of Editing the B-Text', *The Modern Language Review*, 43 (1948), 1–25.

'Review: *The Heresy of Courtly Love* by Alexander J. Denomy', *The Modern Language Review,* 43 (1948), 524–5.

'Review: *The Poetry of Caedmon* by C. L. Wrenn', *The Modern Language Review*, 43 (1948), 250–2.

'Review: *The Impact of French upon English* by John Orr', *The Modern Language Review*, 44 (1949), 95.

'Review: *Annual Bibliography of English Language and Literature. Vol. XX, 1939* by Angus Macdonald and Leslie N. Broughton', *The Review of English Studies*, 25 (1949), 370–1.

'Review: *A Commentary on the General Prologue to the Canterbury Tales* by Muriel Bowden', *The Modern Language Review*, 45 (1950), 363–8.

'The Textual Criticism of Piers Plowman', *Times Literary Supplement* (17 March 1950), 176.

Middle English Literature, A Critical Study of the Romances, the Religious Lyrics, Piers Plowman (London, 1951: repr. 1969; 1970; 1977; 1979).

'The Middle English Verse in MS Wellcome 1491', *London Mediaeval Studies*, 2 (1951), 50–67.

'Review: *The Other World According to Descriptions in Medieval Literature* by Howard Rollin Patch', *The Modern Language Review*, 46 (1951), 475–6.

'Review: *The Audience of Beowulf* by Dorothy Whitelock', *The Modern Language Review*, 47 (1952), 567–8.

'Review: *Annual Bibliography of English Language and Literature. Vol. XXII, 1941* by Angus Macdonald and Leslie N. Broughton and *Annual Bibliography of English Language and Literature. Vol. XXIII, 1942* by Angus Macdonald and Henry J. Pettit, Jr.', *The Review of English Studies*, NS 4 (1953), 399–401.

'Review: *The Seven Deadly Sins* by Morton W. Bloomfeld', *Journal of English and Germanic Philology*, 53 (1953), 98–100.

'Review: *John Lydgate* by Walter F. Schirmer', *Journal of English and Germanic Philology*, 53 (1953), 466–9.

'Review: *Alt- und Mittelenglische Anthologie* by Rolf Kaiser', *The Review of English Studies*, NS 7 (1956), 104–5.

'Review: *Medieval English Poetry: the Non-Chaucerian Tradition* by John Speirs', *The Modern Language Review* (1959), 249–51.

Piers Plowman: the A Version. Will's Vision of Piers Plowman and Do-Well. An Edition in the Form of Trinity College, Cambridge, Manuscript R. 3. 14, Corrected from Other Manuscripts, with Variant Readings ([S.l.]: London, 1960).

'Review: *The South English Legendary* by Charlotte D'Evelyn and Anna J. Mill', *The Review of English Studies*, NS 11 (1960), 311–12.

'Review: *William Langlands 'Piers Plowman' (Eine Interpretation des C-Textes)* by Willi Erzgräber', *The Modern Language Review*, 55 (1960), 264–5.

'Review: *Chaucer: a Critical Appreciation* by Paull F. Baum', *The Modern Language Review*, 55 (1960), 265–6.

'Review: *Piers Plowman* by D. C. Fowler (ed.), in *Medium Ævum*, 33 (1964), 230–1.

'Piers Plowman': the evidence for authorship (London: Athlone Press, 1965). Chambers Memorial Lecture (London, 1965)

The Autobiographical Fallacy in Chaucer and Langland Studies, Chambers Memorial Lecture (London, 1965); repr. in Kane, *Chaucer and Langland* (1989), no. 1.

'Review: Piers Plowman*: A Parallel-Text Edition of the A, B, C and Z Versions: vol. 1, Text* edited by A. V. C. Schmidt', *Notes and Queries*, 43:3 (1966), 315–21.

'Review: *Facsimile of British Museum MS. Harley 2253*', *The Review of English Studies*, NS 19 (1968), 62–3.

'Conjectural emendation', in D. A. Pearsall and R. A. Waldron (eds.), *Medieval Literature and Civilization: Studies in Memory of G. N. Garmonsway* (London, 1969), pp. 155–69; repr. in Christopher Kleinhenz (ed.), *Medieval Manuscripts and Textual Criticism* (Chapel Hill, NC, 1976), pp. 211–25; repr. in Kane, *Chaucer and Langland* (1989), no. 11.

'A short essay on the Middle English secular lyric', in *Studies Presented to Tauno F. Mustanoja on the Occasion of His Sixtieth Birthday, Neuphilologische Mitteilungen*, 73 (1972), 110–21.

Piers Plowman [by William Langland]. [Vol.2], The B version: Will's Visions of Piers Plowman, Do-well, Do-better and Do-best. Edition An edition in the form of Trinity College Cambridge MS. B.15.17, corrected and restored from the known evidence, with variant readings, by George Kane and E. Talbot Donaldson (London, 1975).

'Some reflections on critical method', *Essays & Studies*, 29 (1976), 23–38; repr., under title 'Criticism, Solecism: Does it Matter?' ; in Kane, *Chaucer and Langland* (1989), no. 15.

'Chaucer and the idea of a poet', *Problemi Attuali di Scienza e di Cultura*, 234 (Rome, 1977), 35–49; repr. in Kane, *Chaucer and Langland* (1989), no. 2.

'Outstanding problems of Middle English scholarship', in Paul E. Szarmach and Bernard S. Levy (eds.), *The Fourteenth Century* (Binghamton, NY, 1977), pp. 1–17; repr. in Kane, *Chaucer and Langland* (1989), no. 2.

The Liberating Truth: the Concept of Integrity in Chaucer's Writings: the John Coffin Memorial Lecture delivered before the University of London on 11 May, 1979 (London, 1980); repr. in Kane, *Chaucer and Langland* (1989), no. 4.

'Review: *Piers Plowman: Etudes sur la génèse littéraire des trois versions* by Guy Bourquin', *Speculum*, 55 (1980), 526–9.

'Music "neither unpleasant nor monotonous"', in P. L. Heyworth (ed.), *Medieval Studies for J. A. W. Bennett, Aetatis Suae LXX* (Oxford, 1981), pp. 43–63; repr. in Kane, *Chaucer and Langland* (1989), no. 6.

'Langland and Chaucer: an obligatory conjunction', in Donald L. Rose (ed.), *New Perspectives in Chaucer Criticism* (Norman, OK, 1981), pp. 5–19; repr. in Kane, *Chaucer and Langland* (1989), no. 9.

'Chaucer, love poetry, and romantic love', in Mary J. Carruthers and Elizabeth D. Kirk (eds.), *Acts of Interpretation: The Text in Its Contexts, 700–1600: Essays on Medieval and Renaissance Literature in Honor of E. Talbot Donaldson* (Norman, OK, 1982), pp. 237–55; repr. in Kane, *Chaucer and Langland* (1989), no. 3.

'The perplexities of William Langland', in Larry Dean Benson and Siegfried Wenzel (eds.), *The Wisdom of Poetry: Essays in Early English Literature in Honor of Morton W. Bloomfield* (Kalamazoo, MI, 1982), pp. 3–89; repr. in Kane, *Chaucer and Langland* (1989), no. 8.

'Poetry and lexicography in the translation of *Piers Plowman*', in Frank Tirro (ed.), *Medieval and Renaissance Studies* (Durham, NC, 1982), pp. 33–54; repr. in Kane, *Chaucer and Langland* (1989), no. 7.

'The text of The Legend of Good Women in CUL MS Gg.4.27', in Douglas Gray and E. G. Stanley (eds.), *Middle English Studies Presented to Norman Davis in Honour of His Seventieth Birthday* (Oxford, 1983), pp. 39–58; repr. in Kane, *Chaucer and Langland* (1989), no. 12.

Chaucer (Oxford, 1984).

'John M. Manly (1865–1940) and Edith Rickert (1871–1938)', in Paul G. Ruggiers (ed.), *Editing Chaucer: The Great Tradition* (Norman, OK, 1984), pp. 207–29; repr. in Kane, *Chaucer and Langland* (1989), no. 13.

'The "Z Version" of Piers Plowman', *Speculum*, 60 (1985), 910–30.

'An accident of history: Lord Berners's translation of Froissart's Chronicles', *The Chaucer Review*, 21 (1986), 217–25.

'"Good" and "Bad" manuscripts: texts and critics', *Studies in the Age of Chaucer*, 2 (1986), 137–45; repr. in Kane, *Chaucer and Langland* (1989), no. 14.

'Some Fourteenth-Century "political" poems', in Gregory Kratzmann and James Simpson (eds.), *Medieval English Religious and Ethical Literature: Essays in Honour of G. H. Russell*. (Cambridge, 1986), pp. 82–91.

'Review: *Chaucer's Native Heritage* by Alexander Weiss', *Speculum*, 61 (1986), 1011–12.

Piers Plowman: The A Version: Will's Visions of Piers Plowman and Do-Well (London and Berkeley, CA, 1988).

Piers Plowman. The B version: Will's Visions of Piers Plowman, Do-well, Do better and Do-best an edition in the form of Trinity College Cambridge M.S. B.15.17, corrected and restored from the known evidence with variant reading. Revised edition by George Kane and E. Talbot Donaldson (London, 1988).

'The text', in John A. Alford (ed.), *A Companion to Piers Plowman* (Berkeley, CA, 1988), pp. 175–200.

Chaucer and Langland: Historical and Textual Approaches (London and Berkeley, CA, 1989); includes two previously unpublished papers: no. 5 'Philosophical Chaucer'; no. 10, 'Chaucer and Langland II'.

'Review: *Chaucer: His Life, His Works, His World* by Donald R. Howard', *Albion: a Quarterly Journal Concerned with British Studies*, 21 (1989), 92–4.

'A new translation of the B Text of Piers Plowman', *Yearbook of Langland Studies*, 7 (1993), 129–56.

The Legend of Good Women / Geoffrey Chaucer, ed. Janet Cowen and George Kane (East Lansing, MI, 1995).

'Reading Piers Plowman', *The Yearbook of Langland Studies*, 8 (1995), 1–20.

'Review: *Textual criticism and Middle English Texts*, by T. W. Machan', *Speculum*, 71 (1996), 975–8.

Piers Plowman. The C version: Will's Visions of Piers Plowman, Do-well, Do-better and Do-best: an edition in the form of Huntington Library MS HM 143, corrected and restored from the known evidence, with variant readings, ed. George Russell and George Kane (London, 1997).

'Langland: labour and "authorship"', *Notes and Queries*, 243 (1998), 420–5.

'Review: *Robin Hood: A collection of all the ancient poems, songs and ballads, now extant, relative to that celebrated English outlaw*', *Notes and Queries*, 45 (1998), 114–15.

'An open letter to Jill Mann about the sequence of the versions of *Piers Plowman*', *Yearbook of Langland Studies*, 13 (1999), 7–33.

'Word games: glossing *Piers Plowman*', in Susan Powell and Jeremy J. Smith (eds.), *New Perspectives on Middle English Texts: a Festschrift for R. A. Waldron* (Woodbridge, 2000), pp. 43–53.

'Language as literature', in Christian J. Kay and Louise Sylvester (eds.), *Lexis and Texts in Early English: studies presented to Jane Roberts* (Amsterdam, 2001), pp. 161–71.

'Langland, William (*c.* 1325–*c.* 1390)', *Oxford Dictionary of National Biography* (Oxford University Press, 2004) <http://0-www.oxforddnb.com.catalogue.ulrls.lon.ac.uk/view/article/16021>.

The Piers Plowman Glossary: Will's Visions of Piers Plowman, Do-Well, Do-Better and Do-Best: a glossary of the English vocabulary of the A, B, and C versions as presented in the Athlone editions (New York and London 2005).

'Poets and the poetics of sin', in Daniel Donoghue, James Simpson and Nicholas Watson (eds.), *The Morton W. Bloomfield Lectures, 1989–2005* (Kalamazoo, MI, 2010).

NEIL MACCORMICK

Donald Neil MacCormick
1941–2009

Donald Neil MacCormick was born in Glasgow on 27 May 1941, the son of John MacCormick, a lawyer and leading Scottish nationalist, and of Margaret (née Miller), who was a social worker. He had an elder brother and two younger sisters. Neil showed academic promise at Glasgow High School and went on to obtain First Class Honours in Philosophy and Literature (MA 1963) at the University of Glasgow. He obtained a Snell Exhibition to Balliol College, Oxford in 1963, where he read Jurisprudence (BA First Class Honours, 1965; MA, 1969). He was President of the Union in 1965. Soon after graduation he accepted a teaching post in Jurisprudence at Queen's College Dundee (then part of the University of St Andrews), intending to use it as a stepping stone to legal practice in Edinburgh. However, in 1967 he was elected to a Fellowship in Jurisprudence at Balliol (with a Lectureship at Corpus Christi College). He was called to the English Bar (Inner Temple) in 1971. In 1972, at the age of 31, he was appointed to the Regius Chair of Public Law and the Law of Nature and the Law of Nations at the University of Edinburgh, a position he held with great distinction until his retirement in 2007. Shortly after that he fell ill and was diagnosed with terminal cancer. He died at home in Edinburgh on 5 April 2009 after a long illness during which he saw through the press the last volume of his quartet of books on *Law, State and Practical Reason* (1999–2008) that constitutes the summation of his thought in legal philosophy. In 1965 he married Caroline Rona Barr. They had three daughters. After a divorce in 1992, he married Flora Margaret Britain (née Milne), who survives him. Among numerous honours, including several honorary degrees, he was elected as a Fellow of the British Academy in 1986,

Biographical Memoirs of Fellows of the British Academy, XI, 449–471.

knighted in recognition of 'services to scholarship in Law' in 2001 and was awarded the Royal Society of Edinburgh's Gold Medal for Outstanding Achievement in 2004.

This bare outline says almost nothing about his personality, his achievements or his activities beyond legal philosophy. Nevertheless, it is quite revealing. First, MacCormick's initial grounding in philosophy focused on the Scottish enlightenment, traditional forms of moral theory (including neo-Kantianism), and logic and informal reasoning. This is crucial in interpreting his distinctive place in legal and political philosophy. Second, he studied and taught English law in Oxford. He never formally studied, practiced or taught Scots law (except incidentally), but, largely self-taught, he wrote about it with acumen. Thus, although he was imbued from early on with Scottish history, politics, literature, and philosophy, his legal background was mainly English. Third, his Edinburgh Chair with its sonorous title provided him with a prestigious platform and a congenial and secure base from which he could move out to engage in a wide range of activities—politics, university administration, public service, as a visiting speaker in many places in Europe and North America, and not least as a public intellectual. Neil MacCormick's academic reputation rests largely on his teaching and writing in legal philosophy, but he was highly visible and widely liked and respected as a public figure not only in Scotland but also in the rest of the United Kingdom and in Continental Europe. He was, as one obituarist expressed it, a popular Scottish internationalist.

The many eulogies that poured in after Neil's death tended to emphasise several traits: his energy, formidable intelligence, conviviality, humour, openness to other points of view, and generosity of spirit. In personal relations, with students, colleagues, and politicians of different persuasions, he was much liked, even loved, for his warmth and sympathetic interest. He earned praise for his many contributions to university administration. Popular anecdotes tell of a kilted MacCormick playing the bagpipes at many events, including the funeral of his lifelong friend, John Smith; of instances of professorial absent-mindedness; and of his Scottish accent bewildering foreigners when he waxed eloquent. I was a close personal friend and I witnessed how often, in his own phrase, he 'added to the gaiety of nations'. My first memory is playing energetic Frisbee with the newly appointed Regius Professor of the Law of Nature and the Law of Nations in the grounds of Belfast Castle during a symposium on constitutional law; later, of equally light-hearted games of ping pong, disquisitions on single malts and Scottish history, and prolonged conversations about jurisprudence.

Of course, he had faults. The most commonly voiced criticism was that he was sometimes 'too nice', 'too reasonable', 'too accommodating'. Such generosity of spirit might indeed be a weakness in a captain of a ship or a prison governor or even a vice-chancellor. It could also be a fault in a legal philosopher, so the question arises: was he too accommodating, too generous with his praise, too ready to see other points of view? Or, worse still, was he eclectic? In a posthumously published paper Neil acknowledged that his temperament tended towards the constructive-collaborative rather than the critical-dialectical or confrontational (MacCormick, 2011). He favoured charitable interpretation of other thinkers, openness to differing views and to criticism, sometimes himself presenting a moving target. That he was a synthesiser is not in doubt—his attempts to reconcile Kant, Hume, Smith, and Stair are a prime example. His institutional theory of law is broad enough to accommodate non-state law, supranational law and even some forms of 'soft law'. When I co-examined with him over many years in Edinburgh, Belfast, Warwick and London, I found him concerned to be fair and consistent, willing to listen carefully to contrary opinions, but not soft. Rather he was brisk and decisive. As one of his Ph.D. students put it, as a supervisor he was gentle, but not lenient. As a political speaker, while engaging, he could be robustly critical. Part of his appeal as a philosopher was his willingness both to adopt forthright positions and to change his mind, if persuaded: Hume was wrong about reason being slave of the passions, but many of his insights are worth preserving. Neil's rejection of will theories of rights, his emphasis that state law is only one kind of law, that self-determination is a relative matter, and his initial rejection and later partial defence of Ronald Dworkin's 'one right answer' thesis[1] are all equally robust. His commitment to a gradualist, non-violent form of Scottish nationalism was unequivocal. Throughout his final quartet Neil is concerned to assert clear, coherent positions and to justify them with vigorous arguments. Those positions are nearly always moderate, reasonable and reasoned, but, for the most part, they are neither eclectic nor equivocal.

[1] His final position on this last issue was equivocal; for example, in *Questioning Sovereignty* (1999, p. 6) he suggests that 'sometimes or maybe even often' there is an answer that is objectively better than its rivals.

It is my impression that Neil read, then thought, then wrote largely from his head. Once, when we were collaborating on a joint paper, he came to stay the night. I had struggled for some weeks to produce the first half of a draft. That evening, we discussed what we thought and wanted to say over a bottle of single malt—I think Glemorangie was in favour that year. Next morning I had an appointment. As I was leaving he asked for some rough paper. By the time I returned two or three hours later he had completed the draft—scribbling over forty pages in longhand. When I revised it, I had occasionally to restrain his exuberance, and quietly edit out Scottishisms, but otherwise I altered very little. Many of his essays started as public lectures or conference papers and retain the style of oral delivery. The footnotes tend to be sparse, though carefully constructed. His prose is direct and clear, the mode argumentative rather than expository or interpretive.

One aspect of Neil's outside activities bears directly on his theoretical ideas: his involvement in politics. He was a life-long Scottish nationalist, he stood for election as a Scottish National Party (SNP) candidate in five Westminster elections—showing the flag in hopeless constituencies—and then, more seriously, he served as an SNP Member of the European Parliament from 1999 to 2005. There is ample material for a full-scale biography or even a detailed account of his political career. I shall deal with his ideas on nationalism and sovereignty below. Here his political involvement is immediately relevant in three general respects. First, he developed a theory of social democracy largely through his studies of the political and intellectual history of Scotland. This theory was continuously tested, refined and adjusted through experiences of practical politics. It found expression in many papers,[2] and it pervades all four volumes of *Law, State and Practical Reason*. His political and legal philosophy is all of a piece. Second, his involvement with nationalist politics and the European Union required him to explore fundamental questions about both sovereignty and nationalism. He was often asked how he reconciled his general philosophic position and his enthusiasm for the EU with his involvement in nationalist politics, especially in view of the unhappy history of nationalism in twentieth-century Europe. Third, a concern for 'practicality' underlies all of MacCormick's work: jurisprudence must be about law, not just abstract concepts; law is not merely an inert body of norms; how it is operationalised is a crucial part of understanding legal phenomena

[2] Some of his early essays are collected in *Legal Right and Social Democracy* (1982).

(MacCormick, 2011); legal reasoning is a practice, not just a form of argumentation; sensitivity to both social and political context is crucial.

Intellectual development 1963–1981

Neil's academic career was remarkably stable—he occupied the same Chair for thirty-six years—but the development of his ideas was more complex. In some brief autobiographical notes he summarised his intellectual development as follows:

> Reduced to stages, I would say that 1965–81 was for me a period in which I was most closely engaged with Hart's work, as a follower of his, though one with independent connections derived from other influences. 1981–1995 was a period of re-consideration of main themes and steady distancing from Hart, especially the later Hart. Since 1995 I have developed a rounded account of my own mature thought, having at its centre the post-positivist institutionalism developed in *Institutions of Law*, and ultimately to be underpinned by my book on practical reason in morality and law.

This is a useful rendering, but I shall suggest later that it over-emphasises his relationship with Herbert Hart and the significance of his shift to 'post-positivism'.

Neil first arrived in Oxford as a student in 1963. His main tutors were Donald Harris, a New Zealander, who taught him English law and subsequently became the Director of the Oxford Centre for Socio-Legal Studies, and Alan Watson, a fellow Scot, a specialist in Roman Law and Comparative Law. Oxford was then the home of ordinary language philosophy, which was very different from what Neil had encountered in Glasgow, where W. D. Lamont's lectures on political philosophy had been especially influential. In 1952 H. L. A. Hart had moved from a Fellowship in Philosophy to the Corpus Chair of Jurisprudence. By 1963 Hart's *The Concept of Law* (1961) had become, and has remained ever since, the starting-point for the study of Jurisprudence in Oxford and far beyond. As a student Neil attended two series of Hart's lectures. When he returned to Oxford in 1967 he had quite a lot of contact with him, but they never established a close personal relationship. He also had a close association with John Finnis, Richard Buxton, Brian Simpson, Joseph Raz, and, after Hart resigned his chair in 1968, with his successor Ronald Dworkin. Thus for about twenty years Neil moved in Hart's circles, defended his positivist views, and was considered to be one of his leading disciples.

Neil was a prolific speaker and writer. Until the late 1990s his academic reputation rested largely on his lectures and papers delivered in many countries and on four books that drew heavily on prior oral performances. *An Institutional Theory of Law: New Approaches to Legal Positivism* (with Ota Weinberger, 1986) developed his general theory of law, first expounded in his inaugural lecture in 1973, and most fully developed in *Institutions of Law* in 2007. This was the stable starting-point of his legal philosophy. In *Legal Reasoning and Legal Theory* (1978, 2nd edition 1994) he advanced a general theory of legal reasoning that he claimed was compatible with Hartian positivism. Some viewed it as presenting the kind of view Hart might have developed had he paid more attention to legal reasoning. This was one of MacCormick's most successful works. It was clear, accessible, concrete, taking moderate, reflective positions on a wide range of issues. Students found it accessible and it attracted a lot of attention in Continental Europe. In 1982 he published a collection of essays on *Legal Right and Social Democracy: Essays in Legal and Political Philosophy*, which advanced a rationalist liberal democratic ideology that steered a middle path between 'individualist Whiggery and Marxist collectivism' (MacCormick, 1982: 8). This explored important ideas on social justice, legal rights and obligations, nationalism, the Scottish Enlightenment, and coercion. It was recognised as a significant contribution to political theory. This book foreshadowed several of the central themes in *Law, State and Practical Reason*. Indeed some perceptive commentators suggest that some of these more discursive essays help to make the quartet more accessible.

Towards the end of what MacCormick described as the first phase of his intellectual development, he published an introduction to Hart's ideas. The first edition of *H. L. A. Hart* (1981) was very well-received and for a long time was considered the standard reference. It contained some criticisms on points of detail, but was essentially sympathetic. However, Hart thought that it depicted him as closer to natural law than his own self-perception and he hardened his positivist stance in the Postscript to *The Concept of Law* (1994). The second edition of MacCormick's book (2008), while remaining scrupulously exact and fair, engages with controversies about Hart's works and provides some rather clear clues about MacCormick's own intellectual trajectory.

1981–1997

By the time he was elected to the British Academy in 1986 these four early books, together with his lectures and essays, had established a considerable international reputation for him as a very substantial legal philosopher. In them he had set out carefully argued positions on the nature of law, legal reasoning, political theory, and Scottish nationalism. From 1981 to 1997 he devoted most of his energies to academic administration and nationalist politics. This was hardly a fallow period intellectually, for he continued to lecture and write, but his intellectual agenda was less clear. There were, however, two significant developments in his perspective on legal philosophy. First, he invested a great deal of time in studying and teaching about the thinkers of the Scottish Enlightenment, deepening his study of Hume, Stair and Adam Smith and extending his knowledge of several other figures. Second, largely through the World Congress of Social and Legal Philosophy, he came into contact with leading jurists in Continental Europe. He had met Chaim Perelman (Brussels), the pioneer of 'the new rhetoric' and the precursor of modern argumentation theory. Neil was attracted by his ideas on informal logic and translated some of his work. In 1979 he invested time in improving his command of German. He collaborated with Ota Weinberger (Graz) and worked closely, among others, with Robert Alexy (Germany), Aulis Aarnio (Helsinki), and Aleksander Peczenik (Lund). Later he flirted with the systems theory of Niklas Luhmann and Gunther Teubner. In the late 1970s and early 1980s, in collaboration with Robert Summers and Zenon Bankowski, he became involved in comparative work on legal reasoning and interpretation. This culminated in two outstanding edited volumes of essays on precedent and statutory interpretation, based on a series of workshops, known as the '*Bielefelder Kreis*' (MacCormick and Summers, 1991 and 1997). Thus during this period he returned to his intellectual roots in the Scottish Enlightenment and added a distinctive European and comparative dimension, while experiencing what he called a 'steady distancing from Hart'. In 2008 he summed up his view of Hart as follows:

> Hart's greatest and most enduring insight concerns the need to understand rule-governed conduct from the 'internal point of view'. This is essential to developing a clear and convincing theory of norms—but rules are only one kind of norm. The analysis of law as a union of primary and secondary rules, though full of valuable insight, is in the end incomplete and unsatisfactory. A fresh start is needed. A version of a 'basic norm theory' is more satisfactory than a 'rule of recognition' theory in explaining how a legal system comes together in the

> framework of a constitutionalist state (Rechtsstaat, Estado de derecho). Legal institutions interface with politics and economics and are foundational for the state and also for civil society. Criminal law is one essential part of the foundations of social peace and thus of civil society. All this takes one quite far from the Hartian conception of law, though the development out of a Hartian position is easily traced. Law and morality are indeed conceptually distinct, but it remains also true that minimal elements of respect for justice are essential to the recognition of a normative order as 'legal' in character. (Autobiographical Notes, unpublished, 2008)

The quartet: *Law, State and Practical Reason* (1999–2008)

In 1997 Neil shed his administrative load and started again to concentrate on legal philosophy. He planned to reconsider his position on the main themes of legal, political and moral theory and to develop 'a rounded account of my own mature thought'. He formulated a hugely ambitious project for a work in four volumes on *Law, State and Practical Reason* and applied for and obtained a five-year Research Professorship from the Leverhulme Trust. He completed *Questioning Sovereignty* in 1999, before his tenure of the Leverhulme Fellowship was interrupted by his election as an SNP Member of the European Parliament. From 1999 to 2004 he had almost no time for academic work. Fortunately, when he stepped down as an MEP his Leverhulme Professorship was revived and thereafter he was able to concentrate on *Law, State and Practical Reason*. He did this with renewed enthusiasm and commitment. Two further volumes were completed before his formal retirement in 2007. Shortly after that he fell ill and the final volume was mainly written during that last illness.

This is not the place to attempt a detailed analysis or evaluation of each book in MacCormick's impressive quartet. Instead, I shall briefly describe three of the volumes, give a more detailed account of his ideas on nationalism, sovereignty and self-determination, and then advance an assessment of the distinctiveness and significance of his contributions as a whole.

Institutions of Law

Institutions of Law (2007) was the third in time of the quartet to be published, but it was conceived as its lynchpin in that it set out his theory of law as a contribution to general jurisprudence, with the other three volumes as elaborations of the underpinnings of his philosophy of law and of particular aspects, such as sovereignty, practical reasoning, and a theory of justice.

He first expounded his institutional theory of law in his inaugural lecture at Edinburgh (MacCormick, 1973). Later he developed it in collaboration with Ota Weinberger (MacCormick and Weinberger, 1985, 1986) and he refined and adjusted it over the years in many papers. His central idea, that law is institutionalised normative order, remained constant, but *Institutions of Law* is much more than a restatement and elaboration of his early ideas.

The starting-point for MacCormick's theory was a distinction between 'brute facts' and 'institutional facts', advanced by Elizabeth Anscombe and John Searle (especially in Anscombe, 1958, and Searle, 1959) as part of speech act theory. 'Brute facts' appear to exist in the world entirely independent of human thought or values; they are 'sheer physical facts': 'institutional facts' also exist, but their existence presupposes human thought and institutions. A credit card, a system of scoring in sport, courts, the Scottish law of obligations, and a particular contract all exist—they are facts—but they exist by virtue of human norms.

For MacCormick law is one species of the genus normative order, viz. institutional normative order. This is an 'explanatory definition' which requires the elaboration of three elements—'normative', 'order', and 'institution'. MacCormick uses the example of queuing to illustrate these concepts and to introduce some central themes. In some cultures queuing is a practice that is well-understood by nearly all participants even if they are total strangers. In some contexts, for example waiting for a bus or at a supermarket checkout, people form a line in an orderly way in order to take turns. This is a form of activity that is a mutually coordinated practice, a social-moral institution that is governed by norms. The existence of the practice depends on a fairly high degree of understanding and compliance by the participants. There are norms for turn-taking and against 'queue-barging', with possible exceptions, for example in emergencies or for particular classes of people. The norms may be implicit or they may be informally or formally articulated. They can even be formalised and managed by authority. Queuing is an institutionalised practice, a particular queue is an instance of that practice. In some cultures queuing is a relatively stable normative practice with many variations. The Scottish law of contract and a contract under that law are both institutional facts:

> The existence of the institution as such is relative to a given legal system, and depends upon whether or not the system contains an appropriate set of

> institutive, consequential and terminative rules. If it does, then the occurrence of given events or the performance of given acts has by virtue of the rules the effect of bringing into being the existence of the institution. (MacCormick and Wienberger, 1986: 66)

Legal phenomena as institutional facts are of different kinds: they can be institution-agencies (e.g. courts, legislatures), institution-arrangements (e.g. property, criminal law), or institution things (e.g. contracts, rights to futures). All are normative, institutionalised, and concerned with ordering relations.

Institutions of Law is presented in four parts: Part 1 analyses the central concepts of the theory. Part 2, 'Persons, Acts and Relations', focuses on basic legal concepts (persons, property, rights, powers etc.). This looks rather like a revival of the kind of particularistic English analytical jurisprudence that gave way to the more philosophical approach of Herbert Hart, but it also has echoes of Roman and Scottish institutional writings. Part 3, 'Law, State and Civil Society', explores the constitutive role of law in relation to law and politics, fundamental rights, criminal law and law and economy. Part 4, 'Law, Morality, and Methodology', revisits legal positivism, the relationship between law and justice, and the methodology of analytical jurisprudence. MacCormick claimed that *Institutions of Law* brought his general theory of law up to date in an avowedly 'post-positivistic' form (see below), developing an interpretative approach to analytical jurisprudence that is fully in tune with some major recent developments in the sociology of law and socio-legal studies more generally.

MacCormick uses the example of queuing to introduce some general themes. First, the implicit formalisation by authority, for example in managing a checkout, represents a second tier of institutionalisation of a pre-existing normative practice. Humans are norm-users before they are norm-givers (*Institutions*, 284–8). Second, implicit norms are not the same as hard-and-fast rules. They come into existence in complex ways through human interactions involving expectations, practices, values and mutual understandings. Third, Hart had illuminatingly distinguished between the concepts of 'a habit' and 'a rule'. The former is used to describe actual behaviour, the latter is normative. MacCormick emphasises that rules can exist as institutional facts independently of the extent to which norm users habitually comply with them. There may be a gap between our expectations of queuing and participants' actual behaviour. In respect of the familiar 'gap' between law in books and law in action, a central concern of the sociology of law, he distinguishes between a 'knowledge gap' and an 'efficacy gap' (p. 71). For practising lawyers, knowledge of the law in books is rarely enough and existence of rules is independent of their efficacy or enforcement. Understanding law cannot be solely a matter of rules.

The institutional theory of law addresses basic ontological and epistemological issues about the nature of law and claims explicitly to transcend any sharp divide between analytical and empirical jurisprudence and between doctrinal and socio-legal studies. MacCormick acknowledged to me that it was quite close to the law-jobs theory of the American jurist, Karl Llewellyn. Some of the ideas are controversial (for example, I have reservations about the concept of 'institution' in this context), but the claim is justified. MacCormick's main approach is conceptual, but without espousing extreme versions of 'naturalism' in philosophy, he insisted that analytical, moral, and empirical studies are all necessary to understanding law and are interrelated. He strongly rejected Ronald Dworkin's view that empirical questions about law are neither philosophically interesting nor of practical importance. (e.g. Dworkin, 2006: 98; MacCormick, 2009: 187–90).

MacCormick's principal focus of attention was liberal democratic constitutional states (the *Rechstaat*). They embody the most important form of law and the one that offers the best prospect of realising the Rule of Law, human rights, and other liberal democratic values. However, his conception of law was very broad and explicitly allowed for non-state law. The institutional theory provides conceptual space for treating as 'legal' many different forms of coordination and ordering that are becoming salient at supranational, transnational and subnational levels in an era of 'globalisation'. MacCormick acknowledged, although he did not pursue in detail, the existence and significance of the complex phenomena of legal pluralism, that is the co-existence, from the point of view of norm-users, of two or more legal orders in the same time-space context. Accordingly, his approach to jurisprudence fits modern concerns arising from increasing transnational interdependence far better than narrower, state-centric theories of law.

Rhetoric and the Rule of Law

MacCormick regularly stressed 'the arguable character of law'. He believed strongly in the importance of reason in both morality and law. *Rhetoric and the Rule of Law* is in part a successor to *Legal Reasoning and Legal Theory*, marking a shift from a Hartian towards a Dworkinian view on some much-debated issues. Perhaps because considerable space is devoted to replying to critics, some commentators still prefer the earlier work as being more approachable for non-specialists. However, the changes are significant. First, MacCormick shifts from a robust positivism to a position close to Ronald Dworkin's, notably that there is often a single right answer to a disputed question of law even in the hardest cases and that answer is based on deep probing of underlying moral principles.[3] MacCormick, however, did not go as far as Dworkin in commitment to an objectivist morality. Second, in the later book he clarified his views on the role of deduction in legal reasoning and fruitfully expanded his analysis of three types of argument used in second-order justification—coherence, consistency and consequences. Third, under the influence of the new rhetoric of Chaim Perelman and associates, he gave more attention to the persuasiveness of non-demonstrative arguments and their role in legal justification. He also devoted two chapters to coherence and narrative, important topics which he might have explored much further if he had lived.

Practical Reason in Law and Morality

This last book in the quartet was published shortly before his death. It does not show signs of haste, but he would probably have preferred more time to work on it. The book is the vehicle for the fullest statement of his moral philosophy and the underpinnings of what he called 'post-positivism'.

Practical Reason in Law and Morality can be read as a sequel to *Legal Right and Social Democracy*. It builds on but does not replace the earlier work. Its emphasis is more moral than political and it explores in greater depth issues relating to individual autonomy, universalism and particularism in moral judgements, empathy, objectivity, and the role of reason in public life. It is a contribution to ethics, linked specifically to his legal theory through a comparison of moral and legal reasoning and further probing of the relationship between law and morality. The central question of the book is: can reason be practical? MacCormick (2008: 4; cf. p. 209) answers: 'Most certainly it can!' This book returns to his early engagement with the Scottish Enlightenment and Kant. MacCormick seeks to reconcile Smith's moral sentiments with Kant's categorical imperative and to outline a theory of justice that goes beyond his Scottish precursors to address issues of distributive justice, the environment, and future generations, topics that have engaged late twentieth-century philosophers. A

[3] See above, n. 1.

notable feature of the book is a lengthy examination of the Scottish natural law tradition, exemplified by Stair. MacCormick prefers Stair's version of natural law to Benthamite utilitarianism, but he still rejects the label of 'natural lawyer' for himself.

Nation, nationalism and sovereignty

> My own father used to be set on his grandmother's knee in a humble house in Mull and asked, 'Co tha thu (Who are you?)'; 'Cha n-eil fhios agam (I don't know)'; 'Is tu Iain mac Dhomhunuill 'ic Neill 'ic Iain 'ic Dhughaill… (You are John, son of Donald, son of Neil, son of John, son of Dugald'—and so on went the genealogy up to thirty-three generations). (MacCormick, 1982: 252)

Neil MacCormick's quartet is written in a clear, uncluttered style. However, it is mostly of specialised interest to jurists, political theorists, and moral philosophers. *Questioning Sovereignty* is an exception because it deals with contemporary political issues of general interest and great importance—self-determination, Scottish nationalism, democracy, the decline of sovereignty, and the future of Europe. It is underpinned by Neil's lifelong commitment to Scottish nationalism and his extensive experience of practical politics. I share the view that this is his most important and original book.

Neil was born and bred a nationalist. The MacCormicks came from Mull. Although her husband's exploits sometimes worried her, his mother was also a committed nationalist. But it was his father who was the seminal influence on his politics. John MacCormick (1904–61), popularly known as 'King John', is an iconic but controversial figure in the history of Scottish nationalism. Born in Glasgow, he became involved in politics while he was a law student. He was a founding member of the National Party of Scotland in 1928 and of the Scottish National Party in 1934. In 1942 he split from the SNP to found the broader, non-party Scottish Convention which produced the Scottish Covenant, a moderate document supporting self-government rather than full independence. The Covenant obtained over two million signatories and helped to raise the profile and broaden the base of Scottish nationalism. In 1950–1, while Rector of the University of Glasgow and a respected lawyer, John MacCormick took considerable risks by involving himself in the 'repatriation' of the Stone of Destiny from Westminster Abbey and the aftermath.[4] In 1952–3, with

[4] See J. MacCormick (1955) and Hamilton (2008).

Ian Hamilton, he instituted a famous Scottish legal action (*MacCormick v Lord Advocate*), contesting the right of Queen Elizabeth to be styled Elizabeth II in Scotland. Although the petition was unsuccessful, it succeeded in challenging the idea that the Westminster Parliament could repeal or alter fundamental conditions of the Act of Union. Lord President Cooper in the Court of Session famously expressed the opinion that the principle of parliamentary sovereignty was an English idea that was not part of Scottish constitutional law. John MacCormick was a quiet pragmatic lawyer, deeply committed to an evolutionary approach to self-government rather than the more confrontational, fundamentalist politics favoured by many nationalists. When he had time he wrote poetry and painted. His detractors tended to write him off as an inconsistent compromiser and as a failure, but his role in widening the political base of Scottish nationalism and in furthering the cause of gradualism paid off in the long run. Devolution in 1999, and even aspects of the current policies and style of the SNP, owe much to his influence.

The MacCormick home in Park Quadrant, Glasgow was imbricated with Scottish history, Scottish literature and Scottish nationalist activities. Holidays were spent in the Scottish countryside. Neil was ten when the Stone of Destiny was 'liberated' from Westminster Abbey; he was 12 at the time of *MacCormick v the Lord Advocate*, and during his teens he listened avidly to many conversations about Scottish affairs and politics. It was 'a great political education in a very particular kind of politics'.[5] Later his elder brother Iain represented Argyll for five years as an SNP MP in Westminster. Neil added two dimensions to his political heritage: philosophy as a profession and engagement with Europe.

In politics Neil followed a similar trajectory to his father: he was passionately committed to Scotland, but he was a gradualist, willing to compromise and rejecting atavistic and destructive forms of nationalism. He was fond of quoting his father's friend, the novelist Neil Gunn of Inverness:

> We constantly reaffirmed our faith, not in any narrow and bitter nationalism, but in the capacity of the Scottish people, given the chance, to reconcile in their politics the freedom and human dignity of every individual with such mass organization as modern technocracy has made inevitable.[6]

His family was not the only influence on Neil's nationalism. In addition to his intellectual forebears he was part of a remarkable generation of

[5] Neil MacCormick, Introduction to J. MacCormick, *The Flag in the Wind* (2008)
[6] Cited by Neil MacCormick, *The Scotsman*, 20 Nov. 1974.

politicians and intellectuals, who are becoming recognised as a broader 'Scottish renaissance', that included Ken Alexander, Neal Ascherson, Donald Dewar, John P. Mackintosh, Tom Nairn, and John Smith. All of these have contributed to a climate of opinion that supports a distinctive literature, a sophisticated version of social democracy, and a moderate form of nationalism in Scotland and beyond.

From an early stage Neil had to confront tensions between his commitments to nationalism, political individualism, democracy, and the project for a European Union. In 1979 he published an essay on 'Nations and nationalism',[7] which introduced three themes that form the core of his later writings on the subject: first, explicit acknowledgement and rejection of 'the dark side of nationalism'—exclusive, parochial, playing on hatred of others; second, recognition that moderate love of family, country, colleagues and co-religionists are not only grounds of identity but are also the basis for recognition 'as equally legitimate (because the same in kind) the love others bear for their own' (MacCormick, 1982: 253); and, third, nationalism is historically and conceptually independent of the idea of the sovereign state—a late-comer that 'may have already had its day' (p. 264).

For the next thirty years Neil developed these themes in academic writings, newspaper articles, political tracts and speeches, culminating in *Questioning Sovereignty* (1999). This book weaves together twelve essays on constitutional and political themes, all written in the 1990s, a period that saw important—some would say revolutionary—developments within the United Kingdom and Europe, including moves towards devolution, the seeming abandonment of the doctrine of parliamentary sovereignty,[8] the Human Rights Act 1998, the Maastricht and Amsterdam Treaties (1992, 1997), the aftermath of the fall of the Berlin Wall, and a greatly increased consciousness of 'globalisation'.

Questioning Sovereignty is a philosophical work which intellectualises some heated political issues. A work of political imagination, it sets out a clearly argued vision of the constitutional future for the European Community, Scotland, the United Kingdom and for social democracies generally. It is informed by a passionate commitment to social democracy and the Scottish nationalist cause, but it is presented with remarkable detachment.

The book starts with a restatement of the theory of law as institutionalised normative order and ranges widely over important issues, many of

[7] Reprinted as chapter 13 of *Legal Right and Social Democracy* (1982).

[8] *Factortame v Secretary of State for Transport* [1991] A. C. 603.

them controversial. The core of the book centres on the elucidation and analysis of the relations between five concepts that are captured by the full title: *Questioning Sovereignty: Law, State and Nation in the European Commonwealth*. He summarised his mature philosophical position as follows:

> . . . To [the idea of 'liberal nationalism'] the idea of civic nationalism is strongly material. 'Civic nationalism' identifies the nation in terms of its members' shared allegiance to certain civic institutions. These are understood in broad terms to include, for example, legal norms and institutions, political representative organs, branches of public and local administration, the organization of education, churches and religious communities in their secular aspect, and other like institutions having an understood territorial location to which they refer. Institutions of civil society as much as of the state are relevant here. Territorially located civic institutions can be objects of allegiance, understood as 'ours' by the people among whom they perform their functions. As civic institutions, they are necessarily of great political significance to the community which, to an extent, they define. (MacCormick, 1999: 120)

and

> Naturally, it is possible, and perhaps desirable, for such civic institutions to go the length of including a constitution and the full panoply of statehood. Perhaps without that the civic quality of civic institutions is too precarious. But it would be a mistake to require this by definition, for to do so is simply to endorse the in-principle challenged assumption that the states that currently exist comprise also the totality of nations, at any rate, the totality of nations that can be understood in the civic sense. Whether or not the civic nation is or has a state, or *a fortiori* an independent sovereign state, the point of the idea of a civic nation is that it is in principle open to voluntary membership. The community defined by allegiance to institutions is open to anyone who chooses to dwell in the territory and give allegiance to the institutions. Departure to a different place and different allegiances is also possible, and not traitorous. One is guilty of treachery only if one who remains in place and surreptitiously undermines the institutions of that place while ostensibly giving them respect and allegiance. (MacCormick, 1999: 170)

Questioning Sovereignty addresses a wide range of topics, including: the changing nature of constitutionalism, sovereignty as an outdated concept, the European Union as a *sui generis* form of legal order, jurisdictional competence, legal pluralism, mixed constitutions, democracy, democratic deficits, subsidiarity, individual and national autonomy, self-determination, the *Rechstaat* and the rule of law, and Europe as a Commonwealth of Commonwealths. Highlights include a critique of the idea that the state has a monopoly on political and legal forms, coupled with endorsement of the importance of the democratic constitutional state (*Rechtstaat*), and the relativisation of the concepts of sovereignty, independence and self-determination. His differentiation of four types of subsidiarity—communal, comprehensive, market and rational legislative—has also been widely recognised as a major contribution. The last chapter suggests a new form of Union within Europe with a Council of the British Isles, preserving those elements of cooperation and interdependence that 'have worked', to be achieved through peaceful negotiation and mutual good will. The book ends:

> General principles do not settle concrete cases, and the settlement of this kind of case is a matter for political process, in which the philosopher has no larger a voice than anyone else. (MacCormick, 1999: 204)

Neil MacCormick was a politician as well as a philosopher. *Questioning Sovereignty* was published in 1999, the year in which he was elected to the European Parliament. By then some of his essays and lectures had aroused considerable interest in Europe.[9] So he entered full-time politics *after* he had articulated a coherent political and constitutional philosophy. This informed his activities and greatly enhanced his standing within the European Community. He entered into his role with both energy and enthusiasm. He loved the work and did not mind the acclaim. He served on several committees, represented the SNP on the Convention on the Future of Europe, and involved himself in many specific issues. He was particularly proud of his pamphlet *Who's Afraid of a European Constitution?* (2005). He nursed his constituency, which not inappropriately was the whole of Scotland, fought some important battles regarding ferries for the island communities, and was Vice-President of the SNP from 1999 until 2004. He was voted Scottish MEP of the Year three times. After five frenetic years he returned to academic life, partly because the experience had been exhausting, partly because he missed his students, but mainly to complete his *magnum opus*. However, he was delighted to be appointed Special Adviser to the First Minister, Alex Salmond, after the 2007 Scottish Parliament Elections. He was consulted frequently, but he would probably have been more active in that role had he not been ill.

How far did his political actions reflect his philosophical ideas? This is a complex question, not least because of the extraordinary energy that Neil invested in his role as an MEP. The inventory of the archive of his papers in the University of Edinburgh, which mainly documents his political activities, runs to over 200 pages. There is plenty of scope for detailed

[9] Notably the Chorley Lecture of 1992, 'Beyond the sovereign state' (MacCormick, 1993), and his writings on subsidiarity.

research into how far his practice matched his theory. My general impression is that at a general level they were remarkably close. This is illustrated by some significant changes of position on the ultimate goal of Scottish nationalism: in 1970 he stated that he was 'unconvinced' that full independence should be the ultimate goal for Scotland, even in the long run (*The Scottish Debate*, 1970, Introduction). In 1989 Neil supported The Claim of Right that helped pave the way for devolution a decade later and he strongly opposed the SNP's boycott of a cross-party movement for self-government, thereby repeating his father's gradualism.[10] Yet over time he came round slowly to support the SNP's end goal of independence and was publicly associated with the SNP's draft constitution for an independent Scotland from the mid-1980s. He justified his gradualism on democratic grounds—the Scottish people needed to be persuaded—and he interpreted 'independence' in the relativist terms of his philosophical position on 'post-sovereignty' and interdependence. *Questioning Sovereignty* concludes by acknowledging that while MacCormick the politician had campaigned for independence for Scotland in the long run, MacCormick the philosopher recognised that this is one among a range of reasonable options that can be chosen by the Scottish people.[11]

Conclusion

Neil MacCormick was one of the leading legal philosophers of the twentieth century. His view of philosophy was broad and closely linked to the idea of liberal education in the Scottish University tradition.[12] In his Presidential Address to the Society of Public Teachers of Law in 1984 he endorsed this holistic view and was highly critical of those who restrict the idea of Jurisprudence to abstract philosophy, laying themselves open to the criticism 'that they lack any real interest in real law' (MacCormick, 1985: 181).

He was a prolific writer. Of his many publications, the quartet *Law, State and Practical Reason* stands out as his most distinctive achievement. It is one of the most extensive and intellectually ambitious contributions to jurisprudence in recent times. It advances a general theory of law as institutional normative order, an in-depth study of sovereignty, statehood,

[10] Especially in 'Unrepentant gradualism' (1989).
[11] MacCormick (1999), p. 204.
[12] He greatly admired George Davie's seminal work *The Democratic Intellect* (1961).

and nationalism, a theory of legal reasoning and the role of rhetoric within legal argumentation, and an account of practical reasoning in law and morality. Some final statements at the end of a successful scholarly career add little to earlier work and can even be dismissed as 'old men's books'. MacCormick's quartet, by contrast, is intellectually ambitious, contains much that is new, including significant changes of position, and presents a coherent and distinctive vision of law in today's world. It is a masterly synthesis and much else besides. It does not entirely supercede his earlier works, some of which are more detailed or more ebullient, but it will almost certainly be the main focus of attention for commentators in the foreseeable future.

The institutional theory of law is a distinctive theory about the nature of law. Although it grew out of philosophical concerns, one of his aims was to lessen the divide between analytical and empirical jurisprudence. Herbert Hart had advanced a 'social fact' conception of law, but had retreated from its implications. Moreover he confined his attention to state law. MacCormick sought not only to build bridges with the social sciences, both personally and institutionally,[13] but he also recognised that the models of state legal systems constructed or assumed by most mainstream jurists sit uneasily with forms of law or law-like phenomena with which legal scholars and practitioners are increasingly concerned, especially public international law, regional law, religious law, customary law and various forms of 'soft law'. The institutional theory is one of the most developed attempts to provide an alternative model of legal ordering that is both empirically sensitive and broad enough to encompass ideas of non-state law and legal pluralism, and to provide a theoretical framework for viewing and studying a wide range of phenomena in this era of 'globalisation'.

It is ironic that having embraced an empirically oriented view of law as a species of social institution, the later MacCormick claimed to reject, or at least to move beyond, legal positivism. In the end he called himself a 'post-positivist'. By this he meant that he considered morality and positive law (state law is 'posited') to be conceptually distinct, but there are moral limits to what is conceptually reasonable about the idea of institutional normative order: 'Extremes of injustice are incompatible with law' (MacCormick, 2007: Preface). I have argued elsewhere that he exaggerated the significance of his defection from positivism and that his

[13] He helped to found the Centre for the Social and Philosophical Study of Law in the 1980s and, as Provost, did much to encourage cross-disciplinary work.

post-positivist insistence on a moral dimension to law may fit participant-oriented perspectives suitable for a committed politician or jurist concerned to make her own system the best it can be, but it sits uneasily with outsider perspectives such as those of historians, comparatists or observers of foreign legal orders and regimes that are the products of other people's power (Twining, 2009).

MacCormick's theory of legal reasoning, as developed in *Rhetoric and the Rule of Law*, stands out in a crowded field both for its philosophical sophistication and for its closeness to the actual practices of appellate courts in the common law tradition through the detailed analysis of actual cases. His final position is close to both Ronald Dworkin and Robert Alexy, perhaps the two most prominent thinkers on the topic. Regrettably, he followed convention in restricting his attention almost entirely to reasoning about questions of law, but he did acknowledge that other kinds of reasonings in legal contexts—for example in relation to issues of fact and of disposition (e.g. sentencing)—also merit serious theoretical attention. His ideas on coherence, which he was still developing towards the end of his life, have particular relevance to inferential reasoning from evidence.

Law, State and Practical Reason also contains many specific insights. Of course, not all of MacCormick's moral, political, and jurisprudential ideas are original or distinctive, though even his more orthodox conclusions have a particular Scottish flavour. In addition to *Questioning Sovereignty*, many of his more specific writings on Europe, Scottish nationalism, constitutionalism, and rights are of general interest.

In his autobiographical notes MacCormick defined his intellectual development in terms of his relations with Herbert Hart. But there is a danger that the quartet *Law, State and Practical Reason* will be read and criticised in terms of the narrow perspectives and repetitious debates that have characterised much analytical legal philosophy since the publication of *The Concept of Law*. Neil MacCormick is very much more than a lapsed Hartian and a near convert to natural law. It is important to spell out the reasons for this. First, as we have seen, in Edinburgh he returned to his intellectual roots which were far removed from analytical positivism. Nationalism, the Scottish enlightenment, and, to a lesser extent, Kant and Kelsen were central to his concerns throughout his career. In my view, he was never a 'hard' positivist. Second, MacCormick and Hart were both social democrats with quite similar commitments to democracy, the rule of law, and (Hart less clearly) to human rights. But they arrived at their views by different routes and MacCormick's ethical and political views are much more fully worked out and integrated with his legal theory than were Hart's. Third, MacCormick was much more in sympathy with socio-legal studies and empirical understandings of law than Hart, Raz, Dworkin, or Finnis. Hart shared Oxford's prejudice against sociology and was an ambivalent supporter of socio-legal studies; Dworkin dismisses sociology of law as marginal and philosophically uninteresting; all four take a quite narrow view of what is involved in understanding law. MacCormick, on the other hand, while not himself engaging much in empirical research, was not only strongly supportive of it in Edinburgh (e.g. MacCormick, 1976), but made it part of his institutional theory of law. This was not merely an example of his concern for inclusiveness; it is philosophically grounded in the Scottish Enlightenment, especially Adam Smith, whom he recognised as a forerunner of 'law in context' approaches (e.g. MacCormick, 1982: 116–17). Finally, there is an important European and comparative dimension, which is quite rare in legal philosophy. It was natural for a Scottish jurist educated in English law to transcend the common law–civil law divide.

WILLIAM TWINING
Fellow of the Academy

Note. Detailed assessments and criticisms of MacCormick's contribution and especially of *Law, State and Practical Reason* have only recently begun to emerge. Four books devoted to aspects of his work have recently been published (Bankowski and MacLean, 2006; Menéndez and Fossum, 2011; Del Mar and Bankowski, 2009; and Walker, 2012). There have been numerous articles, with more in preparation. It is to be hoped that there will in time be a full biography that will do justice to Neil MacCormick's contributions not only as a jurist but also as a teacher, politician, public intellectual and citizen of both Scotland and Europe.

I am particularly grateful to Flora MacCormick, Zenon Bankowski, Maksymilian Del Mar and Andrew Halpin for help with preparing this memoir. I am also indebted to many of Neil's colleagues and associates, especially Hector McQueen, FBA, Neil Walker, FBA, and Claudio Michelon. I have been much assisted by some unpublished 'autobiographical notes' and the comprehensive Bibliography by Maksymilian Del Mar, which contains an invaluable appendix on 'Scottish themes'.

References

1. Works by Neil MacCormick[14]

(edited) *The Scottish Debate* (London, 1970).

Law as Institutional Fact, Inaugural Lecture, No. 52, (Edinburgh) (also published in *Law Quarterly Review*, 90 (1974), 102–29).

(edited) *Lawyers in their Social Setting* (Edinburgh, 1976).

Legal Reasoning and Legal Theory (Oxford, 1978: 2nd edn. 1994).

'Nation and nationalism', in C. MacLean (ed.), *The Crown and the Thistle* (Edinburgh, 1970), pp. 97–111.

H. L. A. Hart (London, 1981).

Legal Right and Social Democracy: Essays in Legal and Political Philosophy (Oxford, 1982).

(with O. Weinberger) *Grundlagen des Institutionalistischen Rechtspositivismus*, Schriften zur Rechtstheorie, Heft 113 (Berlin, 1985).

'The democratic intellect and the law', *Legal Studies*, 5(2) (1985), 177–83.

'A moralistic case for a-moralistic law?' *Valparaiso University Law Review*, 20(1) (1985), 1–41.

(with O. Weinberger) *An Institutional Theory of Law: New Approaches to Legal Positivism* (Dordrecht, 1986).

'Unrepentant gradualism', in O. D. Edwards (ed.), *A Claim of Right for Scotland* (Edinburgh, 1989), pp. 99–109.

(edited with R. S. Summers) *Interpreting Statutes: a Comparative Study* (Aldershot, 1991).

'Beyond the sovereign state', (Chorley Lecture) *Modern Law Review*, 56(1) (1993), 1–18.

(edited with R. S. Summers) *Interpreting Precedents: a Comparative Study* (Aldershot, 1997).

Questioning Sovereignty: Law, State and Nation in the European Commonwealth (Oxford, 1999).

A Union of Its Own Kind? Reflections on the European Convention and the Proposed Constitution of the European Union (Edinburgh: Neil MacCormick, personal publication, 2004), 40 pp.

Rhetoric and the Rule of Law (Oxford, 2005).

Who's Afraid of a European Constitution? (Exeter, 2005).

Institutions of Law: an Essay in Legal Theory (Oxford, 2007).

Practical Reason in Law and Morality (Oxford, 2008).

H. L. A. Hart, 2nd edn. (Stanford, CA, 2008).

'MacCormick on MacCormick', in A. J. Menéndez and J. E. Fossum (eds.), *The Post-Sovereign Constellation: Law and Democracy in Neil MacCormick's Legal and Political Theory: the Post-Sovereign Constellation* (Dordrecht, 2011), pp. 17–24.

[14] This selection is extracted from Maksymilian del Mar 'The works of Neil MacCormick: a complete bibliography and a bibliographical essay on Scottish themes', in Walker (ed.) *MacCormick's Scotland* (2012).

2. Works about Neil MacCormick

Z. Bankowski and J. MacLean (eds.), *The Universal and the Particular in Legal Reasoning* (Aldershot, 2006).
A. J. Menéndez and J. E. Fossum (eds.), *The Post-Sovereign Constellation: Law and Democracy in Neil D. MacCormick's Legal and Political Theory* (Oslo, 2011).
M. Del Mar and Z. Bankowski (eds.), *Law as Institutional Normative Order* (Farnham, 2009).
N. Walker (ed.), *MacCormick's Scotland* (Edinburgh, 2012).
W. Twining, '*Institutions of Law* from a Global Perspective', in Del Mar and Bankowski, pp. 17–34.

3. Other references

J. MacCormick, *The Flag in the Wind* (London, 1955: reissued, with an Introduction by Neil MacCormick, Edinburgh, 2008).
G. E. M. Anscombe, 'On brute facts', *Analysis*, 18 (1958), 69–72.
J. R. Searle, *Speech Acts* (Cambridge, 1969).
G. E. Davie, *The Democratic Intellect* (Edinburgh, 1961).
R. Dworkin, 'Hart and the concepts of law', *Harvard Law Review Forum*, 119 (2006), 95–104.
I. Hamilton, *Stone of Destiny* (Edinburgh, 2008).
H. L. A. Hart, *The Concept of Law, second edition* (Oxford, 1994).

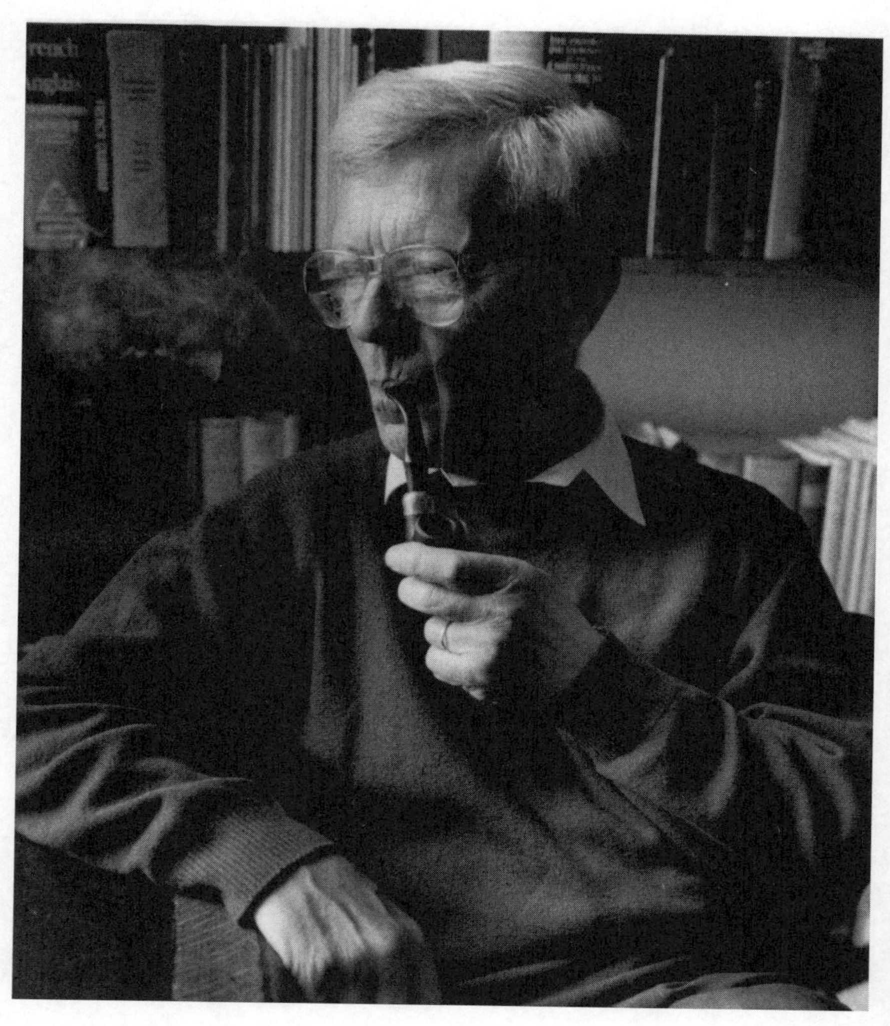

ROBERT MARKUS

Robert Austin Markus
1924–2010

ROBERT MARKUS, who died on Wednesday, 8 December 2010, is known principally for his writings on St Augustine and the history of the early Church. While he wrote as a committed Christian, he always insisted that ecclesiastical history must be written with the same scientific objectivity as secular history, and that ecclesiastical developments can only be understood if they are fully related to changes in society as a whole.

Robert Markus was born on 4 October 1924 in Budapest. His father was director of a heavy engineering firm, which had been founded by Robert's grandfather Markus Lajos, who had started off as a locksmith. Robert's mother Lily, née Elek, came from a Jewish Hungarian family, living near Eszék, which became Osijek, in Croatia, after the 1919 Treaty of Versailles. Her father was manager of an enormous forest. She was an internationally recognised ceramicist winning, amongst other distinctions, a Gold Medal at the 1937 Paris Exhibition. She continued her work in ceramics in England, adding other skills such as wood-carving, cloisonné-enamel work, tapestry-weaving and silver-smithing, until her death in 1962. For her art, she was drawn to Christian themes and, according to Robert's brother Tom, she was Catholic in spirit from an early age. Robert's father converted to Lutheranism as a young man, but amid growing anti-Semitism decided that this was no time for a Jew to leave his community, and so had himself readmitted to the synagogue.

The family came to England in 1939. Robert's father and his uncle Stephen were able to establish 'Ferrostatics', a small engineering works at Hollingworth, near Glossop in Derbyshire. They started off with four employees, making precision machine tools for the manufacture of Spitfires.

Biographical Memoirs of Fellows of the British Academy, XI, 475–489.

Because of this they were exempted from the general policy of sending 'enemy aliens'—including Hungarians—to the Isle of Man. The business grew rapidly under wartime conditions, and moved to larger premises, with more employees. After the war they continued with precision engineering for major industries, such as ICI. Eventually, as neither Robert nor his brother Thomas wished to enter Ferrostatics, and after Stephen, Robert's uncle, had left the firm (he died suddenly in the 1950s), Robert's father sold the business to Chloride Electrical Storage (makers of Exide car batteries) in the 1960s.

From 1939 to 1941 Robert was educated as a boarder at Kingsmoor School, Glossop, which he described as 'a Quaker type school'. He was happy there. He remembered that his main aim, apart from enjoying himself, had been to become thoroughly English and to conform in manners, appearance, language etc. He kept few memories of his childhood, of Hungary or of Hungarian. Although his political views remained left-wing, he continued to think that immigrants have some obligation to conform to the values and culture of their host society.

Robert spent the next eight years at the University of Manchester. He found that city an intellectual powerhouse, and it shaped his life. Robert's father wanted him to study engineering, as a preparation for entering the family firm. He himself wanted to study philosophy. So Robert's undergraduate course was a compromise: Chemistry. Michael Polanyi, a man of very wide interests, was Professor of Physical Chemistry. Robert's scientific training surely influenced his subsequent research in a totally different field. On graduating, Robert spent some time as a works-chemist in a CWS margarine factory under the wartime Essential Works Order. After the war Robert returned to his first choice, and went on to take to take an MA and a Ph.D. in philosophy, being supervised by Dorothy Emmet, to whom Robert thought that he owed more intellectually than to any other person. His MA, then still a research degree, was on Samuel Alexander, Manchester's most famous philosopher. The Ph.D. thesis was a discussion of some Cartesian presuppositions in late medieval and Renaissance philosophy. Postgraduate work resulted in Robert's first academic publications.[1]

Friends were always very important. At Manchester Robert was one of a close circle of friends united by radical socialist ideals. The circle included a student, later a teacher of history, called Margaret Bullen,

[1] 'Alexander's philosophy: the emergence of qualities', *Philosophy and Phenomenological Research*, 11 (1950), 58–74; 'Method and metaphysics: the origin of some Cartesians presuppositions in the philosophy of the Renaissance', *Dominican Studies*, 2 (1949), 356–84.

whose father managed a Cooperative store in the Wirral. Walter Stein became a close friend who introduced Robert to the politics of radical protest. Another member of the group was John (Herbert) McCabe. Like Robert he had transferred from Chemistry to Philosophy, and again like Robert had become a student of Dorothy Emmet. McCabe came from a Catholic family, and was a most impressive personality. He combined strong left-wing views with a highly critical liberal Catholicism and went on to become a noted Dominican priest and theologian. Eric John, already a lecturer in medieval history, and both a Catholic and a socialist, was also a member of the circle.[2] The group was originally very secular. Walter Stein was a Marxist, but in time they all got seriously interested in Christianity. Robert joined university Catholic circles, and eventually the Union of Catholic Students. He decided to convert to Catholicism. According to his brother Thomas, Catholicism helped Robert to harmonise tensions between his inner personal life, his condition as an immigrant, and his social concerns and socialist politics. Fr Vincent Whelan instructed Robert, and in 1946 received him into the Catholic Church. Several others of the group, including Walter Stein, also became Catholics, as eventually also did Robert's parents and his brother Thomas.

Together with Walter Stein, Willy Schenk, Louis Allen and others, Robert founded the journal *Humanitas*, which brought together Catholic faith and a call for personal engagement in the cause of social reform. The journal advocated radical change not only in secular society but also in the Church. It was at the same time strictly non-violent. The journal took a very strong line against nuclear armaments. This was in the aftermath of the atomic bomb. Robert collaborated with Walter Stein in the writing of *Nuclear Warfare and the Christian Conscience*.[3] He went on several demonstrations, including marches to Aldermaston, and took part in TV discussions. He never quite lost this interest.[4] The ideas that motivated that group, and found expression in *Humanitas*, represented an English parallel to the liberal and socially conscious Catholicism which Eduard Mounier advocated in the journal *L'Esprit*, which he had founded in 1932. The

[2] They were later to collaborate in Eric John and R. A. Markus, *Papacy and Hierarchy* (London, 1969).

[3] 'Conscience and deterrence', in W. Stein (ed.), *Nuclear Weapons and Christian Conscience* (London, 1961), pp. 65–90.

[4] 'Work and worker in early Christianity', in J. M. Todd (ed.), *Work: Christian Thought and Practice* (London, 1960), pp. 13–26. 'Christian perspectives on war and peace', in H. A. Haleem, O. Ramsbotham, S. Risaluddin and B. Wicker (eds.), *The Crescent and the Cross: Christian and Muslim Approaches to War and Peace* (London and New York, 1998), pp. 32–6.

French group was the left wing of an important Catholic intellectual revival between the two wars.[5] This revival eventually inspired also the very much more conservative Christian Democratic movement which was to shape Continental politics for several decades after the war, and worked for a European Union.

Fr Vincent Whelan remained a friend. In summer 1949 he and Robert went on a pilgrimage to Rome, for more than half the way on foot, armed with a Latin letter of recommendation from the Dominican provincial to clergy, monks, etc. on their way, who duly provided hospitality. As Robert recalled, 'Whelan was very liberal minded and represented a very liberally construed version of Roman Catholicism: He made me read Newman and Augustine. Pre-Vatican II Catholicism seen from inside was pretty horrifying to most of our circle, including me, brought up as we had been in a liberal tradition. Authoritarian, Rome-centred religion did not appeal: John XXIII and Vatican II were a kind of liberation from a Catholic intellectual ghetto.'[6] Much of Robert's subsequent academic work was concerned with the theme of a more diverse Church, in which Rome has less absolute authority, always in some fruitful tension with other Churches.

In 1949 Robert entered the noviciate of the Dominican order at Oxford, in the same year as John McCabe. His novice-master decreed that he was not to read any philosophy. This was to bring home to him that he was no longer a philosophy student.[7] He allowed him to read Augustine—provided he kept to the scriptural commentaries. Such intellectual narrowness was clearly not to Robert's taste. In due course he was to read every one of Augustine's writings. He more than once told John Moorhead how much he admired Jansenius, who had apparently done so ten times. Robert's academic publications dating from this period were still mainly philosophical, but he was getting interested in the history of the Church.[8] Some weeks before taking final vows he was visited by Margaret Bullen and decided that his future lay in marrying her, which he did in 1955. In

[5] Ph. Chenaux, *Entre Maurras et Maritain: une generation intellectuelle catholique, 1920–30* (Paris, 1999); M. Winock, *'L'esprit': des intellectuels dans la cité, 1930–1950* (Paris, 1975).

[6] 'Papal infallibility, on the importance of not misunderstanding it after a hundred years', *Modern Churchman*, NS 13 (1970), 308–15.

[7] R. A. Markus, 'Evolving disciplinary contexts for the study of Augustine 1950–2000,' *Augustinian Studies*, 3.2.2 (2001), 189–200, on pp. 189–90.

[8] See above, n. 1, also 'Facts, things and persons', *Hibbert Journal*, 48 (1950), 153–8 and 'Hume, reason and moral sense', *Philosophy and Phenomenological Research*, 13 (1952), 139–58; and Robert's earliest writings on Christian themes: 'Pleroma and Fulfilment: the significance of history in St Irenaeus' opposition to Gnosticism', *Vigiliae Christianae*, 8 (1954), 193–224; and 'A note on the meaning of *Via*', *Dominican Studies*, 7 (1954), 239–45.

the same year John (now Herbert) McCabe was ordained. From 1955 to 1974 Markus was at Liverpool, at first as a librarian. K. Povey, the university librarian, was a real scholar-librarian—one of the last of this breed, according to Robert—and he encouraged Robert to carry on with academic research.[9] In 1958 he was appointed to the Department of Medieval History, then headed by Christopher Brooke.[10] There he revealed his great gifts as a teacher. He had been assured that he would be able to keep up Patristic interests, and teach only a little run of the mill medieval history; in fact it turned out to be the reverse. To start with he was given little teaching, and that mainly tutorial, first individually, later to students in pairs. Happy days! He also lectured on Bede,[11] and on ancient and medieval political thought. Towards his students he was benevolent, and totally unauthoritarian. He did not impose knowledge, but helped pupils to recognise and work out problems by themselves. He was interested in education, and particularly in the place in education of theology.[12] According to John Moorhead, he was an ideal supervisor of postgraduates. Not only were all drafts speedily returned, but his comments, which tended to be on general issues rather than facts, were invariably spot-on.

A very strong Classics Department included Hilary Armstrong, who was particularly interested in Later Greek philosophy, especially Plotinus and neo-Platonism. He and Robert became friends and did some work together.[13] Robert became interested in Gregory the Great around 1960, when called on to offer a final year Special Subject (in those days usually two to four students, working intensively on original sources in the original

[9] His publications at that time included: 'The dialectic of Eros in Plato's *Symposium*', *Downside Review*, 73 (1955), 219–30; 'A relevant pattern of holiness: Dietrich Bonhoeffer's "*Ethics*"', *Hibbert Journal*, 55 (1957), 387–92; and his earliest paper on Augustine, 'St Augustine on signs', *Phronesis*, 2 (1957), 60–83.

[10] R. A. Markus, 'Christopher Brooke at Liverpool', in D. Abulafia, M. Franklin, M. Rubin (eds.), *Church and City 1000–1500: Essays in Honour of Christopher Brooke* (Cambridge, 1992), pp. xix–xxi.

[11] 'The chronology of the Gregorian mission to England: Bede's narrative and Gregory's correspondence', *Journal of Ecclesiastical History*, 14 (1963), 16–30; and later *Bede and the Tradition of Ecclesiastical Historiography*', Jarrow Lecture 1975 (Jarrow on Tyne, 1976).

[12] R. A. Markus, 'The study of theology and the framework of secular disciplines', *Downside Review*, 78 (1960), 192–202; also 'Educational principles and university theology teaching', in L. Bright (ed.), *Theology in Modern Education: a Creative Encounter* (London, 1965), pp. 92–6.

[13] R. A. Markus and A. H. Armstrong, *Christian Faith and Greek Philosophy* (London, 1960). R. A. Markus, 'Marius Victorinus and Augustine', in A. H. Armstrong (ed.), Part 5 of the *Cambridge History of Later Greek and Early Medieval Philosophy* (Cambridge, 1967), pp. 327–419; and 'The eclipse of a Neoplatonic theme: Augustine and Gregory the Great on visions and prophecies', in R. A. Markus and H. J. Blumenthal (eds.), *Neoplatonism and Early Christian Thought: Essays in Honour of A. H. Armstrong* (London, 1981), pp. 204–11.

language). One of the first students to take this course was (Sir) Ian Kershaw, who initially went on to lecture in medieval history at Manchester, before changing field to twentieth-century German history and making his name as biographer of Hitler. Robert's interest in Gregory lasted for the rest of his life. As Robert's research was in the field of early Christianity, and his teaching mainly on early medieval history, his interest became focused on the later Roman centuries, to the neglect of later periods. He was fascinated by the radical transformation of classical thought and culture during this period. How precisely, and why, was Gregory's world so different from that of Augustine? Robert thought that as his work developed he owed most intellectually to Henri-Iréné Marrou, whom he was to meet a few times later in his life, admired greatly, and read avidly.[14] From him he learnt the idea that 'Late Antiquity' was a period of history with a special character and identity of its own, which Marrou characterised most illuminatingly in his great book on Augustine.[15] Marrou had been a contributor to Mounier's *L'Esprit*. In his writings Robert encountered an altogether more serene version of liberal Catholicism, and one more respectful of traditions than that of his Manchester friends. In the early 1960s Robert got to know Peter Brown, just before the publication of Brown's *Augustine of Hippo* (London, 1967). Robert felt that he owed a great deal to Peter, and he was to dedicate his *End of Ancient Christianity* to Peter as 'to his teacher'. But according to Brown, the benefits of their friendship were mutual.[16] Perhaps Peter Brown's gift is an intuitive response to what he reads, Robert's the working through of underlying structures of thought.[17]

A widening of Robert's field of interest resulted from his reading William Frend's *The Donatist Church*,[18] with its explanation of Donatism in terms of an analysis of the social structure of North African society. Frend argued that Donatism reflected the aspirations of the under-privileged, that is of the relatively un-Romanised and linguistically Berber population of North Africa. Against this analysis, Robert agreed with Peter Brown that the Donatists were defending pre-Constantinian, uncentralised traditions of the African Church against post-Constantinian centralisation. At the

[14] P. Riché, *Henri Iréné Marrou historien engagé* (Paris, 2003).

[15] H.-I. Marrou, *Saint Augustin et la fin de la culture antique* (Paris, 1938), supplemented by *Retractatio* (Paris, 1949).

[16] Peter Brown, 'Introducing Robert Markus', *Augustinian Studies*, 3.2 (2001), 186.

[17] I owe the comparison to John Moorhead.

[18] *The Donatist Church, a Movement of Protest in North Africa* (Oxford, 1952).

same time he showed that Augustine, the great proponent of Roman centralisation, shared a great deal of theological common ground with his opponents.[19] Donatist dissent, in Robert's view, centred on questions of authority and this for him was, as we have seen, a concern of high contemporary relevance.[20] Robert was a very different personality from Frend in many ways, but the two men shared a sympathy for rebels against authority.

Robert was taking an ever deepening interest in the fascinating richness of the thought of Augustine, and Augustine is at the centre of *Saeculum*, Robert's first major book, which he dedicated to his wife.[21] It is essentially history of thought, but in this, as in all his writings, Robert is careful to interpret philosophical ideas in the light of the context in which they had been expressed. *Saeculum* is essentially an examination of the views on history, on the Roman state, and on the relationship of Church and secular society, which Augustine developed in his *City of God* (*De civitate dei*). Augustine wrote this book after Rome had been sacked by the Goths, and his immediate aim was to defend the Christian religion from the charge that it failed to save Rome from disaster. Augustine argued that in the Roman Empire, as indeed in every human society, the citizens of the 'City of God' and of the 'Earthly City' are inextricably intertwined. States are necessary because sinful man needs to be disciplined if peace and order are to prevail. But this necessary role does not give any state a privileged place in God's scheme of salvation. The role of states and their governments is theologically neutral. This fundamental truth has not been altered by the fact that the Roman state has become formally Christian. It remains an earthly state and therefore cannot expect the privilege of divine protection from its enemies. Rome's capture by the Goths does not therefore in any way discredit Christianity.

When Robert wrote *Saeculum* he focused on Augustine's positive, but theologically neutral, evaluation of secular society. He saw the key to Augustine's mature thought in the following passage:

[19] 'Donatism: the last phase', in C. W. Dugmore and C. Duggan (eds.), *Studies in Church History*, 1 (London, 1964), pp. 118–26; also 'Reflections on religious dissent in North Africa in the Byzantine period', in G. J. Cuming (ed.), *Studies in Church History*, 3 (Leiden, 1966), pp. 140–9; and 'Christianity and dissent in Roman North Africa: changing perspectives', in D. Baker (ed.), *Studies in Church History*, 9, *The Church in Town and Countryside* (Cambridge, 1979), pp. 1–15.

[20] 'The crisis of authority in the Church: its historical roots', *Modern Churchman*, NS 10 (1967), 281–91.

[21] *Saeculum, History and Society in the Theology of Augustine* (Cambridge, 1970, rev. edn. 1988).

> The heavenly city, while on its earthly pilgrimage calls forth its citizens from every nation and every tongue. It assembles a band of pilgrims, not caring about any diversity in customs, laws and institutions whereby they severally make provision for the achievements and maintenance of earthly peace. All these provisions are intended, in their various ways, among the different nations, to secure the aim of earthly peace. The heavenly city does not repeal or abolish any of them, provided that they do not impede the religion in which the one supreme and true god is worshipped.[22]

The last sentence is of course open to a wide range of interpretation, and it was indeed to be interpreted in increasingly restrictive ways. Augustine himself was to become an advocate of religious coercion. Robert acknowledged a tension between Augustine's views on coercion and his views on the autonomy of the civil community, a tension which he even then thought might prove irresolvable.[23] Later, looking back on his life's work, Robert decided that his interpretation of Augustine in *Saeculum* had been one-sided.[24] He had been inclined to see Augustine as one of the founding fathers of a Christian tradition of secularity.[25] His interpretation of Augustine's views had come perilously close to making him a precursor of modern liberalism, reflecting an intellectual tendency of those years, when the influence of Dietrich Bonhoeffer's *Letters and Papers from Prison*, with their emphasis on the 'adulthood of the world', was giving a wide currency to theological attempts to construct a secular theology, or 'religionless Christianity', and to portray secularisation as representing a crucial strand in Christianity itself.[26] This criticism had already been made by M. J. Holerich, who found that Robert's interpretation of Augustine's view of the secular seemed to have been drawn entirely in terms derived from modern individualist Liberalism, in which the state is founded on contract and consent, and lacks any transcendental legitimation, a state which must necessarily be secular, open, pluralistic, and religiously neutral—'freedom plus groceries'.[27] Robert accepted that *Saeculum* reflects the intellectual atmosphere in which it was written, an anxiety about the attitude to be taken by the Christian Church to a society in which Christians were becoming a minority. Returning to this topic in *Christianity*

[22] *The City of God*, 19.17 cited *Saeculum* p. 40

[23] *Saeculum*, p. 66, n. 48.

[24] Robert has provided us with a review of his life's work in the lectures published as *Christianity and the Secular* (Notre Dame, IN, 2006).

[25] Ibid., p. 3.

[26] Ibid., pp. 1–3; D. Bonhoeffer, *Letters and Papers from Prison*, ed. Eberhard Bethgel, tr. Neville Horton Smith (London, 1953).

[27] *Christianity and the Secular*, p. 51.

and the Secular, Robert notes that Maritain had proposed a democratic secular faith which the Church is to advocate in common with non-Christians in public, while it, and each other group, in the semi-privacy of their educational establishments, gives different reasons for it.[28] Robert takes Maritain to mean that the Church proclaims its message to all, but feels morally bound to uphold the consensus on which civilised public order is built, a view with which he agrees.

In his next book Robert carries his examination of the attitude of the Church to secular society into the early history of the Church. *Christianity in the Roman World* traces how Christianity became respectable by adopting large elements of classical culture, and came to accept more and more of the secular realities of the Roman world.[29] Previously hated as the religion of a suspect and outlandish minority, Christianity lost this character in the third century, and could become the religion of emperor and empire. Robert thought that this 'success' created serious new problems for the Church: 'After Constantine the catholic Church lost its link with the past, and had to annex its claim to the past from more plausible claimants like the Donatists. The cult of the martyrs, the ecclesiastical histories, and the ascetic movement were the Church's chief devices for reconciling itself to living in a world which it had assimilated, that is to recreate an identity.'[30]

By now Robert had established an international reputation as a historian of the early Church. In 1974 he was appointed to the Chair of Medieval History at Nottingham. Here he proved an inspiring teacher of both undergraduates and postgraduates. His door was always open to students who had difficulties. To some he offered guidance which changed their lives. He encouraged medievalists from all parts of the university to meet together regularly and discuss their research. As an academic politician he was an effective champion of the humanities. It was largely thanks to him that the Nottingham Department of Classics survived these years of financial stringency to become the thriving academic department that it is today. Meanwhile he continued to think about the Early Church. The question of the Church's relationship with secular society which had long preoccupied Robert is closely related to the Church's view of its essential nature. Post-war scholarship had been preoccupied with the question of

[28] Ibid., p. 68, citing Maritain's *Man and State* (Chicago, 1951), chap. 5.

[29] R. A. Markus, *Christianity in the Roman World* (London, 1974).

[30] *Christianity and the Secular*, p. 33; cf. *The End of Ancient Christianity* (Cambridge, 1990), pp. 24–5.

how it came about that the Christians felt so strongly that they were a distinct group, who had no choice but to reject the religious practices of the rest of society. Was there a unified concept of orthodoxy among the earliest Christian communities?[31] And if, as some have suggested, the earliest teaching did not have the distinction of orthodoxy and heresy, how did this distinction arise? The early history of Christianity, or Christianities, the process involving the creation of hierarchical organisation, definition of doctrine, and the establishment of a canon of sacred writings, is treated by Robert in a stimulating, if not perhaps altogether convincing, paper, as a process of progressive self-definition, the purpose of which was to enable men to recognise the Church, rather than to establish its true doctrine.[32]

In 1982, when it seemed that the University of Nottingham would be forced to make redundancies, Robert took voluntary early retirement, though he continued to do some teaching for a further three years. Retirement proved extremely productive.

He had long intended to write a book on Gregory the Great (540–604). He was struck by the fact that the world of Gregory, and therefore also his problems and his thoughts, were totally different from those of Augustine. So before getting on to the great Pope he felt he had to understand exactly how and why the world, and man's understanding of it, had changed so completely.[33] His efforts to reach that understanding resulted in what is probably his masterpiece, *The End of Ancient Christianity*, published in 1990. What Robert came to see as the decisive difference between the age of Augustine and that of Gregory the Great was a change in the nature of Christianity, a contraction in the scope that Christianity, or rather its clerics, allowed to the secular, to the theologically neutral.[34] Robert's book once again starts with Augustine, and his position in the then current controversy about how a Christian should live. Many were feeling the power of the ascetic ideal, and its call to opt out of everyday life, marriage, and property, and to adopt a life entirely based on the New Testament and Christian perfection. Augustine, like other highly educated young contemporaries, had given up a secular profession and marriage to devote himself first to a life of contemplation, and eventually to the service of the Church. But he came to believe that perfection could never be achieved in

[31] W. Bauer, *Orthodoxy and Heresy in Earliest Christianity*, English Translation (London, 1927).
[32] 'The problem of self-definition: from sect to church', in E. P. Sanders (ed.), *Jewish and Christian Self-Definition, Volume 1, The Shaping of Christianity in the Second and Third Centuries* (London, 1980), pp. 1–15 and 217–19.
[33] *The End of Ancient Christianity*, p. xi.
[34] Ibid., p. 16.

this world, it could only be achieved in the Kingdom. A person could lead a normal life and be a good Christian, as long as he or she was always aware of inherent sin and striving to overcome it. Robert gives a sensitive account of the argument of the advocates of Christian perfection, as well as of Augustine's intellectual struggle with the problem, and the position he finally reached.

There was controversy not only about how men and women should live, but also about the ordering of the social life, the Christianisation of time and place. The progress of the Roman year was marked out by traditional festivals, which had originally been intimately linked to the worship of pagan gods. By the end of the fourth century unambiguously pagan ritual had been largely abandoned, and Christians as well as the remaining pagans enjoyed the occasion simply as public entertainment. By this time there already existed a parallel cycle of Christian festivals: Sundays, Easter, Whitsun and last of all Christmas, and an increasing number of commemorations of martyrs. Now clerics, but also a significant number of laymen, found the pagan survivals represented by the old festivals intolerable. Robert describes the end of the traditional shows in Augustine's Africa, and somewhat later in Rome. Public worship at temples had long ceased. They were now being destroyed, or at least allowed to fall into decay. At the same time the bones of martyrs together with their cult were introduced into cities, where they offered the citizens a Christian medium of communication with Heaven, as well as linking living Christians to the glorious dead of the age of persecutions.

At the same time the ascetic movement was being tamed and directed into the service of the Church, among others by Augustine himself, but perhaps achieving its widest impact in the West through the writings of John Cassian, which were immensely influential in Gaul. Cassian purported to acquaint his readers with Egyptian asceticism but, as Robert shows, with Egyptian asceticism in a significantly modified form. The emphasis was no longer on extremes of austerity, but on communal life, regular ritual and above all the study of the scriptures: 'The image of the monastic community was becoming adapted to making it a model for the Christian community in the world, while the ascetic ideal it proposed to its members was becoming adapted to serve as the model for bishops and clergymen. The stage was set for the wholesale invasion of the Gallic Church by ascetics, and by their ideas of the Christian view of the world, the flesh and the devil.'[35] Monasteries became the nurseries of bishops

[35] Ibid., pp. 197–8: 'the ascetic ideology had moved from the fringes of society to its centre'.

who preached monastic ideas to the laity, and their preaching was all the more influential because many of them belonged to the old ruling class, which in Gaul retained property and influence under the Visigothic and Frankish kings. In Italy the development was rather different, but the eventual result was the same. The monastic movement spread more slowly, and there were fewer aristocratic bishops. But in the middle of the sixth century Justinian's Gothic wars followed by the Lombard invasion and settlement did tremendous damage to the social fabric of Italy. The social and above all the economic bases of the traditional secular culture were destroyed. Cassiodorus lived through these calamities and tried to salvage for the monks of his Vivarium as much of the traditional literary culture as he thought his monks needed for the understanding of the Bible and authoritative patristic texts.

The cumulative effect of all this was enormous. In the two centuries dealt with in this book, and particularly in the second half of the sixth century, the western provinces were being drained of the secular, that is of that sector of life which is not considered of direct religious significance. Above all secular education and culture were running down. Robert sums up the transformation: 'Christian culture in the early medieval centuries became radically and essentially biblical in a way it had not been before. The heterogeneity which had characterised it, at any rate from Augustine to Boethius, and had provided it with a fruitful play of internal tensions for its enrichment and growth had gone; but a good deal of secular learning could, and sometimes did, continue to play an important part within it.'[36]

When he had published *The End of Ancient Christianity* Robert was at last ready to write his book on Pope Gregory I, in which he would describe the life and work of this famous Pope in this transformed world.[37] He records that the whole book was read in typescript by Margaret Markus, and that it owes many improvements to her labours. The title describes exactly what the book is about. According to Robert, we live in two worlds, the material world and the world of imagination, perception and ideas. The two worlds are ever interacting, and Robert has set out to show the two worlds and their interaction in the case of Pope Gregory. He has drawn a very great personality, above all a dedicated pastor, but also a first rate administrator and leader. His culture is the ascetic, bible-based culture whose development Robert has traced in his previous book. Gregory upheld the value of secular disciplines, but in unambiguous subordination

[36] *The End of Ancient Christianity*, p. 225.

[37] *Gregory the Great and his World* (Cambridge, 1997).

to scriptural learning, and only to the extent that they promote scriptural understanding. This had also been Augustine's position in *De doctrina Christiana*, but with the difference that in Augustine's world secular education was flourishing and independent of what bishops said about it.[38] For Gregory to understand the scripture is to be renewed through their power. Gregory believed that scripture could be understood both historically and allegorically. While allegory could express both doctrine and moral teaching, Gregory in practice favoured moral interpretations.[39] Gregory's attitude to allegory was more unquestioning than that of Augustine, revealing the cultural shift that separates the two men. Augustine had been aware that there was a problem about understanding allegories and signs. For Gregory there was no doubt. They are transparent without any need to question.[40]

Gregory's world is the chaotic post-Roman world. He strove hard to do his best for his congregation, but he also had to supervise the administration of the estates which provide the resources for the Church's much needed charitable work. The senate and secular administration of Rome had disappeared so that the Pope had to look after the material as well as the spiritual welfare of its citizens. At the same time the Lombards were a permanent threat, which the Pope had to ward off through his own diplomacy, or by getting the Byzantine exarch at Ravenna to take military action, something which that official was often reluctant to do. Gregory coped heroically.

At the same time Robert shows that Gregory should not be considered the founder of the medieval papacy, and that he had little impact on the development of the papacy as an institution. In Gregory's time the Roman Church was still very much part of the imperial system as established by Justinian.[41] He still relied on Roman order, and legality, and, perhaps over-optimistically, on the Roman army. His sending of Augustine to convert the Anglo-Saxons eventually proved to be an act of far-reaching importance, but his initiative at mission was not immediately continued. He consolidated Roman leadership of the Churches in Byzantine Italy, but the Churches in Lombard Italy refused to accept the condemnation of the Three Chapters,[42] and came to constitute what was practically a Church of

[38] Ibid., pp. 40–1.

[39] Ibid., pp. 41–5.

[40] Ibid., p. 49, see also *Christianity and the Secular*, p. 87.

[41] *Gregory the Great and his World*, pp. 203–4.

[42] See the Introduction and Epilogue which Robert wrote jointly with Claire Sotinel to C. Chazelle and C. Cubitt (eds.), *The Crisis of the Oikoumene, the Three Chapters and the Failed Quest for*

the Lombard kingdom. The see of Ravenna, because that city was the centre of Byzantine administration, resisted Roman jurisdiction. At the same time the African Churches, while recognising the seniority of the Roman Church, insisted on maintaining their own traditions, and were not prepared to take directions from Rome. It was only after North Africa had been conquered by the Arabs, that 'no longer enriched by the creative tensions between a number of great sees ringing the Mediterranean, cut off from Africa and gradually from the Eastern churches, the Roman Church became the unchallenged mistress and teacher of the Western Germanic nations'.[43]

A course of lectures Robert gave during a semester as visitor at Notre Dame University gave him an opportunity to survey his life's academic work and to relate it to his own philosophical concerns and to those of contemporary theology and including a certain amount of revision or, to use Augustine's title, *retractatio*.[44] At the time of his death he was rereading the works of Gregory, and revising his book in the light of his rereading.

Robert was President of the Ecclesiastical History Society in 1978–9. He spent 1986–7 at the Princeton Institute of Advanced Studies. He was Distinguished Visiting Professor at the Catholic University of America in 1988, and Visiting Professor at Notre Dame University in 1993. Robert was President of the International Association of Patristic Studies 1991–5. He was elected a Fellow of the British Academy in 1984, and was awarded the OBE in 2000 for services to ecclesiastical history.

As we have seen Robert Markus was very much concerned with the problem of the place of Christianity, and particularly of the Catholic community, in relation to a multicultural society. He felt that the Church while remaining itself must be open to society, share its concerns, and be ready to discuss them. Another aspect of his thinking, and one which is perhaps less fashionable now, is the belief that in this discussion the Church could draw strength from an understanding of its history and historical texts.[45] Robert's historical studies cover a period of transformation, in the opposite direction to that which was happening in his life-time. In the age of Augustine Christians lived in a world in which the pagan

Unity in the Sixth Century Mediterranean (Turnhout, 2007), pp. 1–14 and 265–78, perhaps Robert's last publication.

43 Ibid., p. 204.

44 *Christianity and the Secular*, Blessed Pope John XXIII lecture series in Theology and Culture (Notre Dame, IN, 2006).

45 Cf. W. E. Klingshirn and M. Vessey (eds.), *The Limits of Ancient Christianity* (Ann Arbor, MI, 1999), p. vii.

culture of the classical world, with its rich variety of traditions, was still fully alive. Augustine engaged in dialogue with a culture which was largely pre-Christian. Roughly two hundred years later, Pope Gregory the Great could assume that everybody who mattered was Christian. The Church now inhabited a culture to a large and ever growing extent of its own making. When he read Augustine, Robert Markus might be said to have gone in search of Christian traditions which did not try to shape, or at least could not hope to shape, surrounding society, and which had a legitimate place for the autonomy of the secular.

Robert Markus's work drew on learning in a very wide field, philosophy, theology, and of course history, both ancient and modern. He was widely read in literature. He was an acute critic of music. Robert and Margaret were an extraordinarily hospitable couple. There were private areas. Visitors remember his pipe and his quiet humour. He was always ready to share his learning, and to give a great deal of his own time to help colleagues with their research. Robert was kind and enormously helpful to his postgraduates. His books have made their impact. But Robert Markus was perhaps most influential through his conversation. His affability and modesty and his warm approachable manner enabled him to assist and inspire very many young scholars at Liverpool and at Nottingham, and in fact all over the world. Robert Markus is survived by his wife and three children.

J. H. W. G. LIEBESCHUETZ
Fellow of the Academy

Note. In preparing this memoir I have been greatly assisted by the 'Notes for Obituarist' that Robert deposited with the Academy. Professor Thomas Markus, Robert's brother, provided information supplementing those notes. I am also indebted for help to Professor Bernard Hamilton, Professor John Moorhead, Professor Jean Porter, Professor Stephen Hodkinson, and Father Mark Brentnall.

A bibliography of Robert's writings between 1949 and 1998 is in W. E. Klinshirn and M. Vessey (eds.), *The Limits of Ancient Christianity, Essays on Late Antique Thought and Culture in Honor of R. A. Markus* (Ann Arbor, MI, 1999), pp. xv–xxv. Robert's most important essays are collected in: *From Augustine to Gregory the Great, History and Christianity in Late Antiquity* (London, 1983), *Sacred and Secular: Studies on Augustine and Latin Christianity* (Aldershot, 1993), and *Signs and Meanings: World and Text in Ancient Christianity* (Liverpool, 1996).

JOHN NORTH

John David North
1934–2008

JOHN DAVID NORTH was the leading British historian of astronomy of his generation. His interests ranged from prehistoric astronomical alignments to modern nuclear physics, but peaked with the Middle Ages and Renaissance, in which he brought out a richness and complexity that hitherto had hardly been seen. In every subject he sought to cast light on the society, culture and literature of the period. His daring interpretations were not immune to controversy, but in everything he published and lectured on he demonstrated intellectual honesty and a mastery of the mathematical detail.

John David North was born on 19 May 1934, in Cheltenham, to John Ernest North, a wool buyer, and his wife Gertrude Annie North (Lobley). His family moved to Yorkshire and he attended Batley Grammar School, where he developed an interest in mathematics and science. In 1953 he went up to Merton College, Oxford as a postmaster (Merton's term for the holder of a college scholarship). He read mathematics, but switched to philosophy, politics and economics (BA 1956, MA 1958). It is perhaps symbolic that this budding historian of medieval mathematics was based at Merton, for in the fourteenth century Merton College was the centre for the Oxford Calculators, a radical group of scholars who applied mathematics to philosophy. North attended the lectures of Gilbert Ryle, John Austin, Paul (H. P.) Grice, Peter Strawson, William Kneale and, most importantly, Alistair Crombie, the first lecturer in History of Science at Oxford (from 1953). Crombie inspired in him an interest in the history of science, and became a lifelong friend. After graduating, North taught in a school in Derbyshire but at the same time he studied for an external degree from London University in mathematics, physics and astronomy, which he passed with distinction (B.Sc. 1958). He then embarked on an Oxford doctorate on the history of cosmology in the first half of the twentieth century, under George Temple, the Sedleian Professor of Natural Philosophy, while simultaneously teaching physics in Magdalen College School. On completing his doctorate in 1963 he obtained a five-year Nuffield Foundation Fellowship. His first book, which started life as his doctoral thesis—*The Measure of the Universe: a History of Modern Cosmology*—was published in 1965, and won many accolades, including that of the astronomer, William McCrea: 'Nothing else like it exists and it will remain a standard work of reference for a long time to come.' It tells a complicated history of rival theories, of battles between scientists, and of claims to priority in the early twentieth century.

In the same year (1965) he discovered, in the Bodleian Library, a description with drawings of a most sophisticated and complicated astronomical clock designed and built by Richard of Wallingford, Abbot of St Albans (1292–1336). The clock itself was described by Leland in his mid-sixteenth-century *De viris illustribus*, but was probably destroyed at the time of the dissolution of the monasteries, and hence these manuscripts are the only record we have of the mechanism. Hardly anyone had noticed this extraordinary example of medieval technology and nobody had realised the significance of the few pages of manuscript, copied, it appears, by the monks of St Albans from Richard's drafts after his untimely death. The St Albans clock, this second 'measurer of the universe', was the link between the microcosm and the macrocosm. It mimicked the courses of the Sun and the Moon and the planets, as well as of the slow movement of the fixed stars; it showed the tides at London Bridge, included a wheel of fortune, and a bell that struck the hours on a 24-hour system. North argued that this clock was the culmination of an English tradition of clock-making going back to the early thirteenth century, and that the mechanical clock itself was an English invention. The St Albans clock was to the Middle Ages what the Antikythera device was to Classical Greece—the most sophisticated astronomical instrument of the time—and similarly it could represent the practical application of a vast body of theoretical work. Much of this theoretical work, on time, on astronomy, astrology and mathematics, was in unpublished texts by Richard of Wallingford himself, and North's merit was to publish, in three volumes, the full range of these writings, with English translations and commentary, in 1976. This involved teaching himself how to handle medieval Latin and acquiring the skills of a palaeographer and editor. This book established North's reputation as a leading historian of premodern science.

At this time he was Librarian and Assistant Curator of the Museum of the History of Science, Oxford (the 'Old Ashmolean'), whose library and rich collection of astronomical instruments, especially astrolabes, attracted his attention. He had been appointed in 1968 by the curator Francis Maddison, who greatly admired his breadth of scholarship and for whom he would later write obituaries in *The Times* and the *Archives internationales d'histoire des sciences*. He assisted Alistair Crombie in his history of science seminars, but when Crombie failed to get the new chair in the subject in 1972 (it went to Margaret Gowing, whose reputation rested on recent history of science[1]) North looked elsewhere to teach the subject. It was thus that he was snatched up by the University of Groningen (in 1977), which immediately appointed him to the 'Chair in the History of Philosophy and the Exact Sciences'. He adapted himself to the university environment, learning Dutch and serving on committees, as well as taking on a full load of teaching and continuing his research (especially during the vacations which he was able to take in Oxford, where he kept his house). He brought together in his work the two main divisions in the Dutch system: the Humanities ('Letterkunde') and the Sciences ('Natuurkunde'). He weathered the storm of student protest and Communist Party infiltration, and served as Dean of the Central Interfaculty from 1981 to 1984 and Dean of the Philosophy Faculty from 1990 to 1993. In the latter year he was awarded the degree of D.Litt. by the University of Oxford, having been elected as a Fellow of the British Academy in 1992. (He was elected as a Corresponding—i.e. overseas-based—Fellow, and in 2001, by which time he was classified as UK-based, he was transferred to the category of Ordinary Fellowship.) In 1979 he travelled to Brazil as part of the Dutch delegation celebrating the tercentenary of Johan Maurits van Nassau-Siegen, governor of the short-lived colony of Dutch Brazil, where the first astronomical observatory in the New World was established. He remained in post at Groningen until his retirement in 1999, when he was appointed Knight in the Orde van de Nederlandse Leeuw for services to education. In this same year a Festschrift was prepared for him by his Dutch colleagues, Lodi Nauta and Arjo Vanderjagt: *Between Demonstration and Imagination. Essays in the History of Philosophy and Science Presented to John D. North*.[2]

[1] See the memoir for her in this volume by Roy McLeod.

[2] This volume (Leiden, 1999) contains a full listing of North's publications up to 1998: it has been updated by Brian Martin—<http://www.ub.edu/arab/suhayl/volums/volum8/paper%207.pdf>.

John North was not afraid to venture onto territory claimed by literary historians, archaeologists and art historians. Through his profound knowledge of astronomy, his boundless inquisitiveness and his keen intuitions, he came up with original and convincing arguments in all these fields.

In the field of literature, in which he had as a ready helpmate and inspiration his wife, Marion, he published *Chaucer's Universe* (Oxford, 1988). Here he showed, by detailed comparison with contemporary astrological texts, almanacs and horoscopes, how the plots of Chaucer's stories were determined by astrological considerations, which also led him to establish dates for their composition and sometimes to propose emendations to the text. North was aware that he might be 'bracketed with those who try to prove that Bacon wrote Shakespeare', but a reviewer in the *Times Literary Supplement* praised the book as 'one of the century's monuments of scholarship'. As well as elucidating Chaucer, the book provides a clear picture of the understanding of the role of heavens by the fourteenth-century man and woman. It includes what remains the most valuable summary to this date of medieval astrological technique, based on the unpublished Medieval English version of Alcabitius's *Introduction to Astrology*. North's own *Chaucer's Universe* showed how the theory of mastership of the planets was applied.

The immediate stimulus for his venture into prehistoric archaeology, according to his Dutch colleague, Johan van Benthem, in the obituary published by the Royal Netherlands Academy,[3] was the presence of the prehistoric 'hunebedden' near his house in Paterswolde. He had noticed that the original timber posts surrounding the Bronze Age mound at Harenermolen were aligned to the rising and setting of the sun and moon. This led him to write his 653-page book on *Stonehenge: Neolithic Man and the Cosmos* in 1996. Within a thorough survey of Neolithic structures in northern Europe, he brought forward detailed evidence that Stonehenge was an astronomical observatory for the setting midwinter sun. He received the approval of archaeologists such as Colin Renfrew, who wrote that 'John North has made a real contribution to our understanding of the henge monuments and of Stonehenge itself', and astronomers such as Patrick Moore, who reckoned that 'it will supersede all earlier works'. His book was taken seriously in university courses and even inspired Bernard Cornwell's novel *Stonehenge, a Novel of 2000 BC* (London, 1999).

[3] <http://www.knaw.nl/Content/Internet_KNAW/publicaties/pdf/20091012_8.pdf>.

His interest in the astronomical instruments of King Henry VIII's German astronomer, Nicolaus Kratzer, and the commemoration of the five-hundredth anniversary of the birth of Hans Holbein the Younger, led North to apply his talents to the study of art—as well as his consummate skills as a detective—in his detailed analysis of Hans Holbein's painting *The Ambassadors* in the National Gallery (*The Ambassadors' Secret: Holbein and the World of the Renaissance*, London, 2002). In the space of over 300 pages he explored the historical occasion of the painting, he described each of the many objects in it—astronomical and musical and religious—and then teased out from their symbolic values and their mutual arrangement the precise day and time of day on which the ambassadors were meeting: Good Friday, April 11, 1533, at 4 p.m., the end of the hour following Christ's death, which had occurred precisely 1,500 years earlier. Moreover, other features of the painting, including the anamorphic skull on the floor between the ambassadors, drew attention to an inclination of 27 degrees, which would have been the altitude of the sun at exactly 4 p.m. on that day. In his review in *The Times*, Frank Whitford commented that North had shown that *The Ambassadors* was 'a highly complex religious allegory about this world and the next, Christ's suffering and triumph over death'. He had achieved the result that 'the painting … and its maker now seem more marvellous than ever'.

Sometimes North's hypotheses have been thought to range too far from the evidence available. Of course, to claim that the Renaissance was a period in which 'people … had an excessive fondness for enigmas' (*The Ambassadors' Secret*, p. 8), gives free rein to find enigmas, secrets and symbols in anything. But, as North writes in the same context, the more deeply one penetrates the mental and spiritual world of the people of the period, the better one can distinguish between likely hypotheses and far-fetched interpretations.

In 1986 North had published with the Warburg Institute *Horoscopes and History*, a book dedicated to his parents, which, besides documenting the different methods used in drawing up horoscopes in the Middle Ages, and giving copious examples of their use, almost entirely from manuscripts, provided a practical way for the modern practitioner to draw up a medieval horoscope, using a computer program which he wrote himself. Anthony Grafton, in his own book on an astrologer—*Cardano's Cosmos* (Cambridge, MA, 1999, p. 14)—wrote that 'John North has laid the technical foundations on which any study of Renaissance astrology must rest.' North was half way through a greatly expanded version of this book until the day before his death. It remains incomplete.

His last major published work was *Cosmos* (Chicago, IL, 2008), a substantial revision in over 900 pages of the *Fontana History of Astronomy and Cosmology* which he had written in 1994. Noel Swerdlow, in his report to the University of Chicago Press concerning *Cosmos*, described it as 'the finest comprehensive history of astronomy and cosmology written, and will remain so for many years to come'. North enlivened the story with wit and anecdotes. A leitmotif of his work is the position of man, whether he be neolithic, medieval, Renaissance, or modern, within the cosmos.

Besides these ground-breaking books, North found time to write general books for a broader public—on *Isaac Newton* (Oxford, 1967), *Mid-Nineteenth Century Scientists* (Oxford, 1969), *Ptolemy* (in Italian, 1968) —and produced a stream of articles for periodicals, conference proceedings, and Festchriften, some of which were collected in two themed volumes: *Stars, Minds and Fate: Essays in Ancient and Medieval Cosmology* (London, 1989), and *The Universal Frame: Historical Essays in Astronomy, Natural Philosophy and Scientific Method* (London, 1989). His facility for finding the right words, for writing with wit, and being critical where criticism was due, made him a popular contributor to the *Times Literary Supplement*. After his death, Maren Meinhardt (Science Editor, March 25, 2009) mentioned both his 'brilliance, wit and terrifying erudition' and his 'modest, courteous and helpful' dealings with the editor. While most science reviewers are listed with their areas of interest or speciality, 'next to John North, it simply said "everything"'.

In addition to the distinctions mentioned already John North was a Fellow of the Royal Astronomical Society (from 1959), a Member of the Academia Leopoldina (from 1992), a Member of the Royal Netherlands Academy of Arts and Science (from 1985), a Foreign Member of the Royal Danish Academy (from 1985) and Member of the Académie internationale d'histoire des sciences (from 1967; administrative secretary 1983–93; perpetual secretary from 1990). He held Visiting Professorships at Frankfurt and Aarhus, Yale, Minnesota and Austin and was awarded the Médaille Alexandre Koyré 1989. He was editor of the *Archives internationales d'histoire des sciences* (from 1971 to 1984), and describes his experiences with his usual humour in an article in that journal (no. 117, vol. 36, 1986, pp. 362–73) entitled 'One of our galleys is missing'.

He died on 31 October 2008, having battled with cancer for the last years of his life, which he endured with exemplary courage, humour and lack of complaint.

He had met Marion Pizzey in Oxford and they had married in 1957. He repeatedly expresses his debt to her, and their personal and intellectual partnership lay at the heart of his work. He was a devoted father and grandfather, inventing stories and games and building computers with his grandchildren. He is survived by his wife, one son and two daughters, and six grandchildren.

CHARLES BURNETT
Fellow of the Academy

Note. I am indebted to obituary notices and appreciations by Johan van Benthem, Lodi Nauta (*The Guardian*), Martin Sheppard (*The Independent*), anonymous (*The Daily Telegraph*), Brian Martin (*The Times*), Owen Gingerich (*Times Literary Supplement*), personal reminiscences of Julio Samsó and Will Ryan, and especially to the help of the North family.

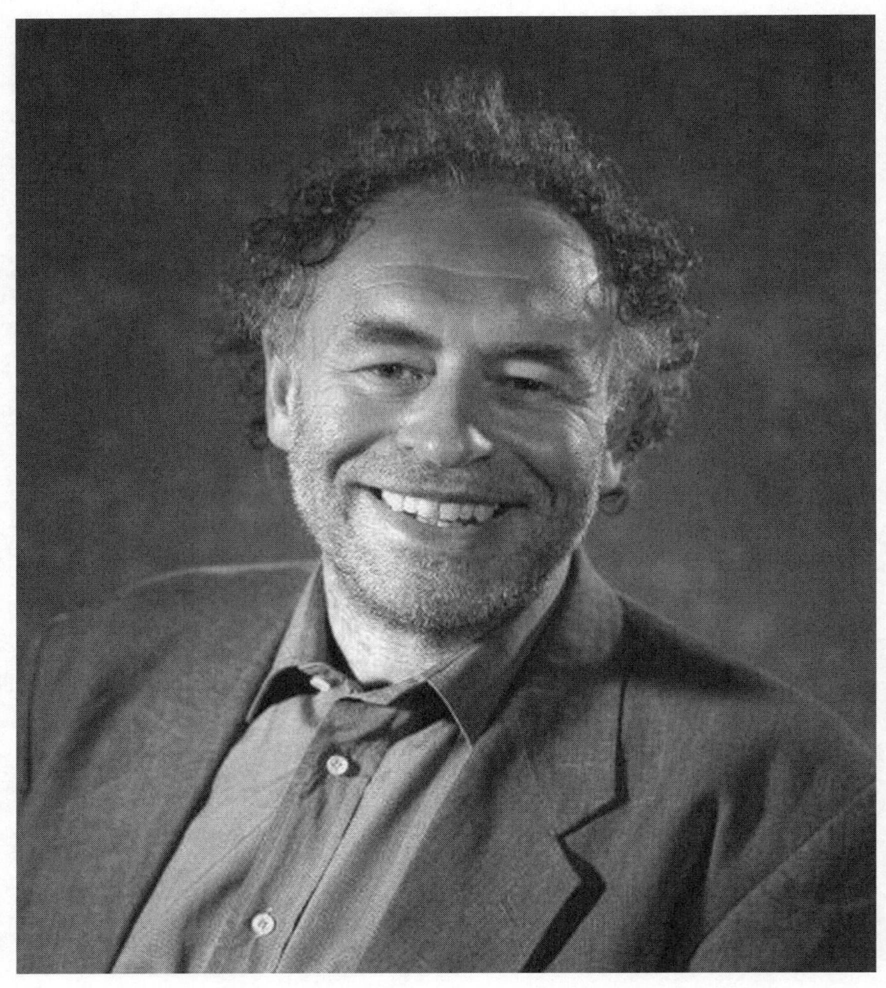

ROY PORTER *Wellcome Library, London*

Roy Sydney Porter
1946–2002

I

WHEN ROY PORTER DIED on 4 March 2002, he had been recognised as an original, prolific and influential historian for a considerable time. He had been preternaturally productive for about three decades; in addition to his numerous and diverse writings, he was a frequent broadcaster and public speaker. Many people knew about him, his writings and ideas far beyond the confines of academia. He was both public historian and public intellectual. Roy worked prodigiously and with a special kind of energy. Since he published so much, it is tempting to list his achievements and to stress the sheer volume of work he produced. But to do so would miss the defining features of the man and of his legacy. In assessing his impact and paying just regard to his ideas and their influence, it is necessary to grasp the drives that lay behind this extraordinary and inspiring man. In writing this memoir I have had in mind those features of his life and work that seem to me to have been most fundamental; they provide the threads that were woven into his existence. I am thinking especially of his work ethic, his dedication to his students, his energy, his attachment to his roots, his capacity to bring people together, to positively exude encouragement and to embrace the tawdry, ugly and desperate parts of humanity's past as well as its more elegant and elevated manifestations.

The broad contours of Roy Porter's life are familiar. Born on 31 December 1946, his early days are briefly sketched, and in moving terms, in his Preface to *London: a Social History* (1994). From a modest working-class background, he was admitted to Christ's College, Cambridge in 1965, and

Biographical Memoirs of Fellows of the British Academy, XI, 503–512. © The British Academy 2012.

joined the talented group of historians for whom Jack Plumb was a powerful patron. A stellar student, he stayed in Cambridge for fourteen years, the last seven as Director of Studies in History at Churchill College. The second part of his career, between 1979 and 2001, was spent in his beloved London, at the Wellcome Institute for the History of Medicine, which no longer exists in the form he knew it. He was elected a Fellow of the British Academy in 1994. When he died he had recently loosened his ties to the Wellcome, not least to spend more time with his adored fifth wife, Natsu Hattori, whom he acknowledged as the love of his life in book dedications. An only child, who was utterly devoted to his parents—his mother survived him—Roy did not himself have any children.

Roy's career was indeed meteoric; for example, he became editor of the major journal *History of Science* while still in his twenties, a post he discharged with distinction and held for an astonishing twenty-nine years.[1] In undertaking such duties, Roy was efficient, imaginative and affable, as he was in the numerous projects he had on the go at any given moment. Many of these were collaborations; like the men of the Enlightenment he wrote about with notable compassion, he believed in betterment through cooperation. In 1982 he published a spirited, readable and influential volume on the eighteenth century in the Penguin Social History of England series.[2] It depicts a dynamic, exuberant period, qualities that he himself manifested. His success was possible thanks to a happy blend of exceptional energy, high intelligence, lively writing, strong curiosity and a honed instinct for attractive, timely subjects.

II

Roy's approach to history and to his professional life, like his awesome productivity, may be understood in terms of deeply felt values. Roy was a worker, who believed in the importance of academic labour, and felt little tolerance towards those who, in his view, had failed to grasp the value of honest, hard toil. He loved life in all its variety, chaos, confusion and richness. He believed it was the task of historians to embrace these qualities, to recast the past in a form that could be grasped by readers without losing its complexity and vitality. Roy believed in generosity as a guiding princi-

[1] *History of Science*, 41 (2003) part 3, number 133 is *In memoriam Roy Porter*.

[2] Roy Porter, *English Society in the Eighteenth Century* (Harmondsworth, 1982); a revised edition appeared in 1990.

ple of life in general and of academic life in particular. He was the master of a number of kinds of generosity. Early in his career he gave many wonderful parties, bringing people together and generally dispensing good cheer, along with food and drink. Thus he was as much cook and nurturer as intellectual and communicator. Roy was perpetually urging people to meet each other and exchange ideas, and bursting with lists of names drawn from his encyclopaedic memory. He wanted to give opportunities to others, to encourage them, to foster their writing, speaking and publishing activities. We should, he made clear, simply get on with it, in a pulling up socks kind of way. Self-pity was not indulged. Roy strove to see the best in others, was keen to collaborate, to give feedback on work, to spread goodwill and, if at all possible, to please others. From the beginning, eager for comments, he shared his own work in draft with many colleagues and students, and distributed his publications as gifts. Nonetheless he remained a private man, whose complex emotional life was known to only a very few. He once shared with me the culture shock he experienced on arriving in Cambridge. The fact that he managed his own two cultures with such integrity is deeply significant. Even his manifest professional achievements defy brief description.

While it is vital not to idealise someone so cruelly cut off in their prime, it is just as important to recognise how rare many of Roy's qualities are in professional life. While he knew many grand people, and was after all a protégé of Jack Plumb, he gave a great deal of his time to those at the beginning of their careers, as he did also to those who felt professionally vulnerable and marginalised. Scholars all over the world remember his kindnesses, his modest, unfeigned enthusiasm, his willingness to take on tasks others found tiresome or demeaning. There is no doubt that Roy was driven, but he was also blessed with self-knowledge. Furthermore, complacence was foreign to him. He had already moved on to the next tasks, hence pride and self-satisfaction played no part in his frenetic working life.

III

To gain an understanding of Roy Porter as a historian, however, one has to attend not just to the unusual personal qualities he brought to his work but also to its content. And his choice of subject matter was shaped, at least in part, by sympathy, a concept of considerable interest to anyone with the sophisticated understanding of eighteenth-century thought that

Roy possessed. He worked on topics of many different kinds, sometimes focusing on periods, at others on people, places, texts, themes or methodological problems. It seems that he was attracted to those who suffered in some way—the mad, for instance—and his work on the eighteenth-century doctor George Cheyne, who wrote about gout in the 1720s, could illustrate the point. Cheyne, whose *The English Malady* (1733) he edited, was a prominent physician, although not a discoverer, inventor or pioneer: he suffered from serious ill health himself.[3]

Roy started out as a historian of geology and came to medicine only later. And it was not only the eminent historian of eighteenth-century England, Jack Plumb, who shaped his education. He was also taught by Quentin Skinner and the radical historian of science Robert M. Young, while he learned the history of geology from Martin Rudwick. His doctoral thesis became his first book, *The Making of Geology: Earth Science in Britain 1660–1815* (1977). The operative term here is 'making'. Roy showed how one specific science was formed through historical processes. There was nothing predetermined or inexorable about such transitions, which took place, the volume reveals, over a long period of time. In tracing the making of a scientific field, in insisting that it was a construct, Roy was addressing lively debates in the history, philosophy and sociology of science concerning the nature of natural knowledge. He was also asserting that the history of science is part of history: 'the history of science is continuous with … economic, social, political and intellectual history'.[4]

Later he demonstrated how the same could be said for the history of medicine, and he deserves considerable credit for helping to put it on the map of general historians. By its very nature medicine prompts the curiosity of most people. Here we can appreciate the wide impact of Roy's writings about medicine and health in the past—they established the history of medicine broadly conceived as both of interest to the general public and fully integrated into the discipline of history. Through his work on science and medicine Roy hoped to attract and engage practitioners in these areas. There were many 'old docs' at the Wellcome Institute, whom he warmly helped and encouraged. He would have none of the facile polarity between supposedly enlightened professional historians and Whiggish practitioners. Yet he was himself fully aware of and sensitive to historiographical trends, and in so many respects a pioneer. Roy has some-

[3] Roy Porter (ed.), *George Cheyne: the English Malady (1733)* (London, 1991); Roy Porter and G. S. Rousseau, *Gout: the Patrician Malady* (New Haven, NJ, and London, 1998).
[4] Roy Porter, *The Making of Geology: Earth Science in Britain 1660–1815* (Cambridge, 1977), p. 9.

times been presented as not theoretically attuned. It is true that he did not present himself as ideologically *parti pris*, and he was indeed highly critical of Michel Foucault on empirical grounds. But it does not follow that he was uninterested either in the political issues that underlie historical practice or in the conceptual frameworks that historians deploy. On the contrary, his critique of Foucault reveals just these concerns. He minded that people bought into a Foucauldian perspective uncritically, when a sharp historical understanding of the history of madness and psychiatry revealed how the English case simply does not fit with Foucault's model. Similarly he was sceptical about the discontinuities Foucault posited.[5]

It was characteristic of Roy's penetrating historical eye that he could spot fashions and trends before they took hold, and develop them as ways into larger historical phenomena. Rather than despising fashion as epiphenomenal, he took it to be a source of historical insight. Diseases that came in and out of focus were grist to his mill. In other words, Roy possessed historical flair, a nose for important, and fun, topics. This account might suggest a historian who was diverted by amusing and entertaining themes. While Roy certainly did respond warmly to an astonishing array of historical questions, he possessed a fine critical mind. Always historiographically acute, Roy had a strong grasp of the philosophical issues that historical practice necessarily generates. His critique of Michel Foucault is a case in point. His engagement with Foucault reminds us of the centrality of the history of mental illness in his writings. He wrote extensively on the subject, and with a kind of humanity that deserves recognition and respect. This underlay too a remarkable book which he co-edited with Sylvana Tomaselli on rape.[6] It may be trite to put it this way, but Roy was genuinely interested in the human condition in all its forms. He relished challenges and was often reluctant to say 'no' when yet another invitation was issued to him. When asked, as he frequently was, why he took on so much, he would say simply, 'I was asked, they wanted me to …'.

One of the most striking features of Roy's work was his attention to language. This is clear in the witticisms and allusions that pepper his writings, in the striking metaphors he used, and his care in casting his thoughts into clear and memorable forms. Just as notable is his engagement with literature. This was a man who loved and often reread *Tristram Shandy*, who appreciated the potential of literary works to nurture historians'

[5] Colin Jones and Roy Porter (eds.), *Reassessing Foucault: Power, Medicine and the Body* (London, 1994).
[6] Sylvana Tomaselli and Roy Porter (eds.), *Rape* (Oxford, 1986).

imaginations and to shed light on past mentalities, and who was an excellent close reader, perhaps inspired by his contact with Quentin Skinner. Here again we find two characteristic features of Roy's thinking: his acceptance of, even relish for, subversion, comedy and satire and his commitment to engaging with as much as possible of what human societies have thrown up without casting himself into the role of moral arbiter. This is precisely the value of his work on quackery, which developed an approach we would now take for granted:

> I shall take as quacks the broad spectrum of those operators who were typically pilloried as such; and in doing so, this being a work of history, the term will convey neither blame nor praise. He (or she) was called a quack who transgressed what those in the saddle defined as true, orthodox, regular, 'good' medicine. . . . quacks [were] those who drummed up custom largely through self-orchestrated publicity; who operated as individual entrepreneurs . . . and who depended heavily upon vending secret nostrums.[7]

In such apparently straightforward claims there is a particular approach to the history of medicine, one that has become so commonplace that there is a danger of forgetting how innovative his way of thinking about early modern medicine was. In the case of the eighteenth century in particular, medicine was generally taken to be in decline—there was a dearth of discoveries and big new ideas. When a progressivist history of medicine prevailed, the period was passed over in relative silence, deemed a dull interlude between Harvey's discovery of the circulation of the blood and the development of pathological anatomy. Roy was altogether more generous and more historiographically sophisticated in attempting to capture the textures of medical activities and ideas in the eighteenth century. Starting from the assumption that prominent doctors of the period, such as William Hunter, Thomas Beddoes, and Erasmus Darwin, deserved our attention even if they were not scientific innovators, Roy was able to show how culturally significant they were, probing the precise nature of their historical importance.

IV

Roy was a brave scholar. It is hard for most of us to grasp his range or to fully appreciate his boldness. An excellent example is his massive tome *The Greatest Benefit to Mankind*, first published in 1997. My understand-

[7] Roy Porter, *Quacks: Fakers & Charlatans in English Medicine* (Stroud, 2000), p. 11.

ing is that he intended the main title to terminate with a question mark. Its subtitle, *A Medical History of Humanity from Antiquity to the Present*, suggests a breadth of understanding that is truly formidable. He knew how to tell a story, how to paint big pictures, trace patterns and conjure up the textures of the past. He found patterns and made generalisations with enviable verve. Roy was also happy to comment, to sum up with a tinge of scepticism. As he pointed out in the last two sentences: 'Medicine has led to inflated expectations, which the public eagerly swallowed. Yet as those expectations become unlimited, they are unfulfillable: medicine will have to redefine its limits even as it extends its capabilities.'[8]

The volume focused on medical thinking and medical practice, about which he could be ironic and critical. Indeed much of his work was from 'the patient's perspective', a notion that will be linked forever to his name.[9] This particular enthusiasm stems from his commitment to social history, and more particularly to a form of it that does justice to the lives of so-called ordinary people. It was nurtured by his wide reading—fast, voracious, and open-minded—in all genres. In fact his interest in how patients viewed their conditions and those they employed to help them was all of a piece with his interest in every form of medical practice, no matter how kooky it appeared in retrospect. He possessed the most lively sense of the range of medical activities, of the importance for historians of being sensitive to the diversity of health-seeking behaviours. His concern with patients and with the varied practices of those from whom they sought assistance were two sides of the same coin.

I take from Roy's work on quackery his understanding that these matters were and are always relational. The very concept 'quack' only makes sense if there are other groups with whom they can be defined by contrast. But the term itself is not stable, and those most wedded to orthodoxy could be vulnerable to the very same accusation. The study of quackery is thus an exceptionally deft way of exposing medical fault lines. The result is a heightened sense of the fragility of medical status, expertise and efficacy, of contests over health and its providers. To convey all this effectively, we need to be thinking about economics, markets and consumption

[8] Roy Porter, *The Greatest Benefit to Mankind: a Medical History of Humanity from Antiquity to the Present* (London, 1997), p. 718.

[9] Roy Porter, 'The patient's view: doing medical history from below', *Theory and Society*, 14 (1985), 175–98; Roy Porter (ed.), *Patients and Practitioners: Lay Perceptions of Medicine in Pre-industrial Society* (Cambridge, 1985), chaps. 1 and 10; Dorothy Porter and Roy Porter, *Patient's Progress: Doctors and Doctoring in Eighteenth-century England* (Cambridge, 1989), especially Part II: Patients.

at the same time. Practitioners, whatever their education and skills, needed to make a living. No matter how orthodox they proclaimed themselves to be, they too had wares to sell, even when there wasn't a pill or potion in sight. Negotiation and contestation in markets is a fruitful way of approaching many aspects of the history of medicine, one which Roy's training in social history made him particularly well qualified to pursue.

There was nothing doctrinaire or preachy about Roy, who never sought to build an empire or create a school. His insistence that historians recognise patients and 'quacks' did not imply that professions and institutions were unimportant. Thus he wrote about the history of psychiatry and mental hospitals, as well as about madness and the mad, fully recognising that these were distinct, if interrelated categories. His remarkable work *Madness: a Brief History* (2001) demonstrates the point. It is remarkable not just because it covered so much so well in a short book, but because Roy negotiated with grace the political minefields that anyone writing about such a delicate and raw topic must cross.

If Roy was notably benign and generous, this does not mean he was uncritical. He could be extremely funny about the shortcomings of those with whom he worked. Beneath the capacity to exude bonhomie was a shrewd understanding of his fellow human beings, especially of their capacity to deliver the goods. This was a valuable skill, given the huge number of collaborations in which he engaged. For instance, he edited and co-edited many volumes of essays, the majority of which were on new topics or approaches. Particularly notable is the suite of books he edited with the distinguished historian of science Mikuláš Teich. These were comparative in nature: each one took a big theme—such as romanticism, drugs and narcotics, or the scientific revolution—and brought together essays upon its manifestation in different settings.[10] The mentality that underlies this, as so many of his other projects, is worth emphasising. I have already noted his exceptional feel for good subjects. Roy co-edited a volume on *Medicine and the Five Senses* before most historians caught on that the senses could provide a generative optic for their field.[11] He consistently demonstrated a generosity of embrace. If considering the Enlightenment, for example, a subject about which he wrote exceptionally well, we should think about Russia and Spain, not just about France and

[10] Roy Porter and M. Teich (eds.), *Romanticism in National Context* (Cambridge, 1988); *Drugs and Narcotics in History* (Cambridge, 1995); and *The Scientific Revolution in National Context* (Cambridge, 1992).

[11] W. F. Bynum and Roy Porter (eds.), *Medicine and the Five Senses* (Cambridge, 1993).

Scotland.[12] These works are highly accessible. He aimed high and got the best people he could, but what they produced could be used by undergraduates. They are veritable treasure troves of ideas. Roy possessed an outstanding capacity to generate fresh projects and to share them with others. The point is made with feeling. When he assigned me a specific task in the book he co-edited about William Hunter, the eighteenth-century Scottish collector and medical man, it changed forever the ways I worked and the subjects I tackled.[13] While he may not have anticipated the lasting impact his invitation would have, it was characteristic of the creative way in which he put people and subjects together.

V

Roy delighted in reaching wide audiences, as the wonderfully readable *Blood and Guts* shows.[14] He practised public history long before the term was common in the United Kingdom. Indeed I think he saw it in moral terms. We, those of us who are privileged to work in universities, *should* share our knowledge and enthusiasm with anyone who is interested. This is why, early in his career when it was possible to do so, he travelled extensively to schools, associations and societies to speak about his work. His recognition of the potential of satirical prints to engage audiences and afford fresh historical insights reinforces these points.

Those encountering him for the first time could not help but be struck by his distinctive personal style, with his open shirts, rumpled trousers and jackets, gold jewelry and stubble. They would quickly be won over by his charm, erudition, and cheerfulness. I have heard it said that a distinguished American academic—a woman—considered him the sexiest man in London. No memoir of Roy would be remotely satisfactory without a discussion of sex, a subject that was, if I may put it this way, close to his heart. His writings on the history of sexuality were innovative and influential.[15] It was a subject he could tackle with wry humour and without a

[12] Roy Porter and M. Teich (eds.), *The Enlightenment in National Context* (Cambridge, 1981); Roy Porter, *Enlightenment: Britain and the Creation of the Modern World* (Harmondsworth, 2000).

[13] W. F. Bynum and Roy Porter (eds.), *William Hunter and the Eighteenth-Century Medical World* (Cambridge, 1985).

[14] Roy Porter, *Blood and Guts: a Short History of Medicine* (London, 2002).

[15] See, for example, Roy Porter, 'A touch of danger: the man-midwife as sexual predator', in G. S. Rousseau and Roy Porter (eds.), *Sexual Underworlds of the Enlightenment* (Manchester, 1987), pp. 206–32.

shred of prudery. In this, as in other respects, he was a liberated man. Roy genuinely liked and appreciated women, nurtured their careers, and took immense pleasure in their achievements. These qualities cannot be taken for granted, and it is greatly to his credit that he applauded all success, and did so much to ensure that others enjoyed as much of it as possible.

Everyone who knew Roy has a favourite anecdote about him.[16] One of mine comes from the time I stayed with Roy and his first wife, the writer Sue Limb, as a despondent and somewhat lost Ph.D. student. Getting up in the middle of the night to go to the bathroom, I discovered Roy, hard at work at the kitchen table. This occurred forty years ago, but I seem to remember he was reading Aristotle. His capacity for work is deservedly legendary. But so is his capacity for many kinds of fun. We can be entirely confident that he would have greatly enjoyed knowing that if, a decade after his death, you google 'Roy Porter', a butcher in Lancashire and an American jazz drummer also come up. What might surprise him, however, is how many of his books can still be obtained from the Amazon website, how many students read and appreciate his work, and how deeply he is missed.

LUDMILLA JORDANOVA
King's College London

Note. I am especially grateful to Sylvana Tomaselli for recent discussions about Roy, and to many other colleagues and friends with whom I have shared memories of him. Above all, I acknowledge Roy Porter as my teacher, friend and mentor, to whom I owe the most profound debt, one of which I am constantly reminded. A full bibliography of his writings can be found in Carol Reeves, *Professor Roy Porter: Bibliography* (246 pages, 2003) in the Wellcome Library <http://encore.wellcome.ac.uk/iii/encore/record/C__Rb1578834__Scarol+reeves__Orightresult__X4?lang=eng&suite=cobalt>.

[16] Some are recounted in Roberta Bivins and John V. Pickstone (eds.), *Medicine, Madness and Social History: Essays in Honour of Roy Porter* (Basingstoke, 2007), pp. 228–35.

ANTHONY QUINTON

Anthony Meredith Quinton
1925–2010

> He always seemed to be in a good mood. He had what many *really* intelligent people have, which is not being serious or solemn. They *know* what they are talking about so they have no need to be earnest about it. (Lucian Freud on Sigmund Freud)

TONY QUINTON (as everyone who knew Lord Quinton called him) had many sides. Here it is appropriate to concentrate on his work as a philosopher and on his career in academic and public life, rather than on the genial polymath who became well known to a wider public as the host of *Round Britain Quiz*. But Tony's personality, his style and wit, are hard totally to repress even in an academic memoir. Opening by borrowing the words of Lucian Freud echoes the start of Paul Levy's obituary in *The Independent:* 'Tony Quinton lit up a room as soon as he entered it.'[1]

He was born on 25 March 1925 In Gillingham, Kent. His father was a naval doctor and the family moved around with him—Tony's earliest memories were of living in Malta; he died in 1935. Despite her reduced income, Tony's mother was determined to get him the best education she could; he went to Stowe School and from there became a Scholar of Christ Church, Oxford, reading history, until this was interrupted by war service as a navigator in the RAF. On returning to Christ Church, and already interested in philosophy, he won a distinguished first in PPE, followed by a Prize Fellowship at All Souls.

He sometimes recalled undergraduate intellectual awakenings, among them reading Ayer's *Language, Truth and Logic*, Ryle's *Concept of Mind*

[1] 25 June 2010.

Biographical Memoirs of Fellows of the British Academy, XI, 515–528.

and Popper's *Open Society*. He was perhaps warmest about J. L. Austin's lectures, for which he, David Pears and Geoffrey Warnock would arrive together early to get good seats. One of Quinton's enduring features was a refusal to see philosophy as separate from the rest of humane letters, or philosophical thought as being quite independent of the style in which it is expressed. The comments on Austin's lectures showed how early this was present. He delighted in the felicities of language and in jokes after the style of P. G. Wodehouse. (Quinton enjoyed Austin's explanation of why every thought needs both a subject and predicate: it would be no use getting an unsigned telegram saying 'Look here, old man, am in an awful hole.')

As an undergraduate, at Elizabeth Anscombe's request, he showed Wittgenstein round Christ Church garden before the famous clash with Prichard at the Jowett Society. (Although Quinton found Wittgenstein an enthusiastic sightseer, years later he did not remember what he had said.)

Quinton's philosophy tutorials were mainly with J. O. Urmson, but also with Michael Foster, J. D. Mabbott and Paul Grice. As well as developing his philosophical skills, they developed his eye for tutors' foibles. One later comment was that Paul Grice had 'spent most of the two and a half hour sessions in silence, but the fragments of conversation were excellent'.

Quinton's distinguished career started with the All Souls Prize Fellowship. (The pleasure of winning it may have been heightened by an overheard comment by another candidate before the exam. He reported Marcus Dick saying to Richard Wollheim, 'Not much competition here, Richard.' Perhaps there was a touch of reciprocity in Tony's later description of Marcus Dick as 'the only professional philosopher I have ever heard of in Oxford who never published a single word'.) On his time in All Souls, as in much of this memoir, I draw on his contribution to the autobiographical volume *Before We Met* (New York and London, 2008), by and about himself and Marcelle Quinton. The account of that period sometimes gives glimpses of other philosophers, as in Quinton having to call on Michael Dummett at ten in the morning to shake him into consciousness so he did not miss breakfast. But some of the inhabitants of the college brought out his comic instinct. His powers of caricature make some of his descriptions into verbal cartoons. The historian John Cooper was 'a human Eeyore, slow speaking and given to banging himself on the head while the conversation oozed out'.

Quinton went on to become a Tutorial Fellow of New College (1955–78) and a Fellow of the British Academy (1977: Vice-President, 1985–6). He was President of Trinity College, Oxford (1978–87). A bronze portrait of him, made by Marcelle in 1980, is in the British Library, near the Chairman's office.

Bronze of Anthony Quinton by Marcelle Quinton, 1980, in the British Library.

His breadth of reading was awe-inspiring, both in philosophy and across the range of the humanities. So there was a symbolic appropriateness in his appointment as Chairman of the Board of the British Library (1985–90). His period of office was at a turbulent period for the Library, the time of the debate over moving from the British Museum to St Pancras.

Some felt that he should have fought to retain the Round Reading Room in the Museum and against the St Pancras move. Others saw the separation from the Museum as being to the advantage of both. The architecture of the new Library was famously attacked by the Prince of Wales, who compared its Reading Room to the assembly hall of an academy for secret police. Fortunately the Royal Assent had not been required for the plans. Some of us think the spacious building, the colour of St Pancras, and in style echoing the Victorian station without imitating it, is one of London's recent architectural glories.

Quinton's polymath side served him well as Chairman of the Kennedy Memorial Trust (1990–5). As a fellow trustee I enjoyed his ability to interview Kennedy Scholarship candidates without preparation. One morning, glancing down at a candidate's papers, he said, 'Ms Robinson, I see your field is Chinese literature. Not a field I know about, except of course the three late Chinese novels everyone has read…' I sat there hoping not to be found out.

He was a member of the Conservative Philosophy Group, sometimes attended by Margaret Thatcher, who made him Baron Quinton of Holywell in 1983. He obviously enjoyed being in the Lords. He did not, as some of us had hoped, use his position to defend the universities from the attempts to remodel them along the lines of commercial corporations as conceived in some dim 'management' textbook. (I forgive him this, just as, if he were able to read the previous sentence, he would forgive this mild hijacking of his memoir to make a political point he would be sceptical about. It was not in his nature to let political disagreement impair friendship.) In the Lords he did campaign against the bad behaviour of some cyclists on the roads and on the pavements. When he first told me this, I thought it was a rather P. G. Wodehouse issue to take up. When I later heard that a cyclist on the pavement had hit Tony's wife Marcelle, causing her serious injury, I thought again.

Other positions that he occupied included being President of the Aristotelian Society (1975–6), President of the Royal Institute of Philosophy (1991–7), President of the Society of Applied Philosophy (1988–91), Fellow of Winchester College (1970–85) and Chairman of the Governors of Stowe School (1963–4).

But this career nearly did not start at all. As a boy in the Second World War, his time at Stowe was interrupted by a planned evacuation (with his mother) to Canada. They went, with many other children, on the *City of Benares*, which was torpedoed and sunk by a U-boat. Many died, but a few, including Quinton and his mother, were rescued and brought back to England. He took all this in his stride. On getting back they went to his grandmother, who looked up from her gardening and said, 'Oh, so you're back, are you?' Describing this later, he wrote, 'I felt that with this kind of sang-froid we were not going to lose the war.' Reading his own unruffled account of the episode suggests he inherited some of his grandmother's war-winning temperament.

His personal life centred round his marriage to the sculptor Marcelle Quinton, with whom he had their children Joanna and Edward. (Joanna, at Tony's memorial service in New College, before reading a passage from his beloved P. G. Wodehouse, gave a vivid account of the noisy, choking and convulsive laughter to which these books could reduce him.)

Marcelle's contribution to their jointly authored book describes how, as a Jewish child, she had escaped Hitler's Berlin with her mother and eventually reached America. Her temperament was artistic, passionate and creative, while he had the calm passions of a twentieth-century English version of David Hume. They made a brilliant combination of opposites, one that included being able to work together on jointly translating Frege's article on 'The Thought'. Marcelle's account of this was, 'I did the German and the translation and Tony did the English and the philosophy.'

They shared a preference for the interesting over the conventional. They met at Sir Keith Joseph's wedding, where Marcelle unconventionally accepted Tony's equally unconventional invitation to go on with him afterwards to another wedding. Just as Tony's career was nearly prevented by the U-boat, their marriage was nearly prevented by Marcelle's father. He knew what English people were like. He had seen English couples in hotels after dinner, reading and not speaking to each other before silently going up to bed. This was surely the only time in his life when Tony was nearly blackballed because he would have nothing to say.

I

Quinton's work in philosophy was marked by its range, its intellectual power, and its clarity. The range was unfashionable in the Oxford of his early days. He was against what he described as 'the market garden school of philosophy', where each person cultivates his own little strip, producing the ultimate account of the influence of Leibniz on Kant, or of proper names.

The clarity and intellectual power made him a stunningly good lecturer. My wife, when reading Biochemistry in the 1960s, went to a Quinton lecture about political philosophy. She still remembers the impression made by the clarity and power of what she called his Rolls Royce mind.

That clarity made him the sworn enemy of all philosophical obscurity and the bad writing linked to it. He detested the darkly portentous style of Heidegger. Noting scholarly disagreements about whether Hegel died of cholera or whether it was 'some kind of upper gastro-intestinal disease', he unkindly remarks that it is somehow typical of Hegel that the cause of his death should be so vague and ambiguous. And style is a matter where he manages to be gloriously unimpressed, at the same time by a great philosopher and by the culture of professional philosophy: 'Kant, with his university post, his regular habits, and the crabbed technicality of his writing, is more the ideal of a philosophy professor than of a philosopher proper.'

Quinton's own main published work consists of his book on metaphysics, *The Nature of Things* (London, 1973), his outline of a conservative political philosophy in *The Politics of Imperfection* (London, 1978), and of books of essays on an astonishingly wide-ranging set of philosophical, historical and cultural topics (*Thoughts and Thinkers*—London, 1982; *From Wodehouse to Wittgenstein: Essays*—Manchester, 1998; and *Of Men and Manners, Essays Historical and Philosophical*—Oxford, 2011.)

II

The Nature of Things was written in conscious reaction against the minutiae of the Oxford ordinary language philosophy, a reaction towards metaphysics, which he defined as 'the attempt to arrive by rational means at a general picture of the world'. It asked—and tried to answer—many of the largest questions in philosophy:

> What is the ultimate stuff or raw material of the world?
> Which of the many kinds of thing that the world seems to contain, really or fundamentally exists?
> What gives a thing—or a person—its identity across time?
> What makes some of our experiences those of a unified object existing independently of them?
> Does empirical knowledge have foundations in immediate awareness (whether of our own sensory experience or of physical objects), on which is built the superstructure of our knowledge of science, the past, other people's minds, and so on?

The answers, reflecting Quinton's sanity of judgement, added up to a materialist picture of the world, with no room left for divine or other supernatural intervention. (Lucretius might not have objected to the appropriation of his title.) The things we perceive without inference go beyond our own mental states to include objects in the world. Experience of these objects is the foundation of our knowledge of everything else. Experiences themselves are states of the brain. Quinton also gives a naturalistic account of values, which guide conduct through their links with desires. Morality is marked off from other values, not by some formal criterion but by its content. And, by the slightly brisk means of the claimed tautology that all desires are for satisfaction, he argues that this content is broadly utilitarian.

The book is a good one, systematic, generally well argued and with sane conclusions, but not one of ground-breaking originality. It shares another limitation with most of the philosophy of forty years ago. It is striking how the discussion of what is the ultimate stuff or raw material of the world has almost no contact with modern physics.

But the book's virtues are substantial. Quinton's large and discriminating familiarity with the history of philosophy liberated it from other forms of parochialism common in the analytical philosophy of its time. The range of reference is remarkable. Gilbert Ryle said it was a *summa.* Indeed it was, taking central questions about the world and our knowledge of it and giving a systematic account of possible philosophical answers to them. In this way it is a kind of Platonic ideal of a philosophy textbook. Yet the thinkers mentioned are never part of a mere historical survey, but always brought under control of an organised argument for Quinton's own naturalist worldview.

Perhaps this 'textbook' aspect is what led Quinton almost entirely to exclude from it his witty and sometimes devastating personal take on thinkers and ideas he opposed. Here his inimitable voice was, probably rightly, subordinated to unadorned argument. *Almost* entirely. Writing of Norman Malcolm's view that dreams are not experiences had during sleep, but are dispositions to tell stories when we wake up *as if* we had had such experiences, he calls arguing for this claim 'the philosophical equivalent of the Charge of the Light Brigade'.

The exclusion of serious reference to the sciences is a real and substantial limitation. But the clarity and verbal economy showed that the metaphysical project of using rational means to obtain a general picture of the world could avoid woolly speculation, and even to some extent be realised.

III

One of the features of both moral and political philosophy is the extent to which the broad rival parties and categories supposed to define the major debates are so blurred or porous. Adherence to a view such as utilitarianism or Kantianism in ethics, or to conservatism, liberalism or socialism in politics, tells so little about the actual content of someone's beliefs. Liberalism may take the form of Mill's principle defended in *On Liberty*, defended by him partly because it would encourage fuller rather than stunted versions of the good life, or it may take the modern American form of political neutrality between different versions of the good life. Utilitarianism takes very different forms according to the possible different conceptions of happiness and of human interests. And a utilitarian philosophy may inspire either political radicalism as in Bentham and Mill or conservatism as in Hume and to some extent in Sidgwick.

Quinton's ethical naturalism took a utilitarian form. And the utilitarianism took a conservative form. The conservatism was explored in his 1976 T. S. Eliot Memorial Lectures on *The Politics of Imperfection.* Characteristically (for Quinton and perhaps for conservatism) the nature of conservative thinking emerges from reflecting on its history. The subtitle of the lectures is *The Religious and Secular Traditions of Conservative Thought in England from Hooker to Oakeshott.* The religious tradition, in England linking conservatism especially to Anglican doctrines and institutions, did not ignite enthusiasm in one whose conservatism was part of a utilitarian outlook linked to philosophical naturalism.

Quinton characterised conservatism by different strands of thought, none of which were distinctively religious, and which found their fullest expression in Burke. One is respect for traditions, and the importance of preserving them. This is sometimes linked to belief in the organic nature of society: a society lives and grows, like a tree or a plant, and is not something like a machine that can be taken to bits and redesigned according to some blueprint. Another strand is scepticism, especially about political theories: political wisdom 'is not to be found in the theoretical speculations of isolated thinkers but in the historically accumulated social experience of the community as a whole'.

Another reason sometimes offered is the practical wisdom of our forebears: our constitutional, legal and political practices were not created out of some abstract doctrine but by wise continuing adaptation of them to give workable results in very different settings. Quinton was sceptical of the 'ancestral wisdom' view. When Evelyn Waugh was asked about how he was going to vote, he replied, 'I would not presume to advise my sovereign on her choice of ministers.' Quinton wrote that 'It is hard to be a conservative in the manner of Burke or Johnson in the present age.' To manage it, he thought, one would have to be either very imperceptive or else fall into the 'combative pretence' of comments like Waugh's. He sees the modern Conservative party as having effectively abandoned ancestral wisdom in favour of a meritocracy in which ability and effort are rewarded: 'The ancient constitutional pieties are invoked only for ritual purposes.'

Another defence of being guided by tradition is that of Michael Oakeshott. Central was Oakeshott's well-known opposition to 'rationalism' in politics, which he interpreted as formulating lists of clearly defined ends and then making technical choices about the most reliable and efficient ways of realising them. The opposition centred round the claim that such a project ignores all knowledge that is not technical, particularly the kinds of knowledge that cannot be articulated, but only imparted and acquired through participation and practice: the kinds of knowledge embodied in a society's traditions.

It is interesting to compare Oakeshott's and Quinton's similar but differently based versions of conservatism. They share the rejection of politics driven by the kind of ideology that tries to realise formulated abstract ends, but their reasons are very different. Quinton says of Oakeshott that his conservatism is much more exclusively epistemological than that of his predecessors. Quinton's conservatism is also to a large extent based on epistemological doubts, though on different ones. Quinton, whose commitment to rationality in *The Nature of Things* had not diminished when he wrote *The Politics of Imperfection*, was clearly a bit pained by Oakeshott's use of 'rationalism' to denote the rejected commitment to abstract ideology, pointing out that the term 'technical rationalism' might have been better. He grants that there is some plausibility in some versions of Oakeshott's claims about the priority of inarticulate practical knowledge, but sees them as too weak to form the basis of conservative thought.

Oakeshott was concerned to confine the activities of the state to such things as the making and enforcement of laws. But Quinton recognised that, while 'the all-engulfing kind of bureaucratic collectivism' was alarming, on the other hand he noted with apparent agreement that 'it has seemed not merely convenient, but imperative, for government to take on itself all sorts of functions that were previously discharged by other institutions, such as the Church or the family, or in a private, non-institutional way'. (One wonders if, at those meetings of the Conservative Philosophy Group, the then Mrs Thatcher heard this bit?) For Oakeshott the need to limit the state's activities came from our traditions. But, as Quinton pointed out, traditions evolve. His question (without mentioning these names) was: could the activities of Lloyd George, Keynes, Beveridge, Attlee and Bevan plausibly be excluded from our traditions? He called

Oakeshott's account of tradition a 'nostalgic illusion'. The vagueness of the appeal to tradition made it too insubstantial to do the work required.

Quinton himself believed that the desirability of setting limits to the more ideologically motivated state programmes came from the conservative's awareness of human imperfection. Because of human intellectual—especially epistemological—limitations, large, abstract projects of political change are likely to come unstuck and so should be avoided. And human moral imperfections mean that abuses need to be guarded against by the restraints of established customs, laws and institutions.

There is obviously considerable truth in both these points. But those of us less sympathetic to conservatism are likely to raise questions about the harm done when bad customs and institutions are among those already established. Was the abolition of slavery a large, abstract project? This problem faces most political positions. Modern conservatives are not sorry slavery was abolished. And modern radicals know that the French and Russian revolutions fell under the control of ideologues who were oblivious or uncaring about the horrendous human costs. Where do we draw the line: what is too large or too abstract a project to risk?

When he was giving a Tanner Lecture followed by a conference in Warsaw, during the communist period, Tony Quinton generously invited some of us to go with him. We were appalled by the secret police at the conference, by the general obstructiveness created in daily life by the bureaucracy, and by such things as the censorship of letters.

In *The Politics of Imperfection*, Quinton quotes Burke saying that no generation should 'think it among their rights to … commit waste on the inheritance, by destroying at their pleasure the whole original fabric of their society; hazarding to leave to those who come after them a ruin instead of a habitation … By this unprincipled facility of changing the State as often, and as much, and in as many ways, as there are floating fancies or fashions, the whole chain and community of the commonwealth would be broken. No one generation could link with the other. Men would become little better than the flies of a summer.' Tony was a conservative and I am not, but I cannot read him quoting this passage without remembering our shared Burkean reaction to a society made more like a ruin than a habitation. But we were also heartened by the wonderfully public disrespect our Polish hosts showed for the easily identifiable secret policeman, and by their determination that soon all this would be overthrown. Perhaps it is harder permanently to ruin a society than Burke thought.

IV

Richard Ellmann once said to me that Tony was a man with his own voice. In his writings, that voice is heard most in his memoir in *Before We Met* and in his books of essays on philosophical and cultural topics. (The final book of essays—*Of Men and Manners*—was posthumously edited by Sir Anthony Kenny.) These collections are perhaps the very best of his writings. A Quinton essay is rather like a good soufflé: enjoyable, easy to consume, and nourishing while being light in texture.

The breadth of these collections is suggested by the title of one of them—*From Wodehouse to Wittgenstein.* And even within a single essay the breadth can be remarkable. The one published in that book on 'Religion and science in three great civilisations' argues that the flourishing of science in the West as against China or India comes from the influence of Christianity as against Confucianism or Hinduism. The essay contrasts Chinese inventiveness in the Han dynasty (paper, magnets, water-wheels, printing and gunpowder) with the Chinese lack of mathematics and of fundamental research. It moves easily from there to the effects on science of the seventeenth-century vulgarisation of Hinduism and then to the seventeenth-century development in Christian Europe of analytic geometry, probability theory and the calculus.

Quinton claims that the naturalistic common sense of Confucianism did not encourage curiosity about any reality behind surface appearances. Chinese mathematics was for measuring land or counting money, not for calculations about the stars. The mindset was for peaceful coexistence with nature rather than any deep exploration of it. Hinduism, on the other hand, was thoroughly otherworldly, seeing nature as a kind of bad dream people should passively submit to in the hope of eventually liberating the soul from it. By contrast, Christianity taught that God had set creation to work according to intelligible laws that were not immediately obvious but which could be explored. This encouraged the idea that the natural world gave mankind the opportunity to explore its underlying nature and ultimately to put it to practical use.

Analogies are drawn with alternative approaches to epistemology and philosophy of science. Hinduism is likened to intuitionism, Confucianism to instrumentalism (the views of Berkeley, Mach and the pragmatists are said to be 'Chinese in spirit'), and the Christian or Western approach to Lockean realism. The latter is endorsed in a way that is consciously slightly comic. H. A. Prichard made a remark, meant seriously, but which has been mocked as absurd: 'In the end, when the truth is known, I think it will turn out to be not very far from the philosophy of Locke.' Quinton quotes this, endorsing it, but in words of self-conscious mild pomposity signalling awareness of the absurd side of Prichard's testimony: 'I must confess that I share the belief attributed to my distinguished Oxford predecessor ...' He loved to tease. One form of this was to say things he really believed in a tone of mock seriousness that might leave people wondering. He knew what he was talking about and saw no need to be earnest about it.

Only someone with a wider range than I have would be in a position to assess the truth of the main claims of the essay. But one question is whether Judaism does not deserve some of the credit here given exclusively to Christianity. Christianity's creation story is taken from Judaism. The idea of the natural world reflecting the mind of a God both immanent and transcendent is shared by the two religions. There is also the history of Jewish contributions to Western scientific and other thought, a contribution surely disproportionate to population size. In any competition between religions about whose believers (or whose secular grandchildren) have done most to look for explanations beneath the surface of things, Judaism would deserve to be at least a finalist. Einstein, Marx, Freud and Wittgenstein would not be a bad opening bid.

The essay encapsulates virtues that are quintessentially Quintonian. The philosophy is not presented as some dry academic argument, but appears in a larger context of religion, science and history. There is the breadth of learning in a small compass. And the learning is not filed away in some antiquarian way. It is put to work to argue for a claim which is clear, important and, above all, interesting.

Even the slighter essays usually have enjoyable touches. In a review of Pinkard's biography of Hegel (published in *On Men and Manners*), Quinton makes the by now platitudinous point that blanket condemnation of Hegel is undiscriminating. But he follows it with the splendid qualification that espousing Hegel's logic would be like buying tsarist government bonds. (Equally obvious, but stylishly so.) And the essay unpromisingly titled 'The tribulations of authors' (in *From Wodehouse to Wittgenstein*), which is partly about original drafts that were lost or destroyed, gave me two bits of miscellaneous information I am glad to have. T. E. Lawrence lost the manuscript of *Seven Pillars of Wisdom* by leaving it in the waiting room at Didcot Station. And the low side of one's nature finds it hard not to laugh on hearing that the manuscript of Carlyle's purple-passaged *French Revolution* was used by John Stuart Mill's maid to light a fire.

Among the more major contributions is a cluster of three essays—also included in *From Wodehouse to Wittgenstein*—about what the point of universities is, and about the relation between them and philosophy. These together add up to a strong defence of a broad and humane learning against the narrowing academic professionalism that is now such a threat to it.

The central essay is on 'The idea of a university: Newman's and others''. As might be expected, Quinton was not an unreserved admirer of Newman's beliefs and writings. He quotes the preposterous claim that 'it would be a gain to the country were it vastly more superstitious', as well as the famously absurd and repellent view Newman attributes to the Church that 'it were better for the sun and moon to drop from heaven, for the earth to fail and for the many millions who are upon it to die of starvation in extremest agony ... than one soul ... should commit one single venial sin, should tell one wilful untruth'. Quinton comments that 'to ascribe such frenzied cruelty to the Church must itself be an untruth, even if hysterical rather than wilful'.

Despite these reservations, he rightly admires much of *The Idea of a University*. What he most admires are two of the book's doctrines about knowledge: that it is a good in itself (though not necessarily an absolute good) and that knowledge is a unity. That knowledge is a good in itself is contrasted with the view that it is *only* of instrumental value, useful for its practical applications. This first doctrine is a platitude, likely only to be denied by Mr Gradgrind or by some of his descendents who, having become politicians and civil servants, managed to stop funding for the humanities in universities.

The second doctrine, that knowledge is a unity, might seem an uplifting vacuity, but Quinton brings out the content Newman gives it. Newman's version of knowledge was intellectual culture. That, in turn, was 'not high expertise in some branch of learning, the attribute of the scholarly specialist, but a just appreciation of the bearing of the different departments of universal knowledge on each other. A scholar who lacks intellectual culture will be the grotesque pedant of traditional comedy.' For Newman this was a justification of institutions like the Oxford colleges, with students and teachers drawn from many different fields and so having the chance to get to know a bit about subjects not their own.

The account of intellectual culture as a just appreciation of the bearing on each other of the different departments of universal knowledge is, to the degree to which it is attainable, not a bad picture of Quinton himself. And he endorses the value of such culture, saying that there is 'no more eloquent and finely judged defence of intellectual culture than Newman's'.

The commitment to Newman's vision of intellectual culture leads, in 'Reflections on the graduate school', to a fairly sceptical view of much graduate study in the humanities and the social sciences. He is broadly against its excessive professionalism. He distinguishes between professional graduate schools (in subjects such as law or medicine) and academic graduate schools, whose function he sees as to train university teachers.

Obviously university teachers need to understand their subject and keep up with developments in it. And, as Newman believed, they should see their subject in the context of some larger intellectual landscape. But, Quinton wonders, do they have to do research, particularly of the kind typical of the Ph.D.? The long period spent on the Ph.D. gives universities a supply of cheap teaching, but 'at the cost of a good deal of distress to those who supply it'. And he doubts whether there is much correlation between successful research in a subject and being good at teaching it. (Possibly remembering Paul Grice's largely silent tutorials, he says that in his own case as an undergraduate he did not see the correlation.)

In the essay on 'Philosophy as an institution', Quinton asks what kind of institution it is, and characteristically his answer draws on philosophy's history. He claims that it has alternated between mainly literary phases and predominantly academic and scholarly periods. From the middle of the nineteenth century it has grown more academic and has 'perhaps unfortunately, more and more addressed itself to an academic, thoroughly professional audience'.

And one bad thing about this professionalisation is that 'academic philosophy tends towards an introversion which is scholastic in the bad sense of the word and from which it can be rescued only by individual initiatives of thought from outside'. In this context he cannot resist (and probably was right not to have resisted) a dig at his own local philosophical environment: 'Scholasticism declined from the mid-fourteenth century, but has remained alive to this day . . . in all Christian countries, Protestant ones included, Aristotle remained the primary philosophical authority in universities until the nineteenth century. I sometimes think he still is in Oxford.'

V

I conclude with a brief personal memory of Tony as a colleague.

When David Wiggins gave up his Fellowship, New College was really looking for another distinguished classical philosopher. I was a Greekless person, but somehow Tony persuaded the College to have a second modern philosopher and to gamble on me. I have been grateful ever since. He was the easiest and most generous of colleagues. Once I was away for several weeks with mumps. I dreaded the amount of teaching there would be to catch up. When I got back, I found that Tony had taken over all my tutorials in addition to his own. He did not tell me this, but the undergraduates did. He would have hated to be held up as an example of moral virtue, but he did manage to do good by stealth.

He also set an example of disregarding conventional opinion, acting and talking with a glorious indifference to all the pressures in academic life towards a grey conformity and professionalism. At a time when most Oxford tutors rode bicycles or drove Morris Travellers, he was the uninhibited driver of a stylish Cadillac.

I loved the wit, and how unrehearsed it was. One year, at the interviews for the Kennedy scholarships, in the early days when *The Independent* was worth reading, I was one of several trustees who turned up carrying the paper. In a flash Tony was expressing pleasure at this herd of independent minds. His stylish but unmalicious teasing was a joy.

Tony died on 19 June 2010. Like Hume, he faced death without wobbling in his scepticism about an afterlife. I don't want him to be wrong about that, and I don't think he was. But, contemplating the bare possibility that there may be an afterlife, there is one cheering thought. Heaven, since Tony's arrival, must be a lot less pious and boring than before.

JONATHAN GLOVER
King's College London

GEOFFREY RICKMAN

Geoffrey Edwin Rickman
1932–2010

Geoffrey Edwin Rickman, Emeritus Professor of Roman History at the University of St Andrews, died on 8 February 2010, aged 77. A man of great wit and humour, he was also a remarkable scholar, an inspiring teacher, a wise administrator, and a major figure in the life of two of great institutions of learning, the University of St Andrews and the British School at Rome.

Geoffrey Rickman was born on 9 October 1932 at Cherāt, a hill sanatorium and cantonment, sixty-five miles from the Khyber Pass and thirty-four miles south east of Peshawar, in what was then Naushahra district of the North West Frontier Province of British India, now the HQ of the Special Service Group of the Pakistan army. His father, Charles Edwin Rickman, was a regular soldier, serving as a Company Sergeant Major in 1st Battalion Hampshire Regiment in Naushahra; he had joined the army under age by lying about his date of birth and during the First World War had fought at Gallipoli and in Mesopotamia, being Mentioned in Despatches. He remained in the army, serving in North Africa in the Second World War, and was invalided out shortly before the landings in Sicily in 1943, by which time he was a Regimental Sergeant Major. The hill station at Cherāt was the closest place to the Afghan border that families were allowed to be and in later life Geoffrey would attribute the fragility of his teeth to the diet his mother experienced in this remote place. His mother, Ethel Ruth Mary Hill, was born in Ely in Cambridgeshire and after school had trained as a dressmaker before going into service, initially as a schoolroom maid and rising to be lady's maid to the wife of General

Biographical Memoirs of Fellows of the British Academy, XI, 533–543.

Sir Peter Strickland when he was Military Governor of Cork in Ireland during the 'Troubles'. It was there she met Geoffrey's father whom she subsequently married in the Lady Chapel of Ely Cathedral. Geoffrey was the third of four brothers, the second of whom died in India.

When Geoffrey was two years old the family returned to England and settled in Winchester, where his fourth brother, Harry, was born. There he attended a local primary school and then, after passing the scholarship examination at the second attempt, Peter Symonds' School, a voluntary controlled grammar school for boys in Winchester, whence he proceeded with a State Scholarship to Brasenose College, Oxford in 1951. There, after a not particularly distinguished performance in Classical Moderations, he took a first class degree in Literae Humaniores in Trinity Term 1955. At Brasenose he was taught ancient philosophy by J. L. Ackrill, who had recently come as a fellow of the college and who (as he later remarked with nostalgic incredulity) for a time led Rickman to believe that he loved Aristotle. Ancient History Geoffrey claimed to have found 'irritating—a sort of difficult crossword puzzle for superior people'—though his interest in Roman history was awakened when, following the death in 1953 of the Brasenose tutor in Ancient History, Michael Holroyd, he was sent to Eric Gray at Christ Church.

After his graduation he did his National Service from 1955 to 1957, most of which was spent in the Joint Services School for Linguists (JSSL), first at Bodmin and then at a disused airfield outside the fishing village of Crail in the East Neuk of Fife. The JSSL was set up after the war to provide intensive courses in foreign languages, especially Russian, for those who showed an aptitude for them in order to provide interpreters for radio surveillance and intelligence work. There Geoffrey achieved a certificate in Russian and also, in occasional respites from the highly pressurised work schedule, his first acquaintance with St Andrews, ten miles northwest of Crail. He was later to recall his first sight of what he described as a magical city from the coastal path, little realising that it was to be his home for nearly fifty years.

In 1957 he returned to Oxford where he studied for the Diploma in Classical Archaeology, which he completed in one year rather than the usual two and which was awarded with distinction in 1958. He was particularly influenced by Bernard Ashmole, the Lincoln Professor of Classical Art and Archaeology, by Ian Richmond, the Professor of the Archaeology of the Roman Empire, and by the newly appointed Reader in Classical Archaeology, William Llewellyn Brown, who was to die at the tragically early age of 34 in 1958. Geoffrey's choice of the classical archaeology diploma marked a significant change in his approach to ancient history, and one which was to characterise his work from then on. Although he had shown himself a skilled practitioner in the style of history which was then dominant, especially in Oxford, of scrupulous investigation and interpretation of the ancient literary sources, he found himself as a result of his two years away from the world of academic scholarship dissatisfied with it as means of discovering the realities of the ancient world. Now, and increasingly over the rest of his career, he wanted to know not only what the literary remains of antiquity could tell us but also what actually happened; and it was this that directed him towards the examination of the archaeological record. Thus, after his success in the Diploma in Classical Archaeology, he proceeded to the British School at Rome (BSR), aided by the award by the Craven Committee of the Henry Francis Pelham Studentship in 1958, to work on the granaries (*horrea*) of the port of Rome at Ostia which was the basis for a D.Phil. thesis, entitled 'The Design, Structure and Organisation of *Horrea* under the Roman Empire', supervised by Ian Richmond.

His year at the BSR was to prove a turning point in many ways. It took him thirty-six hours by boat, train and bus to reach the School, and his first unnerving sight was of Lutyens' magnificent façade atop the great stairs. Inside was a unique world—John Ward-Perkins, the Director of the School, in the midst of one of Britain's truly great archaeological enterprises, the Tiber Valley Survey; his wife Margaret, described by Geoffrey as universal mother, aunt, nanny, nurse and hostess; and scholars of future renown. In Geoffrey's year the latter included not only Peter Dronke, subsequently a great medieval Italian literature expert, but also, unlike Oxford, artists and architects: 'A different non-verbal world of effort and achievement was opened up,' as Geoffrey wrote later in the School's Centenary volume. A photograph in the BSR's collection shows him seated on a row of ancient lavatories at Ostia, and alongside him: Martin Frederiksen, one of Britain's finest ancient historians, who died far too young; Derek Hill, whose beneficence to the artists of the School was remarkable and remains invaluable after his death; and Sir Anthony Blunt, then simply known as one of the world's great art historians. Amongst others who were there was Eric Gray, who had tutored him at Oxford.

Perhaps more importantly still it was in this year that Geoffrey, returning briefly to England, married Anna Wilson, whom he had first met nine years earlier when she was a pupil at St Swithun's School in Winchester, and they took a honeymoon trip to Greece before returning to the BSR. They stayed on in Rome for an extra month, according to Geoffrey because they had had such fun that he had forgotten to do what he said he was going to do, which was measure the buildings of Ostia. Geoffrey's engagement with Ostia was the beginning of an intellectual journey which, like his marriage to Anna, was to last for the rest of his life.

They returned to Oxford later that year, and Geoffrey held a Junior Research Fellowship at The Queen's College, Oxford for the next three years. This enabled him to complete his D.Phil. thesis, which was examined by Sheppard Frere and Russell Meiggs, both of whom were to provide invaluable help in the preparation of the publications which emerged from it. The viva took place in February 1963, but by this time Geoffrey and Anna had moved to St Andrews on Geoffrey's appointment to a Lectureship in Ancient History. This was to be his home for the rest of his life.

Classics at St Andrews when Geoffrey arrived there was flourishing, its student numbers assisted by the requirement for almost all those studying for a degree in the Faculty of Arts to take General Humanity, the name for the first level class in Latin.[1] The Chair of Humanity had just been vacated by the formidable Thomas Erskine Wright and his successor in 1963 was Gordon Williams, formerly a Fellow of Balliol College, Oxford, who was to be himself succeeded ten years later by Robert Ogilvie, another Fellow of Balliol, when in 1974 he moved to Yale. The Professor of Greek was Kenneth Dover, who again had come from Balliol in 1955. One of the foremost Hellenists of his generation, Dover presided over Classics at St Andrews until his departure to become President of Corpus Christi College, Oxford in 1976, and he returned there in 1986 after retiring from Corpus (he had already been elected Chancellor of the University in 1981). Geoffrey told how in Oxford, after he had been appointed at St Andrews but before he had taken up his post, he met Peter Parsons, later to be Regius Professor of Greek at Oxford, in the street, who said to him, 'How brave of you, Geoffrey, to go to St Andrews where Kenneth Dover is. I would not have had such courage.'

When Geoffrey began teaching at St Andrews he was a one-man department, a relatively insignificant island, overlooked by the towering cliffs of Greek and Humanity. However his colleagues in the Classics departments understood better than some in other disciplines the problems he faced. A senior member of the science faculty, to whom Geoffrey

[1] It was some time after I arrived at St Andrews in 1972 that a member of the Department of Humanity explained to me that the name derived not from humanity as opposed to inhumanity but Humanity as opposed to Divinity.

had confessed that he really didn't know what to say to first- and second-level students, advised that for the first couple of years he should simply talk about the topic of his doctoral thesis—Geoffrey observed to me much later that the notion of students whose only exposure to the ancient world was detailed knowledge of the measurements of Roman granaries was too horrendous to contemplate. But it was not only his realisation that the two short periods of history that he had studied so intensely at Oxford would not provide the material for the much broader approach expected at St Andrews that presented challenges: the degree structure was unlike any he had previously encountered, with students being required in the six classes they took in their first two years to cover four different subjects before either completing an ordinary MA (still the norm for many) by taking two further classes or entering two further years of Honours classes in one or both of the second-level subjects taken in the second year to complete an MA (Hons). This broad and flexible structure meant that many students in their first two years took first-year classes unrelated to the main subject they intended when they first matriculated, and some were as a result able to change that original intention without the need of any special permission. The MA, both Ordinary and Honours, was still a degree of the Faculty of Arts rather than of any department. Furthermore the teaching methods in St Andrews in 1962 were very different from those Geoffrey had experienced as an Oxford undergraduate. Whereas in Oxford the main focus of teaching was the weekly tutorial and the essays or other work prepared for it, with lectures providing additional support, in the Scottish universities the lecture was the primary mode, supplemented to an increasing extent over the next years by tutorial groups. All these potential hazards Geoffrey was not only to cope with over the next thirty-five years but to turn to positive advantages as he effectively created the Department of Ancient History.

That is not to say that he began the department. The first lecturer in Ancient History at St Andrews was Peter Brunt, appointed to St Andrews in 1947 and later Camden Professor in Oxford, and he was followed by E. S. Stavely and Ursula Hall, both of whom made important contributions to the discipline. Moreover Geoffrey collected around him a remarkable set of colleagues, some of whom remained in St Andrews in the flourishing and supportive milieu which he established, while others went on to be equally successful elsewhere. It is no disrespect to any of these, however, to say that Ancient History in St Andrews, and the esteem with which it is regarded in the world of classical scholarship across the globe, is Geoffrey's creation.

The first additional member of staff was John Davies in 1965, who returned to Oxford to a Fellowship at Oriel in 1968 and in 1977 took up the Rathbone Chair of Ancient History at Liverpool. He was succeeded in 1968 by Michel Austin. My appointment in 1972 was to the third post in Ancient History. In ten years, Geoffrey had increased the size of the teaching staff by 300 per cent, and with Jill Harries's appointment four years later the department had four lecturers. That increase, in a period which was not favourable to growth in universities, least of all in the study of the ancient world, was attributable almost entirely to Geoffrey's brilliance as a teacher. In those years the first year class grew from some twenty to thirty students to well over a hundred, and the reason for this could be seen in what happened every year. In those days, students enrolled for their classes at the beginning of the session and had four weeks in which they could transfer, if they so wished, into a different class. At the end of the fourth week, the curtain came down and students were fixed in their classes for the rest of the academic session. Year after year, the first-year class in Ancient History began with three weeks of lectures by Geoffrey, and year after year our numbers grew dramatically as those weeks proceeded. Even in week 4, when the class was usually addressed not by Geoffrey but by me, the numbers did not fall sufficiently to dent what was, for a department of our size, remarkably large. Geoffrey was able, through a combination of a passionate understanding of the ancient world (even of a period which was not his speciality), an engaging wit and a careful selection of slides (always including one with Anna alongside an ancient monument), to charm his students into an engagement with peoples and civilisations far distant from their own. The results are well summarised in the preface of the volume of essays presented to him on his sixty-fifth birthday: 'For a whole generation of St Andrews students Geoffrey Rickman brought to his subject a unique style and glitter. A master of the spoken and of the written word, he taught that study of the ancient world was enormous fun as well as a rigorous scholarly enterprise that should address fundamental questions.... Under his direction, the department grew in size and range of courses, and St Andrews was put on the map.'[2] And it continued to do so. Michael Whitby was appointed after my departure to the Chair of Classics at Edinburgh in 1987 and stayed, latterly as Head of Department, until 1996, when he became Professor of Classics and Ancient History at Warwick. In 1992, when Geoffrey took up the

[2] Michel Austin, Jill Harries and Christopher Smith (eds.), *Modus Operandi: Essays in Honour of Geoffrey Rickman* (London, 1998), p. xiii.

major administrative role of Master of the United College of St Salvator and St Leonard, Christopher Smith arrived in St Andrews and remained there until his secondment as Director of the British School at Rome in 2009. Jon Coulston, who joined the department in 1995, brought a new strength in Roman archaeology, and when Geoffrey retired in 1997 the university appointed Greg Woolf to a new Chair of Ancient History.

The success of the department was Geoffrey's doing; but it was not just because he was a fine scholar and a brilliant teacher. He was also astonishingly humane. Academic life in the ancient Scottish universities in the 1970s when I arrived there was still notably hierarchic, a remnant of the time when a department had consisted of the Professor and his (almost always 'his') assistants. Not so the Department of Ancient History, which still in the late 1970s consisted of a senior lecturer and three lecturers. Geoffrey may have been *primus inter pares* but he was more *par* than *primus*. I recall John Davies telling me as I prepared to leave Oxford to move to St Andrews that the department was in theory a hierarchy but in practice a soviet. Geoffrey was always notoriously modest and, if I have a fault to find in this man, it is that he was too modest, too inclined to underrate himself, if not his colleagues. It took considerable efforts on our part to persuade him to assent to being put forward for the professorial chair he was awarded in 1981, and he only agreed then because we insisted that he was undermining our chances of promotion by refusing his.

Within the department, he was immensely generous and concerned about the development of his younger colleagues; and in my case (and, I am sure, that of others) he was hugely influential. As a historian, he was insistent on the significance of the actualities of life in the Roman world, on the *Realien*, the ways in which the ancients actually lived and worked. When I came to St Andrews, I was well-drilled in the methods of ancient history as it was then practised in the University of Oxford, and could analyse the writings of ancient authors and arrange the results into pleasing and not implausible patterns. I remember well Geoffrey's reaction to the first piece that I took to him for advice about possible publication. It was an ingenious article on the silver mines in Spain, dealing in particular with the interpretation of passages in the historian Polybius and the geographer Strabo. 'You have been very clever with the sources,' he said, 'but do you have any idea at all about how they got the silver out of the ground?' My article was radically reshaped and immensely improved by my attempts to find an answer to Geoffrey's question; and since then I have been a determined, if not always effective, follower of the Rickman '*What-actually-happened?*' school of ancient historians, and have attempted to show how

Geoffrey's method should be applied to subjects that I have tried to explore, such as the workings of Roman law and Roman imperialism, though they are quite different from those, such as the investigation of grain-supplies and ports, for which he developed it so successfully.

Outwith St Andrews, Geoffrey's best known academic work is contained in two books and a series of just over a dozen articles. In terms of sheer bulk, this is a not a large output; but its significance is far greater than its size. His first publication, the book *Roman Granaries and Store Buildings* (Cambridge, 1971), was based on his D.Phil. thesis. Such works often reveal their origins only too clearly in a worthy if somewhat stilted style, more suitable for examiners than for subsequent readers, and in a relentless concentration on the topic in hand. These fears were recorded by Peter Salway as he took up the book for review; however, as he went on to say, 'it turned out to be so well written and the author so capable of drawing out the human implications of the buildings that it proved, to the present reviewer at least, one of the most interesting books read recently'.[3] The work was divided into two sections, the first on civil *horrea*, with particular focus on Ostia and Rome, and the second dealing with military *horrea*, especially in Britain and Germany, where most are to be found. Throughout the buildings themselves are described in detail and illustrated by excellent plans (and rather less excellent photographs); but this is far from an archaeological catalogue. At the end of each description a brief section is added which places the building in its context and shows how it worked as a store-building at the various stages of its history. This was supplemented by a chapter on the legal processes involved in the hiring out of civil *horrea* in Rome and another on the organisation of military storehouses in the early and late imperial periods. The reviews at the time were not, of course, uniformly favourable (Geoffrey was particularly mortified by the observation by J. K. Anderson that he hoped that the 'Vale of Strathmore' would not become standard usage: 'Strath' was self-explanatory[4]); but the value of the book was widely recognised both for its subject matter and for its accessibility and it was predicted that it would long remain the standard work on the topic. And so it has remained.

Nine years later he produced a second book, *The Corn Supply of Ancient Rome* (Oxford, 1980), largely written during a three-month spell at the British School at Rome during a period of study leave. Although this is a very different book from his first, covering in a more discursive

[3] Peter Salway, 'Roman storehouses', *Classical Review*, NS 24 (1974), 117.

[4] J. K. Anderson, *Classical Philology*, 68 (1973), 234–5.

style the vast question of the provisioning of the largest city of antiquity across half a millennium, its basic approach is the same. His preface puts it thus:

> This book is a history of the corn supply of ancient Rome. The subject has interested me ever since I was an undergraduate, when I often felt impatient with the traditional topics on which I was asked by kindly tutors to write essays. It was an undeniable exhilaration, in the words of Louis MacNeice: 'to draw the cork out of an old conundrum and watch the paradoxes fizz', but what I wanted to know was how the ancient world really worked.

What he attempted to do was 'to produce a readable narrative, unclogged by too much scholarship but setting out a large selection of the evidence available, and drawing attention to the problems which seem to me particularly important and worth discussion'. In this he undoubtedly succeeded. The book begins with a chapter on the governing factors, following it with three on the Republic, on what he saw as the crucial transition under Pompey, Caesar and Augustus, and on developments in the first two centuries AD. Three chapters on the corn lands, on transport, storage and prices and on corn distributions are followed by another on the late empire and a concluding epilogue. Discussions of a number of detailed questions are included in eleven appendices. This was a remarkable and pioneering piece of work, the first to appear in English on its subject, and has proved its worth, both in giving students access to the complexities of the methods, the politics and the economics of so essential a part of the life of Rome and the Roman world, and in promoting and provoking the studies of other scholars, which have become increasingly numerous in the decades since its publication.

After his work on the corn supply, it was perhaps inevitable that Geoffrey should turn his attention to the ports of the Mediterranean. Between 1985 and 2008 he published ten articles on Roman ports, with the original intention of writing a book on the subject. As time went by (and as he was increasingly engaged with the administration of his university) he became ever more aware of the immensity of his project and, although he has left copious notes as well as the typically vivid and astute accounts to be found in his preparatory publications, it became increasingly unlikely that it would ever be finished. After the onset of the pulmonary fibrosis which led to his death two years later, he wrote no more on the subject. By then he knew (though was surprised to know) the respect in which he was held by his colleagues. He had been a Fellow of the Society of Antiquaries of London since 1966 and twice served on the Council of the Society for the Promotion of Roman Studies (in 1970–2 and 1988–91), but was genuinely astonished to be elected a Fellow of the British Academy in 1989. He was elected Fellow of the Royal Society of Edinburgh in 2001.

In 2002, in his speech at his retirement as Chairman of the British School at Rome Council, Geoffrey Rickman declared 'I have been a very lucky man. I have loved two institutions and one woman in my life, and it has been my good fortune to have spent most of my life with all three—the University of St Andrews, the British School at Rome, and my wife Anna.' The importance to him of the BSR has already been noted but his support and untiring work for the School went far beyond the early years in which he found such inspiration there. A regular visitor at the School and a continuing encourager of those whom he met there, he became a member of the Faculty of Archaeology, History and Letters there in 1979 and Chairman of the Faculty from 1983 to 1987. He also strongly supported one of the BSR's most significant recent archaeological projects, the investigation of the site near Fiumicino simply known as Portus, the Port, and the network of ports connected to it. Following his retiral at St Andrews in 1997, he became Chairman of the School's Council in 1997 and, with the then Director, Professor Andrew Wallace-Hadrill, oversaw and enabled the most significant development of its buildings since the original construction in 1916: a library extension, and a new lecture theatre, internal redevelopment and external improvement, utterly transformed the School.

At St Andrews his acute intelligence and sense of duty, and above all his integrity, made him an outstanding administrator. When the three departments of Greek, Humanity and Ancient History were brought together in a single School in 1990, he was the obvious choice for its first Head; and two years later, he was appointed to the office of Master of the United College, which had in earlier years involved the responsibility for discipline of students in the Faculties of Arts and Science but which now included far wider responsibilities. As such he oversaw major changes in the university, including the restructuring of the teaching patterns, and achieved them with his inimitable combination of tact, incisiveness and good humour.

As a scholar (a word he would have hated), an educator and an administrator Geoffrey Rickman was outstanding; but that gives only a partial picture of the man. Though he always claimed to be inherently lazy, his zest for the exploration of the realities of the ancient world and for communicating them to his students and his love for and practical devotion to the University of St Andrews and the BSR give the lie to this oft-repeated misapprehension of himself. He was cultured in ways that are not always those of a university professor, with a particular and abiding love of opera. He swam whenever he could (including visits to the elderly Infirmary Street baths when visiting Edinburgh as an external examiner); and he would regularly take himself down to the West Sands at St Andrews to walk up and down its two-mile length to clear his head and sort out problems, whether academic or administrative. He was a rich and complex man, and an essential part of that complexity was a simple integrity. He was, to quote again from the preface to his Festschrift of 1997, a connoisseur of life, a man who mastered the art of human relations to an uncommon degree.

JOHN RICHARDSON
University of Edinburgh

Note. In compiling this memoir I have been greatly helped by Mrs Anna Rickman, by Geoffrey's brother, Harry Rickman, and by Professors Jill Harries and Christopher Smith.

BRIAN SIMPSON *Caroline Pannell 1999*

Alfred William Brian Simpson
1931–2011

ALFRED WILLIAM BRIAN SIMPSON (generally known as Brian) died on 10 January 2011 at his home in Sandwich, Kent, aged 79. Brian was a deeply committed scholar who wore his learning lightly. He combined being unequivocally committed to excellence in scholarship with a gift for a good story that made him a superb raconteur and an inspirational teacher. He was tolerant of human foibles except pomposity, self-deprecatingly witty, excellent company, and a natural storyteller. The editors of the Festschrift published in his honour in 2001 confessed in their introduction that they had thought seriously of sub-titling the volume 'Essays in Law, History, Philosophy, *and Fun*'.[1] But there was a darker side to Brian's personality, and there were periods of depression, ill health and marital breakdown. In particular, he retained a degree of self-doubt and he was often his own harshest critic.[2]

[1] K. O'Donovan and G. R. Rubin (eds.), *Human Rights and Legal History: Essays in Honour of Brian Simpson* (Oxford, 2001), p. 6.

[2] A note on sources: in addition to the published sources, cited according to the usual conventions, I have drawn on Brian's own unpublished autobiographical material. These were treated with a degree of caution, given the context in which they were written, near the end of his life when the completion of his final book was a much higher priority. I have drawn on these without further citation; Brian's views, if otherwise unattributed, are derived from these sources. In addition, I have drawn, with permission, on unpublished discussions of Brian's work by Baroness Hale, FBA, Paul Brand, FBA, Nuala Mole, and John Langbein. These were presented at a Memorial Service for Brian held in Oxford on 11 June 2011, and are cited respectively in the form: BHM, PBM, NMM, and JLM.

Biographical Memoirs of Fellows of the British Academy, XI, 547–581.

Early upbringing and education

Brian Simpson was born in Kendal, Westmorland on 17 August 1931, the son of the Revd Bernard W. Simpson[3] and Mary E. Simpson. Apart from the fact that his mother was an Irish Protestant of partly Huguenot descent, little else is known of her background. His father came from a Yorkshire farming family, although he had not been brought up on a farm himself. They were both graduates of Trinity College, Dublin, where presumably they met. He took a BA in the winter of 1915 and a BD in the summer of 1919. After ordination, he became a curate in a Dublin parish between 1915 and 1918 (and so was present in Dublin for the Easter Rising in 1916 and its aftermath). He and his wife subsequently served as missionaries in the Fukien Province of China between 1918 and 1928 (with one extended leave in Ireland between 1924–5), initially with the Church Missionary Society[4] and then the Dublin University Mission. On leaving China in 1928, they returned to Ireland, and his father served as Rector of Borrisokane, County Tipperary until 1930. Under family pressure, he moved back to England, becoming Vicar of Firbank with Howgill, Westmorland, where he was living at the time of Brian's birth. Brian grew up with two siblings: an elder sister, Dorothy, who became a schoolteacher (another sister, Margery, died as a baby in China), and an elder brother, Edward, who became a doctor after military service with the 1/10 Gurkha Rifles. Although they lived in genteel poverty, life in Firbank Vicarage gave Brian an enduring affection for the northern countryside, and in later life he often returned to the area. At times, he claimed that he only felt truly happy when walking on northern hills or fishing in northern rivers.

Once he was seven he was sent away to the private preparatory boarding school, Lancing House, in Lowestoft, Suffolk, to which Edward had been sent. Lancing House was chosen because it sent boys to St John's, Leatherhead, which offered cheap rates for parsons' sons. It was owned by Kenneth and Edith Milliken, who had achieved some celebrity by pioneering the teaching of history through the use of lead soldiers and cardboard models.[5] In 1939 Lancing House closed, possibly connected with the outbreak of war, and Milliken took over the Junior House at

[3] The Revd Simpson subsequently became an Honorary Canon of Bradford Cathedral (1958–61).

[4] See Jocelyn Murray, *Proclaim the Good News: a Short History of the Church Missionary Society* (London, 1985).

[5] They subsequently published a book on the subject: Edith Milliken and Kenneth Milliken, *Handwork Methods in the Teaching of History* second edition (Exeter, 1949).

Oakham School;[6] Brian and his brother were amongst the boys who moved with him. Brian took what was then called the School Certificate examinations when he was twelve, being a precocious child. He then went into the Classical Sixth. Brian stayed in the Classical Sixth until he took Higher School Certificate in Greek and Latin after two years; he performed well but not exceptionally. The standard he then attained would not at this time have been sufficient to give him a chance of a classical scholarship at Oxford or Cambridge.

By now he appreciated the limits of the classical education offered, and moved to the History Sixth under Robert Duesbury, a quite outstanding teacher who came to be idolised by his pupils.[7] He took the Higher School Certificate with history as his main subject when he was sixteen. He then sat for a history scholarship examination in The Queen's College, Oxford (Milliken had been a student there and this may explain his choice of Queen's), and was awarded an Eglesfield Scholarship, which was a closed scholarship only available to natives of the counties of Cumberland and Westmorland. Brian's subsequent academic work always emphasised the complexity of the world we live in. He considered that this approach was significantly affected by his historical studies at Oakham. There he read Arnold Toynbee's *A Study of History*[8] and found his attempts to detect recurrent patterns in the rise and fall of civilisations wholly unconvincing. Instead, he was permanently influenced by the views of H. A. L. Fisher,[9] whom he read at Oakham under the guidance of Duesbury, who was unable to see any pattern in history.

National Service

Brian left Oakham in 1949 for National Service, and was at first placed in the Royal Army Educational Corps. He underwent officer training at

[6] According to David Sugarman, Oakham was 'a direct grant school that had become in effect the boys' grammar school for the county of Rutland, but with an independent boarding element': David Sugarman, 'Beyond ignorance and complacency: Robert Stevens' journey through *Lawyers and the Courts*', *International Journal of the Legal Profession*, 16(1) (2009), 7, 11.

[7] Robert Stevens, another legal historian who attended Duesbury's classes at much the same time, also considered him an inspirational teacher, from whom Stevens received 'a first rate training as a historian'. Sugarman, 'Beyond ignorance and complacency', p. 11.

[8] Arnold J. Toynbee, *A Study of History* (Oxford, 1934–61). Volumes 1–10 of the 12 vols. had been published by that time.

[9] Probably H. A. L. Fisher, *A History of Europe from the Beginning of the 18th Century to 1937* (London, 1952).

Eaton Hall OCTU and was commissioned into the 4th East Yorks Regiment, the 15th of Foot. Officers could express preferences for where they would serve, and Brian claims to have 'opted for units with funny names: the Trucial Oman Levies, the Somaliland Scouts, and the Royal West African Frontier Force'. He was posted to the Nigeria Regiment, part of the Royal West African Frontier Force. He served in Zaria, Enugu, Lagos and finally Abeokuta, where he commanded a company. His subsequent descriptions of National Service rivalled Evelyn Waugh's in capturing the absurdities of military life.[10] (He was once one of the two officers present at a mutiny. Order was restored, he said, 'by masterful inaction'.) There is little doubt that this period contributed to his fascination with the British colonial period and the end of Empire, and that he much enjoyed his time in Nigeria. After leaving the regular army he stayed in the Territorial Army with the 4th East Yorks for some years, eventually being promoted to Captain.

Oxford undergraduate days

In the autumn of 1951, he went up to The Queen's College, Oxford, and decided to read Law (Jurisprudence as it was then termed) rather than modern history.[11] He was fortunate to be tutored by Tony Honoré, a South African Roman law and jurisprudence scholar of great distinction only ten years older than Brian. He found Honoré somewhat intimidating at first, but came to greatly respect him. Honoré insisted on high standards and extensive reading but in his first year at least Brian was not a diligent student, and was threatened with the removal of his scholarship. Subsequently, he had a distinguished undergraduate career. In 1952 he won the Winter Williams Studentship in Law, awarded after a two-day competitive examination (one of the papers he sat was on the history of the law of real property, 1066–1485). In 1953 he won the Gibbs Prize in Law. He became President of the University Law Society, enjoying considerable success in moots. By the end of his undergraduate years he had established a reputation as an up-and-coming scholar or barrister, and was thus presented in *Isis*, the university's student-run paper, as an 'academic idol' in its 'Isis Idols' series. In 1954 he was awarded a first in the Honour School of

[10] Evelyn Waugh, *Sword of Honour* trilogy consisting of three novels, *Men at Arms* (London, 1952), *Officers and Gentlemen* (London, 1955) and *Unconditional Surrender* (London, 1961).
[11] This section draws on PBM.

Jurisprudence, one of only eleven firsts in Law awarded that year, achieving the best Law first of the year. He has elsewhere given an account of the character of the Oxford Law School at this time.[12] He was not impressed.

In his second year, Brian sat the optional paper in the History of English Law, and prepared for that by attending the lectures of Derek Hall (1924–75), then a Fellow of Exeter College, the main Oxford legal historian of this period, and also Brian's tutor for the paper. (Hall went on to become President of Corpus Christi College, Oxford in 1969.) Hall gave lectures on 'Land Law in the Middle Ages' in 1952 and 1953 and also more general lectures on English Legal History in the same years.[13] He soon became a close friend, and greatly encouraged Brian's interest in the history of the law. Hall's interests in legal history were concentrated in the period 1100–1400; he was at this time working on an edition of *Glanvill*,[14] and Brian made some contributions to this edition.

Becoming an academic

Whilst at Oxford, Brian joined Gray's Inn, one of the Inns of Court, with a view to becoming a barrister. (He never took the Bar exams, only becoming a barrister many years later under a scheme which permitted senior academic lawyers to be called without having to do so.) He appears to have considered whether to go to the Bar or to become an academic and for a time he kept his options open. Shortly before taking Final Honour Schools (as the final examinations are termed in Oxford) he was encouraged by his tutors and by Rupert Cross,[15] then law tutor at Magdalen, to apply for a Fellowship at Jesus College; he was short-listed but failed to obtain the job. Soon after graduation he applied for a Junior Research Fellowship at Queen's, but was again unsuccessful. He was then offered a similar post at St Edmund Hall, and accepted it. Soon after that he met and later became engaged to be married to Kathleen Seston, then reading English Literature at St Hugh's College. They married soon after his graduation.

[12] A. W. Brian Simpson, 'Herbert Hart elucidated', *Michigan Law Review*, 104 (2006) 1437–59, 1438–9. See also Nicola Lacey, *A Life of H. L. A. Hart* (Oxford, 2004), pp. 112–78.

[13] He probably also attended Cecil Fifoot's lectures on 'Maitland's *Forms of Action*' in 1952 and perhaps his informal instruction on Year Book studies in Hilary term 1954.

[14] G. D. G. Hall (ed.), *The treatise on the laws and customs of the realm of England, commonly called Glanvill / Edited with introduction, notes and translation* (London, 1965; new edn., Oxford, 1993).

[15] Sir Rupert Cross (1912–80), later Vinerian Professor in the University of Oxford.

Although he has described how he 'in a sense … drifted into becoming an academic, though the career had always been viewed as a possibility', it seems better to describe his choice as a pragmatic way of addressing what he perceived as a significant domestic issue. He thought that marriage ruled out a career at the Bar, in the absence of a private income or other support. He had earlier applied for a Lincoln's Inn scholarship, the Tancred, which would have solved the problem but, though short-listed, he had been not successful. So the offer of the job at St Edmund Hall was in part a welcome solution to a looming financial problem.

Early legal history scholarship

In Michaelmas term 1954, he registered for a doctorate on 'Law reporting in the Sixteenth and Seventeenth Centuries' to be supervised by Derek Hall.[16] The second half of the 1950s and the 1960s has been described by Paul Brand[17] as 'a golden age for the study and teaching of English legal history in Oxford'.[18] Brian's colleagues included not just his doctoral supervisor, but also John Barton (1929–2008) at Merton, Toby Milsom (during his period at New College from 1956 to 1964) who regularly lectured on the history of torts, and Brian's contemporary John Kaye at Queen's (also awarded a first in 1954), who lectured on the history of criminal law. His earliest engagement in legal history scholarship was not, however, a success. His doctoral studies involved considerable archival work in the surviving MS law reports of this period, then mostly to be found in the Bodleian, the British Museum, the Inns of Court libraries, and Cambridge University Library. He describes how he 'floundered about as he sat forlornly in libraries filling in notebook after notebook, and … became increasingly despondent, it becoming clear that he was never going to produce a decent doctoral thesis'.

In the course of 1954–5, Brian was invited to dinner in Lincoln College by the then Rector, Sir Walter Oakeshott (1903–87); he was in fact being inspected, and within a few days was offered a fellowship in the college. So after only a year as Junior Research Fellow at St Edmund Hall he became

[16] This section draws on PBM.

[17] FBA, Senior Research Fellow, All Souls College, Oxford; Professor of English Legal History, University of Oxford; William W. Cook Global Professor of Law, University of Michigan Law School.

[18] PBM.

Fellow and Tutor of Lincoln College, where he remained until 1973,[19] succeeding Robert Goff, later Lord Goff of Chieveley, a House of Lords judge. This position involved a heavy teaching load, often around twenty hours a week, in disparate subjects, a large number of pupils, and considerable involvement in the running of the internal affairs of the college. Despite this, by the end of his Oxford period he had become recognised as a leading historian of the common law. His early work on the history of land, trusts and contract, which continues to be exceptionally influential, illustrated his scholarly method: a profound knowledge of the sources, a willingness to get his hands dirty in original archival work, and an ability to write clearly and persuasively. He was awarded a DCL by Oxford in 1976 and elected a Fellow of the British Academy in 1983.

This success appeared only slowly, however. After becoming a Fellow of Lincoln Brian effectively gave up his doctoral work (although he remained formally registered for the degree until 1958), but retained his academic interest in early English legal history. Brian's contribution to legal history during his period in Oxford consisted initially of a series of lectures on the Year Books. His first university lectures in 1957 were on 'The Ending of the Year Books' and he lectured again the following year on 'The Year Books'. These appear to be related not only to the work he was doing for his doctorate but also to his first publications, all of which were published in the *Law Quarterly Review*. The first of these, a note on 'The reports of John Spelman' appeared in 1956 and identified the reports of the person who was then the earliest known identifiable law reporter.[20] This was followed in the next year by an article on 'Keilway's reports, temp. Henry VII and Henry VIII' identifying John Carell as the compiler of these law reports,[21] and a further article later that year on 'The circulation of Yearbooks in the fifteenth century' refuting Plucknett's theory of a narrow circulation of Year Book MSS.[22] As late as 1971 he produced a provocative *Law Quarterly Review* article on 'The source and function of the later Year Books'.[23] This presented conclusions that he had originally hoped would, in a more elaborate form, contribute towards an

[19] He was elected an Honorary Fellow in 1995.

[20] 'The reports of John Spelman', *Law Quarterly Review*, 72 (July 1956), 334–8.

[21] 'Keilwey's reports, temp. Henry VII and Henry VIII', *Law Quarterly Review*, 73 (Jan. 1957), 89–105.

[22] 'The circulation of Yearbooks in the fifteenth century', *Law Quarterly Review*, 73 (Oct. 1957), 492–505.

[23] 'The source and function of the later Year Books', *Law Quarterly Review*, 87 (Jan. 1971), 94–118.

understanding of the way in which law reports were produced at this period. He never did produce the major work on law reporting himself, however, and he left the thesis unfinished. He did significantly help others. He is thanked by L. W. Abbott in his 1973 work on *Law Reporting in England, 1485–1585*[24] for his assistance in that work, and he prepared the ground for later work by Sir John Baker[25] on later fifteenth- and early sixteenth-century law reporting[26] and his editions of the unedited reports of this period.[27]

Brian's academic breakthrough began about 1959, when he was asked by the Oxford University Press, encouraged by the Oxford Faculty Board, to write a book to replace Sir William Holdsworth's 1927 *Historical Introduction to the Land Law*,[28] which had long been out of print. He responded with *Introduction to the History of the Land Law*,[29] which was written in a very short period in the long vacation in 1960, and published in 1961. It sold well but slowly, and in 1986 it appeared in a revised edition. As the title suggests, it was not a scholarly monograph but an undergraduate textbook, intended to 'make the doctrinal history' of the land law intelligible to law students, although it has copious references to the primary sources on which that doctrinal history is based. This book was mainly a work of exposition, and was assisted by many discussions with Derek Hall; it did not involve any original research into the sources.

Soon after its publication he began work on a doctrinal history of the common law of contract, later published under the title of *A History of the Common Law of Contract: the Rise of the Action of Assumpsit*.[30] This was to become the major original scholarly work that he produced during his time in Oxford (though it did not appear until 1975 and thus after his move to Kent). Brian had begun lecturing on the 'History of Contract' in 1957 and lectured on the subject almost every year thereafter. But he also began (in 1958) publishing a series of articles on the history of contract

[24] L. W. Abbott, *Law Reporting in England, 1485–1585* (London, 1973).
[25] Downing Professor of the Laws of England from 1998 until 2011, subsequently Downing Professor Emeritus.
[26] J. H. Baker, *The Common Law Tradition: Lawyers, Books and the Law* (London, 2000).
[27] Published by the Selden Society.
[28] Sir William Holdsworth, *An Historical Introduction to the Land Law* (London, 1927).
[29] *An Introduction to the History of the Land Law* (London, 1961; repr. with corrs. 1967; second edn., entitled *A History of the Land Law*, Oxford, 1986).
[30] *A History of the Common Law of Contract: the Rise of the Action of* assumpsit (Oxford, 1975; new edn. 1987).

that clearly prepared the way for the eventual book.[31] Notwithstanding its defects, some of which were pointed out in a sympathetic review by Sir John Baker,[32] the book was well received. It is a major *tour de force* covering the development of legal doctrine in the area of contract law during the period of almost five centuries from the later twelfth century down to 1677 (and the Statute of Frauds) and it shows a mastery of the relevant case law, particularly in the printed Year Books and printed and unprinted law reports of the early modern period.

This book was originally planned as a study covering the complete history of the subject up to modern times. It was published in a format that enabled it to be presented as the first volume of a two-volume work in the event that the second volume was ever published. It never was, and Brian confined his writings on the later history of contract law to periodical articles and book reviews. He did indeed begin work on the second volume dealing with the subsequent history of contract law down to the nineteenth century, as can be seen from his paper on 'Innovation in nineteenth century contract law'.[33] But in about 1976 he abandoned the second volume, he said later, 'with guilt, but no regret'; an albatross no longer hung around his neck. He was later to draw on this work in his review of Morton Horwitz's book, discussed below.

His approach to legal history at the time of the first volume was what Paul Brand has described as 'a relatively austere "internalist" view of the subject that saw its proper subject as the development of legal thought and doctrine'.[34] According to his own account, Brian came to lose interest in its completion. He subsequently came to think that a history of contract law based almost exclusively on legal sources, though perhaps tolerable for the early history, would be impossible for the eighteenth and nineteenth centuries, a view reinforced in discussions with Derek Hall. He also increasingly became disillusioned more generally with the study of the evolution of legal doctrine solely through the analysis of the legal sources. He came to view the first volume as belonging to a genre that had become

[31] These are: 'The place of Slade's Case in the history of contract', *Law Quarterly Review*, 74 (July 1958), 381–96; 'The equitable doctrine of consideration and the law of uses', *Toronto Law Journal*, 16 (1965), 1–36; 'The penal bond with conditional defeasance', *Law Quarterly Review*, 82 (1966), 392–422.

[32] *American Journal of Legal History*, 21 (1977), 335.

[33] Given in 1974 to a one-day session of the British Legal History Conference in the Old Hall of Lincoln's Inn, and Subsequently published in *Law Quarterly Review*, 91 (1975), 247–78.

[34] PBM.

unfashionable, being based on the assumption that law can legitimately be studied as an autonomous discipline.

Early jurisprudential scholarship

At the same time as he was building a reputation in the field of legal history, Brian was also part of the discussions that so significantly affected the method and scope of Oxford legal philosophy. Through the influence of Tony Honoré, and because the Professor of Jurisprudence, H. L. A. Hart, had been one of his examiners, Brian was invited to attend the informal jurisprudence discussion group, organised by Hart. This met once a week in Rupert Cross's rooms in Magdalen to discuss issues, many of a philosophical nature, connected with the law. As a result of being a member of the Hart group Brian became a close friend of Rupert Cross, and of Tony Guest[35] and Patrick Fitzgerald,[36] who were also members. He never became a close friend of Herbert Hart. In Hart's time the group provided what Brian had previously lacked, which was a forum at which such issues could be discussed informally and without an intimidating atmosphere. This led to an increased interest in philosophy, and Brian began to read extensively in this area. He attended the Hart discussion group regularly from 1955, an involvement that not only contributed to the lucidity and sophistication of his legal history scholarship but also led to his own original contributions to legal theory.

His initial entry into jurisprudential scholarship arose, however, from his sceptical reaction as an undergraduate to the merits of the then widely read article by Arthur Goodhart[37] on determining the *ratio decidendi* of a case.[38] At this time, the received wisdom was that the doctrine of precedent required courts, appropriately placed in the hierarchy, to follow earlier decisions, which were binding on them, and what this involved was the identification of the reason for the decision, the *ratio decidendi*, which would isolate what aspect of the decision bound subsequent courts. The

[35] Professor Anthony (Tony) Guest, Fellow and Praelector, University College Oxford, 1955–65; Professor of English Law, University of London, 1966–97.

[36] Fellow, Trinity College, Oxford, 1956–60; Professor of Law: University of Leeds, 1960–6; University of Kent at Canterbury, 1966–71.

[37] Master of University College, Oxford, 1951–63; Professor of Jurisprudence, Oxford, 1931–51; Editor, *Law Quarterly Review*.

[38] A. L. Goodhart, 'Determining the ratio decidendi of a case', *Yale Law Journal*, 40 (1930), 161, repr. in A. L. Goodhart, *Essays in Jurisprudence and the Common Law* (Cambridge, 1931), p. 1.

problem, it was thought, was how this was to be done. Goodhart's article had claimed to solve the problem. Brian was unconvinced, and published an article to that effect in the *Modern Law Review*.[39] It generated a considerable three-way debate between Brian, Professor J. L. Montrose of Queen's University, Belfast,[40] and Arthur Goodhart,[41] and came to be widely read. Brian later came to think that, although he was right to be sceptical about Goodhart's theory, his then views as to the process of reasoning used by courts were simplistic. When the Hambledon Press published a collection of his writings he excluded his pieces on the *ratio decidendi* from the collection.[42] They were not a product of his participation in the Hart group, and indeed Hart never showed any particular interest in the controversy.

Brian's early publication on precedent, and his membership of the Hart group, came to suggest that he was likely to develop into a jurisprudence scholar. In 1964 he was invited to be a visiting professor at the Dalhousie Law School in Nova Scotia to teach a jurisprudence course there, not a course in legal history. The perception that Brian was going to become a legal philosopher was enhanced when, together with Harold Cox,[43] the philosophy tutor at Lincoln, he led a seminar in Oxford on Hart's *The Concept of Law*,[44] in which they subjected the text to detailed critical analysis. This seminar ran from around 1965 to 1967, and was attended by undergraduates, graduate students in both law and philosophy, and a number of academics.

Brian largely lacked the self-confidence, however, to publish his views on philosophical issues at that time. Part of his nervousness was a reflection of what he perceived as the arrogance of Oxford philosophers towards members of the law faculty. The Simpson/Cox seminar, for example, did not lead to a book or even an article. Brian's interest in legal reasoning in the common law system did, however, generate two significant articles.

[39] 'The ratio decidendi of a case', *Modern Law Review*, 20 (July 1957), 413–15.

[40] Professor J. L. Montrose, Dean of the Faculty of Law and Professor of Law, Queen's University, Belfast, 1934–63.

[41] J. L. Montrose, 'The ratio decidendi of a case', *Modern Law Review*, 20 (Nov. 1957), 587–95; A. W. B. Simpson, 'The ratio decidendi of a case', *Modern Law Review*, 21 (March 1958), 155–60; A. L. Goodhart, 'The ratio decidendi of a case', *Modern Law Review*, 22 (March 1959), 117–24; A. W. B. Simpson, 'The ratio decidendi of a case', *Modern Law Review*, 22 (Sept. 1959), 453–7.

[42] A. W. B. Simpson, *Legal Theory and Legal History* (London, 1987).

[43] Fellow and Tutor in Philosophy, Lincoln College, Oxford (1929–70).

[44] H. L. A. Hart, *The Concept of Law* (Oxford, 1961). A second edition was published by Clarendon Press in 1994 with a postscript by H. L. A. Hart and edited by Penelope A. Bulloch and Joseph Raz. A third—and the most recent—edition was published by OUP in 2012, with an introduction by Leslie Green, also edited by Bulloch and Raz.

'The analysis of legal concepts' appeared in the *Law Quarterly Review* in 1964;[45] it criticised the idea that legal concepts possessed a special logic of their own, a view which had been put forward by a number of scholars, including Hart. It was discussed in the Hart group somewhat inconclusively, and Hart never responded to it. In 1973 he acted as editor and contributor to the influential second series of *Oxford Essays in Jurisprudence*,[46] but he was particularly nervous about the publication of his own essay in the book on the nature of the common law, 'The common law and legal theory', which nevertheless has come to be seen as one of his most important works.

Both publications reflect the fact that although Brian retained a great respect for Hart and his theoretical work he nevertheless had begun to think that Hart's application of philosophical ideas to the understanding of law had not been wholly successful, and that some of Hart's views were simply mistaken. It was not until much later, however, towards the end of his life, that he returned to consider these concerns in greater detail and ventured into print with his criticisms.[47] It is clear that heavy teaching and other responsibilities combined with a distressing family life also restricted Brian's scholarly output during the 1960s.

Domestic turmoil and itchy feet

The 1960s was a period of considerable career uncertainty and domestic turmoil. His marriage to Kathleen broke up in 1967, when there was an uncontested divorce. In addition, the pay of a law tutor was not good; Brian augmented his income by teaching for the Workers' Educational Association. Around 1963, the University of Liverpool approached him with the offer of a chair, but the salary offered was little better than Oxford, so he declined. In 1964 he applied for, but failed to be elected to,

[45] A. W. B. Simpson, 'The analysis of legal concepts', *Law Quarterly Review*, 80 (1964), 535–58.
[46] *Oxford Essays in Jurisprudence*, 2nd series (Oxford, 1973).
[47] At that time, the only criticism of H. L. A. Hart that Brian published—in a review of Hart's, *The Morality of the Criminal Law* (London, 1965), [1966] *Criminal Law Review*, 124—concerned Hart's view on criminal responsibility. His criticism was of the lecture 'Changing conceptions of responsibility', republished as Chap. VIII of *Punishment and Responsibility* (Oxford, 1967). Hart responded to the criticism in Chap. IX of *Punishment and Responsibility*, 'Postscript: responsibility and retribution', at pp. 222–3. Significantly, however, the review considered, at p. 125, that 'Hart may be over-impressed by the legal rule defined characteristics of lawyers' language.'

an All Souls Readership at Oxford;[48] Guenter Treitel[49] was the successful candidate. He increasingly threw himself into academic administration of various kinds. He served as Junior Proctor (with John Roberts[50] as his senior colleague) at a turbulent period in the University of Oxford's history (during the so-called Oxford 'student revolution'). He began to think that there was little future for him in Oxford, more particularly because he had no wish to move, as other former proctors had done, into full-time university administration.

In 1967, he was asked by Peter Carter, the law tutor in Wadham,[51] if he would like to go to Ghana as Dean of the Law Faculty, helping to found the post-independence law school; Carter was a friend of the then Vice-Chancellor, Alex Kwapong.[52] Brian thus became one of that generation of English legal scholars who spent periods in post-independence Africa during the 1960s.[53] In Ghana he had no time for academic research, but his visit did generate an interest in African customary law, which later led to an article on the colonial civil servant and ethnographer, R. S. Rattray, published in 1986.[54] Attempts were made to persuade him to stay on in Ghana, but he persuaded Kwapong that the law school needed a Ghanaian Dean, and Austin Amissah,[55] then a Court of Appeal judge, was appointed as his successor. The University of Ghana subsequently recognised his services by awarding him an honorary D.Litt. in 1993.

After his return to Oxford from Ghana, Brian found it difficult to settle back into the life of a college don. Soon after his return he was appointed a magistrate with the Bullingdon Bench (the magistrate's court for the area north of the city of Oxford), and he served as a magistrate there and

[48] The Readership was supported by All Souls College but did not bring any other connections with the college.

[49] Sir Guenter Treitel, All Souls Reader in English Law, University of Oxford, 1964–79; Vinerian Professor of English Law, University of Oxford, 1979–96; Fellow of All Souls College, Oxford, 1979–96.

[50] 1928–2003, Merton College, Oxford: Fellow and Tutor, 1953–79 (Honorary Fellow, 1980–4, 1994–); acting Warden, 1969–70, 1977–9; Senior Proctor, University of Oxford, 1967–8; Warden, Merton College, Oxford, 1984–94.

[51] 1921–2004; Fellow, Wadham College, Oxford, 1949–88.

[52] Professor of Classics, University of Ghana, 1962; Dean of Arts, Pro-Vice-Chancellor, University of Ghana, 1962–5, Vice-Chancellor, 1966–75.

[53] For example, William Twining, Robert Stevens, Patrick Atiyah, John Finnis, and Patrick McAuslan.

[54] A. W. B. Simpson, 'R. S. Rattray and Ashanti law', in A. W. B. Simpson, *Legal Theory and Legal History: Essays on the Common Law* (London and Ronceverte, WV, 1987), pp. 403–26.

[55] Director of Public Prosecutions, Ghana 1962–6; Acting Attorney General, Ghana 1966, Attorney General 1979; Judge of the Court of Appeal, Ghana 1966–76; Professor and Dean of the Faculty of Law, University of Ghana 1969–74.

later in Canterbury for some years. He was involved in attempts to break down the rigidity of the Oxford law syllabus, but failed to win the day, and he and Christopher Ball[56] attempted to persuade Lincoln College in 1971 to admit women, but this proposal, which created pandemonium, was lost by one vote.[57] These frustrations were also combined with an increasing sense of intellectual isolation in Oxford, more particularly because his closest Oxford friend, John McMahon, an international lawyer who had become the law tutor (and subsequently Dean) at Hertford College, had committed suicide in 1969 at the age of 32 whilst working at the United Nations in New York. Derek Hall had become a remote figure as President of Corpus. Gareth Jones, who had become a close friend when he held a joint lectureship at Exeter and Oriel Colleges,[58] had long since left Oxford. For Brian, Oxford had become 'a city of ghosts', as he put it subsequently.

In Ghana he had met Caroline Brown, then working as an archaeologist. Her father, Felix, was a consultant psychiatrist, and her mother was a well-known character actress whose stage name was Eileen Way. They married in 1968, and there were to be three children (Tim, Zoë, and Jane) of this second marriage, added to his two children with Kathleen (Charles and Carol). By his death, there were, in addition, twelve grandchildren and five great-grandchildren. Outside his academic work his principal interest was in his family life, and in his children. His love of children, not only his own, was well known among his friends who had children. He had a pied piper-like ability to get into their world and enliven it.

Brian engaged in little research during his post-Ghana years in Oxford. He was approached by Glanville Williams[59] about the possibility of a move to Cambridge, but he was not attracted to the position. By about 1970, however, a decision had been made to leave Oxford, and Brian was short-

[56] Sir Christopher Ball, Fellow and Tutor in English Language, Lincoln College, Oxford, 1964–79 (Bursar, 1972–9); Warden, Keble College, Oxford, 1980–8.

[57] Soon after, he engineered the appointment of Christine Chinkin to a college lectureship, the Governing Body having delegated the power to appoint a lecturer without thinking to limit it only to males. This too created some internal strife. For an account of the admission of women by the college historian, see, Vivian H. Green, *The Commonwealth of Lincoln College 1427–1977* (Oxford, 1979), pp. 551–2. Christine Chinkin's subsequent career (FBA; Professor of International Law at the London School of Economics; William W. Cook Global Professor, University of Michigan Law School) is evidence of Brian's good academic judgement.

[58] Lecturer, Oriel and Exeter Colleges, Oxford, 1956–8; KCL, 1958–61; Trinity College, Cambridge: Lecturer, 1961–75; Tutor, 1967; Senior Tutor, 1972; Vice-Master, 1986–92 and 1996–9; University Lecturer, Cambridge, 1961–75; Fellow of Trinity College, Cambridge, since 1961; Downing Professor of the Laws of England, Cambridge University, 1975–98.

[59] Glanville Llewelyn Williams (1911–97) Rouse Ball Professor of English Law at the University of Cambridge from 1968 to 1978.

listed for a chair at the University of Keele, which he failed to obtain. He also applied for the headship of University College, Durham, but did not get the job. Soon after Brian applied for two chairs then on offer, one at Queen's University, Belfast, and the other in Botswana. Caroline, his new wife, was not enthusiastic about living in Belfast, not least because the Troubles had just recommenced, and his application was withdrawn; Botswana never replied. Claire Palley[60] was at this time about to leave Queen's for a chair at the University of Kent. She took a copy of Brian's file to Kent and Brian was offered an appointment there, which he accepted.

Revolution, rape, pornography, and academic administration at Kent

Brian left Oxford in 1973 to become Professor of Law at the University of Kent. It was not a happy time. The University of Kent had adopted an innovative approach to higher education and there was much questioning of perceived orthodoxies. The Board of Studies in Law was located within the Faculty of Social Sciences. The first Professor of Law was Patrick Fitzgerald, an Oxford friend and former member of the Hart jurisprudence discussion group, who was committed to a progressive approach to the study of law. The board came to be dominated by a group of young academics of radical left wing leanings, influenced by the sociological study of law that was then developing in Britain; the dominant members of this group had been disillusioned by their legal studies at Cambridge. The result was a period of academic turmoil that tested even Brian's tolerance. One can only speculate how far this experience may have affected his subsequent reaction to Critical Legal Studies, when he encountered it in the United States. His description of academic manoeuvrings at lengthy faculty meetings was retrospectively hilarious, but must have been draining at the time. (He recollected how, in frustration, he sowed weeds in some of the Kent's manicured lawns as a token, but highly symbolic, act of revenge.) In order to get away from the 'horrors' of the Law Board ('Collectively the Law Board in session resembled a group therapy session for seriously disturbed teenagers.') Brian agreed to succeed Maurice Vile[61]

[60] Professor of Public Law, 1970–3; Dean of Faculty of Law, 1971–3; Professor of Law, 1973–84, and Master of Darwin College, 1974–82, University of Kent.

[61] Dean of Faculty of Social Sciences, 1969–75; Pro-Vice-Chancellor, 1975–81; Deputy Vice-Chancellor, 1981–4, University of Kent.

as Dean of the Faculty of Social Science in the mid-1970s. He remained Dean for three years. As Dean, Brian felt his only positive achievement had been that of establishing Social Psychology in the Faculty. He had little time for academic work.

His intellectual life largely took place outside the university. He served on an Advisory Group on the law of rape, under the chairmanship of a High Court Judge, Mrs Justice Rose Heilbron.[62] This had been established by the Home Secretary, Roy Jenkins, as a response to public outcry over the House of Lords decision in *D.P.P. v. Morgan*,[63] in which the Law Lords ruled that a genuine belief in the woman's consent, however unreasonable, was a defence to a charge of rape. The issue could not be referred to the Criminal Law Revision Committee, which at the time had sixteen male members and one female. The Advisory Group had a majority of female members, the first such government body ever in Britain. It reported in December 1975[64] and largely affirmed the principles stated by the majority in *Morgan*. The group did not recommend legislation to reverse the *Morgan* decision, which was thought to have little practical as opposed to symbolic significance. The report attracted little criticism, for by the time it appeared public protest over the *Morgan* case had died down. Some of its recommendations were partially adopted, such as that there should be a statutory definition of the crime, subsequently included in the Sexual Offences (Amendment) Act 1976.

More interestingly still, during his time at Kent, he was also a member and deputy chairman of the Williams Committee on Pornography and Film Censorship, which reported in 1979.[65] The Williams Committee meetings 'provided welcome relief from the tedium of existence at Kent', as he subsequently put it. They resembled the best sort of academic seminar, and its chairman, the noted philosopher Bernard Williams,[66] was only one of the impressive members who had been recruited to it; they included David Robinson, the London *Times* film critic,[67] Anthony Storr, a prominent psychiatrist,[68] and Polly Toynbee, a well-known journalist.[69] He was

[62] 1914–2005.
[63] *DPP v. Morgan* [1976] AC 182.
[64] Report of the Advisory Group on the Law of Rape, Cmnd. 6352, Dec. 1975.
[65] Report of the Committee on Obscenity and Film Censorship, Cmnd. 7772, London: HMSO, 1979.
[66] Professor Sir Bernard Williams (1929–2003).
[67] David Robinson, Assistant Editor of *Sight and Sound* and Editor of the *Monthly Film Bulletin*, 1957–8; film critic of *The Financial Times*, 1958–73, film critic *The Times*, 1973–90.
[68] Anthony Storr (1920–2001) psychiatrist and author.
[69] Columnist, *The Guardian*, 1977–88 and since 1998, writer.

an influential member of the committee. The report, which adopted John Stuart Mill's position that legal restrictions on freedom of expression were justifiable only where harm was evident, and that the harm of pornography in general had not been established, proved unpalatable to, and was immediately mothballed by, the incoming Conservative Government led by Margaret Thatcher.

After the report was published Brian was persuaded by Sam Silkin,[70] whose brainchild the committee had been, to write a short book on his experiences on the Williams Committee. This book, *Pornography and Politics* (1983),[71] is an entertaining and perceptive retrospective view of the committee and should be compulsory reading for anyone ever tempted to serve on similar groups. Serving on these committees triggered a continuing fascination with the processes of government, an interest that was further deepened by his experience of dealing with Home Office officials. For a while, he chaired the Home Office Police Promotions Examination Board, for which, he said, the civil servant Secretary produced minutes in advance of the meeting, and gave Brian elaborate advice before each meeting as to how to produce the result the Secretary wanted.

Escape to the United States

Despite these external diversions, by 1978 Brian had more or less come to the conclusion that he had better resign himself to remaining a university administrator at Kent. He had come to the university with high hopes, but by then he was disillusioned. Things were not well on the domestic front either. Brian's second marriage had not proven to be a success, and he ended up living in a mobile home in a caravan park some miles from Canterbury near Petham, Kent.

Brian was 'saved', as he put it, by John Langbein of the University of Chicago Law School.[72] Langbein decided that Brian must be 'rescued from this awful world' and secured him an invitation to visit the Law School, as a visiting professor in the winter of 1979. The experience of joining the intense intellectual community that then constituted the Chicago Law School restored his interest in the academic study of the law,

[70] From 1974 to 1979, he served as Attorney General for England and Northern Ireland under Labour Prime Ministers Harold Wilson and James Callaghan.

[71] *Pornography and Politics: a Look Back to the Williams Committee* (London, 1983).

[72] John H. Langbein, Sterling Professor of Law and Legal History, Yale Law School; Professor of Law, University of Chicago, 1971–90.

notwithstanding the fact that he disagreed with many of the views then current there. He visited again in 1980 and in 1982. The University of Kent had responded to government cuts in funding by encouraging those of its teachers who were readily employable elsewhere to take early retirement. Brian took early retirement. This gave him a lump sum and a modest pension, but it was essential for him to find employment to avoid living thereafter in penury, and he accepted a tenured job at Chicago in 1984. In 1985 Brian was invited to visit the Michigan Law School to teach first year contract law, and was offered a job there, which he only accepted after much thought, since in many ways he liked the Chicago Law School; Brian had made numerous friends there (in particular Richard Helmholz, Richard Posner, and John Langbein), and was sorry to leave. The considerably higher salary at Michigan and an intellectual milieu more sympathetic to his work were strong incentives for this move.

In 1986, he moved to the University of Michigan Law School, where he taught for a quarter of a century, becoming Charles F. and Edith J. Clyne Professor of Law. He remained at Michigan until his retirement in 2009, enjoying the intellectual diversity he found at the Law School. (He also shared with several members of the Michigan faculty a *penchant* for piloting light aircraft, although the enthusiasm of his instructor waned somewhat after he accidentally turned off the engine during a training flight.)

Although his academic career was latterly spent mostly in the United States, and he was a respected member of the American academic community, becoming a Fellow of the American Academy of Arts and Sciences in 1993, and an Honorary Fellow of the American Society for Legal History in 1994, he remained determinedly English, both in his outlook and in the inspiration of much of his scholarship. He never had the least wish to settle in the US, or become an American citizen. Michigan allowed Brian to compact a full year of teaching into a semester, a daunting schedule that enabled him to split each year between his professorship in Ann Arbor and his family and his archive-based research in England. He tended, therefore, to spend the winter and spring in Ann Arbor ('because the Americans understand winter, unlike the English', he was fond of saying), but the summer and autumn would find him back in England, often ensconced in the then Public Record Office in Kew. In 1993–4 he was the Arthur Goodhart Visiting Professor of Legal Science at Cambridge University. He was the general editor of the Oxford University Press series of monographs on modern legal history for many years. After he retired from Michigan, he accepted a Visiting Professorship at Bristol University, which illness prevented him from taking up.

Engaging with American legal ideology

Politically, like his father, he began life as a Conservative, and indeed acted as a Conservative speaker in the Skipton constituency whilst in his late teens. The Suez affair of 1956 permanently alienated him and his father from the Conservative Party, and his views tended to become more left wing as he grew older. An English liberal to his core, however, he viewed the growing extremism of American politics with concern. In his later years, he became somewhat uneasy about continuing to work in a country whose government behaved internationally, he believed, 'in so barbarous a way', although he was comforted by the fact that most of his American friends thought the same way (he considered that the United Kingdom 'behaved almost as badly, though its capacity for doing harm was much more limited'). But he was not a committed person politically.[73] Nor was his work as an academic lawyer driven by political ideology, although it never lacked a passionate commitment.

Brian came on the American law school scene at a time of considerable intellectual ferment about how to think about law.[74] The American legal realist movement had inculcated a pervasive scepticism about legal rules and legal doctrine. Many academics and practitioners purported to regard legal rules as a smoke screen, mere pretexts for what actually motivated judicial decisions. Others had developed more theoretical explanations that were either focused on legal process or avowedly pragmatic. By the late 1970s, when Brian arrived, two newer contending schools of thought were attempting to offer alternative theories. One, called Critical Legal Studies, centred at the Harvard Law School, was New Leftist and frequently post-modernist in tone; its adherents, the so-called 'crits', regarded existing legal rules and legal institutions as instruments of class subordination, but saw the law as capable of being captured to enable a better society to be created. An opposing school, which has been more enduring in the United States than Critical Legal Studies, was the law-and-economics movement, the most influential branch of which was then thriving at the Chicago Law School; these law-and-economics scholars contended that much of what the law does is to apply principles of microeconomics. The result was a fierce contest between the few remaining traditional legal doctrinalists ('black letter lawyers'), the Crits, and Law and Economics.

[73] Late in life his somewhat romantic interest in his partly Irish ancestry impelled him to acquire an Irish passport, and he toyed with the idea of moving to live there, although he did not do so.
[74] This section draws extensively on JLM.

Brian had barely arrived at Chicago before he entered the fray. His most celebrated contribution to the debate was an article that he published in the spring of 1979 in the *University of Chicago Law Review*.[75] Morton Horwitz,[76] then a leading member of the critical legal studies movement, had undertaken to reinterpret the history of contract law, arguing that nineteenth-century capitalists transformed contract law from its originally benign roots into a market-serving tool for exploitation of the weak.[77] Brian considered that Horwitz had, in his view, systematically distorted the historical evidence in order to further his ideological theories of legal evolution. Brian's article was not driven by an opposing political ideology but merely by his astonishment at what he considered to be the loose and deceptive use of evidence, and by his concern that in the world of American law school scholarship it was possible to get away with this. His review ranged across English and American case law and treatise literature of the eighteenth and nineteenth centuries to show that no such transformation had in fact occurred. The Chicago Dean at the time was nervous lest the article should be demolished, and allocated special funds to enable it to be very carefully checked and edited. The article attracted considerable attention, but no rebuttal from Horwitz. It delighted the many academics who detested the crits and caused fury in their camps. This had the 'unfortunate' result, from his point of view, of casting Brian in the role of an ideological enemy of the progressives.

Two years later, in 1981, Brian published in the same journal his path-breaking work on the history of the Anglo-American legal treatise,[78] which this time attacked the American Legal Realists' legacy more broadly. Brian had long been interested in the history of legal literature and of legal education; he saw these subjects in part as windows on legal theory, because the way lawyers write about the law and teach the law reveals how they think about and categorise law. In the 1950s, Brian had already written about the origins of the later medieval yearbooks and their relation to the instructional program of the Inns of Court.[79] Brian's article on the

[75] A. W. B. Simpson, 'The Horwitz thesis and the history of contracts', *University of Chicago Law Review*, 46 (Spring 1979), 533–601.

[76] Harvard Law School: Assistant Professor of Law, 1970, Professor of Law, 1974, since 1981 Charles Warren Professor of American Legal History.

[77] Morton J. Horwitz, *The Transformation of American Law, 1780–1860: the Crisis of Legal Orthodoxy* (Cambridge, MA, 1977).

[78] A. W. B. Simpson, 'The rise and fall of the legal treatise: legal principles and the forms of legal literature', *University of Chicago Law Review*, 48 (Summer 1981), 632–79.

[79] Simpson, 'The circulation of Yearbooks in the fifteenth century'.

history of the treatise developed the theme that the treatise was a prevailingly nineteenth- and early-twentieth-century genre, which came to fruition in consequence of the emergence of university legal education in the common law. Brian concluded his account by pointing to the irony that the tradition of academic treatise writing—which reached its highest expression in the United States in the first half of the twentieth century in the multivolume treatises such as *Wigmore on Evidence* and *Williston on Contracts*—had become largely extinct. Brian blamed the American Legal Realists. The prevailing legal culture of 'cynicism about the significance of legal doctrine' [80] had discredited 'the work of analyzing doctrine and expounding it as the principled science of the law'.[81]

That his concerns about the American approach to legal theorising were not politically ideological was soon demonstrated by his criticism of the work of right-leaning law and economics scholars. His time at Chicago led to an interest in the application of economic ideas to the study of the law, and at Chicago and later Michigan he regularly attended law-and-economics seminars. He had, however, serious doubts as to the validity of some of the claims advanced by devotees of the movement. His principal target in both his critiques of Critical Legal Studies and Law and Economics was the tendency, as he saw it, of academic lawyers to fall in love with simplistic and highly generalised theories of law and legal evolution. The success of the Law and Economics movement in the academy, attempting to explain the whole history of common law development by reference to the concept of economic efficiency, depended in part on this love of all embracing theory.

His scepticism resulted in an article published in 1996,[82] which criticised some of the views of Ronald Coase,[83] regarded as one of the founding fathers of the Law and Economics movement. This enraged Coase, who published an angry reply[84] that failed, however, to address the substantive points that had been made.[85] In the main, Brian's article was ignored by academics committed to the economic analysis of law, much as his criticism

[80] A. W. B. Simpson, 'The rise and fall of the legal treatise: legal principle and the forms of legal literature', *University of Chicago Law Review*, 48 (1981), 632, 677.

[81] Ibid., p. 678.

[82] A. W. B. Simpson, 'Coase v. Pigou reexamined', *Journal of Legal Studies*, 25 (Jan. 1996), 53–97.

[83] Professor of Economics (1964–70), then Clifton R. Musser Professor of Economics (1971–81), University of Chicago; Nobel Prize in Economics, 1991.

[84] R. H. Coase, 'Law and economics and A. W. Brian Simpson', *Journal of Legal Studies*, 25 (Jan. 1996), 103–19.

[85] A. W. B. Simpson, '[Coase v. Pigou reexamined:] An addendum', *Journal of Legal Studies*, 25 (Jan. 1996), 99–101.

of Horwitz was largely ignored by scholars committed to critical legal studies. This phenomenon—the failure to respond to seriously presented criticism of theoretical views—led Brian to adopt a somewhat disdainful attitude to the culture of American law schools, too much of which, in his view, was driven by political ideology.

'Doing a Simpson'

This scholarship, whilst attracting much attention, was nevertheless something of an intellectual sideshow for Brian. His main scholarly efforts were elsewhere. During his time at Kent, but increasingly after he went to the United States, he developed the original idea, as Joshua Getzler,[86] the Oxford legal historian, has pointed out, that the 'leading cases' of the common law deserved the fullest possible study in their historical context.[87] He made this approach his own special area, drawing out new facts, emphasising the contingency of these leading cases, and deepening our understanding of their particular meaning and significance. This genre of scholarship is now commonly known, according to Richard Helmholz,[88] his former colleague at the University of Chicago Law School, as 'doing a Simpson'.[89]

Typically, Brian described his 'eureka moment' in colourful terms. It was, so he said, when he was lying in a bath on his first visit to a wintery Chicago in 1979, trying to get warm, that it occurred to him that the celebrated case of *Rylands v. Fletcher*,[90] in which the doctrine of strict liability for inherently dangerous activities was developed, must have had its origins in some major reservoir failure, a hypothesis he soon found to be true after a visit to Chicago's Regenstein Library. This generated an article that appeared in the Chicago *Journal of Legal Studies* in 1984.[91] This was not the first attempt to study a leading case in its social and political context; the pioneer was Richard Danzig who had in 1975 published an article of

[86] Professor of Legal History, University of Oxford; Fellow, St Hugh's College, Oxford.
[87] J. S. Getzler, 'A. W. B. Simpson, *Leading Cases in the Common Law*', *Journal of Legal History*, 18 (1997), 116–18.
[88] University of Chicago Law School, Professor of Law, 1981–4; Ruth Wyatt Rosenson Professor of Law, 1984–99; Ruth Wyatt Rosenson Distinguished Service Professor of Law, 2000–present.
[89] R. H. Helmholz, 'Brian Simpson in the United States', in Donovan and Rubin *Human Rights and Legal History*, pp. 285, 288.
[90] *Rylands v. Fletcher* [1868] LR 3 HL 330.
[91] A. W. B. Simpson, 'Legal liability for bursting reservoirs: the historical context of *Rylands v. Fletcher*', *Journal of Legal Studies*, 13 (1984), 209–64.

this type on the 1854 contract case of *Hadley v. Baxendale*.[92] But Brian made this approach very much his own, and it was best exemplified in his book *Cannibalism and the Common Law* (Chicago, 1984).[93]

In about 1981 he had written to the Home Office to see if he could obtain access to any surviving papers connected with the notable case of *R. v. Dudley and Stephens* (1884).[94] At this time, the Home Office followed a practice of not releasing files on capital cases for a century; Brian thought that in view of the work he had done for the Home Office on pornography and earlier on the law of rape that he might obtain access a little earlier. At this time he was teaching criminal law at Kent and he thought that access to the file might enliven his teaching. The case concerned the scope of the defence of necessity in criminal law. It dealt with the trial of two shipwrecked sailors who had killed the ship's cabin boy and eaten him to save themselves. The killers survived, were prosecuted for murder, and were ultimately convicted but pardoned. Once he saw the archives, he realised that there was a book in it, and the outcome was *Cannibalism and the Common Law*. Combining these archival with newspaper sources, Brian reconstructed in astonishing detail not only the judicial machinations that led to the conviction, but also the horrific dangers of nineteenth-century maritime life.

Brian's scholarship was closely connected to his general interest in history, which he read voraciously. But his other non-academic interests were also often drawn on in his scholarly writing. *Cannibalism*, in particular, brought together his love of history with his interest in the way law is practised, and with his abiding maritime connections. His first wife, Kathleen, together with her new husband, had earlier disappeared in a yacht that sank without trace in the Pacific. It is probable that the yacht foundered in a tropical storm in October 1978. Brian himself was for many years an intrepid (if somewhat haphazard) sailor who loved messing about in boats. He began with a Gull sailing dinghy, which he towed out to Greece on several occasions, and then progressed to chartering yachts in the Falmouth area and on the Dart. Indeed, partly to equip himself to write about the technical aspects of sailing involved in the *Dudley and Stephens* case that was central to *Cannibalism*, he worked on

[92] Richard Danzig, '*Hadley v. Baxendale*: a study in the industrialization of the law', *Journal of Legal Studies*, 4 (1975), 249.

[93] The book was first published by the University of Chicago Press, and then by Penguin in the UK and reprinted by the Hambledon Press.

[94] *R v. Dudley and Stephens* [1884] 14 QBD 273 DC.

a square-rigger, *Eye of the Wind*, on a voyage from Copenhagen to Southampton; thereafter some reference to futtock shrouds appeared in all his books.[95]

The maritime background to *Dudley and Stephens*, and the ultimate fate of one of the killers, Tom Dudley, as a victim of bubonic plague, made for a good story, but the real subject matter of the book went deeper: the conflict between middle class morality and the practices of seamen; the conflict between notions of the survival of the fittest and the value of the sanctity of human life; the conflict between the rule of law and necessity; and the complexities of the interaction between lawyers, courts and politicians, on the one hand, and elite and working class public opinion, on the other.

The book attracted considerable attention, and sold well for an academic monograph, but it was described by William Twining as 'a magnificent failure' (a phrase Twining later regretted using) and as lacking 'focus'.[96] The 'failure' of the book was that its larger themes did not have a strong intellectual impact within the world of academic law. The claim that the book lacked 'focus'' meant that Brian did not spell out what the book was about, in the sense that there was no attempt to overlay the story with an explicit theory (although *implicitly* the book was centrally concerned with the hostility of state law to legal pluralism), or to point to the moral of the story and that as a result the book came to be read primarily as entertainment rather than for its intellectual content. Nevertheless, with these books and articles, Brian thereafter came to be viewed as something of a pioneer in what some have called 'legal archaeology'.[97] Work on *Cannibalism and the Common Law* involved research in the papers available in the Public Record Office, now The National Archives, and Brian continued to be fascinated by archival research into relatively modern legal history. Extensive use had been made of archives by medievalists and the editors of texts for the Selden Society, but until then virtually no use had been made of them for the study of modern legal history.[98]

[95] On several occasions he worked on a historic Bridgwater ketch, *Irene*, on coastal voyages, and on one trip to the Channel Islands and back. Later in life he bought and sailed *Cosmic Wind*, a decrepit 26 ft Eventide, and *Edelweiss*, an Elizabethan 23 ft yacht. Later still, he gave up solo sailing under pressure from his children, and acquired a sea-going motor launch, *Cheybassa*.

[96] William Twining, 'Cannibalism and legal literature', *Oxford Journal of Legal Studies*, 6(3) (1986), 423.

[97] e.g. Debora L. Threedy, 'Unearthing subversion and legal archaeology', *Texas Journal of Women and Law*, 13 (2003), 133.

[98] With the notable exception of Robert Stevens, who had made extensive use of PRO records in Brian Abel-Smith and Robert Stevens, *Lawyers and the Courts* (London, 1967), Brian Abel-

Brian's next project was suggested by a conversation he had with a Canadian scholar, DeLloyd Guth,[99] who told him that he and Robert Heuston[100] had discovered that Robert Liversidge,[101] the litigant in the important wartime case of *Liversidge v. Anderson* (1942),[102] was still alive and living in the Vancouver, British Columbia area. The case concerned the legality of internment without trial in Britain under emergency powers permitting the incarceration of suspected fascist sympathisers during the Second World War. Out of this came Brian's book, *In the Highest Degree Odious*, which dealt with the detention without trial of British citizens during the First and Second World Wars.[103] The book, favourably reviewed by Richard Posner, his former colleague at Chicago,[104] explored the interaction between the military, the security services, the civil servants, internal governmental committees, the lawyers and the courts, members of Parliament and the media, and the detainees and their families. It was a broad-based study of the working of the British governmental machine in times of stress.

It also allowed him to indulge a long-standing interest in the world of the British security services. He had been, on his own telling, a rather lacklustre talent spotter for them during his time at Oxford. Researching *In the Highest Degree Odious* enabled him to immerse himself more deeply in this world and his account drew on a wide range of sources, including interviews with former members of the British Union of Fascists, members of the Security Service (MI5), and many telephone conversations with Robert Liversidge himself. (His interest in this secretive world remained. He subsequently explored H. L. A. Hart's involvement in counter-espionage during the Second World War,[105] and he assisted in the case that George Blake—the double agent—took to Strasbourg, discussed below.)

Smith and Robert Stevens, *In Search of Justice* (London, 1968), and Robert Stevens, *Law and Politics: the House of Lords as a Judicial Body 1800–1976* (London, 1979).

[99] Assistant Lecturer, Universities of Bristol, 1974–5, and Lancaster, 1975–7; Assistant Professor, University of Michigan, 1966–73; Visiting Associate Professor (Law), University of British Columbia, 1982–93; Professor of Law and Legal History, University of Manitoba since 1994.

[100] Fellow, Pembroke College, Oxford, 1947–65; Professor of Law, University of Southampton, 1965–70; Regius Professor of Laws, Trinity College Dublin, 1970–83.

[101] 1904–94.

[102] *Liversidge v. Anderson* [1942] AC 206.

[103] *In the Highest Degree Odious: Detention Without Trial in Wartime Britain* (Oxford, 1992).

[104] Richard A. Posner, 'Executive detention in time of war', *Michigan Law Review*, 92 (1994), 1675.

[105] A. W. Brian Simpson, 'Herbert Hart elucidated', *Michigan Law Review*, 104 (2006), 1437 at 1443–4.

Brian continued working in this vein of immensely detailed case studies, publishing further studies of leading English cases in tort, contract, and property law. He collected many of these studies in a book published by Oxford University Press in 1995, as *Leading Cases in the Common Law*.[106] In more recent times there has developed in the US legal academic world a story-telling movement, and Brian's work may have had some part in encouraging this development. Articles of his have been included in *Property Law Stories*[107] and *Contract Stories*,[108] recent examples of this type of writing about the law.

There are many strands to Brian's contextualising historical studies; in one dimension, they were part of his reaction against the prevailing anti-doctrinalism of American legal academia. Brian thought rules mattered and, to that end, he wanted to show where important rules came from, and why. The approach he adopted demonstrated a view about the appropriate way of thinking about the evolution of legal doctrine. Brian came to consider that in legal academia there existed a deep reluctance to allow the intricacies of the workings of the real world to get in the way of facile generalisations and the cultivation of romantic theoretical myths. One of the anonymous readers of *In the Highest Degree Odious* for Oxford University Press criticised the draft on the ground that it lacked theoretical analysis, and Brian therefore stitched on a final theoretical chapter which he wrote in two days, but he did it under protest and with distaste.

Human rights scholarship

Although he combined many non-scholarly interests with his scholarship throughout his life, he often appeared sceptical of scholarship driven by political or moral commitments. Brian's next major academic project was somewhat different, therefore, for he was to discover a personal commitment to human rights that was to bring together a strong strand of personal idealism with academic scholarship. During his year at Cambridge (1993–4) he had re-established contact with a former pupil, Nuala Atkinson, later

[106] A. W. B. Simpson, *Leading Cases in the Common Law* (Oxford, 1995).

[107] A. W. B. Simpson, 'The story of *Sturges v. Bridgman*: the resolution of land use disputes between neighbors', in Gerald Korngold and Andrew P. Morriss (eds.), *Property Stories* (New York, 2004).

[108] A. W. B. Simpson, 'Contracts for cotton to arrive: the case of the two ships Peerless', *Cardozo Law Review*, 11 (Dec. 1989), 287–333, in Douglas G. Baird (ed.), *Contract Stories* (New York, 2007).

Nuala Mole,[109] who had established a human rights NGO in London, the AIRE Centre. He was attracted by the idea that Michigan law students might work in the centre as interns, and arrangements for this were in due course set up. Resulting discussions led to a developing interest in the international protection of human rights. This linked naturally to his earlier work on detention without trial in the Second World War.[110]

Brian decided to embark on a study of the genesis of the European Convention on Human Rights (ECHR). He had never studied or indeed shown any particular interest in international law, and had therefore to acquire knowledge of this as he was doing the archival work on which the study was to be based. As this study progressed, Brian decided to relate the story of the development of the Convention to the dismantling of the British colonial empire, and this linked the work to his interest in colonial history. Fascinated as he was by the residue of Empire and its continuing effects in British and Commonwealth law, he showed that the origins and drafting of the Convention needed to be seen from the perspective of a British government obsessed with its colonies, an important corrective to the popular view that the Convention was simply a response to wartime Axis brutalities.

His timing was impeccable, if accidental. The Human Rights Act 1998 came into effect in the United Kingdom in 2000, effectively incorporating the European Convention on Human Rights. In 2001 he published his monumental study *Human Rights and the End of Empire* (Oxford), based on his intensive study of the British and American archives, explaining not only the genesis of the Convention but also the interrelationship between the various persons and entities involved in adapting to the changed world once the Convention came into force and began to have practical consequences that had never been anticipated.

He subsequently published several other pieces on issues of international law,[111] some based on the huge body of archival material in The National Archives. One, on the application of the ECHR to overseas colonial territories, appeared in the *British Yearbook of International Law* in 2007.[112] This was his first joint publication. The co-author, Louise Moor,

[109] Founding director of the AIRE Centre, formerly Director of Interights, St Anne's College, Oxford (1964–7).

[110] *In the Highest Degree Odious*.

[111] See, for example, his important essay, 'Hersch Lauterpacht and the genesis of the age of human rights', *Law Quarterly Review*, 120 (2004), 49.

[112] Louise Moor and A. W. Brian Simpson, 'Ghosts of colonialism in the European Convention on Human Rights', *British Year Book of International Law*, 76(1) (2006), 121–94.

was a New Zealand lawyer working for Amnesty International in London, who had studied for an LLM at the Michigan Law School. The impetus which generated this article was *pro bono* work in which Brian was then engaged with the AIRE Centre in connection with the expulsion of the Chagos Islanders from their homeland in the late 1960s and early 1970s.

Later, Brian was approached by a former Foreign Office Legal Adviser, Sir Frank Berman,[113] who suggested he undertake a comprehensive study of the Foreign Office Legal Advisers. He turned down this suggestion as being a task more appropriate for a younger scholar, given the inevitable scale of such an undertaking. In 2009, Brian collaborated with Dino Kritsiotis,[114] with whom he had run a joint seminar in Michigan, in writing a piece on the international law aspects of the prosecutions of a number of Pitcairn Islanders for offences against the Sexual Offences Act 1956 for inclusion in a volume of essays on the cases.[115] Another international law piece dealt with the Genocide Convention[116] and the Maccabaean Lecture in Jurisprudence (2003) investigated in detail the rule of law in international affairs in relation to the incident of the *Altmark* in 1940, in which a German ship was intercepted by the Royal Navy and boarded in neutral Norwegian waters.[117]

Legal practice: direct and indirect

Brian's interest in human rights was not only academic. He was also deeply committed to the use of law to secure the common good and advance human rights in practical terms. This use of law in practice led him occasionally to regret never having gone into legal practice (although he poked fun at the pomposity of barristers), and he also came to think that he would have greatly enjoyed working in the Foreign Office. His work with

[113] Sir Franklin (Frank) Berman was Legal Adviser to the Foreign and Commonwealth Office from 1991 until 1999.

[114] Dino Kritsiotis is Professor of Public International Law in the University of Nottingham, where he has taught since October 1994.

[115] Dino Kritsiotis and A. W. B. Simpson, 'The Pitcairn prosecutions: an assessment of their historical context by reference to the provisions of public international law', in Dawn Oliver (ed.), *Justice, Legality and the Rule of Law: Lessons from the Pitcairn Prosecutions* (Oxford, 2009).

[116] A. W. B. Simpson, 'Britain and the Genocide Convention', *British Year Book of International Law*, 73(1) (2002), 5–64.

[117] A. W. B. Simpson, 'The rule of law in international affairs', *Proceedings of the British Academy*, 125 (2004), 211–63.

the AIRE Centre during the late 1990s and early 2000s therefore filled something of a gap in his life. He came to be involved in *pro bono* work associated with the London NGO, some related to cases in both the UK courts and Strasbourg.[118]

In 1995, the AIRE Centre asked if he would help in the cases before the European Court of *Hussain and Singh*,[119] which concerned the detention at Her Majesty's Pleasure of juveniles convicted of murder. His advice in *Hussain and Singh* was then used before the House of Lords and in Strasbourg in the more publicised cases of *T and V*, the Jamie Bulger murder case, in which a two-year-old boy was abducted, tortured and then murdered by two ten-year-old boys.[120] The paper submitted to the ECHR in *Singh v. United Kingdom* was cited by Lord Goff (his predecessor as law fellow at Lincoln) in the case of *R v. Secretary of State for the Home Department, ex parte Thompson and Venables*, albeit to disagree with it.[121] He was called on again to provide advice in *Dobbie v. UK*,[122] which concerned the 'date of knowledge' for time to start running to commence litigation. *Dobbie* was followed by *Osman*,[123] which concerned the refusal to recognise a duty of care in negligence in a case where the police had been alerted to the dangerous obsession shown by a disturbed schoolmaster to a thirteen-year-old pupil but did nothing to protect the child. Brian provided a comprehensive account of the genesis of Article 13 of the ECHR, the right to an effective remedy, which won the day for the Osman family. This advice was subsequently also used in the later Strasbourg cases of *Z v. UK* and *TP and KM v. UK*.[124]

Brian was also involved in providing advice in the case taken to the European Court of Human Rights by George Blake, the double agent, challenging the novel legal mechanisms adopted by the British Government to prevent Blake (whom he nevertheless thoroughly disapproved of) from receiving royalties from his book. The Strasbourg court rejected most of the claims, but Blake was partially successful.[125] Brian also assisted the AIRE Centre as a third party intervener in the case of *Hirst v. UK*,[126] the

[118] This section draws on NMM.
[119] *Hussain and Singh v. UK* (1996) 22 EHRR 1.
[120] *T and V v. UK* (2000) 30 EHRR 121.
[121] [1998] AC 407, at p. 481.
[122] *Dobbie v. United Kingdom* (application no 28477/95; declared inadmissible: 16 October 1996).
[123] *Osman v. United Kingdom* [1998] EHRR 101.
[124] *TP and KM v. United Kingdom* (2002) 34 EHRR 2.
[125] *Blake v. United Kingdom* (2007) 44 EHRR 29.
[126] *Hirst v. UK* (2006) 42 EHRR 41.

prisoners' voting case, providing advice to explain how and why convicted felons did not have the right to vote. He put his knowledge of the complex legal relationship between colonial law and the Convention to good use in assisting the Chagos Islanders in their legal claim before the European Court of Human Rights.[127] It was the research he did in connection with his involvement in that litigation that led him to write the scholarly piece with Louise Moor mentioned earlier.[128]

Brian's involvement with the world of the practice of law was also more indirect, most particularly through the influence of his academic writing on the UK highest court.[129] Lady Hale cited *Introduction to the History of the Land Law* in a House of Lords opinion on the scope of possession orders.[130] *In the Highest Degree Odious* has been cited twice in the House of Lords, once by Lord Walker in his dissenting judgment in the *Belmarsh* case, *A v. Secretary of State for the Environment*,[131] and once by Lord Brown in *R (Al-Jeddah) v. Secretary of State for Defence*,[132] both of them cases about detention without trial.[133] *Cannibalism and the Common Law* was cited by Lord Hailsham in *R v. Howe*,[134] and his article on *Rylands v. Fletcher*[135] was cited by both Lord Bingham and Lord Hoffmann in *Transco v. Stockport Metropolitan Borough Council*,[136] when deciding that a burst water pipe was not to be equated with a mill lodge. The respect for his academic work in legal practice was further acknowledged when he was appointed an honorary QC in 2001.

Oxford (and Oxford jurisprudence) revisited

As pointed out earlier, Brian was critical of what he saw as H. L. A. Hart's lack of attention to the workings of the common law tradition, but that

[127] An application was lodged before the ECtHR in 2008 following the defeat of the final British lawsuit before the House of Lords, and that case remains in litigation as of August 2011.
[128] See above, n. 102.
[129] This paragraph draws on BHM.
[130] *Secretary of State for the Environment, Food and Rural Affairs v. Meier* [2009] 1 WLR 2780, para. 33.
[131] [2005] 2 AC 68.
[132] [2007] UKHL 58.
[133] Indeed, his paper 'Europe must go it alone: the European Convention on Human Rights: the first half century' was also cited in *Al Jeddah.*
[134] [1987] 1 AC 417, at 430.
[135] 'Legal liability for bursting reservoirs: the historical context of *Rylands v. Fletcher*', *Journal of Legal Studies*, 13 (1984), 209.
[136] [2004] 2 AC 1, at paras 3 and 28.

his lack of self-confidence in the jurisprudential field when at Oxford meant that he was uneasy about publishing these views. After leaving Oxford, whilst continuing to be interested and to read widely in the area, Brian's subsequent writings did not directly engage with Oxford analytical jurisprudence, until the last decade of his life. His last book, with the title of *Reflections on* The Concept of Law, delivered to Oxford University Press some months before his death and published posthumously, made these reservations public, although some of this material was published earlier in Brian's reviews of Nicola Lacey's illuminating biography, *A Life of H. L. A. Hart: the Nightmare and the Noble Dream*,[137] in the *Times Literary Supplement*,[138] and in the *Michigan Law Review*.[139] *Reflections* revisits Brian's fascination with, and ambivalent respect for, Hart's *The Concept of Law*[140] and analytical jurisprudence more generally (whether of the Oxford variety, or those originating elsewhere).

There are several different ways of reading *Reflections*.[141] At one level, it is an attempt to set out in some detail Brian's understanding of the historical and intellectual context in which *The Concept of Law*, first published in 1961, was written. Lacey had already laid bare much of Hart's life. Brian was able to describe the academic environment from his own experiences as a young don in the Oxford of the 1950s and 1960s. In *Reflections*, Brian also draws out in a more sustained way the diverse, if flawed, jurisprudential traditions that preceded Hart, and the range of intellectual sources that appear to have influenced Hart when he was writing *The Concept of Law*, providing an important supplement to Lacey's account. This is intellectual history of the most engaging kind, not least because it is peppered with classic examples of Brian's famous wit. There is much pleasure to be had from Brian's accounts of post-war Oxford life, irrespective of the background they present to Hart's work; indeed, it is the autobiographical aspects of the book that provide some of the most illuminating and funny moments.

At another level, *Reflections* is an extended critique of Hart's book, elaborating and extending the range of Brian's reservations about the methodology and substantive argument of *The Concept of Law*. From his earlier writings,[142] we know that Brian was critical of what he saw as Hart's

[137] (Oxford, 2004).

[138] A. W. B. Simpson, 'Stag hunter and mole', *Times Literary Supplement*, Feb. 11, 2005, 6–7.

[139] A. W. B. Simpson, 'Herbert Hart elucidated', *Michigan Law Review*, 104 (2006), 1437.

[140] (Oxford, 1961; 2nd edn., 1994; 3rd edn., 2012).

[141] This section draws on the author's Preface to *Reflections*.

[142] 'The common law and legal theory', in A. W. B. Simpson (ed.), *Oxford Essays in Jurisprudence* (2nd series) (Oxford, 1973), pp. 77–99.

lack of attention in *The Concept of Law* to the common law tradition. Hart's emphasis on law as a system of rules was, he thought, more appropriate for the analysis of Continental civil law systems. For Brian, the English common law system 'consists of a body of practices observed and ideas received by a caste of lawyers'.[143] Historically, cohesion was produced through institutional arrangements, such as the way the legal profession is organised, rather than by way of rules, which only developed when the previous consensus based on tradition or custom broke down. For Brian, legal history and legal anthropology were therefore central tools in coming to an understanding of what law is; he considered that, for Hart, they were irrelevant. This earlier critique is developed further in *Reflections*, leading to further criticisms of *The Concept of Law*. The formulation of the rule of recognition, the absence of comparative law analysis, the difficulties with Hart's approach to adjudication, and the book's omission of any sustained discussion of human rights, are all analysed and criticised.

At a third level, *Reflections* comes as close as Brian ever came to setting out his own 'anti-grand-theory' theory of legal scholarship. One of the noteworthy aspects of his scholarship was the determined way in which Brian avoided being drawn into any sustained discussion of abstract legal theory, preferring to allow his books' relevance for legal theory to be drawn out by readers themselves. We know that Brian had in mind a book-length treatment of the common law tradition, along the lines of Merryman's book on the civil law tradition,[144] and this might have addressed more directly his own theoretical views, but sadly it was not completed by the time of his death. In *Reflections,* however, in setting out his analysis of where he and Hart differ, we begin to get a clearer idea of Brian's own approach to legal theory. Agreeing with William Twining's description of Brian,[145] drawing on Isaiah Berlin's famous distinction,[146] as a fox rather than a hedgehog ('the fox knows many things, the hedgehog knows one big thing'), Brian makes clear that his approach to law is essentially fox-like. In

[143] 'The common law and legal theory', in A. W. B. Simpson (ed.), *Oxford Essays in Jurisprudence* (2nd series) (Oxford, 1973), p. 94.

[144] John Henry Merryman, *The Civil Law Tradition* (Stanford, CA, 3rd edn., 2007).

[145] William Twining, 'The *ratio decidendi* of the case of the prodigal son', in O'Donovan and Rubin, 149, 150.

[146] Isaiah Berlin, *The Hedgehog and the Fox: an Essay on Tolstoy's View of History* (London, 1953).

contrast, he regards Hart as an exemplar of a hedgehog's approach to law. For Brian, legal theorising should derive from detailed empirical analysis of what happens in actual legal practice. He was thus deeply sceptical of grand abstract theories that ignore the evidence of such practice. He considered that analytical jurisprudence should build from the practice of law, rather than seek to impose itself on such practice, and that those who espoused analytical jurisprudence had largely ignored the implications of his work in legal history and the challenges it posed for their work. In seeking to engage with *The Concept of Law*, *Reflections* not only pays Hart the ultimate compliment of treating him seriously, but also shines a clearer light than before on Brian's own intellectual development and scholarly approach.

Teaching

Throughout his period in academic life, Brian not only wrote he also taught extensively. In Oxford, he taught a variety of subjects, including jurisprudence, legal history, property law, tort law, contract law and constitutional and administrative law. In Canada he taught jurisprudence. In Kent he taught legal philosophy, legal history, contract, tort and criminal law. For a summer programme run by the T. C. Williams School of Law he taught criminal law and comparative law. In Chicago he taught jurisprudence, property and contract, and on one occasion criminal law. In Michigan he continued to teach a variety of subjects. He taught the basic course in property law, and sometimes contract law as well. He also taught upper-level courses in English and American legal history, jurisprudence, and human rights law; and he offered advanced seminars on special topics, including the history of contract law, the history of tort law, the history of legal education, the history of international law (with Dino Kritsiotis), and (in his view most successfully) a seminar on the boundaries of the market. In general his teaching attracted students, and in Michigan he became something of a pet. Brian was a hugely popular teacher—challenging, helpful, immensely learned, and yet zanily entertaining. His teaching was, indeed, legendary and his influence on those he taught long-lasting; few other academics have a Facebook fan club created by their students. And his teaching was not restricted to academic contexts. His involvement with the AIRE Centre involved teaching human rights to practitioners in Albania, the Balkans, and the Isle of Man.

Conclusion

Brian's scepticism about his long-term scholarly influence only increased with time. History is likely to be kinder to Brian on this front than he was on himself. He is likely to continue to be recognised throughout the common law world as one of the greatest academic lawyers of his generation in the fields of the history of English private law and (more recently) the history of human rights. Long after it was published, his *Introduction to the History of the Land Law* was still considered the best introduction to the long sweep of English land law not just for law students but also for undergraduate and graduate historians; for many students of the common law it was their first insight into how interesting law is, and how good legal writing can be. For the period covered, *A History of the Common Law of Contract* was considered as the most comprehensive analysis of the evolution of legal doctrine in a particular field that had been published in the common law world. His scepticism of American legal writing that ignored inconvenient facts in support of a grand theory, particularly one driven by political ideology, and his impartiality in challenging leading exponents from the American Left and the Right, was an important reminder of the importance of scholarship and rigorous independence in the midst of ideological turmoil. *Human Rights and the End of Empire* represented the most comprehensive study attempted at that time into the genesis and early years of operation of a multilateral treaty. *Reflections* provided an important attempt to link the lessons of legal history with analytical jurisprudence. His use of archival material to study a (relatively) recent case, however, was probably his most significant scholarly contribution. His demonstration of the utility of such scholarship in *Cannibalism and the Common Law* and *In the Highest Degree Odious* contributed to changing modern British and American legal scholarship.

CHRISTOPHER McCRUDDEN
Fellow of the Academy

Note. I am grateful to Thomas Green, David Sugarman, John Langbein, Dino Kritsiotis, William Twining, FBA, Nicola Lacey, FBA, William Miller, Paul Brand, FBA, Joshua Getzler, Bruce Frier and Nuala Mole for comments on earlier drafts.

ROBIN WILSON

Robert McLachlan Wilson
1916–2010

ROBERT MCLACHLAN WILSON was born on 13 February 1916 in Gourock, Renfrewshire. He was the first child of Hugh Jack McLachlan Wilson (1878–1948) and Janet Nicol Wilson (née Struthers: 1882–1965), who later had a younger son Allen (b.1922). Robert was always known as Robin (the name I shall use throughout this memoir), while in print he always styled himself R. McL. Wilson. McLachlan had been the surname of his paternal grandmother Mary Agnes Shanks McLachlan, while Robert was the name of his grandfather Robert John Wilson. Robin's mother Janet was a lady's maid and then seamstress, while his father Hugh was for twelve years a stonemason before making a career in insurance. The family lived in Greenock, where Robin attended Greenock Academy, until his father became a manager of the Royal Liver Friendly Society in Edinburgh. When the family moved to the capital, Robin attended the Royal High School, where he showed particular distinction in Greek, Latin and French, laying the foundations for his later mastery of both classical and modern languages. He became a member of St Anne's Church, Corstorphine.

Robin studied classics at the University of Edinburgh, graduating MA, with first-class honours, in 1939. (It was a distinguished year: of ten students in the class, five gained first-class degrees and three of these were later to become professors.) Robin then trained for ministry in the Church of Scotland at New College, Edinburgh, gaining his Bachelor of Divinity, with distinction in New Testament, in 1942. During these years he showed his academic excellence in this field by winning the Barty Memorial Prize for Hebrew and New Testament Greek, the C. B. Black Scholarship in New Testament Greek, the Brown Downie Scholarship, the Cunningham

Fellowship and the Aitken Fellowship. His teachers included William Manson, John Baillie, Norman Porteous, and A. M. Hunter.

Robin had become seriously deaf at the age of eleven, and so was exempted from war service. Thus he was free to pursue doctoral studies and for this purpose moved to Cambridge, where he was a member of St John's College. His research supervisor was Canon Wilfred L. Knox (one of the famous four Knox brothers, who were all brilliant in quite different ways). Robin's thesis, completed in 1945, was entitled 'Diaspora Judaism in its relation to its contemporary environment, with particular reference to the contribution of Judaism to the development of Gnosticism'. The topic had first been suggested to him by William Manson and was appropriately close to his supervisor's expertise. (One of Knox's major works, *St Paul and the Church of the Gentiles* (Cambridge, 1939), was in large part a significant study of diaspora Judaism as the principal context of the Pauline mission.)

At Cambridge, as well as gaining a Ph.D. Robin also gained a Blue in golf. In view of his later career at St Andrews, it is a little ironic that he captained the English Universities golf team when it was defeated at St Andrews by the Scottish Universities. Golf, which he had first played at school and with his father, was to be a life-long passion.

In 1945 Robin married Enid Bomford (1917–2003), who was a primary school teacher, the daughter of an English Methodist minister. They had met on holiday in the village of Kent's Bank in the Lake District (and later they would name their house in St Andrews 'Kent's Bank') and were married in Barton-on-Sea, near Bournemouth, the last place where Enid's father served as a minister. Robin and Enid were to have two children: Andrew (born 1946) and Peter (1949).

After gaining his Ph.D. in 1945, Robin returned to Scotland to exercise the ministry in the Church of Scotland for which his BD had prepared and qualified him, becoming for nine months an assistant minister at St Stephen's Church in Edinburgh, and then for eight years (1946–54) minister of Rankin Church, Strathaven, Lanarkshire. It has been suggested to me that it was in preaching and presiding at worship that Robin developed his distinctive way of speaking slowly and ponderously. According to one story, the small boys in the church used to have a competition to see how many times they could say the Lord's Prayer before Robin had finished saying it once.

Robin may reasonably have hoped in time for an academic appointment in one of the four Scottish divinity faculties. At the time these served almost exclusively for the education of ministers of the Kirk and it was common for their academic staff to have spent time in parish ministry, during which they would likely also have had time for further study. Perhaps because no such academic post in Scotland was yet forthcoming, Robin applied in 1951 for the Chair in New Testament at Ormond College, Melbourne, Australia, though he was not successful. But in 1954 (by which time he had published three scholarly articles) he was appointed Lecturer in New Testament Language and Literature at St Mary's College (the Faculty of Divinity) in the University of St Andrews. In the same year, Matthew Black (also later a Fellow of the Academy) moved from New College, Edinburgh, to become Professor of Divinity and Biblical Criticism and Principal of St Mary's College. Wilson's expertise in Gnosticism and diaspora Judaism complemented Black's in Aramaic and Palestinian Judaism. They became a distinguished team for many years. Robin was promoted to Senior Lecturer in 1964, and in 1969 was given a Personal Chair in New Testament Language and Literature. When Matthew Black retired in 1978, Robin succeeded to the Chair of Biblical Criticism.

At around the time that Robin completed his doctorate, two brothers from the village of al-Qasr near Nag Hammadi in Upper Egypt made a discovery that was to prove momentous both for the study of early Christianity and for Robin Wilson's own scholarly career. They found a large storage jar containing thirteen leather-bound books (codices) that later came to be known as the Coptic Gnostic Library or the Nag Hammadi Library. Most of the forty-six distinct tractates written in the Coptic language in these codices in the late fourth or early fifth century are Gnostic writings of second- to fourth-century origin. Their importance, which has often been compared with that of the Dead Sea Scrolls, lay in the fact that, almost for the first time, they provided scholars with first-hand access to literature written by Gnostic authors. Until the publication of the Nag Hammadi texts the study of Gnosticism had had to rely very largely on the reports of church Fathers who described Gnostic beliefs in order to refute them, along with the rather unreliable evidence of later religious groups who were indebted to Gnosticism. Robin's Ph.D. thesis had been no exception.

The story of how the Nag Hammadi codices came to scholarly attention and were eventually published is a long and complicated one. Their existence and contents were first made known to the scholarly world in 1948 and 1949. Scholarly publication about the texts really only began in 1954, and only in 1956 was even one complete tractate published. Publication of the rest proceeded frustratingly slowly. (In some correspondence on this matter between Robin Wilson and Rascher Verlag of Zurich in the 1960s, the publishers expressed annoyance at the dilatoriness of the academics.) Not until 1977, when the publication of the facsimile edition was completed and an English translation of all the tractates published, did the whole Nag Hammadi Library become generally accessible.

When Robin revised his thesis for publication (*The Gnostic Problem: a Study of the Relations between Hellenistic Judaism and the Gnostic Heresy*, London, 1958, reprinted 1964) he was able to give an account only of two of the Nag Hammadi tractates: *the Gospel of Truth*, an edition of which had appeared in 1956, and the *Apocryphon of John*, another copy of which had long been known to exist in a Berlin manuscript but was only published (with some information about the two copies in the Nag Hammadi codices) in 1955. But, as already an expert on Gnosticism, Robin was in an unusually favourable position to make use of the new discoveries as they became available. Indeed, he became the only British scholar of his generation who studied and published extensively on the Nag Hammadi Library. By 1955 he had already realised that the Coptic language was now essential for the study of Gnosticism and wrote to the distinguished German Coptologist Walter Till (who had edited the Berlin codex and was then in Manchester) for advice on learning the language. They kept up a correspondence about Coptic and the Nag Hammadi texts until Till's death in 1963.

Robin's own approach to Gnosticism began with his investigation of the possible Jewish origins of the movement. He found important sources of Gnostic ideas in syncretistic forms of diaspora Judaism, including the Jewish philosopher Philo of Alexandria, but there were also Christian and pagan philosophical elements in the eclectic mix that created second-century Gnosticism. Looking for Jewish origins of Gnosticism was unusual at that time, but it has subsequently been vindicated by the Nag Hammadi texts. In 1967 Robin was able to say that the Jewish contribution to Gnosticism was now beyond question and that the danger lay now in neglecting the Hellenistic elements.[1]

Robin's work mediated between the two rather different approaches to Gnosticism that were traditional in German and British scholarship respectively. Whereas the British tended to see Gnosticism as a Christian heresy of the second century, the Germans took a much broader view of *die Gnosis*, seeing it as a vast movement in the history of ancient religion,

[1] 'Addenda et postscripta', in Ugo Bianchi (ed.), *Le Origini dello Gnosticismo: Colloquio di Messina 13–18, Aprile 1966* (Leiden, 1967), p. 693.

whose influence could be identified in many places, including the New Testament. In *The Gnostic Problem* Robin distinguished narrower and broader senses of the term. In the broader sense Gnosticism was 'an atmosphere, not a system', but in the more precise sense of a religious system it did not antedate the New Testament. In the writers of the New Testament or the opponents they refute there may be evidence of ideas related to Gnosticism but not of 'fully-developed Gnosticism'. (Later he was to use the term Gnosis to distinguish the broader sense.)

We see here Robin's characteristic concern for careful definition and his caution about drawing sweeping conclusions not warranted by the evidence. The vexed question of defining Gnosticism frequently occupied Robin in years to come, as it did other scholars in the field, along with the question of the existence of a pre-Christian Gnosticism, for which the Nag Hammadi documents provided a great deal of new and debatable material. It is now widely recognised that too facile a use of the term Gnosticism runs the risk of overlooking the real differences between the groups and writings that have been labelled Gnostic, but Robin was already urging caution in this respect as early as 1955.[2] One of his doctoral students, Alastair Logan, who was himself to contribute significantly to the study of Gnosticism, comments that Robin 'was never carried away with the latest fad or fashion in research, even if his refusal to be dogmatic about any issue infuriated some'.

The most famous of the Nag Hammadi tractates is doubtless the *Gospel of Thomas*, which, as a so-called 'fifth Gospel', captured the public imagination as early as 1959 (when Robin himself wrote an article on it for the *Daily Telegraph*), following the publication of translations and studies of the work in German (1958), French and English (1959). Robin got to work on this text as soon as he was able and, working with remarkable speed, was able to submit his book on it to his publishers in April 1960. It was published the same year with the title *Studies in the Gospel of Thomas* (London, 1960). (American scholars Robert M. Grant and David Noel Freedman were also quick off the mark with their *The Secret Sayings of Jesus*, London, 1960.) The big question, which has still not been fully resolved, was whether this collection of sayings of Jesus preserved genuine sayings independently of the four canonical Gospels. Most New Testament scholars at first saw this Gospel as no more than a compilation made from the canonical Gospels, while those such as Gilles Quispel who argued that there could be independent traditions in *Thomas* were not

[2] 'Gnostic origins', *Vigiliae Christinae*, 9 (1955), 193–211.

taken seriously. Robin magisterially discussed all the research that had been done up to that point and carefully argued his own view of the individual sayings, uninhibited by the consensus among his colleagues in the New Testament field. (Quispel later commented that, from his perspective, Robin in this book 'saved the honour of New Testament scholarship'.[3]) Robin concluded that in some cases the *Gospel of Thomas* probably preserves sayings of Jesus in a more original form than those to be found in the canonical Gospels, a view which has subsequently become common, though not universal.

Einar Thomassen of the University of Bergen, who studied for his doctorate with Robin and is himself an expert on Valentinian Gnosticism, comments that Robin's

> book on Thomas deserves even greater recognition than it has received. It is written in an almost self-effacingly modest style, arguing for and against various propositions in a manner which is more designed to allow the reader to make up his or her own mind than to highlight the author's own position on the issue.

He contrasts this with the 'more self-assertive style' of more recent scholarship.[4] The modesty is typical not only of Robin's published work, which makes its impact much more by meticulous scholarship than by grandiose claims, but also of his personal style, which was characteristically unassuming.

Robin's work on Thomas was soon followed by *The Gospel of Philip* (London, 1962), which included his own translation of this Nag Hammadi tractate from the Coptic as well as introduction and detailed commentary. In the 1960s and 1970s he also collaborated with European scholars (including Puech, Quispel and Till) on editions of the remaining tractates in Codex Jung (Codex I of the Nag Hammadi Library, which, alone of the codices, had found its way to the Jung Institute in Zurich), for which Robin provided or checked the English translations.

Kendrick Grobel, an American Nag Hammadi scholar, invited Robin to spend the first semester of 1965 as Visiting Professor at Vanderbilt Divinity School in Nashville, Tennessee. (Sadly, Grobel died while Robin and Enid were at Vanderbilt.) Enid accompanied Robin on this adventure and they spent three months of the six on a lecturing tour of several uni-

[3] Gilles Quiespel, 'Judaism, Judaic Christianity and Gnosis', in A. H. B. Logan and A. J. M. Wedderburn (eds.), *The New Testament and Gnosis: Essays in Honour of Robert McL. Wilson* (Edinburgh, 1983), p. 46.

[4] Einar Thomassen, 'The contribution of Robert McL. Wilson to the study of gnosticism', unpublished paper read to the celebration of Robin Wilson's ninetieth birthday in St Mary's College, St Andrews, in 2006.

versities and colleges in the United States and Canada, including the University of California at Berkeley, the University of Pennsylvania in Philadelphia and St Andrews Presbyterian College in Laurinburg, North Carolina (owing to its link, in both denomination and nomenclature, with Robin's own institution). The lectures were on Gnosticism and the New Testament and they became *Gnosis and the New Testament* (Oxford, 1968). Surprisingly, Mowbrays, who had published his previous books, were not willing to take another book on Gnosticism, and so he approached Basil Blackwell of Oxford. It was published simultaneously in the USA by Fortress Press, Philadelphia. A French translation appeared in 1969 and a German translation in 1970. Robin's easy mastery of the field is amply evident in this book.

The use of 'Gnosis' rather than 'Gnosticism' in the title (following German practice) stems from the distinction he made between Gnosis as the 'wider and vaguer' phenomenon, which may have influenced the New Testament, and Gnosticism, the developed religious systems of the second century. He is cautious about the usefulness even of identifying Gnosis in the broad sense in New Testament writings, pointing out how often the ideas in question may be Jewish or Hellenistic philosophical notions that Gnostics later adopted. Only in the cases of 1 John and the Pastorals does he allow that there may be traces of 'Gnosticism proper'. This measured critique of the dominant position in German scholarship set a direction that was to be widely followed. As well as the possible influence of Gnosis in the New Testament, the book also dealt with the use of the New Testament by the Gnostic writers of Nag Hammadi tractates, of which however there were still only nine published and translated.

Following the Messina Colloquium on the Origins of Gnosticism in 1966 (in which Robin participated and where he recommended the use of his distinction between Gnosis and Gnosticism), Gnostic scholars, among whom James M. Robinson of Claremont was especially prominent, undertook a fresh initiative to energise a UNESCO plan for publishing a complete facsimile of the Nag Hammadi codices. At the same time Robinson organised a team of scholars working under the auspices of the Institute for Antiquity and Christianity at Claremont Graduate School to prepare a multivolume English language edition of the codices. Robin was the only British member of the international committee for the Nag Hammadi codices that planned the facsimile edition (it began to be published in 1972) and also the only British member of the editorial board of the Coptic Gnostic Library, the English translations that began to appear in the series Nag Hammadi Studies in 1975. Particularly valuable were

Robin's command of German and French and his meticulous eye for detail. His own contributions to the translation project were to prepare the preliminary versions of the *Acts of Peter and the Twelve Apostles*, completed by Douglas Parrott, and the *Gospel of Mary*, completed by George MacRae. He remained a member of the board until 1991.

Robin also undertook the provision of English translations of two major German sources on Gnosticism: the two-volume anthology of texts edited by Werner Foerster (published in German in 1969 and 1971) and Kurt Rudolph's magisterial study of Gnosticism, the best general book on the subject at that time (published in German in 1977, revised edition 1980). While Robin did major parts of these translations himself, he also recruited other translators, whose work he edited. In the case of Rudolph's book, one of these was his St Andrews colleague Peter Coxon, who remembers that this task 'developed into a convivial and lively collaboration between Leipzig and St Andrews, every stage of which progressed under Robin Wilson's scrupulous editorial eye'. The English translation of Foerster's collection (*Gnosis: a Selection of Gnostic Texts*, 2 volumes, Oxford, 1972 and 1974) was more than a translation of the German. It involved much reference back to the sources in their original languages. Robin's fastidious attention to detail, as well as his command of languages, was invaluable in an editor of such projects. The translation of Rudolph's book (*Gnosis: the Nature and History of Gnosticism*, Edinburgh, 1984) was reissued in a paperback edition in 1987 (New York). As well as recruiting translators, Robin liked to use his postgraduate students for help with editing and proofreading large projects such as these.

Robin's work of this kind was not confined to Gnosticism. He realised that the Nag Hammadi literature was also related to that very heterogeneous body of early Christian literature known as 'New Testament Apocrypha'. The well-known English edition of such works, edited by M. R. James in 1924, was now very out-dated compared with the latest edition of the corresponding German collection. This collection had originally been edited by Edgar Hennecke, but the much revised third edition (two volumes, 1959 and 1964) was overseen by Wilhelm Schneemelcher. In 1959 Robin began to plan an English version of 'Hennecke–Schneemelcher' and discussed it with the publishers Lutterworth. It was a particularly complex task (again much more than a mere translation from the German), for which he supervised a team of translators, as well as doing much of the work himself. The first English edition of *New Testament Apocrypha* (London, 1963 and 1965; reprinted 1973–4) became a standard work of reference, but Robin's concern with this work was not over. By the time the German collection reached its sixth edition, much revised and expanded, not least by the inclusion of some Nag Hammadi texts (1989 and 1990), Robin realised that a correspondingly thorough revision of the English version was needed and once again supervised its production (Cambridge and Louisville, KY, 1991 and 1992). Another major project of translating and editing that he undertook was the English version of Ernst Haenchen's important German commentary on Acts (*The Acts of the Apostles*, Oxford and Philadelphia, PA, 1971), following a sorry tale of bad and incomplete efforts at translation that Haenchen refused to approve.

Robin's well-known meticulous attention to detail derived in part from the fact that he read everything thoroughly. In his numerous reviews he always listed minor errors and in writing to fellow scholars about their books he did the same. Authors and publishers took to asking him to read their work before it went to press, when the detection of errors was much more useful. When he sent me a copy of his last book he included a note explaining a minor bibliographical error he had noticed only after publication.[5]

Another direction in which his interest in the Nag Hammadi texts led Robin was into Coptic studies. In 1976, as a member of the international Nag Hammadi committee, he attended the first International Congress of Coptology in Cairo and then edited two volumes of papers given at the congress. In 1977 he was invited to assist the production of a multivolume *Coptic Encyclopedia* (published in eight volumes, New York, 1991) by organising the translation of articles written in German and French. He recruited three other translators (again including Peter Coxon) but, since he was the only one who knew even part of the field, he edited the translations and corresponded with the authors of the articles about the translations. When he deposited the file of his working papers and correspondence on this project in the university archives, he wrote a covering sheet explaining his part in the project. He wrote that he thought the material might be of interest 'as illustrating what (inter alia) a St Andrews professor did with some of his (allegedly!) abundant leisure'. Indeed, surveying Robin's prolific output of books, articles, and reviews, and considering the care with which he worked, it is hard to see how he could have had any leisure time. In fact, he certainly took time for golf and for entertaining at home. Moreover, he typically conducted himself in an unhurried manner, always readily accessible to students and happy to talk with colleagues.

[5] In the same book (Wilson's commentary on *Colossians and Philemon*, p. 376) I myself noted one, faintly amusing typo that had escaped Robin's eagle eye: 'Wedderbum' for 'Wedderburn'.

When he first took up his appointment at St Mary's, he and Enid and the two boys lived for a short period in Crail until the construction of their house at 10 Murrayfield Road, St Andrews, was completed. Robin was to stay in this house for the rest of his life. In the course of time the family had two cats, named Marco (because he was always exploring) and Philo (after the Jewish theologian-philosopher who featured frequently in Robin's work). Robin and Enid were known for the generous hospitality they extended to both colleagues and students. He was a long-term member of the New Golf Club of St Andrews,[6] and was fortunate in sharing his passion for golf with both his colleagues in New Testament at St Mary's: Matthew Black and Ernest ('Paddy') Best (irreverently known to students at St Mary's as 'third Best'). Enid was Secretary of the St Andrews Ladies' Putting Club, and they both putted a lot on the 'Himalayas', as the club's putting course is called. After Robin's retirement and when Paddy Best returned to St Andrews in his retirement, they frequently played golf together.

Robin never forgot that at heart he was a minister of the church or that his job was to teach future ministers of the church. His inaugural lecture as Professor of Biblical Criticism was entitled 'The study, the pulpit and the pew'. He and Enid were faithful and committed members of St Leonard's Church, where he is said to have carried his learning with humility. People of all ages knew him simply as Robin. A year after his death a member of the church told me that he was so integral to the church it felt as though he were still there. He also faithfully attended meetings of the Kirk Session until late in his life, making relevant and succinct contributions. He served the General Assembly as Convenor of the Union and Re-adjustment Committee, a rather thankless task as, for the sake of managing the church's resources better, it required closing church buildings. Church members are rarely happy to see their own church closed so that they can be merged with another. But the painstaking negotiations involved required just the sort of careful attention that Robin's mind naturally gave to whatever he did.

In 1955 Robin was elected to membership of the International Society for New Testament Studies (Studiorum Novi Testamenti Societas), to which Matthew Black had belonged since the first of its annual general meetings in 1947. Also in 1955, the society's journal *New Testament Studies* was launched, with Matthew Black as its Editor. Robin, whose editorial

[6] The New Golf Club was given this name when it was founded in 1902: the 'Old Golf Club' was the Royal and Ancient.

skills must have already been evident, was soon assisting Black in this task. On Black's recommendation, the society's committee formalised his role, appointing him Associate Editor in 1967. He then succeeded Black as Editor in 1977, and at the same time also succeeded Black as Editor of the society's prestigious Monograph Series, which had begun publication in 1965. He was assisted by Margaret Thrall of Bangor as Associate Editor. The two publication series flourished under their guiding hand. At a meeting of the Editorial Board in 1981, it was suggested that members of the Board might play a larger part in assessing material submitted for publication, thus relieving the Editor and Associate Editor of some of the very heavy load they were carrying. But, declining the offer, Robin stressed that he would still feel the need to read everything himself. Among other things, he needed to check the correct use of the English language. Moreover, not all readers of manuscripts reported in sufficient detail. He remained Editor until 1983.

Presidents of the society serve for only one year, which includes one general meeting. Robin was elected President for 1981–2, in recognition both of his outstanding service to the society and of his eminence as a scholar in the field. It cannot have come as a surprise that his presidential address was on 'Nag Hammadi and the New Testament'.[7] (It is a magisterial assessment of the issues, engaging, as his work always did, with the latest as well as the older contributions.) Over the years he and Enid together attended most of the annual meetings of the Society of New Testament Studies, held in various locations in Europe and occasionally elsewhere. Only late in life when he became more deaf and found conferences difficult did he cease to attend.

Other academic honours came to him. He was elected a Fellow of the British Academy in 1977, and was awarded the Academy's Burkitt Medal for Biblical Studies in 1990. He was awarded the honorary degree of Doctor of Divinity by the University of Aberdeen in 1981. When he retired in 1983, St Andrews University made him Emeritus Professor and he continued to take some part in university affairs. To mark his retirement, Alastair Logan, Robin's former doctoral student, and A. J. M. ('Sandy') Wedderburn, Robin's junior colleague in New Testament at St Mary's, edited a Festschrift for him: *The New Testament and Gnosis* (Edinburgh, 1983), a deliberate inversion of the title of his own book *Gnosis and the New Testament*. Those who contributed essays include almost all the leading scholars of

[7] Published in *New Testament Studies*, 28 (1982), 289–392.

Gnosticism, many of whom engage directly with Robin's work and proposals in their essays. It is interesting to note that that Matthew Black and C. K. Barrett of Durham were the only British contributors (neither an expert on Gnosticism). The rest were from Germany, France, the Netherlands, Italy, Canada and the USA. This is testimony that Robin was still a rare, as well as the leading British, scholar in this field. Quite a few of these Gnostic scholars had become friends whom he met frequently at conferences and with whom he continued to keep in touch throughout his life, latterly by email.

Robin's scholarly efforts in the later part of his career were by no means confined to the massive tasks of editing and translating described here. He continued to publish many articles on Gnosticism in journals and reference works. But he also worked on two New Testament commentaries. His commentary on *Hebrews* in the New Century Bible series was commissioned by Matthew Black, who edited the New Testament part of the series, and his commentary on Colossians and Philemon in the new International Critical Commentary series was commissioned by Charles Cranfield, who edited the New Testament volumes in that series.[8] No doubt his particular expertise recommended him for writing on these particular parts of the New Testament: diaspora Judaism in the case of Hebrews, Gnosticism in the case of Colossians.

The commentary on *Hebrews* was published in 1987 (Basingstoke and Grand Rapids, MI). The style of the New Century Bible is to be accessible to the non-specialist reader, though it can hardly be said to be popularising. The commentary is on the English text of the Revised Standard Version without discussion of the Greek (though with students like his own in mind, Robin frequently gives references to the entries in the standard lexicon where information on the Greek words is to be found). Only later did he confess that for 'one accustomed to referring to his Greek New Testament rather than to the English version, the writing of such a commentary can be an exacting task!'[9] Nevertheless he deals with sometimes quite esoteric material (almost unavoidable in a commentary on Hebrews) with his usual clarity. While he discusses the usual introductory questions (authorship, date, place of origin and destination, background of ideas), which are particularly hard to answer in this case, he takes the

[8] The series was informally known as the New ICC, because it emulates and replaces the original ICC, which was never completed.
[9] ICC, p. ix.

view that perhaps they do not make much difference to the understanding of the text, and his exegesis is independent of any particular answers to them. On affinities with Philo and Gnosticism, his particular expertise, he observes that the differences from Philo are as significant as the resemblances, while Gnostic influence must be judged 'at most very slight' (p. 26).

He accepted the invitation to write the ICC volume on *Colossians and Philemon* in 1973, but the fact that it did not appear until 2005 (London and New York) is not unusual in the context of that series. The style of commentary required for the ICC—detailed and rigorously scholarly treatment of the Greek text—made it a considerable undertaking, and many a scholar who signed up to write a volume in this series treated it as largely a project for his or her retirement. With Robin's advancing age, the editors (Cranfield was later joined by Graham Stanton) must have had doubts whether he would finish it (it would not have been the first of the ICC volumes to be left unfinished at the author's death) and I remember Robin himself telling me at one stage that he doubted whether he would. In the event, the commentary was finished and published when he was 89.

A characteristic of the commentary (which is also quite characteristic of his scholarship in general) is Robin's refusal to offer a fresh overall thesis about Colossians (which he thought belongs in a monograph). Instead, he focuses on the detail of exegesis, while in the extensive introduction he surveys and weighs the various proposals on the big questions and reaches only cautious and undogmatic conclusions. On the complex question of authenticity (did Paul himself write this letter?) he finally comments:

> Such tentative and hesitant conclusions will not, of course, satisfy those who must at all costs have a definite and clear-cut answer to every question, but there are times when it is important to recognize the limitations of our knowledge. We do not always have the evidence upon which to face a firm judgment. (p. 34)

He makes the same point about the equally disputed issue of the nature of the 'errors' current in the Colossian church: 'sometimes the simple, clear-cut answer is only found by reading more into the text than is actually there' (p. 233, and cf. 308).

The trend of scholarship has been away from postulating Gnostic influence and towards either some form of mystical-apocalyptic Judaism or (most recently at the time when Robin was writing) popular magical practices. Robin deploys his now well-known distinction between Gnosis and Gnosticism, maintaining, as we would expect, that the evidence cannot support the presence of 'full-blown Gnosticism' of the second-century kind, but that 'some form of incipient Gnosis', ideas of a Gnostic nature without the radical dualism distinctive of later Gnosticism, may be current in the background to the letter. But just as he had long insisted that the roots of Gnosticism were not one but many (including both Jewish and pagan contributions), so he is loath to close the door to any of the recent suggestions about what he still calls the Colossian 'heresy' (but the quotation marks are his): 'It may be that the hypotheses reviewed above are not altogether mutually exclusive, and that eventually more than one of these influences contributed to the final result' (p. 58).

The ICC is not at all a homiletic commentary, being focused on the original meaning of the texts rather than their contemporary relevance, but in his Epilogue to the commentary on Colossians and at the end of his Introduction to Philemon Robin allowed himself some reflections on application to the contemporary scene in church and world (as he did not do in his commentary on Hebrews). For example, commenting on the issue of the church's attitude to slavery in the ancient and later periods (obviously raised by the letter to Philemon), he reflects that the church's ability to effect major changes in society may now be much as it was in Paul's day:

> It may be that the real task of the Church ... is to seek to spread more widely in our own day that same spirit of Christian charity which was eventually to bring about the abolition of slavery. What matters here is not the promulgation of doctrinaire statements as to what 'society' (or some other body, but usually other than the speaker!) ought to be doing; it is what we ourselves are prepared to do, in obedience to Christ our Lord and Master, in our dealings with other people. There can be no evasion of responsibility. (p. 330)

Such an explicitly homiletical comment is unlikely to be found in an ICC volume by a scholar of a younger generation, but it witnesses to the fact that Robin continued to find the scriptural text he studied with such scholarly rigour also an inspiration for faith.

In 1999, at a time when Robin confessed he had given up hope of holding a grandchild in his arms, he and Enid shared the delight of the birth of their granddaughter Ellen. Enid died on Christmas Day, 2003. In the preface to his commentary on *Colossians and Philemon* (2005), which he dedicated to her memory, he wrote:

> she was a good companion and supportive partner through all the years of our married life, and possessed a real flair for getting on with other people, no matter who they might be. Some verses in the last chapter of Proverbs are not relevant (Enid never had a staff of servants to do her bidding, nor did she ever

> purchase a vineyard with the fruit of her labours!), but reading the passage again, as I have done often in recent months, I can only say that I was privileged to have a very capable wife, truly more precious than jewels. I am now beyond the stage of merely grieving, and look back on the years of our married life with proud thanksgiving.

In February 2006 a celebration, attended by former students and colleagues, was held in St Mary's College to mark his ninetieth birthday. Einar Thomassen reviewed his work on Gnosticism and the Nag Hammadi library. Bill Telford, long-term Secretary of the Society for New Testament Studies, chronicled the early days of the society and the role Robin played in them (which he had researched in the society's archive). I spoke about his work on the New Testament Apocrypha and on Colossians. Robin himself concluded the more serious business of the day with reminiscences of his career, and later, amid refreshments and birthday cake, David Parker, another distinguished former student, and Ron Piper, whose own career in New Testament at St Mary's had begun while Robin was Professor, shared memories of Robin as teacher and colleague, both fondly and entertainingly.

He remained intellectually active to the last. He kept abreast of developments in his field, including the appearance (made public in 2006 with absurdly sensational reports in the press) of another long-lost Gnostic work, *The Gospel of Judas*, and the spate of books about it that soon appeared. He reviewed at least one of these, and indeed continued to review books regularly up until he died. Rather unusually for someone of his generation, quite late in life he began using the internet and email, which was particularly useful to him as an alternative to the telephone when he was hard of hearing. He stayed in his own home, regularly visited by his two sons and their families. In June 2010, he suffered a stroke, fortunately while his son Andrew was with him. He died a week later in Ninewells Hospital, Dundee, on Sunday, 27 June aged 94.

RICHARD BAUCKHAM
Fellow of the Academy

Note. There is a Bibliography of Robin Wilson's published works (including reviews) up to 1981, compiled by Ronald A. Piper, in A. H. B. Logan and A. J. M. Wedderburn (eds.) *The New Testament and Gnosis: Essays in Honour of Robert McL. Wilson* (Edinburgh, 1983), pp. 245–58. Unfortunately there is no such bibliography of his later work. There are seventeen boxes of his academic papers and correspondence, dating from the years 1955–84, in St Andrews University Library Special Collections

(MS 38376/1–19). I am grateful to Rachel Hart, Muniments Archivist and Deputy Head of Special Collections, for drawing these to my attention. I am much indebted to Andrew Wilson for information about his father and for letting me see a collection of family documents relating to him. Others who shared information and memories with me include Alastair Logan, Ronald Piper, Robin Salters and Bill Shaw.

BOB WOODS

Robert Ivor Woods
1949–2011

Personal and professional career

IT WAS WITH MUCH SADNESS that colleagues at the University of Liverpool and friends in the population geography community in Britain learnt of Robert (Bob) Woods's premature death on 20 February 2011. The portrait captures Bob's personality well. He was a lovable, humorous and thoughtful professor with a network of research collaborators, the foremost being his Ph.D. students. He gave them great encouragement long after they had 'left the nest'. A few personal memories are appropriate here. Bob and I collaborated in the mid-1980s on an edited book on *Population Models and Structures*.[1] His gentle encouragement to get the job done was much appreciated. Looking back, Bob's contribution to the book represented his goodbye to spatial demography; thereafter he and his students immersed themselves in historical demography. People live on in the memory of those who have lived and worked with them. Bob touched many lives in his time. A small touching moment occurred during a Ph.D. examination I conducted in August 2011 at Liverpool. During the examination conversation the candidate and I were talking about her influences while at the Liverpool department. There was a small tear in her eyes as she mentioned that Bob had found time to talk encouragingly about her research, even though he was not her supervisor.

Born on 17 September 1949 in Birmingham, he was aged 61 when he died in Chester of pancreatic cancer. He is survived and sadly missed by

[1] R. I. Woods and P. H. Rees (eds.), *Population Structures and Models* (London, 1986).

Biographical Memoirs of Fellows of the British Academy, XI, 601–620.

his wife, Alison, who provided a bedrock of support throughout his career, by his daughter Rachel, whose artistic and teaching career he nurtured, and by his son, Gavin, to whom Bob gave paternal support in his rugby and teaching pursuits. He was also survived by his mother Rhoda, who brought him up after she was divorced from her husband Ivor Woods. Ivor maintained contact with his son and so he had joint parental support in his schooling years. Bob attended direct grant Handsworth Grammar School in the 1960s and received an excellent education which prepared him for a successful application to the University of Cambridge.

He joined Fitzwilliam College, Cambridge in 1968 and graduated with a BA in Geography in summer 1971. His Director of Studies was Brian Robson (now a professor at the University of Manchester) who recalls that Bob

> was a very rewarding, larger-than-life undergraduate, full of fun and with a mischievous sense of humour that, I suspect, partly tried to hide his dedication to things academic and his real enthusiasm for his subject and a fascination with the detail of the intellectual puzzles that he set himself. He was very self-deprecating, but above all a very kind and generous man [with] boundless cheerfulness.

Brian Robson published his classic text on urban social geography in 1969,[2] and this probably influenced Bob to apply for a Ph.D. opportunity in the subfield that became available. Although Tony Wrigley was researching and lecturing in Historical Demography at Cambridge while Bob was an undergraduate, it was only later that he engaged with Tony's work in the field.

Bob began his postgraduate studies in 1971 at St Antony's College, Oxford, working on his doctorate for three years with supervisor Ceri Peach (now Emeritus Professor of Social Geography) at the Oxford School of Geography. He submitted his dissertation on *Dynamic Urban Social Structure* (over 800 pages, completed in less than four years) and passed his D.Phil. examination in 1975. The University of Cambridge recognised his achievements with the subsequent award of a D.Litt. degree. Bob added to the spatial perspective of the ethnic segregation work of his supervisor a dynamic temporal perspective: his immigrant groups in Birmingham moved around, left old neighbourhoods, occupied new territory and so transformed socio-geographic space. The importance of analysing population processes simultaneously in space and time continued to be a methodological focus throughout his career.

[2] B. T. Robson *Urban Analysis: a Study of City Structure with Special Reference to Sunderland* (Cambridge, 1969).

At the University of Oxford, Bob was fortunate to be part of an influential group of research postgraduates who went on to greater things. The group that worked in the 'lower room for postgraduates' included Paul White (a colleague at the University of Sheffield, Professor of Geography and Pro-Vice-Chancellor), Philip Ogden (Professor at Queen Mary London and Pro-Vice-Chancellor), the late Dennis Cosgrove (Alexander von Humboldt Professor at the University of California, Los Angeles), Morag Bell (Professor of Geography, Loughborough University) and Eric Pawson (Professor of Geography, University of Canterbury), while in the 'upper room' was Tony Champion (Emeritus Professor of Population Geography, Newcastle University). It would have been fascinating to have eavesdropped on their discussions and debates.

Bob took up his first academic job at the Social Statistics Unit, University of Kent, in 1974, where he started his demographic teaching. Being asked to teach a course in demography in his first postdoctoral job was to influence his subsequent career. He employed the demographic knowledge and skills acquired at Kent in his subsequent research and forged a strong bond between demography and population studies in his subsequent publications.

In 1975, he moved to a lecturer post at the Department of Geography, University of Sheffield. His appointment panel included Ron Johnston, later Professor and Head of Department (now Professor at the University of Bristol), who supported Bob Woods in his developing career, teaching some joint courses and helping in his promotion to Senior Lecturer. It was at the University of Sheffield that Bob met his wife Alison (née Cook), a graduate from the University of Aberdeen who joined the department in 1976 as a lecturer in aerial photography interpretation and analysis. Bob and Alison married in 1977. Their daughter, Rachel, was born in 1979 and their son Gavin in 1982. Alison took up the role of home maker, later taking a Postgraduate Certificate of Education and becoming a secondary school teacher of geography. Key collaborators during Bob's fourteen-year spell at the University of Sheffield were Paul White, with whom he edited a collection on the impacts of migration,[3] and John Woodward, a medical historian who invited Bob to participate in the seminar series of the Department of Social and Economic History there. This awakened Bob's interest in historical demography. John Woodward and Bob Woods collaborated on a successful ESRC grant to pursue research in the area and together they edited an important book on morbidity and mortality

[3] P. E. White and R. I. Woods (eds.), *The Geographical Impact of Migration* (London, 1980).

in nineteenth-century England.[4] At the University of Sheffield Bob also began his career as a supervisor of doctoral students, in which he was to excel.

In 1989 Bob Woods moved to take up a Chair in Historical Geography at the University of Liverpool and in 1996 was appointed John Rankin Professor of Geography. At Liverpool, he established the MA in Population Studies. He served as Head of Department between 1993 and 1996, Faculty Director of Postgraduate Research and Associate Dean for Postgraduate Studies between 1998 and 2002. Later he led the People, Space and Place Research Cluster.

Throughout his time at Sheffield and Liverpool, Bob was a very active supervisor of doctoral students, shepherding twenty-five to a doctorate and engaging actively with many of them in joint publications. Several of his students have progressed to take up posts in Historical Demography and allied fields in British and overseas institutions: Andy Hinde is a Senior Lecturer and Head of Division of Social Statistics and Demography at the University of Southampton; Eilidh Garrett is a Senior Research Associate at the Cambridge Group for the History of Population and Social Structure, University of Cambridge; Chris Galley is a Lecturer and researcher at Barnsley College; Graham Mooney is Professor in the Institute of the History of Medicine at Johns Hopkins University, Baltimore; Catriona Ni Laoire is a Research Officer and part-time Lecturer at University College, Cork; Nicola Shelton is Head of the Health and Social Surveys research group at the University College London Research Department of Epidemiology and Public Health; Chris Smith works in population research at the Office for National Statistics; Mark Brown is a Senior Lecturer in the School of Social Sciences at the University of Manchester; Violetta Hionidou is Senior Lecturer in the School of History, Classics and Archaeology, Newcastle University; and Clare Holdsworth is Professor of Social Geography in the Department of Geography, Geology and the Environment, Keele University. Bob's students were very appreciative of his wise and skilled supervision. Chris Smith wrote his appreciation:[5] 'As a supervisor Bob Woods was simply superb. He was always available, approachable and down-to-earth, calm, and directed me in a very subtle way to focus on particular issues ... He was in every sense

[4] R. I. Woods and J. H. Woodward (eds.) *Urban Disease and Mortality in Nineteenth-Century England* (London, 1984).

[5] Published as part of the programme of the Bob Woods Memorial Symposium held at the University of Liverpool, 9–10 March 2012, p. 20. <http://www.liv.ac.uk/environmental-sciences/bob_woods_memorial_symposium/index.html> (accessed 12 June 2012).

exceptional.' Chris Galley observed in his *Lancet* obituary that 'I cannot recall anyone who worked closely with Woods having a bad word to say about him. When I worked with him I was always keen to please: but you didn't do this by agreeing with him, you did it by telling him something interesting that he didn't already know.'[6] Nicola Shelton testified that '[Bob Woods] was the best boss I ever had; he was always interested in my work and a fantastic mentor.'[7]

Bob Woods gave generously of his time to learned society activities. He served on the committee of the Royal Geographical Society, with the Institute of British Geographers' Population Geography Research Group (POPGRG) in various capacities which has, in his honour, established the 'Bob Woods Prize' for Best Postgraduate Dissertation in Population Studies at a UK university, with a first call for nominations in 2012. I am sure Bob would have been very pleased with this initiative. On behalf of the POPGRG, he was founding co-editor with Huw Jones of the *International Journal of Population Geography* from 1997 to 2002. The journal continues to go from strength to strength as *Population, Space and Place*. In 2003 he became one of the co-editors of the journal *Population Studies*, until illness intervened. He was an active member of the British Society for Population Studies, serving as its President in 1991.

His contributions to knowledge were recognised by election to a Fellowship of the British Academy in 2003 (section S4, Sociology, Demography and Social Statistics with cross-membership in section S3, Anthropology and Geography). He was later elected to the Academy of Learned Societies for the Social Sciences. He received the Royal Scottish Geographical Society's Newbigin Award in 2005, was awarded Research Fellowships by the Nuffield Foundation in 1984–5 and the Wellcome Trust in 2005–7, and took up a Visiting Fellowship at All Soul's College, Oxford in 2005.

Themes of his four decades of scholarship

Bob's career was a journey across a landscape of subdisciplines within geography. As a research postgraduate he was a social geographer who used spatial demographic methods to understand the dynamics of rapidly

[6] Chris Galley, 'Robert Ivor Woods', *The Lancet*, 377(9774): 1312, 16 April 2011, doi:10.1016/S0140-6736(11)60529-1.

[7] Quoted in Chris Galley's *Lancet* obituary.

growing immigrant subpopulations in a major metropolis. Then as a teacher he had to prepare a lecture course in formal demography and embraced these techniques in his subsequent research, following the precept that if you want to learn a subject thoroughly, then teach a course on it. He developed an abiding interest in population theory, which requires viewing population change and its drivers across decades and centuries. At first his empirical explorations in the 1970s and early 1980s were into contemporary population developments. Then, inspired by the reading of Tony Wrigley's important book on historical demography,[8] and the publication of Wrigley and Schofield's seminal work on the history of the population of England in 1981, he applied his intellectual curiosity and formidable theoretical and empirical analysis skills to the field of historical demography. Spending time reading and interpreting the historical records of the population in the archives, in his study at home or in cafés on field trips suited his personality. Understanding the patterns, transitions and causes of mortality of nineteenth-century England was the main focus of his work from the early 1980s to the 2000s. In the last decade he added to his meticulous quantitative analysis an interest in the contributions of individuals to the reduction of mortality and in the emotional impact of mortality on Victorian society at a time when death rates were, from a contemporary viewpoint, truly horrendous. His book *Children Remembered* is a unique combination of demographic and literary analysis, replete with poetry and painting, which demonstrated that parents, even in an age of large families, were still deeply moved by the death of their children.[9] His colleague Paul Williamson has reviewed Bob's career in scholarship in a piece in *Progress in Human Geography,* which includes a listing of his publications.[10]

Bob Woods authored many books: an influential textbook which provides an excellent introduction to population analysis methods, including standard, abridged and model life tables and the Coale fertility indexes;[11] a textbook on population theory which places the techniques of the first book into a wider explanatory framework;[12] and a set of research mono-

[8] R. I. Woods, 'Textbooks that moved generations—E. A. Wrigley, *Population and History* (1969)', *Progress in Human Geography*, 30 (2006), 405–8.

[9] R. I. Woods, *Children Remembered: Responses to Untimely Death in the Past* (Liverpool and Chicago, IL, 2006).

[10] P. Williamson, 'Robert I. Woods (1949–2011)', *Progress in Human Geography*, 2012, doi: 10.1177/0309132511408274.

[11] R. I. Woods, *Population Analysis in Geography* (London, 1979).

[12] R. I. Woods, *Theoretical Population Geography* (London, 1982).

graphs in the field of historical demography, covering population history, mortality, and infant and fetal health and mortality.[13] Bob's books set a new course for population geography in adopting more rigorous methods of analysing population change. Description of static population geographies would no longer be enough in future. Bob was comfortable with the mathematics of demographic analysis and felt that population geographers should understand the basics. In this we shared a common belief, though today only a minority of population geographers are comfortable navigating the algebra and graphics of formal demography.

Bob wrote fifty-four articles in peer-reviewed journals, starting in 1976 with a paper on the effect of spatial scale on the computation of segregation indexes[14] and ending in 2009 with a paper on disease environments in Victorian England and Wales.[15] He also wrote up his research output in book chapters in edited collections, of which he produced five with colleagues.[16] Some of these chapters are context setting pieces;[17] others are important syntheses of knowledge and insights into the demographic transition in the West.[18] Edited books are important means of research dissemination because they bind together outputs by leading researchers on a particular theme and together have more impact than if published individually in journals. His publications start with his 1975 D.Phil. thesis (874 pages!),[19] from which some of his early publications were derived,

[13] R. I. Woods, *The Population History of Britain in the Nineteenth Century* (London, 1992; republished Cambridge, 1995); R. I. Woods and N. Shelton, *An Atlas of Victorian Mortality* (Liverpool, 1997); R. I. Woods, *The Demography of Victorian England and Wales* (Cambridge, 2000); Woods, *Children Remembered*; and R. I. Woods, *Death before Birth: Fetal Health and Mortality in Historical Perspective* (Oxford, 2009).

[14] R. I. Woods, 'Aspects of the scale problem in calculation of segregation indexes: London and Birmingham, 1961 and 1971', *Tijdschrift voor Economische en Sociale Geografie*, 67 (1976), 169–74.

[15] R. I. Woods and N. Shelton, 'Disease environments in Victorian England and Wales', *Historical Methods: a Journal of Quantitative and Interdisciplinary History*, 33 (2009), 73–82.

[16] White and Woods, *The Geographical Impact of Migration*; Woods and Woodward, *Urban Disease and Mortality in Nineteenth-Century England*; Woods and Rees, *Population Structures and Models*; D. Noin and R. I. Woods (eds.), *The Changing Population of Europe* (Oxford, 1993); and E. Garrett, C. Galley, N. Shelton and R. I. Woods (eds.), *Infant Mortality: a Continuing Social Problem* (Aldershot, 2006).

[17] R. I. Woods and P. H. Rees, 'Spatial demography: themes, issues and progress', in R. I. Woods and P. H. Rees (eds.), *Population Structures and Models* (London, 1986), pp. 1–3.

[18] R. I. Woods, 'The spatial dynamics of the demographic transition in the West', ibid, pp. 21–44.

[19] R. I. Woods, 'Dynamic Urban Social Structure: a Study of Intra-Urban Migration and the Development of Social Stress Areas in Birmingham', D.Phil. thesis, University of Oxford, 1975.

and one 1975 departmental paper,[20] a medium he subsequently avoided, believing that the rigour of peer review was essential before publication, a process which he oversaw as editor or co-editor of journals.

What *themes* did Bob Woods cover and how did they change over time? A simple classification is suggested here, though a more detailed reading could lead to a more refined typology. Bob's work covered all the components that determine demographic change: fertility (eight publications), mortality (seventeen), migration (five) and international migration indirectly via studies of immigrants (ten), though most of this latter work concerned the population distribution and migration within the country of international immigrants. But this account underweights his interest in mortality, which should also include his publications on infant mortality (thirteen), fetal mortality (six) and the emotional aspects of child death.[21] He also published more general works on aspects of population development.[22] His early papers focused on the spatial distributions of immigrant populations[23] and how those changed over space and time.[24] 'Immigrant' has been a contested term for populations with origins outside this country as the available census data for monitoring the changing spatial locations of immigrants were based on country of birth in the 1961, 1971 and 1981 Censuses and therefore excluded the descendants of persons who had immigrated in the past. There is also confusion between 'immigration' used as a demographic accounting term, which includes returning UK citizens, residents or natives, and 'immigrants' used as a term to distinguish persons with a different race, ethnic origin or culture from the majority

[20] R. I. Woods, *The Stochastic Analysis of Immigrant Distributions*, Research Paper 1, School of Geography, University of Oxford (1975).

[21] Woods, *Children Remembered.*

[22] R. I. Woods, 'Urbanisation in Europe and China during the second millennium: a review of urbanism and demography', *International Journal of Population Geography*, 9 (2003), 215–27; D. Baines and R. I. Woods, 'Population and regional development', in R. Floud and P. Johnson (eds.), *The Cambridge Economic History of Modern Britain, Volume II: Economic Maturity, 1860–1939* (Cambridge, 2004), pp. 25–55.

[23] C. Peach, S. Winchester and R. I. Woods, 'The distribution of coloured immigrants in Britain', in G. Gappert and H. M. Rose (eds.), *The Social Economy of Cities* (Beverley Hills, CA, 1975), pp. 395–426; Woods, 'Aspects of the scale problem': R. I. Woods, 'A note on the future demographic structure of the coloured population of Birmingham, England', *Journal of Biosocial Science*, 9 (1977), 239–50; R. I. Woods, 'Ethnic segregation in Birmingham in the 1960s and 1970s', *Ethnic and Racial Studies*, 2 (1979), 455–76.

[24] R. I. Woods, 'Population turnover, tipping points and Markov chains', *Transactions of the Institute of British Geographers*, NS 2 (1977), 473–89; R. I. Woods, 'Migrations and social segregation in Birmingham and the West Midlands region', in White and Woods, *The Geographical Impact of Migration*, pp. 181–97; R. I. Woods, 'Spatiotemporal models of ethnic segregation and their implications for housing policy', *Environment and Planning A*, 13 (1981), 1415–33.

White British population. After much debate this led to the introduction of the broader concept of ethnicity. An ethnic identity question was proposed for the 1981 Census and implemented in the 1991, 2001 and 2011 Censuses. Bob Woods wrote on these issues in 1983.[25] Outside these core themes, Bob wrote about fertility (making intensive use of the Coale indexes as an aid to understanding the drivers of fertility change) and its links to class and geography,[26] morbidity in Victorian England,[27] and, with his Liverpool colleague Bill Gould, on the Human Immunodeficiency Virus/Acquired Immunodeficiency Syndrome (HIV/AIDS) on a world canvas,[28] as well as about medical history[29] and nuptiality.[30] He also published works on methods[31] and extensively on population theory (fourteen publications). A later section of the memoir returns to some of these themes in discussing some of his important contributions through a review of selected publications.

What *time periods* were of interest to Bob Woods? Here we use a broad-brush temporal classification. He was interested in the long run of several centuries and, in the case of one paper, a millennium. He dipped his toe into the eighteenth century but his main focus was the nineteenth

[25] P. E. White and R. I. Woods, 'Migration and the formation of ethnic minorities', *Journal of Biosocial Science*, Supplement 8 (1983), 7–24.

[26] R. I. Woods, 'On the long term relationship between fertility and the standard of living', *Genus*, 39 (1983), 21–35; R. I. Woods and C. W. Smith, 'The decline of marital fertility in the late nineteenth century: the case of England and Wales', *Population Studies*, 37 (1983), 207–25; R. I. Woods, 'Social class variations in the decline of marital fertility in late nineteenth-century London', *Geografiska Annale*r, *Series B*, 66 (1984), 29–38; R. I. Woods and P. R. A. Hinde, 'Variations in historical natural fertility patterns and the measurement of fertility control', *Journal of Biosocial Science*, 16 (1984), 309–21; R. I. Woods, 'The fertility transition in nineteenth-century England and Wales: a social class model?', *Tijdschrift voor Economische en Sociale Geografie*, 76 (1985), 180–91; R. I. Woods, 'Approaches to the fertility transition in Victorian England', *Population Studies*, 41 (1987), 283–311; R. I. Woods and C. Wilson, 'Fertility in England: a long-term perspective', *Population Studies*, 45 (1991), 399–415; and R. I. Woods, 'Working class fertility decline in Britain', *Past and Present*, 134 (1992), 200–7.

[27] Woods and Shelton, 'Disease environments in Victorian England and Wales'.

[28] W. T. S. Gould and R. I. Woods, 'Population geography and HIV/AIDS: the challenge of a "wholly exceptional disease"', *Scottish Geographical Journal*, 119 (2003), 265–81.

[29] R. I. Woods, 'Physician, heal thyself: the health and mortality of Victorian doctors', *The Society for the Social History of Medicine*, 9 (1996), 1–30; R. I. Woods, 'Dr Smellie's prescriptions for pregnant women', *Medical History*, 52 (2008), 257–76.

[30] R. I. Woods and P. R. A. Hinde, 'Nuptiality and age at marriage in nineteenth-century England', *Journal of Family History*, 10 (1985), 119–44.

[31] Woods, *Population Analysis in Geography*; R. I. Woods and P. H. Rees, 'Demographic estimation: problems, methods and examples', in Woods and Rees, *Population Structures and Models* (London, 1986), pp. 301–43; C. Galley, N. Williams and R. I. Woods, 'Detection without correction: problems in assessing the quality of English ecclesiastical and civil registration', *Annales de Demographie Historique*, 2 (1995), 161–83.

in which twenty-five of the forty-four publications assigned a definite time reference are located; twelve are located in the twentieth century. Bob started off as a population geographer using contemporary census, register and administrative data sources but then refocused in the 1980s and thereafter as a historical demographer on the nineteenth century or more precisely the Victorian and Edwardian eras when census information along with vital events data was available for the whole population.

What *locations* interested Bob Woods? He started off in his home city of Birmingham in which his immigrant studies were placed, along with a couple of excursions to London. Then his geographical horizon expanded to England, England and Wales and Britain as he developed his historical demographic research. 'Britain' means that Scotland was added to England and Wales as a country of interest. Note that these scales refer to the study 'universe'. He was very interested in the variation within the universe by detailed spatial unit, as befits a population geographer. The studies of Birmingham used small areas from the 1961, 1966 and 1971 Censuses, which were called enumeration districts (EDs). For operational reasons (land use changes, shifting populations and efficiency measures) the boundary definitions of a large proportion of EDs changed between censuses and so the population counts from successive censuses are for areas which cannot be directly compared. Bob solved this problem by using uniform one kilometre grid cells to which the ED populations were assigned. His studies of the geography of demographic processes in the nineteenth century were based on the Registration District. England and Wales were divided into forty-five registration counties and varying numbers of registration districts. These were harmonised in the *Atlas of Victorian Mortality*,[32] which he and colleagues reduced to a comparable set of circa 614 common registration districts for some analyses so that time series analysis could be carried out across successive censuses. Bob's international studies outside Britain were based on countries or groups of countries, drawing on international sources and a wide range of previous studies.[33]

[32] R. I. Woods and N. Shelton, *An Atlas of Victorian Mortality* (Liverpool, 1997).

[33] Noin and Woods, *The Changing Population of Europe*; Gould and Woods, 'Population geography and HIV/AIDS'; Woods, 'Urbanisation in Europe and China during the second millennium'.

Contributions as a model builder

While the bibliographic analysis is helpful in showing the broad expanse of Bob Woods's opus, it is useful to look in detail at particular outputs to identify his unique and important contributions to demographic and geographic knowledge. I concentrate on 'models' (in the broadest sense) used and developed by Bob Woods, as suggested by Bill Gould.[34] Others will be able to review Bob's contribution to historical demography more thoroughly.

'Model' is a contentious term with lots of different meanings for different people. My understanding is that a model is a representation of reality using various devices (words, graphs, equations, numbers, materials, roles, pictures or computer program logic). Inevitably a model is a simplification of reality but is something that can be tested against reality. Often the model embodies a set of testable hypotheses in a way that shows how variables to be accounted for are linked to explanatory factors. The variables that are often included in a demographic model come in several layers—for example: population structures and the components determining the pace of population change; the factors that directly influence the components; and the system variables that affect the factors and their relationship with the variables to be explained. The variables to be included in an explanation can be demographic, social, economic, cultural, behavioural and political (affected by policy). I think Bob would agree with this catholic definition, to judge from his frequent employment of variables of all these types. I exemplify his contribution by looking at five selected publications.

A graphical model: conceptualisation of the demographic transition

In a book chapter, Bob outlines a framework that we should use to understand the demographic transition model as a representation of demographic regime changes that play out differently depending on context (e.g. Britain from the 1870s versus India from the 1950s).[35] He uses a set of six carefully constructed graphs to convey his arguments. One of these

[34] Bill Gould organised a Bob Woods Memorial Symposium, 9–10 March 2012, University of Liverpool, <http://www.liv.ac.uk/environmental-sciences/bob_woods_memorial_symposium/>. I gave a talk entitled 'Bob, the model builder'.

[35] R. I. Woods, 'Spatial and temporal patterns', in Woods and Rees, *Population Structures and Models*, pp. 7–20.

summarises his characterisation of demographic regimes, particular combinations of fertility and mortality levels and structures (Fig. 1). Previous representations had just plotted the birth rate and death rate against time. Bob uses the two components, mortality and fertility, as two axes of the same graph in which empirical observations of the Crude Birth Rate (CBR) and Crude Death Rate (CDR) can be plotted. Lines of equal rates of growth (actually natural increase rates) can be represented on such a CBR versus CDR graph as diagonal lines which show increasing growth as you move towards the top right corner and decreasing growth as you move in the opposite direction towards the bottom left corner. No lines are added beyond the –1% (or –10/1000) line to indicate that demographic regimes in that region are rare and are likely to disappear fast. Bob uses this basic construction in his text books and in his historical demography papers, with refinements of the variables plotted on the two axes. So the total fertility rate or the gross reproduction rate may be used on the fertility dimension (*y*-axis) and variables such as life expectancy at birth on the mortality dimension (*x*-axis).[36] On these graphs lines of equal growth are curved reflecting non-linear relationships between the variables plotted. Note that the direction of the mortality axis is reversed in Figure 1 with high values on the left-hand side and low values on the right. When life expectancy is used as the mortality indicator, this reversal is not needed as low life expectancies correspond with high mortality and high life expectancies with low mortality.

Bob was not content with just plotting the distribution of populations for a particular time period but extended this to plot the paths through time of particular populations. In Figure 1 clusters of populations are represented by circles which move to new positions in fertility-mortality space over time. So cluster *A* contains countries where natural fertility prevails subject to high mortality; these experience, at a first stage of the demographic transition, a reduction in mortality accompanying an increase in fertility linked to improving maternal health prior to any limitation on the number of children. The countries move to larger circle *B*, which suggests more dispersal of demographic regimes. Fertility and mortality then decline in tandem so the cluster of populations moves along the same growth line until a steeper decline in fertility sets in. The arrow from circle *B* to circle *C* curves back, indicating that CDRs increase in the later stages of the demographic transition because the age structure becomes older.

[36] Figure 3.2 in R. I. Woods, 'The spatial dynamics of the demographic transition in the West', in Woods and Rees, *Population Structures and Models*, pp. 21–44.

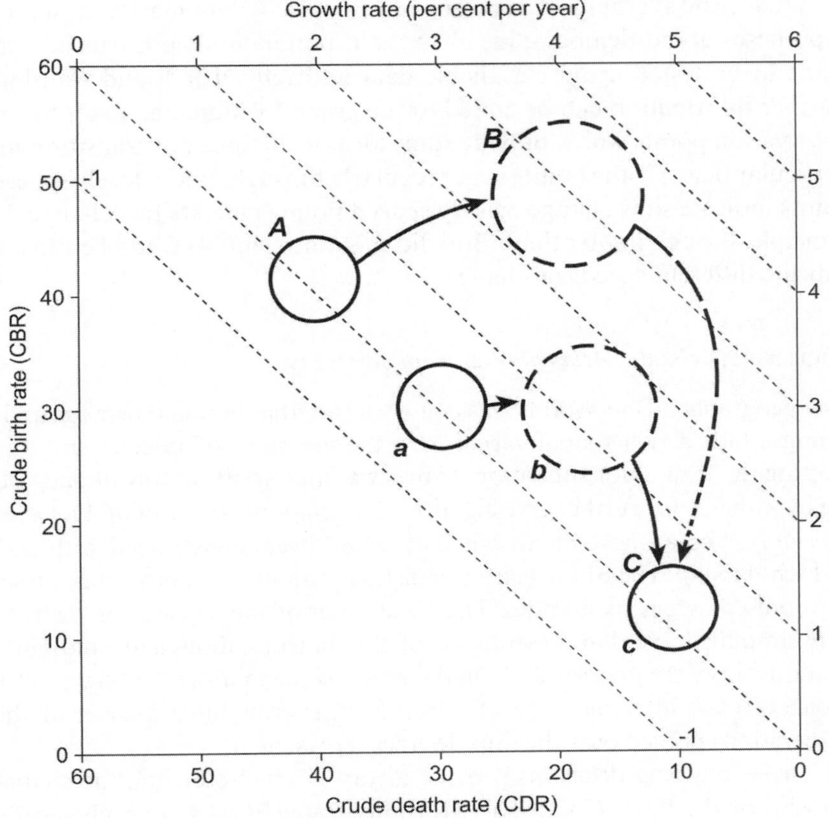

Figure 1. A definition of demographic regimes.
Source: Figure 2.3, p. 12 in R. I. Woods, 'Spatial and temporal patterns', in R. I. Woods and P. H. Rees (eds.), *Population Structures and Models* (London, 1986), pp. 7–20.

This curve back does not happen when life expectancy is used as the indicator for mortality, although there may be some slowing of the increase in life expectancy as very high levels are approached (this is the subject of current debate). The different regimes through time for European populations are indicated by the smaller circles *a*, *b* and *c*. The starting position of European countries is different because of the role of marriage postponement on fertility. Over time fertility increases only for some countries but not for others so circle *b* is larger than circle *a*. European populations then see substantial decline in fertility and a small decline in mortality moving them to circle *c*.

What Bob's graphical representation does is summarise a set of hypotheses about demographic changes in populations in a fruitful way that can be tested against available data and refined if found wanting. Further information can be added to the graph by attaching dates to the observation points which provide some idea of the speed of transition for particular places if the points occur regularly through time. Closely spaced points indicate slow change; widely spaced points indicate fast change. In principle, though I don't think Bob did this, line symbols could be used to indicate different speeds of change.

Maps as models: the *Atlas of Victorian mortality*

As a geographer, Bob Woods was acutely aware that national demographic averages hide a rich spatial variation in the measures of interest and that plotting those rates for subnational areas was an important way of suggesting hypotheses for further investigation. The maps in *An Atlas of Victorian Mortality*,[37] co-authored with Nicola Shelton, were constructed with skill and scholarship. The 614 registration districts employed were a common set harmonised across six decades. The boundaries of the registration districts were simplified to aid in presentation of the statistics, though all contiguity relationships were preserved. A final feature of the maps is the very careful choice of class intervals, each of which contains roughly a quarter of the observations pooled over the four decades represented.

These mapping decisions provide a way of characterising the spatial patterns of the Early Childhood Mortality Rate (ECMR) in each decade and enable comparison across decades (Fig. 2). So looking at the distribution of shades on each map we can see immediately that the relative spatial structure of ECMR persists over four decades.[38] The dense urban, industrial and mining districts of the North West, North East, Yorkshire, South Wales, West Midlands and London have the highest rates in each map. However, the levels of ECMR shift downwards steadily because the lighter shades grow in importance in rural and southern England. The authors then go on to analyse the geographical patterns of the causes of death in early childhood, linking many diseases to the effects of high urban population densities and overcrowding which meant the rapid spread of measles, whooping cough and scarlet fever. The decreases in

[37] Woods and Shelton, *An Atlas of Victorian Mortality*.

[38] The original maps are in colour. In Figure 2 the colours have been converted to grey scale shades.

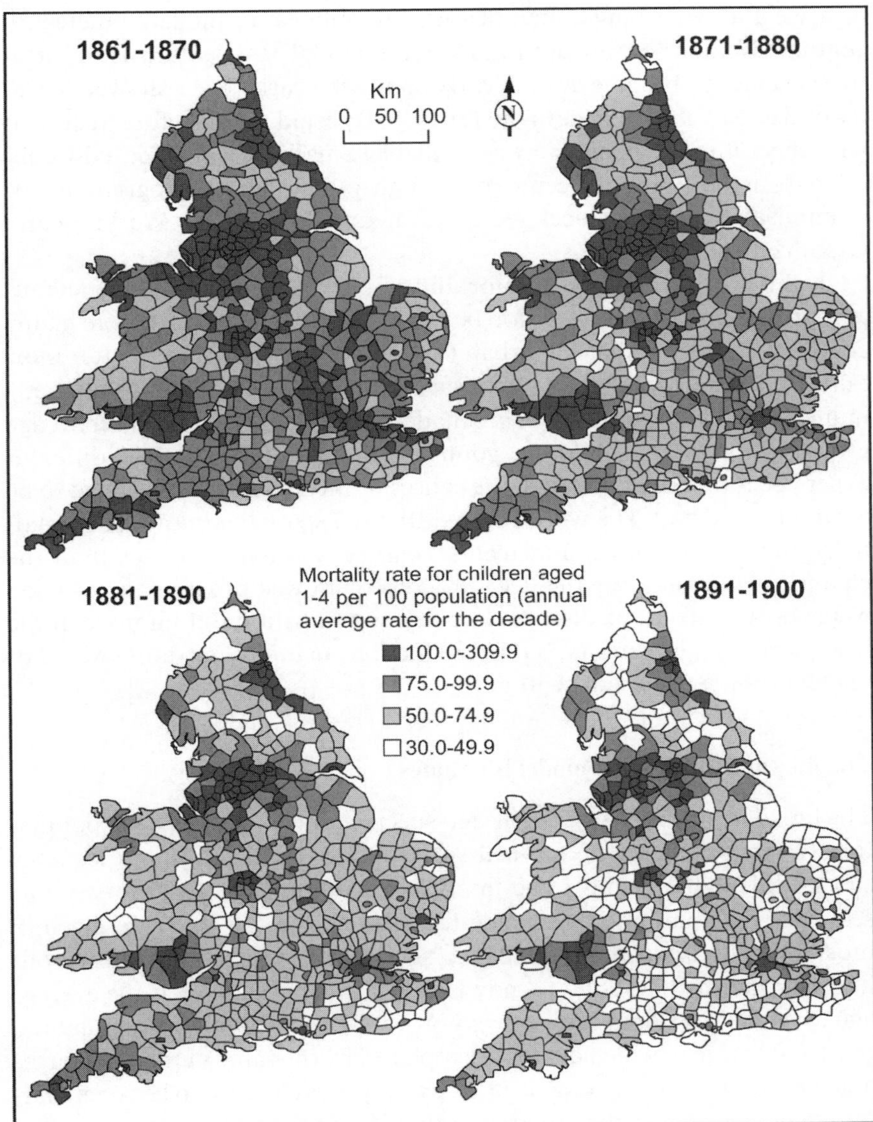

Figure 2. Early childhood mortality rates for ages 1–4, registration districts, England and Wales, 1861–1870 to 1891–1900.

Source: Map 11a, p. 67 in R. I. Woods and N. Shelton, *An Atlas of Victorian Mortality* (Liverpool, 1997). Reproduced with the permission of Liverpool University Press.

measles and whooping cough deaths were modest in the late nineteenth century. We had to wait until the second half of last century for protective vaccines to become available. By contrast, scarlet fever showed a dramatic decrease in virulence in the 1861–1900 period,[39] well before treatment with the antibiotic penicillin was available. Smallpox was essentially conquered in the twentieth century through public health programmes of immunisation and was declared eradicated in 1977 by the World Health Organization.

In his work on Victorian mortality, Bob Woods shows that previous accounts of change need revision because the processes at work were highly complex. He shows that the urban (worse mortality) to rural (better mortality) gradient meant that urbanisation slowed down the improvements in life expectancy that were being made. He stresses that the different age groups (infants and children, young adults and the old) had different experiences processed through the causes of mortality, which needed to be examined in detail. His work showed that the spatial variation in mortality in any decade in the nineteenth century was much greater than the changes occurring over the decades. Yes, there was progress in reducing water-borne infectious diseases in cities and nutrition did improve in the last quarter of the century, but big reductions in infant mortality were not made until the twentieth century.

The life table model and model life tables

The life table model uses a set of age-specific mortality rates for a population to compute a set of survival variables from which a life expectancy can be calculated, using some important assumptions. Accounts of the sequence of equations that generate the life table variables are given in most introductory demographic texts such as those written by Bob Woods himself[40] and by his student Andy Hinde.[41] Life expectancy is the average age to which the population can expect to live in a stationary population, one fixed in size in which deaths are replaced by the same number of births and whose age structure is dependent on only the relationship between mortality and age. An important assumption is that the age-specific mortality rates observed in a period of interest persist for the lives of those for whom we generate the life expectancies—that is, the mortality rates are fixed over

[39] Woods and Shelton, *An Atlas of Victorian Mortality*, Map 16a, p. 85.

[40] Woods, *Population Analysis in Geography*.

[41] A. Hinde, *Demographic Methods* (London, 1998); D. T. Rowland, *Demographic Methods and Concepts* (Oxford, 2003).

time. In reality, mortality rates vary over time and in recent decades in most European countries have been steadily declining, apart from some minor rises for young adult males associated with the HIV/AIDS epidemic that started in the 1980s. So if we were to use the mortality rates actually experienced by a cohort born in a year or set of years, then we would compute a higher life expectancy, which is termed the cohort life expectancy. We should label the conventional life expectancy as the period life expectancy. The data demands of the period life table are small, just mortality rates for one to five years; for the cohort life table we need one hundred years of deaths data after a cohort has been born.

We tend to regard the life table model results as 'reality' but of course they are not. The results depend on the quality of the input mortality rates (which depend in turn on the accuracy of death registration and the estimation of a corresponding population at risk). There are assumptions about the force of mortality between ages, and about the time spent alive between ages by those who die, which have important influences on development of birth-first age survival probabilities and which affect how we finish off the life table after the last age (in the final open-ended age group). Bob Woods and Andy Hinde tackled the problems of estimating accurate life tables for registration districts in the Victorian period, given known age misreporting at older ages,[42] using Model Life Tables (MLTs) building on methods used by Wrigley and Schofield,[43] who in turn used the empirical MLTs of Coale and Demeny.[44] MLTs were used to smooth out implausible empirical values or to fill in where complete data were absent. The Woods-Hinde model life table functions largely coincide with those of Wrigley and Schofield at the same mortality levels. However, curves associated with higher life expectancies were needed for estimating life expectancies by district after 1871 because they showed a different age pattern, with lower survival at younger ages and higher survival at older ages. It would have been interesting to have discussed with Bob these historical methods for estimating small population life tables and compared them with contemporary methods.[45]

[42] R. I. Woods and P. R. A. Hinde, 'Mortality in Victorian England: models and patterns', *Journal of Interdisciplinary History*, 18 (1987), 27–54.

[43] E. A. Wrigley and R. S. Schofield, *The Population History of England, 1541–1871: a Reconstruction* (Cambridge, 1981).

[44] A. J. Coale and P. Demeny, *Regional Model Life Tables and Stable Populations* (Princeton, NJ, 1966).

[45] P. Rees, P. Wohland and P. Norman, 'The estimation of mortality for ethnic groups within the United Kingdom', *Social Science and Medicine*, 69 (2009), 1592–1607; M. P. Grayer, 'Analysis of

Simulation models: representations of shifting populations

The graphs, maps and life tables which Bob Woods employed in his work were used in the main to develop a better understanding of the past. However, early in his career he published two important pieces of work which simulated the development of population systems forward over time: the first used Markov Chain analysis to project the distribution of primary schools in Birmingham by immigrant/native composition,[46] and the second used spatial simulation methods to project the populations of immigrant groups at small area scale (one kilometre squares) across Birmingham.[47] Population simulation is the process of implementing a model of a demographic system over time and space. Sometimes the system is specified at the macro-scale (counts of people in classes or at locations) or sometimes the population is represented at the micro-scale of individuals or households. The macro-simulation uses average probabilities of transition between system states whereas micro-simulation involves a method for deciding whether individuals make transitions or not.[48] Alternatively, a set of rules can be specified that lead to a decision or not to make the transition in situations where you have poor information about the probabilities of transition or about the determinants of those transitions. Simulation models normally derive the information for driving the model from one historical period, then use a second to test the validity of the simulations and in a third period allow the model to predict the future.

In his paper on 'Population turnover, tipping points and Markov chains' Bob uses data from Birmingham primary schools on immigrant/native pupil composition and classifies them into twenty percentage classes in 1961 and 1971.[49] He then counted the number of schools in each of the 400 cells to demonstrate how the country of birth composition of school pupils had changed. These tables were developed for pupils born in the New Commonwealth, in Ireland, in the West Indies and in India, Pakistan and Ceylon. Similar tables for 'coloured' pupils as a whole were assembled for 1966 to 1971 and for 1970 to 1971. He then derived transition prob-

Variation in Small Area Life Expectancy within London, 2000–2008', Ph.D. thesis, Queen Mary University of London, 2011.

[46] Woods, 'Population turnover, tipping points and Markov chains'.

[47] Woods, 'Spatiotemporal models of ethnic segregation'.

[48] Van Imhoff and Post show that macro-simulation and micro-simulation are two different representations of the same underlying model. E. van Imhoff and W. Post, 'Microsimulation methods for population projection', *Population: an English Selection*, 10 (1998), 97–138.

[49] Woods, 'Population turnover, tipping points and Markov chains'.

ability matrices from all these tables and used them in a simple Markov chain model to explore how school immigrant/foreign composition might change up to 2061.

This was an interesting and innovative analysis. It has been picked up in subsequent reviews but the methodology has not been applied subsequently for two reasons. Firstly, the projections referred to aspatial classes (primary schools in groups according to immigrant concentration) rather than to particular schools or school catchment areas, which would have been of greater interest to managers, heads and teachers. Secondly, change in the school ethnic composition is a symptom of underlying process of neighbourhood ethnic population change, school catchment area design and the respective roles of state and private schools. There is a growing literature on the ethnic composition of schools in England, on its potential effect on performance and community relations, the results of the Schools Census (National Pupil Database) which provides longitudinal data on the schools and residences of pupils of different ethnicity, and on demographic projections of ethnic group populations at different spatial scales. However, these have not yet come together to provide better forecasts than the ones Bob Woods attempted back in 1977.

In his paper on 'Spatiotemporal models of ethnic segregation and their implications for housing policy'[50] Bob Woods did take up part of the challenge. He projected the spatial distribution of New Commonwealth immigrants in Birmingham taking into account both internal migration within Birmingham and assumptions about the distribution of new immigrants. The models build on work by Hägerstrand[51] and Morrill,[52] in which people living in grid cell areas migrate to other cells through the application of a field of probabilities that reflects decay with increasing distance from origin. Bob developed several refinements of the basic model, changing the rules of migration behaviour in various ways and introducing new variables. Significantly, he subjected his simulations to careful tests by rolling forward the simulation from the 1961 Census to 1971 and then comparing outcomes with the 1971 Census using detailed maps. Simulation carried forward into the future is called 'projection'. Ideally, projections should be subject to the kind of validation exercise that Bob carried out but this is rather rare.

[50] Woods, 'Spatiotemporal models of ethnic segregation'.

[51] D. Hannerberg, T. Hägerstrand and B. Odeving (eds.), *Migration in Sweden: a Symposium* (Lund, 1957).

[52] R. L. Morrill, 'The Negro ghetto: problems and alternatives', *Geographical Review*, 55 (1965), 339–61.

This work has been cited not just in review papers but also in recent work on 'complexity' theory applied to urban residential populations.[53] This involves agent based micro-simulation modelling, which is useful when empirical data to power the simulation model are either lacking or flawed. This is the case for intra-urban migration which Bob simulated. He used surrogate marriage distance data to estimate the distance-decay parameter needed in the simulation model, for example. Bob's model of the population of his native city was both innovative and complex, so he would have been pleased with the interest from contemporary complexity modellers.

Lessons from Bob's research

This memoir has touched on only a few aspects of Bob Woods's extensive work in population geography and historical demography over thirty-seven years. Each paper, book or edited collection was characterised by a thorough grasp of the relevant literature, by a scholastic diligence in citing sources and by an engagement in issues and debates of the topic being discussed. He had a deep interest in the theory and methods which informed his empirical work. He desired to test conventional wisdom and often found it wanting. He taught himself and used the most refined methods employed in historical demography, work which can inform contemporary demographic analysis. He realised that a well-constructed graph or map could convey a great deal of useful information in a compressed format. He gave attention to the detail of empirical measurement and index construction. To quote the words of two of his students, 'he was the pre-eminent historical demographer of his generation'[54] and 'the foremost demographic historian of later-19th century Britain'.[55] His work will continue to be read by new researchers in his chosen fields as guides to excellent analysis of issues that continue to be important.

PHILIP REES

Fellow of the Academy

[53] For example in I. Omer, 'Demographic processes and ethnic residential segregation', *Discrete Dynamics in Nature and Society*, 3 (1999), 171–84; H. Yizhaq and E. Meron, 'Urban segregation as a nonlinear phenonenon', *Nonlinear Dynamics, Psychology and Life Sciences*, 6 (2002), 269–83; and J. Barkley Rosser, *Complex Evolutionary Dynamics in Urban-Regional and Ecologic-Economic Systems: from Catastrophe to Chaos and Beyond* (Berlin, 2011).

[54] Chris Galley's obituary in the *The Lancet*.

[55] Eilidh Garrett, quoted in Galley's *The Lancet* obituary.